NAZI GERMANY AT ITS GREATEST EXTENT

Maximum extent of Axis control

— · — · — 1938 boundaries

NORWAY
Oslo
SWE

NORTH SEA

IRELAND

DENMARK
Copenhag
BALT

Invasion of Norway
and Denmark Apr 9, 1940

Hamburg
Amsterdam
Berlin
Elbe R.
Oder R.

ENGLAND
London

NETH.
Brussels
GERMANY

CHANNEL ISLANDS
BELG.
LUX.

Invasion of Sudetenland
Oct 1-10, 1938

Invasion of Czechos
March 10-16, 19

ATLANTIC OCEAN

Paris

Invasion of France
and the Low Countries
May 10, 1940

Rhine R.

Prague

Loire R.

Saar to Germany
by plebiscite
Jan 13, 1935

Invasion and annexation
of Austria
Mar 12, 13, 1938

Vienna

CZE

FRANCE
Vichy
Bordeaux

Munich
AUSTRIA

SWITZ.
Milan
Po R.

Invasion of Yugoslavia
April 6- 17, 1941

Y

Rhône R.
Marseilles

ITALY

PORTUGAL
Ebro R.
Tagus R.

Barcelona

CORSICA

Rome

Lisbon

SPAIN

SARDINIA
Naples

Invasion of Alba
April 7, 1939

TANGIER
Strait of Gibraltar

SPAN. MOROCCO
Casablanca
Oran
Algiers

MEDITERRANEAN

SICILY

Tunis

MOROCCO
(Vichy)

ALGERIA
(Vichy)

TUNISIA
(Vichy)

0   500 miles

LIBYA

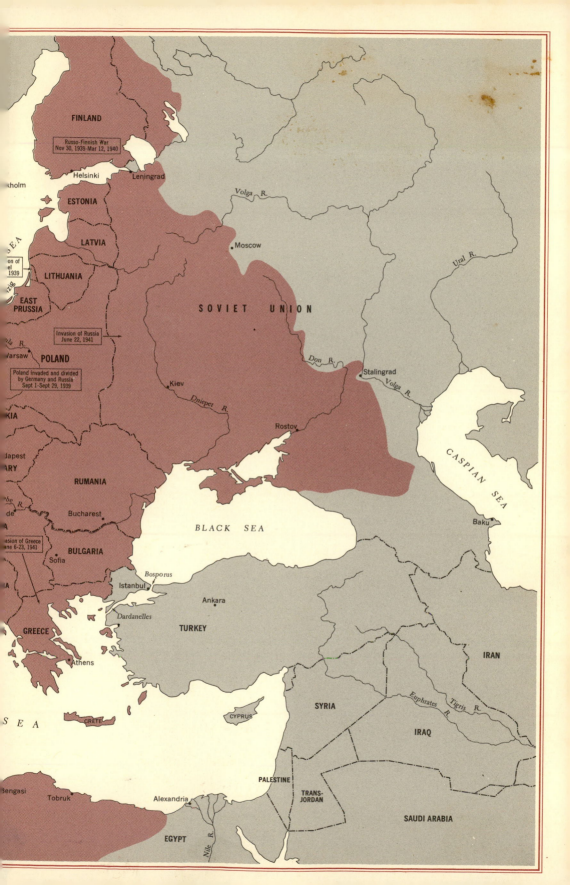

FINLAND

Russo-Finnish War
Nov 30, 1939-Mar 12, 1940

kholm

Helsinki

Leningrad

ESTONIA

Volga R.

LATVIA

Moscow

on of
el
1939

LITHUANIA

Ural R.

EAST
PRUSSIA

S O V I E T   U N I O N

zig

la R.

Invasion of Russia
June 22, 1941

Warsaw

POLAND

Don R.

Stalingrad

Poland invaded and divided
by Germany and Russia
Sept 1-Sept 29, 1939

Kiev

Dnieper R.

Volga R.

KIA

Rostov

CASPIAN SEA

dapest

ARY

RUMANIA

de

R.

A

Bucharest

BLACK   SEA

Baku

asion of Greece
ne 6-23, 1941

BULGARIA

Sofia

Bosporus

Istanbul

Ankara

GREECE

Dardanelles

TURKEY

IRAN

Athens

SEA

CRETE

CYPRUS

SYRIA

Euphrates R.

Tigris R.

IRAQ

Bengasi

Tobruk

Alexandria

PALESTINE

TRANS-
JORDAN

SAUDI ARABIA

EGYPT

Nile R.

HITLER'S WAR AIMS

THE ESTABLISHMENT OF
THE NEW ORDER

By the same author

The Age of Nationalism and Reform, 1850–1890
Friedrich Von Holstein: Politics and Diplomacy
    in the Era of Bismarck and Wilhelm II
The Holstein Papers (edited with M. H. Fisher)
Hitler's War Aims: Ideology, the Nazi State, and
    the Course of Expansion

HITLER'S WAR AIMS

THE ESTABLISHMENT OF
THE NEW ORDER

by Norman Rich

II

W · W · NORTON & COMPANY · INC ·
NEW YORK

Copyright © 1974 by W. W. Norton & Company, Inc.

FIRST EDITION

Library of Congress Cataloging in Publication Data
Rich, Norman.
    Hitler's war aims.

    Bibliography: v. 1, p. 313–342; v. 2, p.
    CONTENTS: v. 1. Ideology, the Nazi State, and
the course of expansion.—v. 2. The establishment of
the new order.
    1. Hitler, Adolf, 1889–1945.   2. Germany—Foreign
relations—1933–1945.   3. World War, 1939–1945—
Occupied territories.   4. National socialism.
5. World War, 1939–1945—Germany.   I. Title.
DD256.5.R473   943.086′092′4   [B]   78-116108
ISBN 0-393-05509-4 (v. 2)

This book was designed by Robert Freese.
The types are Caledonia and Bodoni Book.
The book was manufactured by Vail-Ballou Press, Inc.
Printed in the United States of America.

1 2 3 4 5 6 7 8 9 0

To the Memory of my Father
Robert Louis Rich.

Contents

CONTENTS

List of Photographs

Hinrich Lohse
Erich Koch

List of Maps

Preface

In his ideological textbook *Mein Kampf,* Hitler had set forth clearly and unequivocally his plans for the future of Germany and Europe. Very simply, these plans amounted to the establishment of a pan-German racial state from which non-Aryans were to be excluded and whose future was to be secured by the conquest of *Lebensraum* in Eastern Europe, largely at the expense of Russia. Before the conquest of Russia could be undertaken, however, the military power of France was to be eliminated, for Hitler believed he could never risk a major military commitment in Eastern Europe while France remained in a position to stab Germany in the back.

In the policies he actually pursued after he came to power, Hitler seemed to adhere to his original ideological program with terrifying consistency. He set out at once to eliminate non-Aryans from German national life; he launched a massive program of remilitarization to prepare Germany for its career of conquest; with the annexation of Austria and the Sudetenland, he laid the foundations for his pan-German state; he began the process of German expansion into Eastern Europe with the conquest of Poland; he destroyed the military power of France; and at last he embarked on what he had declared to be the major goal of his expansionist program, the conquest of Russia.

Yet many of Hitler's policies, far from being part of a consistent ideological pattern, not only failed to fit into that pattern but seemed an outright repudiation of his ideological program. He had advocated an alliance with England, but instead went to war with England. He had championed the concept of Germanic solidarity, yet he ruthlessly attacked Denmark, Norway, and the Netherlands. He had repudiated the policies of former German rulers who had sought to extend German territorial dominion to the south and west, yet he sent his own armies to the frontiers of Spain and to North Africa, to Yugoslavia and Greece. He had denounced the folly of William II's diplomacy which had forced Germany to wage a war on two fronts, yet he himself gratuitously plunged into a war on two fronts. He formed an alliance with Japan, which not even the most skilled Nazi propagandist could represent as a Germanic nation. And in partnership with Japan he declared war on the United States, a Europeanized if not necessarily a Nordic country, which had not figured at all in his original plans for conquest. Finally in 1943, with the surrender of his Italian allies, he sent his armies into Italy and the Italian-occupied areas of the Balkans. By that time it was evident that Hitler's ideological blueprint for expansion, if it could ever have been regarded as a blueprint, had become very distorted indeed. So frequently and finally so completely was Hitler diverted from his ideological course that many students of the Nazi era have questioned whether such a course had ever existed, or if it did exist whether it was of any importance whatever in determining his strategy and objectives. They argue that Hitler's expansionism, instead of adhering to some ideological pattern, was in reality little more than a series of improvisations.

In my opinion, such underestimation of the influence of Hitler's ideology goes too far. In the first volume of this study I tried to make the case that Hitler did indeed have a definite expansionist program which derived from his ideological conceptions, and that deviations from that program were the result of efforts to anticipate the moves of his opponents, of ambitions inflated by easy successes, or of political, military, and economic necessities. Whatever the merits of this theory, the fact remains that major deviations from Hitler's original ideological program did take place, and that these constitute valid reasons for questioning the significance of that program.

Besides the record of Hitler's diplomatic and military activity, however, there exists another body of evidence on which to base an estimate of his purposes and the role of ideology in his political calculations: the policies he pursued in the territories that came under his dominion. This evidence is all the more important because, in the realm of government and administration, in contrast to diplomacy and war, Hitler was not constantly obliged to adjust his policies to the moves, or suspected moves, of other powers, but had a relatively free hand to implement his own programs. Here too, of course, his policies were bound to be affected by the exigencies of politics, economics, and war. Yet it is here, if anywhere, that one might expect to find a reliable guide to his war aims.

This evidence assumes even greater significance in view of the fact that Hitler's ideological writings and pronouncements contained only broad general guidelines for future policies, that the details of those policies and the methods for implementing them still had to be worked out. Hitler had expressed his intention to remove non-Aryans from his pan-German racial state, to eliminate the Jews and to make use of the Slavs and other lesser breeds as menial labor for the German master race until they too could be removed. But did Hitler really propose to put such preposterous ideas into practice? Students of the Nazi era who question the importance of his ideology would presumably feel compelled to doubt it. Indeed it is difficult to believe, in view of Hitler's willingness to commit all kinds of racial heresies in the interest of political or military expediency and the manifest inexpediency of his proposed racial policies, that he could have taken his racial theories seriously. Quite apart from their inherent absurdity, how could such theories ever be transformed into practical policy? How was anyone to define an Aryan? Even if defined, how would it be possible to isolate Aryans from non-Aryans in the incredible hodgepodge of peoples and nationalities that made up the population of Europe? And how could any government be foolish enough to undertake the politically disastrous, economically ruinous, not to mention supremely inhuman task of removing the millions of Jews and tens of millions of Slavs and other non-Aryans from the territories under its control?

With respect to the Jews and Slavs Hitler had at least provided ideological guidelines for future Nazi policies. But what about the other nationalities that came under Nazi rule in the course of the Second World War? Presumably the Germanic peoples such as the Scandinavians, the Dutch, or the Flemings were to share in the benefits of Hitler's New Order. But what was to be the nature of their association in the Germanic empire? On this subject Hitler had said very little. Nor had he made any specific pronouncements about the future fate of the French. Their military power was to be eliminated before the war for *Lebensraum* in Russia was launched, but where did the French fit into Hitler's racial-political scheme? Did he intend to accord a privileged status to these descendants of ancient Germanic tribes and fellow members of the Carolingian Empire? Or were the French, too, to be relegated to a menial role? The Italians, another racial anomaly, were originally conceded a predominant position in the Mediterranean area, but Hitler's intentions toward Italy changed radically after the Italian surrender. His plans also fluctuated in considering the future of the peoples of Southeastern Europe, who had played an insignificant role in his ideological calculations. And what of the nations which did not come under his immediate control, the peoples of Finland and the neutral countries of Europe, of Sweden, Switzerland, or Spain? Of the Arabs, whose aid Hitler attempted to enlist in his war against Britain? Of the peoples of the Western Hemisphere, above all the Americans, whom he regarded as the chief arsenal of British strength and a major obstacle to his avowed aim of an accord with Britain? What were his ultimate intentions with regard to his Japanese allies?

The answers to all these questions, if indeed there were answers, could only be found in the record of Hitler's actual government and administration of the peoples who came under his rule, and in the plans he formulated in dealing with the constantly shifting political, military, and economic situation with which he was confronted.

In placing such emphasis on Hitler's government and administration, it might have been logical to begin the present volume on the establishment of his New Order with a description of the policies he pursued in Germany itself, for Germany was the first country to come under his rule. But, even though Hitler's government of Germany must be regarded as the prototype of the New Order, it was essentially a government to ensure his control over the German state and people. In this respect it differed little from other totalitarian regimes and in itself offers few clues to Hitler's war aims except (and it is a very important exception) in the manner in which it was organized to provide the wherewithal to fulfill his expansionist ambitions. Consequently the discussion of Hitler's government of Germany is included in the previous volume because it seemed essential to an understanding of his efforts to fulfill those ambitions.

But one crucial function of Nazi rule was not discussed in connection with the Nazi government of Germany: the treatment of non-Aryans, notably the Jews, in German society. The reason for this omission was that Hitler's Jewish policy was not confined to Germany but was to be extended to all territories that came under Nazi rule, and that the significance and scope of that policy can only be grasped when it is considered in its entirety. The elimination of the Jews from his pan-German racial state, however, began directly after Hitler came to power in Germany, long before he had occupied or conquered a single foreign country. Appropriately, therefore, the discussion of Hitler's establishment of his New Order begins with a description of his policy toward the Jews.

The succeeding chapters (the greater part of this volume) are devoted to an analysis of Nazi policies in the countries which came under German occupation before and during the Second World War. As the Nazi administrations in each of the occupied countries differed widely, there seemed no practicable method for dealing with occupation policies in general categories. I have therefore considered the case of each occupied country separately, and, with a few minor exceptions, according to the chronological order in which it was brought under Nazi control. Finally, to round out the story, I have dealt with Hitler's intentions toward countries and continents which never came under German occupation, a subject for which the evidence is necessarily fragmentary and inconclusive.

For the study of Hitler's policies in the countries actually occupied by the Nazis, however, the amount of documentary evidence available is overwhelming, and there is hardly any part of this book about which another book could not be—or has not already been—written. In the present volume I have tried to put together a comprehensive survey of Nazi occupation policies so as to be able to view them in their entirety and in perspective, and, in fine, to construct a picture of the kind of world which would have existed if Hitler had won the Second World War.

For financial assistance which made it possible for me to do research in European and American archives, I am indebted to the generosity of the John Simon Guggenheim Memorial Foundation, the American Philosophical Society, and to Michigan State and Brown universities.

I am indebted further to the librarians of Michigan State and Brown universities, especially those in charge of interlibrary loan services; to Dr. Hans-Günther Seraphim of the Staatliches Archivlager, Göttingen; and to Dr. Jan Stepan of the Harvard Law Library, who was enormously kind and helpful.

Among the friends and colleagues who read various sections of this book and offered valuable advice and comments, I would like to express special thanks to Abbott Gleason, Robert Herzstein, Thomas Knight, Bryce Lyon, William O. McCagg, Jr., Anthony Molho, Charles Neu, Donald Rohr, Dennison Rusinow, and above all Paul Sweet, who read almost the entire manuscript.

For editorial assistance, I am deeply grateful to Mary M. Shuford, Anne Thomas Stevens, and Donald Lamm; to James Mairs, who helped with the collection of photographs; and to Harold Faye, who prepared the maps.

As always, my most profound debt is owed to my wife for help and support on every front.

HITLER'S WAR AIMS

THE ESTABLISHMENT OF
THE NEW ORDER

CHAPTER 1

The Jews

Hitler never made any secret of his ultimate intentions with regard to the Jews. During the years of his struggle for power, he had fully expounded his anti-Semitic theories in his speeches and writings. His party program contained a provision denying Jews the right of German citizenship, and he had stated frankly that the ultimate aim of his movement was the removal of the Jews from Germany altogether.[1] Hitler, however, had made wild statements about a large number of things, and many people, Germans and foreigners alike, found it as impossible to believe that he actually intended to put his racial theories into practice as to believe in a literal interpretation of his plans for German *Lebensraum*. To such people it was simply inconceivable that, after more than two centuries of scientific enlightenment and humanitarian reform, the head of a civilized European state could take these preposterous racial theories seriously, much less make them the basis of an actual program of national policy.

But Hitler, although he might belittle the exaggerated racial cultism of Heinrich Himmler and Alfred Rosenberg, not only believed in his racial theories but was convinced of his obligation to world civilization to draw the necessary conclusions from them. It is now only too clear that from the time he came to power he intended to carry out the removal of Jews from Germany and all territories that might in the future come into the German sphere of influence. The only change in this, perhaps the most fundamental of his political aims, was how the expulsion of the Jews was to be effected.[2]

In his campaign to drive the Jews from Germany, and subsequently from German-occupied Europe, Hitler resorted to three distinct, if overlapping, methods. The first of these was emigration, either voluntarily or under political and economic pressure, the method in general use before the war. The second, deportation to territories that had come under di-

1

rect or indirect German control, was adopted at the beginning of the war after the principal avenues of foreign emigration were closed. This included the project proposed after the fall of France of shipping the Jews to the French island of Madagascar, a scheme which soon gave way to the more practicable program of sending them to Eastern Europe. Finally there was the system of outright extermination, a method applied on a large scale in Eastern Europe from the beginning of the war, and then extended to include Jews deported from the Old Reich and all other territories in the German power sphere. The few part-Jews, Jews in mixed marriages, or special cases who were allowed to remain were to be rendered incapable of reproduction through sterilization.

The basis of the whole process was Hitler's definition of Jews in racial rather than religious terms. By this he meant that Jews differed from ethnic Germans in a physical sense, and that no repudiation of Judaism or conversion to Christianity could eliminate the fact of their Jewishness. "Anti-Semitism as a political movement neither can nor should be based on fleeting emotions, but on the acceptance of the fact that Judaism is a matter of race and not of religion," he wrote in a letter of September 16, 1919. "The final aim of such anti-Semitism must be, unquestionably, the expulsion of the Jews." [3]

After Hitler came to power, Nazi racial specialists sought in vain a satisfactory racial definition of a Jew. Because of their inability to formulate such a definition, Nazi lawmakers who first attempted to define non-Aryans in drawing up anti-Semitic legislation were compelled to revert to the criterion of religion. A decree of April 11, 1933, defined a non-Aryan as anyone who had a Jewish parent or grandparent, with the crux of the definition in the provision that the parent or grandparent was presumed to be Jewish if he or she adhered to the Jewish faith. Otherwise, "if Aryan descent is doubtful, an opinion must be obtained from the expert on racial research [Sachverständiger für Rassenforschung] commissioned by the Reich minister of the interior." The law did not specify what standards the government racial expert was to apply in making his decision.[4] Subsequent Nazi laws attempted to define Jews in terms of skull measurement, nose size, and other physical characteristics; but all such definitions proved unsatisfactory. In the end the Nazis were compelled to resort to the expedient of defining a Jew as anyone who regarded himself as a Jew or who was considered to be a Jew by the Nazi official in charge of his racial evaluation.

Their failure to concoct a satisfactory racial definition of a Jew did not prevent the Nazis from adhering to a racial concept of Jewishness or from enacting a large body of legislation directed against persons considered to be Jewish. Most notorious were two laws promulgated during the party congress at Nuremberg on September 15, 1935: the "Law for the Protection of German Blood and Honor," which prohibited marriage and sexual relations between Jews and ethnic Germans; and the "Reich

Citizenship Law," which deprived the majority of Jews of their German citizenship.[5]

The attack on the legal status of the Jews was accompanied by an attack on their economic status. The Nazi boycott of Jewish economic enterprises launched on April 1, 1933, was the beginning of a long series of legal and extraordinary measures designed to drive the Jews from the German economy, the idea being that by depriving them of all means of earning a livelihood they would be forced to leave the country. Jewish economic enterprises had to be clearly identified as such and could not be disguised by transferring management or shares to non-Jewish partners; licenses were withdrawn from Jewish doctors, dentists, lawyers; Jews were forbidden to act as salesmen, brokers, real estate or patent agents.

Jews were barred from studying or teaching at German schools and universities; they were excluded from museums, theaters, concerts, and all other places of public entertainment. In many areas they were forbidden to use public transportation and forced to observe stringent curfew regulations. Jewish name changes granted after January 30, 1933, were revoked, Jewish men were required to add the name Israel, Jewish women the name Sara to their regular names to ensure their immediate identification as Jews. All Jews over fifteen were required to register and carry identity cards, their passports and other documents had to be stamped with a J or the word *Jude*.[6]

Despite the political, social, and economic pressure brought to bear against the Jews and the actual physical violence to which many of them were subjected, only about one hundred fifty thousand of Germany's five hundred fifteen thousand Jews had left the country by 1938. With Germany's annexation of Austria in March 1938 an additional two hundred twenty thousand Jews were brought into the Reich, making for an actual increase in Germany's Jewish population since 1933. Even now most Jews could not comprehend the implacable quality of Nazi anti-Semitism, and many were still reluctant to leave the country they regarded as their homeland or to abandon the fruits of their lifework. Moreover, stripped of most of their property by the German government, the Jews had difficulty securing permission to settle in a foreign land.

The assassination of a German diplomat by a Jew in Paris on November 7, 1938, gave the Nazis a pretext to step up the pace of their anti-Semitic action. Hitler himself set the objective of the campaign by demanding that the Jewish question now be dealt with in its totality and brought to a conclusion. Joseph Goebbels responded with a propaganda barrage designed to whip German public opinion into a frenzy of righteous indignation. But lest that indignation fail to reach the proper pitch, Nazi officials were instructed to organize and carry out popular demonstrations against the Jews in such a manner that they would appear as the "spontaneous reaction of the German people." This was the background of the events of the night of November 9, 1938, later called the *Kristallnacht* or "night of the broken glass," when the shop windows of thousands of Jewish stores were smashed and synagogues in cities all over the Reich were burned. When the extent of the riots against the Jews became apparent, Himmler instructed his police not to interfere with such popular demonstrations except to protect German life and property and prevent the indiscriminate looting of Jewish property (which the state proposed to do in more systematic fashion). Further, the police were to prepare for the arrest of twenty to thirty thousand Jews in the Reich, preferably wealthy Jews.[7]

Hermann Göring, who had been a prime mover in the economic campaign against the Jews and who still had confidence in the efficacy of economic measures, issued a decree on November 11, 1938, "For the Elimination of Jews from German Economic Life," which was designed to close the remaining channels of Jewish economic activity. According to its provisions Jews were prohibited from owning or operating retail or wholesale businesses; they were compelled to sell their interests in all business enterprises and real estate; and they were forbidden to seek employment with non-Jews. To get at whatever assets the Jews still possessed, Göring imposed on them a massive "atonement tax" to pay for crimes the Jews had allegedly committed against the German people.[8]

With all legal channels of Jewish economic activity closed, the SS journal *Das Schwarze Korps* predicted that the Jews would soon find themselves in such desperate straits that they would be compelled to resort to crime. "In that case we shall be faced with the stern necessity of rooting out the Jewish underworld in the interest of law and order, just as we root out ordinary criminals: with fire and sword. Then we shall see the final and utter collapse of Judaism in Germany—its total destruction." [9]

Still the emigration of Jews from Germany did not proceed rapidly enough to suit the Nazi authorities. On January 24, 1939, Göring instructed Dr. Wilhelm Frick, the Reich minister of the interior, to set up a central Reich office to co-ordinate measures to speed up the emigration of Jews. This office was to be comparable to that already established in Austria for the same purpose. The result was the Central Reich Office for the Emigration of Jews (*Reichszentrale für die jüdische Auswanderung*), which was established in the Ministry of the Interior under the direction of Reinhard Heydrich, the head of Himmler's security police. As deputy director of this office, Heydrich selected Heinrich Müller, a senior officer of the Gestapo and security police. When Müller was made chief of the Gestapo within the newly organized Central Office for Reich Security (*Reichssicherheitshauptamt*, or RSHA) in September 1939, his successor as deputy director of the Jewish emigration office was Adolf Eichmann, the head of the RSHA's department for Jewish affairs.[10]

The Jews themselves were now organized under a single agency, the Reich Union of Jews in Germany (*Reichsvereinigung der Juden in Deutschland*), which was to provide the money for the emigration of indigent Jews and assume responsibility for Jewish welfare services while Jews still remained in the country.[11]

With the coming of war in September 1939, the problem of where the Jews should go after they left Germany—always a major obstacle to the emigration program—was rendered even more difficult by the British naval blockade, which cut off almost all previous havens of refuge.

The fall of France in the spring of 1940 seemed to offer new possibilities. At a conference with his naval leaders on June 20, 1940, Hitler announced his intention to settle Jews on the French island of Madagascar. To implement this policy, a representative of the German Foreign Office proposed that a future peace treaty with France contain a provision placing Madagascar at Germany's disposal for the solution of the Jewish problem. The twenty-five thousand French living there were to be compensated (nothing was said about what was to become of the black population), and the island was to be transferred to Germany as a mandate under the administration of a police governor responsible to the Reichsführer SS, Heinrich Himmler. The Reich would retain a few harbors and air strips as naval and air bases, but otherwise the entire island was to be set aside as a "reservation" for Jews. Apart from the German supervisory administration, the Jews were to have complete political autonomy, with their own mayors, police, postal service, transportation system, and the like. All Jewish property in Europe was to be placed in trust in a European bank to finance the settlement of the Jews in Madagascar, who were to serve as hostages for the good conduct of Jews in America and other areas not under Nazi control. The Madagascar scheme was considered preferable to the proposed settlement of Jews in Palestine, which had a dangerous symbolic significance.[12]

Until the German attack on Russia, the term *final solution of the Jewish question*, insofar as it concerned German Jews, still referred to their emigration from German territory or their deportation and resettlement in Madagascar or elsewhere. In Eastern Europe, however, other solutions had already come into widespread use. After a conference in Berlin on September 21, 1939, dealing with the problem of the Jews in Eastern Europe, Heydrich issued instructions to his task forces in Poland which left little doubt that the final solution there, at least, was to be the outright extermination of the Jews. "I should like to emphasize once more," Heydrich said, "that the *total measures planned* (i.e., the final aim) are to be kept *strictly secret*." Meanwhile a distinction had to be made between the final aim, which would take some time, and measures to achieve the final aim, which could be carried out in the near future. The first of these measures would be the roundup of Jews in the countryside and villages and their concentration in a few big towns. These concentration centers were to be chosen for their location on a railway, preferably a railway junction, to facilitate the transportation of Jews to these centers and their subsequent removal.

In every Jewish community, a Jewish council of elders was to be set up which was to be responsible for the exact and punctual fulfillment of all instructions from German authorities. The Jewish councils were to undertake an interim census of the Jews in their community, and they would be held responsible for the removal of the Jews under their jurisdiction to the concentration centers. Within these centers the councils of elders were to be responsible for the accommodation of Jews who had been relocated there and for preserving order in the Jewish community.

At this time economic considerations still played a role in Heydrich's plans, and his task forces were instructed not to endanger the economy of the occupied territories or the delivery of supplies to the *Wehrmacht* through their anti-Jewish measures. At the same time, however, the task forces should consider how Jewish workers could be replaced by non-Jews in the shortest possible time.[13]

The experience gained by his task forces in Poland formed the basis of Heydrich's preparations for the Nazi racial campaign in Russia. Already in Poland, faced with the manifold difficulties of roundups, transportation, and resettlement, his men had dealt with large numbers of Jews by the simple expedient of shooting them, allegedly because they represented a security risk. In Russia this shooting of Jews was to be applied not as an exceptional measure but as a general rule. Shortly before the attack on Russia was launched Heydrich's task forces were given secret orders by word of mouth to kill all Jews. Soon the Nazis did not even bother to keep such orders secret. On August 1, 1941, "specific orders of the Reichsführer SS" were telegraphed *en clair* to the Second Cavalry Regiment of the *Waffen*-SS that "all Jews must be shot; Jewish females [*Judenweiber*] driven into the swamps." One of Heydrich's task forces reported in October 1941 that "in accordance with instructions received" the security police were working "to solve the Jewish problem decisively and by all available means," that the "cleansing operations" now being carried out had as their objective "the total elimination of the Jews." [14]

The German Jews were still exempt from such drastic measures; but, during the summer of 1941, with Madagascar still unavailable as a relocation area because the British controlled the sea lanes to Africa, Hitler decided that the German Jews should be sent east instead.[15] On September 18, 1941, Himmler informed Arthur Greiser, Gauleiter and Reichsstatthalter (governor) of the Wartheland (Polish territory incorporated into the Reich), that the Führer wanted the Old Reich and other territories under German control to be cleared of Jews "from west to east." "I am therefore doing all I can to see that the deportation of the Jews from the Old Reich and the territories assimilated into the Reich during the past two years is completed during this year as a first stage, preparatory to their being sent further east early in the new year." [16]

In October 1941 Himmler officially put an end to the emigration phase of Germany's anti-Jewish campaign by specifically prohibiting further Jewish emigration to foreign countries. "Only in exceptional cases, if, for instance, a positive advantage to the Reich would be likely to accrue therefrom, will the emigration of Jews be permitted with the prior approval of the RSHA." [17]

Large-scale deportations of Jews from the Reich began in the autumn of 1941; but now it was necessary to decide what was to be done with these Jews after they had been shipped east. Heydrich, who on July 31, 1941, had been charged by Göring with making all necessary preparations "to bring about a complete solution of the Jewish question in the German sphere of influence in Europe," proposed on November 29 that a conference of all officials concerned with the evacuation of Jews be convened to discuss this problem, "because already since October 15, 1941, Jews from Reich territory, including the Protectorate of Bohemia and Moravia, have been evacuated to the east in continuous transports." [18]

After several postponements, the proposed conference was held in Wannsee, near Berlin, on January 20, 1942. Heydrich opened the meeting by reminding the assembled officials that he had been placed in charge of preparations for the final solution of the Jewish question, and by reviewing the progress of the anti-Jewish campaign thus far. In the past, he said, Jewish emigration had run into numerous difficulties because of foreign immigration restrictions. Even so, a total of three hundred sixty thousand Jews from the Old Reich, one hundred forty-seven thousand from Austria, and thirty thousand from Bohemia and Moravia had been removed in this manner. In October 1941, however, the Reichsführer SS had forbidden the further emigration of Jews because of the danger they might represent to the Reich in foreign countries; since that time the policy of emigration abroad had been replaced by the evacuation of Jews to the east. "These actions are of course to be regarded only as a temporary substitute," Heydrich said. "Nonetheless, here already the coming final solution of the Jewish question is of great importance."

The policy now being pursued, Heydrich continued, was to send Jews capable of work to the east in large labor gangs, with the sexes separated. It was expected that as a result of the process of "natural selection" the majority of these Jews would soon die. The remainder, who would represent the strongest and, therefore, the most dangerous Jewish elements, would have to be "dealt with accordingly [entsprechend behandelt werden]." For the time being, Jews in essential war industries were not to be evacuated.

The planned evacuation measures were not to be confined to the Reich or territories annexed to the Reich, but were to be carried out in all areas within the German sphere of influence. Heydrich anticipated no difficulties in Slovakia, Croatia, or Rumania, or in occupied and unoccupied France. In Hungary the government would have to be compelled to accept an adviser for Jewish affairs, and in Italy better liaison was needed with the police. On the whole, however, no organized opposition to the evacuation program was expected in Southeastern and Western Europe. In Northern Europe, on the other hand, the Germans feared serious complications, and because there were so few Jews in Northern Europe in any case the representative of the Foreign Office at the Wannsee conference advised postponing action in that area.[19]

As in previous stages of their anti-Semitic campaign, the Nazi authorities devoted a great deal of attention to the problem of defining the term *Jew* and in deciding what should be done about mixed breeds and Jews in mixed marriages. Eventually Himmler brushed aside such technicalities with impatience, "I urgently request that no ordinance regarding the definition of the word 'Jew' be issued," he wrote on July 28, 1942. "We are only tying our hands by establishing these foolish definitions." The Führer had charged him with the execution of this extremely difficult task, and he would tolerate no interference. "The occupied territories will be purged of Jews," Himmler said, and that was that.[20]

It is uncertain when the decision was made that those Jews sent to the east who were incapable of work should be killed, or when it was decided to carry out the mass execution of Jews in gas chambers instead of by firing squads. Both programs, however, appear to have been under consideration well before the Wannsee conference.

The first experiments in execution by gas had been undertaken early in the Nazi era in connection with the mercy killing (euthanasia) programs of the insane or incurably ill, a process in which large numbers of Jews in German concentration camps had already been involved.[21] According to the testimony of Rudolf Hoess, the first commandant of the Auschwitz (Oswiecim) concentration camp (which was to become the largest of the killing centers), he received instructions from Himmler in the summer of 1941 to establish the Auschwitz camp as part of the final solution program. But at this time it would appear that Auschwitz was simply to be another major evacuation center for the housing of Jewish labor gangs.[22]

The first direct evidence of an intention to use gas for the mass killing of Jews is contained in a communication of October 25, 1941, from Dr. Ernst Wetzel, an official of Rosenberg's Ministry for the East, to Hinrich Lohse, the head of the German civil government in the Ostland (the Baltic States and White Russia), informing him that *Oberdienstleiter* Viktor Brack of the Führer Chancellery had agreed to co-operate in providing the necessary accommodations (*Unterkünfte*) and gas appliances (*Vergasungsapparate*) for the final solution of the Jewish problem. As gas appliances were in short supply, Brack had suggested manufacturing them on the spot instead of ordering them from the Reich, and he had volunteered to send a number of experts to Riga for that purpose. Adolf Eichmann, then head of the Jewish section in the RSHA, had agreed with this procedure, and had informed Wetzel that camps were to be established in Riga and Minsk to which Jews from the Old Reich would eventually be sent.

> In our present position, [Wetzel said,] we cannot afford to have scruples about taking advantage of Brack's facilities for the elimination of Jews who are not fit for work, as these will provide a way of avoiding any possible recurrence of the events which occurred, according to a report I have in front of me, at the shooting of the Jews in Vilna. Incidentally, I see from the report that the shootings took place in public, which can hardly have been approved. Jews fit for work, on the other hand, are to be transferred further east for use as labor. It goes without saying that the men are to be separated from the women.[23]

Despite the co-operation of Brack and the intentions of Eichmann, the major gas killing centers in the east were not established in the Ostland but in the former territories of Poland. The first to go into operation, in December 1941, was located near Kulmhof (Chelmno) in the Wartheland, where killings were at first performed in mobile units with carbon monoxide gas generated by trucks. Subsequently four permanent killing centers were established in rump Poland, the so-called Government General: Belzec, the first camp to be equipped with permanent gas chambers (March 1942); Sobibor (May 1942); and Maidanek (autumn 1942), all in the Lublin district where the majority of Polish Jews were located; and Treblinka, near Malkinia on the Bug (July 1942), which handled the Jews from the districts of Warsaw and Bialystok. The largest of the killing centers, Auschwitz, was located in the former Polish district of Kattowitz, which had been incorporated into the Reich province of Silesia. In the permanent killing centers carbon monoxide gas was eventually replaced by hydrogen cyanide (prussic acid), which was given the commercial name Zyklon B.[24]

By the spring of 1942 the Nazis had begun to apply their "special treatment" (*Sonderbehandlung*) program—the Nazi euphemism for the killing of Jews—not only to Jews incapable of work, but to all Jews in Eastern Europe, including the German Jews who had been sent there. In April 1942 Himmler approved a request from Arthur Greiser in the Wartheland to apply the special treatment to one hundred thousand Jews in his province. Himmler also agreed with the proposal of Odilo Globocnik, the head of the SS and police in Lublin, that the special treatment of all Jews should now be carried out as completely and rapidly as possible in order to avoid the danger of having the program interrupted in mid-passage by unexpected difficulties. Himmler placed special emphasis on the desirability of speed "if only for reasons of secrecy [*schon aus Gründen der Tarnung*]." [25]

The desire to keep the extermination of Jews secret appears to have been a major reason for the development of gas chambers. It had gradually become evident to Nazi leaders that the mass execution of Jews by firing squads, which could not be kept secret, was having a deleterious effect on the morale of German troops in the east, and was giving rise to serious difficulties in dealing with the local populations.[26] To avoid such problems in the future, Nazi officials ordered that henceforth all publicity about Germany's Jewish policy was to be avoided. According to Globocnik the special treatment program was now considered to be "one of the most secret matters there is at the moment, one could even say the most secret. Anyone who talks about it is to be shot on the spot." Bormann's office deplored the circulation of rumors by men on leave in the Reich about what was happening to the Jews, because the majority of Germans did not understand the necessity for such measures.[27] Finally Hitler himself had to issue an order prohibiting all mention of a future total solution of the Jewish problem. If questions were asked about what had become of the Jews, people were to be told that they had been drafted for labor purposes.[28]

Viktor Brack, the expert from the Führer Chancellery on gas killing procedures, assured Himmler that he was in complete agreement with the ultimate aims of the total solution program. But even Brack wondered whether, of the ten million Jews still in Europe, two or even three million men and women capable of work should not be allowed to survive to carry out essential services for the Reich. Of course these Jews would have to be rendered incapable of reproduction, and for this purpose Brack recommended mass sterilization by X ray, a method that recent experiments had demonstrated could be both quick and effective.[29]

Himmler, however, although he himself was employing large numbers of Jews in his various SS economic enterprises, disliked the idea of exempting Jews from extermination on economic grounds. He suspected that many German firms, and especially the German army, were using the excuse of essential war work to protect Jewish workers or to continue making large profits through the use of cheap Jewish labor. SS and police officials were instructed to get on with the job of clearing out the Jews, regardless of their economic status.[30]

Under pressure from Himmler, Wilhelm Keitel issued an order on September 5, 1942, that all Jews employed by the Wehrmacht for armament production or military services of any kind were to be replaced immediately by non-Jews.[31] But the men who ran these war industries proved to be far from co-operative, and they received considerable support in resisting orders to give up their Jews from German military and civilian officials.[32]

Himmler regarded such conduct as nothing less than treasonous. In an order of October 9, 1942, he referred contemptuously to the "so-called armaments workers," who were in reality employed in shoemaker, tailor, or similar establishments. All these Jews were to be removed at once and sent to concentration camp factories east of the Government General; but those Jews, too, were to disappear eventually in accordance with the orders of the Führer. All persons who objected to these measures on the grounds that Jews were essential to the German war economy were in reality secret supporters of the Jews, or profiteers of cheap Jewish labor. Such persons were to be investigated and proceeded against ruthlessly. Henceforth the Wehrmacht should place all its orders for materials previously manufactured by Jews with the economic offices of the SS, and Himmler personally would guarantee their delivery.[33]

In March 1943 the Nazi government began a drive to remove what was left of the Jews, not only from areas directly under German occupation, but from all territories within the German sphere of influence. Orders were issued on March 5 and 24 requiring the evacuation to the east of all stateless Jews (which, since the Nuremberg laws of September 1935, included all German Jews), as well as Jewish citizens of the former Poland, the former Luxembourg, Slovakia, Croatia, Serbia, Rumania, Bulgaria, Greece, the Netherlands, Belgium, France, the former states of Estonia, Latvia, and Lithuania, and Norway. Jewish citizens of Italy, Switzerland, Finland, Spain, Portugal, Sweden, and Denmark (which was still nominally independent) were to be given until March 31, 1943, to return to their home countries, unless German authorities decided to detain them for reasons of security. Jewish citizens of all other countries, including Britain and the United States, were not to be subjected to anti-Jewish measures, but were to be held for purposes of exchange, or ransom. In September 1943 the evacuation order was extended to cover Jewish citizens of Italy, Switzerland, Spain, Portugal, Denmark, Sweden, Finland, Hungary, and Turkey. Since the evacuation of these Jews to the east could not take place immediately for reasons of foreign policy, they were to be housed temporarily in concentration camps in the Old Reich, with the women and children in Ravensbrück and the males over fourteen years of age in Buchenwald. Italian Jews were to be removed at once, Turkish Jews on October 20, Jewish citizens of all other countries mentioned in the decree on October 10. Jews of foreign citizenship mentioned in previous decrees who had not yet been evacuated to the east were to be removed immediately.[34]

The evidence is absolutely clear that by 1943 Hitler and the chief executors of his policies were determined to kill or sterilize all Jews within their power sphere, with the possible exception of those Jews who might be used for purposes of exchange or barter. Moreover, this operation was to be carried out, insofar as humanly possible, in the course of the war, while the attention of the German people was focused elsewhere, and with an almost total disregard for political and economic consequences. Hitler's greatest fear was that the German people, and perhaps even his immediate successors as rulers of Germany, would not understand the vital necessity of a radical solution of the Jewish problem.[35]

There is a horrible irony in the fact that this program continued to be carried out—that it indeed reached its most extreme phase—at a time when even Hitler must have realized that the war was irretrievably lost.

It has been suggested that it was precisely because the war was lost that Hitler was determined to wreak this last grim vengeance on the people whom he held responsible for his defeat. But this thesis is surely untenable. Had Hitler won the war, the more fortunate Jews might have been sent to Madagascar or used as objects of barter, but his intention of clearing all Jews out of the German power sphere was at all times certain.

Hitler's attitude, and that of his more fanatic followers, was summed up in a Goebbels diary entry of March 1942.

> One simply cannot be sentimental about these things. If we did not fight the Jews, they would destroy us. It's a life and death struggle between the Aryan race and the Jewish bacillus. No other government and no other regime could marshal the strength to undertake a general solution of this question. Here too the Führer is the resolute leader, both in word and deed, in the fight for a radical solution, which is necessitated by present conditions and therefore seems impossible to evade. Thank God we now have a whole series of possibilities during the war which would be denied us in peacetime. These we will have to exploit.[36]

CHAPTER 2

The Ethnic Germans

Hitler's denunciation and vilification of the Jews played a role second only to his glorification of the ethnic Germans in his pronouncements on racial questions. In his ideological world view the Germans were the master race, the supermen, the sole creators of true culture, the source and shield of the highest forms of human civilization. Ostensibly it was to provide security for these ethnic Germans (and, with them, for world civilization) that he was establishing his New Order. They were to serve as his chief instruments in creating and ruling it, but they were also to be its major—and in the long run its sole—beneficiaries.[1]

Hitler's solicitude for ethnic Germans was not confined to the inhabitants of Germany; in theory at least it extended to Germans in every part of the world. "Common blood belongs in a common Reich," he wrote on the first page of *Mein Kampf*, with specific reference to the ethnic Germans of his Austrian homeland; but he made it clear that this principle was not to be restricted to Austria, and that one of his major political objectives would be to bring all Germans together into a Greater German Reich.[2]

After coming to power, Hitler skillfully exploited the principle of self-determination propounded by the Allies in drawing up the peace treaties following the First World War. On the basis of the claim that ethnic Germans should have the right to self-determination in territories where they constituted a majority of the population (by which he meant that he should have the right to incorporate them into his racial state), and by the application of brutal diplomatic pressure backed up by the threat of war, Hitler succeeded in annexing Austria, the Sudetenland, and Memel to the Reich. Danzig, which he had hoped to acquire in the same way, finally had to be won by conquest. The peaceful acquisition of Austria and the Sudetenland enormously enhanced Hitler's personal prestige and brought about a striking improvement in Germany's strategic and economic position, which undoubtedly had a decisive influence on the Nazi leader's subsequent calculations about the timing and future course of his expansionist policy.[3]

An evaluation of Hitler's ultimate intentions in these territories, however, must be based on the evidence of the policies he actually pursued. During the initial stage of the German occupation of Austria Hitler made some effort to disguise his intentions to avoid offending Austrian pride. However, official German records show plainly that from the beginning his policies for dealing with Austria, and indeed with all territories annexed on the basis of their ethnic German population, were both purposeful and consistent, and fully in line with his ideological conceptions.

Austria

When German troops marched into Austria on March 12, 1938, Hitler had realized the first major territorial objective set forth in *Mein Kampf*. "If providence once summoned me from this city to the leadership of the Reich," Hitler announced to passionately cheering crowds from the balcony of the city hall of Linz on that evening, "then it must have assigned me a task. And it can only have been *one* task: to restore my dear homeland to the German Reich!"[4] In a speech in Vienna three days later, Hitler poured ridicule on the rulers of post-1918 Austria who had presumed to speak of the special mission of an independent Austria. The only mission of this creation of Germany's enemies, he said, was to prevent the formation of a great German Reich and to bar the way to the future of the German people. "I herewith proclaim a new mission for this land," Hitler declared.

> It corresponds with the commandment that once summoned German settlers here from every Gau of the Old Reich. The oldest eastern march [Ostmark] of the German people shall from now on be the newest bulwark of the German nation and therewith of the German Reich. For centuries during the turbulent times of the past, the storms from the east have broken up on the borders of this ancient march. For centuries and for all time to come, it shall once again become an ironclad guarantee for the future and freedom of the German Reich and therewith a pledge for the happiness and freedom of our great people. . . . It will be our task, through labor and industry, by standing together and working together, to solve the great social, cultural, and economic problems, but above all to develop and build up Austria to an ever greater extent into a bastion of National Socialist consciousness and National Socialist willpower. . . . As Führer and Chancellor of the German Nation and Reich, I herewith announce before German history the entry of my homeland into the German Reich.[5]

Two days before Hitler made this announcement, the machinery for Austria's entry into the Reich had already been set in motion. On March 13, 1938, the Austrian federal government, under the leadership of Dr. Arthur Seyss-Inquart, issued a law "On the Reunion of Austria with the German Reich." Austria was henceforth to be a state (*Land*) of the Reich, and on Sunday, April 10, a free and secret plebiscite would be held for German men and women of Austria over twenty years of age on the reunion question.[6]

The Reich government acknowledged the Austrian reunion law of March 13 by making it a law of the Reich, with the added provision that the existing body of Austrian law should remain in effect until further notice. Reich law would subsequently be introduced by the Führer and Reich chancellor, or by Reich ministers delegated by him. Meanwhile the Reich minister of the interior was empowered, after consultation with the other Reich ministers concerned, to issue legal and administrative decrees to implement and supplement the March 13 law.[7]

Hitler made no pretense of waiting for the results of the plebiscite of April 10 before beginning the *Gleichschaltung* of German and Austrian institutions.[8] His first act following the promulgation of the reunion law was the incorporation of the Austrian army into the German army under his personal command, with the requirement that all members of the former Austrian army immediately swear an oath of allegiance to himself as their supreme commander. General Wilhelm Zehner, the last Austrian defense minister and a resolute opponent of the *Anschluss,* was dismissed at once, as were twenty other senior officers, one-third of the Austrian general staff, and large numbers of officers of lower rank. Austrian military units were not allowed to remain identified with the Austrian army, but were distributed among German army units throughout the Reich. Thus the Austrian army as an entity ceased to exist.[9]

Simultaneously the Germans undertook a large-scale purge of the Austrian civil service, with particular emphasis on the police. Six thousand Austrian officials were dismissed immediately, most of them from key positions in the ministries of Public Safety and Education. Already on March 12, with the appointment of Seyss-Inquart as chancellor of Austria, Dr. Ernst Kaltenbrunner, head of the illegal Austrian SS, had been assigned to the chancellor's office to deal with problems of security. Kaltenbrunner at once opened the door to the agents of Himmler and Heydrich who had accompanied the Wehrmacht into Austria and who immediately undertook mass arrests of Jews and persons suspected of political unreliability, especially potential leaders of opposition to the Nazi regime.[10] A few days later Himmler was empowered by a Reich law to take all necessary steps in Austria to preserve order and security "including those outside customary legal boundaries." [11]

On March 15, 1938, Seyss-Inquart, whose position as chancellor of Austria had been eliminated with the promulgation of the law uniting

15

Austria to the Reich, was appointed provisional Reich governor (Reichs-statthalter) of the Austrian state government. He was given the power to reorganize the Austrian administration in co-operation with the Reich Ministry of the Interior, which was made the central Reich authority for carrying out the reunion of Austria with the Reich. All Austrian public officials were required to swear an oath of loyalty and obedience to Hitler. Those who refused to do so were to be dismissed. There followed a succession of decrees providing for the co-ordination of the German and Austrian administrations, their legal and banking systems, currency, railroads, post and telegraph services. The entire apparatus of the Four-Year Plan was introduced, and a Reich Propaganda Office was established in Vienna—all this before the plebiscite to record the will of the people on the question of reunion even took place.[12]

The Austrian Nazi party was co-ordinated in the same way as the Austrian state. On March 13 Josef Bürckel, a member of the German Nazi party and, since 1926, Gauleiter of the Palatinate, was entrusted with the control and reorganization of the Nazi party in Austria. At the same time Bürckel, who had conducted the German election campaign during the Saar plebiscite of 1935, was placed in charge of the forthcoming plebiscite in Austria.[13]

Bürckel did his job well, for the plebiscite held in Austria under his supervision on April 10, 1938, produced a 99.73 per cent vote in favor of union with Germany, a figure which suggests that his agents also exercised close supervision over the counting of the votes. Simultaneously with the plebiscite, the Austrian Germans were allowed to vote for deputies from the Nazi party list to represent them in the German *Reichstag*. As a result of this election seventy-three Austrian deputies took their seats in what was shortly to be called the parliament of the Greater German Reich.[14]

Following the plebiscite, the co-ordination of German and Austrian institutions, or rather the imposition of Nazi measures on Austria, continued apace. The compulsory Reich Labor Service was introduced on April 19, compulsory military service on June 16. On May 20, 1938, the Nuremberg racial laws were extended to Austria, thus legalizing the persecution of Jews which was already well under way. On July 3, 1938, all racially suitable citizens of the former Federal Republic of Austria were officially designated citizens of the German Reich.[15]

In all these measures for the incorporation of Austria into the Reich there was nothing that could be considered in any way unexpected. But there was one arresting feature of the annexation process: It was soon obvious that Hitler's reorganization of the administration of Austria, like his reorganization of the Austrian army, was designed to put an end to every kind of centralized Austrian authority and to eliminate the very concept of an Austrian state.[16]

On April 23, thirteen days after the plebiscite, Hitler appointed Gauleiter Bürckel Reichskommissar for the Reunion of Austria with the German Reich with the task of undertaking "measures for the political reconstruction and for accomplishing the political, economic, and cultural reincorporation of Austria into the German Reich." His headquarters were to be in Vienna; he was to be directly and personally responsible to Hitler with authority to issue instructions to all Austrian state and party offices. His consent had to be secured for all measures proposed by the Reich government, especially questions of legislation. Bürckel's assignment was to terminate on May 1, 1939, by which time it was expected that the work of reunion would be completed.[17]

Informing Seyss-Inquart of Bürckel's appointment, Hitler explained that the new Reichskommissar was to act as the Führer's liaison officer (*Verbindungsmann*) in Austria in order to facilitate the tasks of Seyss as Reichsstatthalter as well as his own as head of the German government. It would be Seyss-Inquart's mission to implement the legislation for the reunion of Austria and the Reich. If within a year this task was essentially completed, Hitler proposed to make Seyss a member of the Reich government (*Reichsregierung*), in which capacity he would carry on his activity on behalf of Austria within the Greater German Reich. Thus Hitler provided that both Seyss and Bürckel, the sole remaining representatives of a centralized Austria, were to be removed from their positions within just over a year.[18]

On May 22, 1938, four weeks after Bürckel's appointment, Hitler named seven party Gauleiters for the Ostmark, as Austria was now officially called. Many of these men had served as illegal Gauleiters before the Anschluss. The boundaries of several of their party districts, however, were changed and each Gauleiter was now also made *Landeshauptmann*, or head of local state administration, in which capacity he came under the Reich Ministry of Interior.[19]

Appointed in the first instance were old-guard leaders of the Austrian Nazi party who now received their reward for their loyalty to the Nazi cause: Franz Hofer for the Tyrol; Dr. Friedrich Rainer for Salzburg; August Eigruber for the Upper Danube; Dr. Hugo Jury for the Lower Danube; Odilo Globocnik for Vienna; Hubert Klausner for Carinthia; and Siegfried Uiberreither for Styria. In the critical post of Vienna, Globocnik was shortly relieved of his duties, allegedly at his own request, and was succeeded on January 30, 1939, by Bürckel, who retained all his other positions as well.[20] When, after the fall of France, Bürckel was appointed Reichstatthalter and Gauleiter of the newly created *Westmark* (made up of the French province of Lorraine, the Saar, and the Palatinate), he was succeeded in Vienna by the Reich youth leader and perennial boy scout, Baldur von Schirach, who held the position until the end, despite the fact that at least as early as November 1943 Hitler was trying to find a more competent and energetic administrator for Vienna.[21]

Hitler did not even wait a full year after Bürckel's appointment as

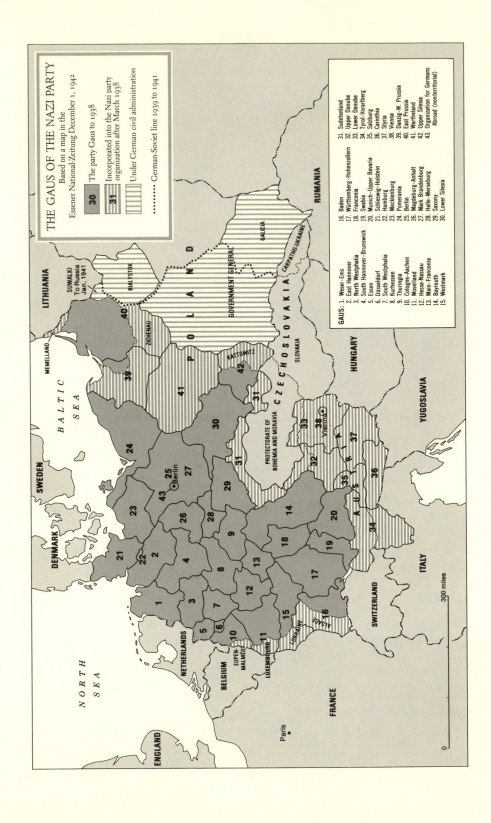

THE GAUS OF THE NAZI PARTY

Based on a map in the
Essener National-Zeitung December 1, 1942

30 The party Gaus to 1938

31 Incorporated into the Nazi party
organization after March 1938

Under German civil administration

········· German-Soviet line 1939 to 1941

GAUS: 1. Weser–Ems
2. East Hannover
3. North Westphalia
4. South Hannover–Brunswick
5. Essen
6. Düsseldorf
7. South Westphalia
8. Kurhessen
9. Thuringia
10. Cologne–Aachen
11. Moselland
12. Hesse-Nassau
13. Main-Franconia
14. Bayreuth
15. Westmark

16. Baden
17. Württemberg–Hohenzollern
18. Franconia
19. Swabia
20. Munich–Upper Bavaria
21. Schleswig–Holstein
22. Hamburg
23. Mecklenburg
24. Pomerania
25. Berlin
26. Magdeburg–Anhalt
27. Mark Brandenburg
28. Halle–Merseburg
29. Saxony
30. Lower Silesia

31. Sudetenland
32. Upper Danube
33. Lower Danube
34. Tyrol–Vorarlberg
35. Salzburg
36. Carinthia
37. Styria
38. Vienna
39. Danzig–W. Prussia
40. East Prussia
41. Wartheland
42. Upper Silesia
43. Organization for Germans
     Abroad (nonterritorial)

Reichskommissar before undertaking the final obliteration of Austria as a political entity. On April 14, 1939, he published a decree putting an end to the existing administrative boundaries of the so-called Ostmark. "The aim of the reorganization," the Nazi government candidly explained, "is the establishment of a very close bond between the former individual provinces of the Ostmark (including the city of Vienna) and the Reich, while eliminating the central administrative offices of Vienna." The seven party *Gaue* set up by the law of May 22, 1938, were now designated *Reichsgaue*, and each Gauleiter, in his capacity as Landeshauptmann, was elevated to the rank of Reichsstatthalter, with all the duties and powers heretofore exercised by the Reichsstatthalter of Austria. Thus each chief of administration in the former provinces of Austria, in his dual capacity as party and state leader, came under the direct authority of Hitler. Austria as such ceased to exist.[22]

The law of April 14, 1939, was later described by Minister of the Interior Frick as "an outstanding milestone in the constitutional reconstruction of the Third Reich," for it had established an entirely new state organization, the Reichsgau. A decree of that same date made the Sudetenland, too, a Reichsgau, a status which was to be conferred on all conquered territories subsequently incorporated into the Reich. The laws of April 14, 1939, for Austria and the Sudetenland were to serve as models on which all such future incorporations were based.[23]

In carrying through his reorganization of Austria, Hitler knew precisely what he was doing and for what purpose. "As regards Austria," he told his associates in August 1941, "it was the proper solution to destroy the centralized state, to the detriment of Vienna, and reestablish the provinces. In this way innumerable points of friction were removed. Each of the Gaus is happy to be its own master."[24]

Hitler protested that he felt no hostility to Vienna. On the contrary, he was filled with admiration for Vienna's cultural monuments and considered it to be a more beautiful city than Paris. Nevertheless, Vienna could not be allowed to continue its unrivaled cultural dominion in the Danube area.

> For Vienna to become the sole center of attraction for the Austrian portion of our territories would be dangerous for the whole Reich, [Hitler said.] For that reason I feel impelled to take steps to counteract any such possibility; and for that reason, too, I am anxious to create other centers of culture in Austria. . . . Therefore, all that Vienna has drained from its neighboring provinces must be channeled back into the Gaus. Furthermore, I will not tolerate any rivalry between Vienna and Berlin. Berlin is the capital of the Reich and will remain the capital of the Reich.

In the former territories of Austria, Hitler intended to build up Graz and above all Linz, the city of his youth, into rivals of Vienna. Linz, in fact, was to be made the most important city on the Danube and transformed into a modern metropolis with splendid buildings on both banks of the river. "Linz owes all it possesses, and all it will possess, to the Reich. For this reason Linz should become the personification of the Reich." [25]

In January 1942 Hitler took a further step in his campaign to destroy the concept of Austria by forbidding the use of the term *Ostmark*, which implied that the territorial entity of Austria still existed. Henceforth only the names of the individual Gaus created out of the former territory of Austria were to be used. Lammers duly forwarded this order to Reich and party administrators, but was obliged to confess four months later that it had been impossible to avoid all references to the area that had once been Austria. To take the place of the term *Ostmark*, he proposed that this region be called the Reichsgaus of the Alps and the Danube (*Alpen-und Donau-Reichsgaue*), but he recognized that even this designation was dangerous and warned that it should be used as little as possible. [26]

In Austria as in Germany, and indeed in all territories subsequently occupied by the Nazis, one of the first moves of the Nazi government was to take action against the Jews. According to Himmler's statisticians there were two hundred and twenty thousand Jews in Austria at the time of the Anschluss, a large number of whom lived in Vienna. [27]

Directly after the Anschluss, Göring stated publicly that one of the most important tasks in the Ostmark would be to make Vienna a German city again, which meant that the Jews would have to be removed from the former Austrian capital. Confident that economic measures would suffice to persuade the Jews to leave, Göring issued orders designed to ruin the economic base of the Jewish community and deprive the Jews of their means to earn a livelihood. All such measures were to be carried out strictly in accordance with the letter of the law—legally, but inexorably. [28]

Despite Göring's directives, the Nazi campaign against the Austrian Jews was never restricted to legal, or to economic, measures. Already on the first day of the German occupation large numbers of Jews were arrested; by October 1939 the first deportations of Austrian Jews to the newly occupied eastern territories had begun, although as yet on a very small scale. [29]

The statistics compiled in Himmler's offices tell the terrible story in bald outline. Of the 220,000 Jews in the Ostmark at the time of the Anschluss, only 94,270 remained by May 17, 1939, and by the end of December 1942 there were only 8,102. Of these 149,124 had emigrated, 14,509 had died of natural causes, 47,555 had been evacuated, and 710 had been removed by other (unspecified) means. Early in 1943 Himmler's officials assured their chief that in a short time Austria would be completely cleared of Jews. By the end of the war they had not yet succeeded in accomplishing this task, but their ultimate intention to do so was horrifyingly clear. [30]

The Sudetenland

Hardly had Hitler completed the peaceful annexation of Austria, justified by the principle of self-determination, than he began to make demands on the basis of the same principle in the name of the ethnic Germans living in the border areas of Czechoslovakia, the so-called Sudetenland.

The peaceful cession of the Sudeten German territories to Germany through the Munich agreement of September 29, 1938, almost seems to have taken Hitler by surprise, for he had made no preliminary plans for their organization and administration.[31] As was the case with Austria, however, he was obviously determined from the start to incorporate this area into the Greater German Reich. It is hardly surprising, therefore, that his policies in the Sudetenland were almost identical to those he had adopted in Austria.

The principal difference between the Sudetenland and Austria, and from an administrative view it was an important one, was that this region had never been the center of a great empire and that it contained no cities to rival the capital of the Reich or even one which might serve as the administrative center for all the Sudeten territories. Hitler's problem here, then, was not to destroy the traditions and institutions of an ancient state, as in Austria; but, on the contrary, to find an effective system for administering these widely scattered lands. There was the further difference that the Jewish population of the Sudetenland was comparatively small, and that a large number of the region's thirty thousand Jews had managed to flee before the Nazi occupation began.

On October 1, 1938, the first day the German troops began their occupation of the Sudeten territories, Hitler issued a decree appointing Konrad Henlein, the head of the Sudeten German party and the chief agent of Nazi policy in the Sudetenland prior to the Munich settlement, to the position of Reichskommissar and head of the administration of the Sudeten German territories. His appointment was to take effect as soon as the military occupation of the territories had been successfully completed and they could be withdrawn from the administration of the German army. The Reichskommissar was to be directly responsible to Hitler and, working according to his general directives, was to ensure the political, economic, and cultural reconstruction of the Sudetenland. He was empowered to give orders to all state and party offices in territories under his administration and to supervise their operations and activities. The Reich Ministry of the Interior was to act as the central Reich office for the transfer of the Sudeten German territories.[32]

In a speech from the balcony of the civic theater in Karlsbad (Karlovy Vary) on October 4, Hitler greeted the citizens of the Sudetenland as racial comrades (*Volksgenossen*) and informed them that they were now citizens of the Reich. "We are proud to take over this land in all its beauty, and are determined to undertake immediately the task of improving what has to be improved, of building up what can be built up, and to heal all the wounds of the past." [33]

By October 10, according to the timetable arranged by the Munich treaty, all Sudeten territory demanded by Hitler had been occupied by German troops. On October 21 supreme administrative authority in the Sudetenland was officially transferred from General Walther von Brauchitsch, the commander in chief of the army, to Henlein, the newly appointed Reichskommissar.[34] Already on October 10, however, the Four-Year Plan had been introduced in the Sudetenland, and the Reichsmark had been made legal tender in addition to the Czech crown. On October 22 Himmler was authorized to take all administrative measures required to maintain security and order in the newly occupied territories, including any extralegal measures he considered necessary. By the end of the month the financial and judicial offices of the Sudetenland, the railroad system, the post and telegraph offices, had all been integrated with those of the Reich.[35]

In the following month Hitler initiated a territorial reorganization of the Sudetenland comparable to the one he had carried out in Austria, only in this case the reorganization was undertaken not to destroy a rival political tradition but to provide greater administrative efficiency. The Sudeten territories, extending as they did along a great part of the lengthy frontiers of Czechoslovakia, constituted an unwieldy administrative agglomeration.[36] By a Hitler order of October 30 the Nazi party's territorial organization in the Sudetenland was reorganized in a manner that clearly foreshadowed its future political organization within the German Reich. A Reichsgau Sudetenland was created out of a large bloc of Sudeten territory along the western and northern frontiers of Czechoslovakia. The rest of the Sudeten territory, however, was assigned to other Gaus: an area in the northeast to the Gau of Silesia; in the southwest to the Bavarian Ostmark; in the south to the Gaus of the Upper and Lower Danube. The capital of the new Reichsgau Sudetenland was to be at Reichenberg (Liberec). Its Gauleiter was to be Konrad Henlein, its deputy Gauleiter Karl Hermann Frank, the deputy leader of the Sudeten German party, who was destined to play a major role in the Nazi administration of the Czech provinces of Bohemia and Moravia.

As leader of the Sudeten German party, Henlein was to arrange immediately for the incorporation of his organization into the German Nazi party in accordance with the instructions of the Führer's deputy and to inaugurate the build-up of the Nazi party and its organizations. On November 5, 1938, the Sudeten German party was duly absorbed into the NSDAP, and on December 11 the Sudeten German territories assigned to other Gaus were officially incorporated in their new party administrative districts.[37]

All this time no plebiscite of any kind was held in the territory yielded by Czechoslovakia to Germany as had been required by the terms of the Munich agreement. An international boundary commission to determine the final frontiers between Germany and Czechoslovakia, set up in accordance with the provisions of that agreement, exercised no authority whatever. "It might as well be dead for all the use it is," the British chargé d'affaires reported on November 11, 1938. "All questions arising out of the Munich agreement have been and will be decided at German Nazi dictation." And indeed, on that same day a final boundary treaty was arranged directly between the German and Czechoslovak governments. By demanding that the boundaries be determined on the basis of the population census of 1910, the Germans were able to claim, on ethnic grounds, territories which included virtually all of Czechoslovakia's frontier fortifications. In fact, however, this treaty did little more than confirm the Germans' right to territory they had occupied already. The treaty was subsequently communicated to the international boundary commission, which ratified it and then ceased to function altogether.[38]

On November 21, 1938, the Sudeten areas surrendered by Czechoslovakia were officially incorporated into the German Reich and the ethnic German inhabitants were proclaimed citizens of the Reich, although subject to more specific provisions on this point.[39] Guidelines for dealing with this difficult problem had been laid down by Hitler in the previous month. German citizenship was to be given only to those inhabitants of the Sudetenland and their immediate descendants who had resided there before January 1, 1910, because after that date the policies of the Habsburg archduke, Francis Ferdinand, designed to promote the cause of the Czechs in the region, had begun to take effect. Non-Germans who had moved into the Sudetenland after January 1, 1910, would have to leave the area if ordered to do so by the German government. Conversely, the Czechoslovak government would have the right to order the departure of Germans who had moved into the Czech provinces after that date. All ethnic Germans with Czech citizenship who did not receive German citizenship *ipso jure* were to have the right to opt for German citizenship, with the exception of German or Austrian citizens who had become citizens of Czechoslovakia after January 30, 1933 (when the Nazis came to power in Germany).[40]

On December 4, 1938, a plebiscite of sorts was held in the Sudeten territories. Voting rights were restricted to German citizens, who were asked to acknowledge Adolf Hitler as the liberator of the Sudetenland and to vote for candidates selected by the Nazi party to represent them in the Reichstag of Greater Germany. This election resulted in a 99.8 per cent endorsement of the policies of Hitler and sent forty-one new Reichstag deputies to Berlin.[41]

The *Gleichschaltung* of law took place soon afterward. On December 27, 1938, the Nuremberg racial laws were introduced. During the following February the entire body of Reich law officially became the law of the Sudeten territories.[42]

Laws for the territorial reorganization of the government of the Sude-

23

tenland, foreshadowed in the party reorganization of the previous October, were promulgated on March 25 and April 14, 1939. On May 1 the Reichsgau Sudetenland was made an administrative district of the Reich, and Gauleiter Henlein, until now Reichskommissar in his capacity as head of the state administration, became a Reich provincial governor (Reichsstatthalter.) The other sections of the Sudetenland which had previously been assigned to party Gaus were now officially assigned to the state governments of those districts and were thereby incorporated into provinces of the German Reich.[43]

Memel

The old Hanseatic city of Memel and its surrounding territory, part of the German Empire before 1918, was another area which the Nazis claimed for the Reich on the basis of its large proportion of ethnic German inhabitants. Placed under Allied control in 1918, the Memel territory was seized by Lithuania in 1923 and was allowed to remain under Lithuanian authority, although as a separate administrative entity. In March 1939, following a German ultimatum, Lithuania yielded the territory to Germany.[44]

The German annexation of the Memel territory was a comparatively minor episode in the turbulent months preceding the Second World War, but it had a special significance in that it was to be Hitler's last peaceful territorial acquisition.

By a law of March 23, 1939, the Memel territory was incorporated into the Greater German Reich as part of the state of Prussia and the province of East Prussia. The entire body of German and Prussian law was to go into effect May 1 subject to reservations of particular Reich or Prussian government departments. All inhabitants of the Memel territory and their descendants who had lost their German citizenship on July 30, 1924, because of the separation of this area from the Reich, were to become German citizens.

As elsewhere, the Reich Ministry of the Interior was to be the central office for the reunion of the Memel territory. Here, however, the supreme local commissar for reunion was to be the head of the administration (Oberpräsident) of East Prussia, Gauleiter Erich Koch. Dr. Ernst Neumann, the head of the Germans in Memel, was made his deputy.[45]

Danzig

On September 1, 1939, the first day of the war, another area which the Nazis claimed on the basis of its predominantly ethnic German population was annexed to the Reich. This was the city of Danzig, formerly part of the German Empire, which, since the First World War, had been a free city under the trusteeship of the League of Nations.

On the same day the Nazis annexed the city, they laid down the principle that all ethnic German citizens of Danzig were automatically to become Reich citizens. All existing laws, apart from the constitution of the free city, were to remain in force temporarily until January 1, 1940, when the entire body of Reich and Prussian law was to go into effect. Meanwhile all legislative and executive power was to be invested in the head of the state government of Danzig, a position held since August 23, 1939, by the Nazi Gauleiter of Danzig, Albert Forster.[46] On September 7 Hitler appointed Forster head of the German civil government in Danzig. The Reich minister of the interior was declared responsible for all matters dealing with the reunion of Danzig and the Reich and was authorized to issue any decrees that might be required for this purpose.[47]

The economy as well as the territory of Danzig was incorporated into the Reich. The German mark became legal currency, together with the Danzig gulden, and the Bank of Danzig was merged with the Reichsbank. On September 4 all Polish public and private property in Danzig was confiscated and declared the property of the Reich.[48]

On October 8, Hitler issued a decree making Danzig a district of a new Gau of West Prussia (later called the Reichsgau Danzig-Westpreussen) that was to be made up of former Polish territory to be annexed to the Reich, a decree that came into effect on October 26.[49]

By the time the Second World War began (in the case of Danzig by the end of the second month of that war), the main features of Hitler's intentions with respect to the ethnic German territories and their inhabitants had already been clearly established. These territories were to be incorporated into the German Reich, their ethnic German population was to be given the same favored position in the New Order as the ethnic Germans of the Old Reich, while the non-Aryan inhabitants, like those of Germany, were to be deprived of all rights and eventually removed. Meanwhile every conceivable source of opposition to Nazi control, including every suspect person, every institution, and every tradition, was to be co-ordinated, eliminated, or otherwise brought low. This intention was most strikingly demonstrated in Hitler's Austrian homeland, where he had purposefully set about destroying the very concept of an Austria and had divided the country into new state and party administrative districts. By so doing he believed he had succeeded to a great degree in destroying Austrian separatist tendencies and had made it easier to integrate the Austrian population into his Greater German Reich.

The significance of Hitler's policies toward Austria extended far beyond Austria itself, for so satisfied was he with their success that he proposed to make them the model for his future program in dealing with other Germanic or Nordic countries. In analyzing the policies he had pursued in Austria, Hitler took some pride in having profited from the example of Bismarck, who had realized in 1871 that the Bavarians would have resented being annexed to Prussia, but they had accepted incorporation into a German Reich and had subsequently become loyal and even passionate supporters of that Reich. Following the lead of Bismarck, Hitler had not allowed the Austrians to feel that they were simply being annexed to Germany in 1938, but had integrated them with the Germans of the Old Reich with absolute equality in an entirely new state structure, the Greater German Reich.

Hitler intended to adopt a similar method in dealing with the Germanic peoples of Western and Northern Europe. Instead of annexing them outright to Germany or even to a Greater German Reich, he would make them part of yet another entirely new state structure, the Germanic Reich, in which the former state of Germany would enjoy no preferential status, but merely would be the most powerful source of military and ideological strength. As the symbol of this new Germanic union, the flag of the old German Reich could not be imposed on other Germanic countries any more than the flag of Prussia could have been imposed on Bavaria in 1871. It was for this reason that Hitler had given the NSDAP, as the bearer of the concept of a Germanic union, an emblem which could serve as the symbol for all Germanic peoples and hence for the new Germanic empire: the swastika flag.[50]

CHAPTER 3

The Slavs: Czechoslovakia

Until March 1939 Hitler had justified his expansionist program on the basis of the principle of self-determination for ethnic Germans. This principle was brazenly cast aside when, on March 15, 1939, German troops occupied the Czech provinces of Bohemia and Moravia.

Hitler had done his best to provide plausible reasons for this action by mounting a propaganda campaign that the Czech provinces were in a state of anarchy and the entire Czecho-Slovak state in the process of dissolution. At the same time he had used all the political and diplomatic means at his command to foster such developments. His success in fomenting unrest in the Czech provinces had been meager, but on March 14, following German threats to turn the country over to Hungary and Poland, Slovakia declared its independence from the Czecho-Slovak union, as did the Carpatho-Ukraine, the easternmost province of the country. Dismayed by these developments, the inexperienced president of Czechoslovakia, Dr. Emil Hácha, journeyed to Berlin to take counsel with Hitler. Here he too was subjected to savage German threats; in the early morning hours of March 15 he yielded to Hitler's demand that he ask for German aid to restore order in his country.

Hitler's elaborate propagandistic and political maneuvers failed completely to convince world public opinion of the justification of the German occupation of the Czech provinces. On the contrary, by this flagrant violation of the Munich agreement and invasion of lands inhabited by a Slavic people, Hitler had demonstrated beyond all doubt that his word could not be trusted and that his ambitions went beyond securing justice and self-determination for ethnic Germans. But just what those ambitions were, how they applied to the lands of Bohemia and Moravia, and what Hitler proposed to do with the Czechs who had now come under his dominion remained to be seen.[1]

27

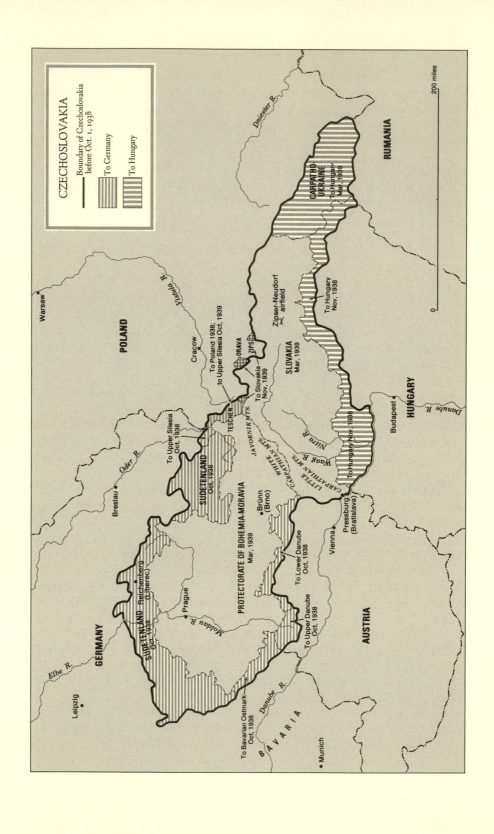

CZECHOSLOVAKIA

Boundary of Czechoslovakia
before Oct. 1, 1938

To Germany

To Hungary

200 miles

0

POLAND

Warsaw

Cracow

Breslau

Leipzig

GERMANY

Prague

Munich

B A V A R I A

AUSTRIA

Vienna

Pressburg
(Bratislava)

Budapest

HUNGARY

RUMANIA

Dniester R.

Vistula R.

Oder R.

Elbe R.

Moldau R.

Danube R.

Danube R.

Nitra R.

Waag R.

CARPATHO-
UKRAINE

To Hungary
Mar. 1939

SLOVAKIA
Mar. 1939

Zipser-Neudorf
airfield

To Hungary
Nov. 1938

To Hungary Nov. 1938

LITTLE CARPATHIAN MTS.

WHITE CARPATHIAN MTS.

JAVORNIK MTS.

ODRA

ZIPS

TESCHEN

To Poland 1938;
to Upper Silesia Oct. 1939

To Slovakia
Nov. 1939

To Upper Silesia
Oct. 1938

SUDETENLAND
Oct. 1938

Reichenberg
(Liberec)
Oct. 1938

SUDETENLAND
Oct. 1938

To Bavarian Ostmark
Oct. 1938

PROTECTORATE OF BOHEMIA-MORAVIA
Mar. 1939

Brünn
(Brno)

To Upper Danube
Oct. 1938

To Lower Danube
Oct. 1938

The Protectorate of Bohemia and Moravia

In his unpublished sequel to *Mein Kampf*, Hitler had written that the National Socialist movement "knows no Germanizing or Teutonizing . . . but only the spread of its own people. It will never see in the subjugated Czechs or Poles a national, let alone folkish, strengthening, but only the weakening of our people." [2] Hermann Rauschning reports that Hitler said in 1932 that he intended to colonize the Bohemian-Moravian basin with German peasants; the Czechs would be transplanted to Siberia or the Volhynian regions. "The Czechs must get out of Central Europe." [3] This was still his view a decade later. "The Czechs are a foreign body in the midst of the German community," he told his associates in January 1942. "There is no room both for them and for us. One of us must give way." [4]

It was one thing, however, to contemplate the eventual resettlement of Bohemia and Moravia with Germans and another to disrupt the society and economy of this productive region by the immediate application of radical racial theories, especially after the outbreak of war. Moreover, in contrast to his attitude toward the Poles and Russians, Hitler consistently acknowledged the need to preserve the productive capacity of the Czechs; [5] his policies in Bohemia and Moravia reflected this awareness. For an evaluation of Hitler's war aims, these policies also raise a number of significant questions. Was Hitler's pragmatic attitude toward the Czechs simply a matter of cynical calculation? Did it indicate a higher regard for the Czechs than for other Slavic peoples? Or, far more significantly, did it reveal that Hitler was in fact primarily a pragmatist and that his racial doctrines with respect to the Slavs, as a race, did not really have to be taken seriously? As the first predominantly Slavic land to be occupied by Hitler, the Protectorate of Bohemia and Moravia is an interesting, although not necessarily typical, test case.

In his first official decree for Bohemia and Moravia following their occupation by German troops, Hitler stated baldly that these provinces had belonged to the *Lebensraum* of the German people for a thousand years.[6] They had been torn arbitrarily from their ancient setting by force and folly, and ever since had been centers of instability and unrest. Germany could no longer tolerate the continuation of such conditions in areas vital to its peace and security. It was therefore in accordance with the laws of self-preservation that the German Reich had resolved to intervene decisively to rebuild the foundations of a reasonable order in Central Europe. "The territories of the former Czechoslovak Republic occupied by German troops in March 1939 from now on form part of the territory of the Greater German Reich," Hitler declared, "and, as the Protectorate of Bohemia and Moravia, come under its protection." All residents of German origin were declared to be German nationals and German citizens, subject to the jurisdiction of German courts. All other residents were declared to be citizens of the Protectorate and subject to the laws of that country. The autonomy and self-government which Hitler had so grandly promised President Hácha on the fateful morning of March 15 [7] was to be an autonomy exercised "in conformity with the political, military, and economic interests of the Reich." The head of the Czech government was expected to enjoy the confidence of the Führer, and the government itself was to be placed under the supervision of a German administrative authority.

To carry out this supervision and serve as his personal representative in the provinces, Hitler announced his intention to appoint a Reich protector for Bohemia and Moravia who would be "guardian of the interests of the Reich" and "assure compliance with the political instructions issued by the Führer and Reich chancellor." All members of the Czech government, all its official acts, laws, administrative measures, and judicial decisions were subject to the approval of the Reich protector. The foreign affairs of the Protectorate, its transportation systems, post and telegraph offices were to be taken over and administered directly by the German Reich. Its military security, too, was to be provided by Germany, and for this purpose the Reich was to maintain garrisons and military establishments in the Czech provinces. The Czech government for its part was to be allowed to maintain its own military units for the maintenance of domestic peace; but their organization, size, and armaments were to be determined by the German authorities. The German supervisory government was empowered to promulgate laws for the Protectorate. It could incorporate departments of the Czech government in its own administration or set up new Reich offices for special tasks. Finally, to make certain that all possible avenues of authority were covered, the German government was permitted to "take all measures necessary for the maintenance of security and order." [8]

On March 21, 1939, the territorial organization of the Nazi party was extended to Bohemia and Moravia. In contrast to the Nazi government, the Nazi party ignored altogether the frontiers of the Protectorate. The entire territory was divided into four sections, and each section was assigned for party administrative purposes to four adjacent Gaus of the Reich: the Sudetenland, the Bavarian Ostmark, and the Upper and Lower Danube.[9]

During the first four weeks of the German occupation of Bohemia and Moravia, supreme executive authority was delegated to the German army, which set up a separate administration in each of the two provinces, with headquarters at Prague and Brno (Brünn) respectively. Attached to each military commander was a chief of the civil administration (Henlein in Bohemia and the ubiquitous Bürckel in Moravia), who was responsible for all nonmilitary matters. Each military commander was also assigned a military economic staff, whose principal task was to take over the property of the Czech army and ensure the continued operation of the Czech economy.[10]

On April 16, 1939, supreme civil authority was transferred to the Reich protector, as envisaged in Hitler's proclamation of the previous month. The German civil government was to be responsible for the maintenance of law and order, the continued operation of the economy, and the fulfillment of the demands of the Reich government. Supreme military authority continued to be exercised by the local German military commander, who was responsible for the military security of the area and who remained independent of the Office of the Reich Protector. He was represented by a military plenipotentiary, who acted as liaison officer between the German civil and military administrations.[11]

To fill the important post of Reich protector, Hitler selected Constantin von Neurath, a member of an old aristocratic family from Württemberg who, since 1901, had made his career in the German foreign service. After many years as ambassador in Rome and London, Neurath became Germany's foreign minister in 1932, a post he retained under the Nazis until his displacement by Joachim von Ribbentrop in February 1938.

On learning of Neurath's appointment as Reich protector, Goebbels expressed the disgust of an old-guard party man. Everyone knew Neurath was a weakling and a sneak, he said. "But what is needed in the Protectorate is a strong hand to keep order. This man has nothing in common with us; he belongs to an entirely different world." Hitler disagreed. He believed that, on the contrary, Neurath was the ideal person for the job. "In the Anglo-Saxon world he is considered a man of distinction. The international effect of his appointment will be reassuring because people will see in it my decision not to deprive the Czechs of their racial and national life." And indeed, Neurath's appointment was evidently intended by Hitler to cover German rule in Bohemia and Moravia with a mantle of respectability, for he was known abroad as a statesman of the old school who might be expected to exercise his powers with decency and restraint.[12]

Neurath was given what appeared to be unlimited authority. He was named sole representative of the Führer, and in this capacity was to be directly responsible to him and subject to his orders only. He alone was to administer the affairs of the Reich; all branches of Reich offices in the Protectorate were subordinated to him, all relations between them and corresponding offices in the Reich were to be conducted through him.[13] Neurath, however, lacked the strength of character and will to exploit these powers or insist on exercising them, as Hitler was well aware.

At the advice of Himmler and without bothering to consult Neurath, he appointed the Sudeten German leader Karl Hermann Frank to the position of Neurath's deputy and executive director (state secretary) of the Office of the Reich Protector.[14] Frank, who had been Henlein's second in command in the Sudeten German party, was born in Karlsbad into a family deeply influenced by the idea of the pan-German nationalist Georg Schönerer and by the so-called dauphin of the Schönerer movement, Karl Hermann Wolf, after whom Frank was named. He studied for a year at the law school of the German university in Prague, but after the war failed to complete his education and worked as a poorly paid clerk in a number of business establishments. As was the case with so many semieducated and unsuccessful members of the German middle class, he was attracted to Nazism and eventually set up a bookstore specializing in Nazi literature. When the Nazi organizations in Czechoslovakia were threatened with dissolution in the early 1930s, he joined the Sudeten German party. Ambitious, shrewd, and ruthless, Frank quickly won a prominent position in the party, was elected to the Czechoslovak parliament in Prague, and as the party's deputy leader he demonstrated far more drive and initiative than Henlein. While Hitler still needed the more moderate Henlein to represent the grievances of the Sudeten Germans to foreign and particularly to British observers, he retained him as the chief agent of Nazi policy in Czechoslovakia. But he evidently recognized in Frank the qualities of a Nazi leader more to his own taste, a man fanatically dedicated to the Nazi cause and one who could get things done quickly and effectively without being excessively scrupulous about the methods he employed in achieving his objectives.[15]

Himmler obviously also found Frank to his taste. Not only did he recommend him to Hitler as deputy Reich protector, but on May 5, 1939, he appointed him senior SS and police officer in the Protectorate, a position which put him in control of the entire SS and police apparatus in the Czech provinces and which also brought him under the direct command of Himmler. Although Frank in this new position was still officially subordinate to Neurath and immediately responsible to him, he at once began to use his combination of offices to build up his personal power at Neurath's expense. In the process he received steady encouragement and support from Himmler, who saw in every increase in Frank's power an extension of his own influence in the Protectorate.[16]

A decree of September 1, 1939, removed even Neurath's nominal authority over Frank and the local German police offices. The decree began by confirming the authority of the Reich protector over all Reich offices in the Protectorate; but it then went on to say that officials of the Gestapo in the Protectorate were to be under the direct authority of the central Reich administration and that "in all political problems which concern the police, the German agencies under the jurisdiction of the Reich protector and all officials of the Protectorate of Bohemia and Moravia must comply with the directives of the central offices of the state police." As the concern of the police could be extended to all problems, this decree in effect empowered Himmler to issue orders directly to every branch of the German and Czech administrations in the Protectorate.[17]

Neurath loathed Frank, and his relations with his deputy were strained from the beginning; but he neither asserted his authority over Frank nor did he resign. At the end of the year 1939 General Johannes

Blaskowitz, who had directed the German invasion of the Czech provinces, told a friend in Berlin that Neurath gave magnificent hunting parties "but in reality served only as an 'extra.'" [18]

Under the direction of State Secretary Frank, the Office of the Reich Protector, if not the Reich protector himself, was the central agency of German rule in Bohemia and Moravia throughout the occupation. Although reorganized on several occasions, it always consisted of three main sections: (1) a central office which dealt with personnel, budget, and general problems of the German administration; (2) the offices to supervise the Czech central government, organized to correspond to Czech administration divisions; and (3) the offices to supervise Czech local government. [19]

The German officials in Bohemia and Moravia took care to emphasize, at least in the beginning, that they were merely a supervisory body and that the real government of the country was the "autonomous" Czech administration. [20] In a very significant sense this was true, for the main agents of German rule in the Protectorate, as in almost every area they were to occupy, were the local inhabitants themselves—not only the government officials, cabinet ministers, and heads of departments, but also the clerks, policemen, and rubbish collectors, the factory owners, shopkeepers, peasants, and industrial workers, and indeed anyone who in any way helped to keep the government and the economy going.

The Germans clearly recognized their dependence on such co-operation. The first order issued to the Czech people by the supreme command of the German army on March 15, 1939, required that the public administration, including the police, post office, railroads, and all state-owned enterprises, should continue to operate, and that all business life should go on as usual. "Everyone is to remain at his post and continue to work," the order stipulated. "Cessation of work will be regarded as sabotage." [21] Throughout the occupation Czech authorities were held responsibile for carrying on the government and the economy, and for performing routine administrative and police duties. For this purpose the importance to the Germans of the existence of a Czech government can hardly be overemphasized.

The government of Czechoslovakia had undergone significant changes since the Munich crisis. President Eduard Beneš had resigned on October 5, 1938. Shortly thereafter Slovakia and the Carpatho-Ukraine were conceded a quasi-independent status in a newly constituted, federally organized Czecho-Slovak Republic. In domestic affairs the Czech government in Prague remained responsible only for the Czech provinces of Bohemia and Moravia. On December 15, 1938, this government secured parliamentary approval of a law which authorized the government (the president and cabinet) to take extraordinary measures in an emergency situation and to issue decrees without consulting parliament. The government almost immediately made use of these powers, so that even before the German invasion the Czech provinces were being ruled in an authoritarian manner. After the occupation this law assumed far greater significance, for it provided the basis for the entire body of legislation promulgated by the Czech government at German dictation, and thus gave this legislation a technical legality.[22]

The appearance of legality was enhanced by the behavior of the leaders of the Czech government. The appeal by President Hácha in March 1939 for German help to restore order in his country had obviously been made under duress and fooled no one, except perhaps German public opinion. More impressive for German purposes was the fact that Hácha remained in office after the occupation, and that the membership of the first Czech cabinet formed under German rule was almost identical with that of the previous cabinet. It no longer included the ministers of foreign affairs, transportation, and national defense, whose functions had been taken over by the Germans, and the premiership had been transferred from Rudolf Beran, the head of the Agrarian party, to General Alois Eliáš, a professional soldier without previous political experience. But all other members of the government were experts in their fields, and some of them had played important roles in Czech public life. That men of this caliber were willing to enter a government under German auspices lent support to the German claim that Czech autonomy and rights of self-government had been preserved.[23]

Hácha and his ministers were neither willing nor witless collaborators. They stayed in office because they saw how much the Germans needed them, they believed this need gave them a strong bargaining position, and that this strength would enable them to do much on behalf of the Czech people. Perhaps they were indeed able to do more for their fellow countrymen than a government appointed by and entirely dependent on the Germans. The advantage to the Germans, however, of a legally constituted Czech government as an instrument for carrying out their orders was without doubt inestimably greater.

The Germans kept a tight control over the Czech government. All Czech official personnel, including the president and members of the cabinet, were subject to German approval. Every Czech administrative department was supervised by a comparable department in the office of the Reich protector and could be placed under immediate German direction or incorporated altogether in the German administrative apparatus. For the supervision of Czech local government, the Germans divided Bohemia and Moravia into administrative districts under German district commissioners (*Oberlandräte*) attached to the Office of the Reich Protector. In local as in central government they exercised absolute authority over Czech administrative personnel; they could appoint Germans to any Czech regional council or municipal office, or replace Czech with German officials.[24]

Under Neurath and Frank the staff of the German administration in the Protectorate expanded rapidly until by the autumn of 1941 it consisted of almost 10,000 German officials to supervise approximately 400,000 Czech officials. In proportion to the number of local officials, the German staff in the Protectorate was far larger than in other occupied territories, 20 times larger than in occupied France, 53 times larger than in Denmark. Moreover these figures do not take into account the 4,706 German officials who were technically employed by the "autonomous" Czech administration as of May 1940.[25]

On the fundamental question of what policy Germany should pursue in Bohemia and Moravia, there were as many views among German leaders as there were attempts to seize some share of the wealth and power of these provinces for themselves and their organizations. The Sudeten Germans, the army, Göring, Himmler, Neurath, Frank—all had short- and long-term programs which they believed should serve as guidelines for the German administration.

Göring was almost exclusively concerned with the incorporation of the Czech provinces into the German economic area and their exploitation for the German war economy.[26] Other Nazi leaders, whether out of conviction or calculation, placed their primary emphasis on the racial question.

As early as November 1937 Henlein had informed Hitler that the Sudeten German party "desires nothing more ardently than the incorporation of the Sudeten German territory, nay of the whole Bohemian, Moravian, and Silesian areas within the Reich." And by 1938 the Sudeten German party was calling for the complete Germanization of the Czech lands. "The long-range aim must be to smash Czech national consciousness, settlement of hitherto Czech linguistic territory by Germans, conducting (also partly through resettlement) the Czech part of the nation into an indissoluble spiritual and physical connection with Germany."[27]

Himmler, the most ardent exponent of Hitler's colonization plans for Eastern Europe, proposed in May 1939 that the Germans of the South Tyrol, who were to be evacuated from this region in accordance with Hitler's promises to Mussolini, should be resettled in Bohemia and Moravia "which must once again become entirely and completely German." In October Himmler was put in charge of the entire German resettlement program, but by that time the Germans had conquered Poland, which, fortunately for the Czechs, became the prime target of Himmler's colonizing endeavors.[28]

Not to be outdone by party leaders, General of the Infantry Erich Friderici, the representative of the Wehrmacht in the Office of the Reich Protector, prepared a memorandum shortly before the outbreak of the war in which he argued that the Germans should settle the Czech question once and for all now that they were undisputed masters of Central Europe. "There is only one solution," he said. "To dissolve this Czech community spatially and spiritually, and for this purpose to expel in the first place its leading stratum from the area of Bohemia and Moravia."

As the radical measure of physical extermination was not feasible under ordinary circumstances, Friderici proposed that Czech intellectuals be encouraged to emigrate, either to distant continents or to Germany itself, where they could be absorbed into the German community. The mass of the Czech population, the workers and peasants, should be won over to Germanization by raising their living standards and by a thorough program of re-education. If these policies were pursued vigorously,

> it should be possible in the foreseeable future, without severe shocks or international complications, to link the Bohemian-Moravian area organically with Greater Germany for all time. Thus the healing of the thousand-year-old wound would not take place by covering it over with a thin skin of Germanization, whereby the pus in the wound would continue to fester and break out again when opportunity offers, but by a final healing from within after the pernicious bodies have been removed permanently.[29]

Hitler himself had always opposed a program of Germanization of the Czechs and Poles on the ground that the assimilation of inferior Slavic races could only lead to the bastardization and deterioration of the superior German race. As we have seen, his own program called for the expulsion of the Czechs from Central Europe and their replacement by Germans. But in marked contrast to his rule in Poland and Russia, he laid down no guidelines for carrying out radical racial measures in Bohemia and Moravia. Indeed, his entire attitude toward the Czechs was marked by a curious and quite unusual indecisiveness which was reflected in the conduct of his administrators. It was not until student demonstrations against German rule in the autumn of 1939 had produced a situation of potential crisis that Hitler provided his representatives in the Protectorate with specific directives for the conduct of German policy in the immediate future.

Hitler responded to the crisis situation itself with the only methods he understood for dealing with popular unrest: force and terror. At his orders nine students identified as ringleaders were shot, twenty-five hundred were sent to concentration camps, and the Czech universities and higher technical schools in Prague and Brno were closed.[30]

In the first part of December, after the disturbances in the Protectorate had been brought under control, Hitler summoned Neurath to Berlin and at last provided him with definite instructions. Every sign of Czech defiance was to be crushed at once with the harshest measures, he said. Otherwise, however, the German authorities were to avoid any action likely to provoke mass unrest. The existing system of governing through the Czech administration was to be preserved, if only because there were not enough German officials available for direct administration. There were to be no large-scale resettlements of the Czech provinces by Germans; Germanization of the new German east had precedence, and there were scarcely enough German settlers available for that project.[31]

The apparent reluctance of the German administration in the Protectorate to initiate radical racial policies against the Czechs provoked bitter criticism on the part of Nazi extremists, who knew nothing of Hitler's directives. They realized, or some of them did, that it would hardly be practical to deport the entire Czech population during wartime, but they saw no reason why Czechs should continue to exercise any kind of political authority, and they wanted to abolish both the Czech government and the German supervisory administration.

Particularly active in this kind of agitation were local Nazi party leaders, among them the familiar figure of Konrad Henlein, Gauleiter of the Sudetenland, whose party administrative district (Gau) had been extended to include the greater part of northern Bohemia and the city of Prague. Embittered by not having been appointed to high political office in the Protectorate, he now tried to recoup his political fortunes through the party administration. Equally prominent, and considerably more able, was Dr. Hugo Jury, Gauleiter of the Lower Danube, whose Gau had been extended to include a large part of Moravia and the city of Brno. Both men advocated the transfer of political authority from the government of the Protectorate to party leaders, and the reorganization of administrative boundaries to correspond with party district boundaries "so as to destroy for all time the fiction of the union of the 'historic' lands of Bohemia and Moravia." [32]

In response to pressures of this kind and in defense of their own positions, Neurath and Frank prepared long memoranda for Hitler in August 1940. As the arguments in the memoranda were almost identical, it is possible, as Neurath contended at Nuremberg, that Frank, or officials in Frank's office, prepared both of them. Neurath nevertheless endorsed them and sent them under his signature to Hans Lammers in the Reich Chancellery with the request that they be forwarded to Hitler and that a date be arranged for a personal conference for himself and State Secretary Frank. He had heard, Neurath said, that individual party and other offices intended to submit proposals for dividing the Protectorate and he wanted the Führer to be informed of the opinions of his personal representatives before all sorts of plans were suggested to him by other people.[33]

Neurath's memorandum was clearly intended to fit in with Hitler's own views, and began by emphasizing that German policy in the Protectorate had to be considered from both a political and racial point of view. "Politically the only possible goal can be: complete incorporation into the Greater German Reich; racially: populating the area with Germans." The political goal, Neurath assured the Führer, was well on the way to fulfillment under the present system of government. Peasants and industrial workers were on the whole co-operating loyally and making substantial contributions to the German war economy; the government machinery was with few exceptions operating satisfactorily. "Even by the most stringent standards it can therefore be said that this country . . . has fulfilled its duties as part of the Greater German Reich." This did not mean that the Czechs had abandoned their desire for independence or that they regarded the Germans as anything but tiresome intruders. They were co-operating primarily because they feared the results of disobedience, and their attitude of fundamental hostility would continue for a long time to come. Given this situation, how could the racial goal of populating the area with Germans be fulfilled as rapidly and as thoroughly as possible?

The most radical and theoretically the most perfect solution would be the expulsion of all Czechs and the settlement of the area with Germans, but this would not be feasible in the foreseeable future because there were not enough Germans available. Nor would it be in the interests of the Reich to leave this important industrial and agricultural region depopulated for a long period of time. To achieve the desired racial goal, however, the radical measure of expelling the entire Czech population was in no way necessary, for during the thousand years of their association with the Germans, the Czechs themselves had become predominantly Germanic. The objective of the German policy, then, should not be to expel these racially valuable elements but to regain them for the Germanic community. This was a difficult task that would require many years, during which time racially undesirable elements and unregenerate opponents of Germanism could be expelled from the area.

Because of the difficulty of the task and the consequent need for consistency and steadiness of purpose, Neurath believed it could be carried out best by a centralized administration under the immediate direction of the Führer. For this reason both he and Frank urgently recommended that the geographic unity of the Protectorate and the present system of government be maintained.[34]

The arguments of Neurath and Frank convinced Hitler. Early in October 1940 he summoned both men to a conference in Berlin, where, after considering the various political alternatives available to Germany, he decided in favor of the Neurath-Frank plan. Bohemia and Moravia were to be Germanized by Germanizing the Czechs; all racially undesirable or anti-German elements were to be eliminated (*sei auszumerzen*). The program of Germanization was to be carried out by the Office of the Reich Protector, which was to be maintained in its present form in the interests of a uniform German policy. To emphasize this point, Hitler instructed Lammers to quash all proposals for either administrative or geographic changes in the Protectorate.[35]

Through their representations to Hitler, Neurath and Frank had temporarily beaten back all attacks on their government. Neurath's chief purpose in advocating a long-term program of Germanization, apart from staying in office, may have been to sidetrack the whole issue. This was his defense at Nuremberg, and contemporary evidence suggests that he did his best to avoid taking action on the racial question.[36] Frank, however, was serious about Germanization. His great worry in the past had been that other Nazi officials would supersede him in this vital sphere of activity. "What has remained open to question," he complained to Himmler in the previous June, "is who is to become the instrument of the new settlement." [37]

This question was answered by Hitler's decision of October 1940, which Frank evidently regarded not only as a victory over rivals in the Nazi government and party, but as a victory over Neurath as well. On October 9 he took it upon himself to inform the higher officials in the Reich protector's office of the results of the conference with Hitler.[38] Three days later he saw Hitler again, this time without Neurath. On this occasion Hitler confirmed his earlier decision to maintain the present system of government, including the Czech administration, at least for the duration of the war. "On the other hand," he said, "preparations are to be made for the prospective Germanization of the area and its inhabitants." [39]

Frank was already busy with such preparations. To put an end to the haphazard nature of the German acquisition of Czech land, he had proposed to Himmler's Central Office for Race and Resettlement (RuSHA) that Germany build corridors of German settlement which would leave the Czechs isolated and cut off from each other. The Germans should then go to work on these racial islands, compile a register of racially unacceptable elements—probably about half the population—and deport them to areas to be decided by the Führer. The remaining Czechs were to be Germanized by all practical means.[40]

To lay the groundwork for this undertaking, Frank as early as May 1939 had sequestered the Czech Land Office, which had been in charge of land reform programs under the Czech republic and possessed detailed records of land ownership. The Czech staff was ousted and replaced by a German staff under SS Oberführer Curt von Gottberg, who proved to be an unfortunate choice. His domineering manner and crude behavior alienated even his SS supporters, and his position was weakened further when it was discovered that he had misappropriated over one million marks of Land Office funds. Altogether his activities aroused such resentment that by the end of the year Neurath and his supporters succeeded in having him removed and replaced by an appointee of their own, Theodor Gross, the head of the agricultural section of the Reich protector's office, who was instructed to curtail the Land Office's operations. "This measure," Frank informed Himmler on December 19, "delivers the land policy of the Protectorate definitively into the hands of the bureaucracy and removes it from the control of the SS." After his conference with Hitler in October 1940, however, Frank evidently decided the time had come to restore the Land Office to the control of a reliable SS man, but on this issue Neurath showed quite unusual firmness. Gross was not removed until Neurath himself left the Protectorate a full year later.[41]

Because Hitler had specifically forbidden all activities likely to provoke mass unrest, Frank saw that it would be impossible to push his resettlement projects. But the Führer had encouraged him to make preparations for Germanization, and one essential step in this process could be undertaken safely if it were done without arousing suspicion. This was the compilation of a racial register of every member of the population to determine which persons were suitable for Germanization and which should be eliminated or deported when the final solution of the Czech problem took place.[42] For this project Frank received vigorous support from Himmler, who in October 1940 ordered the preparation of a special racial questionnaire for Bohemia and Moravia disguised as a health examination. Besides such routine items as weight, height, vision, the questionnaire asked for data considered crucial for the determination of race: size and shape of the body, color of the eyes, hair, and skin, and the shape of the skull. Two photographs of each examinee were to be included with each completed form, one frontal, the other in profile. On the basis of the data which would be provided by this questionnaire, Himmler confidently predicted that his racial experts would be able for the first time to compile a systematic and accurate "racial inventory" of Bohemia and Moravia.[43]

A preliminary racial survey undertaken shortly afterward yielded the surprising result that the population of Bohemia and Moravia was considerably more Germanic than that of the Sudeten area, whose predominantly Germanic quality had been trumpeted so loudly by the Nazis prior to the Munich crisis. Whereas in Bohemia and Moravia 45 per cent of the population was classified as predominantly Nordic, 40 per cent the product of mixed marriages with predominantly eastern racial characteristics, and 15 per cent racially alien, the corresponding figures in the Sudetenland were 25, 55, and 20 per cent. Nazi authorities explained the poor racial quality of the Sudeten territories by the fact that "for a century they had received no infusion of healthy blood from the German mother country, while during this same period they had lost much valuable blood as the result of emigration." [44]

The results of the racial survey confirmed Frank's belief that approximately one-half of the Czech population of Bohemia and Moravia were suitable for Germanization, and he put forward various plans for winning this group over to a proper racial point of view. Suitable Czechs, especially unmarried men of talent, were to be encouraged to work in Germany, where their assimilation could be brought about by natural means. In the Protectorate proper such persons should be given a privileged status, they should be maneuvered into the best jobs, taxes should be manipulated for their benefit, and they should be treated with special favor by the German authorities. The entire campaign should be con-

40

ducted in such a manner that the Czechs should come to regard acceptance in the Germanic community as the highest possible honor.[45]

On October 29, 1940, Frank secured the passage of a marriage law designed to promote marriages between Germans and racially suitable Czechs. Both parties were obliged to sign certificates expressing willingness to allow their children to be educated in German schools and to be brought up as Germans. A secret memorandum sent out to German officials in the Protectorate explained that "in each case it is to be shown whether, in view of the general situation, it can be assumed that the Czech party, by marrying a German national, will be permanently won for Germanism."[46]

Frank realized that there would always be racially valuable Czechs who would refuse to accept Germanization. These would be persons of principle, and on the whole far higher types than those who became Germans for reasons of expediency. Such persons would have to be killed to prevent them from assuming the leadership of anti-German movements, but their children should be saved and brought up as Germans. As for the other half of the population, the people unsuitable for Germanization, they would in the course of time have to be "weakened, eliminated, and moved out of the country by every conceivable means," in accordance with the orders of the Führer.[47]

Although Nazi racial programs were supposed to be a closely guarded secret, many German officials took little trouble to disguise their intentions. Neurath even had to issue an order forbidding them to discuss these programs in public.[48] German indiscretions gave new impetus to the already strong Czech fear and dislike of German rule. The comparative calm which had persisted throughout most of 1940 gave way to growing unrest in the following year, which increased significantly after the German attack on Russia. Czechs in general saw renewed reason to hope that Germany might yet be defeated in the war; and Czech Communists, long skilled in underground operations, joined forces with existing opposition groups. German police officials reported more numerous cases of sabotage, terrorist activity, and willful destruction of the harvest, which they believed could only be the work of a large-scale and well-organized resistance movement.[49]

Alarmed by reports about the deteriorating situation in the Protectorate, Hitler summoned Neurath to his headquarters on September 23, 1941, and accused him of excessive leniency toward the Czechs. To restore order in Bohemia and Moravia harsher measures were required, and for his purpose he was sending Reinhard Heydrich to Prague as acting Reich protector. Neurath was to retain the title of Reich protector —Hitler may have thought his name was still politically useful—but he was to take a leave of absence "for reasons of health." Neurath kept this title until August 1943, but never again resumed his official functions in the Protectorate.[50]

SS Obergruppenführer Reinhard Heydrich was the deputy director of the Central Office for Reich Security (RSHA) and second only to Himmler in the hierarchy of the dreaded Nazi secret police. There has been a good deal of speculation about why Heydrich allowed himself to be transferred from the center of the Nazi power structure to the provincial post of Prague. It has been suggested that he wished to escape vassalage to Himmler by taking a position which gave him direct access to Hitler. It is also possible, if the story was true that Heydrich had a Jewish grandmother,[51] that jealous rivals found out about it and that simple blackmail played a part in his move to Prague. In fact, however, there was nothing very mysterious about Heydrich's acceptance of the Prague appointment. His colleagues and rivals suspected that, with his burning ambition, he aspired to nothing less than supreme power in the Third Reich, and that he regarded the position in the Protectorate as a means of proving himself a suitable successor to the Führer. In this they were almost certainly correct. Heydrich obviously saw in Bohemia and Moravia an admirable opportunity to demonstrate his talents not only as a grand inquisitor but as an administrator and political leader. After going to Prague, moreover, he took care to keep in close and constant contact with the power centers of the Reich.

On September 27, 1941, Heydrich was officially installed in Prague as acting Reich protector. Frank, although deeply disappointed at not having been offered the post himself, stayed on as executive director of the Office of the Reich Protector and senior SS and police officer.[52]

Three days after taking office, Heydrich informed German leaders in the Protectorate of Hitler's most recent directives for the conduct of German policy. These remained the same as before: The ultimate aim was to recover Bohemia and Moravia for Germany, racially and territorially; the immediate tasks were to preserve order and ensure maximum economic production. To this end the native population was to be treated firmly and all opposition was to be ruthlessly suppressed.[53]

In setting forth his own views in this and subsequent conferences, Heydrich sounded a new note in demanding greater self-discipline from the Germans. Under no circumstances should they allow the Czechs to suspect their long-range aims, so as not to drive them to desperate actions or open revolt; in their daily relationships with the native population they should avoid all behavior likely to arouse unnecessary hostility. To calm the nerves of the Czechs and make certain that they would continue to work for the Germans, the policy of firmness was to be tempered by concessions and incentives. As a first step, Heydrich proposed to increase the fat rations for Czech workers sufficiently so that the threat of lowering them again would have a powerful coercive effect. German policy in general was to be conducted with greater finesse, the propaganda line should be more subtle, more attention should be paid to psychological factors in dealing with national questions. Instead of suppressing the Czech veneration for King Wenceslas, for example, the

Germans should divert it to their own purposes by pointing out that his greatness lay in his realization that the existence of the Czechs depended on their living in harmony with the Germans.

While indulging in these subterfuges in carrying out their immediate tasks in the Protectorate, German authorities should at all times keep the long-term aims firmly in mind and make all possible preparations for the final solution of the racial problem. The compilation of the racial register was to continue, but on the basis of more stringent standards of selection and better disguised to conceal its real purpose. Similarly the Land Office, which already managed Czech estates confiscated by the Germans, should go on with its classification of all land on a racial basis and draw up plans for systematic resettlement until complete Germanization had been achieved.

Certain steps in the Germanization program were to be undertaken immediately. The evacuation of Jews was to be carried out at regular intervals until all Jews had been removed from the Protectorate. Under no circumstances was anything to leak out to the public about this plan until the actual evacuations had taken place.

Frank's project of sending young Czechs capable of Germanization to work in Germany was to go on; but instead of keeping this program on a voluntary basis Heydrich intended to use the Czech government's compulsory labor service program (the equivalent of the German *Arbeitsdienst*) for this purpose. Czechs sent to Germany were to be persuaded to remain there permanently. Their places in the economy of Bohemia and Moravia would be taken by Germans from the Reich.

Heydrich attached particular importance to the problem of education, which should be removed from Czech control and made to serve the interests of Germanization. The Czech universities and higher technical schools, closed for three years in November 1939, were never to be reopened. Czechs suitable for Germanization who desired a higher education should be sent to Germany for that purpose, a procedure which would contribute to the Germanization of Czech intellectuals. In the Czech schools the main problem was the teachers, who constituted a veritable training corps for opposition. "We must obviously smash them, and at the same time abolish Czech upper schools," Heydrich said. To remove Czech children from the pernicious influence of their teachers, they would have to be organized outside the schools, perhaps in athletic societies under German leadership.

Older Czechs would not be subject to ordinary educational influences and could probably never be won over to a reliable pro-German attitude in any case. In dealing with them the Germans could only attempt to neutralize them politically by turning their attention to religion, the quest for material advantages, or other nonpolitical matters. To deprive the Czechs of a political organization or rallying point of any kind, the authority of the Czech government should be steadily undermined. However a well-functioning Czech administration was to be preserved as long as the Germans needed it. Meanwhile Czech government organizations, administrative offices, and laws were to be brought as closely into line with those of Germany as possible.

The ultimate goals of German policy were firm, Heydrich said, but he impressed upon his staff the need to be practical in attempting to realize them. If a particular plan did not work, then it just would not work and it would be necessary to try some other method.[54]

Heydrich's actual policies in the Protectorate followed closely his ideas on the subject. There was never any doubt about his intention to deal firmly with the Czechs. On the day after his arrival in Prague (September 27) he proclaimed a state of emergency, put a large part of the country under martial law, introduced a curfew, and transferred jurisdiction on political cases to *Standgerichte* (drumhead courts) where persons accused of treason could be tried immediately and condemned without further legal formality. Alois Eliáš, the Czech prime minister, was arrested, accused of high treason, and later executed. The state of emergency lasted until January 3, 1942, during which time some 10,000 persons were arrested, 1,134 handed over to the Gestapo, and 394 executed.[55] These measures effectively put an end to large-scale, organized Czech resistance during the period of Heydrich's administration.[56]

Ruthless repression was accompanied by carrot and stick tactics, or what Czechs in exile called a policy of "bullying, blackmail, and bribery." Seeing in the Czech intelligentsia his most dangerous and uncompromising opponents, Heydrich sought to isolate this group from the rest of the population and concentrated his efforts on the workers and peasants. On a broad scale he introduced social welfare programs that had won the Nazis such favor at home. On October 28 he increased the fat ration for two million industrial workers, two hundred thousand pairs of shoes were distributed to armament workers, wages were raised significantly. The peasants benefited from a rationalized agricultural program and higher food prices. At his offices in the Czernin palace Heydrich received deputations of workers and peasants, listened patiently to their complaints, and treated them with respect. The result of these policies was that production was maintained at a satisfactory level, the industrial peace was undisturbed by strikes, and acts of sabotage declined so as to be only a minor irritation.[57]

Heydrich also carried out his plan to undermine the authority of the Czech government in order to eliminate this last bastion of Czech political life as a potential focal point for political action. It was not a particularly difficult task. Various members of the Czech government, including the prime minister, Alois Eliáš, were involved in the anti-Nazi underground, but the Czech man-in-the-street saw only that his government appeared to be doing nothing more than administering the country in the German interest. Throughout the occupation it had never taken a strong public stand against any German measure, and even the arrest of Eliáš failed to produce a dramatic gesture of protest. The cabinet met to

44

consider the possibility of mass resignation, but by a majority of four decided to remain in office to prevent the appointment of a ministry of Quislings. The decision of the Czech cabinet suited Heydrich's purposes admirably. "The policy line in all measures," he informed Bormann on November 6, 1941, "is to pretend that there is autonomy, but simultaneously to liquidate this autonomy from within. We must demand that the Czechs take those measures which will arouse indignation while we adopt measures which are popular." [58]

The decision of the Czech ministers to remain in office was a vain sacrifice. Hardly had they served their purpose as a partial cover for Germany's ruthless policies during the state of emergency than Heydrich highhandedly dismissed most of them, reorganized the Czech cabinet offices to correspond with ministries of the Reich, abolished the post of prime minister, and put an end to the operation of the Czech cabinet as a collective policy-making body. On January 19, 1942, a new cabinet was formed in which an actual Reich German, Dr. Walter Bertsch, became minister of economics and labor, and Colonel Emanuel Moravec, one of the few Czech leaders to co-operate actively with the Germans, was made minister of education and head of a new Department (later Ministry) of Public Enlightenment. In each Czech ministry the German head of the corresponding department in the Office of the Reich Protector was installed as deputy director. [59]

While endeavoring to co-ordinate German and Czech political and administrative organizations and procedures, Heydrich took similar steps in the field of law. At his instigation the Czech government issued a decree on April 16, 1942, providing that the entire body of Czech criminal law be adapted to that of the Reich. [60]

In May 1942 Heydrich's powers in the Protectorate were reconfirmed and extended to permit him to carry out a radical reorganization of the German administration. Since the establishment of the Protectorate government there had been two parallel bodies of officials, Czech and German, most of whom performed identical functions. Heydrich now eliminated most of the German offices, especially those involved in local government, and assigned their functions to Czech administrative agencies which were in any case either tightly controlled or actually under the direction of the Germans. The Czech administration now received the name *Reichsauftragsverwaltung* (an administration by mandate of the Reich), and a large number of officials in the German administration, desperately needed in other parts of the Nazi empire, were made available for duty elsewhere. By the end of 1942 the number of German administrators in the Protectorate had been cut from almost 10,000 to 738, the number of German supervisors of other Czech administrative agencies from 4,706 to 1,146. The size of the German army and police forces remained approximately the same. [61]

Meanwhile Heydrich consistently pursued Germany's l[ong-range] goals. New methods were introduced in compiling the all-imp[ortant] cial register. Questionnaires and medical examinations were supplemented by an X-ray examination disguised as a massive antituberculosis campaign to "provide scientific data needed for subsequent Germanization," presumably evidence about body structure. In March 1942 Heydrich issued decrees requiring all inhabitants of Bohemia and Moravia to have a nationality identity card, which could only be obtained by producing documents establishing family background, national origin, and other pertinent information about each applicant. Thus the Czechs themselves were forced to aid in the process of racial classification.[62]

Fresh encouragement was given to the activities of the Land Office in confiscating property of "enemies of the Reich" and in planning future resettlement programs. As head of the office, Theodor Gross, the appointee of Neurath, was replaced a few days after Heydrich's arrival by a Heydrich man. Two major resettlement programs were approved and launched, though on a very limited scale. The plan was to build a solid belt of German farms which would link Prague with the German border, and a similar belt along the Slovakian border to separate Czech from Slovak territory permanently.[63]

Heydrich followed up his ideas about sending Czechs to Germany for purposes of Germanization by forcing the Czech government to issue a decree on December 18, 1941, providing that all single persons could be called up for work in the Reich. In May of the following year the Czech government issued a second decree extending the possibility of work in the Reich to all citizens.[64]

In the field of education, on which Heydrich laid such stress, Emanuel Moravec, installed by Heydrich as Czech minister of education, soon proved his value to the Germans. Until January 1942 they had made little progress in breaking down the Czech educational system. When Moravec took over the Czech Ministry of Education, it was described by a German-controlled Czech newspaper as "the strongest bastion of Benešism." Moravec began at once to "clean up" the Czech school system and to eradicate what he called "the last vestiges of the liberal democratic ideal of universal education." Henceforth Czech standards were to be based on the National Socialist ideal of selective education for gifted children only. This rejection of the principle of universal education served two purposes: It supplied an excuse to close large numbers of Czech schools at all levels and to increase the number of German schools, which were fully integrated into the school system of the Reich.

Some time later Hitler issued instructions that special efforts should be made to train Czechs capable of Germanization at German universities. Upon completion of their studies these students should be encouraged to remain in the Reich, while German students should go to the Protectorate. As a member of Himmler's Germanization office defined the program, "The whole complex is an attempt which at present still keeps within narrow limits and aims at preparing the Germanization of the intellectual class." [65]

In May 1942 the German administration began to carry out Heydrich's plan to separate Czech children from their teachers by putting them into special training camps under German control. By Czech government decrees of May 28 and 30, all non-Jewish Czech children between the ages of ten and eighteen, male and female, were declared subject to duty in compulsory youth service organizations, which were to supplement school education by "physical, mental and moral education." A little over a year later Göring's *Essener Nationalzeitung* could report that "over a million Czech boys and girls are being systematically educated in German camps according to German views with the object of bringing about a change in the attitude of Czech youth." [66]

The Nazi leadership in Berlin was enthusiastic about the effectiveness of Heydrich's administration. Heydrich had mastered the crisis there with ease, Goebbels wrote in his diary, and he was winning over the rank and file by popular measures such as the complete elimination of the black market. The intelligentsia remained hostile, but "the danger to German security from Czech elements in the Protectorate has been completely eliminated." [67]

Heydrich's success, or apparent success, proved to be his undoing. The British government and the Czech government in exile were observing with increasing uneasiness the effectiveness of Heydrich's policies, the crushing of the underground, and the apparent decline in the Czech will to resist. To reactivate the opposition and at the same time strike a blow at Nazi prestige, they resolved to attempt the assassination of Heydrich, an action which would be certain to provoke brutal Nazi reprisals and once again expose the true nature of German rule. The chances that such an attempt might succeed were good, for Heydrich, whether out of vanity, fatalism, or genuine confidence in the success of his pacification efforts, took almost no precautions about his personal security. He walked unescorted through the streets of Prague, and drove each day from his residence outside the city to his office in the Czernin palace along a fixed route in an open car driven by one chauffeur-guard.

There was a good deal of controversy among Czech and British leaders about the assassination plot, for they were well aware that they would be exposing the Czech population to the risk of extreme Nazi reprisals, and it is uncertain who was ultimately responsible for the decision to go ahead with the project. The decision was made, however, and in December 1941 Czech parachutists trained in Britain were dropped on Czech territory. After numerous difficulties and delays they made their way to Prague. Here they observed Heydrich's movements and his daily drive through the city to his office. On May 27, 1942, two of them took their stations at a sharp bend in the road where Heydrich's car habitually slowed down. As the car approached, the first assassin raised his gun to fire, but the gun failed to go off and Heydrich passed by unharmed. The second assassin, however, still had time to hurl a grenade at Heydrich's retreating car, and succeeded in blowing a hole in the back of the vehicle. Heydrich and his bodyguard-chauffeur leaped out, firing at the assassins as they fled on bicycles, their mission apparently a failure. But splinters from the explosion had entered Heydrich's back, and soon afterward he collapsed on the pavement. He died on June 4, one week later.[68]

The assassination of Heydrich produced exactly the reaction the British and the Czech government in exile had anticipated: ruthless Nazi reprisals. Hitler decided to use this occasion to teach the Czechs—and everyone else—what opposition to German domination could mean. Immediately after the attack on Heydrich he gave orders to Frank that "as a measure of atonement, ten thousand suspect Czechs, or people who have been guilty of anything political in the past, are to be arrested, or if already detained, shot in concentration camps." This was followed by an order from Himmler: "Among the ten thousand hostages which are to be seized, the entire Czech opposition intelligentsia is to be arrested first of all. The hundred most important opponents from this Czech intelligentsia are to be shot this very night." [69]

Frank was unable to carry out these orders to the letter, but he did his best. He immediately proclaimed a state of emergency, the assassins and their accomplices were hunted down and massacred, there was a mass roundup of all persons suspected of any connection with the event. During the next thirty-seven days 3,188 Czechs were arrested, 1,357 sentenced to death by German courts-martial and shot. The villages of Lidice (ninety-five houses) and Ležáky (eight houses), which were suspected of harboring the assassins, were leveled, the male inhabitants shot, the women and children sent to concentration camps from which children suitable for Germanization were later removed and sent to Himmler's re-education orphanages in the Reich.[70]

Hitler informed his associates that his primary objective in demanding such harsh measures was the restoration of order in a country which contained two of Germany's most important armaments factories. The Czechs were industrious and intelligent workers, and for the time being Germany needed them badly. To keep them in line they should be so filled with terror that they would never again dare to lift a finger against the German authorities. During the memorial service for Heydrich in Berlin, Hitler told President Hácha and members of his government that further acts prejudicial to the interests of the Reich would result in the deportation of the entire Czech population. Hácha's reaction convinced Hitler that the threat had worked and that it had much to do with the fact that after Heydrich's death the Czech government continued to carry out its tasks "in a manner that can only be described as 100 per cent pro-German." [71]

On July 3, 1942, the state of emergency was lifted, and by September the new acting Reich protector, SS Obergruppenführer and General of the Police Kurt Daluege, could report to the Führer that peace and order had been re-established, the armaments industry was working at full capacity, and the autumn harvest was secure. "The continuation of our previous policy proved to be correct," the report stated. "The ruthless measures, the individual political actions, the state of mind we artificially induced, and our systematic screwing-up of Czech nervous tension —all this led to a steady increase of terror which went so far as rumors that the entire population was going to be wiped out." [72]

The appointment of Daluege to succeed Heydrich was a blow to Karl Hermann Frank, who informed Hitler that he regarded himself as the guarantor of the political line of the Führer and the SS in the Protectorate. Unlike Heydrich, however, Daluege remained more concerned with his position in central Reich offices than with affairs in the Protectorate. In a short time Frank found that his personal authority was even greater than it had been in the days of Neurath.[73]

In August 1943 this authority was given a solid legal basis. Dr. Wilhelm Frick, whose position as Reich minister of the interior was being taken over by Himmler, was appointed to succeed Neurath as Reich protector, and Daluege was relieved of his duties as his stand-in. These personnel changes were accompanied by an administrative reorganization. A decree of August 29 transformed the Office of the Reich Protector into the German Ministry of State for Bohemia and Moravia, which was no longer to be under the direction of a state secretary but a minister of state with the rank of Reich minister. The Reich protector became a figurehead and the real power transferred to the minister of state, who was entrusted with "the affairs of government relating to safeguarding the interests of the Reich in the Protectorate." All German administrative officials and liaison officers of Reich organizations in the Protectorate were accredited to him. The August 29 decree clearly established the minister of state as the chief Reich authority in the Protectorate. With that Frank's ambitions were at last fulfilled, for it was he who was appointed to this position.[74]

The changes in leadership and organization in the German government in the Protectorate after the death of Heydrich did not make for any significant changes in German policy. By now all efforts had been abandoned even to disguise the fact that Germany intended to make Bohemia and Moravia an integral part of the Reich. On October 18, 1942, Frank had announced in a public speech in Prague that Hitler's decree of March 16, 1939, had meant nothing less than the constitutional reincorporation of these areas into the Reich. The task that remained was "the complete mental and spiritual reconquest of Bohemia and Moravia and its people for the Reich idea." [75]

In 1943 the German government published a handsome book about the Protectorate which was dedicated to all those who had sacrificed their blood for the German cause in this area over the centuries—a sacrifice crowned by the death of Heydrich "whose brief but immortal endeavors guarantee that the flag of the Reich will wave over the Prague castle for all eternity." In a brief introduction Frank stated that the purpose of the book was to explain to the inhabitants of both the Old Reich and the Protectorate the age-old connection of these areas with each other. The better this was understood the more obvious would become the right of the Reich to reincorporate the Bohemian-Moravian area into its exclusive sphere of political responsibility. Walter Bertsch, the German minister of economics and labor in the Czech government, was equally frank in the chapter he contributed to the volume. "That the lands of Bohemia and Moravia are part of the *Lebensraum* of the German Reich," he said, "has been established without the shadow of a doubt by their geographical position, their historical development, and by the political decisions of the past few years." [76]

What the Germans did not reveal was the radical nature of their plans for the final solution of the Czech problem. Still top secret were such items as Himmler's order for Germanizing racially valuable Czech children whose fathers or parents had been executed as members of the resistance movement. "We will not show our hand prematurely," said the deputy Gauleiter for the Lower Danube, "but in two or three years perhaps we will see to it that we employ the harshest and most public kind of brutality in taking care of the Czechs." [77]

Yet by their actions the Nazis revealed clearly enough their more sinister intentions. Although resettlement projects were never carried out on so vast a scale as in Poland, they were nevertheless sufficiently extensive to allow the Czechs to perceive the pattern and purpose of German expropriations. In February 1943 Frank announced publicly that almost five thousand German resettlers had been installed in the Protectorate. Another thirteen hundred appear to have been moved there by the end of September 1944, at which time, incredible as it seems in view of the German military situation, resettlements of German peasant families were still being carried out.[78]

Great as were the sufferings of the Slavs in the Protectorate, the chief victims of Nazi racial theories and the most obvious examples of the radical nature of their racial policies were the Jews. In March 1939 there were 118,310 Jews in Bohemia and Moravia, many of them refugees from Germany, Austria, and the Sudetenland. Large numbers of Jews left the Czech provinces after the Germans moved in, an emigration which the German authorities did their best to encourage. By October 1939, according to a German census based on a racial rather than religious definition of Jewishness, 90,847 Jews remained in the Protectorate, of whom 9,828 were not Jews by religion.[79]

The first German anti-Semitic legislation in the Protectorate was primarily economic. A German decree of June 21, 1939, defined the term *Jew* in accordance with the Nuremberg laws of 1935 and ordered the registration of all Jewish property. Then came a series of laws from September 14, 1940, through 1941 to eliminate Jews from the economy.

Each law extended the range of economic prohibition so that in the end there was almost nothing Jews were permitted to do legally except manual labor under official supervision. In every case German authorities were allowed to make exceptions to permit the employment of Jews whose special skills were still essential to the economy.[80]

To encourage Jews to leave the Protectorate, the Germans established a Central Office for Jewish Emigration in July 1939, whose functions were extended in March of the following year to include the supervision of all Jews and Jewish organizations. Jewish communities were assigned the task of aiding all Jews to emigrate, and were empowered to levy contributions on other Jews to support this activity.[81]

In order not to bear sole responsibility for the campaign against the Jews, the Germans brought pressure to bear on the Czech government to pass anti-Semitic legislation of its own. The Czech ministers made some effort to resist. Their law of July 4, 1939, restricting Jewish participation in certain professions, followed the Nazi practice of defining Jews in racial rather than religious terms, but they succeeded in delaying its publication until the following year. It was not until after the reorganization of the Czech government under Heydrich in January 1942 that a full set of Czech anti-Jewish laws was passed, among them a provision for the protection of "Czech blood and honor" based on Germany's 1935 Nuremberg legislation.[82]

With the arrival of Heydrich, the German campaign against the Jews in the Protectorate entered a more extreme phase. The policy of encouraging voluntary Jewish emigration was abandoned in favor of organized, large-scale deportations. Heydrich explained his intentions to his staff in a speech of October 17, 1941.

> First a transport of five thousand Jews will be evacuated to Litzmann-stadt [Lodz, in the German-annexed section of Poland]. One part has already been sent off. . . . Then there should be a short interval so as not to impede the preparations for further evacuations, that is ghettoization. In the meantime the Jews from Bohemia and Moravia will be concentrated for evacuation purposes in each case in one transit camp. For this purpose Theresienstadt [Terezín] has been completely evacuated [by its present inhabitants] . . . fifty thousand to sixty thousand Jews can easily be housed in Theresienstadt. From there the Jews will be taken to the east. . . . After the complete evacuation of all Jews, Theresienstadt will be settled by Germans in accordance with perfect planning and will become a center of German life. . . . In no case must even the smallest detail leak out to the public about these plans.[83]

There was no need for leakage, for German actions made their intentions plain. The first great roundup and deportation of Czech Jews took place the day before Heydrich made this speech and similar roundups went on regularly thereafter. The old Habsburg fortress town of Theresienstadt became a major evacuation center not only for Czech Jews but for Jews from every part of Europe. From there the majority were sent to extermination camps in the east.

On January 1, 1943, according to the statistics compiled in Himmler's office, 15,550 Jews remained in the Protectorate. Of these 6,211 were partners in mixed marriages. The rest were still considered essential to the economy, but all were scheduled for eventual deportation.[84]

German economic aims in the Protectorate as such were never expounded with such authority as programs for racial and territorial Germanization; they generally formed part of broader expositions of Nazi planners. Hitler stated clearly in his original decree for the Protectorate that its government would have to conform to the economic as well as the political and military interests of the Reich, but he did nothing more to define what he meant by economic interests.[85]

For many Germans in the Protectorate these interests were at all times predominantly practical. The control of Bohemia and Moravia promised to establish German economic predominance in Central and Southeastern Europe once and for all, and government agencies as well as private firms engaged in vicious competition to exploit the situation to their own advantage, whether for profit, power, or both.[86]

Motives of greed merged with those of national interest. Göring admitted candidly some weeks before the war began that one reason for the occupation of Bohemia and Moravia had been to exploit the industry there for military purposes. This remained the overriding concern of German economic policy throughout the occupation, and was clearly expressed by the head of the economic section of the Office of the Reich Protector early in 1941. "Today the aim that stands in the forefront of economic policy in the Protectorate is the demand brought forward by the Führer's clear decision completely to adapt the economy of the state to the war necessities of the Reich and to exploit it for this purpose."[87]

Interwoven with personal and military motives, yet giving a special direction to German economic policies, was the long-term aim of the total Germanization of the Bohemian-Moravian area. The transfers of land ownership, the uprooting and resettlement of peasants, the exclusion of the Jews, could hardly be regarded as practical policies during wartime except by fanatic ideologists who were convinced that the ultimate practicality lay in obeying the dictates of their beliefs.

For both ideologists and pragmatists, however, the programs of Germanization provided a convenient rationale for the seizure of Czech economic assets.[88] With the entry of German troops into Bohemia and Moravia on March 15, 1939, the German army had promptly seized all Czech military property, while agents of Göring's Four-Year Plan had hastened to establish control over the major Czech industries. Control was the principal characteristic of Germany's economic policy in the Protectorate throughout the occupation. During the four weeks of German military administration this control was exercised through special economic sections of the military government. But even after the establishment of the German civil government the German army retained an independent economic staff in the provinces to represent its interests and keep direct control over property deemed essential to military security.[89]

The German civil government was empowered to control all aspects of the Czech economy and represent the interests of all Reich offices, public and private, with the exception of the army. Each Czech economic department was supervised by a corresponding department in the Office of the Reich Protector. Also established in the Reich protector's office were special economic offices corresponding to economic offices in the Reich which were responsible for controlling entire sectors of the Czech economy. The German coal office (*Kohlenwirtschaftsstelle*) in the Protectorate, for example, was the counterpart of the Reich Coal Office (*Reichsstelle Kohle*); there were similar offices for oil, motor vehicles, transportation, agriculture, public contracts, and consumer co-operatives, each of which imposed Reich policies for production, distribution, and consumption in their respective fields in the Protectorate.[90]

But the most important instrument of German control over the economy of the Protectorate was the native Czech administration. Under pressure from the German authorities, the Czech government issued a series of decrees giving the Czech ministries the power to reorganize the entire Czech economy; to liquidate, merge, or otherwise transform individual enterprises; and to compel all enterprises performing similar functions to become members of government-controlled associations. All industry, for example, was organized in a Central Union of Industry for Bohemia and Moravia, which was subdivided on a regional and professional basis. This method of control culminated in a Czech government decree of September 1940 "for the co-ordination of the economy of the Protectorate of Bohemia and Moravia with that of the Greater German Reich" whereby agencies of the Czech government were to ensure that the use of raw materials, production, and distribution were all adapted to the requirements of Germany.[91]

Apart from Czech economic ministries, the most important Czech departments for economic control were the Price Control and Supervisory offices. The Price Control Office, established in May 1939 as an autonomous agency directly under the Czech prime minister, controlled all prices except wages and salaries. In 1943 the German head of the price control section in the Office of the Reich Protector was made head of this office in the Czech government.

The Supervisory Office, set up in June 1939 as an autonomous department in the Ministry of Industry, Trade, and Commerce, was empowered to prescribe the methods of manufacture of goods and to direct and control their use to ensure the most effective exploitation of raw materials. Its main task at first was the control of imports; but so important was this function that it soon controlled the bulk of manufacture and trade in the Protectorate and became the principal agency for the integration of the Czech and German economies. These latter powers were given legal recognition by a decree of June 26, 1943, which charged the Supervisory Office with the regulation, production, distribution, marketing, consumption, and finishing of all goods. German control was assured through a special delegate of the Reich protector, who was given a staff of economic experts, and through deputies of other Reich offices permanently attached to the Supervisory Office.[92]

In January 1942 the Czech Ministry of Industry, Trade, and Commerce was reorganized as the Ministry of Economics and Labor and placed directly under a Reich German, Dr. Walter Bertsch. This direct control was considered necessary by the German authorities because of the deteriorating military situation and the demand for greater production which could no longer be achieved by supervision alone. Under Bertsch the Czech economy was reorganized, thousands of enterprises of all kinds not directly connected with war production were closed and their workers and facilities funneled into war industries.[93]

While establishing a large measure of control over the Czech economy through German and Czech supervisory agencies, the Germans also employed more direct methods, such as securing outright ownership of Czech property and economic enterprises and acquiring dominant positions in these enterprises. This was accomplished by a variety of means ranging from direct to indirect expropriation.

Direct expropriation included the seizure of Czech government property (gold reserves, military equipment, military training areas), the levying of charges on the Czech government to pay for the costs of German "protection," the confiscation of the property of Jews and "enemies of the state." It included the drafting of men and women for compulsory labor service in the Protectorate or the Reich, the lengthening of working hours for all labor, and the control of wages and salaries.[94]

The techniques of indirect expropriation were more varied and occasionally more subtle. Taxation schedules were drawn up to favor German or German-controlled enterprises. The manipulation of the currency permitted the purchase of Czech goods and securities cheaply and forced the Czechs to pay correspondingly high prices for imports from the Reich or other parts of German-controlled Europe. Currency manipulation played a large role in the establishment of German control over the Czech banking system, which was also hit hard by the loss of assets in the Sudetenland, the elimination of government patronage, and the confiscation of Jewish investments. The banks, and indeed most Czech economic enterprises, found it necessary to sell securities on a large scale, usually at prices far below their actual value, and this gave the Germans their opportunity to move in.[95]

It was splendid business for the Germans, so splendid that government offices and private firms engaged in savage rivalries to purchase Czech securities and thereby establish their control over some of the most important business establishments in Central Europe. The process was not so systematic as some German leaders would have liked, however. Heydrich complained in 1942 that the purchasing of shares was not enough; Germanization could only be achieved by the actual installation of Germans in key economic positions. But in industry as on the land, there were simply not enough Germans available.[96]

Systematic or not, a substantial transfer of property to German ownership and control took place. Within two years the almost complete integration of Bohemia and Moravia into the German economic sphere had been achieved. The transportation and communication systems, railroads, river and canal shipping, the post and telegraph offices, were all incorporated into the systems of the Reich. And as early as October 1, 1940, after several delays to allow time for economic adjustments, the provinces were made part of the German customs union.[97]

Until the last days of the war, the Germans remained in firm control of Bohemia and Moravia. There was mass discontent, but no mass revolt or even serious local revolt. By that time the pattern of Nazi policy and Hitler's aims with respect to the Czech provinces were clear: They were to be incorporated into the Greater German Reich. As early as March 1939 Bohemia and Moravia had been divided into party administrative districts and assigned to adjacent Gaus of the Reich. Within two years the economy of the provinces had been almost completely integrated with that of the Reich, they had been included in the Reich customs union, they had been declared part of the Reich for purposes of international law,[98] and all preparations had been made for the eventual complete Germanization of the population.[99]

The major problem that remained to be resolved was whether and to what extent the Czechs themselves could be Germanized. In the course of the German occupation, Hitler appears to have approved a population policy based on the assumption that a large proportion of the Czech population was in fact suitable for Germanization. But he also issued strict orders that all those who could not be Germanized, as well as all anti-German elements, were to be eliminated. Thus the Czechs and other Slavic inhabitants of Bohemia and Moravia who refused to be Germanized, or who were considered unsuitable for Germanization, would sooner or later have suffered the same fate as the Jews.[100]

The Satellite State of Slovakia

Since the formation of the state of Czechoslovakia in 1918, there had always been a substantial number of Slovaks who had resented their incorporation in the Czechoslovak union. In fact, the popularity of the biggest political organization in Slovakia, the Slovak People's party, was based in large measure on its opposition to Czech dominion.

The Slovak People's party, which drew its support largely from the rural, Roman Catholic population, had been founded in 1905 by a Roman Catholic priest, Andrej Hlinka, to fight for Slovakia's independence from Hungary when it was still part of the Austro-Hungarian Empire. Dissatisfied with the role conceded the Slovaks in the Czechoslovak union formed after the First World War, Hlinka and his party continued to struggle for Slovakia's independence, but now against the Czechs instead of the Hungarians. With the exception of a brief period from 1927 to 1929, when it entered the national government in return for promises of greater regional autonomy for Slovakia, the Hlinka party consistently opposed the Prague regime. Upon his death on August 16, 1938, Hlinka was succeeded as acting head of the party by Monsignor Jozef Tiso, another Roman Catholic priest, who had served as minister of health in the national government in 1927. After the Munich agreement of September 29, 1938, with the national government demoralized and the Czechoslovak union apparently on the verge of dissolution, Tiso conducted negotiations with Prague which led to an agreement of October 7, 1938, granting Slovakia far-reaching autonomy over its internal affairs and Tiso's appointment as Slovakia's prime minister.[101]

In February 1939, after Hitler had evidently made up his mind to destroy the Czecho-Slovak state, the Nazis began to exert pressure on Slovak nationalists to sever all connections with Prague. The Czechs for their part, alarmed by the growing intransigeance of the Slovaks, sought assurances from the Slovak government that it would not secede from the Czecho-Slovak union. When these assurances were not forthcoming, the Prague government on March 12 dismissed Tiso and jailed leading advocates of the Slovakian independence movement. It was this crisis over Slovakia that gave Hitler the opportunity to arrange the final breakup of Czechoslovakia and the excuse to occupy the Czech provinces of Bohemia and Moravia.[102]

On March 14, under brutal German pressure, the Slovak parliament declared Slovakia's independence and Tiso again became prime minister. On the following day, as his first official act, Tiso asked Hitler to take Slovakia under Germany's protection, a request the Nazi leader at once granted.[103]

The new state was in dire need of protection. Slovakia had already been shorn of much of its territory. Immediately after the Munich agreement Poland, as a reward for its tacit support of Germany during the Sudeten crisis, had been encouraged by Hitler to take the Těšín (Teschen) region at the junction of the Czech and Slovak provinces. One month later, on November 1, 1938, a German-Italian court of arbitration had compelled Slovakia to turn over a broad strip of territory along its southern border to Hungary. What was left of the country now maintained a precarious existence at the sufferance of Germany, always subject to the threat that any refusal to yield to German demands might result in Slovakia's complete subjugation to Hungary, a fate which had

56

already befallen the Carpatho-Ukraine, which the Germans had delivered up to Hungary on March 15, the day after the Carpatho-Ukraine had proclaimed its own independence.[104]

Too late, Tiso tried to make a compromise of sorts with the Czechs by appointing Karol Sidor, prime minister of Slovakia under Czech auspices from March 12 to 14, to the critical post of minister of the interior in his new government, but Sidor remained in office for only one day.[105] Tiso now evidently saw no alternative but to staff his cabinet exclusively with Slovak nationalists who were known to favor co-operation with the Germans. To take the place of Sidor as minister of the interior he appointed Dr. Vojtěch Tuka, whom he had previously named deputy prime minister; as minister for foreign affairs he selected Ferdinand Ďurčanský. Both men had played leading roles in severing Slovakia's connections with Prague, and it was Tuka who in February 1939 had been entrusted by Hitler with a message to Slovak leaders advising them to demand complete independence. With the exception of the minister of war, Ferdinand Čatloš, a political independent, all members of Tiso's cabinet belonged to the Slovak People's party.

This cabinet was to remain in office until October 26, 1939, when, in a reorganization of the Slovak government, Tiso was elected president of the Slovak Republic and a new cabinet was formed with Tuka as prime minister.[106]

Hitler's promise to Tiso of March 15, 1939, to take Slovakia under his protection was followed by a formal treaty of protection between Germany and Slovakia, signed on March 18 and 23. By the terms of this treaty the German Reich guaranteed the political independence of the Slovakian state and the integrity of its territory. To do so effectively the German Wehrmacht was to have the right to set up military installations along Slovakia's western frontier, generally delineated by the eastern edge of the Little Carpathians, the White Carpathians, and the Javornik Mountains, and to man them with such forces as it considered necessary. Slovakia was to organize its own military forces and to conduct its foreign policy in close consultation with the German government.

In a supplementary protocol on economic and financial co-operation between Germany and Slovakia, particular emphasis was placed on agricultural production, the development of mines and industry, communication and transport. Slovakia was to have its own currency, with a Slovak National Bank to supervise the country's financial policies. This bank was to have the benefit of an adviser from the German Reichsbank, who was to be consulted by the Slovak government in drawing up the national budget and whose consent had to be obtained for all government loans. Future trade agreements between Germany and Slovakia were to be concluded on the principle that Germany would purchase Slovakia's agricultural products and raw materials and would supply finished or semifinished goods and capital equipment in return. Slovakia was not to conduct economic negotiations with other states before the conclusion of such agreements with Germany. A customs union between Germany and Slovakia was not envisaged, but for the time being there was to be no customs barrier between Slovakia, the Protectorate of Bohemia and Moravia, and the Sudeten German territories.[107]

Even after the conclusion of the treaty of protection, Hitler was undecided about what to do with Slovakia. Two days after his government signed the treaty, he briefed the commander in chief of the army on the international situation. The staff officer recording Hitler's views noted,

> How long the Führer will adhere to the treaty concluded with Slovakia is doubtful. The High Command of the Army has the impression that when the time comes the Führer will rid himself of this, and will use Slovakia as a political bargaining counter between himself, Poland, and Hungary. For the time being, however, Hungary is to be kept in check. The Führer agrees with the proposed frontier delimitation (line of the Waag) [the river Váh, presumably the military frontier between Slovakia and the Protectorate]. Should Slovakia be partitioned, the eastern frontier (Nitra line) is to become the frontier and Pressburg [Bratislava, the capital of Slovakia] is to be included.[108]

While the fate of Slovakia was still under discussion, the German army proceeded to occupy an area along the Czech border considerably larger than that provided for by the treaty of protection. In this so-called zone of protection, it demanded control over all economic establishments involved in war production, the power to take all measures considered necessary for the defense of the area, and the exclusion of all Slovak forces. Elsewhere in Slovakia, German occupation forces were to remain until all "Czech" arms and materiel had been removed.[109]

Hitler was annoyed by Slovak government protests against these demands as well as by its reluctance to sign a treaty acknowledging the German army's sovereign rights in the zone of protection. "The Führer said he wished the negotiations to be conducted energetically and resolutely which, together with our concrete offers, *must* lead to early success," an aide recorded on June 20. "The prerequisite for the proposed support of Slovakia is the complete acceptance of our demands, the more so as Slovakia is dependent on our military, economic, and financial aid." [110] Despite Hitler's pressure, it was not until August 12, 1939, that a treaty on the zone of protection was finally signed defining the extent of the German occupation zone and Germany's rights there. The Slovaks were conceded token representation of their troops in the zone; but apart from that they had been forced to concede all along the line.[111]

Hitler's decision to attack Poland ended all possibility that he might use Slovakia in bargaining with that country. This decision, in fact, led to a reversal of the previous situation, for the Germans now proposed to use Poland as bait to secure greater co-operation from Slovakia. On August 24, 1939, the German Foreign Office informed the Slovak government that "according to information available here, Polish operations against the Slovak frontier can be expected at any time." To guard against surprises, Germany asked that Slovakia allow the commander in chief of the German army to assume immediate control of the Slovak army in order to safeguard Slovakia's northern frontier, and that the German Luftwaffe be allowed to occupy the airfield at Zipser-Neudorf (Spišská Nová Ves). If the Slovak government provided the co-operation Germany expected, the German government was prepared to guarantee Slovakia's frontier with Hungary, and, in the event of war between Germany and Poland, to work for the return of the regions Slovakia had lost to Poland in 1938. The Germans promised further that if it should come to war, Slovak forces would not be employed outside Slovakia.[112]

The Slovaks yielded to these German requests immediately, without protest or reservation. They expressed their extreme satisfaction with the proposed guarantee of their Hungarian frontier, and asked only that the Reich government support their claims to territory lost to Poland in 1920 as well as 1938, even if there should be no war between Germany and Poland.[113]

At 11:45 P.M. on August 27 the German minister in Bratislava handed the Slovak government a note (prepared six days earlier) stating that the Reich government was in possession of definite information that Polish units were about to cross the Slovak frontier. To carry out the obligations undertaken in the treaty of protection of March 18–23, the German government had therefore ordered German troops into Slovakia to protect the independence of the Slovak state and the integrity of its territory. Executive power was to remain formally in the hands of the Slovak government, but all Slovak officials were instructed to comply with the orders of German military authorities.[114] German troops had received the strictest instructions to base their conduct on the fact that Slovakia was a friendly state which had voluntarily made its territory available for the deployment of German troops.[115] On the morning of August 28 the mass deployment of German forces along Slovakia's northern frontier began. When the German offensive against Poland was launched on the morning of September 1, 1939, Slovakia joined in the conflict against Poland.[116]

On October 21, following the victorious conclusion of the Polish campaign, the Slovak minister to Berlin brought Hitler the congratulations of his government. "He had wished to present a request which in the meantime, however, had probably become unnecessary, since he had been told just an hour ago that the areas lost to Poland would now definitely be united with Slovakia. . . . The only thing he could do now was to thank the Führer that his request had already been fulfilled." Hitler was very gracious. He promised to confirm this territorial rectification in writing, and declared that "Slovakia had behaved very decently in the recent dispute—in contrast to another power, by which he meant Hungary. "Your conduct has definitely established the Slovak state," he said. From now on Germany would no longer permit anyone to infringe on the rights of Slovakia. Germany itself had no territorial interest there, and was only concerned with defending the line of the Carpathians.[117]

If Germany had no territorial interests in Slovakia, it had very decided political, military, and economic interests there. Because Slovakia was nominally a sovereign state, the German agency primarily responsible for Slovakian affairs was Ribbentrop's Foreign Office, and the principal representative of German interests was consquently the German diplomatic mission in Bratislava. Attached to that mission were representatives of the German army and police, who were later supplemented by a group of official advisers to the Slovak government.

In July 1939 the German diplomatic mission in Bratislava was raised from the status of a consulate to a legation; at the same time, Ernst von Drüffel, German consul general in Bratislava since 1932, was replaced by Hans Bernard, who held the necessary rank of minister. In July of the following year Bernard was succeeded by Freiherr Manfred von Killinger. But only five months later Killinger, previously inspector of German diplomatic missions in the Balkans, was transferred to the strategic post of Bucharest. In January 1941 the assignment as German minister in Bratislava went to Hanns Elard Ludin, who held the post to the end.[118]

Killinger and Ludin were the first of a series of SA (*Sturm Abteilung*) men Ribbentrop appointed to diplomatic posts in Eastern Europe in his campaign to replace members of the professional diplomatic corps by party men—but party men who could be trusted not to become the agents of Himmler, Ribbentrop's rival for power within the party. Because old-guard SA men had not yet forgotten the role Himmler and his SS had played in the purge of their organization in June 1934, the SA served as something of a reservoir for anti-Himmler personnel.[119]

As conceived by the German Foreign Office, Germany's policy toward Slovakia should be designed to impress not only Slovakia but all the countries of Southeastern Europe with the rewards accruing to those states which entrusted their destiny to the Reich. "I am assuming," Drüffel reported to Berlin on March 25, 1939, "that it is our intention to create, with respect to Slovakia, a classic example of our conception of a protective relationship with a Southeastern Slav state." This policy was endorsed by the German Foreign Office; and, when Bernard succeeded Drüffel as head of the German diplomatic mission in Bratislava in July 1939, he was given specific instructions along these lines. Slovakia was to be regarded as a calling card Germany was holding out to the small countries of Southeastern Europe, particularly to the Slavic peoples: This was how a small country could live that placed itself under the protection of the Greater German Reich. On arrival in Slovakia, Bernard found that, apart from the zone of protection, the country had been allowed to retain complete independence in the political and economic fields. It was "a country with which Germany *was negotiating* as with any other country. . . . In all *negotiations* with the Slovak government, I had to be discreetly mindful that this calling card remained clean." [120]

Calling card or no, the Germans did not hesistate to satisfy their basic military and economic needs in Slovakia. The treaty on the zone of protection of August 1939 gave the German army sovereign rights in Slovak territory as far as the Váh River. In December the Slovak government was obliged to conclude a treaty permitting the hiring of Slovak laborers for work in Germany; the following January it agreed to a treaty "on the exploitation of war economy enterprises in Slovakia for the purposes of the German war economy." The Slovak National Bank was forced to co-operate in financing huge German armament orders; the Slovak transportation and communication networks were placed under German supervision; the press and radio put at Germany's disposal for propaganda purposes.[121]

The Nazi government also saw to it that a special status was accorded the German minority in Slovakia. On October 25, 1938, Franz Karamsin, the leader of Slovakia's ethnic Germans, had been appointed to a newly created post of state secretary for German affairs in the Slovak government. Subsequently Slovakia's ethnic Germans were conceded the status of a legal corporation; the Slovak government fulfilled their every demand, including the right to maintain their own educational system, to acknowledge themselves as National Socialists, and to opt for service in the German rather than the Slovak army. They represented, in fact, a state within a state.[122]

Still the Germans were not satisfied. They were concerned about the reliability of the Slovak government and the lack of enthusiasm of many Slovak leaders, including Prime Minister Tiso, for the German cause. When the Slovak government was reorganized in October 1939 and Tiso was made president of the Slovak Republic, he was succeeded as prime minister by Vojtěch Tuka, the most openly pro-German among Slovak leaders. Tuka's appointment was regarded by the Germans as a step in the right direction. Early in 1940, however, they were dismayed to learn that Šaňo Mach, another protagonist of co-operation with Germany and head of the Slovak government's propaganda department, had been removed from the leadership of the Hlinka Guards, the military arm of the Slovak People's party, and replaced by a candidate of President Tiso's. Even more alarming from the German point of view was the changed attitude of Ferdinand Ďurčanský, minister of the interior and of foreign affairs in the Tuka cabinet, whom they suspected of having become a tool of anti-German forces in Slovakia—Jews, Freemasons, and Anglophiles—and who appeared to be staffing his ministries with persons of dubious loyalty to Germany.[123]

By the summer of 1940 Bernard thought a change in Germany's policy toward Slovakia was in order. All along it had been obvious, he said in a report of June 25, that there was a time limit to holding out the Slovakian calling card, depending on developments in the political situation in Europe. With Germany's dramatic victories in the north and west, the situation had now changed sufficiently to warrant the withdrawal of that calling card. "The time had come to make perfectly plain once again, particularly with reference to the countries of Southeastern Europe, that Slovakia is in our *Lebensraum,* that is, that our wishes alone count." [124]

Bernard followed up this report with a dossier of German grievances against Slovakia: In a recent note to the Italian government, the Slovak Foreign Office under Ďurčanský's direction had emphasized Slovakia's status of neutrality and had asked that the British be informed of this "in order that England may recognize *Slovakia's neutrality and all its consequences.*" As minister of the interior, Ďurčanský had failed to coordinate Slovakia's internal policy with its treaty commitments to Germany; the Jewish question had in no sense been brought nearer a solution. President Tiso had publicly and unequivocally professed his adherence to a policy of political Catholicism and had declared, among other things, that Slovakia "must have full autarky in spiritual matters" and that "Catholicism must guide politics . . . any other politics is gangster politics." Taken altogether, Bernard believed, these personalities and their policies presaged the establishment of a state comparable to Schuschnigg's pre-Anschluss regime in Austria.[125]

Bernard's criticisms were reinforced by the reports of other German observers in Slovakia. Martin Bormann contemplated sending Gustav Wächter, the district governor of Lvov in the Government General, as resident general to Slovakia, an appointment that would have signaled an intention to curtail Slovakia's status of independence. But the German government, engaged in delicate negotiations designed to win over those states of Southeastern Europe not yet committed to the German cause, could not afford so obvious a move. It is possible that Bernard's obtuseness in this regard was the major reason for his recall a month after his appeal for a change of policy in Slovakia.[126]

What the German government did do was arrange a reorganization of the Slovak government in an effort to make it a more reliable instrument of German policy. Toward the end of July 1940, Tiso, Tuka, and Šaňo Mach were summoned to Germany, where Ribbentrop confronted them with a demand to remove Ďurčanský from the government. Tuka was to assume responsibility for foreign affairs and Mach was to be appointed minister of the interior and restored to the leadership of the Hlinka Guards. When the Slovak leaders had agreed to these terms, they were rewarded with a reception by Hitler at the Berghof on July 28. On this occasion he repeated his assurances that Germany had no territorial interest in Slovakia and was only concerned with the defense of the Carpathians. Germany had guaranteed the political independence and territorial integrity of Slovakia without requiring any military contributions from the beneficiary of the guarantee. "In return, Germany demanded that Slovakia adhere loyally and unequivocally to the German cause in her domestic politics." No coercion would be used. If the Slovak government desired, Germany would confine itself to defending the Carpathian frontier and withdraw from Slovakia as it had withdrawn from the Baltic states (which a week earlier had been annexed by the Soviet Union). Tiso understood. He assured Hitler that Slovakia would remain as a nation under the protection of Germany and would gladly participate in the New Order as the Führer had planned it; he himself would continue to work enthusiastically for collaboration between the two countries.[127]

The reorganization of the Slovak government took place on July 30, 1940, after the return of the Slovak leaders from Germany. On the same day Killinger was named to succeed Bernard as German minister to Bratislava.[128] Killinger arrived in Slovakia armed with instructions from Ribbentrop to do everything possible to strengthen German influence over the Slovak government. In the first instance he was to secure the appointment of German advisers in critical sectors of the Slovakian administration and economy—the police, propaganda, and economic offices, the Hlinka Guards, and that section of the Ministry of the Interior concerned with the Jewish question. Ever mindful of his own authority and prerogatives, Ribbentrop emphasized that these advisers were to be directly responsible to Killinger, and thus to the German Foreign Office, and that they should under no circumstances be allowed to receive instructions from other German offices. In dealing with Tuka, Killinger was to impress upon him that he could count on Germany's full support, but that he must on no account yield to his opponents in dealing with political Catholicism, Jews, Freemasons, Panslavs, or the Ďurčanský clique.[129]

The government reorganization imposed on Slovakia in July 1940 seemed to achieve what the Germans desired. Upon his return, after seeing Hitler at the Berghof, Tuka announced his intention to reorganize Slovakia along National Socialist lines. In November 1940, while in Berlin on the occasion of Slovakia's accession to the Tripartite Pact,[130] Tuka told Ribbentrop that the German advisers in Slovakia had all done an excellent job and had conducted themselves so well that they had dispelled all fears that Germany intended to turn Slovakia into a protectorate. Even more advisers were now needed, especially in the army, where Czech influence was still strong among the officers. General Paul Otto, the head of the German military mission to Slovakia, had tried to get things done by kindness, but Tuka was afraid that surgical measures were necessary. Meanwhile Tuka was going ahead with the reorganization of the police on the German model, and was purging the twenty-four thousand Czech officials still working for the Slovak state. He could promise the Reich foreign minister that there would be no more political upsets in Slovakia. "The President [Tiso] was a shrewd man and in line with our policy." [131] Slovakia gave further evidence of its willingness to remain in line with German policy by joining in the war against the Soviet Union on July 24, 1941.[132] Despite the problems arising from the Russian campaign, the political situation in Slovakia remained relatively stable.[133] In October 1943 a confidential agent of the SS could report that, of all the states of Southeastern Europe, Slovakia was most strongly and directly under German influence.[134]

The situation in Slovakia remained calm for another ten months until, in August 1944, Slovak partisans launched what they hoped would develop into a large-scale popular rebellion. They ambushed and killed General Otto and members of his staff, seized control of several provinces from Tiso's forces, and persuaded a number of regular Slovak army units to come over to their side. Germany responded by sending German troops into Slovakia under the leadership of Himmler's henchman, Gottlob Berger, who was supposed to supervise political as well as military operations.

Berger's first moves were to disarm the Slovak army and to purge the Slovak government of unreliable elements, including General Čatloš, the minister of defense. The Slovak security police were placed under the command of Jozef Kubala, the chief of staff of the Hlinka Guard, which Berger proposed to make the nucleus of a small but reliable Slovak army.[135] As so often when the SS was involved, SS officials seemed more concerned about SS interests than about German national interests. Berger made certain to enroll Kubala into the Waffen-SS to ensure that his force should be under SS command. Further, Berger refused to have anything to do with the Wehrmacht commander in Slovakia and would deal only with Count Pückler, the head of the SS contingent. "I have told him that only one could command," Berger informed Himmler on September 2, "and that was the deputy of the Reichsführer SS." In reorganizing the Slovak government, Berger worked with President Tiso and sanctioned the overthrow of Prime Minister Tuka, until then the principal agent of German policy in Slovakia, in all likelihood because Tuka had been the instrument of Ribbentrop, the rival of Himmler. On September 2 a new government was formed under Štefan Tiso, a third cousin of the president who, in addition to the prime ministership, took over the ministries of Foreign Affairs and of Justice.[136]

On September 12 Himmler himself appeared in Bratislava. He must have decided that German military leadership (including Berger's) was incompetent, for the revolt in Slovakia, which the Germans had expected to suppress in a few days, was still out of control. On September 16 he appointed SS Gruppenführer Hermann Höffle to succeed Berger, and additional reinforcements were sent into the country, including the notorious Dirlewanger Brigade which consisted of officers and men previously court-martialed for misconduct.[137]

By the end of October the rebellion in Slovakia was broken, its leaders killed, captured, or in flight. An estimated seventy thousand persons had died in the conflict, and German forces now occupied the entire country.[138] The Tiso government remained in office, but Slovakia was now subjected to a more direct form of German control and exploitation than it had heretofore experienced. Himmler was convinced that the Slovak revolt had been the result of Germany's previous conciliatory policy. The Slovaks were after all Slavs, he said, and their basic sympathies would always be with their fellow Slavs, including the Russians. Although it might be temporarily necessary to show respect for the Slovak president for the sake of appearances, it was fundamentally wrong to treat Slovakia as a sovereign state or as an actual ally of Germany. Like all other non-German countries, it was to be exploited with utter ruthlessness in the German interest.[139]

But by the autumn of 1944, when a more radical policy was actually inaugurated in Slovakia, time was running out for the Germans. The greater part of Slovakia was cleared of German troops in January 1945, although Bratislava did not fall until April. Tiso and his government were evacuated to Austria on May 5, 1945, two days before Germany's final surrender.

Whatever existence the Nazis may have been willing to concede the Slovak people in their New Order did not extend to the Slovak Jews. According to a population census of December 31, 1938, after the cessions of Slovak territory to Hungary and Poland, there were 87,487 Jews in Slovakia, about 4 per cent of the population—a percentage surpassed only in Poland among the countries of Europe.[140]

After the Munich crisis the new Slovak government of Jozef Tiso proclaimed its opposition to Jewish Marxism, and Ferdinand Ďurčanský, deputy prime minister and minister of the interior, promised Göring that the Jewish problem in Slovakia would be solved as in Germany.[141] In accordance with this promise, the Slovak government issued its first anti-Semitic decree in April 1939. In contrast to German legislation, the Slovak law defined Jews in a religious rather than a racial sense, and its chief aim was to reduce Jewish influence in Slovak economic life. Jewish membership in the professions, which in many cases amounted to well over 50 per cent, was to be restricted to the percentage represented by the total Jewish population. The same percentage principle was to be applied to Jewish ownership of economic enterprises, although Jews might continue to manage such enterprises if 51 per cent of the ownership passed to non-Jewish Slovaks.[142]

The April decree was supplemented by further legislation restricting Jewish economic activity in Slovakia, but the Germans were not satisfied with such measures. Following the reorganization of the Slovak government at the end of July 1940, SS Hauptsturmführer Dieter Wisliceny of Himmler's Central Office for Reich Security (RSHA) was sent to Slovakia as adviser for Jewish affairs. Attached to the German legation, he worked closely with Šaňo Mach, the new Slovak minister of the interior, and with Anton Vašek, the head of the ministry's Jewish department.[143]

65

Wisliceny's appointment did not bring about any immediate change in Slovakia's policy toward the Jews. Indeed, for over a year after his arrival, nothing of major significance was done on the question. On September 9, 1941, however, the Slovak government issued a new Jewish law, which a German counselor of legation in Bratislava described as even more severe than Germany's Nuremberg laws on which it was based. Jews were now defined by race rather than by religion. They were deprived of all political and legal rights, excluded altogether from government service and the professions, obliged to register and to wear the Star of David. All Jews between the ages of sixteen and sixty were subject to conscription for labor services. The only loophole in this law was that it gave President Tiso (who refused to sign it) the right to exempt anyone he chose from its provisions.[144]

Tiso made ample use of this right, but he employed it primarily on behalf of wealthy or influential Jews who could bring their cases to his attention. Because of the large number of Jews deprived of employment by the anti-Semitic laws passed since 1939, the Slovak government agreed in the spring of 1942 to send seventeen thousand male Jews from Slovakia to Poland as "workers." Soon afterward the Slovak government arranged with the Germans to send the families of these Jews to Poland as well, about thirty-five thousand additional persons. The Slovak officials involved in these transactions were promised that the Slovak Jews were to be settled permanently in the area around Lublin. "Families will stay together. The international legal and civic status of the Jews will be that of protégés [*Schutzbefohlene*] of the German Reich. . . . The German government will take care of the Jews as humanely as possible." [145]

If Slovak officials honestly believed such promises and were ignorant of the real fate that awaited the Slovak Jews in Poland, the refusal of the Germans to allow them to see these Jews and the letters of protests they received from abroad soon forced them to recognize the truth. What was more, they did something about the situation. On May 15, 1942, the Slovak government issued a decree that once again defined Jews in religious rather than racial terms and extended exemptions to Jews from labor service on a broad scale. By late June 1942 the German minister in Bratislava complained that the evacuation of Jews from Slovakia had almost ground to a halt. As of June 26, fifty-two thousand Jews had been deported, but because of clerical influence and official corruption the remaining thirty-five thousand Jews had been provided with certificates of exemption. During the last six months of 1942 and throughout 1943 the Germans succeeded in deporting just over five thousand Jews from Slovakia. An estimated seven thousand fled to Hungary, so that at the end of 1943 about twenty-three thousand Jews remained in Slovakia.[146]

In December 1943 the German Foreign Office trouble shooter Edmund Veesenmayer arrived in Bratislava with orders from the Führer to speak bluntly to Tiso about the Jewish question. In response to Veesenmayer's pressure, Tiso agreed to place the remaining sixteen to eighteen thousand "unconverted" Jews in concentration camps by April 1, 1944. Tuka promised to do the same for baptized Jews. A large proportion of the Slovakian Jews still at liberty were now rounded up, but no Jews were deported until the outbreak of the insurrection of August 1944. The Germans took advantage of this opportunity to send one of Eichmann's agents, SS Hauptsturmführer Anton Brunner, to Slovakia. Without informing the Slovak government, Brunner sent about fourteen thousand Slovakian Jews to Auschwitz during the autumn of 1944. When the new Slovak prime minister, Štefan Tiso, protested, Ludin told him that the Jewish question "had to be solved radically under all circumstances." [147]

In the spring of 1945, after Auschwitz was no longer available for deportations, another small group of Slovakian Jews was evacuated to Terezín (Theresienstadt) in northern Bohemia. By the end of the war approximately eighty thousand of the eighty-seven thousand Jews living in Slovakia in December 1938 appear to have perished.[148]

While the Nazi intentions toward the Jews in Slovakia, as everywhere else in Europe, are unmistakably clear, the same thing cannot be said about their intentions with respect to the Slavic population of the country. In October 1944 Himmler had bitterly criticized Germany's previous conciliatory policy toward the Slovaks, which he held responsible for the current uprising against the Germans. In his opinion it had been a fundamental error to treat Slovakia as a sovereign state, to concede the Slovak people a status of quasi equality with the Germans, or to believe that the Slovaks would or could ever be loyal allies of the Germans. These people were, after all, Slavs; they could always be expected to join forces with their fellow Slavs against the Germans; therefore they would always have to be considered a menace to German security. They might be allowed to remain in the German power sphere so long as they were needed for labor or other services, but meanwhile they should be accorded the same treatment as other Slavs; and once their usefulness was at an end the Germans would have to deal with them in such a way that they could never again pose a threat to the Greater German Reich.[149]

The policy recommended by Himmler may have corresponded with Hitler's real intentions in Slovakia. Until the autumn of 1944 the Tiso government had saved the Slovak people from the worst rigors of Nazi oppression, but it is possible that all along he had been doing nothing more than buying time for his people, and that the Nazis, as soon as there was no longer any reason for restraint, would have adopted a radical racial policy in Slovakia comparable to the policies they were already pursuing in Poland and Russia.

CHAPTER 4

The Slavs: Poland[1]

Immediately following the German occupation of Bohemia and Moravia in 1939, Hitler mounted an intensive propaganda and diplomatic campaign against Poland designed to isolate that country, as he had previously isolated Czechoslovakia, and to reduce it to a similar condition of helplessness. But the Poles refused to be intimidated and the British and French governments, instead of abandoning Poland as they had Czechoslovakia, provided the Poles with renewed pledges of support. On August 23, 1939, Hitler astounded the world by concluding a nonaggression pact with the Soviet Union, which he had heretofore denounced as the archenemy of Nazi Germany. With this move he evidently expected to put an end to whatever intentions Britain and France may have had to stand by their commitments to Poland. To his dismay, however, Britain and France responded to the Nazi-Soviet pact by ratifying treaties of mutual assistance with Poland.

Unable to coerce or isolate the Poles, Hitler found himself confronted with the alternative of backing down in the demands he had made on Poland or of going to war against that country and its Western allies. Hitler chose the course of war; on September 1, 1939, German troops launched the attack on Poland which marked the beginning of the Second World War.[2] On September 17, with the main centers of Polish resistance already shattered, Russian troops invaded Poland from the east, and eleven days later Germany and Russia signed a treaty dividing Poland between them and fixing their respective zones of occupation.[3]

The Fourth Partition of Poland

Although Hitler had advocated a war of expansion into Eastern Europe in his earliest statements on politics and had actively prepared for war

SWEDEN

BALTIC
SEA

LATVIA

• Riga

Memel

LITHUANIA

REICHSKOMMISSARIAT OSTLAND

Kaunas

• Königsberg

EAST PRUSSIA

Danzig

SUWALKI

REICHSGAU DANZIG-
WEST PRUSSIA

Marienwerder

Bromberg ✗ Kulmhof

ZICHENAU
To East Prussia
Zichenau

BIALYSTOK
To East Prussia
after invasion of Russia

Hohensalza

GERMANY

Treblinka ✗

Posen
(Poznań)

REICHSGAU
WARTHELAND

• Warsaw
WARSAW DISTRICT

REICHSKOMMISSARIAT UKRAINE

• Kalisch
(Kalisz)

GERMANY

Leipzig

Sobibor •

GOVERNMENT GENERAL

SILESIA

• Radom

✗ Maldanek
LUBLIN DISTRICT

To Upper Silesia

RADOM DISTRICT

KATOWITZ

Belzec •✗

Auschwitz ✗

Cracow •

CRACOW DISTRICT

Lemberg •
(Lvov)

To Poland 1938;
to Upper Silesia Oct, 1939

ORAVA
ZIPS

TESCHEN

GALICIA
To Government General
after invasion of Russia

To Slovakia Nov, 1939

CZECHOSLOVAKIA

RUMANIA

Vienna

Danube R.

• Budapest

HUNGARY

YUGOSLAVIA

Belgrade •

SWEDEN

GERMANY

SOVIET UNION

0 — 200 miles

POLAND

⎯⎯⎯ Boundary of Poland before
Sept. 1, 1939

• • • • • Russian-German line, 1939

▮▮▮ Annexed by Germany

▬▬▬ Under German civil administration

✗ Killing centers

since he became head of the German government, his attention had been focused on the conquest of Russia and he had devoted surprisingly little thought to the problem of Poland, whose territories lay across his path to Russia. Detailed administrative plans had been prepared by the German army as part of its overall preparations for the Polish campaign, and it was the army which assumed responsibility for the government of Poland in the first instance. But Hitler soon made it clear that he had no intention of leaving the administration of this Slavic country in the hands of his conservative generals and that he intended to conduct German policy in Poland through reliable National Socialists. On September 8, 1939, he issued guidelines for German rule in the conquered Polish territories which provided for the establishment of a civil administration in each military administrative district. Dr. Hans Frank, *Reichsminister* without portfolio, *Reichsleiter* of the National Socialist party, and president of the Academy of German Law, was appointed supreme civil administrator for all occupied Polish territory, and specifically for the province of Litzmannstadt (Lodz). Albert Forster, Gauleiter and now head of the German civil government of Danzig, was named head of the civil administration for the district of West Prussia; and Arthur Greiser, the Nazi president of the Danzig Senate, was made head of the civil administration for the district of Posen (Poznań). These men in turn were to nominate officials to fill the major posts in city and provincial administration in the conquered territories.[4]

With the signature of the partition treaty with Russia, Hitler announced his intention to regulate the political status of the former Polish state lying in the German sphere of interest and to annex a substantial part of it to Germany. The new political frontier of the Reich in the east would include the "former area of German colonization," plus those areas which had special military or economic value. All higher Reich officials were invited to express opinions as to where the final boundaries should be drawn.[5]

When the news of the final surrender of the Polish forces reached him on October 6, Hitler ordered a decree to be drawn up providing for the incorporation into the Reich of the entire area to be united with Germany. The decree, issued two days later, was to go into effect October 26.[6] Out of the former Polish territory, two new provinces (*Reichsgaue*) were to be formed and annexed to Germany: West Prussia (later called the Reichsgau Danzig-Westpreussen), comprising the administrative districts of Danzig, Marienwerder (Kwidzyn), and Bromberg (Bydgoszcz); and Posen (Poznań) (later called the Reichsgau Wartheland), which included the administrative districts of Hohensalza (Inowroclaw), Posen, and Kalisch (Kalisz). Both provinces were to be organized and governed according to the provisions of the decree of April 14, 1939, which had been drawn up to regulate German rule in the Sudetenland. Each province was placed under a Reich governor (Reichsstatthalter)—Albert Forster in West Prussia and Arthur Greiser in Posen—who, in contrast to the governors of the Ostmark (Austria) and the Sudetenland, were given full control of all branches of the administration, including the departments of justice, finance, railroads, and post office. Residents of the provinces of German blood were to become German nationals (*Staatsangehörige*) in accordance with provisions to be issued later; residents of German origin were to become Reich citizens (*Reichsbürger*) in accordance with the Reich citizenship law. The Reich Ministry of the Interior was to act as a central office for the organization of the newly annexed eastern territories, with the power to introduce Reich and Prussian law by decree in agreement with the responsible Reich ministers concerned. Annexed to the Reich in addition to these new provinces were the Polish districts of Kattowitz (Katowice), which was incorporated into the German province of Silesia, and Zichenau (Ciechanow), which was joined to East Prussia.[7]

The fate of the Polish territory not incorporated into the Reich, which Hitler had evidently thought might be used as a bargaining counter with the Western powers, was settled by a decree of October 12.[8] This area was to be placed under the authority of a German governor general, who was to be directly responsible to Hitler and in control of all branches of the civil administration. To this position Hitler appointed Dr. Hans Frank, heretofore supreme civil administrator for all occupied Polish territory. This decree, like the October 8 decree for the incorporated areas, was to come into effect on October 26.

Thus the Polish territory occupied by the Germans in the first stage of the war in the east was divided into two main sections: the areas incorporated into the Reich, and the nonincorporated territory of the Government General (*Generalgouvernement*). The actual boundaries between the various German provinces and between the incorporated and nonincorporated territories were not to be determined for many months; in fact, they remained a subject of dispute among the German authorities until the end of the war.[9]

The Incorporated Territories

Well before October 26, the day when the October 8 decree setting up civil governments in the Polish provinces to be annexed to the Reich was to come into effect, German currency, emergency laws, postal and communications systems had been introduced in these territories, and provisions had been made for the confiscation of the property of the Polish state.[10]

In the months that followed, the German administrative system for provincial and local government, the entire body of Reich and Prussian law, the German educational system, and almost all other features of German government were imposed on the new provinces, as were the German police, the Four-Year Plan, and a multitude of other German

71

government and party organizations.[11] The German language was made the official language of government and education. All place names and public signs had to be rendered into German. All Polish organizations were dissolved, all religious organizations subjected to state control and supervision. All property of the Polish state, all Jewish property, and the property of all persons who had left the country was confiscated by the German state or placed under trusteeship. The customs boundary of the Reich was extended to include the newly incorporated provinces; but at the request of Himmler the police border remained as before to prevent unrestricted immigration to the Old Reich and to enable German authorities to carry out a racial examination of the population. Only the city of Danzig and the district of Upper Silesia were excluded from this police restriction because these areas were held to be Germanic already.[12]

The basic Hitler decree of October 8, 1939, on the organization and administration of the incorporated eastern territories was supplemented by a decree from Wilhelm Frick, the Reich minister of the interior, of November 2, 1939, which laid down guidelines for the organization of the office of the Reichsstatthalter in the new provinces.[13] According to section one of this law, the Reichsstatthalter's office was to be headed by a president of the administration (*Regierungspräsident*) and was to be divided into departments to deal with all major sectors of the administration. In this respect it differed little from similar offices in the Reich. More significant was section two which provided that "a senior SS and police officer shall be attached to the office of the Reichsstatthalter and shall be personally and directly subordinate to him. He shall at the same time serve as the agent of the Reichskommissar for the consolidation of the German people." [14]

In a speech commenting on this decree, Frick placed great emphasis on the fact that the new eastern provinces, like the provinces of the Ostmark and the Sudetenland, had been made into Reichsgaus. As such, the administration of each of these Gaus was entirely a Reich administration; its offices were Reich offices, its personnel were Reich personnel, and the Reichsstatthalter was the focal point of the administration. "The entire administration of the Reichsgaus of Posen and West Prussia is subordinate to the Reichsstatthalter. There are to be no separate or special administrations." [15]

This was a brave pronouncement, but as Frick himself must have realized, separate administrations already existed in the new eastern provinces. His own law of November 2, with its provision that the senior SS and police officer should serve as the agent of Himmler in his capacity as Reichskommissar for the consolidation of the German people, left open the possibility for establishing another one. The military commanders in these provinces, although deprived of their civil administrative authority, were still empowered to enact measures for the execution of their military tasks and the security of their troops.[16] And Göring, in

72

a decree of September 28, had already reserved for himself the right to exercise co-ordinated supervision over the economy of all areas under German occupation, an authority he later extended to include the right to issue general directives and specific decrees in the economic field.[17]

Not content with these powers, Göring issued a directive on October 19, 1939, setting up an entirely new economic office under the Four-Year Plan which was to ensure unified and co-ordinated economic exploitation of the conquered territories and to seize and administer all economically desirable Polish and Jewish property. This was the Main Trustee Office East (*Haupttreuhandstelle Ost,* or HTO), which Göring placed under his immediate and personal direction. The management of this office he delegated to Max Winkler, a leading government financial authority and member of the advisory board of the Reichsbank. Headquarters of the new office were to be in Berlin, but there were to be branch offices in each eastern administrative region. "In the future, confiscations may be decreed only by the Main Trustee Office East, with the concurrence of the administrative leaders concerned," Göring's directive stated. "I expect fullest support of the measures carried out by the Main Trustee Office and the [local] trustee offices from the heads of the administrative districts." [18]

Göring was not permitted to exercise jurisdiction over the economy of the occupied eastern areas without challenge. Frank, in the Government General, objected vigorously to this encroachment on his own authority; and Himmler, who had economic ambitions of his own in the east, raised another and far more serious challenge to Göring's economic omnipotence. On November 15, 1939, Frank established his own Trustee Office to administer Polish property in the Government General,[19] and in December Himmler claimed control over all economic assets necessary for his population resettlement programs—a claim which admitted an indefinitely elastic interpretation.[20] Ultimately Göring capitulated completely to Frank and restricted the authority of the HTO to the incorporated territories. With Himmler he reached a compromise in June 1940 whereby he gave up the greater part of his claims over agricultural property.[21]

Faced with ever-growing competition from Himmler, Göring in February 1941 attempted to gain the support of the local administrative leaders by naming them heads of the local HTO offices; [22] but Himmler neatly countered this move by giving the administrative leaders a similar position in his own offices in the east. All local governors, with the exception of Forster, a long-time opponent of Himmler's, accepted Himmler's offer and thereby came under his control, which by this time was a good deal more effective than Göring's. As Himmler, through his various agencies, exercised some kind of control over the majority of higher officials in the incorporated territories, including the leaders of Göring's own HTO organization, it was he who eventually profited most from Göring's economic empire in the east.

Well before 1941, however, Himmler had established himself as a dominant influence in the new provinces. As head of the SS and German police he had exercised broad authority there from the beginning. But his greatest accretion of power came when Hitler appointed him Reichskommissar for the consolidation of the German people on October 7, 1939, therewith assigning him primary responsibility for carrying out his racial program in the east.[23]

Although Hitler had made no detailed preparations for the occupation and administration of the occupied Polish territories, he had very definite ideas about the general line of policy he intended to pursue there. In *Mein Kampf* and subsequent writings he had rejected the nationalities policies of earlier "bourgeois" governments, which had sought to Germanize non-German peoples in territory under German control. The National Socialist state, he wrote in 1928, "should under no circumstances annex Poles with the intention of making Germans of them." On the contrary, it "must either seal off these alien racial elements to prevent an ever-recurring corruption of the blood of our own people, or remove them without further ado and hand over the territory made available in this way to members of our own racial community."[24]

Hitler had refrained from publishing anti-Polish pronouncements after coming to power, especially after concluding his nonaggression pact with Poland in 1934; but in 1939, even before the conquest of Poland was completed, he made it clear that his previous restraint with regard to Poland had been tactical only, and that his earlier writings embodied his fundamental views on dealing with the Polish racial question.

At a conference with his army and intelligence officers on September 12, 1939, Hitler announced that he intended to carry out large-scale executions of Poles, and that the nobility and clergy in particular were to be exterminated (*ausgerottet*). After this conference Admiral Wilhelm Canaris, the chief of the German counterintelligence, protested to Wilhelm Keitel, the chief of the OKW (High Command of the Armed Forces), that the German army could not and should not condone such atrocities. Keitel replied that objections were useless. General Walther von Brauchitsch, the commander in chief of the army, had already protested to Hitler and had been informed that, if the army refused to carry out these racial policies, the job would be performed by the SS and the Gestapo. For this purpose Hitler was establishing a civil government in each military district which would be entrusted with the task of racial extermination (*volkstümliche Ausrottung*) and political housecleaning (*politische Flurbereinigung*).[25]

Hitler meant what he said. Directly behind the troops of the regular army came SS and police battalions, which in the name of the pacification of the conquered territories proceeded to carry out mass arrests and mass executions, for the most part quite arbitrarily and in full view of the Polish population and the German troops. German army leaders continued to register protests. As appeals to humanity and common decency seemed to carry no weight with Hitler, they pointed out that these brutal racial policies were shattering the morale of their soldiers in Poland and had seriously imperiled the economic productivity of the conquered territories. These arguments had some effect. On September 22 Hitler agreed that economic requirements should henceforth take precedence over all other considerations, and that all racial measures be postponed until after the conclusion of military operations.

Reinhard Heydrich, who had been delegated by Himmler to implement National Socialist racial policies in Poland, interpreted Hitler's instructions about postponing racial measures in his own way. Orders to shoot insurgents had been withdrawn, he said, but nothing could be allowed to interfere with measures against potential leaders of the resistance among the Polish nobility, priesthood, and teachers, whose economic importance was in any case negligible. These few thousand persons would be arrested at once and sent to a concentration camp. Heydrich also intended to proceed with the transfer of Jews from the countryside to the cities, where they could be more easily controlled. These tasks could not be left to army leaders, who were filled with prejudices and had no understanding of their importance.[26]

Hitler's postponement of radical racial measures in Poland did not mean that his views about the necessity for such measures had been modified in any way. If anything they had become more extreme as a result of his own observations in the conquered territories. The Polish population consisted of a thin layer of Germanic leaders, he told Alfred Rosenberg toward the end of September, but beneath that layer the human material was horrifying. As for the Polish Jews, it would be impossible to conceive of anything more loathsome. Only firm leadership with the clearest possible objectives could deal with the situation in Poland. In talks with Rosenberg and Keitel, Hitler described his plans to colonize the greater part of the conquered Polish territory with Germans, to remove all Poles and Jews to a Polish rump state, and to construct an impregnable defensive wall along the Vistula. The territory of the Old Reich and the areas to be annexed had to be cleared of Jews, Polacks, and other trash (*Polacken und Gesindel*). It would be necessary to conduct a brutal racial war (*Volkstumskampf*) which would admit no legal restrictions.[27]

Hitler clung to these ideas with fanatic consistency, and throughout the war insisted on the need for a ruthless racial policy in Poland. Otherwise Germany would go through the same experiences as after the partitions of Poland of the eighteenth century. After ten years he expected his Gauleiters to report that the eastern provinces were utterly and completely German. He would not question them about the methods they employed in carrying out this policy, nor did he care whether at some time in the future these methods might be criticized as being not altogether beautiful or defensible from a legal point of view. It was his aim to put one hundred million Germans into this area so that it should remain German for all time.[28]

As we have seen, Hitler had assigned primary responsibility for putting his racial theories into practice to Heinrich Himmler who, in his capacity as Reichskommissar for the consolidation of the German people (an office created by a secret Hitler decree of October 7, 1939, shortly after the conquest of Poland), from the first gave top priority in the Germanization program to the newly incorporated Polish territories. Under his supervision detailed memoranda were prepared to serve as theoretical and practical guidelines for his officials in these areas.[29]

Himmler believed there were two fundamental tasks to be accomplished in the east: the ruthless segregation of German from alien blood and the settlement of Germans in this ancient German territory. During the coming winter Himmler expected well over half a million Jews to be evacuated; thereafter the aim would be to introduce a steady stream of German settlers into the area and gradually to squeeze out the Poles.

Himmler's resettlement plans for West Prussia and the Wartheland resembled those he had drawn up for Bohemia and Moravia. A belt of German farmers was to be established on the border of the Government General to separate those Poles who remained in the Reich from the hinterland; another broad belt should tie the border area to the Reich; while a network of narrower belts over both provinces should isolate the Poles and leave them, so to speak, on racial islands.

Himmler envisaged a German population density of about one hundred per square kilometer in the new provinces, about 30 to 40 per cent higher than in East Prussia and Pomerania but roughly the same as in Bavaria, with an equal proportion employed in agriculture and industry according to local conditions. As usual in Nazi theory, the main emphasis was on agriculture. "The decisive and most important element in the reconstruction of the eastern provinces is the peasantry. The consolidation of the German people and the final conquest of the land won by the sword depends on its work in the soil." Thus the entire future of the German people in the east depended on the success of the agricultural resettlement program.

It was essential to impress on the new German peasants in the east their role as political warriors, as civilian troops which would consolidate for all time the military conquests of the German army. The new peasants should be given enough land to assure them not only economic security, but to provide them with the means to support large families and to permit them to associate on a level of cultural, social, and economic equality with other groups of workers. This did not mean that a class of large landowners or gentleman farmers was to be created; the German peasant should continue to till his own soil and not depend on foreign or hired labor. Poles were to be employed only temporarily until enough German agricultural workers were available.

The owners of the new German farms should be pioneers and leaders, they should inspire by their example a new pride in labor on the land. But to ensure balance and variety in their lives, they should be encouraged to engage in farm and village handicrafts, folk dancing, music, and other arts.

Special attention was to be paid to the architecture of the new farms. "Farm houses in the east should not merely fulfill practical requirements, but also be a visible expression of a new German peasant culture. The farm complexes should conform to the landscape and to the customs of their inhabitants. While a mere copying of traditional architectual forms was to be avoided, good and proven structural styles were to be carried over into the new era." Each farm house should be roomy and contain a bath and a shower, and in every case dignified accommodation for the elderly was to be provided. Only the best construction materials were to be used, as befitted the importance of the undertaking. Building materials and colors should be suitable to the area, wires hidden as much as possible, signs and advertising kept to a minimum.

The new German villages in the east were to be grouped around a main village, which would contain the community halls of the party, sport areas, warehouses, stores, and repair shops. In each smaller village there would be a party center, buildings for education and physical training, an inn, a community hall, and a bell tower.

Around the farms and villages the peasants were to be encouraged to plant trees and shrubs, and in general to contribute to the beautification of the landscape, while higher Reich authorities should see to it that highways, waterways, and all major construction projects would be aesthetically attractive. To avoid unnecessary construction, local sources of power such as wind and water should be developed wherever possible.

With all the emphasis on agriculture, Himmler still proposed that 50 per cent of the German population in the new eastern provinces should consist of persons employed in industry, which was to be shifted to the east on a large scale to relieve the pressure on the Old Reich. But industries in the east should be rigidly confined to big cities; in rural districts only those industries should be permitted which were definitely associated with agriculture, such as sawmills, dairies, or sugar-beet factories.

The new cities in the east were to be built with German traditions in mind, but their principal function should be to take care of modern needs. Thus only living traditions should be carried on. In old cities, entirely new city centers might have to be created, although the old centers should be preserved as an organic part of city life.

The office and business area was to be the functional center of the city, the city hall the architectural focus. Industry was to be located in a separate but easily accessible area and to be given a form corresponding to the importance and dignity of industry in city life. Residential areas were to be arranged so as to provide easy access to places of work and to cultural and social centers, with ample room for parks, playgrounds, and schools. City dwellers should be given every encouragement to own their houses, so as to give each individual pride of ownership and at the same time a stake in the community. Residential housing should be protected as much as possible from noise and smoke, all houses should have access to gardens for the planting of vegetables and flowers.

Around each city there was to be a green belt consisting of a network of parks, playgrounds, and cemeteries. The various districts within the city were to be connected by woods, waterways, and any other natural scenic attraction to be found in the area. Every part of the city should be accessible by foot and bicycle paths. Railroads and major highways, on the other hand, should lead only to the city center, and should be kept as far as possible from the residential districts. Bypasses were to be built around each city for all traffic wishing to circumvent it. In every part of the city ample parking space was to be allocated well in advance of all building programs.

It was important to plan the new cities in relation to the environment in which they were to be located, and to make them as aesthetically satisfying as possible, both for the sake of the well-being of their inhabitants and because they were to be regarded as monuments of German cultural enterprise.

Of far greater immediate importance for Himmler than city planning and construction, however, was the racial program and the need to begin at once with the segregation of Germans from non-Germans. As it would be impossible to remove all alien racial elements from the new provinces immediately, Himmler had special studies prepared for dealing with this problem. One such study, which Hitler approved as "very good and correct," [30] proposed the systematic breakup of non-German communities into national splinter groups, a process that should continue until their ultimate extinction. It was to be hoped that over the years the very concept of Kashub, Ukrainian, or Pole would be destroyed.

The non-German peoples were to be allowed only local leaders, mayors, heads of villages, and police. Their education was not to go beyond the fourth grade. It would be enough if they learned to do simple arithmetic and were taught that it was the law of God to obey Germans, be honest, industrious, and behave themselves. Children who showed German racial characteristics were to be sent to school in Germany. Their parents too might be sent to Germany where their anxiety for the welfare of their children would guarantee their good behavior. Their names were to be Germanized, they should be treated as Germans and made to feel welcome in the German ethnic community. The rest of the population would be a leaderless class of workers who could be brought to Germany to perform menial tasks and aid in building the German cultural monuments of the future.

The newly annexed eastern provinces should be the first to be Germanized. Then would come the turn of the Government General. With the final Germanization of that area the Polish nationality would be entirely snuffed out.

Himmler did not wait for the preparation of elaborate plans before putting the Nazi racial program into practice. SS and police units under the command of Heydrich were sent into Poland immediately behind the troops of the regular army and at once began their grim work of removing Jews and eradicating the leaders, or suspected leaders, of the Poles.[31]

At the end of October 1939, Himmler drew up a schedule for the first stage of evacuations from West Prussia and Posen which called for the removal by the end of February 1940 of all Jews (well over half a million), of Poles who had migrated to the provinces since 1918, and of Polish leaders and intellectuals. All these racially and otherwise undesirable elements were to be dumped in the Government General. At the same time all racially valuable families in the Government General were to be brought to the Reich and settled individually so as to separate them more completely from their Polish background. The RSHA in Berlin was entrusted with the central planning of the operation, while the actual removals were to be carried out by local authorities under the direction of local SS and police officers. All persons resisting evacuation were to be shot.[32]

Simultaneously with the evacuation of Jews and Poles from the newly incorporated eastern provinces, Himmler's agencies were faced with the problem of resettling ethnic Germans from the Baltic states and the Polish territories that had been turned over to the Russians.[33] On September 28, 1939, Hitler ordered that the evacuation of ethnic Germans from Estonia and Latvia should begin at once, and Himmler proposed to resettle them in the new eastern provinces.[34]

To provide for the new settlers and at the same time to establish his right to a substantial share of Poland's economic assets already claimed by Göring, Himmler ordered the confiscation of all agricultural property of the former Polish state and of all private persons who had been evacuated, executed, or who had fled the country. These confiscations were to be undertaken by SS and police officers in co-operation with the officials of Göring's HTO organization, and the entire property thus acquired was to be placed at the disposal of the RKFDV (Reich Commission for the Consolidation of the German People).[35]

The new German settlers were not assigned new farms or homes immediately. The majority were housed in temporary relocation centers run by the local SS and police offices where they were expected to remain over the winter. Himmler did not intend to act hastily in a matter he considered vital to the German future. In the coming months his various resettlement offices were to survey the property made available through confiscations and screen the persons who were to be the vanguard of the new wave of German migration in the east. By spring he expected plans for urban and rural settlement to be completed. "After that the systematic resettlement of city and country, which will continue for many years, perhaps for decades, is to take place." [36]

In carrying out evacuations and resettlements, Nazi officials faced one major complication, which was to be a chronic problem in all their resettlement operations: How were they to identify an ethnic German? [37] There had been no screening of the persons evacuated from the Baltic states and eastern Poland, whose only claim to German nationality was that they had identified themselves as Germans and had opted to come to Germany. But were they in fact Germans? Was it not possible that they had chosen to leave their homelands for political, economic, or other reasons which had nothing to do with nationality? And what of the large numbers of blond, blue-eyed, handsome people the Nazis encountered in Poland who passionately adhered to their Polish nationality and regarded the Germans with hatred and contempt? Could these people be anything but Germanic? Their very fidelity to their Polish nationality was evidence of the worth of their blood, for lesser breeds would have been prepared to renounce their nationality for personal advantage.

Several procedures were proposed to cope with these problems, but Himmler soon came to the conclusion that it would be necessary to undertake a detailed racial examination of every individual in the area. "The removal of all persons of alien race from the annexed eastern territories is one of the most important aims to be achieved in the German east," Himmler said. But it was just as indispensable to regain for Germanism the German blood in these districts even when the bearer of such blood had become Polish in feeling, language, and religion. "It is therefore an absolute national-political necessity to 'screen' the annexed eastern territories and later also the Government General for such persons of Teutonic blood in order to make this lost German blood available again to our own people."

Understandably enough no altogether satisfactory racial examination system was ever developed; local boards differed widely on procedure, and to the end of the war German authorities were experimenting with new techniques. In fact, the entire racial examination business was at all times a hopeless muddle and confusion, and the steady flow of new guidelines and directives which were designed to standardize criteria and procedures did nothing to improve the situation. In very general terms the fundamentals of the system can be described as follows.[38] There were two main categories of persons to be examined: (1) all ostensible ethnic Germans, who were to be inscribed in a German National Register (*Deutsche Volksliste*) and then classified further according to political-national reliability and (2) the Polish population, from which racially valuable elements were to be removed and re-Germanized.

To deal with the first group the German authorities ordered all ethnic

Germans to apply for inclusion in the German National Register. As a large number of ethnic Germans who were presumably eligible for inclusion failed to apply, increasingly severe penalties were decreed for those who refused to do so.[39]

After a person had applied for enrollment in the German National Register, he came before a racial examination board (*Zentralstelle für die deutsche Volksliste*), which was set up in all principal administrative centers to decide on the racial qualities of each candidate. Decisions were based on physical appearance, the documentary evidence submitted by the candidate, and on such considerations as language, religion, Christian and family names, marriage ties, and the quality of the applicant's local sponsors. Only persons who had been citizens of Poland or Danzig as of October 26, 1939, were eligible to apply.

Successful applicants were then divided into four groups: (1) ethnic Germans who had taken an active part in the nationality struggle while living under foreign rule; (2) ethnic Germans who had not played an active role but who could prove their adherence to their German nationality; (3) ethnic Germans, or racially related persons, who had established strong ties with Poles over the years, but who showed promise of becoming racially valuable members of the Germanic community; and (4) ethnic Germans who had become Polandized (renegades). Persons belonging to the first and second groups were to be accorded both German nationality and citizenship and employed in the reconstruction of the east, although for the time being only members of the first group were to be allowed to join the Nazi party. Persons belonging to the third and fourth groups were to be removed to the Old Reich where they were to be subjected to an intensive program of re-Germanization. Members of this group were to be accorded German nationality but not German citizenship, and for members of the fourth group even German nationality was conditional. The names of persons sent to the Old Reich for Germanization were to be Germanized and were to resemble their old names as closely as possible. If this could not be done, they were to be given new names, but "of course not names with a religious connotation." Exaggeratedly Nordic names were also to be avoided.[40]

Variations in procedure and conflicts in authority among the local examination boards led in October 1941 to the establishment of a Supreme Examination Tribunal for Nationality Questions (*Oberste Prüfungshof für Volkszugehörigkeitsfragen*), which was to be run by the Central Office (*Stabshauptamt*) of Himmler's RKFDV under Himmler's chairmanship.[41] As the final authority for all Germanization questions, this court gave Himmler yet another instrument to assert his authority in the east. But the real purpose of the court—to impose unity and rationale on a basically irrational system—was never fulfilled.

The racial examination of the Polish population was conducted in the Central Immigration Offices (*Umwandererzentralstellen*, or UWZ) by officials of the Central Office for Race and Resettlement (*Rasse-und*

81

Siedlungshauptamt, or RuSHA). Their task was to screen out all Germanic elements so as to deprive the Poles of their leadership class and regain this blood for Germandom. Germanic types were to be sent to the Old Reich to undergo re-Germanization under the supervision of the local senior SS and police officers. Because these people could not be left as potential leaders among the Poles, those who refused re-Germanization were to be shot, but their children were to be sent to Germany. All other Poles were to be evacuated to the Government General, where they were to remain unless needed for menial labor in the Reich or until their lands were required for German settlements. Then they too were to be eradicated.[42]

Lack of personnel and the unwillingness of many local officials to disrupt the economy of their administrative districts made it impossible for Himmler's officials to impound the entire Polish population in immigration centers in order to determine their racial quality. The more determined of Himmler's agents were eventually compelled to resort to such methods as ordering local officials to pick out persons and families of German appearance for purposes of re-Germanization. In the end the only standard that came to be applied to racial selection was that a person was German if, in the opinion of the selector, he looked like a German. It was as good a standard as any.[43]

Statistics on the evacuations and resettlements in Poland were not always reliable, as Himmler himself often complained; but the records compiled in his own office from official reports and checked by inspectors in the field are probably as accurate as figures on such subjects can ever be.

The number of persons involved in these population movements differed widely from province to province according to the degree of co-operation of the local German administrator. Most co-operative was Arthur Greiser, Reichsstatthalter of the Wartheland (Posen), while Albert Forster in Danzig-West Prussia and Erich Koch in East Prussia tended to drag their feet. Frank in the Government General was least co-operative. Himmler's resettlement programs played havoc with the economy of his province; the large numbers of displaced persons set adrift there represented a serious threat to internal security. Moreover, as Frank's pretensions to build himself up as leader of a semiautonomous state grew, so did his resentment that his administrative preserve should be treated as a dumping ground for racially undesirable elements from which all racially valuable persons were to be removed.[44]

Statistical records of the RKFDV of December 1940, after the evacuation of Germans from the Russian sphere of influence and their resettlement during the summer and autumn of 1940, show that some 70,000 ethnic Germans from the Baltic states, 130,000 from Soviet-occupied Poland, 90,000 from the Government General, 90,000 from Bessarabia, 90,000 from North and South Bukovina, and 14,000 from the Dobruja (occupied by Bulgaria)—a total of almost 500,000 persons—had been moved to the Old Reich and to the newly incorporated eastern provinces.[45] During this same period almost 300,000 Poles—234,620 from the Wartheland, 30,758 from Danzig-West Prussia, 14,636 from East Prussia, and 14,322 from eastern Upper Silesia—had been evacuated to the Government General, together with some 9,000 Jews and gypsies from the Old Reich, Austria, and the Protectorate.[46]

Evacuations and resettlements did not cease with the attack on Russia in June 1941. Despite the army's desperate need for transportation to carry troops and supplies to the eastern front, another 175,000 ethnic Germans, their household goods, livestock, and farm equipment were moved into old and new provinces of the Reich by the end of 1941.[47] Increasing difficulties were being encountered in the actual process of resettlement, however. Forced evacuations were leading to a disastrous decline in production in all parts of the conquered east; but even more dangerous was the fact that, to an ever-increasing extent, evacuees of every age and sex were joining guerrilla bands in swamps and forests. As a result of the activity of these guerrillas, the new settlers frequently found themselves in serious physical danger. The guerrillas burned crops, killed livestock, and systematically terrorized not only the new German settlers but the Polish peasants who continued to cultivate their fields. So grave did the situation become and so serious were the protests registered by German military leaders and local administrators, that in May 1943 Himmler was obliged to instruct Ulrich Greifelt, the head of the central office of the RKFVD, that for the time being no further Poles were to be evacuated.[48]

By this time 300,000 additional ethnic Germans had been transported from Russian and Balkan territory conquered since the spring of 1941, bringing the total number of candidates for resettlement from the east alone to almost 800,000, a figure that did not include resettlers from Austria, Bohemia and Moravia, the north, or the west. Of this number, 408,000 had been successfully resettled in newly annexed eastern provinces, 74,000 in the Old Reich, while well over 300,000 had not yet been resettled or were not deemed worthy of resettlement. The labor of all these people was at least partially and in many cases totally lost to the Reich; the majority of farms from which the owners were evacuated fell into ruin and neglect, most of their livestock perished. In addition there were the losses resulting from the activities of the guerrilla bands.[49]

The losses in production did not concern Himmler who, in the summer of 1943, was busy with plans to move the 500,000 Saxons from Rumania, the ethnic Germans from Serbia and Croatia, and a maximum number of Germanic persons from the conquered western territories into the new eastern provinces. In December 1943 he told a conference of naval officers about his plans for bringing back all Germans who had emigrated to North and South America. He had come to the sober conclusion that every drop of German blood in the world, or at least in Europe, must either belong to Germany or be eradicated. To carry this racial revolution to its successful and logical conclusion was the goal of the SS.[50]

The Government General

On October 26, 1939, Dr. Hans Frank, until now supreme civil administrator for all German-occupied Polish territories, assumed his duties as head of the Government General, the administration for that part of German-occupied Poland that was not annexed to Germany.[51] Born in Karlsruhe (Baden) on May 23, 1900, Frank at the age of nineteen had joined the German Labor party, the forerunner of the NSDAP. He enlisted in the Nazi SA in 1923, took part in the November Putsch, but not until 1927 did he become a formal member of the Nazi party. Having taken his law degree in the previous year, he served principally as the party's legal adviser and demonstrated considerable skill in conducting the defense of Hitler and other party members in the numerous law suits in which they became involved. In 1929 Hitler appointed Frank head of the party's legal department and a member of the party directorate. After the Nazis came to power, Frank served briefly as minister of justice in Bavaria and as Reichskommisar of justice, in which capacity he was responsible for reforming the German legal system in the spirit of National Socialism as well as for the *Gleichschaltung* of justice in every state of the Reich. In 1934 he was appointed Reich minister without portfolio and president of the Academy of German Law, an institution founded by himself.[52]

But Frank's ambitions were as yet unfulfilled. He was bitterly disappointed at having been passed over for the post of Reich minister of justice or any other high-ranking position of real power. His appointment as governor general in Poland, while not perhaps so influential as he may have desired, at least provided him with an independent sphere of action, and one he clearly intended to make into a personal administrative empire.[53]

Hitler gave him every encouragement to do so. He had set up the Government General as a temporary Polish rump state, one that might serve as a bargaining counter with the Western powers, and he intended that its administration should be completely independent of Berlin. "We do not want to do anything there that we do in the Reich," Hitler said. "The Berlin ministries bear no responsibility because no German administrative unit is involved." Frank was made immediately and personally responsible to Hitler, he was given authority over all branches of the administration, the power to legislate by decree and to draft his own budget.[54]

Frank endeavored to take full advantage of the powers conferred on him. Preening himself as supreme legate of the Führer, he so flaunted his authority that the senior German military commander in Poland de-

84

scribed his behavior as that of a "megalomaniac pasha." But with all his efforts to appear a strong man, Frank was not a strong character. Goebbels complained that he vacillated between brusque outbursts of anger and a sort of spiritual self-mortification (qualities he was to display during his trial at Nuremberg), and that he lacked the self-assurance which alone can inspire confidence in others.[55]

Certainly Frank inspired neither confidence nor loyalty among his colleagues or in the subject Polish population. His temper tantrums and brutal displays of self-importance made him an object of contempt; and his use of his position to enrich himself and his friends and to indulge his sexual appetites exposed him to outright blackmail. His personal conduct and sporadic opposition to a radical racial policy in the Government General eventually lost him the confidence of Hitler. Without a personal following of any kind or an administrative organization on which he could count, he found himself unable to take a firm stand on any issue and proved to be no match for Himmler and his agents. Even so, although frequently on the verge of dismissal, he retained his position in the Government General to the end and, by the nature of that position, he remained the central figure in the German occupation government.

When Frank took over supreme administrative power from the German army in the Government General on October 26, 1939, he had already assembled a team of officials to staff the central administrative office he established for the province. This office was organized along typical departmental lines and was placed under the direction of a state secretary, Dr. Josef Bühler, a long-time associate who had been head of the bureau Frank had maintained as Reich minister without portfolio. Arthur Seyss-Inquart, who had been appointed deputy governor general by Hitler, exercised little influence under the jealously authoritarian Frank. In May 1940 he was withdrawn from Poland to become head of the German civil government in the Netherlands.[56]

As the capital of his administrative domain Frank selected Cracow, which Nazi theorists regarded as an ancient German city (in contrast to the predominantly Polish Warsaw, a city they proposed to relegate to relative insignificance). The official language of the Government General was German; but out of necessity the Polish language was permitted and continued to be used for most administrative functions. Polish law was to remain in force for the Polish population until superseded, or unless it proved contrary to the interests of the occupation government. All cases involving German citizens or German interests were to come before German courts and be judged according to German law.[57]

For purposes of regional administration the Government General was divided into four major districts: Cracow, Lublin, Radom, and Warsaw. A fifth, Galicia, was added on August 1, 1941, after the attack on Russia. Each district was under a German district chief (later called governor), who was immediately responsible to the governor general, from whom he received his orders and policy guidelines. The major districts in turn were subdivided into rural and urban counties (*Kreise*) under local county leaders. The German administrative units were much larger than those organized by the Polish government, because the Germans lacked the personnel to staff smaller administrative subdivisions.[58]

Frank soon found, as did other German administrators in occupied territories, that the absolute authority ostensibly conferred on him by Hitler was in fact severely limited, and that he had been made part of a typical Nazi balance of power mechanism. Although civil administrative power had been transferred from the army to the Government General after October 26, 1939, the army was still authorized to take all measures it considered necessary in the interests of military security, including the commandeering of transport and communications facilities, factories, installations, and anything else it might require.[59] The governor general was empowered to legislate by decree, but so too were the Ministerial Council for the Defense of the Reich and the plenipotentiary of the Four-Year Plan; all "supreme Reich authorities" were to make whatever arrangements were required "for the planning of German life and the German economic sphere" in the territory subject to the authority of the governor general. The budget required the approval of the Reich Ministry of Finance; the railways of the Government General (with nine thousand German and one hundred forty-five thousand Polish employees) were to be operated by the Ostbahn as a subsidiary of the German Reichsbahn; and, finally, the Reich minister of the interior was named the central authority for the occupied Polish territories. Thus from the start Frank's powers were subject to serious encroachment from many sides.[60]

Frank's position in the Government General was not made any easier by the policies of Hitler. Shortly before the transfer of the conquered Polish territories from a military to a civilian government, Hitler told General Wilhelm Keitel that the Wehrmacht should be glad to be relieved of administrative duties in Poland, because many of the tasks to be carried out there would be far from pleasant. The German civilian administration would not be expected to make Poland a model province along German lines, or to clean up the country economically and financially. "All attempts to establish orderly conditions in Poland must be avoided, 'Polish chaos' [*die 'polnische Wirtschaft'*] must be allowed to flourish." Germany's only interest lay in exploiting the area economically and retaining it as an advance glacis for future military deployment purposes. To that end the railroads, highways, and lines of communication were to be kept in order and utilized for Germany's needs.

In his first policy directives to Frank, Hitler insisted that the Government General was to be regarded solely as an object of booty and was to be ruthlessly exploited in the German interest. All raw materials, machines, and any other products that might be of any use whatever to the

German war economy, including labor forces, were to be shipped off to Germany, and the economy of Poland itself was to be so throttled as to reduce the local population to a minimum level of subsistence. All educational institutions, especially technical schools and universities, were to be closed to prevent the development of a Polish intelligentsia. "Poland is to be treated as a colony, the Poles are to be the slaves of the Great-German World Reich."

Apart from that, the Government General was to serve as a dumping ground for undesirable elements from the Reich and the newly annexed provinces. It was to be a home for Poles and Jews, who were to be deprived of leadership and reduced to an elementary cultural and economic level. The population should be nothing more than a reservoir of menial labor for the Reich.

To carry out this policy, a tough racial war would have to be waged that would admit of no legal restrictions, nor would the methods employed be compatible with "our usual principles." The purpose of the entire operation in Poland would be to spare the Germans for all time the need to do battle on account of this country again.[61]

This line of policy was all very well for a Hitler intoxicated with victory and the apparent confirmation of his racial theories through the quick collapse of Polish military resistance; but it was another matter to govern a province with the maintenance of chaos as the sole guiding principle. "We had not been in this territory long," Frank confessed later, "before we saw that this path led to totally negative results, and that it was the German Reich itself that suffered most."[62]

There was the further problem that Hitler never clearly defined the territorial extent or status of the Government General. In November 1939 he expressed his intention of keeping this territory permanently under German control, but Frank was left without further guidelines. He told his senior officials in December that Hitler had not yet determined the final form of the Government General, or whether it would even be a permanent institution. He knew only that it was the will of the Führer to make this area the first colony of the German nation.[63] And indeed it fit the condition laid down in *Mein Kampf* that the only colonies of lasting value to the Reich were contiguous territories in Eastern Europe.

Until the fall of France Hitler evidently still thought he might use "the Government General for the Occupied Polish Territories" as a bargaining counter in making peace with the Western powers. Long before this hope had been permanently dashed he had made it clear in his private conversations that he had no intention of setting up a permanent Polish rump state; when the opportune moment came, the Government General, like the rest of Poland, was to be used as an area of Germanic colonization and absorbed into the Greater German Reich.[64] Frank understood these long-range plans well enough; but meanwhile the indefinite status of the Government General made it difficult for him to make even short-range plans and deprived his administration of any real sense of direction.

After the fall of France, when there was no longer any question of setting up even a sham Polish state, Frank thought the time had come to persuade Hitler to give precise definition to the status of the Government General and its administration. For this purpose he asked Hans Lammers to arrange a conference with the Führer. He wanted to discuss the question of incorporating the Government General into the Reich and to stress the economic importance of extending the boundaries of the province to include the coal fields of the Dombrawa region. At the same time he also hoped to convince the Führer of the need to stop the indiscriminate dumping of Poles and Jews in the province, which was already dangerously overcrowded.[65]

Frank was granted his conference early in July. Hitler refused to extend the boundaries of the Government General, nor would he consider its incorporation into the Reich at this time. He did, however, agree that the name of the Government General could be changed from the Government General for the Occupied Polish Territories to the Government General or the Government General, Poland, and that Frank's own title could be changed accordingly. Hitler agreed further that "naturally there could no longer be any question of relinquishing the territory of the Government General, and that therefore it would become and remain German Reich territory for all time." The province was not to be divided, Cracow was to remain its capital; Warsaw was not to be rebuilt as a Polish metropolis but was to be reduced to the status of a provincial city. "Very significant too is the decision of the Führer, which he made at my request," Frank told his staff afterward, "that there shall be no more transports of Jews to the Government General." The program for the Jews was to move them all to an African or American colony, perhaps Madagascar, where they could begin a new life. This would mean the elimination of an enormous burden for the administration of the Government General.[66] On July 24, 1940, Frank changed the name of his province to The Government General. In a public speech soon afterward he stated frankly that the area would remain permanently under German leadership "so that peace and order might be preserved there for all time." [67]

In September 1940 Hitler informed Frank that the Government General was no longer to be treated as occupied territory but as part of the German Reich; and in the following month he designated the province as a *Nebenland* (adjunct) of the Reich. At the same time he emphatically rejected Frank's request for a customs or currency union with the Reich, a measure which would achieve the opposite of what he intended, namely, to preserve this area as a gigantic labor reservoir.[68]

A year later Frank was gratified that Hitler had allowed him to bring out a postage stamp with the inscription "Deutsches Reich—

Generalgouvernement." That the Führer had made a territory under occupation a part of the German Reich only two years after a German administration had been established there he regarded as an enormous distinction, he told a colleague.[69] But Hitler never took the final step of actually incorporating the province into the Reich. To the end of the war Frank had to be satisfied with his postage stamp.

News of the imminent attack on Russia stimulated Frank, like every other Nazi leader, to seek an extension of his power base. He asked that the area of the Pripet Marshes, with Brest-Litovsk and the Goryn River valley, be attached to the Government General. "I would then have the possibility to undertake a gigantic improvement program [*Meliorationswerk*] with the Polish and other labor forces that would be available to me." All Frank received, however, was the province of Galicia, which was made part of the Government General by a Hitler order of August 1, 1941.[70]

With the German occupation of immense additional areas in Eastern Europe in the summer of 1941, Frank claimed a new and vastly greater significance for his administrative preserve. Instead of being an advance outpost of German rule in the east, it had become the very hub of Germany's eastern activity. Frank was certain that there could now no longer be any question that the Government General would have to become a German province, as free of Jews as the Reich itself, and that all Poles and Ukrainians, too, would eventually have to be cleared out completely.[71]

When German administrators in Russia drew up plans for creating a Gau of the Goths in those areas once inhabited by Gothic tribes, Frank expressed the intention of making the Government General into a Gau of the Vandals (*Vandalengau*) to commemorate these most misunderstood and maligned of all Germanic peoples. This was their country of origin, here they had built up their *Kultur*. This Gau of the Vandals would one day help to repay the terrible debt the world owed to one of the most noble of Germanic tribes, whose name had been synonymous with evil for two thousand years—a fact which was, incidentally, a masterpiece of anti-German propaganda. Just how and when the area would be Germanized and incorporated into the Greater German Reich the Führer had not yet decided, but one thing was clear, this area was and would remain German for all time.[72]

Frank's own policies in the Government General fluctuated with the shifts in the status of his province and with the need to adjust to the actual problems confronting his administration. In contrast to Hitler, he realized that to operate any kind of government in a territory inhabited by an overwhelming majority of Poles, the co-operation of the Polish population was essential. In his first proclamation to the Polish people on October 26, 1939, he spoke of his desire to develop neighborly relations with the Poles and of incorporating them into the world Reich of the German nation. "You will be allowed to conduct your life in accor-

dance with your age-old customs, to retain your Polish identity in all aspects of communal life." [73]

This proclamation was not mere propagandistic hypocrisy. Lack of
trained German personnel would have made it impossible for Frank to
carry out Hitler's program in the Government General even if he had
desired to do so. In late 1939 his entire German staff for both central
and local government consisted of fewer than eight hundred persons,
many of them inexperienced. He was thus obliged to employ Poles to fill
not only the lower administrative positions, but many of the higher
ranks as well. With his government almost entirely dependent on Poles
to carry out its orders, Frank was hardly in a position to conduct a policy of ruthless repression and exploitation.[74]

There was the additional factor of Frank's personal ambition. An economically devastated land, the dumping ground for Jews and Poles expelled from other parts of German-occupied Europe, was hardly the
ideal basis on which to build up his own power in the Reich. Instead of
merely exploiting the Government General, therefore, he sought to establish orderly conditions there. By January 1940 he thought he had
won Hitler over to his point of view. As a result of their educational experiences in Poland during the past months, he told his staff, the official
attitude in Berlin toward the Government General had changed completely. "Today the territory of the Government General is regarded as a
valuable part of the German *Lebensraum*. The principle of absolute destruction has changed into the principle of fostering this territory in its
present status in every way that may bring advantage to the Reich." The
two central tasks were: (1) to prevent any revival of Polish power and
eliminate Poland permanently as a threat to the Reich; and (2) to put a
maximum amount of the human and material resources of the area at
the disposal of the German war economy.[75]

To ensure maximum productivity in the Government General, Frank
insisted that it was essential to secure the labor of Poles and other non-
German nationalities. Hence he demanded that they be accorded decent
treatment so long as they behaved themselves. Mass executions and the
policy of naked exploitation would have to cease; the Poles were to be
reassured about their future status in a German-ordered world. The
Jews, too, who were both more industrious and able than the Poles,
should be allowed to continue in their present occupations.

To implement his conciliatory policy toward the non-German peoples,
Frank proposed to give the Poles greater cultural opportunities, to allow
medical and technical students to complete their studies, to re-establish
Polish technical schools which would provide training up to the lowest
grade of a German technical secondary school. Polish workers were to
be given better treatment and assurances of personal and economic security. Even greater concessions were to be made to the Ukrainians in
the Government General, as part of the German policy of playing the
subject nationalities off against each other. They were to be promised

cultural autonomy and were to be allowed to open secondary schools, a university, and seminaries for priests.

Frank turned aside the complaints of fanatic Germanizers, who deplored the fact that the Polish language was still tolerated in official transactions in the Government General, or that the Poles were allowed to live according to their own laws and to exercise a limited amount of self-government. He went further, and openly denounced Germanization policies such as those of the Ostbahn, which published its instructions and timetables exclusively in German. Such policies accomplished nothing but to make it more difficult for the Poles to co-operate with the Germans.

For the Germans it was absolutely essential to secure such co-operation. How else could they expect to keep millions of Poles in order and productive for the Reich with a minimum investment of German personnel? All measures injurious to a policy of working with the Poles jeopardized the interests of the Reich and were contrary to the wishes of the Führer. Frank reassured his German colleagues that if he, as governor general, were treating the Poles decently and even giving them a friendly pat on the back now and then, he was not doing so out of love for the Poles or because of misguided humanitarian sentiments, but solely in the expectation that as a result of such treatment they would produce more for the benefit of the Reich. This was not a racial but a tactical-strategic problem, and he requested all his officials in the Government General to recognize it as such. Frank made it clear that if his conciliatory policies failed to produce results in the form of increased productivity, he would not hesitate to apply Draconian measures. He intended to keep a watchful eye on the Polish intelligentsia, the Roman Catholic Church, and other possible centers of resistance, and to proceed against them ruthlessly if necessary. The Jews on the other hand constituted no danger. "There was therefore no need to introduce the racial legislation of the Reich in the Government General." [76]

By the summer of 1940 Frank was able to draw on the authority of Hitler to forbid the further dumping of undesirable racial elements in the Government General, and to oppose all programs of Germanization as well. The Führer had ordered that for the time being at least the Government General should be set aside as a homeland for the Poles and that it was to be regarded as "a sort of reservation." Frank would therefore allow no further resettlement or Germanization programs to be conducted there. Besides, there was already ample territory available for the resettlement of ethnic Germans. As Germany still needed Polish labor, it made no sense to Germanize the Government General until the Warthegau, West Prussia, Danzig, and the other incorporated areas had been Germanized according to the principles laid down by the Führer. This naturally should not prevent German officials in the Government General from doing everything possible to further the German cause. And for this purpose, if only because of their paucity in numbers, the

Germans living and working in the province should present a united front.[77]

One of Frank's greatest problems was that the Germans in the Government General did not in fact present a united front, and that other German officials had been given broad and independent authority in his administrative domain. Frank did his best to override competition by dealing highhandedly with the army and other Reich agencies. "In questions of large-scale planning he alone would make the decisions and he would duly inform the Reich offices about them," he told representatives of the army at the time of his appointment.[78] But assertions of authority were not enough, and Frank found himself engaged in a constant power struggle throughout the years of his administration.

By the end of 1939 Frank had won something of a victory over Göring, who as head of the Ministerial Council for the Defense of the Reich and plenipotentiary of the Four-Year Plan had been empowered to legislate by decree in the Government General. Seeing in Frank an ally against Himmler, Göring appointed him his deputy as plenipotentiary of the Four-Year Plan and Reich defense commissar in the Government General. The following February he agreed to restrict the activities of his Main Trustee Office East, which had been organized for the confiscation of Polish property, to the territories to be annexed to Germany, and in general to work through the offices of the governor general in implementing his own economic programs.[79]

Frank was less fortunate in dealing with other Reich authorities. In his contest with the army he was at a grave disadvantage because of the small size of his staff and his consequent need to rely on army administrative personnel. So great was this reliance that during the autumn and winter of 1939–40 much of the administration of the Government General was actually carried on by army administrative and economic officials, who were in large part responsible for the re-establishment of some semblance of order in the country, an achievement for which Frank later took full credit.[80]

Frank attempted to compensate for the weakness of his position by securing repeated confirmation of his authority from Hitler, and he constantly reminded local military commanders and other German officials of the powers that had been conferred on him. He and he alone was the representative of the Reich and the personal deputy of the Führer in the Government General; orders coming from the Reich had to be discussed with him and required his personal approval before they could be carried out. This included orders for the army and, so far as he was concerned, the powers granted to the army to take independent action in certain situations were for all practical purposes null and void.[81]

By the spring of 1940 Frank had gained an apparent victory over the army. Through personal intervention with Hitler he succeeded in securing the removal of General Johannes Blaskowitz, the supreme military commander in the Government General, who had consistently opposed

Frank's effort to impose National Socialist principles in the province. After Blaskowitz's departure in May, the army gradually withdrew from its administrative role. But Frank was not to fill the void thus created, for the place of the army was almost entirely usurped by Himmler's SS and police who, in the Government General as everywhere else in the Nazi empire, had been building their influence with steady persistence.[82]

Frank had done his best to ensure his authority over Himmler's forces. A decree issued on his first day in office, October 26, 1939, provided that the senior SS and police officer in the Government General was to be directly subordinate and responsible to himself and that, before issuing any important orders, especially those involving questions of principle, he had to obtain Frank's specific approval.[83]

Himmler, however, was a master at circumventing regulations of this kind. On October 31, Frank was persuaded to sign a decree "to combat acts of violence," which in effect gave the senior SS and police officer in the Government General (SS Obergruppenführer Friederich Wilhelm Krüger) unlimited authority to act as he saw fit in the name of preserving security and order.[84] Krüger took full advantage of the power this decree permitted him to exercise, securing control over the Polish police forces, which were allowed to remain in existence to carry out routine police functions under the direction of German officials.[85]

After the ouster of Blaskowitz in May 1940, Frank was virtually helpless in dealing with the German police. Armed forces were necessary for purposes of security. By turning against the army Frank in effect delivered himself into the hands of Himmler, who controlled the only other armed forces in Poland. Frank tried to counter the influence of Himmler's police by setting up a task force of his own, which was to be composed of "exemplary men of German nationality" in the Government General. Unfortunately for Frank, most men of German nationality, exemplary or otherwise, were engaged in other occupations. His task force never assumed any real significance, and in May 1942 he was obliged to submit even this group to Himmler's control.[86]

Himmler was even more successful in encroaching on Frank's authority in the field of race and resettlement. Shortly after his appointment as RKFDV in October 1939, he demanded the removal from the newly annexed provinces of all Jews, gypsies, Poles who had migrated there since 1918, and other "trash." These people, about one million in all, were to be dumped in the Government General by the February of the following year. At the same time some four million racially valuable persons now living in the Government General were to be moved to the old and new provinces of the Reich. The transportation for this mass resettlement job was to be organized by SS Obergruppenführer Krüger, who declared that after November 15 the entire railway network of the Government General would be devoted to the resettlement operation. His schedule called for the shipment of ten thousand Jews and Poles into the province daily.[87] Because of the powers Hitler had conferred on Himmler as RKFDV, Frank was forced to agree to these measures and even give the necessary orders to Krüger to carry them out. Unable to prevent Himmler's incursion into his administrative domain, he could only express his resentment and attempt to save face by belligerently reasserting his claim to exclusive political authority. Neither the Wehrmacht, the SS and police, the party, or any other Reich or party agency had the right to exercise any political influence whatever in the Government General, he told his department heads early in 1940. "Here there is no state within a state. Instead we are the representatives of the Führer and the Reich." [88]

When, in the summer of 1940, Frank succeeded in obtaining assurances from Hitler that no further resettlement or Germanization programs were to be carried out in the Government General [89] he appeared to have won a significant victory over Himmler. But he soon found that he had accomplished nothing. Transports of Poles and Jews continued to arrive in the Government General; on November 4, 1940, Hitler blandly contradicted his previous assurances to Frank by stating that the evacuation of non-Germans from Reich territory was part of his policy. Moreover these evacuations were to be carried out while the war was still in progress, because later such operations would encounter all kinds of international difficulties.[90]

At a conference on January 8, 1941, Reinhard Heydrich, who was in charge of planning the entire evacuation and resettlement program, informed the German officials involved in the operation that about eight hundred and thirty-one thousand Poles and Jews would have to be removed shortly from the newly annexed eastern provinces to make room for ethnic Germans from Wolhynia, Lithuania, and other areas. Another two hundred thousand were to be removed from territory needed by the German army for military training grounds, bringing the total to be evacuated during the current year to well over a million. Heydrich's schedule called for the evacuation by May 1 of two hundred and thirty-eight thousand Poles and Jews from the newly annexed provinces plus ten thousand Jews from Vienna. These persons were to be deposited in the Government General at the rate of two thousand a day.[91]

Frank and his staff were in despair, especially as no provision was being made for taking care of the evacuees. The influx of so many people would inevitably create security and health problems. Plans were considered to set up enormous work camps for the Poles, to house the Jews in existing ghettos, to send large numbers of Polish workers to the Reich to make room for the new arrivals. One aide suggested that Frank try to reduce the number of persons to be evacuated, but Frank said it would be easier to accept them all—and then send one hundred and twenty to one hundred and fifty thousand back by special transports. It was hardly an efficient use of manpower, or of German transportation facilities.[92]

Frank made further representations to Hitler, received further assurances that mass evacuations to the Government General would cease, but the dumping process went on until the eve of the Russian campaign. By October 1941 Frank feared that Hitler's attitude toward the Government General had reverted to what it had been in the first months of the war, and that the province was again being regarded as nothing more than an object of spoliation.[93]

As Frank's influence declined, the Himmler forces stepped up their demands. In November 1941 SS Obergruppenführer Krüger claimed absolute and sole authority over all police, race, and resettlement problems in his capacity as Himmler's representative. "All racial-political activity in the Government General will be co-ordinated and directed by me and by me exclusively as deputy of the Reichsführer SS in his capacity as RKFDV," Krüger wrote to the head of the RKFDV central office. This included supervision of the work of all other agencies involved in the racial-political program.[94]

When Frank balked at conceding Krüger these powers, Himmler resorted to other tactics. In some way he got at State Secretary Bühler, Frank's long-time associate, who sent Himmler a detailed report about the disgraceful personal conduct of officials in the Government General including that of the governor general himself.[95] This report was forwarded to Lammers, who summoned Frank to a conference in Himmler's private train on March 5, 1942, where he was confronted by Himmler, Lammers, and Bormann. Lammers opened the meeting by informing Frank that serious charges had been leveled against his regime and that he had been invited to discuss these problems in a friendly spirit without having to disturb the Führer about them. Frank had been accused of nepotism and corruption, his sister had negotiated with Jews, his brother-in-law had renounced his German nationality and become a citizen of Sweden.

The March 5 meeting accomplished all that Himmler could have desired. Frank accepted all conditions imposed upon him. Krüger was made state secretary for security and the consolidation of the German people in the administration of the Government General. Frank conceded him full responsibility for all police and racial questions, and he agreed to place his own recently recruited police force under Krüger's command. Lammers would secure from the Führer a decree empowering the RFSS to issue orders directly to the new state secretary, although decrees based on these orders would continue to be issued in the name of the governor general.[96]

Frank put up a brave front. Upon his return to Cracow, he informed his staff that on all essential questions his conference with Himmler had ended in complete victory for himself. The principle had been established that racial questions were not the responsibility of the police (Frank did not mention that they were to be the responsibility of the deputy of the RKFDV). Krüger, in his new capacity as state secretary, was to be subordinate not only to the governor general but to Bühler, the senior state secretary. And all SS and police officers were to remain under the authority of the governor general.[97]

It was a futile effort to save face. On March 7, 1942, Lammers sent Himmler the draft of a Führer decree embodying the administrative changes to be introduced in the Government General which, after being approved by Himmler, was published in the *Reichsgesetzblatt* (*RGBl*) on May 7.[98] After the publication of the May 7 decree, according to Frank's testimony at Nuremberg, Krüger never obeyed a single one of his orders and never bothered to obtain his approval for measures carried out by the SS and police.[99] In this case Frank appears to have told the truth.

Frustrated by the diminution of his authority and the pursuit of what he regarded as a mistaken policy in the Government General, Frank submitted his resignation to Hitler on August 24, 1942. The fact that Hitler refused to accept his resignation did not reassure Frank. He was convinced that the Himmler faction had resolved to oust him in any case, and that the policies now being pursued in Poland were disastrous. "For it is clear . . . that the Führer's present course of brute force, the complete abolition of legal guarantees, of government based on concentration camps and police despotism, represented the greatest possible danger for the Führer and his Reich." The current German policy was a hopeless paradox. "You should not slaughter the cow you want to milk. But the Reich under the pressure of circumstances wants to milk the Government General and slaughter it as well." [100]

Following his triumph over Frank, Himmler's own policy toward the Government General changed. Having heretofore used the province as a racial dumping ground, he decided in the spring of 1942 to initiate a program of Germanization in accordance with his policy of Germanizing those regions he planned to make into border marches or connecting links between the provinces of the Germanic empire. On May 14, 1942, he established a branch of the Central Office for Immigration (*Einwandererzentralstelle,* or EWZ) in the Government General to undertake those racial examinations which were the essential prelude to resettlements.[101]

The first area of the Government General Himmler had singled out for Germanization was the province of Lublin. By mid-June 1942 the Jews had been removed from the city of Lublin, and all other Jews in the province had been herded into the ghettos of smaller towns. State Secretary Krüger reported that plans for the final evacuation of all Jews had been prepared and that his men were only waiting for the necessary transportation facilities to be made available.[102] In November Himmler ordered Krüger to begin the Germanization of the Zamość region in the southern part of the Lublin province. The EWZ was to conduct the seizure (*Erfassung*), examination, and naturalization of the persons to be resettled, while the German Resettlement Trusteeship Corporation

(*Deutsche Umsiedlungs-Treuhandgesellschaft,* or DUT) was to be responsible for working out property compensations and providing the settlers with basic necessities. The first resettlements began shortly before Christmas, when four thousand Wolhynian Germans were established in Zamosć. As there was no transportation available to evacuate the Poles, they were simply driven out of their homes and herded into camps.[103]

German administrators, who continued to be dependent on the Polish population to carry on the routine work of running the country, now found the entire situation in the Government General dissolving into chaos. The effects on the native population of resettlements and rumors of resettlements were summed up in the bitter criticisms of Ernst Zörner, the governor of the Lublin province. The chief results, he told Frank in a letter of February 1943, were the flight of the Polish peasants to avoid being sent as forced labor to Auschwitz or Germany, and a sharp decline in production. The supply of milk had declined 75 per cent or more in some areas. The peasants, women and children included, were joining guerrilla bands and either took their livestock with them or slaughtered them because they saw no hope for the future. Driven by the fury of despair, they were ravaging the country, killing, burning, sabotaging. And the German police, fully occupied with resettlement operations, were not available for the preservation of order when disorder was growing at an alarming rate. The new German settlements themselves were under constant attack, the settlers fearful and for the most part dissatisfied because they were often established in farms far worse than those they had been compelled to leave. This resettlement business during a time of total war, when every bit of manpower and every kernel of grain was so desperately needed, was totally irresponsible, and he called upon Frank to put an end to the operation once and for all.[104]

Frank agreed entirely, but he was powerless. Zörner resigned in May 1943. Other Nazi officials in high places were equally powerless. "It makes you want to tear your hair out when you encounter such appalling political ineptitude," Goebbels wrote in his diary when he heard of Zörner's resignation. "In the occupied areas affairs are being conducted as though we were living in profound peace." [105]

Even Himmler's officials were obliged to recognize the growing restlessness of the population. However, they attributed it not to their own activities but to the perverse nature of the Pole. Himmler's trusted lieutenant Gottlob Berger regretted the withdrawal of Oskar Dirlewanger's special SS task force composed of convicted criminals. This should be a warning, Berger said, "that a savage country cannot be ruled with kid gloves and that the motto of the task force: 'better shoot two Poles too many than one too few' was right." What was needed in Poland was more Dirlewanger units.[106]

Himmler himself held grimly to his course. When State Secretary Hans-Joachim Riecke, head of the food and agriculture section of the German economic staff in the east, protested that resettlement was causing serious damage to agricultural production, Himmler ordered that Riecke be forbidden to make use of tendentious reports to cover up his own responsibility for agricultural failures. The resettlement programs were to go on, and as rapidly as conditions would permit. Particularly urgent was the removal of the three to four hundred thousand [sic] Jews still remaining in the Government General; but preparations should also be made for getting hold of the three to four hundred thousand ethnic Germans in the area, more than half of whom would probably be worthy of Germanization. It was particularly desirable to undertake as many resettlements as possible during the war, when they could be carried out as a sort of joint operation. After the war there would be too many other grandiose tasks to perform.[107]

Overwhelmed by the problems his government was facing, Frank again attempted to persuade Hitler of the catastrophic consequences of Himmler's population policies. As a good National Socialist, he said in a letter of May 25, 1943, he understood the importance of these measures, but he questioned whether they should be undertaken in the midst of Germany's fight for existence. The evacuation of Poles was being carried out by the German police in the most ruthless way, people were often given no more than ten minutes and never more than two hours to pack, everyone was herded into mass camps. The result had been economic chaos, the mass flight of the population to partisan bands, and a sharp increase in violence and terrorism. In reprisal the German police were carrying out mass shootings of innocent people, including children and the aged, which only led to further unrest. The state secretary for security and Germanization was requisitioning buildings, hospitals, and moveable property with total disregard for the needs of the German administration in the Government General. To give him a chance to deal effectively with this unbearable situation, Frank appealed to Hitler to clarify his authority over the state secretary for security.[108]

Unfortunately for Frank, his letter to Hitler crossed the desk of Lammers, who sent a copy to Himmler with the request for his opinion "so that I may be in a position to give the Führer an objective picture of the situation in my forthcoming conference with him on the subject." Receiving no reply to his appeal of May 25, Frank tried again on June 19, with a forty-page letter describing in even greater detail the deplorable situation in the Government General.[109] In response to this effort, Lammers again bypassed Hitler by arranging another personal confrontation between Frank and Himmler at Himmler's field headquarters on June 23.[110] At this conference verbal agreement about the entire resettlement procedure in the Government General was reached.

Himmler recorded his version of that agreement in a letter to Frank. "Our first aim must be to populate the eastern frontier of the Government General with Germans. For this purpose the Lublin district and the former German villages of Galicia have been considered." Resettlements during wartime should of course not be allowed to interfere seri-

ously with domestic peace and economic productivity, but excessive ti-
midity was also undesirable. Accordingly, Himmler was going ahead
with resettlement operations. The plan for the district of Lublin called
for the Germanization by 1944 of the Zamosć region and of the old
Hansa city of Lublin itself. A large-scale resettlement project (Operation
Werewolf) had recently cleared an area south of the Bilgoraj forests, to
which the present Polish inhabitants of Zamosć and Lublin would be
moved. This area was also to be resettled with an equal number of
Ukrainians, to permit Germans to govern on the divide and rule principle. "From now on Germans will be settled continuously on the farms
which have become vacant as a result of the departure of the Ukrainian
and Polish population of the Zamosć region. Among these Germans are
ethnic Germans, some of whom are already Germanic peasants, artisans,
or entrepreneurs; further, there are the Alsatians and Lorrainers, who
are to be settled in the east in accordance with a Führer order; and
Slovenian settlers from Upper Carniola and Lower Styria, who are on
the whole very good. Simultaneously with the settlement of the countryside, the relentless Germanization of the city of Zamosć must be carried
forward."

Himmler believed it would be possible to have a German population
of 20–25 per cent in Lublin by the beginning of 1944, and 30–40 per
cent by the following year, at which time Lublin would be declared a
German city and be given a German lord mayor. "The prerequisite for
all these measures is the complete co-operation which we discussed between the administration on the one hand and the SS and police on the
other, and an absolutely unbureaucratic procedure in the execution of
our common purposes." [111]

As in 1941, Frank claimed that he had won a major victory in his conference with Himmler. Himmler was quick to set the record straight,
however. "I hear through various circles that you boast of having scored
the biggest political success of your life in your talk with me," he wrote
Frank on August 16. But Frank was seriously deceiving himself. Himmler had only wanted to clarify their relationship so as not to injure
German interests in the Government General. "Rest assured that I can
continue my activity in the Government General without consulting you
in any way, and that I shall be pleased to represent my point of view to
the Führer. I know that the Führer will agree with me, just as he did in
the case when you tried to interfere with my justifiable measures in the
Warsaw ghetto." [112]

As Himmler had long been carrying on his activity in the Government
General without consulting Frank, his threat was of no significance.
What was significant was that Krüger, whose authority Himmler had
consistently enlarged, began to feel strong enough to defy his creator.
He was soon shown the limits of his strength. On October 22, 1943, Himmler stripped him of all his offices in the Government General and appointed Wilhelm Koppe to take his place. [113]

The ouster of Krüger led to something of a reconciliation between Himmler and Frank, who reported to Lammers on November 22 that he had had a very satisfactory talk with the Reichsführer SS. He was well pleased with Koppe and believed that a satisfactory working relationship with the police had now been permanently established.[114]

In fact very little changed in Frank's relationship with the Himmler organization. What did change was the position of the Government General itself, which by the autumn of 1943 had once again become an outpost of the Nazi empire as Russian troops advanced all along the line of Germany's eastern front. By July 1944 the Russians had broken into the Government General itself and set up a provisional Polish government at Chelm (afterward moved to Lublin) to offset the anti-Communist Polish government in exile in London. As the Russians approached Warsaw a Polish underground army, organized under the auspices of the London exile government, launched a major uprising in the city on August 1, 1944. Instead of pressing their offensive, the Russians, evidently fearing that the underground revolt was directed against themselves as much as against the Germans, stood by while the Germans crushed the Polish forces, who surrendered on October 2. This was to be the last German success in Poland. The Russians entered Warsaw on January 11, 1945, and by mid-March they were in control of all Polish and German territory east of the Oder.[115]

Already by July of the previous year, Frank had been making preparations for the evacuation of his government. He was still in Cracow to celebrate the victory over the Polish underground army, but his appeals to exploit the anti-Russian sentiment of the Polish population went unheeded. Hitler refused to sanction the use of Polish forces against the Russians, and to the end backed up the measures of his racial extremists.[116]

The late start of the Germanization program in the Government General, the opposition of Frank and other German administrators, and finally the rapid advance of the Russians made it impossible for Himmler to meet his resettlement schedule. By January 1944 only some thirty-three thousand persons had been relocated in this territory, many of them Germans with most dubious racial qualifications.[117]

Meanwhile far more had been accomplished with respect to the Jews, who had been the subject of special legislation from the day the Government General was established. On October 26, 1939, a Frank decree introduced compulsory labor for Jews not otherwise employed in jobs the occupation authorities considered useful.[118] In subsequent decrees the term *Jew* was defined, Jews were required to wear the Star of David emblem, Jewish enterprises had to be identified as such, and all Jewish property had to be declared. The Jews were organized under Jewish councils, which were held responsible for the implementation of ordinances pertaining to Jews. At first forbidden to change their places of residence, they were later compelled to live in special areas (ghettos) "in the interests of public order and security." [119]

In October 1939 Himmler inaugurated his program of dumping Jews from Germany and other parts of German-occupied Europe in the Government General. Because of transportation difficulties, however, the actual shipment of Jews did not begin until December 1, and even then not so many were evacuated as Himmler had planned. Nevertheless, by the spring of 1940 the original Jewish population of the Government General of 1.4 million had been increased to almost 2 million.[120]

Faced with a housing shortage in his capital of Cracow, Frank decided in April 1940 to take advantage of the general evacuation project to remove the Jews from that city. If the Reich intended to send almost half a million Jews to the Government General anyway, then the fifty thousand Jews from Cracow could also be moved. To justify this action, he proposed to point out that it was absolutely intolerable to have thousands upon thousands of Jews slinking about and inhabiting houses in a city which the Führer had honored by making the seat of a major Reich office. It was his plan to have Cracow completely freed of Jews by November 1, 1940, leaving only some five to ten thousand Jewish workers whose skills were essential to the local economy. After that the ghetto was to be cleaned up to make room for decent German housing in which a German air could be breathed. "What was to be done with the Poles was a question reserved for the future; for the time being at any rate they were to remain here." [121]

Faced with ever-increasing administrative difficulties connected with the relocation of Jews, Frank persuaded Hitler in the summer of 1940 to order a halt to further Jewish transports to the Government General. Informing his department chiefs of Hitler's decision, Frank said, "In general political terms I would like to say on this point that the plan is to transport the entire Jewish clan in the German Reich, the Government General, and the Protectorate in the shortest possible time after the conclusion of peace to an African or American colony. Madagascar is being considered, and is to be given up by France for this purpose." [122]

On September 12 Frank told his department chiefs that he had agreed to the sealing off of the Warsaw ghetto, above all because of the danger of allowing half a million Jews to mill about freely, but also because these Jews were essential to the economy of the country. "We cannot teach the Poles either the initiative or the ability to enable them to take the place of the Jews." [123]

Meanwhile, despite Hitler's assurances, Jews continued to be shipped to the Government General. Early in 1941 Frank was faced with a massive new evacuation project that would dump approximately one million additional Poles and Jews in his province in the course of the year.[124] Frank's protests were largely disregarded, but with the beginning of the Russian campaign the Reich officials concerned with the Jewish problem also began to have doubts about their Jewish policy. The temporary resettlement of the Jews until they could be evacuated permanently to Madagascar or elsewhere outside Europe was growing increasingly difficult. It would be both simpler and safer, they reasoned, to destroy the Jews altogether.[125]

Some time toward the end of 1941 Frank appears to have been informed of the new policy for dealing with the Jewish problem, for in a conference on December 16 he confided to the leaders of his government, "As for the Jews—this I will also tell you openly—they will have to be finished off in one way or another [*Mit den Juden . . . muss so oder so Schluss gemacht werden*]." Frank had opened negotiations to send the Jews farther east, but all plans had to await the results of a major conference on the subject which was to be held in January at the RSHA under the chairmanship of Heydrich.

> At all events, a great Jewish migration is to take place. But what is to be done with these Jews? Do you think they will settle them in resettlement villages in the Ostland?[126] In Berlin they told us: Why all this fuss; we can't use them in the Ostland or the Reich Commissariat [of the Ukraine] either. Liquidate them yourselves! Gentlemen, I must ask you to arm yourselves against all considerations of pity. We must destroy the Jews wherever we find them and wherever possible.

This policy would require new and extraordinary measures, but the means for carrying it out would have to be found "and I have my own ideas on the subject." Moreover the Jews were consuming vast quantities of food.

> We have in the Government General an estimated 2.5 million Jews; perhaps, counting the Mixed Jews and their various hangers-on, 3.5 million Jews. We cannot shoot these 3.5 million Jews, we cannot poison them, but we nevertheless can take measures which will somehow lead to successful annihilation in conjunction with the great measures to be discussed in the Reich. The Government General must become as free of Jews as the Reich. Where and how this is to be done is the task of the agencies which we will have to introduce and create here, and of whose activities I will inform you at the appropriate time.[127]

The "great measures" to which Frank referred were discussed at the Wannsee conference of January 20, 1942, when the decision was made to round up all Jews in areas under German control and send them to the east in large labor gangs where the majority were expected to perish through a process of natural attrition. Those who did not die were to be "dealt with" later.[128]

State Secretary Bühler, Frank's representative at the Wannsee conference, urged that the final solution be initiated in the Government General immediately. He explained that the transportation problem was negligible, and that the Jews in the Government General, the majority of whom were unfit for work in any case, represented a serious danger as bearers of disease and, through their black market activities, as disrupters of the economy. Bühler had only one request: that the Jewish problem in the Government General be solved as quickly as possible.[129]

As Bühler already knew, various plans had been under consideration for some time for solving the Jewish question, and in March 1942 the first of four permanent centers in the Government General was established for the purpose of killing the Jews in gas chambers. The Nazi authorities continued to speak of sending these Jews east, but in fact all permanent gas chamber installations were located in the former territories of Poland.[130]

Goebbels, who appears to have been well informed about what was happening to the Jews, wrote in his diary on March 27, 1942,

> Starting with Lublin, the deportation of Jews from the Government General to the east has been set in train. It is a pretty barbarous business— one would not wish to go into details. Not much will remain of the Jews. I should think that about 60 per cent of them will have to be liquidated and about 40 per cent can be used for forced labor. The former Gauleiter of Vienna [Odilo Globocnik, the head of the SS and police in the Lublin province of the Government General], who is in charge of the operation, is carrying it out with a good deal of circumspection, and his methods do not seem to be attracting much publicity.[131]

On July 19, 1942, Himmler ordered Krüger to see to it that the "resettlement" of the entire Jewish population of the Government General be completed by December 31, 1942. After that date no person of Jewish extraction would be allowed to live in the Government General; those who remained would have to be confined in the collection centers of Warsaw, Cracow, Tschenstochau (Czestochowa), Radom, and Lublin.[132]

The evacuation of Jews from the city of Lublin had already been completed by mid-June, 1942. Their removal from the Warsaw ghetto began on July 22. Some time later Himmler was informed that "a train containing five thousand Jews has been leaving Warsaw for [the gas chamber camp of] Treblinka every day since July 22; in addition a train containing five thousand Jews has been leaving Przemyśl for Belzec twice a week."[133]

Although the removal of Jews from Warsaw was undertaken on a large scale, the pace was not rapid enough to suit Himmler. Early in 1943 he complained to Krüger that there were still forty thousand Jews left in Warsaw. Of these, thirty-two thousand were employed in so-called armaments industries contrary to his orders. Economic considerations, Himmler said, should not be allowed to interfere with the evacuation of Jews, and he set a deadline of February 15, 1943, for the dissolution of all private firms employing Jews. Already in September of the previous year he had persuaded Keitel to order the Wehrmacht to get rid of all Jews employed in military armaments establishments or auxiliary services.[134]

By April 1943 the approximately half million Jews who had been herded into the Warsaw ghetto over the past four years had been reduced to just over sixty thousand—which was still twenty thousand more than the number estimated by Himmler. On April 19 these Jews, having received weapons from the Polish underground army and other sources, decided to fight rather than allow themselves to be led to the slaughter like cattle. Despite their inadequate equipment they held out for over a month against the Germans and their Polish and Lithuanian auxiliaries, but by May 16 the fifty-six thousand-odd Jews still alive in Warsaw surrendered. The Warsaw uprising, although a heroic chapter in the history of the Jews, was for the Nazis only an awkward interruption in their campaign of annihilation. With the Warsaw uprising suppressed, Himmler ordered that the former Warsaw ghetto be razed and the entire area converted into a city park.[135]

Elsewhere in the Government General the evacuation of Jews was carried out just as systematically as in Warsaw. The objections of those who considered the labor of Jews essential to the war economy were regularly overridden. Frank, although he himself had frequently objected to the removal of Jews on economic grounds, boasted on August 2, 1943, that of the three and a half million Jews who had been in the Government General in December 1941, only a few labor battalions remained. "All the rest have—let us say—emigrated." Early in 1944 he estimated that the total Jewish population in his province was now perhaps one hundred thousand. At least half of these appear to have been exterminated before the Germans were finally driven out of the country in 1945.[136]

In none of the areas occupied by the Germans were Hitler's intentions more clearly delineated than in the Polish territories annexed to the Reich. Even before their formal annexation on October 26, 1939, he had begun the process of co-ordinating their institutions with those of the Reich and had inaugurated a radical program of Germanization. On the Germanization question Hitler had adopted a surprisingly liberal attitude in dealing with the Czechs. Given the general German prejudice against the Poles, however, it is probable that a far smaller percentage of Poles than Czechs would ultimately have been found suitable for Germanization and that consequently a far larger proportion would have been expelled or exterminated.

Less clear were Hitler's goals in the Polish territories not annexed to Germany, the so-called Government General. His original policy guidelines had called for the ruthless exploitation of this area and its use as a dumping ground for undesirable elements expelled from the Reich and other occupied territories. In the spring of 1942 Himmler had reversed this policy by inaugurating a Germanization program in the Government General, but this is one of the few cases when his actions may have run ahead of the intentions of his leader. For Hitler, this non-German Polish rump state remained a necessary and desirable political institution, precisely what he had envisaged in his ideological program for the lesser breeds of Europe: a powerless political entity which could not possibly pose a threat to the security of the Reich and which would serve as a sort of reservation where lesser breeds might continue to exist while they were still needed by the German master race as menial labor for the gigantic construction tasks which lay ahead.

Over the years, as German peasants settled the lands already selected for Germanization and new generations of Germans required additional lands for colonization, the territory of the Government General, too, would undoubtedly have been annexed to the Reich, whether as the Gau of the Vandals or under some similar designation. When that time came, it may be assumed that the non-Aryan peoples in this last bit of Poland would have been subjected to the same Germanization-expulsion-extermination treatment already accorded them in every other part of the former state of Poland.

CHAPTER 5

The Nordics: Scandinavia

In contrast to the lands of Eastern Europe, which from the beginning had been his prime territorial objective, Hitler had no immediate plans for the invasion and occupation of the countries of Scandinavia, although there can be no doubt that he intended to bring them into his greater Germanic realm at some time in the future. But until his major adversaries had been crushed, Hitler was primarily concerned with preserving the neutral status of the Scandinavian countries to avoid extending his theater of military operations unnecessarily. It was only after he had become convinced early in 1940 that these countries were about to be occupied by the British, a move that would have dealt a crushing blow to his strategic and economic position, that he resolved to occupy them himself.[1]

Besides making detailed military plans for the invasion of Denmark and Norway, Hitler prepared a careful political campaign. The governments of these states were to be convinced that resistance to Germany's armed might was useless, that the more smoothly and quickly the German occupation was allowed to proceed, the more certain it would be that their countries would not be drawn into the war. The sole purpose of the German action was to protect the neutrality of the Scandinavian countries, which had been threatened by the British. As evidence of its good faith, the German government was prepared to make agreements with the Danish and Norwegian governments guaranteeing the future integrity of their territories, the liberties of their peoples, and the inviolability of their present systems of government, including their armies and navies. On the other hand, if the existing governments failed to accept the German conditions, Germany would be forced to take all necessary measures to safeguard its own interests and would not be responsible for the consequences.[2]

The German political campaign and the assurances that accompanied

106

it were not altogether a matter of cynical calculation. The Danes and Norwegians were after all Nordics, and in dealing with them the Nazi government appears to have been influenced as much as ever by ideological considerations. Certainly Hitler's secret directives for the invasion of Denmark and Norway differed strikingly from those that hurled a National Socialist nation in destructive fury against the lesser breeds of Poland. In all of them he emphasized the necessity of safeguarding the welfare and securing the good will of the local population. This attitude was reflected in the preinvasion directives of the German army. "Every member of the Wehrmacht must be aware that he is not going into enemy territory, but that the army is entering Denmark for the protection of the country and the security of its people." [3]

Denmark

The German political campaign in Denmark was a complete success. On April 9, 1940, the first day of the German invasion, the Danish government accepted the German conditions of occupation, although under protest, and ordered that no resistance be offered to the German invasion forces. The Danish cabinet was reorganized immediately after the occupation to include leaders of parties representing over 90 per cent of the population. Once this had been done, the king, cabinet, and parliament continued to function with every appearance of normality. [4]

The Germans intended to preserve this convenient arrangement. The aim of German political measures, Wilhelm Keitel informed the highest Reich authorities, was to persuade the Danish government to tolerate the German occupation and to co-operate loyally with German civilian and military officials. The mission of the Wehrmacht was exclusively military. The German military commander in Denmark was to be responsible for the defense of the occupied territory, but was to exericse no executive power. In nonmilitary matters, the demands of the Reich would be submitted to the Danish government by Germany's diplomatic representative in Denmark or by a plenipotentiary appointed by the German Foreign Office. It would be the task of this official and his staff to supervise the work of the Danish government in fulfilling German demands and living up to its promises of co-operation. [5]

The German ethnic minority in North Schleswig, which for years had received German government support in agitating for frontier rectifications in favor of Germany, was instructed to cease all anti-Danish demonstrations. Denmark had been promised territorial integrity. The frontier question should therefore not be raised by the Danish Germans; nor should they engage in provocative acts or excessive fraternization with German occupation troops. At all times they were to maintain a correct attitude toward the Danish authorities. [6]

In conformity with the policy he had laid down for Denmark, Hitler appointed his regular diplomatic representative to Copenhagen, Cecil von Renthe-Fink, as the chief representative of German interests in Denmark with the title of minister and plenipotentiary. In this capacity he was to remain under the direction of the German Foreign Office and be responsible in the first instance to Joachim von Ribbentrop. The office organized under his direction had the task of supervising Denmark's foreign relations, of co-ordinating the Danish and German economies, and above all of supervising the entire Danish administration, including the Danish police and law courts.[7]

The royal Danish government was to retain, at least in theory, unrestricted control of the Danish administration and all public establishments. German relations with this government were conducted through regular diplomatic channels by the plenipotentiary and his assistants. There was no direct German control of the Danish administration, which was not subject to German orders. German law was introduced only for members of the German armed forces, and, except in unusual cases, Danes were to go before Danish courts even when their crimes involved German military personnel.[8]

In comparison with most occupied countries, Denmark was fortunate in its German administrators. The first German military commander in Denmark, General Leonhard von Kaupisch, was succeeded after two months by General Erich Lüdke, a jovial, sociable man from Hamburg, who had retired from active service before the war. Lüdke had little sympathy with National Socialist ideology, he kept his relations with Nazi members of the legation staff to a minimum, and he did his best to avoid friction with the local population.

Renthe-Fink, the head of the legation, was himself no Nazi but a career diplomat who had represented Germany in Denmark before the Nazis came to power. He believed it was in Germany's interest to live up to its bargain with Denmark by preserving the appearance of Danish independence and political autonomy. With a total German staff of fewer than one hundred persons, he was fully aware of the extent of his dependence on Danish co-operation in administering the country.[9]

Renthe-Fink was nevertheless a sound German nationalist anxious to advance the interests of his country. While willing to respect Denmark's nominal independence, he sought the establishment of the closest possible political, military, economic, and cultural ties between Denmark and the Reich. To this end he proposed the negotiation of a treaty with Denmark which should serve as a model for Germany's relations with other neutral countries. This treaty would include a permanent mutual assistance pact making Danish bases available to Germany and assigning Danish forces a role in the defense of the greater German area. Danish foreign policy was to be oriented exclusively toward Germany, there would be a permanent liaison between the German and Danish foreign offices, and Danish representatives abroad would be selected in agreement with the Reich. Finally, Denmark should become part of the German economic sphere and enter into a customs and currency union with the Reich.[10]

Renthe-Fink had no illusions that such a one-sided treaty could be negotiated with the present Danish government. He therefore endeavored to secure the appointment of ministers favorably disposed toward Germany and the dismissal of hostile elements. He appeared to be well on the way toward the realization of this program when, in July 1940, the ostensibly pro-German Erik Scavenius replaced the pacifist Peter Munch as foreign minister, the member of the cabinet chiefly responsible for negotiation with the Germans.

The appointment of Scavenius did not produce so great a change in Danish policy as Renthe-Fink had anticipated. Scavenius had at first seemed to be the ideal collaborationist minister. He assured the German plenipotentiary of his personal desire to co-operate closely with Germany to enable Denmark to take its place in the new European order under German leadership. By making public statements to this effect he brought upon himself the wrath of Danish patriots. But Scavenius's collaboration appears to have been more a matter of tactics than conviction. After the collapse of France, he shared the belief of most Europeans that Germany had won the war and that Denmark would have to make the best bargain it could. He also knew that many Germans were agitating for direct German control of the Danish administration, or the establishment of a government under Frits Clausen, the leader of the Danish Nazis. With the examples of Norway and the Netherlands, not to mention Poland, before him, Scavenius had reason to believe that the preservation of a buffer government in Denmark was worth a good many concessions. In his actual negotiations with the Germans he gave away as little as he could, and he constantly warned them not to demand too much from his country or interfere in its internal affairs; any attempt to install an outright pro-German or Nazi government would mean revolution and the establishment of a regime that could only be supported by bayonets.[11]

Renthe-Fink passed Scavenius's arguments along to Berlin with his own endorsement. Clausen could not be brought to power by legal means, he said, and imposing him on the Danes would only provoke passive resistance and lead to a decline of production. In his annual report on the situation in Denmark, written in March 1941, he described his policy in Denmark as a compromise: an unrelenting maintenance of German military and economic interests, balanced by a consideration for Danish sovereignty and integrity. The occupation authorities were having no difficulties, he said, although feelings toward the Germans were anything but friendly. He attributed the present sensible behavior of the population solely to opportunistic considerations, and believed that this attitude was not likely to change until after the final German victory.[12]

The relative calm in Denmark continued even after the German attack on Russia. At the behest of the Germans, the Danish government interned Danish Communists, outlawed the Communist party, and prohibited all Communist activity; in November 1941 Denmark adhered to the Anti-Comintern Pact.[13]

> Results of co-operation with the Danish government, utterly alien though it may be to us from an ideological point of view, by and large, have been satisfactory, [Ribbentrop informed Hitler.] None of the countries occupied by us is as peaceful or is offering so close and virtually trouble-free co-operation by its authorities as is Denmark. Maintenance of peace in the country requires only small German military forces. The Danish government has to date always complied with our military demands and even approved the transfer of a number of Danish torpedo boats to the German navy. The results of co-operation with the Danish government are especially good in the economic field.

Ribbentrop's greatest disappointment in Denmark was the poor showing of the Danish Nazi party, whose leader, Dr. Frits Clausen, a physician from Bovrup in Schleswig, seemed to lack personal magnetism and organizing ability. Despite substantial financial and advisory support from the Foreign Office and other Reich agencies, the party remained small and ineffective. Ribbentrop, however, was confident that this situation would soon change. The policy being pursued in Denmark, he said, "aims at achieving a synthesis of our present-day need for exploiting all economic resources to the fullest extent possible in Denmark, which will be the more effective the better we succeed in maintaining tranquillity in the country, and the necessity for providing for the future politcal evolution of Denmark by effectively assisting the Clausen movement." As Clausen was opposed by a majority of the Danish people, Ribbentrop believed it would be dangerous to take any hasty action on his behalf. He nevertheless wanted a directive from the Führer as to whether he should adhere to the present policy of caution, or step up the support of the National Socialist movement in Denmark. On November 17 the Foreign Office was informed that Hitler had expressed his satisfaction with German policy in Denmark and that he believed his officials should continue along their present course.[14]

Although Hitler might approve the cautious policy pursued by his Foreign Office in Denmark, he did not really like it. He resented the presence of professional, old-fashioned diplomats like Renthe-Fink in positions of leadership in German missions abroad and wanted them replaced as soon as possible by reliable Nazis.[15] He also hoped to get rid of the Danish king. "We already have the successor. That's Clausen." The Danish Nazi leader had sinned so much that he would have to remain loyal to Germany no matter what happened. In a less cynical mood Hitler expressed confidence that "even in Denmark" the youth could be drawn away from the views of the older generation and be persuaded to adopt "the German way of thought, for they feel they spring from the same racial origins." By systematically working with youth movements, he believed he could undercut the king and draw his people away from him, just as he had separated the people of Austria from the Dollfuss-Schuschnigg regime.[16]

The summer of 1942 brought the first serious unrest in Denmark. Members of the Danish Free Corps who had volunteered for service on the Russian front returned to their homeland on leave. Angered by their cool and frequently insulting reception, they engaged in demonstrations and various kinds of provocative behavior, which further aroused the local population. Clausen, who had long looked for an opportunity to stir up trouble and thereby force the Germans to turn to him in their hour of need, threw his Danish Nazis into the fray to add to the turmoil. The unrest was never dangerous and was soon brought under control by German troops, but it was enough to convince Hitler that a change in German policy toward Denmark was in order.[17]

In September 1942 the easy-going General Lüdke was succeeded as commander of the German troops in Denmark by General Hermann von Hanneken, chief of the raw materials division of the Reich Ministry of Economics and plenipotentiary for iron and steel production in Göring's Four-Year Plan. He was described by the Foreign Office official in charge of Northern Europe as a crude and ignorant Praetorian Guard captain.[18] In October Renthe-Fink was replaced as Reich plenipotentiary by SS Gruppenführer Dr. Karl Rudolf Werner Best.

Hitler received Hanneken on October 1 to give him oral instructions before he took up his duties in Denmark. He had long considered the conditions governing Germany's relations with Denmark to be unsatisfactory and unsuitable, the Führer said. German policy had been based on the expectation of a short war, but now it would have to be changed. It was no longer possible to maintain a democratic regime under a monarchy in the new European order under German leadership. Hitler therefore proposed to lay down new guidelines for German policy in Denmark. As plenipotentiary he intended to appoint a National Socialist "with a hard fist." The aim of German policy would be to establish a Danish regime under National Socialist leadership as soon as possible. Whether Clausen had a large or small following was completely unimportant. "The Führer needed a puppet government in Denmark which would do everything he required of it." Hanneken, as military commander, should bear in mind that the German army was not in a friendly but an enemy country, and he should conduct himself accordingly. All resistance, even the slightest, should be suppressed by force. If Danish police forces were inadequate or undependable, German police and troops would be made available.

For the future, Hitler told Hanneken, he definitely intended to abolish the Danish monarchy and the parliamentary system of government. Nor did he have any intention of allowing Denmark to retain its present independent status. That country, like Norway, was essential to Germany

111

for strategic reasons. "Denmark would have to become a German province." [19]

Hitler issued similar instructions to Best, who assumed his duties as minister and Reich plenipotentiary in Denmark on November 5, 1942. He was to arrange a complete transformation of the Danish government, and secure the inclusion of Danish National Socialists in the cabinet.[20]

Best had no success whatever in securing the appointment of Danish Nazis to the Danish government, but he did get the king's consent to the dismissal of the Socialist prime minister Vilhelm Buhl and the formation of a new government under Scavenius, who retained his post as foreign minister. Best assured Ribbentrop on November 8 that the new Danish government corresponded exactly to the wishes of the Führer, for Scavenius had neither parliamentary nor popular support and would thus be exactly the kind of German puppet that Hitler desired. Further, Best had persuaded the government to pass an enabling law (the Power of Attorney Bill) which permitted the state to take emergency measures legally for the maintenance of order and security.[21]

With the appointment of Best, the official status of the Reich plenipotentiary was changed. Instead of being Reich plenipotentiary with the Danish government, he was named Reich plenipotentiary in Denmark. As such he was no longer merely the Reich representative to the Danish government, but the supreme civilian authority in Denmark. In practice, however, the position of the plenipotentiary remained very much the same. All his orders still went through the Danish government, he was not authorized to issue orders directly to Danish officials, and he remained directly responsible to the Foreign Office, not to the Führer.[22]

Best was not generally regarded as the National Socialist with the hard fist Hitler had promised to send to Denmark, although his credentials were impressive enough. Trained in the law, he had served as a judge since 1929, joined the Nazi party in the following year, and after the Nazis came to power he became chief of police in Hesse. In January 1935 he was appointed senior counselor and department chief for administration and law in the Berlin office of the Gestapo. From 1936 to 1940 he served in the department of the Security Police in the Reich Ministry of the Interior. In 1940 he left the police to enlist in the regular army, and was made chief of the civil administrative department of the German military commander in France.[23]

Yet despite his background in the Nazi party and police, Best managed to avoid the appearance of brutality and ruthlessness. Hans Gisevius, Best's colleague in the Gestapo and later a member of the anti-Nazi resistance, denounced Best in his memoirs as one of the worst of the Nazi crew "precisely because he behaved in a fashion so disarmingly decent." But the Danes, who had every reason to expect the worst from Hitler's most recent appointee, were evidently pleasantly surprised by the new plenipotentiary. A Danish secretary of legation in Berlin, while otherwise condemning Nazi policies, thought Best seemed to show a certain understanding for the problems of Denmark. He was systematically eliminating the influence of the despicable Danish Nazis, and on the whole seemed to be avoiding the mistakes of Renthe-Fink, who had lived in abject fear of the party. This favorable opinion of Best was shared by the German Foreign Office official in charge of Danish affairs, who regarded him as a thoroughly reasonable man but unable to counter the half-diabolical, half-stupid directives from "upstairs." Goebbels, on the other hand, criticized Best as an official who sought to rule with a velvet glove, and condemned his policies in Denmark as lax and feeble.[24]

Himmler, too, had a poor opinion of the new Reich plenipotentiary, although it was he who had originally recommended Best to Ribbentrop. Best had served Himmler in a variety of positions since 1933; but over the years Himmler had come to distrust and dislike him. So strained did relations between the two men become that in 1940 Best resigned from the police and joined the regular army. It was, therefore, a curious quirk of fate that two years later, when Hitler demanded the rapid replacement of career diplomats by qualified Nazis, Himmler, at the request of members of his staff, included Best's name in a list he submitted to Ribbentrop, evidently never expecting that Ribbentrop would select anyone recommended by himself, much less give him so important a position as that of Reich plenipotentiary in Denmark.[25]

Once installed in Denmark, Best set about trying to regain Himmler's favor. He asked to be made his deputy for Germanization work in Denmark so as to be able to use his position to further this important task. Himmler scornfully turned aside Best's proposal. He did not want Germanic work carried out by an official of the Foreign Office, he said. But Best persisted. He let Himmler know that, although he was nominally subordinate to the Foreign Office, he always regarded the Reichsführer SS as his real superior. He not only communicated with him directly on Danish affairs, but sent him copies of his official communications to the Foreign Office.[26]

Himmler was evidently won over. On January 19, 1943, he assured Best that he would give him his full support and prevent all outside interference, including that of his own agents, with Best's activities. Best was to act at all times as though he had absolute power in Denmark. At a conference on Germanic work on January 20, Himmler's faithful deputy Gottlob Berger expressed his satisfaction about the situation in Denmark, where SS Gruppenführer Dr. Best had taken over the leadership. He was confident that Best's work would be a model of Reich racial policy.[27]

As it proved, Himmler's original distrust of Best had been justified. Although Best paid abundant lip service to Himmler and his theories, the new Reich plenipotentiary signally failed to carry out Himmler's policies in Denmark. In fact, he pursued a course very similar to that of his predecessor Renthe-Fink. Before his appointment he had concluded a long report on the situation in Denmark, "Subjectively the Danes will adjust to the new order in Europe as the people of Iceland once did to Christianity: not as a result of force or propaganda, but through the cold-blooded realization that this course cannot be avoided and that in the long run it will also be of advantage to the Danes." [28] In a memorandum for the Foreign Office written shortly after his arrival in Denmark—a document he certainly did not submit to Himmler—Best advised strongly against Himmler's plan to initiate the "special treatment" of the Jews in Denmark.[29]

In March 1943, as a gesture of conciliation to the Danes—and perhaps to demonstrate to overeager German Nazis how little support Clausen enjoyed—he permitted free parliamentary elections to be held. That the elections were free could not be denied even by the most anti-German Danes, for they resulted in a crushing defeat for Frits Clausen's Nazi party, which polled just over 2 per cent of the vote, the same percentage it had registered before the war in 1939. Clausen was thoroughly discredited. In an order of the day to his followers of March 25, he confessed that after the disastrous elections it would be impossible to hold party meetings in public and that even party insignia could no longer be worn in public.[30]

Best showed no concern or regret about Clausen's defeat. The present Danish government, he told Himmler shortly after the elections, was serving Germany's needs very well. All that could be expected by way of military and agricultural supplies was being sent to Germany; the Danish National Bank had made heavy contributions to support the German army of occupation; Danish dockyards were working almost exclusively for Germany. In addition, one hundred twenty-four thousand Danes had gone to work in the Reich, two thousand were working for the Luftwaffe, and thirty-three hundred had joined the Waffen-SS. The Danish administration was operating effectively, a Danish police force of fifteen thousand men was serving loyally under German supervision. Best admitted that the Danes did not like the Germans, that they regarded the occupation as unlawful and oppressive, but on the whole they had refrained so far from outright resistance and sabotage. This was all the more remarkable in view of the fact that the German administrative staff in Denmark consisted of a mere 27 senior and 188 junior officials.[31]

This favorable situation deteriorated rapidly in the summer of 1943, a circumstance Best attributed to events in Italy. (The Allies had landed in Sicily in July, Mussolini had resigned on July 25, and most Danes seemed to believe that the collapse of Germany itself was imminent.) Early in August a strike among Danish dock workers in Odense set off a wave of strikes, riots, and sabotage in other parts of the country.[32]

Best was alarmed by the disturbances in Denmark, but he was even more alarmed by the reaction of General von Hanneken, who called for vigorous repressive measures, an end to the present relationship with the Danish government, and the establishment of direct German control. Fearing that Hanneken might succeed in undermining both his policy and his position in Denmark, Best wrote to Himmler on August 22 recommending caution and moderation. If German policy in Denmark were to be changed, however, he pleaded with Himmler to allow him to remain in charge of the German administration and to prevent his being supplanted by Hanneken, the agent of the Wehrmacht in Denmark. Best implied that he, unlike Hanneken, was seeking to implement Himmler's policy of preparing for the ultimate co-operation of all Germanic peoples; to foster this ideal it was essential to avoid arousing unnecessary bitterness between the Danes and the Germans.[33]

Best's appeal for restraint was disregarded. On August 24 he was recalled to Berlin by Ribbentrop and reprimanded because everything in Denmark was now topsy-turvy (*dass alles drunter und drüber ginge*). He returned to Copenhagen on August 27 with orders to submit specific demands to the Danish government which would certainly be rejected. After that a state of military emergency was to be declared and stringent measures were to be taken.[34]

Best carried out these instructions faithfully. An ultimatum to the Danish government of August 28 was duly rejected, the government resigned on August 29, and the Germans proclaimed a state of military emergency in Denmark. The Danish army and navy were disarmed, the king placed under guard, five hundred hostages seized from among the prominent members of the population; and the Communists, who had been interned since the beginning of the Russian campaign, were deported to Germany.[35]

August 29, 1943, marked a decisive turning point in the German occupation of Denmark. The Danish government (king, cabinet, and parliament) never resumed its functions. The Danish bureaucracy continued to operate, but it now took its orders directly from the Germans. The buffer of the Danish government between the Germans and the Danish people had been removed, a change that proved to be of greater significance than even Best had anticipated, for the naked authority of Germany was now exposed and Danish resistance at last began in earnest.

Best was dismayed by the new course of German policy. He complained to Himmler that such stringent measures had not been necessary, and he criticized Hanneken's methods of carrying them out, in particular the manner in which he had disarmed the Danish forces, which had resulted in the scuttling of what was left of the Danish fleet. Moreover, as a result of the proclamation of a state of military emergency, Hanneken, the representative of the Wehrmacht, rather than Best, the representative of the Reichsführer SS, had become the supreme German authority in Denmark. If the primacy of German civil authority were to be restored, heavy German police reinforcements would be required. This was a situation Best had always hoped to avoid, but now that the Danish government was out of the picture there was nothing else to be done. The "Danish political show horse" had been killed, doing irretrievable damage to the policy of Germanic co-operation.[36]

Himmler's response to this request for police reinforcements was undoubtedly greater than Best had anticipated—or desired. Instead of merely providing support for the German civil administration, and incidentally support for Best against Hanneken, Himmler sent enough police into Denmark to create an entirely new power center in the country. Prior to this time there had been very few German police in Denmark. At the beginning of the occupation they had been attached to the German legation. In February 1941 Himmler set up a special police office under SS Oberführer Dr. Paul Kanstein. Even then the German police force remained small and, although Kanstein was also entrusted with the supervision of Germanic work in Denmark, he exercised little influence. Himmler's agent Gottlob Berger complained in July 1941 that Kanstein's work was being maliciously and treacherously undercut by the Foreign Office.[37]

Now, in September 1943, Himmler sought to take advantage of the changed situation in Denmark to ensure the influence of his own organizations in the country. Whether he was still suspicious of Best or had become convinced of his ineffectiveness, he sent SS Obergruppenführer Günther Pancke, the former head of his Central Office for Race and Resettlement, to Denmark as senior SS and police officer, making him independent of the authority of the Reich plenipotentiary. In informing Best of Pancke's appointment, Himmler expressed the hope that he would not be unhappy that Pancke had not been subordinated to him and that he would co-operate loyally with the new German police chief. Pancke took up his duties on November 1.[38]

Best was very unhappy indeed about the independent position conceded to Pancke, and so was Ribbentrop's Foreign Office. After much negotiation between representatives of the Foreign Office and Himmler, a compromise was arranged which provided that the senior SS and police officer should receive his political directives from the Reich plenipotentiary, but that his "professional instructions" (fachliche Weisungen) should come from the Reichsführer SS and his agencies. This arrangement meant, of course, that Pancke remained as independent of Best as before. As a result there were now three separate and independent authorities in Denmark: Best, the Reich plenipotentiary; Hanneken, the commander of the German troops; and Pancke, the police chief.[39]

The establishment of this triumverate failed to improve the German position in Denmark. The state of military emergency was lifted on October 6. But, despite the German police reinforcements and the continued application of stringent controls, disorder, sabotage, and resistance in general steadily increased.[40] At the end of December 1943 all three leaders of the German administration in Denmark were summoned to Berlin where Hitler took them to task for their failure to apply sufficiently ruthless measures. He ordered that Danish resistance forces be smashed by any and every means, that the German police launch a program of counterterror, that prominent Danes be assassinated in retaliation for the assassination of Germans or collaborators, and that Danish property be destroyed in retaliation for all acts of sabotage. To aid in carrying out these orders, Hitler sent a commando group to Denmark specially trained in counterterror tactics.[41]

Terror and counterterror now became the order of the day. According to the testimony of the leading German police officials in Denmark, Best protested against many of the actions taken by the German police, but he was powerless to stop them. On January 20, 1944, Hitler authorized the Reich plenipotentiary to issue emergency decrees.[42] In May, presumably under pressure from the police, Best asked the Foreign Office to agree to an SS demand for full judicial powers in Denmark, a proposal which encountered the interesting objection from Ribbentrop that such a move might create the impression "that we regarded Denmark as an integral part of the Reich." [43]

Toward the end of June 1944 a new German curfew order provoked a general strike in Copenhagen, which Hitler ordered suppressed with "ruthless and brutal vigor." Best proclaimed a state of martial law, Copenhagen's water, gas, and electric supplies were cut off, and German police fired on people in the streets who disobeyed the curfew regulations. When, as a result of these measures, Danish production virtually came to a standstill, Best felt obliged to yield to the demands of a Danish Freedom Council to lift the curfew; to prohibit the counterterrorist activities of Danish-Nazi military units; and to forbid Danish Nazis, the police, and the SS to carry out independent arrests and house searches. The strike ended on July 4.[44]

Best's concessions infuriated Hitler, who called him to Berlin and personally abused him for his moderation. Best could only argue (and with Ribbentrop, not with Hitler) that his policies in Denmark had been successful. Agricultural production had increased; in the past year meat deliveries to the Reich had risen from seventy-four to one hundred fifty thousand tons; the country was making large monetary contributions to finance the German army of occupation; the fortifications of Jutland had been completed on schedule.[45]

Although Best was left in Denmark as Reich plenipotentiary, the real authority during the last stage of the German occupation was exercised by Pancke and Hanneken. In September 1944 these two officials, anticipating an Allied invasion through Denmark, decided to disarm the Danish police force, which they feared might turn against the Germans as soon as the Allies landed. Without consulting Best, Pancke submitted his plan to Himmler, whose written approval, together with that of Hitler, arrived on September 12. On September 19 Pancke declared a state of police emergency, the entire Danish police force was disarmed and interned, and about two thousand policemen were deported to Germany. The result was the immediate outbreak of new disorders, for the Germans lacked the manpower to police the entire country themselves. To take the place of the regular police, they mobilized Danish Nazi units and other pro-German organizations, while many ordinary Danish citizens, anxious to prevent the disintegration of their society, assumed special constabulary duties. It was a difficult situation for the Danes, but the biggest losers were the Germans, whose economic interests suffered in proportion to the increase in disorder. On October 15 Pancke lifted the state of police emergency and the majority of Danish rural and small-town police was reinstated in their positions.

The chief result of the police action, apart from its blow to German economic interests, was the consolidation of Pancke's influence in Denmark. The country was now divided into four SS and police administrative districts, each headed by an SS and police officer responsible to Pancke. SS and police courts took over the major responsibility for dealing with the opponents, or suspected opponents, of the German occupation. Denmark, which the Germans had once boasted of as their "model protectorate," had become a police state, which was rapidly being reduced to a condition similar to that of other countries under German occupation.[46]

The Allied landings in Denmark, the chief justification for the police action, never took place. The Germans remained in the country until their general surrender in northwestern Europe on May 4, 1945.

Until the last months of the war the Danes had been comparatively immune from the more extreme manifestations of Nazi policy. This was especially evident in the economic field. As Denmark was not technically an occupied country, the Danes were not obliged to support the German army of occupation or to pay a war indemnity. Throughout the war they managed to maintain a standard of living comparable to that of Germany.

Yet Denmark did not escape German exploitation. The country was, after all, in a position of constraint, cut off from its markets and sources of supplies outside the German sphere of influence. The majority of Danish industries, entirely dependent on Germany for raw materials, found themselves obliged to work for the German account or close down. Almost the entire Danish agricultural surplus went to Germany.[47]

The Germans paid conscientiously for their purchases in Denmark. The rate of exchange was fair, the Germans even agreeing to a rise in the value of the Danish crown to offset the generally lower prices obtaining in Denmark. Exploitation took place chiefly through the various devices the Germans used to finance their purchases. The Germany army at first paid with *Reichskreditkassenscheine* (military currency certificates), which were nothing more than promissory notes. When the Danes protested against this procedure, the Germans arranged that the Danish National Bank maintain a credit account for German military purchases, promising to draw on it only for the maintenance of the German forces in Denmark. Army maintenance was interpreted very freely, however, and by the end of 1944 the Germans had drawn on their credit account with the Danish National Bank for some seven million crowns. The Danish government endeavored to prevent this drain on the economy by restricting sales to Germany. Although several laws were passed for this purpose which were often temporarily effective, the Danes simply lacked the power to withstand German pressure. In the last months of the war even the fiction of German purchases was abandoned and gave way to outright confiscation.

Even so, Denmark was more fortunate than most other occupied countries. The policy of outright confiscation began much later than elsewhere. More important, at no time during the war was a system of compulsory labor recruitment introduced in Denmark, although well over one hundred thousand Danish men and women volunteered for work in Germany (the wages offered in the Reich being much higher than those in Denmark). Many more worked for the Germans in Denmark itself, either in war industries or the construction of fortifications.[48]

The Germans always hoped to establish a much closer economic relationship with Denmark than the system of disguised extortion that was actually adopted. In the first months of the occupation the Foreign Office, with Hitler's approval, proposed to negotiate economic treaties with Denmark that would lay the basis for a complete economic union with the Reich. After Scavenius's appointment as foreign minister in July 1940, the Germans initiated discussions for a customs and currency union, but the Danish government refused to be lured into such a relationship. So successfully did the Danes procrastinate that, by August 23, the German diplomats were forced to concede that the negotiations had for all intents and purposes broken down. The program of a Danish-German economic union never got any further.[49]

The Germans were even less successful in promoting a program of Danish-German racial co-operation. In May 1940 Hitler authorized sending SS detachments to Denmark to recruit for the Waffen-SS and to work for the solidarity of the Germanic nations. In February of the following year Himmler authorized SS Oberführer Paul Kanstein to take charge of the Germanic program in Denmark. After the beginning of the Russian campaign a Free Corps Denmark was formed to fight against Bolshevism.[50]

But the fruits of such efforts were meager. Despite German political and financial support, the Danish Nazi party under Frits Clausen remained a political pariah. As small as it was, it broke into various feuding splinter groups, which in turn feuded with members of the Free Corps Denmark and its successor, the Schalburg Corps, named after a commander of the Free Corps who fell on the Eastern front in 1942.[51] The Free Corps, which was severely decimated in the fighting in Russia, attracted little more than a thousand volunteers. Recruiting for the

Schalburg Corps proved somewhat more successful, perhaps because it was never sent to Russia; but even enlistments in this organization soon dried up. Berger complained to Himmler that the brutal methods employed by General von Hanneken in disarming the Danish army in September 1943 had ruined his recruiting program, and that as a result of mistakes of other Reich agencies "we are now at the end of our rope in the Germanic countries." [52]

In their campaign against the Jews, too, the Germans were largely frustrated in Denmark. No action of any kind was undertaken against the seven thousand Jews living in Denmark during the first three years of the German occupation. On September 24, 1942, however, the chief of the Gestapo, SS Gruppenführer Heinrich Müller, drew up a list of persons to be arrested in Denmark (*Festnahmekartei*) and recommended to Himmler that the Danish Jews be included. Himmler agreed, urging that the arrest of Jews begin as soon as possible. [53] With the appointment of SS Gruppenführer Best as Reich plenipotentiary in Denmark in November 1942, Himmler evidently expected that action against the Jews would soon be carried out, but Best refused to co-operate. In a confidential report to Ribbentrop he explained that such a move would mean the resignation of the Danish government and the ruin of Germany's present occupation policies. [54]

During the crisis of August and September 1943, however, Best himself appears to have suggested the possibility of "solving" the Jewish problem in Denmark while the country was under martial law. This suggestion was eagerly followed up by Hitler, who on September 18 ordered that the deportation of all Jews from Denmark should be undertaken at once and that Best should make proposals as to how this could be done most effectively. Best tried to pass the job along to the police and the army, but Hanneken would have nothing to do with the matter and protested to his superior officers that the consequences of the proposed action would be disastrous. Germany would no longer be able to count on the collaboration of Danish officials or the Danish police in administering the country, the delivery of agricultural and industrial products to Germany would be seriously endangered, and there would almost certainly be widespread unrest and violence which would require the intervention of the German army. [55]

Hanneken's objections were overridden by Himmler, who undertook to have his own men carry out the Jewish action. For this purpose he transferred two additional police battalions to Denmark. As German police forces were still inadequate, their leader, Dr. Rudolf Mildner (Pancke, the new senior SS and police officer, had not yet arrived in Denmark) appealed to Hanneken for support, but the military commander refused all assistance on the ground that the High Command of the Wehrmacht had forbidden the army to participate in actions against Jews. Hanneken's refusal was reported to Berlin and drew a sharp reprimand from General Keitel, but even so only a small detachment of military police eventually participated in the Jewish action, and that indirectly.

When the roundup of Jews in Denmark finally took place on the night of October 1–2, 1943, the operation was a fiasco. The German police not only lacked sufficient manpower, but they were hampered by an order from Best forbidding them to break down the doors of Jewish dwellings. Thus only those Jews were arrested who were foolish enough to open their doors voluntarily. Moreover several German officials, including Best himself, appear to have leaked information about the pending Jewish action, giving the Jews ample warning, and that night only 284 Jews were arrested, for the most part people too old to hide or escape. Arrests during the next few days brought the total figure to 475. Thanks to the halfhearted measures of the Germans, but above all to the courageous attitude of the Danish people, who at the risk of their lives aided in hiding and smuggling out the Jews, well over six thousand Jews or part-Jews (and thus almost the entire Jewish population of Denmark) succeeded in escaping to Sweden.[56]

Norway

Preliminary German political plans for the occupation of Norway were the same as those for Denmark. The flight of the king and government was to be prevented and everything was to be done to give the German action the character of a peaceful occupation. It would be the task of Germany's diplomatic representative in Norway to persuade the government to refrain from armed resistance, to co-operate loyally with German military and civilian authorities. To this end the Norwegian government was to be assured that the sole aim of the German occupation was the protection of Norway's neutrality, which was being threatened by Britain and France. Germany had "no intention of infringing by its measures the territorial integrity and political independence of the kingdom of Norway now or in the future." If the Norwegian government accepted the German conditions, it was to be allowed to function as before under the protection of the German Wehrmacht. If it refused or was unable to prevent resistance, the German minister in Oslo should seek to form a new, pro-German, government.[57]

Before dawn on April 9, 1940, Dr. Curt Bräuer, the German minister to Oslo, submitted Germany's demands to the Norwegian government. But the Germans were less fortunate in Norway than in Denmark. Because of the late arrival of German military forces, the king and other high-ranking members of his government succeeded in evading capture and leaving the capital. The Norwegian foreign minister, Halvdahn Koht, to whom Bräuer presented the German demands, consulted briefly with the members of the council of ministers still in Oslo. In a few moments he returned with his government's reply: "We will not submit voluntarily. The struggle is already under way." [58]

Instead of following his instructions to form a new, pro-German, government, Bräuer addressed renewed appeals to the existing government and sought to get in touch with the king. But before anything could come of these efforts, the head of Norway's authoritarian Nasjonal Samling party, Vidkun Quisling, evidently with the connivance of Alfred Rosenberg's representative in Norway, was allowed to make a radio address to the Norwegian people on the evening of April 9 in which he announced that the old government had fled and that the Nasjonal Samling now had the duty and the right to take over governmental authority "in order to defend the vital interests of the Norwegian people and safeguard the country's security and independence." He announced a list of ministers (without consulting them about their willingness to serve in his government), and called for an end to Norwegian resistance.[59]

Shortly afterward Bräuer received telephone instructions from Hitler personally to seek royal sanction of the Quisling regime. His primary task, however, would still be to persuade the king to call for an end to Norwegian resistance. On the afternoon of April 10, after many delays and difficulties, Bräuer managed to see the king at Elverum, north of Oslo, where he had temporarily taken refuge. The German emissary appealed to him to stop the fighting and stressed Germany's desire to maintain the existing dynasties in both Denmark and Norway. Germany, however, could have no confidence in the former Norwegian government, which had pursued a demonstrably pro-British policy. A ministry had now been formed by Quisling, whose Norwegian patriotism and regard for Germany were well known, and Bräuer thought it proper that he should be entrusted with the responsibility of government in these times. After consulting with members of his cabinet, the king sent word to Bräuer that he would never appoint a government headed by Quisling. Neither would he appeal to his subjects to lay down their arms. "Resistance will continue as long as possible," Bräuer was told.[60]

Quisling's assumption of authority in Norway was premature and proved to be a serious political error. On April 11 Bräuer drew his government's attention to the fact that a Norwegian government not only had to have the confidence of Germany, but also that of its own people. "This confidence was not, however, enjoyed by Herr Quisling, a lone wolf [*Einzelgänger*] without followers, who was rejected by the country." Quisling's orders were not being obeyed, and even the ministers he had named had failed to rally round him.[61]

Bräuer had feared all along the consequences of co-operation with Quisling. With more honesty than survival instinct he reported to Berlin on April 13 that he had carried out the Führer's instructions to maintain contact with Quisling and to propose to the king that he be entrusted with the formation of a new government. "In doing so," Bräuer said, "I disregarded completely my own private misgivings as to the person and position of Quisling." It was now evident that, despite the absence of a legal government and the support of German bayonets, Quisling was quite unable to form a government which could control the Norwegian administration or be of any use to the Germans in their occupation of the country.[62] On his own initiative Bräuer now proceeded to form an administrative directorate in co-operation with the Norwegian Supreme Court, which in the absence of the king and parliament was empowered by the constitution to take emergency measures to carry on the administration of the country.[63]

Ribbentrop was dismayed by the developments in Norway. His political campaign to eliminate military resistance to the German invasion had failed, and now his minister to Norway was questioning Hitler's political judgment. Ignoring Bräuer's pessimistic reports, Ribbentrop sent Under State Secretary Theodor Habicht as a special envoy to Oslo to undertake the support of the Quisling regime. But Habicht was as unfavorably impressed by Quisling as Bräuer. "I found Quisling in a frame of mind which makes it seem absolutely impossible that he could assert himself," he told Ribbentrop on the evening of April 14. "He is at bottom entirely unstable and weak. . . . Nothing can be done with him. He lacks all control." [64]

Confronted by the combined opinions of Habicht and Bräuer, Ribbentrop gave in and consented to negotiations with the Norwegian Supreme Court. Anxious to get rid of Quisling, the president of the Supreme Court, Paal Berg, suggested the appointment of an Administrative Council to carry on the government of the country until normal conditions were restored. This council would pledge complete loyalty to the German occupation authorities, each member would be personally responsible for the maintenance of peace and order and for carrying out the instructions of the occupation officials. Everything would be done to save Quisling's face, but Berg refused to tolerate him as a member of the council.

These conditions were accepted by the Germans, who imposed them on a reluctant Quisling. On April 15 the Norwegian Administrative Council was formed and installed in office by Bräuer, the German minister. At the same time the Supreme Court issued a proclamation that, since the Norwegian government was unable to fulfill its functions in districts occupied by the German forces and since it was absolutely necessary to keep a civil administration in being, the Supreme Court had set up the Administrative Council to conduct the civil administrtration in the occupied areas.[65]

This council was composed of seven members, all of them reputable and distinguished men. Its president, Ingolf Christensen, was the governor of Oslo and a leading figure in the Conservative party. Bräuer was well satisfied with the results of his activity. The formation of the council was generally regarded as a return to constitutional conditions, he

wrote in a memorandum of April 17, and "the pacification which has en-
sued is more complete than was to be expected." Moreover the possibility had been created for the return of the king, which would not have
been the case under Quisling or any other usurper government.[66]

But the king did not return. In fact, on April 19 he disavowed the
governmental authority of the Administrative Council just as firmly as
he had previously rejected that of Quisling. He remained with the Norwegian troops fighting the Germans in the northern part of the country;
when all organized resistance came to an end in early June he sought
refuge in England, assuming the leadership of a Norwegian government
in exile.

On the evening of April 19 Hitler telephoned General Nikolaus von
Falkenhorst, the commander of the German invasion forces, informing
him that a state of war now existed between Germany and Norway and
conferring on him supreme executive power in the occupied areas. On
the same day he appointed Josef Terboven, Gauleiter of Essen and head
of the administration of the province of the Rhine, to the position of
Reichskommissar for Norway. Bräuer, whose political efforts had seemingly ended in failure, was recalled in disgrace. The Administrative
Council he had established, however, remained, and was to be of enormous value to the Germans in their subsequent administration of the
country.[67]

Reichskommissar Terboven was a pale, spectacled former bank official
from Essen who had made his way to his present position through the
ranks of the National Socialist party, which he had joined in 1923. No
reliable evidence has so far come to light as to why Hitler selected Terboven for the post in Norway. Perhaps Göring, a long-time friend and
political ally, had something to do with his appointment. It must be recalled, however, that Hitler had to make a quick personnel decision
with regard to Norway—until mid-April he had still counted on using
his diplomatic representative in Oslo as his chief civil plenipotentiary—
and in such cases he tended to resort to tried and true Gauleiters who
had administrative experience and who had proven their personal loyalty to himself.

Terboven was described by a member of his staff as an energetic, brutal, dangerous fellow, who kept an eye on his goal. It was soon evident
that his goal in Norway was maximum power for himself and possibly a
permanent position as German governor of that country. An ambition of
this kind was common to the majority of German administrators in the
occupied territories, but Terboven succeeded better than most in fulfilling it.[68]

The official announcement of Terboven's appointment to Norway was
made on April 24, 1940. As Reichskommissar he was to be the protector
of Reich interests and to exercise supreme governmental power in the civilian sector. He was empowered to make use of the Norwegian Administrative Council, the Norwegian civil service, and the German police

forces for the execution of his orders. The existing body of Norwegian law was to remain in force insofar as it was compatible with the purposes of the occupation, but the Reichskommissar was given the authority to issue new laws by decree. "The Reichskommissar is directly responsible to me and receives his political guidelines and directives from me," Hitler's appointment order stated. The commander of the German army in Norway was to continue to exercise supreme military authority, but all his requests in the civilian sector were to be carried out exclusively by the Reichskommissar.[69]

Because of the continued existence of a Norwegian administration, the Germans were able, as in Denmark, to govern the country with a supervisory administration only. As late as September 1941, the entire German civil administrative staff in Norway, including personnel to supervise both central and local government, the economy, and propaganda, consisted of fewer than three hundred persons. The central office of the Reichskommissar was divided into departments to supervise the various sectors of the Norwegian administration, together with a liaison department to deal with the central offices of the Reich, and a special task force to advise Quisling's Nasjonal Samling.[70]

From the beginning Terboven's relations with the German military commander in Norway were strained, but Falkenhorst did nothing to extend his own authority or to curb the influence of the civilian governor. Indeed, he specifically ordered the men under his command to stay out of political affairs. He was, according to Ulrich von Hassell, "the usual general, without political will or courage." [71]

In the economic sphere, army economic officials had immediately taken charge of all economic assets needed for the conquest and occupation of the country; they were instrumental in keeping the Norwegian economy going. After Norwegian resistance had ended, however, the army co-operated closely with the office of the Reichskommissar in economic affairs. Other Reich economic authorities, including Göring, were on the whole willing to allow Terboven's staff to carry out their instructions without interfering directly in Norwegian affairs.[72] Göring presumably thought his interests would be adequately defended through his friend Terboven. But on the whole it would appear that Norway was simply too poor a country to stimulate the greed of the more powerful Nazi officials or their agencies.

Even the influence of Himmler was kept at bay, although the Reichsführer SS professed a special interest in Norway as a Germanic country. Despite the large size of the German SS and police administrative staff in Norway and the fact that the Reichskommissar was not given direct authority over them, neither SS Obergruppenführer Fritz Weitzel, the first senior SS and police officer in Norway, nor his successor, SS Obergruppenführer Wilhelm Rediess, ever seriously challenged Terboven's authority. He gave them ample scope for their activities, and managed to convince them that they had his full support. In April 1943 Himmler's lieutenant Gottlob Berger wrote his chief of Terboven's undeniable efforts to maintain close relations with the Himmler forces "because he knows very well that without our co-operation no long-term rulership is possible." [73]

The greatest threat to Terboven's position came, strangely enough, from the man whom the Germans had originally eased out of the leadership of the Norwegian government, Vidkun Quisling. Quisling's strength derived not from his qualities as a politician and certainly not from the esteem he enjoyed among his compartriots, but from the fact that he still played a role in Hitler's calculations. When Quisling was dropped as head of the Norwegian government on April 15, 1940, Hitler demanded that he be accorded every honor and that he be held in reserve until the Norwegian people had been conditioned to accept his leadership. The accomplishment of this political-educational task was to be left primarily to the Norwegian Nazis themselves, and the German administration in Norway was instructed to give them every possible support.[74]

Himmler issued similar instructions to his senior SS and police officer in Norway. The existing Administrative Council was merely a temporary expedient and could not be used to get at the Norwegian people, Himmler said. This could only be accomplished through a party modeled on German National Socialist lines. As the Nasjonal Samling party was the sole Norwegian organization dedicated to the conversion of the Norwegian people to the Greater Germanic ideal, everything was to be done to further that party's cause.[75]

The Germans did indeed do much to inject life into the Nasjonal Samling. Funds were poured into the party treasury. One of the largest sections of the Reichskommissar's office was almost exclusively concerned with advising and supporting the Quisling movement. In every province and at every level German National Socialists worked beside members of the Nasjonal Samling to strengthen the party's organization, plan strategy, and assist in propaganda campaigns. Newspaper, radio, and every other communication facility was placed at the party's disposal. In a major speech of May 1941, Terboven declared that the New Order in Norway would be established exclusively through the Nasjonal Samling party of Vidkun Quisling, thereby enabling the Norwegians to determine their own future.[76]

The record of Terboven's administration in Norway makes it clear, however, that he was far from enthusiastic about either Quisling or his party, and that whatever public or private support he gave them was the result of pressure from Berlin. He worked with Quisling, he appointed members or adherents of the Nasjonal Samling to top administrative positions in the country; in February 1942 he elevated Quisling himself to the minister presidency. But he always saw to it that the real power in Norway remained in his own hands. According to the testimony of Admiral Erich Raeder after the war, the Reichskommissar actually sabotaged Quisling's work. "Terboven's chief motive was, in my opinion, to remain Gauleiter of Norway." [77]

The Norwegian armed forces formally surrendered on June 10, 1940, and almost immediately afterward Terboven set out to create a Norwegian government which would not merely be a stop-gap administration, such as the existing Administrative Council, but one which would have a greater appearance of legality and might command a larger measure of popular support. Significantly, he did not propose to do anything for Quisling, who complained often and at length to Hitler and other Reich authorities about his exclusion from the Norwegian government.[78]

On June 13 Terboven called upon the Norwegian Administrative Council to approve a resolution which was to be submitted to the Norwegian parliament (*Storting*) calling for the deposition of the king, the repudiation of the Norwegian government in exile, the cancellation of the mandates of members of the Storting no longer in the country, and the election of a new Norwegian parliament and government within three months after the end of the war.[79] Meanwhile the Storting was to pass an enabling act to give emergency powers to the interim Norwegian government. Once these resolutions and measures had been passed by a majority of the present Storting in accordance with the provisions of the Norwegian constitution, the Führer would recall the Reichskommissar for the occupied Norwegian territory and appoint a special plenipotentiary as his personal representative to the "State of the Kingdom of Norway (*beim Staate Königreich Norwegen*)"—in other words Norway was to be governed in the same way as Denmark, as Hitler had originally intended. Until a new plenipotentiary had been named, Reichskommissar Terboven was to serve as acting special plenipotentiary.

It is possible that Terboven himself inspired the last part of this proposal. With the German armies sweeping through France and the collapse of the Allied armies imminent, he realized that there might soon be new realms to administer and he had evidently been led to hope that he would shortly be invited to exchange his post in Norway for one in the lusher countries of Western Europe. Terboven may therefore have intended to create a political situation in Norway which would make him available for assignments elsewhere. But nothing came of these maneuvers. Terboven remained in Norway until the end of the war.

Terboven applied heavy pressure on the Norwegians to accept the conditions of June 13. They were given four days to reply, and were warned that rejection would mean the suspension of the powers of the Administrative Council and the installation of Germans as heads of the various Norwegian ministries. The Norwegians were operating in an atmosphere of despair. Rumors were rife that rejection of the German conditions might be accompanied by other dire consequences: the installation of a Quisling government, the conscription of Norway's entire youth population for service in Germany, or the outright annexation of Norway to the Reich. Nor could the Norwegians hope for aid from abroad. The last Allied forces had withdrawn from Northern Norway on June 7, the Allied armies were in full retreat in Western Europe, and a final German military victory seemed imminent. The Norwegians nevertheless did their best to evade the German demands, in particular the repudiation of the king and the government in exile. Instead they proposed that the Norwegian Supreme Court be allowed to appoint a new State Council (*Riksråd*), which should serve as an interim government until after the war when a new Norwegian government would be elected.

The Germans were adamant on the question of the king and the government in exile, but by July 18 they reached a sort of compromise with the Norwegian negotiators: If the Norwegian parliament would call upon the king to abdicate and withdraw recognition from the government in exile, the Germans would allow the steering committee of the Storting to appoint a Riksråd whose degree of authority would be determined by the Storting itself. On June 27, in accordance with this agreement, the steering committee of the Storting sent the king in London a formal request to abdicate. Not unexpectedly the king refused.

The king's refusal did not deter Terboven, who continued his negotiations with Norwegian political leaders in an attempt to establish a Norwegian government with a greater appearance of constitutional legality. These negotiations were based on the agreement of June 18, which provided for the formation of a Riksråd to govern the country until the end of the war. Difficulties began at once when it became evident that the Germans had no intention of allowing the steering committee of the Storting a free hand in selecting the members of this council or the Storting a decisive voice in determining its authority. In particular the Germans wanted their own nominees to head the critical ministries of police, propaganda, the interior, and foreign affairs. To make these conditions more palatable to the Norwegians, Terboven suggested men for these posts who were on the whole able and respected Norwegian officials. More important, he pointed out that, although the German nominees were known to hold authoritarian political views, it was also known that none was a follower of Quisling. The Germans asked only that "for the sake of appearances" an insignificant member of the Nasjonal Samling be included in the council as head of the Ministry for Sport. When the Norwegians balked at this they were told that, in return for this token concession, the Reichskommissar was prepared to ship Quisling off to Germany and to remove him from the leadership of the Nasjonal Samling. It was suggested further that on the day the new Norwegian government took office the Germans would declare a general amnesty. If the Norwegians refused the German conditions, on the other hand, they might be deprived of all administrative authority or an outright Quisling government might be installed.

The Norwegians yielded to this combination of threat and promise. On June 29 they reached agreement with the Germans on the establishment of a Riksråd consisting of sixteen members, all Norwegians, under the leadership of Ingolf Christensen, the head of the present Administrative Council.

Terboven lost no time in keeping his word with respect to Quisling. On the very day agreement was reached with the Norwegians, he elicited a promise from Quisling to accept an invitation to Germany and "temporarily" to relinquish his leadership of the Nasjonal Samling. Terboven took some pride in this accomplishment. It had been no simple matter to ease Quisling out of Norway, he told German military leaders on June 30, but an honorable pretext had been found. "A sledge hammer and plenty of schnaps" had done the rest.[80]

But the Riksråd, which was to have been the product of Terboven's negotiations with the Norwegians, never came into existence. In arranging affairs in Norway the Reichskommissar had seriously underestimated the influence of Quisling who, through the mediation of Rosenberg and other pro-Quisling (or anti-Terboven) forces in Berlin, was able to transmit to Hitler his version of what was going on in Norway. On July 21 Terboven informed his staff that the Führer had endorsed all his policies—but that Quisling was to return to Norway and be reinstated as leader of the Nasjonal Samling.[81]

On August 16 Quisling was given the opportunity to present his case to Hitler personally. The Norwegian leader did not spare his criticism of Terboven. He complained that the Reichskommissar continued to work with leaders of the old system, that he gave only token support to the Nasjonal Samling, that his policies were inconsistent and mistaken. When Hitler asked what political course he would recommend in Norway, Quisling called for the formation of a government dominated by members of the Nasjonal Samling, the elimination of all former leaders from positions of influence, "and then clear-cut and decisive work for future collaboration with Germany."

Hitler expressed complete agreement with Quisling's ideas, assuring him that he was mistaken about the attitude of the Reichskommissar. Terboven had always said that the Nasjonal Samling was the only movement with which Germany could possibly co-operate in the future. Hitler would, however, summon Terboven to Berlin and discuss the situation with him. The new Norway was only conceivable under the leadership of the Nasjonal Samling and indissolubly connected with the person of Quisling. "Quisling could rely on him." [82]

Hitler kept his word, or so it would appear. In accordance with Quisling's recommendations he gave orders toward the end of August to secure for Quisling the leadership of the administration of the Norwegian state. In the office of the Reichskommissar it was expected that Hitler's decision would lead within a week to the dissolution of the Norwegian Administrative Council, the prohibition of all parties with the exception of the Nasjonal Samling, the founding of a "German" party, and the appointment of Quisling's followers to head the Norwegian government departments. "In this way the taking over of the leadership of the state by Quisling is to be prepared and secured." [83]

These changes in the Norwegian government did not take place as rapidly as anticipated, perhaps because of the objections of Terboven, who made frequent appearances at the Führer's headquarters at this time. Whether or not as a result of Terboven's arguments, Hitler authorized his Reichskommissar early in September to resume negotiations with the Norwegian parliamentary leaders to see if they could not be cajoled or coerced into accepting a Riksråd which included followers of Quisling. The advantages of such negotiations to the Germans were obvious. If they succeeded, the new Norwegian government with its Quisling contingent would acquire that appearance of legality by which Hitler always set such store; if they failed, the Norwegian parliamentarians would have only themselves to blame for compelling the Germans to turn exclusively to Quisling.

Whatever Hitler's own intentions with regard to Quisling may have been at this time, it looks very much as though Terboven now took advantage of the Führer's authorization to work for a "legal" Norwegian government to continue his sabotage of the Quisling cause.[84] When negotiations with the Norwegians were resumed in the first part of September 1940, the chief of Terboven's administrative office informed them that Hitler had consented to the establishment of a Riksråd, in accordance with their own recommendations, and that the "Quisling danger" was over. The situation, to be sure, had changed somewhat since the agreement of June 29. Quisling was to remain in Norway and several additional members of the Nasjonal Samling would have to be included in the new government council, although Quisling himself would not be a member. The Reichskommissar, too, was to remain in Norway and would operate at the side of the Norwegian government council.

In attempting to persuade the Norwegians to accept such a radical departure from the agreement of June 29 and the "several additional members of the Nasjonal Samling" in the new government, Terboven resorted to the same tactics he had employed successfully in his earlier negotiations. The Norwegians were asked to accept candidates for the council who had authoritarian political leanings, who were even members of the Nasjonal Samling, but who were not necessarily supporters of Quisling and who in some cases were well known to be his bitterest rivals within the party. Specifically Terboven proposed a thirteen-member Riksråd under the leadership of Ingolf Christensen which was to be composed of four members who were "direct" adherents of the Nasjonal Samling, four who were "sympathetic" to the Nasjonal Samling, and seven others who represented the four largest political parties in Norway. Thus the Nasjonal Samling would have a nominal majority in the Riksråd, as desired in Berlin, but since only two of the candidates proposed by Terboven could be considered actual supporters of Quisling his influence would be minimal.

Quisling and his lieutenants immediately saw through Terboven's game, and in view of the support they enjoyed in Berlin and the attitude of Hitler toward the Nasjonal Samling it is doubtful whether the Reichskommissar would have been allowed to carry it through to a successful conclusion under any circumstances. But the Norwegian parliamentarians gave him no opportunity to try. Justifiably suspicious of the new and more onerous German proposals, they refused to make the required personnel concessions and demanded definite assurances about the membership and status of the Riksråd in return for any further co-operation. By the last week of September 1940 it was evident that Terboven's negotiations with the Norwegians had failed, and that if a new Norwegian government were to be established along the lines desired by Hitler it would have to be promulgated without benefit of a mantle of legality.

Final Norwegian rejection of the Reichskommissar's proposals came on September 25. That same evening Terboven announced the abolition of the monarchy, the deposition of the Norwegian government in exile, and the termination of the activities of the Administrative Council. To take the place of these institutions he was setting up a commission of state councilors, each of whom was to be in charge of an administrative department and given broad legislative powers. Of the thirteen new state councilors, nine were members or adherents of the Nasjonal Samling.[85]

At the same time Terboven issued a decree dissolving all political parties and organizations with the exception of the Nasjonal Samling, which was henceforth to be the sole legal party in Norway. "For a future Norwegian national solution to the present political situation," Terboven said, "meaning a solution designed to allow the Norwegian people to regain a large measure of their freedom and independence, there is now only one way and that is through the Nasjonal Samling. It is now up to the Norwegian people to decide." [86]

Terboven thus carried out Hitler's orders to form a Norwegian government dominated by members of the Nasjonal Samling. This did not mean, however, that either Quisling or his party was conceded any genuine authority. Quisling had assured the Germans that to him it was a matter of indifference whether he himself were made a member of the government. Terboven took him at his word and did not include him in the new commission. Quisling remained the head of his party, nothing more. To undermine Quisling's position still further, Terboven resorted to the strategem of appointing Quisling's rivals within the Nasjonal Samling to the new state commission. Jonas Lie, for example, who was selected to head the crucial Department of Police, had only recently joined the Nasjonal Samling, and at the time of Quisling's banishment to Germany had been Terboven's candidate to succeed Quisling as leader of the movement.

The councilors themselves, however, were conceded little enough power. Like the members of the Administrative Council whom they replaced, they were simply heads of the various Norwegian government departments and as such little more than agents of the Reichskommissar. They were appointed by him, supervised and controlled by him, and obliged to carry out his instructions. Even their legislative power was a sham, for all proposed legislation had to be submitted to the Reichskommissar before it could go into effect.[87]

The councilors did their best to broaden their authority. Those among them who were loyal members of the Nasjonal Samling used their positions to improve the status of their party in the country, systematically attempting to install party members in important administrative positions.[88]

As head of the Department of the Interior, Albert Viljam Hagelin, Quisling's former go-between in Germany, began a reorganization of provincial and local government in the interest of greater administrative centralization. Administration was to be based on the *Führerprinzip*, and all officials were expected to co-operate loyally in the establishment of the new political order. Those who failed to do so were to be removed, a process that did not proceed so rapidly as Hagelin may have wished because of the lack of qualified personnel among Nasjonal Samling party members. It took over a year, for instance, before all eighteen provincial governorships could be filled by party men.

In charge of the critical Department of Religion and Education was a former professor of electrical engineering at the University of Trondheim, Dr. Ragnar Skancke, who introduced fundamental changes in the educational curriculum to bring Norwegian schools into line with National Socialist ideas. To purge teachers antagonistic to the New Order, he decreed that the appointment of teachers as well as the curriculum should henceforth be controlled by his department.

The resignation of the Norwegian Supreme Court on December 21, 1940, gave the government an opportunity to reorganize the Department of Justice and to appoint members of the Nasjonal Samling to the vacated positions on the Supreme Court. Early in the following year the large-scale resignation of members of the clergy, including the majority of bishops and deans, afforded an opportunity to reorganize and control the state church.

The most powerful member of the new Norwegian government was Quisling's rival, Jonas Lie, head of the Department of Police. Lie, a writer of popular detective stories, had headed the international police force which supervised the Saar plebiscite in 1934–35 and was an able and experienced police officer. Through a vigorous recruiting program and the elimination of unreliable elements, he succeeded in building

132

the Norwegian police force into the strongest organization under Norwegian control.[89]

Almost all other leaders of the new Norwegian administration were notably lacking in experience, yet the administration itself continued to function with reasonable efficiency thanks largely to the fact that the experienced bureaucrats who staffed the various government departments remained at their posts. But the reorganization of the government failed to produce the political results that Hitler and the supporters of the Nasjonal Samling had hoped for. Despite the monopoly status of the party, the installation of its members in strategic positions in the government and society, its control of all legal channels of communication, and the financial and political support it received from the Germans, the Nasjonal Samling failed to win the allegiance or respect of the majority of the Norwegian people. The party was held in contempt by almost all intellectuals and the old ruling groups; efforts to enroll town laborers and peasants in the party or its subsidiary organizations were on the whole a sorry failure.

Quisling placed much of the blame for the unpopularity of his movement on the Germans, particularly on Terboven, whose degrading treatment of himself and refusal to concede his party any real authority he believed was responsible for the general lack of respect for the Nasjonal Samling. But he also blamed the German government for its refusal to grant Norway a separate peace treaty guaranteeing its future status within the new European order. Without such a treaty Quisling saw little hope for his movement; for only by proving to the Norwegian people that he could offer them solid advantages for the future could he expect to win their allegiance.[90]

The kind of treaty Quisling had in mind was one that would specifically reaffirm Norway's status of neutrality and independence. For, although Quisling was willing enough to enroll his country in some kind of future Nordic confederation, he insisted that it should continue to enjoy a considerable degree of national autonomy. Within Norway itself he demanded the immediate establishment of an independent Nasjonal Samling government, with the leader of the party as chief of state, and the replacement of the Reichskommissar by a plenipotentiary or some other diplomatic representative of the Reich.[91]

Quisling's demands did not help his cause in Norway—or in Germany. Hitler had no intention of allowing Norway to lead an independent existence during or after the war. Other Nazi leaders who were not already disillusioned by Quisling's political incompetence were now seriously annoyed by his political pretensions. The Germans, however, had trapped themselves into a position of dependence on the Nasjonal Samling, a dependence which increased after the beginning of the Russian campaign. For, in Norway as in other occupied countries, the war against Russia stimulated the activity of resistance forces.

Strikes, sabotage, and growing disorder during the summer of 1941 led to the promulgation of emergency laws and the beginning of the familiar pattern of reprisals, mass arrests, executions, terror, and counter-terror. On September 17 Terboven issued a decree extending the jurisdiction of German SS and police tribunals to cover violations by Norwegians of all legislation promulgated by the Reichskommissar, a decree amplified by a succession of more stringent measures in the months that followed.[92]

The entry of the United States into the war in December 1941 once again focused Hitler's attention on Norway as an area of crucial strategic importance. An Anglo-American invasion of Norway and subsequent pressure of the Allies on Sweden and Finland might be decisive to the outcome of the war, he told his naval commanders. Germany's freedom of movement in the Baltic would be ended and its supplies of Swedish ore and Finnish nickel would be cut off. "The Führer is convinced that Norway is the 'zone of destiny' in this war," a naval aide recorded on January 22, 1942.[93]

The combination of the growing unrest in Norway and Hitler's fears of an Anglo-American invasion persuaded the Germans to concede Quisling the greater measure of authority and prestige he had so long requested, in the hope that such a gesture might indeed enable him to govern the country effectively. Already on September 25, 1941, the first anniversary of the formation of a government dominated by members of the Nasjonal Samling, the councilors who composed that government were given the title of ministers. On February 1, 1942, Quisling was appointed minister president of Norway at the head of a "national" government and invested with all the authority formerly exercised by the king, cabinet, and parliament. The order announcing his appointment, however, included the significant qualification that the activity of Reichskommissar Terboven would not be affected by Quisling's new position and that the Reichskommissar would continue to act as the Führer's representative in Norway.[94]

Quisling now faced the dual problem of establishing his own authority in Norway and emancipating his government from the influence of Terboven. One of his first moves was to issue a law against attacks on the state and the party. This was followed by a law making the Nasjonal Samling the "fundamental party of the state" and endowing its "Fører" with sole responsibility for its organization, activities, and membership.[95]

Well aware of the unpopularity of his movement with older Norwegians, Quisling aimed to get at Norway's youth. For this purpose he issued a decree requiring that every boy and girl between the ages of ten and eighteen years serve in the youth organization of the Nasjonal Samling. A further decree required that all active teachers become members of the party's teachers association and that they adhere to the policies dictated by the government.[96]

But domestic legislation alone was not enough, Quisling realized, to consolidate his own position in Norway or to undermine that of the Reichskommissar. It was with the view to accomplishing both these purposes that, shortly after his appointment as minister president, he again appealed to Hitler, personally and in writing, to grant Norway a separate peace treaty guaranteeing its future neutrality and independence.[97]

Hitler was scornful of Quisling's naïveté in believing that he would be permitted to build up an independent Norway with all the trappings of national sovereignty; during a conference with Quisling on February 13, 1942, he replied evasively to the claims of the Norwegian leader. Hitler's own ideas with respect to Norway were in no way fixed. Soon after the conclusion of the Norwegian campaign he spoke of making Trondheim into a naval base that would far outshine Singapore, and he had thoughts of converting other Norwegian ports into permanent German naval stations. At the time of Quisling's appointment as minister president, Hans Lammers had the impression that Hitler saw no need for hurry in determining the future of Norway and that he was still undecided whether it should be governed by a German Reichskommissar or a plenipotenitary; whether it should be given a status comparable to that of the Protectorate of Bohemia and Moravia, of a satellite state such as Croatia, or whether it should be placed under the jurisdiction of the Foreign Office like Denmark. One thing was certain, however. The Germans would never withdraw from Norway, which was to become an integral part of the Greater Germanic realm.[98]

Hitler appreciated the difficulties connected with such a program. It would obviously be hard for a young Norwegian to give up his old national loyalties and join with other Germanic peoples in the framework of a Reich, but they would not be called upon to do more than had been asked of Germanic tribes at the time of the great migrations, or of the German states that formed the Second Reich. To win over the young people of the Germanic countries, he approved of Himmler's plan to set up Reich schools in Norway (and the Netherlands) which should serve as training grounds for those men and women who would lead their peoples into the new Germanic era.[99]

Hitler's disillusionment with Quisling gave new strength to the position of Terboven, who conferred with the Führer in May 1942. Afterward Hitler praised Terboven as "a man capable of assuming control of Norway, the most difficult commissarship of the Reich. As he told me himself . . . if he relaxes his authority for a single day, he feels as though he were standing on quick-sands." [100]

Fresh from the impression of his conference with Terboven, Hitler met Quisling's next request for a separate peace treaty for Norway with a categorical refusal. In September 1942 Lammers informed Quisling that Hitler had definitely decided that the final relationship between Germany and Norway could only be settled after the war. Quisling was to discuss all political questions concerning Norway exclusively with the Reichskommissar. Meanwhile he was to see to it that all discussion about the future status of Norway be stopped. With that Quisling's direct access to Hitler was cut off and Reichskommissar Terboven was left in command.[101]

The hapless Quisling had no alternative but to continue to co-operate with the Germans, but he still did not give up his attempts to consolidate his own authority. In the months that followed he issued a succession of emergency decrees, culminating in a law of September 1943 which gave him the power to declare a state of emergency in any part of the country and which provided the death penalty for encouraging strikes, sabotage, or public disturbances, for failing to carry out official orders, and indeed for every kind of opposition to the "governing power."[102]

These Draconian measures succeeded neither in preserving order nor in enhancing the authority of Quisling; but they did strengthen the position of the Norwegian police minister, Jonas Lie, who used the emergency decrees to purge political opponents from the police and to enlist the paramilitary units of the Nasjonal Samling under his command as police auxiliaries. Well aware that Terboven had long preferred him over Quisling, Lie undertook to ingratiate himself still further by appearing to co-operate unconditionally with the German authorities. By 1943 he had gone far toward displacing the more intractable Quisling as the principal agent of German policy in Norway.[103] He fell from favor early in 1944, however, when he saw that the German cause was lost and attempted to pursue a more independent policy. In December of that year Senior SS and Police Officer Wilhelm Rediess told Himmler that Lie, who had at first worked secretly against German influence in Norway, was now doing so more and more openly; he urged that Hitler order Quisling to get rid of him. By this time Hitler was fully occupied with other concerns. Both Lie and Quisling, as well as Reichskommissar Terboven and Rediess, remained in their positions in Norway until the final German surrender in May 1945.[104]

German economic policies in Norway closely resembled those pursued in Denmark, the principal difference being that, in Norway, which had resisted the German occupation and was therefore officially an enemy country, there was never so great a need to disguise the German policies of exploitation.[105] Norway was obliged to bear the costs of the German army of occupation, all Norwegian military assets were requisitioned, the transportation system was placed under German control. Purchases were made, as in Denmark, with military promissory notes (Reichskreditkassenscheine). In July 1940 these were absorbed by the Bank of Norway, which henceforth made credit available for German purchases.[106]

As in other occupied countries, the Germans demanded that all Norwegian economic enterprises continue to operate and made refusal to work punishable by fines or even death. Wages and prices were frozen, rates of exchange between Norwegian and foreign currency fixed by the

Germans. While legislation was quite unable to control prices, which almost doubled in the course of the occupation, wages remained relatively stable, with corresponding hardship for the Norwegian population. Because of the higher wages offered by the Germans and the temporary unemployment caused by wartime economic dislocation, many Norwegian laborers went to work in Germany. Many more worked for the German army or German construction projects in Norway itself. When still more labor was required, a compulsory labor service law was introduced on February 3, 1943, making all men from eighteen to fifty-five and all women from twenty-one to forty liable for the "national labor contribution." [107]

According to a German war economy directive of April 1940, Norwegian industry was to be put at the disposal of the German armament industry in the shortest possible time, with special emphasis on mining plants, chemical industries, armaments and related industries, shipyards, and power stations. The one resource Norway possessed in abundance was hydroelectric power, which the Germans attempted to turn to account to augment the Norwegian production of aluminum, already the third largest in Europe despite Norway's complete dependence on foreign supplies of bauxite. Hitler envisaged developing the country into the electrical center of Northern Europe. "In that way the Norwegians will at last find a European mission to fulfill." A German-Norwegian company for the development of hydroelectric power was founded in February 1941 which planned to increase Norwegian production by ten billion kilowatt hours. Development projects soon had to be scaled down drastically because of difficulties in getting equipment to Norway; by the autumn of 1942 these projects virtually came to an end.[108]

Although the economic burden Norway was compelled to bear during the war was immense in proportion to its small population and national wealth—the German occupation cost Norway approximately three-quarters of its national income annually—its total contribution to the German war economy was insignificant in comparison with that of the more wealthy countries of Western Europe. Strangely enough, there is almost no evidence of German plans for an economic union with Germanic Norway. The Germans were evidently in no hurry to include this poverty-stricken country in their common market.[109]

The Germans showed far more interest in persuading the Norwegians to accept membership in their Greater Germanic Reich. Because of the Norwegians' undeniable status as a Germanic people, the Germans had been dismayed by the necessity of having had to fight them at all. "This development was much regretted by the Reich from its National Socialist racial-political point of view," the official Nazi journal on German occupation policies stated. "For the German Volk sees in the Norwegian Volk a Volk of the same race and the same blood." It was Germany's political goal "to achieve the closest possible friendly relationship with Norway." [110]

In line with this policy, the Nazis not only encouraged the activities of Quisling's Nasjonal Samling party in attempting to further the cause of Germanic solidarity, but engaged in the outright recruitment of Norwegians in German organizations. Among the more obtrusive of these endeavors were the activities of Himmler's agents in recruiting for the Waffen-SS Regiment Nordland, which was to be composed of volunteers from Denmark and Norway. Its members were required to take an oath of loyalty to Hitler and Himmler, and they were expected to learn German, the future lingua franca of the Germanic world. The Nazis clearly intended that volunteers for this regiment should play an important part in Norwegian affairs in the future, for a one-year term of service gave a volunteer a claim to a Norwegian government post, two years entitled him to German as well as Norwegian citizenship, while three years entitled him to a farm. All volunteers were expected to return to their native land as "champions of the Greater Germanic idea." [111]

With the disappointingly small number of enlistments in the Regiment Nordland, the Nazis endeavored to combine an appeal to local patriotism with the Germanic ideal. On May 21, 1941, they founded the SS Norge, whose members were to take an oath of loyalty to both Hitler and Quisling. Quisling professed to be enthusiastic about the new organization, which not only restored the honor of the Norwegian people by giving them the right to bear arms, but which constituted the first expression of the free and equal association (*Gleichordnung*) of the Germanic peoples.[112]

After the German attack on Russia, Norwegian volunteers were sought for the crusade against Bolshevism, and the Norwegian SS was given an even more national character to dramatize the association of this Nordic nation in the common struggle. In July 1942 the name of the SS Norge was changed to Germanske Norge SS, and Quisling, now minister president of Norway, assumed direct command of these troops as part of his program to enhance his personal authority. This unit was to be composed of soldiers of Nordic origin and ideology; as a subsidiary of the Nasjonal Samling, it was to be directly subordinate to the Fører of the NS movement. At the same time it was to be a part of the SS of Greater Germany, and "was to contribute in demonstrating to the Germanic people the path to a new future and create the bases of a Germanic community." [113]

Just over a year later, under German pressure, Quisling allowed members of the paramilitary organizations of his party to be used as special police auxiliaries, a move which brought the Germanske Norge SS under the command of his chief of police, Jonas Lie. Lie's fall from grace in 1944 stemmed in part from his failure to promote the cause of the Norwegian SS legion. Early in 1945 the Germanic SS was given a new and presumably more reliable commander.[114]

The overall significance of the Germanic movement in Norway was not great, except perhaps as a record of failure. The Quisling party was notably unsuccessful in winning popular support. During the entire war only six thousand Norwegians joined the Regiment Nordland and its various successors. Considering Himmler's heavy investment of money and personnel in his recruiting program, this was not an impressive monument to Germanic solidarity.[115]

An integral part of the Nazis' ideological program in Norway, as everywhere else in occupied Europe, was the campaign against the Jews. When the Germans invaded the country, there were fewer than two thousand Jews in Norway, many of them German refugees living in Oslo.

Until the autumn of 1942 no serious measures were undertaken against the Norwegian Jews. On the night of October 25, however, the order went out that all male Jews over the age of sixteen were to be arrested. Forewarned by rumors of an impending anti-Jewish action and by what had happened in other occupied countries, the majority of male Jews succeeded in evading capture and either went into hiding or fled across the border into Sweden. A Quisling government decree of November 17, 1942, required all Jews to register. Eight days later German and Norwegian police forces began a systematic roundup of Jewish women and children.

But most of these Jews, too, succeeded in evading capture, and by the end of 1942 the Germans had managed to seize only 532 Jews, most of them old or sick, who were shipped to Auschwitz and exterminated. By the end of the war only an additional 238 Jews had been seized and sent to Auschwitz. Thus well over half of Norway's Jews had managed to survive. As in Denmark, the courageous aid of the local population and the convenient proximity of the Swedish border had been their salvation.[116]

After approximately five years of rule over Denmark and Norway, the Nazis had been notably unsuccessful in promoting their ideal of Germanic brotherhood, much less that of a Greater Germanic union. The original aim of Cecil von Renthe-Fink to establish the closest possible political, military, economic, and cultural ties between Denmark and the Reich had been frustrated by the procrastination and ultimately by the outright resistance of the Danes; the Norwegians had shown themselves equally recalcitrant. Neither Frits Clausen in Denmark nor Vidkun Quisling in Norway had managed to build native Nazi parties into political organizations of any size or prestige. On the contrary, these leaders and their adherents were held in general contempt and despised as traitors. The Nazis were even less successful in advancing their cause through German agencies; long before the end of the war even the most sanguine Nazi enthusiasts were compelled to acknowledge that in these Nordic states their Germanic program had been a sorry failure.

Nazi failures in Denmark and Norway, however, do not appear to have had any effect whatever on Hitler's aims in these countries, or on his conception of the role these Germanic peoples should play in his New Order. Hitler regarded the situation of the Danes and the Norwegians as comparable to that of the Bavarians before 1871 and the Austrians before 1938, and he remained convinced that in time they could be won over to the Germanic idea and converted into enthusiastic members of the Germanic community. Although he might order that all unrest and opposition in Denmark and Norway be suppressed with ruthless severity, at no time did he or his henchmen suggest that the Danish or Norwegian people should be destroyed. He did propose to send many of them to Eastern Europe, to be sure, but not for purposes of extermination, as in the case of the Jews, but as Germanic settlers of lands that were to be gained permanently for the Germanic cause.

In the course of the German occupation, little was done to integrate either Denmark or Norway into the German political or economic system, but Hitler had stated on several occasions that he intended to make these countries part of his Greater Germanic Reich and there is no reason to doubt that this was indeed his intention. He had, however, recognized the necessity to proceed carefully in dealing with these Germanic peoples, and believed that several transitional stages might be required before they could be fully incorporated into his Germanic union. That either Clausen or Quisling would have been selected to lead one of these transitional governments seems unlikely, for Clausen was too obviously incompetent and Quisling too much a Norwegian nationalist for Nazi purposes. It is more probable that Denmark as well as Norway would have been made a *Reichskommissariat,* and that such reliable German National Socialists as Günther Pancke and Josef Terboven would have been left in charge of the administration to carry on a program of *Gleichschaltung* and the spiritual re-education of the population on behalf of the Germanic idea. The process of amalgamation would presumably have taken a good deal longer than in Austria. But when the stage of the actual annexation of the Scandinavian countries to the Reich had been reached, it can be taken as certain that, as in the case of Austria, they too would have been broken into smaller state and party administrative units, and that a systematic campaign would have been conducted to destroy the very concept of a Denmark or a Norway.[117]

CHAPTER 6

The Nordics:
The Netherlands
and Luxembourg[1]

As in the case of Denmark and Norway, the Low Countries had not figured in Hitler's initial plans for the conquest of German *Lebensraum*,
but it became part of those plans when this area was included in the
German army's grand strategy for the campaign in the west.

Hitler's political tactics for dealing with the Low Countries resembled
those he had adopted in Scandinavia. An appeal was addressed to the
governments of the Netherlands, Belgium, and Luxembourg to prevent
all resistance to the German troops, who were entering the Low Countries solely to forestall an invasion by Britain and France. The Germans
for their part declared they had no intention of encroaching, now or in
the future, on the sovereignty of the Netherlands, Belgium, or Luxembourg, or on any of their European or extra-European possessions.

The Netherlands

The refusal of the Dutch government to respond to Hitler's appeal to
prevent resistance, the flight of Queen Wilhelmina and her cabinet, and
the establishment in Britain of a Dutch government in exile, frustrated
whatever hopes the Nazis may have had to occupy the Netherlands
peacefully and to administer this land of fellow Nordics through a government with all the outward symbols of legitimacy, as they had been
able to do in Denmark.[2] A German military government assumed responsibility for the administration of the country;[3] but as early as May

141

18, 1940, Hitler signed a decree providing for the establishment of a German civil administration, the Reichskommissariat of the Occupied Netherlands, which took over the government of the Netherlands on May 29.[4]

The head of the German civil administration, the Reichskommissar, was to be the personal representative of the Führer, directly responsible to him and subject to him for his specific instructions as for his general policy. The existing laws of the Netherlands were to remain in force insofar as they were compatible with the purposes of the occupation, but the Reichskommissar had the power to promulgate new laws by decree. He was authorized to employ the German as well as the Dutch police to enforce his orders. In effect, he was made deputy dictator of the Netherlands and was specifically named guardian of the interests of the Reich.

Hitler's creation of a German civilian government in the Netherlands was undoubtedly a gesture to the Germanic character of the Dutch people, but there were also sound political reasons for his action. He had no intention of permitting the establishment of a uniform system of government in the occupied territories which would furnish the basis for some individual or organization to build up power to rival his own. In this case he prevented the military leadership from organizing an administrative empire in the west which would have given the army a dangerous amount of power and independence.

As his personal representative in the Netherlands Hitler selected Arthur Seyss-Inquart, still prominent in the popular memory for his aid to the Nazi cause in Austria.[5] A number of contemporary writers have suggested that Hitler's appointment of an Austrian was an effort to side-step Dutch hostility to the stiff and uncompromising Prussian officialdom, and instead to engage Dutch sympathies for a more genial German tradition. Austria, however, had an impressive imperial heritage of its own, as Goebbels recalled in praising Seyss-Inquart's administration in 1943: "a master in the art of alternating the carrot and the stick, at putting severe measures through with a light touch. One can tell that he has had a good Habsburg schooling." [6]

Seyss-Inquart was an able jurist, he had gained administrative experience in the governments of both Austria and Germany. Most recently he had been the deputy of Hans Frank in the Government General of occupied Poland.[7] Hitler believed that Seyss-Inquart had the ideal qualities of leadership: He was extraordinarily clever, supple, amiable, but at the same time thick-skinned and tough.[8] But Hitler did not always select his officials for their ability or experience. His most important consideration in this case may have been that Seyss-Inquart had proved himself a dedicated Nazi, but one who had neither a personal following nor organizational support. He was therefore entirely dependent on Hitler for his power and position, and consequently obliged to remain loyal to him.

Seyss-Inquart was supplied with clear directives about his tasks in the Netherlands. Above all the country was to be made secure. All other activity was subordinate to this fundamental consideration. Scarcely less imperative was the duty of the Reichskommissar to funnel a maximum of the productive capacity of the Netherlands into the German war effort. "Under the Führer the German people are fighting a decisive battle for their survival or destruction, a struggle which the hatred and envy of their enemies have forced upon them," Seyss-Inquart said in his first proclamation to the Dutch people. "This struggle compels the German nation to exert all its strength and gives it the right to avail itself of all means within its reach. This compulsion and this right of necessity also affect the life of the Dutch people and their economy." With this statement the Reichskommissar wished to warn the Dutch of possible unpleasant measures, but he had no desire to alarm them unnecessarily. It was the concern of the Reichskommissar that the Dutch people, akin in blood to the German nation, should not be subject to living conditions less favorable than those necessitated by the community of fate and the destructive intentions of Germany's enemies. "There is nothing which should prevent us from meeting each other on a plane of mutual respect." [9]

The blood relationship between the Dutch and the Germans, which Seyss-Inquart had emphasized in his first proclamation to the Dutch people, was to remain a central theme of Nazi policy in the Netherlands and was given far more emphasis by Nazi theorists than the similar relationship which they presumed to exist between the Germans and the peoples of Scandinavia, perhaps because of Germany's closer historical and cultural ties with the Netherlands. According to these theorists, scientific investigation in anthropology and prehistory had proven the Teutonic origin of the people inhabiting the territory of the Netherlands.[10] Nazi writers maintained further that for many centuries this blood relationship had also been a political relationship. From the year 925 the Netherlands had formed a part of the German Reich until foreign rulers, unable to comprehend the spiritual aspirations of this Germanic folk, had driven the Dutch to revolt.[11] At the German Reichstag of 1578 the Dutch poet Philipp van Marnix had addressed an impassioned appeal for aid to his fellow Germans: "Reflect how much it concerns Germany that these provinces are not torn from the heart of the Holy Empire," he had cried.[12] But the criminally negligent German princes failed to rally to the cause of the Dutch. The Peace of Westphalia detached the Netherlands from the body of the Reich, and after 1648 the Dutch pursued an independent political course. Fundamentally, however, they remained a part of Germandom. Dutch culture remained Germanic culture; the Dutch nature remained a Germanic nature. A people could not dissociate itself from its racial foundation. "To build on these existing unities and to go back to this common origin in order to create new commonalities within the framework of the new European order is the task in this area," Seyss-Inquart said.[13]

It was one thing for National Socialism to acclaim the Dutch as brothers, but quite another for the Dutch to welcome National Socialist domination and exploitation in the same spirit. Instead of finding the warm welcome they had been led to expect in a Nordic country, the German invaders faced general hostility and disgust. Nazi theorists were forced to explain. The long political separatism of the Dutch nation and the gradual adoption of foreign modes of thought had, they reasoned, resulted in the spiritual cleavage which prevented the Dutch from generally recognizing and acclaiming the mission of the National Socialist movement. In the course of the last three hundred years the Germanic Netherlands had moved into ever-closer spiritual and cultural relations with the West. The rulers of Holland had gained their great wealth and maintained their dominant position at home largely through their overseas enterprises. The dependence of the ruling strata of Dutch society on foreign trade and colonial exploitation had forced Holland into the orbit of capitalist and free-trade countries, particularly into subservience to the sea power of the British Empire.[14] The point of view of the Dutch ruling strata, imposed for centuries on the mass of the Dutch people, had caused the present lack of comprehension for the National Socialist renaissance. This same ruling group had maneuvered the Netherlands into a criminal international position during the present war. Only the alertness of the German Führer and the speed of the German armies had prevented the use of the Netherlands as a base for Anglo-French aggression against Germany.[15]

Seyss-Inquart grandly swept aside the idea that his government should restrict itself to the prosaic functions of preserving order and carrying out the economic exploitation of an inconsiderable patch of territory in Western Europe. As the representative of the Führer, he considered it to be his duty to work toward the highest purposes of National Socialist leadership. The totality of the war being fought by the Germans was not restricted to material activity. The war was but the visible expression of a national striving toward a higher spiritual plane. That the Reichskommissar should aid to his utmost the military phase of this German struggle was a matter of course. But beyond and above the clash of arms, the Reichskommissar intended to initiate a policy which should bring about such conditions as would eventually begin to express the spiritual significance of the National Socialist revolution.[16] "Several times it has been held against me that I have let National Socialism come to the fore in all phases of public life," Seyss-Inquart said in 1943 in reply to critics of his policy in the Netherlands. "So far as I am concerned that is no reproach. That is the historic mission I have to fulfill here." [17]

Within that mission, Seyss-Inquart believed his most significant task was to regain the Dutch for Germandom, and in describing this task he and his propagandists indulged in an effusion of National Socialist rhetoric. They observed with dismay that the flame of burning idealism had

144

flickered low in the Netherlands. There was no longer the same unrelenting drive toward noblest *völkisch* expressions, no effort to live according to highest principles pressed to their ultimate demands. Through the centuries an atmosphere of tolerance and liberalism had permeated all phases of Dutch existence, blurring the distinctions between the false and the true, the base and the beautiful. The tensions of human relationships had been harmonized on a plane of comfortable mediocrity. It was a way of life, said the Nazis, which smothered every genuine *völkisch* revival movement. The National Socialist yearning after higher stature, this convulsive struggle between ideal and reality, between soaring spiritual potentiality and earthbound striving, this tension which was testing the German spirit to the breaking point—all this was as yet foreign to the constricted and materialistic Hollander. The Dutchman's ideal of balance in spiritual as well as in political life, his attachment to material well-being, his bovine satisfaction in a calm existence—all this now had to be altered.[18] "The present war is not being waged for the possession of this or that bit of land or for any dynastic interest," a Nazi theorist wrote with specific reference to the Netherlands. "It is a war for the racial configuration of a part of the earth in the sense of a *Weltanschauung*. There is, therefore, hardly a sphere of human existence in which the government of an occupied territory must not interfere." [19]

Seyss-Inquart's lofty conception of his mission in the Netherlands was not without its practical side. His initial report to Berlin gave an attention to earthly calculations which would have impressed the most materialistic Hollander, and which certainly would have alarmed him. The Reichskommissar recommended that the Netherlands retain a nominal sovereignty for the purpose of preserving all possible ties with the Dutch overseas possessions. Propagandistically the German Reich could appear as the protector of Dutch property against the encroachments of Japan or the United States, and politically the colonies would serve as valuable hostages for a correct attitude on the part of numerous Dutch leaders. For the future, Seyss-Inquart candidly remarked, the Dutch colonies would prove valuable assets to the Greater German Reich. The Reichskommissar also had plans for the reconstruction of Rotterdam, which the Germans had bombed during their attack on the Netherlands, with a view toward making it one of the major seaports of the Germanic area. Rotterdam's natural harbor facilities and its strategic location at the mouth of the Rhine already made it the most convenient harbor for Central Europe. With the completion of the Rhine-Main-Danube canal its sphere of service would extend from the Atlantic Ocean to the Black Sea.

These considerations, Seyss-Inquart admitted, were dreams of the future. For the present the German administration would seek to bind the Netherlands as closely as possible to the Reich, particularly in the economic sphere. This task could be solved most conveniently by creating a political situation which would make it possible for German measures to appear as the will of the Dutch people themselves.[20]

In pursuing this policy the Germans were aided by the fact that, although the queen and cabinet had fled, the majority of professional civil servants, including the permanent heads of the main administrative departments (the secretaries-general) had remained at their posts. Thus the Germans were able to carry on a large part of the administration of the country through the regular Dutch bureaucracy. General H. G. Winkelman, the acting head of the Dutch government after the departure of the queen, was speedily removed from office, as were the deputies of both houses of the Dutch parliament (the States General), on the ground that both Winkelman and the elected parliamentary deputies were part of the executive branch of the Dutch government whose purpose had been eliminated by the establishment of the German executive power. The secretaries-general, on the other hand, were given a substantial increase in authority, including the power to issue new laws by decree—subject of course to the agreement of the Germans.[21] Local elected assemblies, too, were dissolved, and their power transferred to individual officials—mayors and provincial commissioners—whose activities could be more easily controlled and supervised.[22]

To foster the illusion that the Dutch people were being left a considerable amount of political independence and self-government, the Germans at first permitted the existence of all political parties except the Marxists. Such tolerance was helpful in retaining the service of bureaucrats of widely different political affiliations. "The occupying power has . . . been satisfied to place a staff of German leaders next to the central Dutch governmental bodies," Seyss-Inquart said. "It is their duty to look after the interests of the occupying power according to the needs of the moment. In other words: the people of the Netherlands are governed by their own authorities and civil servants."[23]

Seyss-Inquart assured the Dutch that he would not force National Socialism on anyone. It might be his hope to lead administrators to National Socialism, but membership in a National Socialist organization was absolutely voluntary. "It is immaterial what political views the individual has so long as he fulfills his duties in his particular profession."[24] The Reichskommissar was probably sincere in this pronouncement. He took considerable pride in ruling the Netherlands through a native administration with a minimum investment of German manpower, he had little confidence in the abilities of the Dutch Nazis. Gradually, however, as German demands grew more onerous, an increasing number of Dutch officials resigned rather than co-operate any longer with the occupation authorities. Gradually the Germans, too, began to replace leading officials by ideologically more trustworthy candidates. By 1943 only three of the original eleven secretaries-general remained in office and almost all important city and provincial posts had been given to Dutch Nazis.

146

But for German purposes the important thing was that a large majority of rank and file Dutch civil servants stayed at their jobs, so that until the end of the war the routine administrative functions were performed by the Dutch themselves. The savings to the Germans in terms of manpower were immense.[25]

For the German direction of the Dutch bureaucracy, Seyss-Inquart divided his government into four departments: administration and justice, economics and finance, security, and special affairs, each of which was placed under the direction of a German Generalkommissar. To supervise provincial and local affairs, Seyss-Inquart appointed a number of special commissars who were given considerable autonomous authority to enable them to deal flexibly with the different conditions in the various sections of the country.[26]

Seyss-Inquart's rule in the Netherlands was not left uncontested. The Nazi administration in this country, as in all German-occupied territories, reflected the struggle for power and position waged among Hitler's henchmen in every sphere of activity in every part of the Nazi empire. It was not that Hitler's authority in the person of his representative was being challenged, but that subordinate Führers intended to establish and extend the influence of their departments while conditions in the occupied areas were still in flux. Because Hitler actually encouraged this competition for power, Seyss-Inquart was unable to withstand the challenge of other Nazi leaders; in the course of the occupation the representatives of the Nazi party, the Four-Year Plan, the SS and police, the Labor Front, the Foreign Office, and numerous other organizations gained their niche in the government of the Netherlands. His Generalkommissars, too, persistently sought to broaden their spheres of authority, at the expense of their chief and of each other.

The most obvious competitor for power in the Netherlands was the Wehrmacht, which had conquered the country and remained primarily responsible for its military security. An ambitious military commander might well have contested Seyss-Inquart's authority, but General Friedrich Christian Christiansen, German supreme commander in the Netherlands, was not an ambitious man. Nor did he have the full confidence or support of the German army leaders, for he was a general in the Luftwaffe and his appointment had been recommended by Göring. Moreover his power was limited by Hitler's decree of May 18, 1940, which required that all orders relating to the civil domain be enforced by the civil government. This restriction might have been evaded by attaching a broad interpretation to the concept of military security, but Christiansen confined himself strictly to his military sphere, apparently glad to leave the enforcement of the more onerous German regulations to the Reichskommissar and the German police. He soon was to find himself involved in the roundup and shooting of hostages and similar actions, but he never used these activities to extend his authority.[27]

Among his Generalkommissars, Seyss-Inquart had least competition from Dr. Friedrich Wimmer, a fellow-Austrian and close friend. Although head of the department of administration and justice, which involved the supervision of the Dutch administration, the law courts, education, public health, and other critical fields, Wimmer was not a power in the occupation government. One by one he allowed his functions to be taken over by more ambitious and unscrupulous colleagues, so that in the end he was left with very little influence.[28]

A far greater threat was Fritz Schmidt, the Generalkommissar for special tasks and the only non-Austrian among the top German civilian officials in the Netherlands (he was born in Münster, Westphalia). At first Schmidt's tasks included little more than party and ideological matters. Schmidt, however, was ambitious and worked steadily and effectively to broaden his influence. Moreover, as the representative of the party in the Netherlands, he had behind him the Nazi party organization and the leading spirit in that organization, the ruthless and power-hungry Martin Bormann. So great was Schmidt's energy and ability that Seyss-Inquart came to depend on him as a political adviser and to entrust him with some of the more difficult tasks of administration. He was placed in charge of the provincial commissars and became the chief force in provincial government. When the great German drive for foreign labor began in 1942, he was selected as Fritz Sauckel's deputy for the Netherlands. On the strength of his responsibility for ideological indoctrination he rapidly assumed most of Wimmer's authority in the field of education; as supervisor of propaganda, the press, radio, and the theater, he became the deputy of Joseph Goebbels. To win local support he took the lead in promoting the interests and ambitions of the Dutch National Socialist party and its leader, Anton Mussert. Early in 1943 he was entrusted by Lammers, the chief of the Reich Chancellery, with the overall direction of political affairs in the Netherlands. The unfortunate Wimmer was almost completely frozen out.[29]

The success of Schmidt in extending his authority brought him into conflict with Heinrich Himmler and his multifarious organizations, and it is possible that Himmler succeeded in turning Bormann against him. For on February 16, 1943, Bormann wrote to an official of the Party Chancellery in Munich, "I have heard that Schmidt is not pursuing a clear and purposeful policy, but is instead constantly playing off persons and groups against each other. . . . I should like to make unequivocally clear that I bear no responsibility for what the Münster *Parteigenosse* Schmidt considers to be policy or for what he does, nor do I care to do so." [30]

Schmidt's career came to a sudden end when he was killed in a fall from a train in June 1943, a death so providential that it was widely believed Himmler's men had done the job. The evidence suggests that Schmidt, an unbalanced personality, committed suicide, perhaps as a result of reprimands he received from Bormann. So rife were the rumors that Himmler felt obliged to order his chief representative in the Netherlands to attend Schmidt's funeral to allay suspicion. Schmidt's death was a loss to Seyss-Inquart, who had found him a useful ally against Himmler's agents. His successor, Wilhelm Ritterbusch, a colorless man of mediocre ability, soon lost most of the authority Schmidt had won.[31]

The most serious encroachments on the authority of the Reichskommissar came in the fields of economics and security. The powers of the Reichskommissar in the economic sphere had been undercut before he even arrived in the Netherlands. On May 19, 1940, the day after the civilian government in the Netherlands had been created, Hitler issued a supplementary secret decree empowering Göring, as plenipotentiary of the Four-Year Plan, to give orders directly to the Reichskommissar to ensure the unified direction and planning of the German war economy. Thus Seyss was subject to the immediate orders of Göring as well as Hitler.[32]

Göring at once proceeded to send members of his own staff into the Netherlands to perform tasks almost identical to those Seyss-Inquart had entrusted to his own Generalkommissar for economics and finance, Dr. Hans Fischboeck, a former bank president from Vienna. Göring, however, proved unable to establish effective control over Dutch economic affairs. He faced the competition of the economic agencies of the army, which were already engaged in securing the resources of the Netherlands; and from the Reich came members of the offices of finance and economics, armaments and munitions, agriculture and labor, as well as representatives of a multitude of private firms, to claim a share of the spoils or the power to distribute them.[33]

To co-ordinate the efforts of the many competing German economic agencies, Göring, in collaboration with the Ministry of Economics and the economic offices of the Wehrmacht, set up Central Order Offices (*Zentralauftragstellen*, or Zast) in all the occupied countries of the west. These were to act as clearing houses for all orders over five thousand marks placed by any German agency, and were to go into operation on September 15, 1940. Orders placed by the Wehrmacht were to have priority, but otherwise the decision as to how the demands of the German economy were to be met were left to the local Zast offices.[34] As the tasks of Zast soon widened to include the requisitioning of economic resources, their distribution, and the overall supervision of the economy of the occupied countries of the west, the Central Order Offices became very powerful indeed. But they never developed into centers for the extension of the authority of the Office of the Four-Year Plan, as Göring may have hoped. Established at the seat of the German government in the occupied territories and staffed by officials of the Ministry of Economics and various army economic offices, they became adjuncts of the occupation governments and operated with a good deal of independence.[35]

The system of economic exploitation through the Central Order Offices was never very efficient in any case. By simply placing German orders with local firms, the Zast offices permitted the continuation of quasi peacetime methods of production. Moreover the system of priorities established by the individual offices often varied widely and bore little relationship to the needs of the Reich. Various efforts were made to impose more rigorous controls, especially after Albert Speer became minister of armaments and munitions in 1942. But it was not until December 3, 1943, that a decree was issued which initiated such elementary procedures as the standardization of production in war industries, the rationalization of manufacturing programs, and the establishment of a uniform and rigid system of priorities. By that time the Allied air raids and the constant threat of invasion had made it almost impossible to put the new regulations into effect; thus a genuinely efficient system of economic exploitation was never established.[36]

Meanwhile Göring's power had slipped badly, especially after the beginning of the Russian campaign. In 1942 Speer's Ministry of Armaments and Munitions took over many of the duties and powers of the Office of the Four-Year Plan. Officially Speer worked in the Netherlands through the German Generalkommissar for economic affairs, but in fact he dictated policy to him. By the end of 1943 Speer had brought most economic agencies in the Netherlands under his control.[37]

In the field of labor, too, power and responsibility changed hands. Göring, as head of the Four-Year Plan, was responsible for supplying manpower to German industry and agriculture; but on the whole he refrained from radical recruitment measures in Western Europe so as not to disrupt the sophisticated and productive economy of this region. In the Netherlands he left labor recruitment largely in the hands of Generalkommissar Fischboeck, local officials, and private hiring agencies. The government of the Reichskommissariat took several steps to speed the flow of workers to Germany, but until April 1942 enlistment for work in the Reich remained voluntary.[38]

By that time the German labor shortage had become acute and the large-scale program for drafting foreign workers was inaugurated under the direction of Fritz Sauckel. In the Netherlands Sauckel bypassed Fischboeck and placed the labor recruitment program in the hands of the more energetic Fritz Schmidt, whose agents at once began a rigorous selection of men to be drafted for work in Germany. As this method did not produce manpower fast enough to suit the German authorities, a decree was issued on May 6, 1943, requiring all males between the ages of eighteen and thirty-five to register for work in Germany; shortly thereafter entire age groups were called up for labor service.[39]

The German labor recruitment program was as inefficient as most other aspects of their economic policy. The drafting of skilled laborers for work in Germany crippled many Dutch industries and agricultural enterprises and forced the Germans to set up an elaborate system of exemptions. The Dutch soon became skilled in evading the draft, and the total number of laborers sent to Germany dropped from a high of 162,-

800 in 1942, to 148,900 in 1943, and to a mere 20,000 in the first seven months of 1944. In desperation the Germans resorted to massive raids to round up workers, a method that produced impressive results statistically but dealt a further blow to the Dutch economy and the overall German position in the country.[40]

Amid all the confusion, diversity, and inefficiency of German economic activity in the Netherlands, however, all Nazi policies possessed two common features: They were all concerned with exploiting the Netherlands for the German war economy and with integrating the Dutch economy into that of the Reich. German economic exploitation followed the familiar pattern of direct and indirect expropriation, the outright confiscation of Dutch military supplies and strategic raw materials, wage and price controls, and currency manipulation.

More interesting, and from a long-term point of view more significant, were the measures to integrate the German and Dutch economies which, according to policy guidelines laid down by Göring, was the major goal of German economic policy in the Netherlands. As part of this policy, Göring instructed Dr. Friedrich Landfried of the Reich Ministry of Economics to send German banks a circular on principles for investment in the Netherlands: They should buy into key economic enterprises, secure a dominant position in their management, and eliminate undesirable elements, especially Jews, with the ultimate objective of establishing maximum German control over Dutch business.[41] On January 1, 1941, the customs barriers between Germany and the Netherlands were removed; on March 31 the currency barriers were eliminated.[42] These steps were fundamental in the whole relationship of the Netherlands to Germany, as Göring intended that they should be. In September 1941 Seyss-Inquart reported proudly to the Führer that one of the main tasks assigned the German administration in the Netherlands—that of integrating the German and Dutch economies—had been accomplished. So close had the economic co-ordination of the two countries become that, from an economic point of view, there would be no difficulty in treating the Netherlands as a Gau of the German Reich.[43]

The most successful usurper of authority in the Netherlands, as in almost every other part of the Nazi empire, was the Reichsführer SS and chief of the German police, Heinrich Himmler. In the appointment of a Generalkommissar for security in the Netherlands, Seyss-Inquart was not even consulted. Two men were under consideration for the post, both evidently proposed by Himmler: SS Brigadeführer Hanns Albin Rauter and SS Gruppenführer Erich von dem Bach-Zelewski. On May 22, 1940, Hitler decided in favor of Rauter, who was subsequently named senior SS and police officer in the Netherlands by Himmler. Thus Rauter owed a dual allegiance: As Generalkommissar for security he was under the jurisdiction of Seyss-Inquart; as senior SS and police officer he was subject to the authority of Himmler.[44]

Born in Klagenfurt in 1895, the son of a master forester, Rauter had served in the Austro-Hungarian army throughout all four years of the First World War. After the war he had joined the pro-Anschluss Styrian Home Guard, as Seyss had done; but when the Austrian government banned all overt pro-Anschluss organizations he emigrated to Germany. Here he became the head of a group called the Circle of Fighters of German-Austrians in the Reich and an officer in the SS, whose personnel files describe him as a firm adherent of National Socialist ideology, "an able fighter, tough, energetic, and experienced in the ways of the world." [45]

With the steady support of Himmler, Rauter succeeded in establishing a virtually autonomous administration in the Netherlands. His responsibility for the security of the realm in itself gave him almost unlimited jurisdiction. His police supervised the removal of Jews from the Dutch national body, they established and administered the concentration camps, they operated the hostage system for controlling the recalcitrant portion of the Dutch population. Rauter was also head of all Dutch state and municipal police, and in this capacity he could exercise decisive influence within the German-controlled Dutch bureaucracy.

The degree of independence achieved by the police officer in the Netherlands can be seen from a decree of March 19, 1941, which empowered him to take all measures he considered necessary "for the maintenance or restoration of public order and security." [46] This ambiguous phraseology left the sphere of influence of the police officer restricted only by his choice of interpretation. The police officer, the law went on to say, was authorized to promulgate regulations having the force and effect of law in fulfilling his duties and to deviate from existing laws. Thus Himmler, through Rauter, was in a position to issue decrees of his own in the Netherlands and to disregard those of the Reichskommissar.

In addition to his police powers, Rauter was Himmler's agent in dealing with the various SS units organized in the Netherlands.[47] The right to recruit, train, and indoctrinate a body of specially selected men was an important one, and Himmler clearly intended to use it to create a group of leaders who would rule the Netherlands according to his own interpretation of National Socialism—and under his control. But the SS in the Netherlands never came up to Himmler's expectations. Enlistments were meager despite a vigorous recruiting program; among those who did join no forceful leaders ever emerged. After the beginning of the Russian campaign, the majority of Dutch SS men volunteered or were drafted for service in the east, and with that their immediate usefulness came to an end. Their time was to come later. According to Rauter's plan for the future of the Netherlands, the country was to be incorporated into the Greater German Reich and divided into Reichsgaus administered by SS men, preferably those who had fought in Russia.[48]

Rauter was also Himmler's deputy in his capacity as Reichskommissar for the consolidation of the German people (RKFDV), which for

Himmler represented not only a further source of power and influence, but made him responsible for what he considered the most critical part of the entire National Socialist program. On January 1, 1941, in the course of a routine controversy over questions of authority, he reminded Seyss-Inquart that it was he who had been entrusted by the Führer with the historically important task of regaining the nine million Germanic people from the Low Countries, separated for centuries from Germandom, for the Germanic community. "That this task of creating a community of 110 million [Germanic people] is fundamental to the establishment of a truly great Germanic Reich is surely absolutely clear to both of us," Himmler said.[49]

Spurred on by his chief, Rauter soon began to usurp Seyss-Inquart's authority as the official with primary responsibility for the racial reunification of the Dutch with their Germanic brothers. Himmler's agents did not underestimate the difficulties of the problem. Ulrich Greifelt, the head of the RKFDV's central office, despaired of working through the present leading classes in the Netherlands, imbued as they were with liberal, Freemason, and English ideas. He recommended instead that the Germans seek to win over the less educated lower classes. In a letter to Himmler of June 11, 1940, he proposed that, for a start, two to three million Dutch laborers be brought to Germany for purposes of indoctrination. The outstanding personalities from this group should then be returned to the Netherlands as leaders in the work of Germanization. This process could begin at once by recruiting Dutch laborers for work in the Reich and by an intelligent indoctrination of prisoners of war. Himmler professed interest in Greifelt's scheme and it was, in fact, initiated on a small scale.[50]

Of far greater interest to Himmler, however, was the settlement of large numbers of racially pure Netherlanders in Eastern Europe, for in his view these were the ideal colonists for those eastern areas conquered by the German sword which should be won permanently by the German plow. From the beginning of the German occupation Himmler's agents tried to lure Dutch peasants to the east by promises of large tracts of land. But Himmler knew he could never carry out his grandiose resettlement projects on a voluntary basis alone and plans were made for large-scale compulsory migrations. There is evidence to suggest that Himmler was dissuaded from putting plans of this nature into effect in the spring of 1941, but he definitely intended to carry them out after the war. "I think the right thing to do later on will be to settle the Flemings and Dutch in the east on the greatest possible scale," he wrote to one of his officials on January 7, 1941. "On the one hand that will relieve the pressure of excess population in the central German realm; on the other it will bring incredibly valuable sources of strength into the east. The orders for initiating this policy will be issued after the war."[51]

The failure of the Dutch people to react favorably to his Germanization policies was a disappointment to Himmler, but he realized that it

153

would take time to overcome centuries of ideological error. This could only be done by skillfully conceived indoctrination programs. With the loss of the greater part of their overseas empire to the Japanese in 1941, he believed the psychological moment had come to convince the Dutch that their future lay in the continent of Europe, in the Reich, and in their membership in the Germanic world. They should be made to see that the loss of their colonies had meant the salvation of their racial substance, and be persuaded to revert with heart and soul to their Germanic heritage.[52]

Himmler was dismayed by Seyss-Inquart's failure to launch a propaganda program along these lines, and through personal confrontations and forcefully worded letters he attempted to persuade the Reichskommissar to change his tactics. His efforts were unsuccessful, but he acknowledged in a letter of June 1943 that on the fundamental issue he and Seyss-Inquart had always been in agreement: The Netherlands were to become equal partners in a Germanic Reich.[53]

Seyss-Inquart and Himmler were in agreement on another point: their poor opinion of the majority of Dutch National Socialists and their leaders. When the Germans moved into the Netherlands they did not seek the collaboration of native Nazis in their government. Their experience with Quisling in Norway had not been encouraging in this respect, and, having succeeded in preserving the services of the existing Dutch bureaucracy, they had no desire to disturb the smooth functioning of the government machinery which made possible the administration of the country with a minimum of German personnel. The Dutch Nazis were divided among themselves, they were regarded by their countrymen as traitors, and they would have lacked all prestige and authority as government leaders.

The largest of the Dutch Nazi parties was the National Socialist Movement in the Netherlands (*Nationaal-Socialistische Beweging*, or NSB), founded in 1931, which at the time of the German occupation claimed about fifty thousand members.[54] The leader of this group was Anton Adriaan Mussert who, until his dismissal for political activity in 1934, had been chief engineer of the public works department of the province of Utrecht. A large, heavy-set man, given to posturing in the manner of Mussolini, Mussert lacked the drive and will power of a successful authoritarian leader, and his political competence was evaluated by Seyss-Inquart as being somewhat lower than that of the average Gauleiter. "Mussert is a typical Netherlander," he wrote to Hitler on September 21, 1941, "with the inferiority complex typical of most Netherlanders, but in addition also very mistrustful; further, he is personally ambitious [*Geltungsbedürftig*], not to say conceited." The major objection to Mussert, however, was that he was not a National Socialist in the German sense at all, but a Dutch nationalist whose ideal was Holland's golden age of the seventeenth century and who wanted to secure German support in restoring Holland's greatness—under the leadership of Mussert. He opposed the annexation or even the close integration of the Netherlands with the German Reich. On the contrary, he favored the creation of a Greater Netherlands (a Gross*dietsch*es as opposed to a Gross*deutsch*es Reich), which was to include the Flemish sections of Belgium and France and would control both the Dutch and Belgian colonial empires.[55]

To make his ideas more palatable to Hitler, Mussert drew up a plan for a league of Germanic peoples which was to be made up of Greater Germany, the Greater Netherlands, and a Scandinavian union. Hitler was to be head of the league, but each member was to have its own, independent, National Socialist government and military establishment.[56]

It was a naïve scheme which ignored both Nazi ideology and Nazi greed; there can be little doubt that the Germans would have jettisoned Mussert in short order had they won the war quickly. Mussert, however, was the only Dutch leader sympathetic to the German cause who had anything like a sizable following, and the longer the war dragged on the more the Germans needed him. Over the years members of his party were called upon increasingly to fill posts from which more scrupulous men had resigned and to carry out unpopular German measures such as property confiscations and labor recruitment.

The usefulness of the NSB stepped up sharply after the beginning of the Russian campaign, as German manpower was drained off to the east and as Dutch resistance to German rule began to stiffen. The Germans soon felt obliged to give the party active support. In July 1941 they dissolved all political parties except those in line with Nazi principles, and all these were shortly afterward merged with the NSB.[57]

The improved status of the NSB did not mean that its leader had become more popular with the Germans. Rauter, the SS police chief, complained that Mussert was still intent on creating his Greater Netherlands, despite the fact that Hitler had forbidden all propaganda on the subject. So persistent was Mussert's agitation that Rauter found it necessary to close the border between Belgium and the Netherlands in the autumn of 1941 and to refuse NSB members travel permits to Belgium.[58] Himmler shared his deputy's views on Mussert and was particularly incensed by Mussert's efforts to seek direct access to Hitler to press his Greater Netherlands idea. The candidate of Rauter and Himmler for leadership in the Netherlands was M. M. Rost van Tonningen, the Dutch Nazi head of the Department for Special Economic Affairs, who advocated the complete integration of the Netherlands into the Reich. But his usefulness was limited because of his lack of popular support. In June 1942 Himmler announced that so far as he was concerned Mussert was "finished," but he did not intend to let things come to a break. He would continue to work with Mussert as long as he remained at all useful.[59]

Both Seyss-Inquart and Fritz Schmidt were convinced that Mussert's usefulness was still considerable. In October 1942 they attempted to persuade Hitler to give Mussert a position comparable to that of Quisling as minister president in the Netherlands. The Germans intended to recruit three hundred thousand Dutch as police troops in the east, and they wanted a native government to undertake this unsavory task. Schmidt had yet subtler motives. He had no intention of leaving Mussert in the position of minister president permanently, but believed that a few years under such a man as Mussert would soon bring the Dutch around to pleading for annexation to the Reich "as the lesser evil." [60]

Hitler rejected the proposal to make Mussert the head of a native Dutch government. He had no fear that the Dutch leader would desert the Germans—Mussert had sinned so much that he would be obliged to remain faithful no matter what happened.[61] He did, however, consent to see Mussert and at a conference on December 10, 1942, he explained to him the principles governing German policy toward the Netherlands. He countered Mussert's plea to be made head of the Dutch government by pointing out that this government would shortly be called upon to take particularly severe measures, and that Mussert's position would be seriously weakened if he were associated with them. "For Quisling it would have been better if he had never become head of the government." Hitler also rejected Mussert's idea of a union of Germanic states, which he predicted would fall apart in the first crisis. Hitler proposed instead a firm consolidation of the Germanic peoples, an absolutely essential condition for holding the line against the hordes of the east now and in the future; but such consolidation could be achieved only if the German Reich were the strongest factor. The Netherlands would play an important role in the security system of the New Order, but Mussert could not expect Hitler to do more for the Netherlands than he had done for his native Austria. Vienna, the capital of the German Reich for five hundred years, had been conquered by him in the interest of the Reich idea and Reich consolidation. Just as he had co-ordinated his own country with the Reich, so must Mussert co-ordinate the Netherlands. To aid Mussert in this task, Hitler was recognizing him as "Führer of the Dutch people," and authorizing him to organize a Political Secretariat of State which was to advise the Reichskommissar on all important political matters. When the time came to build the new Europe, Mussert would be called to the Führer to discuss the whole question. Meanwhile he was to aid in administering the Netherlands and to represent the political will of the Dutch people.[62]

Mussert was appalled by Hitler's frank demand for co-operation in reducing the Netherlands to the status of a province of the Reich, but Hitler was correct in his belief that Mussert would not abandon the German cause. Instead, he took advantage of what small concessions had been made to him and proceeded to organize the Political Secretariat of State, in which he tried to include the most able Netherlanders with authoritarian sympathies. To curry favor with the Germans he even

156

tried to win recruits for the war in Russia. A large Dutch contingent on the Eastern front would be strong proof of the desire of the Netherlands to assist in the realization of the New Order. There was talk of augmenting the trickle of recruits by shipping off the greater part of the militia of the NSB, but this project met with but feeble acclaim from NSB members themselves.[63]

Despite his new prestige and elaborate preparations, Mussert was conceded little actual authority. "The Germans will continue to control the country as long as the war lasts," Seyss-Inquart told the petulant Dutch Führer. Himmler was even more emphatic. In July 1943 he made a special journey to the Netherlands to condemn Mussert's ideological errors and put an end to his dream of a Greater Netherlands. The only future of the Netherlands lay in its inclusion in a Greater Germany," Himmler said. "It was clear that a Germanic Reich of the German Nation would be created here." [64]

The nullity of Dutch National Socialism as a mass movement forced the Germans to find other means of getting at Dutch popular sentiment. "It can be said with some confidence," Seyss-Inquart predicted in 1940, "that it is only a question of time until the Dutch people can be won over to a program of close connection between the Netherlands and the Reich." [65]

Basic in a long-range program of ideological indoctrination was the training of youth. "If we cannot get the parents, we will win over the children," promised Generalkommissar Wimmer, the German chief of the Netherlands educational system.[66] The school was to become the center for the instruction of Germanism, the teacher the chief bearer of the Germanic idea.[67] The difficulty here was the lack of teachers willing and able to give Dutch youth a proper National Socialist education. In peacetime the Germans might have supplied this lack themselves, but during the war literate Nazis were needed elsewhere.

Under the guidance of Dr. R. van Genechten, a member of the NSB and public prosecutor at The Hague, an Educators' Guild was founded which was to include all teachers willing to educate Dutch youth in the National Socialist spirit. The old League of Netherlands Teachers was then incorporated into the Netherlands Federation of Trade Unions (the NVV), an agency which the Nazis were using to pull all trades into a single, easily controlled organization. A Dutch Nazi was appointed leader of the education section of the NVV. An order of April 10, 1941, placed the selection of every new teacher in Dutch primary and secondary schools in the hands of Jan van Dam, the Dutch Nazi secretary general for education. By July 1941 van Dam was able to announce that the curriculum of Dutch schools had been "brought up to date." In January 1942 Seyss-Inquart gave van Dam full control over Dutch teachers and professors. He had the power to transfer them, dismiss them without salary or pension; he could have them fined or imprisoned if they exercised their duties in a manner "detrimental to the fruitful development of

Dutch education." In the field of higher education Dutch universities were brought into line with those of Germany. Dutch students were to be admitted to German universities, and Germans into those of the Netherlands. The degrees conferred by Dutch and German institutions would be mutually acceptable.[68]

On the question of education Himmler was in full agreement with the Reichskommissar. There was to be no compromise with the Dutch over schools, he wrote to Seyss-Inquart on March 5, 1942. "The schools must be schools of the Reich." [69] To implement his educational theories, however, Himmler again appears to have bypassed the authority of the Reichskommissar, for in April he informed Hitler that he had established three "Reich Schools" in the Netherlands to further the cause of Germanization. One-third of the pupils in these schools were to be Dutch, two-thirds German. After a certain time the Dutch pupils were to attend similar schools in Germany, where they were to be exposed to further programs of indoctrination. "If we want to prevent Germanic blood from penetrating into the ruling class of the peoples whom we dominate, and subsequently turning against us, we shall gradually have to subject all the precious Germanic elements to the influence of this instruction," Himmler said. According to Bormann's record of Himmler's conversation with Hitler, "the Führer approved of this point of view." [70]

The Nazis originally expected much from the introduction of a prototype of their labor service organization, the Arbeitsdienst, in the Netherlands, which they intended as another vehicle for ideological indoctrination. The Dutch administrators of the service were un-co-operative, however, and by the time the Nazis had reorganized it for their purposes, labor was desperately needed elsewhere, so that its importance remained negligible. More promising was the activity of the NSB's youth organization, the National Youth Storm. Never large in comparison to some Dutch youth groups (its prewar membership of one thousand five hundred attained a mere maximum of eighteen thousand by 1943), it served as a useful nucleus for intensive ideological indoctrination. Relations with its model, the Hitler Youth, were close and continuous, and the Nazis boasted of the fusion of understanding that seemed to be taking place between the members of the two organizations. Vacations of Dutch Nazi children were filled with training courses for leadership similar to those which occupied the free time of Germany's youth.[71]

A prominent feature of Nazi administration in all occupied territories was the procedure of bringing together related activities into single, easily controlled organizations. In the Netherlands this was not done simply to effect a more efficient administrative control. In the case of labor, for instance, Seyss-Inquart explained another purpose to Hitler: "If we succeed in retaining the people belonging to free trade unions and to the Socialist party organizations (that is, if we can get control of these organizations and at the same time prevent their members from deserting them), and if the NSB makes further progress, one-fourth to one-third of the Dutch people will be going the same road as the Reich in well-organized form, whereas other groups will be split and undecided." [72]

Early in June 1940, Dr. Robert Ley installed Dr. Hellwig at The Hague as the representative of the German Labor Front (the Dienststelle Hellwig). Hellwig announced that the Germans did not intend to meddle with old Dutch trade organizations, but that they must not engage in politics, strike, or work against the Germans. On July 16, 1940, Hellwig called together the leaders of the largest trade union organization, the NVV, whom he accused of Marxist leanings and promptly dismissed. To replace this group of leaders he appointed a single man, H. J. Woudenberg, a Dutch Nazi, who proceeded to pull all other labor groups into the NVV and to remold that organization in the image of the German Labor Front. In April 1942 the NVV officially became the Netherlands Labor Front.

Dutch industry and commerce was similarly organized. In July 1940 a National Committee for Economic Collaboration was established for the "co-ordination of Holland's economic life." This co-ordination was further advanced in November 1941 with the formation of an Organization Committee, which was to take all preparatory measures "fit and necessary to establish an independent organization for the development of Dutch industry and commerce." The arrangement was almost identical to the 1936 organization of commerce and industry in Germany. Six main divisions were set up: industry, crafts, commerce, banking, insurance, and transportation, each of which was subdivided further along regional and functional lines to cover every aspect of Dutch commercial and industrial life.[73]

A decree of November 1941 required that everyone in a creative field (writers, architects), or anyone who presented anything before the public (artists, actors, journalists), as well as everyone who participated in the production, maintenance, or sale of such presentations, should become members of guilds for the creative arts. These guilds were all part of a Netherlands Chamber of Culture, whose president had the right to expel any member "if the facts reveal that the person in question does not possess the trustworthiness or attitude required in the exercise of his activities." Jews were a priori excluded. In similar fashion members of all economic groups, whether they were shipowners, insurance brokers, fishermen, or professional football players, were obliged to become members of national associations and were thus brought under yet another form of centralized control.[74]

Particular attention was devoted to Dutch agriculture, for here in the Netherlands was the kind of sturdy Aryan peasantry which the Nazis regarded as the very foundation of their New Order. During the summer of 1940 the Germans ordered the NSB to establish an Agrarian Front to bring together all farming societies and all farmers into a single organization. E. J. Roskam, the leader of this organization, took his ideological cue directly from *Mein Kampf*. Only a revival of a strong peasantry could restore the ancient vigor of the Netherlands, he said. "Then and only then will our nation regain its old character and face the new times with self-reliance and straight-forwardness." Despite this pretentious program for a rustic renaissance, few farmers joined the movement. Membership at first was voluntary, and so long as it was the success of the Agrarian Front was far from gratifying to its founders. The situation was soon rectified by making membership compulsory.

On October 25, 1941, Seyss-Inquart formed the *Nederlandsche Landstand*, an equivalent of the German Agrarian Union. Everyone active in the fields of farming, horticulture, fishing, or forestry automatically became a member. All associations of workers in any of these fields, as well as the Agrarian Front itself, were dissolved into the Landstand. The leader of this new and inclusive society was again E. J. Roskam.[75]

To dramatize their confidence in the Netherlands' basic Teutonism, the Nazis made much of the fact that they were offering the Dutch peasant his share in the newly won soil in the east. The peasant of the Low Countries had in the past done his part in the Germanic *Drang nach Osten*. It was only right therefore that he should be allowed to continue that tradition. As stated by Roskam, "racially pure generations of our peasants and land workers must possess and work 40,000 farms of their own within the living space which will be yielded to us in the framework of a New Europe."[76]

The recognition of the Dutch as Germans was reflected in the laws concerning Dutch and German citizenship, a distinction the Nazis sought to blur as much as possible. Dutch citizens were allowed to acquire German nationality, while still retaining their Dutch citizenship. In this manner a privileged class of Netherlanders was created who enjoyed all rights of Dutch nationals and at the same time were protected by their German status. The Dutch who joined the Anti-Bolshevik Legion to fight in Russia were automatically given German citizenship, and the Dutch law was abrogated which deprived anyone serving in a foreign army of Dutch citizenship.[77]

The Jews alone were to enjoy no status whatever in the Netherlands. Seyss-Inquart made no secret of his attitude. "The Jews are the enemy of National Socialism and the National Socialist Reich. From the moment of their emancipation, their methods were aimed at the destruction of the national and moral values of the German people and the replacement of national and responsible ideology with international nihilism. . . . The Jews for us are not Dutch. They are enemies with whom we can neither make an armistice nor peace."[78] In the course of the German occupation the Jews in the Netherlands were systematically eliminated from every political, economic, and cultural activity, and in the end they were removed physically from the body of the Dutch nation.[79]

160

The sequestration of Jewish economic assets began almost immediately. The first "voluntary Aryanization" processes were soon supplemented by official decrees requiring that all Jewish property and economic enterprises be Aryanized, liquidated, or placed under trustees to be appointed by the occupation authorities. A law of November 28, 1940, expelled Jews from the civil service and the professions. Jewish government officials, professors, teachers, doctors, lawyers—all were dismissed or forbidden to practice. The general indignation in the Netherlands against this law forced the Nazis to make an explanation. "The dismissals have taken place," they said, "because of the world action of the Jews against the German nation. . . . It does not in the least matter whether these Dutch Jews have or have not played a part in the activities of international Jewry. We consider them capable of doing so, and it is our right and our duty to act preventively." In the end the only employment available to Jews, as a law of October 22, 1941, made specific, was manual labor under German or Dutch police supervision.[80]

A decree of January 10, 1941, required all Jews or part-Jews to register, a procedure that resulted in their enrollment on registration lists which were to be a major aid to the Nazi authorities in their subsequent roundup and deportation of Jews.[81] The initial mass arrest of Jews in February 1941 provoked the first serious demonstrations on the part of the Dutch people against Nazi rule. In that same month the Nazis ordered the establishment of a Jewish Council in the Netherlands, as they were doing in other parts of Europe, to secure the co-operation of Jewish leaders in the administration of Jewish affairs. It was a particularly vicious system, for Jews were persuaded to become members of the council in the belief that they could thereby help their people, whereas in fact they were used to carry out Nazi programs.[82]

In September 1941 the RSHA established a Central Office for Jewish Emigration (*Zentralstelle für Jüdische Auswanderung*) in Amsterdam to plan and ultimately to carry out the deportation of Jews from the Netherlands. In the following June this Central Office informed the Jewish Council that the Reich government had decided to put large numbers of Jews to work in Germany, and the council was ordered to aid in the selection and collection of Jews to be deported. In fact the majority of these Jews were to be sent to Auschwitz, as Eichmann informed the German Foreign Office in a letter of June 22. Forty thousand Jews from the Netherlands, another forty thousand from occupied France, and ten thousand from Belgium were to be sent east by train at the rate of one thousand a day. Only Jews capable of work were to be selected, for at this stage the Jews were still really wanted for labor.[83]

The hostility of the Dutch people to Germany's anti-Jewish measures seriously worried Generalkommissar Rauter, but he informed Himmler with some pride that he had no intention of curtailing his program or canceling a single Jewish transport "because what is gone is gone." He expected the registration of Jewish partners in mixed marriages and of

Jewish workers in armament and diamond cutting industries, all of whom were to be exempted from deportation, to be completed by October 15, 1942. After that the big "cleanup" in the Netherlands could begin. By that time two big Jewish internment camps would have been constructed, each capable of holding forty thousand persons. Everyone was to be sent to these camps who was proved to be Jewish or who looked Jewish. The camps would be closed as soon as all their inmates had been deported. In all, some one hundred and twenty thousand Jews, including part-Jews, were to go.[84]

To speed the roundup of Jews, Rauter was urging Jews to enter special work camps voluntarily for their own protection, because so far no work camp inmates had been deported. By this ruse he hoped to lure eight thousand Jews into work camps by October 1. On that day he planned to occupy the camps, arrest the inmates as well as their twenty-two thousand relatives and dependents outside the camps, and to deport the lot. If possible the number of deportation trains would be increased from two to three a week. By Christmas of 1942 some fifty thousand persons, almost half the total Jewish population of the Netherlands, would be gone.

Rauter reported to Himmler that he was receiving the full co-operation of the Netherlands police and party members in his campaign against the Jews. He had special praise for the zeal of the Dutch police, his only complaint being that they tended to enrich themselves through their confiscations of Jewish property. He had a far more serious complaint against the German commissar for Jewish affairs in the Netherlands, Heinrich-Johann Böhmcker, who had seen fit to criticize his harsh treatment of the Jews, an impudence that had given Rauter the opportunity to get rid of this "Judenkommissar." Seyss-Inquart, too, had protested against Rauter's unnecessary cruelty, but he had now wisely agreed to leave the whole Jewish business in the hands of the police.[85]

Himmler fully supported the actions of his police officer. "The evacuation of Jews is to continue without interruption," he told Rauter early in 1943. These measures were authorized by the Führer, who demanded "no compromise of any kind . . . harshest measures." The campaign against the Jews also had the complete support of Seyss-Inquart, despite his objections to unnecessary cruelty. Germany was waging a war to the finish against the Jews, he said, and that war had to be waged in the Netherlands as in every other part of Europe.[86]

Although many Jews had been protected during the early years of the occupation by their service in essential industries or as partners in mixed marriages, they too lost their immunity. Of the 20,000 Jews in mixed marriages, well over half were deported by February 1944, and of those who remained 2,256 had submitted proof of sterilization. Despite the desperate shortage of labor, Himmler's agents worked steadily to root Jewish workers out of Dutch industries. In November 1942 the armaments industry lost hundreds of its Jewish fur and textile workers, and in the following month the diamond cutters were brought under the direct control of the SS. They were deported en masse in March 1944.[87]

By the end of the German occupation, approximately 115,000 of the 120,000 Jews and part-Jews scheduled for deportation by Rauter in 1941 had actually been deported to the east. Those who remained were Jews in mixed marriages who had been sterilized, and Jews who had succeeded in going into hiding. The Nazis left no doubt, however, that in the end all Dutch Jews were to be removed. "The Führer has declared that the Jews have played their final act in Europe," Seyss-Inquart said, "and therefore they have played their final act."[88]

Luxembourg

The Grand Duchy of Luxembourg, like the Netherlands, was regarded by the Nazis as a Germanic country and one which was to be given the same preferential treatment as Denmark. As in the case of the Netherlands, however, the Luxembourg government refused to yield to German demands to prevent all resistance to the German occupation forces, and the Grand Duchess Charlotte and her ministers went into exile. With that the Germans declared that Luxembourg had forfeited its right to preferential treatment, the country was proclaimed to be enemy territory, and a German military government was installed.

Despite the flight of the grand duchess and her ministers, the Germans found that a native administration was still in operation in Luxembourg when their armies overran the country. On May 16, 1940, the Luxembourg Chamber of Deputies had placed executive authority in the hands of Albert Wehrer, secretary general and the ranking permanent civil servant in the Luxembourg government. Wehrer in turn had appointed counselors of state to direct the various branches of the government, who together formed an administrative commission under his leadership. When a German military commander took over executive authority in Luxembourg on the afternoon of May 16, he successfully appealed to Wehrer and his colleagues to remain at their posts in their administrative capacities to aid in the restoration of orderly conditions in the country.[89] So effective were these officials that in the initial stage of the occupation the German military government did little more than supervise the Luxembourg administration, which undertook the difficult tasks of re-establishing order, dealing with returning refugees, and getting the economy going again.[90]

This situation did not endure for long, however. On August 2, 1940, Hitler replaced the German military government with a civilian government under the leadership of Gustav Simon, the Gauleiter of Koblenz-Trier.[91] He was made directly responsible to Hitler, from whom he was to receive his directives for specific measures and general policies. As the deputy of the Führer he was to have sole responsibility for the civil sector of the administration. The military sector remained the responsibility of the army.[92]

To fill key positions in his government of Luxembourg, Simon drew upon the staff of his German Gau, but he lacked sufficient personnel to make any large-scale changes and was on the whole obliged to follow the precedent of the military government in carrying on the administration of Luxembourg through local officials. These officials were carefully screened for their political reliability, and Simon insisted that all appointments and assignments receive his personal approval.[93]

Hitler made no secret of his intentions in Luxembourg. "Luxembourg shall be regained for German folkdom in the shortest possible time," he announced in a decree defining the tasks of the German civil administration. "In order to reach this goal quickly and without friction, the initiative for all administrative measures in Luxembourg must in principle emanate from the chief of the civil administration, who is directly under my command . . . and who is responsible to me alone for the administration of Luxembourg."[94] In a proclamation of his own, Simon informed the ethnic Germans of Luxembourg that he intended to conduct his administration on the principle that "Luxembourg is a German land." There was no need to remodel it, but simply to free it from previous remodelings that had changed its German character. Later, speaking to a group of Luxembourg workers, he candidly admitted that Luxembourg would never have a plebiscite to decide whether its people wanted to join the Reich. That decision had been made on May 10, 1940, when German soldiers had crossed the frontier and protected the country from destruction. "On the day when the first grave for a German hero-soldier was dug we made the following decision: 'This land was won and will be kept by German blood and therefore will remain German for all eternity.'"[95]

Public proclamations were accompanied by official actions. On August 6, 1940, Simon issued a decree making German the exclusive language of Luxembourg, with the justification that "the language of the land of Luxembourg and of its inhabitants is and always has been German."[96] In a public statement commenting on this decree, Simon said, "From now on no Luxembourger will be expected to use the language of a nigger nation [*einer verniggerten Nation*]. Luxembourg is too proud of its heritage and its native language to be the *parrot of France* and to blabber French noises." Luxembourg was no longer to be *"the lackey of a culturally degenerate France. . . . Away with this foreign gibberish. Your language shall be German and only German."*[97] According to the decree of August 6, German was to be the sole language of government, law, and education, as well as the only language to be used in all aspects of economic life. All periodicals had to be in German, as did all advertising and public announcements. By September 30 all place names in Luxembourg were to be Germanized and all signs, names of stores, and inscriptions on buildings were to be rendered into German. A subsequent decree required that all citizens of Luxembourg should Germanize their names.[98]

Shortly after the establishment of the German civil government, all political organizations in Luxembourg, with the exception of the Nazi party, were abolished, and the Luxembourg parliament was dissolved. On August 28, 1940, Simon appointed *Oberreichsleiter* Franz Schmidt to a position with the resounding title of commissar for the regulation and control of all organizations within the jurisdiction of the chief of the civil administration in Luxembourg. All activities of all associations, organizations, leagues, foundations, and groups, whether incorporated or unincorporated, were declared illegal until they had received a special license from the commissar. Every change in an organization likewise required a license. On October 23 the commissar was ordered to see to it that all organizations were set up and conducted according to National Socialist principles. He was empowered to dissolve or reconstitute all organizations, dismiss their leaders or appoint new ones, confiscate their property, and otherwise control every aspect of their activities. Simon took care, however, not to encroach on the powers of Himmler's agents in Luxembourg, for his order stated specifically that "the authority of the Security Police to seize and dissolve associations, organizations, and leagues was to be in no way affected by this order." [99]

In November 1940 the entire administrative system of Luxembourg, including local and district government, the police, and the tax structure, was reorganized and brought into line with German administrative procedures. In that same month Luxembourg law courts and tribunals were abolished and replaced by new ones organized along German lines. In the spring of 1942 the entire body of German civil law was introduced.[100]

The Luxembourg educational system, too, was Germanized and education was made compulsory for all persons of German or related blood. Not only was German made the sole language of instruction, but in the lower schools (*Volksschulen*) French could no longer be taught at all. New textbooks were introduced which presented the German and Nazi points of view. Teaching in both public and private schools was rigidly supervised; teachers suspected of educational sabotage or un-co-operative attitudes were sent to Germany for indoctrination, or jailed.[101]

Germanization also proceeded at a forced pace in the economy. A decree of May 10, 1940, the day the Germans entered the country, made the Reichsmark legal tender at a rate of exchange fixed by the Germans. This decree was supplemented by later orders fixing wages and prices and introducing German occupation currency which allowed the Germans to buy in Luxembourg but made it almost impossible for Luxembourgers to buy in the Reich, assuring a one-way flow of goods. In the interests of Germanization this favorable situation was changed on January 29, 1941, when all Luxembourg, Belgian, and French francs, and all German occupation currency were called in, and the Reichsmark became the exclusive currency in Luxembourg for Germans and Luxembourgers alike.[102]

The Luxembourg economy, like that of other occupied areas, was centralized to facilitate German control and exploitation. An order of November 12, 1940, empowered the chief of the civil administration to establish organizations embracing all major sectors of the economy in which membership was to be compulsory. He was to determine which sectors of the economy should be organized, to make bylaws for the new organizations, define their objectives, and select their leaders. This order was supplemented on February 19, 1941, to allow the chief of the civil administration to dismiss all entrepreneurs who were insufficiently zealous in the promotion of Germanism or who had violated the general principles of the National Socialist labor community, and to appoint commissioners to take their places.[103]

The Nazi paramilitary labor organization, the Reich Labor Service, was introduced in Luxembourg on February 12, 1941. All men and women born between 1919 and 1922 were urged to volunteer. Prerequisites for membership were German or related blood and Luxembourg citizenship. On May 23, 1941, the labor service was made compulsory for both men and women. A decree on compulsory membership of all Luxembourg boys between the ages of sixteen and eighteen in the Hitler Youth followed on August 25, 1942. Boys who refused to join were sent to the SS educational center at Burg Stahleck. On August 30 all men of draft age were subjected to compulsory service in the German Wehrmacht.[104]

Full German citizenship was conferred on all Luxembourgers drafted into the German armed forces, on members of the police who took an oath of allegiance to the Führer, and on all persons who had rendered special service to the German cause, as well as on their wives and children. Provisional German citizenship went to all Luxembourgers who joined the German Folk Movement (*Volksdeutsche Bewegung*), an organization created in January 1942 to be the "bearer of the *Volksdeutsch* idea in Luxembourg and an advance fighting unit of National Socialist ideology." The badge of membership was similar to that of the Nazi party, but bore the additional legend "*Heim ins Reich*" (home to the Reich). Provisional citizenship was also conferred on all persons who joined the Nazi party. This meant that the majority of adult males received such citizenship, for wage earners in every walk of life, from civil servant to factory hand, were required to join and pay dues to the movement.[105]

With the German occupation of Luxembourg, the usual swarm of Nazi officials arrived in the country to ensure a maximum influence for themselves and their organizations. Typically prominent were the representatives of the many offices of Heinrich Himmler, whose influence in Lux-

166

embourg was assured with the appointment of Simon as head of a civil administration. Simon had no pretensions about establishing a personal power base in so small a territory as Luxembourg, and he actually welcomed Himmler's co-operation in the Nazification and Germanization of his new province. Himmler was therefore able to establish his authority and play his game of racial shuffleboard in Luxembourg almost without hindrance.

In response to a request from Simon, Himmler ordered his deputy, Werner Lorenz, chief of the Liaison Office for Ethnic Germans (*Volksdeutsche Mittelstelle*, or VoMi), to prepare a draft of guidelines for handling the racial question in Luxembourg. Lorenz concluded that "as Luxembourg is a German racial area, the goal must be to see to it that the area is inhabited by persons of German stock." Therefore all foreigners and persons of mixed blood were to be evacuated as soon as political and economic conditions allowed. The large number of Italians working in Luxembourg were to be returned to Italy at the end of the war. The French, a category which included all French citizens and "anyone who calls himself a Frenchman," were to be removed as soon as possible. The Walloon Belgians were to be seized but were not to be returned to Belgium until a final boundary for that country had been drawn up.

Himmler did not give a blanket endorsement to Lorenz's proposals, his main objection being that "anyone who calls himself a Frenchman" might well be a person of German blood, and such persons should under no circumstances be lost to Germany. He agreed, however, that all Italians should be returned to Italy after the war, and that all French and other foreign elements should be sent back to France or otherwise evacuated unless they were considered suitable for Germanization. The prerequisite for all these policies, however, was the compilation of a racial register of all persons living in Luxembourg, and Himmler instructed Lorenz to get in touch with Heydrich for this purpose.[106]

By September 1942 Himmler was ready to launch his program of Germanization in Luxembourg. With Germany's transportation facilities already desperately overburdened in supplying the needs of the Wehrmacht in Eastern Europe, he ordered the immediate resettlement of seven thousand Luxembourg peasants, with their household goods and livestock, in Poland and the Protectorate. These were persons who were considered to be racially valuable but politically unreliable, and they were to be resettled among other ethnic Germans in the same racial-political category. At the same time Germans from South Tyrol, who were evacuated to fulfill treaty commitments to Mussolini, were resettled in Luxembourg. Resettlers were supplied from the proceeds of the confiscated property of Jews and of those Luxembourgers who had fled at the time of the German invasion and had not returned. This included the property of the Grand Duchess.[107]

With regret the Nazis were forced to observe that many Luxembourgers, despite their Germanic character, reacted with anger and hostility to the occupation government. In July 1943 Simon decided that it would be necessary to remove all Luxembourg families of doubtful loyalty to the Old Reich in order to establish an absolutely reliable population in this crucial border area, and to educate the evacuees in the light of the greater German ideal. Their evacuation was not to be considered a punishment, but a necessary measure for the security of this Germanic border area. Their property would be placed at their disposal, and they would be granted provisional German citizenship.[108]

Reliable Nazi official that he was, Simon did his part in the campaign against the Jews. There were only about three thousand Jews in Luxembourg before the war, and most of these had fled to France and Belgium at the time of the German invasion. Simon moved quickly against those who remained. In August 1940 he submitted proposals for action against the Jews to Hitler, who agreed to the introduction of the entire body of German anti-Jewish legislation in Luxembourg. Shortly afterward all Jewish property was confiscated, Jewish businesses and farms were taken over by or sold to Luxembourg ethnic Germans.

In 1941 the Jews were forbidden to attend public functions or to appear in most public places. They were forced to wear the Jewish star and to adopt German-designated Jewish names. In the autumn of that year the transports to Eastern Europe began. Although a few Jews, indispensable to the economy, were allowed to remain in the country temporarily, the Nazis made it clear that their ultimate intention was the removal of all Jews from this Germanic area.[109]

Hitler's plans for the future of the Netherlands and Luxembourg do not appear to have differed in any way from his plans for Denmark and Norway. In contrast to the Scandinavian countries, however, the Nazis had pursued policies in the Netherlands and Luxembourg which made their intentions unmistakably clear.

In the case of the Netherlands, although Nazi leaders might disagree about tactics and engage in vicious struggles for power among themselves, they were unanimous on one thing: The Netherlands was to be annexed to the Reich.[110] Well before the end of the war most of the conditions for the union of the Netherlands to the Nazi empire had been created. The distinctions in citizenship had been eliminated, the Jews were gone. In the economic sphere the customs and currency barriers had been removed, and a large degree of integration with the economy of the Reich had been achieved. The Nazification of the educational system, cultural, labor, and all other organizations was well under way. There remained very little to do except to settle with Mussert and to decide how many Dutch peasants were to be drafted for the colonization of the east. The Netherlands was ready to take its place beside Austria, the Sudetenland, and West Prussia as a province of the Greater German Reich.

Conditions for the incorporation of Luxembourg into the Reich were even more advanced than in the Netherlands. Although Luxembourg was not officially annexed to the Reich during the war, it was attached to the Nazi party administrative district of Koblenz-Trier to form the Gau Moselland, and the Germans left no doubt of their intention to make the country an integral part of the Reich after the war. Meanwhile all possible preliminary steps had been taken. The German language, currency, law, education had all been imposed on the country. The population was conscripted into the German youth organizations, the labor service, and the German army. The people were forced to adopt German names, and all ethnic Germans—the only persons allowed to remain in the country—had already been given definite or provisional German citizenship.[111]

CHAPTER 7

The Limes of Lebensraum:
Belgium and Northern France[1]

Hitler's renunciation in *Mein Kampf* of the Germans' ancient drive to the south and west did not prevent other Nazis—and even Hitler himself—from speculating about German claims to territory in these areas after their conquest by the Wehrmacht.

Some of the most interesting theories on this subject were put forward in a publication called *Westland,* a periodical devoted exclusively to the problems of Germany's western frontiers. The articles in *Westland* may be considered more authoritative than the usual expansionist rhapsodies of Nazi theorists because the journal was edited by Dr. Arthur Seyss-Inquart, the Reichskommissar for the occupied Netherlands. Its contributors included Nazi experts on racial and geopolitical questions whose views had upon occasion been endorsed by Hitler.[2]

By Westland was meant the region bounded on the west by the watershed of the Meuse and the Seine and on the east by the Rhine axis. Since the establishment of the Roman Empire, according to Nazi theorists, this territory had been the frontier of Roman dominion, the broad border region separating the Roman from the Germanic world. "Its symbol is the *Limes,* the limits [of Roman rule] to the east." [3] During the period of their ascendancy the Franks had converted this border territory into the very heartland of Merovingian and Arnulfing power. But the Frankish attempt to alter the natural condition of this border region had inevitably ended in failure. Their artificial creation broke apart into its natural racial components, and the Westland reverted to its natural position as a borderland. Throughout the entire Middle Ages it was to remain the Westmark of the German Reich, a fact remarkable in itself considering how many other territorial fluctuations took place during this period.

After the fall of the Hohenstaufen, the French, welded into a powerful political-military structure by a Germanic ruling class, had hammered constantly against this border region in a futile *Drang nach Osten.* In spite of all their efforts, they failed to secure the coveted Rhine frontier because this region was bound by natural racial as well as geopolitical ties to the Germanic realm. These same ties prevented the establishment of an independent political structure in the Westland as contemplated by the dukes of Burgundy, Philip the Good and Charles the Bold. The marriage of Charles's daughter to a German Habsburg was not merely the result of diplomatic necessity, but was yet another expression of the natural racial and geopolitical orientation of this region.

It was finally England which, by exploiting Franco-German hostility, wrenched the Westland from its natural place in the Germanic world and, for over three centuries, made the Low Countries an instrument in its balance of power politics. With the entrance of England into the destiny of the Westland a whole series of sorry figures appeared on the historical stage, leaders who played an ignominious role as England's puppets or dupes. These men tried to alter the natural racial and geopolitical position of the Westland, and in the name of national interests they followed the political leadership of England, a policy they tried to disguise as neutrality.

Nazi theorists agreed that the goal of the present struggle must be to restore the Westland for all time to its position dictated by natural law. The Reich would once again have to take up its watch at the mouths of the Rhine, the Meuse, and the Scheldt. This had to be done not for the sake of power or even for military or strategic reasons, but in obedience to those eternal laws of blood and space which were more enduring than the absurdity and tragedy of historical accident. These same principles held true for Luxembourg, Lorraine, and Alsace. This entire complex of territory would now be charged for all time with the task assigned to it by natural law: to be the Westmark for the Germanic center of Europe. Never again was this region to be an outpost for French aggression; never again should it become the tournament ground for English balance of power diplomacy. To make certain of this decision, all the social, cultural, and racial problems which such a solution demanded would have to be attacked and solved.

The articles in *Westland* appeared to present a comprehensive Nazi program for the west. But what, in fact, did all these distortions of history and effusions about natural law amount to? Germany intended to retain control of the mouths of the major rivers of the Low Countries, and presumably German influence was to replace that of France and England. But what, in precise terms, was to be the future political and economic status of these western border regions? Above all, what did

171

the Nazis mean when they spoke of attacking the social, cultural, and racial problems so as to exclude Anglo-French influences and ensure the domination of their own for all time?

The answer to all these questions appears to be that the Nazis themselves did not know what they meant, at least in any precise terms. Certainly Hitler did not. For all evidence indicates that, no matter how elaborate the theories or how inflated the ambitions of other Germans may have been with respect to Western Europe, Hitler himself had no firm preconceived plans for a large part of this area at the time the German occupation began, and that in Belgium as well as France he pursued a policy of improvisation.

There was never any doubt about Hitler's intentions in three of the provinces conquered from Belgium in 1940, however. On May 18 he issued a decree providing for the reunion with Germany of Eupen, Malmédy, and Moresnet, which had been awarded to Belgium after the First World War. "The districts separated from the German Reich by the Versailles dictate and incorporated into Belgium are once again in German possession," Hitler said. "At heart they have always remained united with Germany. They are therefore not even temporarily to be regarded and treated as occupied enemy territory." The districts were attached to the Prussian province of the Rhineland, Aachen. All ethnic German inhabitants were accorded full or provisional German citizenship, the entire body of Reich and Prussian provincial law was to become valid by September 1, 1940. On February 4, 1941, the people were granted representation in the Greater German Reichstag through deputies appointed by the Führer "in order to give visible expression to the reunion of the territories . . . with the Greater German Reich."[4]

While the status of Eupen, Malmédy, and Moresnet was fixed by Hitler almost immediately after the German conquest, the fate of the rest of Belgium—and of France—was left in doubt. For administrative purposes he joined the two northwestern departments of France (Nord and Pas de Calais) to Belgium, and placed the entire area under a military government.

There were obvious reasons for this procedure. Belgium and northwestern France were closely related economically, they were of supreme importance as a jumping-off place for an attack on Britain and as a defensive shield for the vital industrial districts of the Ruhr and the Rhineland. But the main reason they were placed under military administration may have been Hitler's own indecision about the future of both Belgium and France.[5]

Belgium did not fit conveniently into Nazi racial conceptions. In a total population of 8.4 million, about 45 per cent were French-speaking Walloons, who were generally considered to be sympathetic to France, and about 53 per cent were Flemish, who spoke a language closely related to German and were regarded by Nazi theorists as Germanic. Before the German invasion the more radical Nazi leaders were confident that the Flemish would acknowledge their Germanic heritage and support the German cause, as many of them had done during the German occupation of Belgium in the First World War. Hitler was not so sure. In a directive to the army of November 4, 1939, he expressed doubts about the attitude of the Flemish. He had no desire to alienate the Walloons by premature commitments and ordered that for the time being no distinction should be made between the two peoples. Above all, everything should be done to avoid the impression that Germany intended to impinge on Belgium's independence. Further directives would be issued based on the situation as it developed.[6]

As we have seen, at the time of the German invasion of the Low Countries in May 1940, Hitler addressed an appeal to the governments of the Netherlands, Belgium, and Luxembourg to prevent all resistance to the German forces, promising at the same time to respect the sovereignty of these countries as well as all their territorial possessions in Europe and overseas.[7] All three countries did resist, Belgium holding out the longest; but at midnight on May 27 the Belgian army capitulated. Instead of going into exile, like Queen Wilhelmina of the Netherlands or Grand Duchess Charlotte of Luxembourg, King Leopold of Belgium decided to share the fate of his soldiers and go into military captivity, evidently believing that he could do more for his people by remaining in the country than by setting up a Belgian government in exile. His expectations on this score were vain, however, for Hitler conceded him no influence whatever in the Belgian administration operating under German auspices and no opportunity to affect the policies of the German occupation government.

In conferences with Hitler soon after the occupation of Belgium, Himmler urged the establishment of a German civil government similar to the one in the Netherlands; but Hitler rejected the proposal. He wanted to reserve his decision on the ultimate status of Belgium, and he evidently decided that a military government was the least compromising that could be established.[8] On May 31, 1940, General of the Infantry Baron Alexander von Falkenhausen was officially appointed military commander (*Militärbefehlshaber*) for Belgium and Northern France.[9]

Falkenhausen had a more cosmopolitan background than many of his military colleagues. A member of the German expeditionary force in China at the time of the Boxer Rebellion, he was subsequently appointed military attaché in Tokyo. During the First World War he became chief of staff of the Turkish army, and at the end of the war he remained in Turkey as chargé d'affaires in Constantinople. After serving on various military missions to Poland, he returned to China in 1930 as military adviser to the national government of Chiang Kai-shek. Recalled in 1938 when the Nazi government began cultivating better relations with Japan, he was living in retirement when he was appointed supreme military administrator in the Low Countries in May 1940. Like many Prussian officers he had far-ranging intellectual interests, he was a student of philosophy, a devotee of the novels of Stendahl, and an admirer of the teachings of Lao-tzu. There can be no doubt of his loathing for the Nazi regime, and his appointment appears to have been due in large measure to the fact that he was the nephew of Germany's military commander in Belgium in the later stages of the First World War. During his own four years as military governor, he did what he could to prevent the introduction of the worst aspects of Nazi rule in Belgium. In 1944 he was implicated in the July 20 plot to assassinate Hitler and was thrown into a concentration camp.[10]

According to Ulrich von Hassell, who was to play a leading role in the anti-Nazi resistance, Falkenhausen was a physical phenomenon, able to drink enormous quantities in the evening and to appear at his office shortly after eight the following morning apparently none the worse for wear. Hassell thought his years abroad had knocked out any parade-ground mentality he might have acquired in the army and given him a broad view of military and political problems. "He is intelligent, clear-headed, sober (that is in judgment)," Hassell said, and in the course of the war he came to depend on Falkenhausen as a key figure in the military conspiracy against Hitler. At one time Falkenhausen was even considered as the head of a future anti-Nazi government.[11]

Appalled by Nazi occupation policies in Poland, Falkenhausen was determined to pursue a different political course in the territory under his jurisdiction; he recognized that the essential precondition for doing so was to establish strong and exclusive control over his own administration. The powers he was given as military governor seemed to give him all the authority he required. Unlike the civil governor of the Netherlands, the military governor of Belgium was not directly responsible to Hitler, but to the commander in chief of the army. He was given full executive power and, in a statement issued immediately after his appointment, Falkenhausen made it clear that he intended to exercise it. There was to be no delegation of authority to other Reich offices and no division of responsibilities and tasks, as in other occupied areas. The military governor was to be the supreme and the sole representative of the Reich within his administrative sphere. Other offices and organizations were to function only with his permission, and in case that permission were granted they would have to adapt themselves to the policies of the military government.[12]

Falkenhausen's assertion of his prerogatives as military governor was a brave attempt to stave off the encroachments of Nazi functionaries and their various departments; but he could not escape the fact that he was operating under a Nazi regime and that, in Belgium as in Germany, the ultimate authority was Hitler. Moreover, Hitler made it clear that he regarded the military administration as at best a caretaker government, which would be replaced as soon as he thought the time had come to establish different or more permanent institutions. Falkenhausen and his staff were instructed to make no long-range political decisions or plans. Their primary task was to safeguard the security of the country and to mobilize its resources for the German war economy. No special privileges were to be given to the Walloons, although they were to be treated sufficiently well to preserve their economic usefulness and wean them away from French influences. The Flemings were to be favored as much as military necessity would allow, but never in a manner that might prejudice a future solution of the Belgian problem. The Führer, and the Führer alone, would determine the future status of the country.[13]

Hitler's attitude toward the military administration in Belgium did not make Falkenhausen's position easier, nor did that of other Nazi leaders, who agitated persistently for the replacement of the military administration with a civilian government run by dependable party men. Falkenhausen's efforts to safeguard his authority only increased the antagonism of party officials, who found him an awkward obstacle to the extension of their own influence. Falkenhausen was accused of failing to rule with a sufficiently strong hand, of extracting too little from the Belgian economy for the German war effort, of allowing the Belgian people too much freedom and independence. But above all he was attacked as being ideologically untrustworthy, as a man who could not be counted on to impose Nazi principles in Belgium with vigor or conviction.[14]

The speed with which the military government re-established order and reactivated the economy in Belgium temporarily silenced Falkenhausen's critics, but he remained on the defensive. Four months after taking office he felt called upon to write a seventy-nine-page report explaining the reasons for his political moderation. The Belgians should become accustomed gradually to the idea of a Germanic community and the need to fit into a German-ordered world, he said. After victory Belgium would certainly become a German border district (*Vorland*) in one form or another, but if this was to be done to the maximum benefit of the people involved, an atmosphere of confidence had to be created. Instead of striving for dramatic and largely illusory effects, the military government was working steadily to establish this atmosphere of confidence.[15] Falkenhausen expressed dismay that despite the success of the methods he had employed so far, "there was as yet no general understanding [in the Reich] that a people making a maximum contribution to the German war economy and whose inclusion in the greater German sphere of influence had to be prepared both materially and psychologically could not be ruled with a truncheon." Nor could the country be ruthlessly exploited, as many German officials were advocating. Germany was fighting for the creation of a new European order, and for this purpose it was necessary to win over the Walloons as well as the racially related Flemings. It would be impossible to create an understanding for German aims and conceptions if Belgium were simply subjected to economic spoliation and ruin.[16]

Although his pleas for political moderation found little sympathy or understanding among Nazi extremists and opportunists, Falkenhausen was relatively successful in pursuing the kind of policy he recommended. This success was due in large measure to the fact that he was presiding over a military government, which was more amenable to his direction than a civil administration dominated by party members might have been, and that the principal Nazis assigned to his staff were as anxious as Falkenhausen himself to prevent the enroachments of political rivals.

The German military government in Belgium was divided into two main sections: a military staff (*Militär-oder Kommandostab*), which was primarily concerned with problems of military security; and an administrative staff (*Militärverwaltungsstab*), which was in charge of the actual government of the country.[17] The head of the latter section was SS Obergruppenführer Eggert Reeder, an early member of the Nazi party, who was evidently expected to wield the real power in the military government in the party's interests.

The son of a Schleswig-Holstein landowner, Reeder fought four years in the First World War and later as a member of a free corps. After the war he studied jurisprudence at the universities of Halle and Kiel, and in 1924 he entered the German civil service. His career flourished after the Nazis came to power. On May 16, 1933, he was made head of the administration (Regierungspräsident) of the provincial district of Aachen; he subsequently held similar posts in the districts of Cologne and Düsseldorf.[18] Appointed chief of the administrative staff of Army Group B in 1940, he was instructed to work out guidelines for a German military administration in Belgium in case the occupation of that country should become necessary. After studying the history of the German administration of Belgium during the First World War, Reeder came to the conclusion that Germany's major error at that time had been to assume too much direct control, that in the future every effort should be made to govern the country through Belgian administrative personnel. At the same time the Belgian government should be thoroughly transformed by centralizing the administration along German lines, a change that would have the added advantage of facilitating the eventual incorporation of Belgium into the administration of the Reich. Representatives of the army studied and approved Reeder's guidelines, and with the actual German occupation of Belgium in May 1940 he was appointed chief of the military administrative staff.[19]

Reeder proved to be an able administrator, and for over two years he firmly backed Falkenhausen's policy of defending the military government against the encroachments of Reich and party functionaries. He insisted that the representatives of the various Reich departments concerned with Belgian affairs should operate through the military occupation government, and that their representatives in Belgium should be subject to the orders of the leaders of that government. Otherwise Germany would be doomed to repeat the mistakes of the First World War, when competition for authority among the various German offices had resulted in the establishment of several separate and conflicting German governments in Belgium.

A strong central authority was all the more necessary, Reeder argued, because Belgium was the most difficult country in Europe to govern. There was no centralizing administrative apparatus, the country was divided on religious, cultural, linguistic, and racial lines. In the course of centuries of domination by foreign powers, the Belgian people had become highly skilled in evading authority of any sort, whether it was Spanish, French, Austrian, or Dutch. This tradition of insubordination had been reinforced by the slogans of the French Revolution and by intimate contact with irresponsible liberal capitalism. Whereas the German took a certain pride in his discipline, the Belgian took a positive pride in his lack of it. His one object in studying the law at all was to discover its loopholes or means of turning it to his own advantage.

Reeder expressed lofty views about the purpose of the military government in Belgium. The opinion sometimes heard that it had no national-political tasks to fulfill was false, he said. The safeguarding of the fundamental interests of the Reich was in itself a political task of the first importance. This was especially true of the present conflict, which grappled at the roots of every aspect of life and society. It was the supreme duty of the military government to prepare the Belgian people for a position in the new European order, and to bring all aspects of the political, economic, and cultural life of the country and its inhabitants into harmony with National Socialist conceptions.[20] But beyond these high-sounding—and thoroughly routine—pronouncements Reeder did not go. He had no intention of incurring the wrath of Hitler by making definite statements regarding Belgium's future, but neither did he intend to open the door to political rivals.

As already seen, Himmler had begun agitating against the German military government in Belgium even before it was officially established. On May 22, 1940, he had urged Hitler to install a German civil government in Belgium under a Reichskommissar, and he had suggested reliable SS men such as Hanns Rauter or Erich von dem Bach-Zelewski for the position.[21] But Hitler refused to commit himself. While acknowledging the desirability of a civil government in Flanders, he thought it necessary to retain a military government in Wallonia, and he feared the effects on the Belgian population if the two provinces were separated without an extended period of propagandistic preparation. Despite considerable pressure from Himmler and other members of his entourage, he decided on July 20, 1940, that "Belgium is to be administered by a military governor until further notice."[22]

In the summer of 1941, when the Russian campaign had temporarily put an end to preparations for a landing in England, Hitler informed Hans Lammers that he had now decided to install a civil government in Belgium and in October he instructed him to draw up the necessary decrees. He was considering appointing Gauleiter Josef Grohé (Aachen) head of the new government, with the title either of Reichskommissar or chief of the civil administration. But Hitler was still uncertain about the expediency of dividing Belgium; and if it were to be done, whether a civil administration for Belgium should be established in Wallonia only and whether Flanders should be transferred to the jurisdiction of the Reichskommissariat for the Occupied Netherlands.[23]

The Wehrmacht, the Ministry of the Interior, and the Office of the Four-Year Plan all objected strongly to the proposed reorganization of the German administration in Belgium. General Wilhelm Keitel pointed out that army, navy, and air bases in Belgium were needed for the defense of the continent, for a future attack on England, and for submarine and aerial warfare. On the political level, Keitel wondered what was to become of the two French departments now under the German military government of Belgium. If they were attached to present Belgian territory in any reorganization of the Belgian government, the French would consider this a further step in their permanent separation from the mother country. On the other hand, if they were placed under the German military government in France, the great political effect on France that such a move might have if it were made at the right moment would be completely lost, whereas the Flemings would regard such a transfer of authority as a permanent renunciation of territory they regarded as "French Flanders." An administrative reorganization of Belgium was also undesirable for economic reasons. Belgium and the two departments of northern France now formed a single economic unit, whose productivity would be seriously jeopardized by a division of the country.[24]

Wilhelm Stuckart of the Reich Ministry of the Interior opposed a change in the status of Belgium on similar grounds. Belgium and the two French departments were producing almost 45 per cent as much coal as the Ruhr and supplying 16 per cent of the Reich's iron and steel requirements. Thirty thousand men were working in Belgian war industries, two-thirds of them Walloons. Of all occupied countries, Belgium was the one most fully harnessed to the German war economy, a situation that should not be disturbed. A change of administration and a division of the country would also have serious administrative drawbacks. The Belgian administration was undeniably incompetent, but the German military government had just succeeded in bringing it up to a level of moderate effectiveness. Another administrative change would result in renewed disorder, and Germany did not have the personnel available to replace the Belgian civil servants. Most dangerous of all in Stuckart's opinion would be the administrative union of Flanders and the Netherlands, which would simply encourage the advocates of a Greater Netherlands.[25]

Hermann Göring raised much the same objections on behalf of the Four-Year Plan. In contrast to the First World War, he said, Belgium was producing to the utmost of its capacity under the military administration; it constituted one of the most important economic areas under German control. As Germany needed all the production it could get, any change likely to curtail Belgian production would be a major error.[26]

Hitler was not to be put off by such rational arguments. He refused to read Keitel's objections to his proposed administrative changes in Belgium, and there is no indication that the opinions of Stuckart and Göring were even submitted to him. He seems to have held back chiefly because he could think of no suitable candidate for the position of civil governor of Belgium. There could be no question of sending a brutal North German martinet there, he told his associates in February 1942. He needed someone clever, supple, amiable, but at the same time thick-skinned and tough. Seyss-Inquart was such a man, tempting Hitler to turn once again to his Austrian compatriots: perhaps to Hugo Jury, the Gauleiter of the Lower Danube, or to Siegfried Uiberreither in Styria—but the latter was still too young.[27]

By May of 1942 Hitler's attitude toward Wallonia and Northern France had taken a more precise form, for he was now convinced that these lands were as fundamentally German as Flanders. The abundance of Germanic place names and the prevalence of Germanic customs, "all these prove, to my mind, that these territories have been systematically detached, not to say snatched, from the Germanic territories. If there are territories anywhere which we have every right to reclaim, then it is these." Hitler spoke in much the same vein to Goebbels: It was now self-evident (*eine Selbstverständlichkeit*) that Belgium should one day be annexed to the Reich and reconstituted as the Reichsgaus of Flanders and Brabant.[28]

Still Hitler did nothing to change the status of Belgium. Lammers noted on May 13 that he did not yet wish to concern himself with the question of establishing a civil government; he nevertheless continued to talk about the problem. In June he observed that Mussolini, in discussing the future of Europe, had placed the Flemings in one category and the Walloons and French in another. Hitler no longer regarded such a solution as practicable within the framework of a Greater Germanic state. "I am pleased, therefore, that there exists neither in Holland nor in Belgium any government with which we should have to negotiate. This will enable us to impose whatever we feel is politically expedient and obviously useful. I propose solving the problem of these small states by means of brief and decisive declarations." [29] Hitler did not elaborate on these ideas, but by October 1942 he had decided one thing: There was to be no administrative union of Flanders and the Netherlands. The

fears expressed about the dangers of encouraging the Greater Netherlands idea had evidently convinced him that this solution to the government of the Germanic peoples in the Low Countries was undesirable.[30]

Rumors of an impending change in the government of Belgium had
meanwhile alarmed Eggert Reeder. Heretofore a staunch supporter of
the military administration, he now joined the advocates of change, perhaps as a means of saving his own position. In September 1942 he informed Stuckart that he was thinking in terms of a civil Reichskommissar for Belgium who would be directly responsible to the Führer, but
who would at the same time be chief of a military administration for the
two French provinces and as such under the German military government in France. By this time Stuckart was inclined to agree with Reeder
about the desirability of administrative change in Belgium. He told
Lammers that the military government was not keeping in sufficiently
close touch with the leadership of the Reich and appeared to have out-
lived its usefulness; a strong personality immediately responsible to the
Führer was needed to restore the proper measure of Reich control. He
would be willing to bring the problem to the attention of the Führer
and was thinking of recommending Gauleiter Grohé or Reichskommissar
Josef Terboven (Norway) for the position—proposals that probably
would have shocked Reeder, who obviously had himself in mind for the
job.[31]

All this time Himmler had not ceased his own agitation against the
military government in Belgium, and in the autumn of 1942 he began to
sense victory. His agent Gottlob Berger suggested on October 21 that
the delicate problem of the nomenclature of the head of a new civil government in Belgium could be resolved most easily by calling him simply
the plenipotentiary of the Führer. "The title is harmlessly neutral. Under
this title *anything* can be covered up." Berger considered Terboven the
most suitable candidate for the position, especially since the latter had
long desired to exchange Norway for a post in the west.

> He has come over to us, [Berger said, meaning that he had joined the
> Himmler faction,] and would be eternally grateful to the Reichsführer
> SS. His assignment in Flanders would be quite simply to begin, cau-
> tiously but clearly [*in klarer Form*] to put the Reichsgau Flanders on its
> feet, and to lay the foundations of the Reichsgau Wallonia. With that
> there would be an end to the activity of all those who, because of per-
> sonal interests or hostility to the work of the Reichsführer SS, have put
> obstacles in our path heretofore.[32]

But Himmler was doomed to disappointment. Lammers informed him
on October 25 that the Führer was not inclined to release Terboven
from Norway. Himmler thereupon proposed the appointment of his senior SS and police officer and chief of police in Vienna, Ernst Kaltenbrunner. Hitler, however, refused to be pushed. On October 28 Lammers let it be known that the Führer did not consider the present

moment opportune for a change of government in Belgium; with that the matter rested. Not until July 13, 1944, did Hitler at last take the step so persistently advocated by Himmler and establish a German civil administration.[33]

In their government of Belgium the Germans were as successful as in other occupied countries in securing the co-operation of the local professional bureaucracy for the administration of the country. The Belgian ministers had fled, the king was a prisoner of war, but a large majority of the civil servants in Belgium and Northern France remained at their posts and conducted the routine affairs of government in the German interest throughout the war.[34]

Following the precepts of his own guidelines,[35] Reeder made skillful use of this Belgian manpower and bureaucratic machinery. Instead of imposing a German bureaucracy on the country, he set up a German supervisory administration. In this way, with a minimum investment of German manpower, he was able to govern the country, carry out the orders of the multitude of Reich agencies, and keep the representatives of those agencies at bay with a considerable degree of success. At the time of the German attack on Russia the German administrative staff in Belgium consisted of no more than 204 officials of all ranks. The figure rose in later years, but the staff remained a small one, especially when compared with the staff of 10,000 German officials sent into Belgium during the First World War.[36]

In governing the country through the Belgian civil service, the Germans were aided by an emergency decree passed by the Belgian legislature on May 10, 1940, which delegated executive power to the highest ranking civil servants in case the responsible ministers were compelled to abandon their posts. Thus when the ministers fled following the German invasion, the executive power passed legally to the secretaries-general, the permanent civil service heads of their respective departments, who operated on the assumption that executive power included legislative power and hence the right to issue government decrees. This interpretation of the law of May 10 was very convenient to the Germans, who had only to direct their orders through Belgian officials to introduce their own measures legally. Only when immediate German interests were involved did the military government issue decrees in its own name. Immediate German interests proved to be very numerous, however, and over the years a substantial body of legislation was published over the signature of the leaders of the military government.[37]

The situation was somewhat different in the former French departments, where no local officials assumed the right to exercise either executive or legislative authority. In these areas the military governor delegated his legislative powers to his deputy in Lille, who published decrees specifically affecting the French provinces in a separate law book. Yet here too the actual administration of the area was carried on by the local officialdom.[38]

Having secured the co-operation of the Belgian civil service, the Germans undertook to make that service, and especially its leadership, as reliable as possible. The military government conducted a thorough investigation of all members of the Belgian bureaucracy, undesirable elements were removed from their positions, and all new appointees were carefully screened. On the assumption that officials who had left the country at the time of the German invasion were likely to be unreliable, a decree was issued on July 18, 1940, prohibiting their re-employment in the government service, although exceptions could be made at the discretion of the military government. A decree of October 28, 1940, required the removal of all Jews from the civil service by the end of the year. And by a decree of March 7, 1941, all officials over the age of sixty were compelled to retire, a measure designed to eliminate the large number of older and generally higher-ranking civil servants who were suspected of passive resistance. Again provision was made for exceptions. As a result of this decree some twenty-eight hundred civil servants, including four secretaries-general, were dismissed, and the decks were cleared for a sweeping introduction of German appointees in key positions.[39]

Routine internal security was maintained by the Belgian police, who received their orders from the military government through the Belgian secretary-general of the interior. External security was in the hands of the Wehrmacht; but an important order of May 22, 1940, gave the Wehrmacht the right to exercise police powers as well. By using the regular army for special police duties, the military administration was able to escape dependence on Himmler's police officials, who played a minor role in Belgium during the first years of the German occupation.[40] For Falkenhausen, the most unfortunate aspect of this situation was that the military government itself was charged with such tasks as the roundup of laborers for the Reich, economic confiscations, the arrest and execution of hostages, and the removal of the Jews. Its failure to carry out some of these assignments to the satisfaction of Nazi authorities eventually opened the way to the increased influence of the Himmler forces. As late as August 1943, however, Falkenhausen rejected the claim of SS General Bach-Zelewski to direct operation against guerrillas in Belgium as he was doing in other parts of the Nazi empire. "The maintenance of order and security remains my task, as it has always been," Falkenhausen said.[41]

The German military government also retained a surprising degree of control over the administration of the Belgian economy. This was possible because German economic interests in Belgium were represented in large measure by the economic department of the military government and by the economic offices of the army, which worked together in close co-operation.[42]

The first German economic legislation in Belgium, as in other occupied territories, was concerned with the reactivation of the economy, and required that all persons remain at their jobs and that all economic enterprises continue in operation. There followed the familiar pattern of direct and indirect exploitation: the outright confiscation of military equipment and scarce raw materials, currency manipulation, taxation to finance German occupation costs, wage and price controls.[43] Once order had been re-established, however, the Germans did their best to give their economic policies an appearance of legality and to make them acceptable to the Belgian population. Their primary concern was to keep the Belgian economy operating as productively as possible, and for this purpose they realized that the co-operation of the Belgian population was essential.

The goal of German economic policy was defined by the chief of the economic section of the military government as the integration of the economy of Belgium and Northern France into the German war effort and the preparation of these areas for their incorporation into the Greater German economic sphere. In the initial stages of the occupation, German economic experts hoped that this "secret goal" could be achieved simply by making co-operation with the Germans profitable and leaving Belgian entrepreneurs a good deal of freedom and initiative. The main problems were to shift the orientation of the Belgian economy from overseas to the continent, and to bring production methods in line with those of the Reich. This private enterprise phase of German economic penetration was reflected in policy guidelines laid down by Göring. German influence in Belgium was to be strengthened by purchasing a controlling interest in the more important enterprises of the motherland and the colonies, and by fostering the closest possible reciprocal involvement between the German and Belgian economies.[44]

In August 1940 Göring ordered the establishment of Central Order Offices (Zast) in Belguim to co-ordinate and establish priorities for the purchases and requisitions of the many German agencies competing for Belgian products.[45] The Zast system produced the same inefficiencies and illegalities in Belgium as it did in the other occupied countries of Western Europe.[46] Private German firms did their best to avoid placing orders through Zast by making direct arrangements with Belgian companies. The same tactics were used on a much larger scale by the Wehrmacht, especially the Luftwaffe, the Organisation Todt, and the Reichsbahn, which openly ignored regulations in order to bypass the cumbersome and slow procedures of the Zast system.

By the end of 1940 Göring, and indeed almost all German government and private organizations involved in the Belgian economy, had come to realize that if an intermediary organization was wanted in Belgium at all, their most effective instrument was the economic office of the military government with its network of economic officials. Thus it was that until July 1944 German economic policy, including the labor recruitment drives of Fritz Sauckel and the economic mobilization program of

Albert Speer, were entrusted to the Falkenhausen regime. The price of administrative independence was high.[47]

Despite the official assistance given to German entrepreneurs, German economists were forced to confess by May of 1941 that their economic penetration in Belgium was not nearly so successful as in the Netherlands. They ascribed this to the fact that the most important Belgian industries were controlled by two Belgian banks, the Société Générale and the Banque de Bruxelles. The former alone controlled over eight hundred enterprises which, with their affiliated firms, dominated almost 40 per cent of the Belgian economy. As German attempts to buy into the Belgian economy were left largely to private enterprise, German businessmen were finding it difficult to make headway against the giant Belgian corporations, which were in no way anxious to sell out to the Germans, especially at German-controlled rates of exchange.[48] The Germans might have taken a harder line in Belgium and either compelled the Belgians to sell the controlling interest in their corporations or confiscated their property outright, but they remained aware of their dependence on the Belgian population to keep the economy going, and therefore continued to preserve a façade of legality in their economic measures.

Although private German business interests found it difficult to gain a controlling interest in the major Belgian corporations, the German military government succeeded in establishing a considerable degree of control over the Belgian economy in general. This was done in much the same way as it had established control over the Belgian administration: The Belgians themselves were allowed to run their economy, but all aspects of economic life were centralized and brought under German supervision. In conducting this policy, the German military government took advantage of the fact that Belgian industry was controlled by a few major corporations. It was, therefore, only necessary to appoint German supervisors to the offices of these corporations in order to gain a "unified influence" over Belgian industry as a whole.[49]

As early as May 20, 1940, the Germans had attempted to regulate the production and distribution of industrial products and raw materials in short supply. On September 2 the various measures taken for this purpose were supplemented by the establishment of a Central Commodities Office (*Les Offices centraux de marchandises*), which regulated and controlled the entire field of industrial production. A decree of April 29, 1941, provided for the appointment of "management commissioners" for any industry where supervision or control was considered necessary. Their task was to regulate production and distribution, and to do everything possible to increase production.[50]

A supervisory board for banking was created on June 14, 1940, with the right to inspect all books, demand information, and pass on all important business transactions. The German director of this board was also made banking commissioner for Belgium and head of a new Bank of Issue (established June 27, 1940) to issue Belgian currency. This combination of positions enabled him to gain a large measure of control over the Belgian financial system.[51]

In August 1940 the Belgian department of agriculture was persuaded to set up a special National Corporation of Food and Agriculture (*Corporation nationale de l'agriculture et d'alimentation*) to control the production and distribution of food, the most critical item in the Belgian economy. The new organization was charged with the enrollment of all enterprises engaged in the production, processing, and sale of agricultural products; it was empowered to impose quota systems on producers, to create new agricultural organizations, and to suspend economically superfluous enterprises. Subsequent ordinances brought the entire Belgian agricultural system into a tight organizational network. These controls were supplemented early in 1941 by a corps of "economic advisers" who were to make certain that Belgium's economic resources were being exploited effectively.[52]

Labor came under control with the establishment in June 1940 of a government labor department (the *Office national du placement et du control*, later called the *Office national du travail*). This office compiled a card index of all registered workers to enable the government to make certain that skilled workers were being employed to the best possible advantage for the war effort, and, if this was not the case, to assign them to other jobs. The Union of Manual and Intellectual Workers (*Union des travailleurs manuels et intellectuels*) was established in November 1940 to embrace every variety of worker: miner and stevedore, teacher and civil servant. This new egalitarian superunion was allegedly founded to put an end to class conflict, to ensure a just social policy for all; but in fact it was just another instrument of control. Within a year, all other Belgian labor unions were either incorporated into this organization or dissolved.[53]

The most comprehensive measure in the process of economic centralization was a decree of February 10, 1941, which authorized the head of the Belgian government's department of economic affairs "to give any and all orders for the regulation of economic matters and to take all steps necessary to enforce such orders." Specifically the department was empowered to create new economic organizations on an occupational or regional basis which should be the sole representatives of their spheres of economic activity and have the status of agencies of public law. Further, the department was to establish the objectives, powers, rights, privileges, and obligations of these organizations and their members, and to appoint—and dismiss—their leaders.[54]

The Germans took some pride in their success in securing the economic co-operation of the Belgian population, especially Belgian labor. During the First World War the head of the German occupation government, General Moritz von Bissing, had operated on the theory that it was not possible to force men to work, especially not skilled laborers. Of the one hundred ten thousand Belgian laborers sent to work in Germany during the First World War, the majority had to be sent home because they had caused more trouble than they were worth.

This situation was completely changed in the Second World War because of the application of "modern" methods of persuasion. In case of refusal to work a man's means of support were cut off, he received no wages, and, even more important, no ration cards for himself and his family. There were also "correctional institutions" for agitators or recalcitrants. Thus, although hours were longer and wages comparatively lower than before the war, the majority of Belgian workers stayed on the job. Again in contrast to the First World War, greater care was taken to channel labor into essential industries and to put the right man in the right job. All in all, the Belgian workers' rate of production ranked among the highest in Europe, despite the fact that Belgium had the lowest food ration of the occupied countries of Western Europe.[55]

The period of voluntary labor in Belgium ended in March 1942, when labor was made compulsory for all people not hitherto employed in essential work. In October all men between eighteen and fifty, and unmarried women between twenty-one and thirty-five, were made subject to compulsory work in Belgium or Germany "according to their capabilities and physical fitness."[56] Sauckel, in charge of labor recruitment for the Reich since March 1942, was not satisfied with these measures. In August 1943 he arranged for the recruiting of one hundred fifty thousand Belgians for work in the Reich, and the transfer of another one hundred thousand from nonessential work to war industries in Belgium itself. Early in 1944 he secured approval for the recruiting of another two hundred fifty thousand Belgian workers. But until July 1944 Sauckel depended on the co-operation of the German military government for the success of his activities, and that government withheld its support whenever it felt that security of Belgian economic productivity would be threatened by Sauckel's policies. As a result Sauckel's recruiting drive fell far short of its goal. Altogether, according to Belgian statistics, a total of two hundred seventy-five thousand Belgians volunteered or were drafted for work in Germany during the entire course of the war.[57]

The "secret goal" of preparing Belgium and Northern France for integration into Germany's economic New Order was carried on in every sphere of activity. None of these, according to Falkenhausen's report to Berlin of July 31, 1940, was of greater significance than the field of education.

In Belgium the German program of re-education was designed to serve a double purpose: to replace factional strife and false political ideologies with a responsible sense of national-political unity and order; and to create an appreciation of German cultural and intellectual values to take the place of Western, and especially French, influences. These goals were to be achieved by ridding schools and libraries of anti-German propaganda, by introducing new textbooks, by taking politics and

"Jews not wanted in this town." A typical sign in German streets and shops during the Nazi era.

Jews being slaughtered in Lithuania by local inhabitants and "auxiliary police," while German SS and police forces stand by.

Josef Bürckel, Gauleiter and Reichsstatthalter of the Saar-Palatinate, chief of the civil administration for Lorraine, and co-ordinator of the annexation of the Saar and Austria to the Reich, delivering a speech on the occasion of the reunion of the Saar with the Reich.

Constantin von Neurath and the Czech president Emil Hácha in the Hrad-schin palace in Prague on the occasion of Neurath's installation as Reich pro-tector of Bohemia and Moravia.

Vojtěch Tuka (left) and Jozef Tiso (right), leaders of the puppet government of Slovakia, talking with Field Marshal Wilhelm Keitel.

Reinhard Heydrich, acting Reich protector of Bohemia and Moravia, speaking to Czech journalists in his office in the Hradschin palace in Prague. At his side, Karl Hermann Frank.

Dr. Hans Frank, governor general of occupied Poland. At his right, Heinrich
Himmler.

Reich Plenipotentiary Dr. Werner Best (right) with the Danish minister Erik Scavenius.

General Erich Lüdke (left) greeting the chief of the German navy in Denmark. In the center, Reich Plenipotentiary Cecil von Renthe-Fink.

Hitler and Göring (far right) as witnesses at the wedding of Josef Terboven, Reichskommissar of occupied Norway.

Vidkun Quisling, during an interview.

From left to right, Arthur Seyss-Inquart, Reichskommissar of the occupied Netherlands; Hanns Albin Rauter, senior SS and police officer; and Karl Demelhuber, commander of the Waffen-SS in the Netherlands.

religion out of the school curriculum. There was to be a thorough reform of the "completely disorganized liberal educational system" and a reorganization of research principles and aims. A major campaign was to be launched to regain the Flemish for the Germanic world. Flemish universities were to be transformed into "a Germanic bastion against Western Europe in which the Flemish, who had been made aware of their Germanic tasks, should co-operate with available German forces in common labor toward common goals." [58]

Whether these views actually represented the opinions of Falkenhausen or of members of his staff is impossible to determine. The important thing is that the policies based on them were in fact pursued by the German occupation authorities. Textbooks and curricula were changed, and in time school and university faculties were purged of teachers who refused to co-operate with the new educational line.

Although the reports of both Falkenhausen and Reeder were frequently permeated with National Socialist sentiment—it is never certain who wrote these reports or how much party jargon was purposely introduced to satisfy official scrutiny in Berlin—they were unusually reticent about the problem which for most dedicated Nazis was the most important of all: the campaign against the Jews.

On the eve of the German invasion there were approximately ninety thousand Jews in Belgium, almost half of them refugees from Germany or Eastern Europe. When the Germans invaded Belgium a large number of Jews fled. How many remained in the country cannot be determined with any accuracy. The German estimate was fifty-two thousand, but there may have been many more.[59]

The first major anti-Jewish laws in Belgium were published on October 28, 1940. They required the registration of all Jews over fifteen and of all Jewish economic enterprises. Jews who had fled were forbidden to return. All Jews in official positions, including schools and universities, were to be dismissed by December 31. By the end of the year forty-two thousand Jews had registered. As only four thousand of this number were of Belgian nationality, it is obvious that the majority of Belgian Jews had refused to register.[60]

The military government did not press the search for unregistered Jews. Toward the end of 1941 a Belgian *Judenrat* was formed, the *Association des Juifs en Belgique,* which had local committees in the larger Belgian cities and to which all Jews were subject. In May 1942 large numbers of Jews were rounded up for labor in the Organisation Todt. But it was not until August of that year, when the agents of Adolf Eichmann arrived in Belgium, that the mass deportation of Jews to Eastern Europe began. The original quota for Belgium was ten thousand persons.[61]

The German military administration was far from co-operative. Reeder pointed out to Himmler that there was a lack of understanding for the Jewish question among the Belgian people, and he drew attention to the shortage of German police for an operation of this kind. It was finally arranged that only Polish, Czech, Russian, and other Eastern European Jews should be deported. With some annoyance Martin Luther, the head of the Jewish section of the German Foreign Office, complained to Eichmann that the Jewish program in Belgium was being blocked by the military government, which had doubts about deporting the Belgian Jews. These were doubts, Luther said, which the Foreign Office did not share.[62] The transport of Jews from Belgium to Eastern Europe began in August 1942, and by the end of November about fifteen thousand had been removed. With the exception of a few Belgian Jews who refused to wear the Jewish star, the deportees were all non-Belgians.[63]

Luther now urged that Belgian Jews be included in the evacuation process because "Belgium must be thoroughly cleansed of Jews sooner or later in any case." There was no reason whatever to postpone an action in Belgium that had already been carried out in the Netherlands. Luther's proposal had the full approval of the SS deportation experts, who complained that delay had already caused serious difficulties. The Jews had been alerted to their danger. Many had found refuge in non-Jewish homes or had equipped themselves with false identification papers and passports. It would now be more difficult than ever to locate the Jews in Belgium, and large numbers were succeeding in escaping to Switzerland.[64]

The military government was finally forced to agree to the evacuation of Belgian Jews, but it never supported the action with vigor. Only one large-scale roundup of Jews was carried out, and that came as the result of heavy pressure from Reich authorities. When the Allies freed Belgium in September 1944, about twenty-five thousand Jews had been deported. More than half, including a large majority of the Belgian Jews, had evidently succeeded in evading the Nazi net. But the success of many Jews in escaping deportation is of no consequence in a consideration of Nazi war aims. Had the Germans won the war, all Jews and part-Jews would have been captured and deported to the work gangs and gas chambers of Eastern Europe "sooner or later." [65]

The removal of large numbers of undependable or un-co-operative persons, and of all Jews, from government offices, economic enterprises, and the educational system, forced the Germans to find people to take their place. For this purpose they turned to authoritarian political groups in Belgium; but, above all, they looked to the Flemish nationalist movement.

Following the instructions of Hitler, the leaders of the military government did their best to support and exploit Flemish nationalism. They made holidays of the anniversaries of great Flemish figures, they held festivals to celebrate Flemish achievements. Flemish was made the only language in the schools of Flanders. By a German decree Brussels was designated a Flemish city, as were the border towns of Renaix, Menin, and Enghien, where everything French was gradually to be eliminated. After October 1940 Flemish prisoners of war, but not the Walloons, were released. "Our efforts have all along been directed primarily toward finding and furthering forces of value to Germany," Falkenhausen said, "and to give them a chance to prove themselves in the tasks of public life that now confront us." The immediate goal was to discover and make use of those persons "who can be guaranteed to stand by Germany unconditionally in a future political New Order." [66]

The Germans were to find that Flemish nationalism was more easy to support than to exploit. The movement was badly divided by party and factional strife, and the political aims of its leaders often differed substantially from those of the Germans. A few Flemish nationalists advocated the outright incorporation of Flanders into the Reich, but most of them wanted independence for Flanders; their programs ranged from vague proposals for cultural autonomy to demands for complete political autonomy and a revival of the old empire of Burgundy under Flemish leadership.[67]

The most important of the Flemish nationalist parties during the occupation was the Flemish National Union (*Vlaamsch National Verbond,* or VNV), which acknowledged the close racial kinship between the Flemish and the German peoples and favored closer political ties with Germany. The Germans hoped to transform the VNV into a sound National Socialist political organization, and the attitude of Staf de Clercq, the leader of the party, seemed to justify their expectations. In public and private statements he expressed his admiration for Germany and the National Socialist movement, and his belief that the Flemish people constituted an integral part of the greater Germanic community.

The views expressed by Staf de Clercq gave promise of an ideal ideological partnership between the VNV and the Nazis, but co-operation between them broke down the moment any attempt was made to define the future role of Flanders in the new Germanic order. De Clercq and most of his followers shared the territorial aspirations of Anton Mussert and his National Socialist party of the Netherlands. Their ideal was a Greater Netherlands, which was to include the Netherlands, Belgian Flanders, and French Flanders—plus the Belgian and Dutch colonies. The geographical triangle formed by these areas in Europe was the symbol on the party banner of the VNV. VNV leaders were to find that they could not abandon this territorial goal without the risk of losing a great part of their following.[68]

The most simple procedure for the Germans would have been to promise the VNV anything in order to secure its collaboration. But the VNV was not the only party in Flanders or in Belgium, and the Germans could not afford to alienate the entire Walloon population or the large number of Flemings still loyal to the Belgian state by making defi-

nite promises to a single Flemish minority party. Their success in retaining the co-operation of a majority of Belgians in key positions depended
on keeping a maximum number of conflicting hopes alive.

In Wallonia the only political group of any importance that favored
close collaboration with the Germans was the Rexist party, founded in
1935 by Léon Degrelle. Rexism appealed to patriotic, royalist, and religious sentiment, with the religious issue predominant, at least in the
early years of the movement. The name Rexist was not derived from the
royalist part of the party program, but from *Christus Rex.*

Degrelle had the support of members of the nobility, businessmen,
and army officers who feared social and economic upheaval and wished
an improvement in their own status while maintaining the *status quo* for
everyone else. Before the war Rexism resembled Italian Fascism much
more closely than German National Socialism. It was organized as an
all-Belgian party and tried to resolve the differences between Flemings
and Walloons on the common denominator of Belgian patriotism. The
party enjoyed a brief success shortly after its foundation by winning 21
of 202 seats in the Belgian Chamber of Deputies; after that its appeal
steadily declined. In April 1939 only four Rexist deputies were elected.[69]

When the Germans occupied Belgium, Degrelle put his services at the
disposal of the military government. The organization and ideology of
the Rexist party was remodeled along National Socialist lines, and its
leader publicly expressed his willingness to assist in building the new
European order under German leadership.[70] The co-operative attitude
of Degrelle did not win him favor among the Germans. Reeder had
nothing but contempt for him, and dismissed his public statements as a
"speculative expression of confidence in the builder of Europe from
whom he expects the preservation of the Belgian state." The Rexist party
itself was useless, Reeder said, because its members were so much disliked that their appointment to important administrative positions
would have caused more trouble than they were worth.[71]

Degrelle, however, proved to be a sincere and valuable collaborator.
After the invasion of Russia he helped organize a Walloon brigade,
which he himself joined as a private. Twice he volunteered for service
on the Eastern front, where he fought with bravery and distinction. But
it was not until 1943, after long disillusionment with the Flemish nationalists, that the Germans at last gave any real support and recognition to
Degrelle and his Walloon Nazis.[72]

For fanatic Nazis the sponsorship of Flemish and other Germanic
groups in Belgium was more than a matter of securing administrative
collaborators or popular support; for them the regaining of these peoples
for the Germanic community was the primary task of German policy in
Belgium. This was certainly the attitude of Heinrich Himmler, whose
devotion to the cause of Germanization was intertwined in Belgium, as

everywhere else, with a campaign to establish and extend his own authority.

Against the stubborn resistance of Falkenhausen, Himmler found it difficult to gain a foothold in Belgium. During the first year of the German occupation his powers were restricted almost exclusively to recruiting for the Waffen-SS, but this was all Himmler needed as an entering wedge. In September 1940 he secured Hitler's authorization to recruit a Flemish SS unit, and his trusted agent Gottlob Berger was sent to Belgium to take charge of the operation. Berger proposed to build the Flemish SS into an organization that would control all other collaborationist groups in Belgium. It was to be recruited from racially suitable Flemings, who were expected to dedicate themselves to the creation of a greater Germanic realm and to the union (Anschluss) of Flanders with the Reich, by force if necessary.[73]

Considering the nature of Berger's program, it is little wonder that he received scant support from Flemish nationalist groups in his recruitment drive. The immediate response of the VNV to Berger's efforts, for example, was public repudiation of the policy of union with Germany and a restatement of its determination to work for an independent Greater Netherlands. The leaders of the party nevertheless recognized that the only way they could retain some influence in determining the future fate of their country after a final German victory (and few in the summer of 1940 had any doubt about such a victory) would be to convince the Germans of their willingness to collaborate in the formation of a new European order. Accordingly, in the name of his party, Staf de Clercq addressed a memorandum to Hitler toward the end of the year professing belief in National Socialism and assuring the Führer of his unconditional loyalty and his desire to see Flanders bound closely to the Reich. De Clercq did not specify in what way Flanders was to be bound to Germany, but his later activities indicate that he intended that relationship to be as loose as possible, and that he proposed to strike the best bargain he could for his country. At the very least he desired cultural autonomy for Flanders, but he continued to work for a maximum amount of political autonomy and to keep alive the concept of a Greater Netherlands. De Clercq's bargaining position depended very much on the fluctuations of the military situation; thus over the next two years his demands rose and fell in relation to the fortunes of the German Wehrmacht.

Himmler and his lieutenants saw little reason for concern about the attitude of the VNV leaders. When Germany had won the war they would do what they liked with Flanders; they were convinced that with the proper combination of pressure and propaganda the Flemish people could be persuaded to accept their rightful place within the Greater German Reich. In February 1941, after consultation with Reeder, they agreed to recognize the VNV as the sole political representation of the

Flemish people and to incorporate in it all other nationalist and pro-German parties, including the Flemish branch of Degrelle's Rexist movement.

The Germans soon found that they had made a political error in granting the VNV a political monopoly status in Flanders. Once they had placed themselves in a position of dependence on the VNV, the leaders of the movement began to take a more independent line. There were frequent demands for a clear definition of the future status of their country, and the program of an independent Greater Netherlands was put forward with fresh insistence. The position of the VNV was strengthened further after the beginning of the Russian campaign, for, with the drain on their manpower in the east, the Germans became more dependent than ever on the co-operation of local forces. Berger found himself obliged to agree to subordinate his SS unit in Flanders to the VNV in return for the party's support in recruiting men for service in Eastern Europe. Even this concession availed him little. Instead of the seven thousand men promised, the VNV produced a mere 212 men for the Waffen-SS and 489 for the Flemish Legion.[74]

In reporting to Himmler in September 1941, Berger ascribed his lack of success to the food shortages in Flanders and to the growing effectiveness of British and clerical anti-German propaganda. But Berger also blamed the German authorities for the deterioration of the situation in Flanders. The Organisation Todt and other German employment agencies were subjecting the Flemish people to compulsory and often brutal methods of labor recruitment. "Both in Northern France and Flanders methods are used which cannot be applied to Germanic nations related by blood ties." Nor did the German leaders of the occupation government clearly understand the new roads to be followed. "Most of them are opposed to the idea of a reorganization of Europe on a racial basis. They cannot abandon their ideas based on international law." Falkenhausen was adhering rigidly to the Führer's instructions to maintain order and to exploit the Belgian economy. "Everything else, especially the strengthening of the Flemings, is a matter of indifference to him." Reeder was giving the SS all possible help, but he was constantly obliged to overcome the objections of his superior officer. The SS men Berger had succeeded in recruiting in Flanders were splendid material, thoroughly imbued with the Greater Germanic idea and "unreservedly dedicated to union with the Reich." But as yet there were not many of them.[75]

Had Berger been able to recruit systematically for his SS formations, subject their members to a thorough training and indoctrination program, and leave them in Belgium, there can be little doubt that the SS would have become a major influence in Flanders in a comparatively short time. But these men were not left in Belgium. They were sent to fight—and die—in Russia. Thus the most dedicated advocates of the union of Flanders with the Reich were removed from the scene, and the field was left open for opportunists and outright opponents of a Greater German Reich.

Berger resorted to a variety of expedients to increase SS influence in Flanders at the expense of the VNV. He revived a pro-German Flemish political party called the Society for German-Flemish Co-operation (*Dietsch-Vlaamsche Arbeidsgemeenschap*, or Devlag) to foster closer ties with the Reich and provide the indispensable corps of Belgian officials to administer the country. He founded a pro-German organization for Flemish women, and a similar organization for Flemish men unfit for military service. He fostered the development of counterparts of the Reich Labor Service and the Hitler Youth movement and arranged for the training of Flemish youth and labor leaders in Germany.[76] When Staf de Clercq died in October 1942, Berger arranged the selection of Dr. Hendrick Elias, the mayor of Ghent, as his successor in the belief that he was the Flemish leader most amenable to German influence. Again he was to be disappointed, for Elias proved to be as stubborn as de Clercq had been in defending Flemish interests.[77]

More than ever Berger now urged the replacement of the excessively soft and unpolitical military government by a National Socialist civil administration. The installation of a dedicated and energetic party man as head of the German occupation government was the essential prerequisite for converting Flanders and Wallonia into Reichsgaus, and for strengthening the foundations of the Germanic realm as a whole. This was all the more important because Berger, who was responsible for Himmler's Germanization and recruitment programs in all the occupied territories, could devote only a small part of his attention to Belgium.[78]

The military government was not replaced, but in April 1942 Himmler succeeded in arranging for the appointment of SS Brigadeführer Richard Jungclaus as his permanent deputy in Belgium. Jungclaus, recently returned from the Russian front, had served briefly on the staff of Hanns Rauter in the Netherlands.[79]

Shortly after the appointment of Jungclaus, Himmler and Berger began a campaign to oust Reeder and put Jungclaus in his place. Reeder had long been tolerated by the SS leadership because he had appeared to support their efforts in Belgium. But by the autumn of 1942 they had become impatient with his failure to assert himself against Falkenhausen or to take forceful measures against the recalcitrant leaders of the VNV. In February 1943 Himmler accused Reeder of negligence, disloyalty, and disobedience. "I have to object to certain things to which I am not accustomed from SS leaders," he said. Taking his cue from Himmler, Berger charged Reeder with failure to conform to the "policy of the Reich" in Flanders. "Perhaps I am one-sided," he said, "but a promise given to the Reichsführer SS will be carried out even if the world is laid in ruins as a result." [80]

Reeder defended himself by pointing out that Germany still needed the help of the VNV in governing Belgium. Berger's various organizations in Flanders, including the Devlag party, were simply not strong or popular enough to supply the necessary Belgian administrators or create any kind of general support for the German cause. The VNV was after all still collaborating, Reeder argued, and German officials reported that the co-operation of its members was beyond reproach. "The VNV is still providing qualified candidates for the positions of mayors, city managers and other offices," Reeder said, and he pleaded with Himmler to give Flemish leaders the guarantees they desired concerning Flemish cultural autonomy. Berger dismissed Reeder's plea as an example of his milksop (*pflaumenweiche*) attitude. Had he been in charge, he said, he would simply have jailed the recalcitrant VNV leaders, and he predicted that Reeder would soon be compelled to adopt this tactic if present tendencies continued.[81]

Himmler's attempt to oust Reeder failed. Falkenhausen loyally supported his chief of administration, and as long as Hitler persisted in maintaining the military government in Belgium there was nothing Himmler could do to alter the situation. On November 9, 1943, Reeder was promoted to SS Gruppenführer, a move which marked the end of Himmler's efforts to get rid of Reeder and the beginning of a new campaign to regain his loyalty.

Nazi disappointments with the Flemish in Flanders created an opportunity for Léon Degrelle to win recognition for the status of the Walloons in the new European order. From the beginning of the occupation fanatic Nazis had tended to treat the Walloons as second-class citizens, an attitude that persisted despite the gallant service of the Walloon legion in Eastern Europe.[82]

Degrelle returned from the Russian front in mid-December 1942; after taking stock of the political situation at home, he approached Jungclaus with the request to establish a Walloon SS unit.[83] In a speech in Brussels on January 17, 1943, he claimed a Germanic background for the Walloons. Wallonia itself was a Germanic country, he said, and had been part of Germany for a millennium. He now looked to Germany to unite all peoples of Germanic origin, including the Walloons, in one great Germanic community.[84]

Himmler scoffed at Degrelle's speech and the Walloons' "sudden decision to become Germanic," but by this time the Germans could no longer afford an excessively strict line in racial matters. The decisive push on behalf of the Walloons came from Hitler, who in February 1943 ordered the German authorities to support Degrelle's efforts. Himmler took the cue. He allowed a Walloon SS legion to be raised, which was incorporated into the Waffen-SS as the Germanic Volunteer Legion (*Germanishe Freiwillige Legion*).[85]

After a personal inspection of the legion in May, Himmler conceded that it included many fine racial specimens who had proved themselves in battle. He agreed with Hitler in regarding the Walloon SS "as the renaissance movement of a basically Germanic people (*als die Erneue-*

rungsbewegung einem in Kern germanischen Volkes)." The Walloons and above all the Flemings were two racial groups (*Volksstämme*) "which were subjectively best prepared for a very clever and delicately managed future process of amalgamation (*die innerlich am reifsten für eine sehr kluge und mit weicher Hand einmal vorzunehmende Eingliederung sind*)." [86]

In July 1944 Hitler at last took the step Himmler had been recommending for four years and replaced the military administration in Belgium with a civil government. As head (Reichskommissar) of this new government he appointed Josef Grohé, the Gauleiter of Aachen, who was made directly responsible to himself and was given all the powers accorded to Terboven in Norway and Seyss-Inquart in the Netherlands.

The transfer of authority took place on July 18. Grohé retained Reeder as his deputy for administrative affairs, which meant that the official position of Reeder remained unchanged. The same was true of all other officials of the military government, who were simply transferred to the civil administration.

The big difference in the new government was the increased influence of Himmler, who was authorized to appoint a senior SS and police officer for Belgium with responsibility for all matters relating to internal security. This appointment went to Richard Jungclaus who, with the support of Himmler, immediately began to exploit his new authority to establish himself—and through him the Himmler organizations—as the principal power factor in the occupation government.[87]

The change of government was greeted enthusiastically by Léon Degrelle, who urged Jungclaus to make Belgium feel at last the full force of the German fist. The policies of the military government had been too soft altogether, Degrelle said. His own brother and many of his best men had been killed by terrorists. The time had come for a complete change of policy, for a large-scale roundup of hostages and shootings as reprisals. Both Jungclaus and Himmler were in full agreement, and Degrelle was assured that a fundamental change in German policy was imminent. Jungclaus was ordered to initiate a radical counterterror movement. No time was to be lost by setting up courts of any kind. All culprits were to be shot at once without trial.[88]

The full effect of the new policies was never felt in Belgium. German resistance was rapidly disintegrating before the Allied advance. On August 13, 1944, Himmler put Jungclaus in charge of the regular army in Belgium as well as the police, but this desperate measure did nothing to stem the tide. On September 3, 1944, the Allied forces entered Brussels.

Whatever doubts Hitler and his principal collaborators may have had about the future status of the Belgians in the Nazi New Order when Germany first occupied the country were completely resolved by 1942. The Nazis had always recognized the Flemish as a Germanic people. Once

195

Hitler had decided that the Walloons were Germanic as well, there was no longer any question as to what was to be done with Belgium: The country was to be annexed to the Reich and was to be divided into two new Reichsgaus, Flanders and Brabant. From these lands all undesirable political and racial elements were to be removed, in accordance with procedures already adopted in other parts of the Greater German Reich.

As in the case of Denmark and Norway, not a great deal had been accomplished in the course of the Nazi occupation to integrate Belgium into the Reich politically and culturally, and German attempts at economic integration had fallen far short of expectations. But in Belgium, too, the stubborn resistance of the population to the Nazi Germanization campaign had little effect on Hitler's plans. Here as well he was confident that in the course of time the Flemish and the Walloons, like all other Germanic peoples, would learn to have pride in their Germanic blood and racial heritage, and become stalwart supporters of the Greater Germanic union.[89]

Territorially the one question that remained to be decided was the fate of the two French departments which the Germans had attached to Belgium for administrative purposes. Even here, however, there can be little doubt about what their future status would have been. Unless the Nazis had found compelling reason to restore them to France in return for a French military alliance or some similar advantage, it seems probable that these departments, which the Flemish regarded as French Flanders, would have been made part of the Reichsgau Flandern, and, with Belgian Flanders, would have been incorporated into the Germanic Reich.

CHAPTER 8

France: The Mortal Enemy

"The German people's irreconcilable mortal enemy is and remains France," Hitler wrote in *Mein Kampf*. "It does not matter who ruled or will rule in France . . . the final goal of her foreign policy will always be to hold the Rhine frontier and in so doing to guarantee a disintegrated and dismembered Germany. England desires no German world power, but France desires no power at all called Germany."

The aim of German policy toward France, Hitler said, should be to break France's power to throttle German national aspirations. For this purpose "a final, decisive settlement" with France was necessary. But such a settlement, he insisted, would only be meaningful if it were not regarded as an end in itself, but as "a means of subsequently and finally giving our nation a chance to expand elsewhere." By elsewhere Hitler made clear that he meant the territories of Eastern Europe. Thus German expansion at the expense of France was not originally one of the primary goals of Nazi Germany.[1]

Hitler's belief in the necessity of knocking out France before attacking in the east was restated on numerous occasions before and during the war, but he never made any precise pronouncements about what was to be done with France after its conquest.

The actual defeat of France in the spring of 1940 produced a more concrete program. Even before the armistice, Hitler was talking in terms of a peace treaty that should restore to Germany "all the territory robbed from the German people during the past four hundred years."[2] The army was to make it a special point of honor "to capture as rapidly as possible the former German Reich territories up to the line of Verdun, Toul, Belfort, as well as the coastal towns of Cherbourg and Brest, and the Le Creusot armaments center."[3] Soon afterward Hitler ordered his Ministry of the Interior to draw up plans for a new boundary with

France that should incorporate into Germany those territories in northern and eastern France which for historical, political, ethnic, geographic, strategic, and any other reasons appeared to belong to Central rather than to Western Europe. The line drawn up in response to these orders corresponded approximately to the western boundary of the Holy Roman Empire at the time of Charles V, except that it did not run so far south but stopped at the old Duchy of Savoy. This line was approved by Hitler in general, but he wanted the area included in Germany to be extended, especially along the Channel coast. The final boundary, approved by Hitler in full, ran from the mouth of the Somme River eastward along the northern ridge of the Paris basin and Champagne to the Argonne. It then turned south through Burgundy along the western boundary of the Franche-Comté to the Lake of Geneva.[4]

Later Hitler decided it would be necessary to claim even more territory. "If we are to ensure our hegemony on the continent, we must also retain military strong points on what was formerly the French Atlantic coast. Further, we must not forget that a large portion of German history took place in the old kingdom of Burgundy, and that this land is therefore age-old German soil, which the French stole from us in times of our weakness." When a German workman on the Atlantic fortifications expressed regret that Germany should give up these strongholds after investing so much work in them, Hitler saw a wealth of wisdom in his remark. "I need hardly say that nothing on earth would persuade us to abandon such safe positions as those on the Channel coast, captured during the campaign in France and consolidated by the Organisation Todt."[5] Where Hitler's greed would have stopped will never be known. The only thing certain is that large territorial annexations would have been made at the expense of France had Germany won the war.[6]

What was to be done with what was left of France remained indefinite; it is probable that Hitler himself had no fixed ideas on the subject. He had no desire to incorporate all Frenchmen into the Reich, he told his associates in 1942. He was willing to include those who dwelt on the borders of Germany and who had been Germans four hundred years ago. But the others? "The real question one must ask oneself is this," he said. "Can we absorb them with advantage—do they by blood belong to our race? And then one must act in accordance with the answer one gives oneself."[7]

In practice, Hitler's wartime policies toward France varied according to the military and political needs of the moment. In September 1941 he declared that he would postpone any final decision until after the Russian campaign so that he could approach the French problem with a clear mind (mit freiem Kopf).[8] He never had the opportunity to do so, but in the course of the German occupation of France a fairly clear picture emerges of the position France was to occupy in Hitler's New Order.

NORTH SEA

GREAT BRITAIN

London •

ENGLISH CHANNEL

The Hague • NETHERLANDS

Brussels •

BELGIUM

GERMANY

Rhine R.

LUXEMBOURG

CHANNEL
ISLANDS

PAS-DE-CALAIS

NORD

SOMME

AISNE

ARDENNES

MEUSE

LORRAINE

Strasbourg

MEURTHE
ET-MOSELLE

Seine R.

Paris •

OCCUPIED FRANCE

VOSGES

HAUTE-
MARNE

HAUTE-SAÔNE

Montoire •

Loire R.

DOUBS

JURA

SWITZERLAND

L. Geneva

BAY OF

BISCAY

Vichy •

ITALY

VICHY FRANCE
Occupied Nov. 1942

Rhône R.

Nice •

Garonne R.

Hendaye •

Marseille •

Toulon •

SPAIN

MEDITERRANEAN
SEA

FRANCE

Boundary of France before May 10, 1940

Under German civil administration; attached to
Nazi party administrative districts

Closed zone

Under German military administration
for Belgium

0   300 miles

The German Administration

All captured territory in the west was first placed under military administration. "The military administration will be conducted so as to avoid giving the impression that it is intended to annex the occupied territories," Hitler said in a directive of May 9. "The provisions of the Hague Convention on Land Warfare will be observed. The population will be protected and economic life maintained." Hostile acts by the population, on the other hand, including passive resistance and stoppage of work as a political gesture, were to be suppressed with the utmost severity.[9]

On June 12 a separate military government was created for the occupied territory of France, with the exception of the departments Nord and Pas de Calais, which were placed under the military commander for Belgium and Northern France.[10]

The armistice treaty of June 22, 1940, concluded with the plenipotentiaries of the government of the Third Republic, divided France into two parts, an occupied and an unoccupied zone. The occupied zone, about three-fifths of the country, included the northern half of France, with Paris, and the entire Channel coast—France's most valuable industrial and agricultural regions.[11]

The French government was to continue to exercise jurisdiction over Frenchmen in both the occupied and unoccupied zones, but not in the departments Nord and Pas de Calais, nor, as it proved, in the provinces of Alsace and Lorraine, or in the so-called closed zone (*Sperrzone*), an area east and northeast of the demarcation line which corresponded roughly to the territory Hitler intended to annex permanently.[12] According to the terms of the armistice agreement, the French government was to be permitted to return to Paris, but the Germans blocked every attempt that was made to do so and in the end the French government found itself established permanently at Vichy.[13]

From the German point of view, the division of France and the provision that the French government should exercise authority over its citizens in both zones was a remarkably clever arrangement. It obliged the French to continue to assume routine administrative duties for the entire country, yet it permitted the Germans to retain direct control over the most important strategic and economic areas. By leaving a large part of France unoccupied the Germans were able to reduce the size of their army of occupation. At the same time the existence of an unoccupied area gave the French an illusion of independence and the Germans a means of exercising pressure on the French government by threatening to impinge on that independence. The line of demarcation itself was an admirable instrument of pressure, for by tightening border restrictions between the two zones the occupation authorities could cause serious human hardship and cripple the economy of the unoccupied zone, which depended on the north for agricultural and industrial products. But most important of all was the fact that the arrangement ensured the existence of a French government which could command the services of the French bureaucracy and thus immeasurably ease the burden of the German administrators.[14]

To govern the occupied zone of France created by the armistice agreement, the Germans established the Office of the Chief of the Military Administration in France, which was directly under the commander in chief of the army.[15] The first head of the new office was General of the Infantry Alfred Streccius, who had been recalled from retirement to active service at the beginning of the war. He assumed his duties on June 30, 1940. Like Alexander von Falkenhausen, the head of the military government in Belgium, Streccius had served as a military adviser in China, where he too had become an admirer of the philosophy of Taoism; he was fond of quoting the saying of Lao-Tzu that nonaction was preferable to action. Altogether, he and Falkenhausen were curious choices to be heads of National Socialist military governments.[16]

A thoroughgoing reorganization of the German military administration in France took place on October 18, 1940. The military and administrative leadership were now united in a military commander (Militärbefehlshaber) who was invested with supreme executive power (*vollziehende Gewalt*) and who took over the functions of the chief of the military administration. He remained directly responsible to the commander in chief of the army, but his control of military as well as administrative affairs gave him a greater degree of power and independence.[17]

The man selected to head the reorganized German military government was General Otto von Stülpnagel, an officer of the old imperial army, who held the position until February 1942. At that time, demoralized by Hitler's orders to shoot hostages and other Nazification measures, he used the excuse of poor health to ask to be relieved of his duties. He was succeeded after a short interval by his cousin, General Karl Heinrich von Stülpnagel, the former head of the German Armistice Commission for France.[18]

Ulrich von Hassell, the anti-Nazi resistance leader, regarded Otto von Stüpnagel as a man of intelligence but little moral fiber, a judgment he believed confirmed when Stülpnagel carried out Hitler's orders for the mass shooting of hostages in December 1941. "[Stülpnagel] is, of course, in a most disagreeable situation," Hassell noted in his diary. "His staff had implored him, as he told me himself, not to shoot hostages but to resign, which he unquestionably should have done. He offered the usual excuse that by not resigning he could 'prevent worse things happening.'"[19]

Hassell had a much higher opinion of Stülpnagel's cousin and successor, General Karl Heinrich von Stülpnagel, who had been involved in abortive anti-Nazi revolt plans of the army in 1938, and who, like Falkenhausen in Belgium, became one of the key figures in the resistance movement during the last years of the war. As military governor of

201

France he collected a group of anti-Nazi officers on his staff, and held his forces in readiness to assist in the overthrow of the Nazi regime. He was in a cruel situation, for he was confronted regularly with onerous orders from the Nazi leadership which he could not reject outright for fear that his attitude would lead to his dismissal, a blow the anti-Nazi opposition could ill afford. His solution to the dilemma, if solution it may be called, was to insist on a "clear separation of military and political affairs" before taking over his new office. In this way he escaped responsibility for Nazification measures, but at the same time he opened the way to the appointment of a senior SS and police officer for France who could be expected to carry out such measures far more energetically than the ordinary professional army officer. What Stülpnagel accomplished by this device, however, was to remain in a position to withhold the co-operation of regular army troops in such programs as the roundup of Jews, and to be in a post of crucial importance when the signal was given for the overthrow of the Nazi regime. When that signal finally came on July 20, 1944, Stülpnagel placed Himmler's police agents under arrest and put the forces under his command at the disposal of the new anti-Nazi German government. Upon hearing the news of the failure of the attempt on Hitler's life and the collapse of the resistance movement, he tried unsuccessfully to kill himself. He was saved to appear before the Nazis' "Peoples' Court" and then hanged.[20]

The German military government in France consisted of three separate staffs: military, administrative, and supply (the staff of the quartermaster). Of these it was the administrative staff that was primarily responsible for the actual government of the country.

The administrative staff was headed by Dr. Jonathan Schmid, a former minister of economics in Württemberg, and was divided into two main sections, administrative and economic. The administrative section dealt with general domestic problems, the supervision of the French police, refugees, education and culture, finances, health, justice, propaganda, communications, buildings, the post office, art, and archives. The economic section, under Dr. Elmar Michel, an appointee of Göring's, exercised general supervision over the French economy and included departments of raw materials, industry, food and agriculture, labor and social questions, transportation, foreign trade, currency and price regulations.[21]

The German military administration in France was assigned tasks similar to those of all occupation governments in the west. Above all it was to create favorable conditions for carrying on the war against England, and for this purpose it was expected to re-establish order and security, to reactivate the economy, and to exploit it for the Wehrmacht and the German war effort.[22] By the terms of the armistice treaty, the French government had agreed to support by every means orders issued by the Germans in exercising their rights and to instruct French officials to comply with such orders.[23] The Germans were thus in a position to direct their orders to three different groups of officials: to their own personnel; to French officials directly; or to the French government at Vichy, which in turn transmitted German orders to French officials.

The German military administration regarded itself primarily as a supervisory rather than as an administrative agency, and it took some pride in its ability to restrict its personnel and its activities to a minimum. In late October 1940 the entire German administrative staff consisted of only 489 persons of all ranks, including 162 employees of the Wehrmacht.[24]

For purposes of their own administration, the Germans divided occupied France into four military administrative regions, with a special administration for Paris and the departments of the Seine. These main regions were divided and subdivided to form a German administrative network. But the Germans also made use of the French administrative network. In every French department a German military commander was established beside the French prefect and German officers were attached to the heads of the various French departmental subdivisions as well as to the mayors of the more important cities and towns.[25]

All French government departments and official personnel, especially police officers and bureaucrats in critical positions, were kept under close control. In addition the Germans exercised close supervision over the French economy; in cases where vital German interests were involved they assumed control directly. German laws were introduced for all matters affecting German security—a broad area—and new laws were promulgated to cover special cases. Deeds punishable under these laws were to go before German courts.[26] In the routine business of administration, however, the German military government did its best to leave the greatest possible amount of responsibility—and work—to the French authorities.

The German military commander in France had been given "supreme executive power," but this did not mean that he was able to exercise it. As in other occupied areas, there was in France a bewildering overlap of authority among the various German administrative agencies and a vicious competition for power. On a visit to Paris in February 1941, Hassell noted that the military governor was obviously suffering from the mad administrative confusion and the conflicts among the various German agencies. The Vichy statesman Jacques Benoist-Méchin summed the situation up nicely: "After having been a federation of states, Germany has become a federation of administrations." [27]

Among the more important of these administrative organizations was the German Armistice Commission, with its headquarters in Wiesbaden, which had been empowered by the armistice agreement with France to regulate and supervise the execution of that agreement until a final peace treaty had been signed. A delegation of the French government was attached to this commission "to represent French wishes and to receive the executive orders of the German Armistice Commission." [28]

Thus the armistice treaty had already assigned to the Armistice Commission many of the functions and powers which were later delegated to the military government—but without any corresponding curtailment of the functions of the Armistice Commission.

There was the additional complication that the Armistice Commission was responsible to the High Command of the Wehrmacht (OKW), and hence in the first instance to Hitler or Keitel, whereas the military government was responsible to the High Command of the Army (OKH), and thus to General Walther von Brauchitsch. Serious conflicts were generally avoided because the leaders of both organizations were army officers—the head of the Armistice Commission was Karl Heinrich von Stülpnagel, who later became head of the military government. The Armistice Commission remained a separate political force in France and an important independent channel of communication between the French and German governments until the end of 1941, when both governments came to rely increasingly on other agents and agencies to carry on their negotiations.[29]

Within the Armistice Commission itself, a separate agency had been created to deal with economic problems which was assigned exactly the same economic task as the military government, namely, to exploit the French economy in the German interest. This special commission for economic questions was composed of representatives of the Four-Year Plan, the Foreign Office, the plenipotentiary for the Reich administration, the High Command of the Wehrmacht, and the military government in France. After a struggle with Göring, Ribbentrop succeeded in getting one of his own men, Hans Richard Hemmen, an economic expert of the Foreign Office, named head of this commission. Göring consented to Ribbentrop's candidate only on condition that Hemmen be subordinate to himself in his capacity as head of the commission, a condition Ribbentrop vigorously contested. Hemmen himself tried to steer a course between the two Nazi leaders to gain maximum independent authority in his own right.[30]

Ribbentrop's claim to authority in France was based on the assumption that France was still a foreign country and that German relations with a foreign country should be conducted primarily if not exclusively through the Foreign Office. To press his claim Ribbentrop sent a Foreign Office delegation to France immediately after the armistice under the leadership of Otto Abetz, since 1935 a member of Ribbentrop's personal staff (the Dienststelle Ribbentrop) and since March 1940 a regular official of the Foreign Office with the title of minister. Under Ribbentrop's auspices Abetz had made many trips to France before the war. In the summer of 1939 the French government denied him permission to return on the grounds that he had been engaging in illegal political activities. This incident only enhanced Abetz in the estimation of Ribbentrop, who regarded him as his foremost expert on French affairs.[31]

Abetz was sent to France in June 1940 without any definite assignment, and his staff was little more than an appendage of the German military government. By August, however, Ribbentrop had succeeded in persuading Hitler to accept his views about the position the Foreign Office should occupy with respect to France. Abetz was raised to the rank of ambassador and was assigned the task of advising the military government on political matters and maintaining continuous liaison with the Vichy regime. He was also given powers that went far beyond those of an ordinary ambassador and which conflicted directly with the authority of the military government. In announcing Abetz's appointment to General Keitel on August 3, Ribbentrop said, "The Führer has expressed directly in this connection that Ambassador Abetz be solely responsible for dealing with all political questions in occupied and unoccupied France. Insofar as his functions affect military interests, Ambassador Abetz will act only in conjunction with the military commander in France." [32]

Hitler's assignment to Abetz meant that there were now three separate authorities responsible for German policy in France, the military government, the Armistice Commission, and the Foreign Office. As is customary in such cases, the actual exercise of power depended largely on the ability and tenacity of the personalities involved. Abetz began with grave disadvantages. His ambassadorial position was in itself highly irregular, he was never accredited to the French government, he maintained his residence in Paris rather than in Vichy, and the Vichy government had no comparable representative either in Paris or Berlin. He did not have strong personal or organizational backing in the Reich —Ribbentrop and the Foreign Office were in no way comparable to Göring or Himmler and their organizations in this respect. And in France he lacked the staff through which to exercise the power he had been given.

That Abetz nevertheless succeeded in creating a strong position for himself in France was due above all to his ability to form close connections with the French politicians who became prominent leaders of the Vichy regime. Abetz's outstanding success in this respect was Pierre Laval, whose cause he consistently supported in both German and French official circles, and who repaid this support handsomely by dealing with Abetz as the foremost German official in France. This favored status with Laval gave Abetz his influence and forced the military government to work with him and through him while Laval was in power. Even so there were long gaps between his periods of influence. With the failure of the Vichy government to prevent the defection of the French colonies in November 1942, the loss of North Africa, and the scuttling of the French fleet, Abetz was recalled to Berlin in semidisgrace and was not sent back to Paris until a year later, by which time other forces had appeared on the scene.[33]

The military government, the Armistice Commission, and Abetz were primarily concerned with the administration of France and with relations with the Vichy government. Far more important in determining France's future in a German-dominated world were the various German economic agencies and the organizations of Heinrich Himmler.

Göring, still flying high in the summer of 1940 before the defeat of his Luftwaffe in the Battle of Britain, demanded unified control of economic affairs in France, especially as they concerned preparations for the final peace treaty with that country. "The economic portion [of the treaty] will, in any case, definitely be decided by me," he told the Foreign Office on July 2, 1940.[34]

As head of the Four-Year Plan, Göring was empowered to issue orders directly to the German military government. The weakness of his position was that he was dependent on the staff of the military government to carry out these orders, and, despite his claim to unified direction over economic affairs, he was but one of several economic authorities operating in France. The various economic agencies of the Wehrmacht also worked through the military government, as did the economic section of the Armistice Commission, the Reich ministries of Economics, Commerce, and Finance, the Organisation Todt, and in later years the Speer ministry and Sauckel's labor recruitment office. To emphasize the urgency of their particular requirements, government economic offices as well as private firms sent their own agents into France, thereby creating further complications in an already confused economic situation. In addition there were the special economic branches of Himmler's various organizations, Rosenberg's office for the seizure of Jewish and enemy property, and the agents of numerous German private firms, all of them competing for a share of the spoils.[35]

Various efforts were made to unify German economic policy in France. Göring's Central Order Offices (Zast) were set up in September 1940 to centralize German requisitions in France.[36] Two years later Walther Funk, Keitel, and Speer ordered the establishment of the Economic Procurement Office (*Beschaffungsamt*) to increase efficiency in exploiting the French economy and to integrate it into German methods of production. But throughout the occupation the army economic offices remained the chief agents for carrying out German economic policies in France, and throughout they remained conscious that their main task was the exploitation of the French economy for the German war effort.[37]

As in other occupied territories, numerous methods of direct and indirect exploitation were available to the Germans: the outright seizure of goods and raw materials, insofar as this could be justified by a broad interpretation of the armistice agreement; charging exorbitant rates for German occupation costs; the sequestration of enemy property, including the property of Jews and refugees who had failed to return; or the manipulation of the currency to permit purchases at favorable rates of exchange.[38]

More significant than any of these methods of exploitation, however, were the German efforts to revive the French economy and to co-ordinate it with that of Germany so as to ensure maximum French production for German military requirements. For this purpose the German military administration established a tight system of supervision and control over all French economic activity.[39] France was covered with a network of German economic as well as administrative agencies. Economic as well as administrative officials were installed beside French administrators at almost every level of government and in all major French economic enterprises. In July 1940 a German supervisory commission was appointed to control French banking, especially the central Bank of France. Soon afterward similar commissions were created to supervise agriculture, industry, and labor. In April 1941 the economic office of the military government in France reported that "as regards raw materials, the economy of occupied France has been incorporated into the German order." A year later Hitler was informed that the French war industry was working almost 100 per cent for Germany.[40]

This supervisory role did not satisfy the Germans, who wanted not only to gear the French production to the needs of the German war effort but to establish permanent German control over the French economy as well. This was to be done by purchasing controlling shares in French economic enterprises both at home and abroad. By 1942 the Germans, according to their own statistics, had been far more successful in France than in Belgium or the Netherlands in gaining the economic dominion they desired.[41]

The German economic penetration of unoccupied France, which was in any case far less valuable from an economic point of view, went more slowly. In November 1942 this area, too, was overrun by the German armies,[42] and after that the German program to establish permanent ascendancy over the French economy was applied to the entire country.

Himmler's influence in France was slight at first. All German police in France were originally under the direct authority of the military government. Of these the most important were two branches of the military police, the Secret Military Police (*Geheime Feldpolizei*) and the Military Gendarmerie (*Feldgendarmerie*). As both military police forces had very little manpower at their disposal, the military government was obliged to rely heavily on the French police for the routine preservation of order and security in the country. From the beginning of the German occupation, however, there was a representative of Himmler's police organizations in France, a position held until May 1942 by SS Sturmbannführer Dr. Helmut Knochen. Within his office, although in an almost independent capacity, was a department for Jewish affairs under SS Obersturmbannführer Theodor Dannecker.[43]

The supervision of the French police was carried out with a stringent economy of means.[44] During the first year of the German occupation the entire police section of the military administrative offices consisted of one police chief, two or sometimes three senior specialists, and three junior specialists. Regional administrative offices were assigned only one police specialist. The commander of greater Paris had but two high-ranking police specialists and five or six inspectors to supervise a French police force of over thirty thousand men.

In dealing with the French police the military government, conscious of its position of dependence, operated with tact and restraint. Orders to the French police were issued almost exclusively through French authorities, either the Vichy government or local French officials, and every effort was made to keep such orders to a minimum. The only direct interference with the French police was in personnel, which was carefully screened in an attempt to remove what the Germans considered to be unreliable elements, in particular Jews, Freemasons, and Communists. "The control of personnel was one of the most important methods of German supervision," a German staff specialist wrote in an analysis of German security measures.[45] The policy of the military government was remarkably successful. On the whole the French police served the Germans reliably and efficiently throughout the occupation.

The attack on Russia in June 1941 was accompanied by a marked increase in terrorist activity against German rule, for not only did Russian resistance provide some hope that the previously invincible Germans might be defeated, but French Communists, long skilled in underground operations, joined forces with other opposition groups. The Germans now found themselves obliged to increase their supervision of the French police and to depend more heavily on their own police forces. The steady deterioration of the security situation in France gave Himmler the opportunity to press for a greater role for his own organizations, and during the summer of 1941 the military government was obliged to agree to the large-scale reinforcement of the Himmler police.

The security situation did not improve with the strengthening of Himmler's organizations. Their presence was as usual accompanied by programs of Nazification and Germanization, and an intensified campaign against the Jews. As everywhere else in the occupied countries, these attempts to carry out ideological campaigns in conjunction with security measures only increased the difficulties in maintaining order.

Toward the end of 1941 Stülpnagel was compelled to delegate to Himmler's police the task of dealing with Jews, Communists, and refugees. But he insisted that the supervision of the French police and all counterespionage work, especially against the French resistance, be left in the hands of his own military police, whose strength was increased from twenty-five hundred in June 1940 to over six thousand by the end of 1941.[46]

This arrangement did not satisfy Himmler or his chief lieutenant, Reinhard Heydrich, who wanted complete control of all German as well as French police forces, and who in France as in Belgium had agitated persistently for the replacement of a military head of the occupation government by a sound Nazi, preferably a senior SS and police officer.

Early in 1942 part of Himmler's program was realized. On March 9 a special senior SS and police officer was assigned to France with full powers over both the German and French police. According to the terms of the assignment given him by Hitler, he was to receive orders on military affairs from the military governor; but all orders concerning police questions, including reprisals against the French population, hostage policies, and the Jewish question were to come from Himmler. The Himmler police were confident that this meant the transfer of the entire police power and executive authority from the military governor to their organizations. "This new regulation will have an especially good effect on the final solution of the Jewish question," a security police official predicted.[47]

On April 28, 1942, SS Gruppenführer Karl Albrecht Oberg, up to this time SS and police officer in Radom (Poland), was appointed senior SS and police officer in France, and in May Heydrich himself accompanied him to Paris to install him in his new office. "General Oberg is responsible for all matters affecting public order and internal security in the occupied zone," Heydrich informed the French secretary-general of police. "He will carry out his duties with the assistance of the German police and the SS divisions. The French administration will obey the orders given them by the German authorities in conformity with the rights appertaining to the occupying power." At the same time Heydrich demanded the complete reorganization of the French police, especially its leadership and personnel. "Men must be appointed to the head of the police force who have given evidence of their sincere adherence to a policy of Franco-German collaboration." Heydrich's instructions were backed up by Hitler. In notifying the French of Oberg's appointment, he issued the injunction, "The French government must immediately give the necessary orders to the French administration to collaborate effectively with the German administration under pain of the most serious sanctions."[48]

The transfer of control over the police had still wider implications. By decrees of October 10, 1940, and October 2, 1941, the military commander had been given judicial power to deal with exceptional security cases and to remove them from the jurisdiction of ordinary German or French law courts. On August 22, 1942, the military commander was obliged to turn these powers over to the senior SS and police officer so that, in effect, both police and judicial authority in France came under Himmler's control.[49]

Although Oberg was Himmler's man and had been a colleague of Heydrich's since the founding of the SD, there existed a better understanding between him and the military governor, Karl Heinrich von Stülpnagel, than was generally the case between SS and military officials. Oberg had been a member of Stülpnagel's division during the First World War, and he retained a deep respect for the older general. Whether under the influence of Stülpnagel or because Oberg himself found such measures distasteful, there was a sharp decline in the execution of hostages in the first six months after he took office. Oberg, however, remained primarily an SS man. As French resistance mounted, reprisal actions were undertaken on an ever-increasing scale. Moreover, after Oberg's appointment there was less reliance on the French police and a steady reinforcement of German police units. The Germans themselves now took the lead in hunting down and wiping out members of the French resistance.[50] But beyond such measures, which can still be considered as efforts to preserve order and security, the Himmler police indulged in other activities which were purely National Socialist in conception and purpose.

In December 1942 Himmler launched a campaign against the French intelligentsia and "criminal types," which included Communists, homosexuals, Freemasons, gypsies, and other elements marked for destruction by the National Socialist state. At the command of Hitler, he ordered the total destruction of the "criminal quarter" of Marseille and the roundup of one hundred thousand persons from that area into concentration camps.[51] For Himmler, however, the major tasks in France, as everywhere else in Europe, were the programs of Germanization and the total destruction of the Jews.

The campaign of Germanization was conducted primarily in Alsace and Lorraine and in the so-called Closed Zone, a broad strip of border territory from the mouth of the Somme to Lake Geneva. The French peasants who had fled from this area at the approach of the German armies were forbidden to return, and an attempt was made to resettle it with Germans. The organization originally entrusted with this task was Himmler's *Ostdeutsche Landbewirtschaftungs Gesellschaft*, generally called simply the *Ostland Gesellschaft*, which had been founded in February 1940 to colonize the conquered territories in Eastern Europe.[52] In November 1940 this office was called upon to supervise colonization in the west, and its name was changed to Westland to correspond with its new functions. The headquarters of the organization were in Paris, with regional offices in Amiens, Laons, Mézières-Charleville, Nancy, and Dijon.

The primary task of the Westland organization, according to an order of November 22, 1940, was to take charge of the cultivation of lands occupied by German troops which had been abandoned by their owners, or of lands which were "not being cultivated with German methods." A year later the *Berliner Börsenzeitung* defined the Westland organization as a veritable school of agrarian policy. "An elite of German agriculturalists is learning here to think in broad terms and to work in a European scope." But the work of the Westland organization proved to be a failure. Not enough German settlers could be found to cultivate the lands made available in the Closed Zone, and on May 20, 1943, the Vichy government was authorized to issue a circular permitting the return of French peasants to this area so that the lands here could once again be brought under cultivation.[53]

As for the rest of France, although Hitler might still talk occasionally of giving the French an honorable place in the New Order, it is clear that Himmler, his Reichskommissar for racial affairs, had no intention of conceding France such a future, but intended to use that country as a dumping ground for politically and racially undesirable elements. Basically Hitler must have agreed with this attitude, for he gave Himmler steadfast support in pursuing such a policy. The Jews, of course, even in France, were to be removed entirely.

Neither Hitler's nor Himmler's conception of the future of France was known to the leaders of the French government at Vichy, whose policy of collaboration was based, at least in part, on the belief that self-interest alone would force the Germans to bid for French support and thus open the way for negotiation and bargaining. This policy might have worked had the French been dealing with rational opponents. But National Socialist leadership was not motivated by rational principles, as the Vichy leaders were to discover, and Hitler's political judgment had by now been disastrously distorted by political and military successes which had given him a sense of invincibility as well as infallibility.

The Germans and the Vichy Government

The French government at Vichy was yet another rival authority in France, and an important one, for it ensured the continuation of a French administration through which the Germans ruled the country. But the Vichy regime is also significant in considering Hitler's war aims, for it represented what was left of France. Consequently, his treatment of this government gives some indication of the position France was to occupy in a Nazi-ordered Europe.[54]

On June 16, 1940, with the French armies in full retreat and their military situation seemingly hopeless, the aged French marshal Henri-Philippe Pétain, the hero of the Verdun campaign in the First World War, succeeded Paul Reynaud as minister president of France. On the following day Pétain appealed to the Germans for an armistice; on June 22 an armistice between France and Germany was signed.

The problems confronting the French government at this time extended far beyond the conclusion of an armistice agreement. As a result of the recent military campaigns and the panic engendered by the rapid German advance, some four million persons had fled from their homes and were now wandering about the country as refugees. A large proportion of the French people, in particular the urban population, was threatened with starvation as a result of food shortages and the breakdown of the transportation and communications systems. Moreover, difficult negotiations with the Germans still lay ahead in which the very future of France and its inhabitants were at stake. Clearly drastic measures were needed to cope with the situation. On July 9 the French legislature voted to give Pétain dictatorial powers to enable him to act quickly and authoritatively in this period of national emergency. Thus, almost from the beginning, the French government (known as the Vichy government after its move to the spa of Vichy on June 30) was an authoritarian regime, with Pétain having the right to rule by decree.

According to the terms of the armistice agreement, the authority of the French government was to extend over both the occupied and unoccupied zones; but, as has already been seen, this authority did not extend to the departments Nord and Pas de Calais, to the Closed Zone, or to the provinces of Alsace and Lorraine. Moreover the Germans were shortly to demand the right to see all French legislation before it was promulgated, thereby giving them supervisory control over one of the most important powers of the Vichy regime.

Despite the fact that the Germans dominated France militarily, the powers of the Vichy regime were by no means negligible. In 1940 Vichy still controlled the greater part of France's overseas empire, which included important bases for potential German and Italian military operations against the British Empire and Britain's economic lifelines. It still controlled one of the world's finest navies and a large merchant fleet, both of which the Germans wanted to keep out of the hands of the enemy and which they themselves badly needed to carry on the war against Britain. Further, it still had the power to sabotage or at least seriously disrupt German rule in France according to the degree of its co-operation or non-co-operation with the German authorities.

Once the leaders of the Vichy government recovered from the initial demoralization of defeat, they began to recognize the strength of their bargaining position. However different their characters and methods, however selfish their personal motives may have been, it can be said of most of them that they collaborated with the Germans in the expectation that this strength could be exploited to ease the burden of the occupation for their fellow countrymen and to gain the most favorable possible place for France (and for themselves) in a German-dominated Europe. A majority of Europeans in the summer of 1940, certainly most Frenchmen who lived under the shadow of the German guns, were convinced that Germany had already won the war. The Vichy leaders believed that they, in contrast to those who had joined French resistance organizations, were facing the situation realistically, and they regarded it as the task of responsible Frenchmen to seek the best possible adjustment for their country under the circumstances.

That the Vichy leaders gained so few real advantages for France was not due so much to their own spinelessness or incompetence, but was far more the result of Hitler's arrogant refusal to appreciate the importance of bargaining in his own and Germany's interests. His crude application of pressure, his refusal to make timely concessions, and his open disregard of the terms of the armistice agreement left Vichy little room to maneuver. But to the end of the war some Vichy statesmen do not appear to have realized that they were dealing with a dictator who was neither amenable to reason nor even responsive to the dictates of his own self-interest. The German tactics undercut the prestige and consequently the influence of the Vichy regime, whose support Germany desperately needed in the conduct of the war and for the administration of France. By the end of 1942 the greater part of the French overseas empire was lost, the fleet was scuttled, and the authority of Vichy was being challenged on an ever-wider scale in France itself.

It will probably never be possible to form an accurate or generally accepted judgment about the policies and motives of the leaders of the Vichy government. They were caught in a situation which undermined honor and loyalty, they were surrounded by spies, they could trust no one altogether and most people not at all. In this malignant political atmosphere their every statement and action was made with a calculation of the effect it would produce on others. Nothing they said or did can be taken at face value. So devious did their activity become that they themselves undoubtedly were often lost in the maze of their own involutions.

Marshal Pétain, the titular head of the Vichy regime throughout the years of the German occupation, intended to lead a French national revival similar to the one that had taken place in Prussia after its defeat by Napoleon.[55] The Third Republic was blamed for the loss of the war, and parliamentary democracy was rejected as a form of government. "The State, bloated and debilitated, has collapsed more from the weight of its own weaknesses and mistakes than under the blows of the enemy," Pétain declared. In its place an authoritarian regime had been established which purported to draw on France's greatest historical traditions, primarily those of the period before 1789, but which clearly sought to emulate the success of more recently established authoritarian regimes in Germany and Italy. The slogans of Work, Family, and Fatherland replaced Liberty, Equality, and Fraternity. The emphasis was on moral and physical fitness. The Roman Catholic Church was restored to a prominent place in French national life. Education was to indoctrinate youth with sound principles rather than mere information. There was to be no more "cramming of the mind (*Plus de barrage de crâne*)." [56]

With this program Pétain undoubtedly struck the right note in 1940. The French were disillusioned and demoralized, ready to accept strong leadership that promised moral and national rehabilitation. In all parts of the country the old marshal was acclaimed as the man who would save France in the Second World War as he had once saved it in the First.

In the first months of the German occupation, Pétain appears to have believed that some kind of honorable working arrangement with the

Germans could be achieved and that he could do more than any other man to aid France and its people in this time of crisis. But beyond the desire to help his countrymen there may have been profounder calculations which kept Pétain on the path of collaboration and prevented him from resigning even after it became evident that honorable co-operation with Hitler was impossible. On the issues that really counted, the issues that might have changed the course of the war—the use of France's African colonies, the use of the fleet, actual military collaboration with Germany—the old man dug in. In the face of massive German pressure he resisted not only with courage and determination, but with skill and guile. Throughout the occupation his basic consideration may have been that a successor, a Laval for example, might have neither the prestige, the ability, nor the principle to make what Pétain thought to be the right decision at the crucial time.

Laval himself, however, is no simple case. A lawyer from the Auvergne, several times minister president and foreign minister in the governments of the Third Republic, he was quite the most important personality in the Vichy regime next to Pétain, and in the last years considerably more important. With some justification he has been considered the most pro-German among the leaders of the Vichy regime and the outstanding advocate of collaboration. There is consequently some irony in the fact that, before the war, he had built up a reputation as an advocate of a hard line against Germany.

As his rationale for collaboration with Germany after 1940, Laval offered the convincing argument that France had no other choice. The fundamental political fact for France was that it had been defeated by Germany; the fundamental geographical fact, that it was located directly on Germany's western frontier. So long as France maintained an attitude of irreconcilable hostility to Germany, it would always be a temptation to the Germans to destroy France utterly in order to eliminate the French threat to German national security. As Laval saw it, the only possibility for France to save its national identity was through a policy of reconciliation, hence of collaboration with Germany. Such a policy, however, if skillfully conducted, might achieve even more, for, given time and opportunity, French genius and French civilization would surely gain for France a position as the foremost partner in Germany's new European order. Laval was sufficiently vain—and blind—to believe he was the man who could successfully manipulate his country into that position.[57]

Whether Laval was actually prepared to take France into the war against Britain will never be known for certain. He was essentially a man of peace. The dominant motive in his policy of holding the line against Germany and appeasing Mussolini in Africa in the 1930s appears to have been to keep Germany weak and to retain Italy as an ally against Germany, a policy designed to preserve the *status quo* and therewith the peace of Europe. Even so, he might have taken France over the brink in pursuit of his ideal of collaborationist-reconciliation, just as he sacrificed Jews, French laborers, French economic assets, and with them honor and decency in a vain effort to satisfy the insatiable appetites of the Nazi conquerors. With the government of a Bismarck, even of a William II, his policy might have worked. In dealing with the government of a Hitler, his policy was not only dishonorable but futile.

Pierre Flandin, who succeeded Laval as the dominant influence in Vichy in December 1940, was willing to make the most far-reaching verbal promises of collaboration; but he used all his skill as a trained lawyer to avoid making concrete concessions to the Germans. The Germans responded to these tactics by making life even more unpleasant for French prisoners of war and by tightening controls at the line of demarcation. Pétain succumbed to this pressure. Within two months Flandin was dropped and Admiral Jean François Darlan was made vice-president of Vichy's Council of Ministers.[58]

Darlan was above all an opportunist. "We should not let ourselves be guided by sentiments, we should determine our conduct according only to France's interests," he said. While Germany was winning, or when German pressure was great enough, he was willing to collaborate. Indeed he went farther than any other Vichy minister along the road to actual military collaboration with the Germans in Africa. The prospect of a German victory did not alarm him unduly. "Even if Germany wins the present war," he told an American representative in Vichy in December 1940, "France will, given the strength and character of her people and German weaknesses, eventually be the dominating continental force." Shortly afterward he assured Admiral William D. Leahy, the newly appointed American ambassador, that the Nazi regime could not long survive the passing of Hitler and that the French people would then attain a position of great influence or actual control of the new Europe that would emerge after the war. As German difficulties grew in the autumn and winter of 1941–42, so did Darlan's resistance to their demands. German pressure brought about his removal in April 1942, and from that time to the end of the occupation the Vichy government was dominated by Laval.[59]

The Vichy leaders may have saved France from a government of extreme collaborationists who wanted active French participation in the war on the side of Germany; they may have spared the French people some of the extremes of suffering endured by non-German peoples in other parts of Europe. Whether these services to France and the French outweighed the services the Vichy government rendered the Germans in facilitating their rule and exploitation of France; whether they were worth the shame and dishonor which collaboration so often involved is another matter. The Vichy leaders attempted to sup with the devil, but their spoon was not nearly long enough.

While the Germans still expected the quick surrender or collapse of Britain, they did not follow any definite line in dealing with the Vichy regime. Hitler undoubtedly intended to use France and the French Empire as bargaining counters in peace negotiations with Britain. As long as he could get everything he thought he needed from France he saw no reason to commit himself in any way about his policies toward that country.

The defeat of the Luftwaffe in the summer of 1940 and the failure of German bombings to bring Britain to the conference table forced Hitler to consider other means of overcoming British resistance, and, like Napoleon, he began to consider the possibility of cutting Britain's supply lines in the Mediterranean.[60] Germany's Mediterranean plans, especially the project to block Britain's access to the Mediterranean by the capture of Gibraltar, suddenly made Spain a key factor in German calculations.[61] They also increased the importance of the Vichy government, which still controlled critical areas of North Africa, a navy, and a merchant fleet.

That Pétain was anything but the dupe or tool of the Germans was revealed the first time they tried to extract concessions from him which he was still in a position to withhold. On July 15, 1940, the Germans demanded eight airfields in the Casablanca area, the surrender of France's African weather stations, the use of the Tunis-Rabat railway, and the use of French merchant vessels to transport supplies across the Mediterranean. These demands were rejected by Pétain as being incompatible with the terms of the armistice. From his rejection the Germans got the impression that "the French want to derive from this the right to conduct separate negotiations on this question with the aim of transforming their position with relation to Germany to one of a negotiator with equal rights." [62] Whether or not this was Pétain's intention, he persisted in his refusal to give up bases in North Africa despite mounting German pressure.

In October Hitler decided to intervene personally. He proposed to confront Pétain and Franco directly in order to persuade or pressure them into agreeing to the passage of German troops through their territory, and if possible to secure their active co-operation in the war against England. A major problem in dealing with France and Spain was that France demanded concrete guarantees concerning its continental and colonial territories in exchange for any kind of co-operation, whereas Spain demanded the cession of substantial amounts of French territory as its price for entering the war. Then there was Mussolini, who was fearful that Hitler might attempt to buy French or Spanish support with territory already claimed by Italy as its share of the postwar spoils.[63]

Well aware of Italian fears, Hitler conferred with Mussolini before holding his talks with Pétain and Franco. At a conference at the Brenner Pass on October 4, he assured the Duce that Germany would never conclude peace with France without satisfying Italian claims. Italy was promised the area around Nice, Corsica, Tunis, and French Somaliland; Germany would take Alsace and Lorraine, the ore basins of Longwy and Briey, and territory that would improve its strategic border in the west. In Africa, Germany wanted bases in Agadir or Casablanca, the return of its former colonies, and a rounding out of German possessions in central Africa. Hitler hoped to compensate France at the expense of Britain, primarily in Nigeria.[64]

In the last week of October Hitler held what may have been the most important diplomatic conversations of the war: with Franco at Hendaye on the Franco-Spanish border on October 23; and with Pétain at Montoire on October 24. In both he expressed the desirability of European co-operation against Britain, "the enemy of the continent." In both he brought forward impressive statistics to demonstrate Germany's military might and prove the inevitability of a German victory. In both he warned of the dire consequences for Spain and France if they failed to join Germany in time. In dealing with the French, Hitler used the further argument that France should join in the war against England so that England, not France, would be forced to pay the cost of the war.[65]

Hitler employed all the eloquence that had succeeded so often in the past in overcoming the opposition of opponents; but his efforts in this case were a failure. Both Franco and Pétain procrastinated, and Hitler received none of the concessions he needed to carry out his Mediterranean projects.

An even greater blow, as it proved, was dealt Hitler at this time by his ally Mussolini who, on October 28, 1940, four days after the Montoire meeting, launched his ill-fated attack on Greece. The problems arising from this move, especially the possibility it afforded the British to establish bases in the southern Balkans and thus get within easy striking distance of the Rumanian oil fields, seriously alarmed the Germans, whose diplomatic and military projects in every sector were endangered by the Italian action.[66]

But the Germans had little reason to complain about Italian blunders. At the very time the Montoire talks were taking place, Hitler himself ordered the deportation of over five thousand German Jews from Baden and the Saar-Palatinate to unoccupied France without consulting or even informing the French government. And only a few days after Montoire Hitler agreed to the far more drastic proposal of Gauleiter Josef Bürckel, his civil governor for Lorraine, to deport one hundred thousand pro-French Lorrainers to unoccupied France. Meanwhile, between July and December 1940, about one hundred and five thousand Jews, Francophiles, and other "undesirable elements" were removed from Alsace to unoccupied France.[67]

Hitler was seemingly oblivious to the effect these actions would have on the French government and French public opinion. In reporting the results of his talks with Franco and Pétain to Mussolini, he expressed

217

complete confidence that German pressure and French fears would be enough to secure French co-operation. If France expected anything like a favorable peace, Hitler told the Italian leader, "she must first prove herself worthy of it by rendering special service, namely by making herself available for the fight against England." Hitler did not intend to ask France for direct military aid, but it should make bases available to the Luftwaffe and commit parts of its fleet, above all submarines based in North African ports, against the English. With France in the anti-English camp, French West and North Africa would be secured, new bases against England acquired, and Gibraltar could be taken with a very small force. The other end of the Mediterranean, the Suez Canal, could be closed by German mines. Thus England would be excluded altogether from the Mediterranean area.[68]

Hitler formulated his ideas about France in a directive to the leaders of his armed forces on November 12. The aim of his policy toward France, he said, was to co-operate with that country in the manner most effective for the future conduct of the war against England. For the time being France would have to tolerate German military measures in territories under its sovereignty, while the chief task of the French themselves would be the defense of their African possessions against England and the de Gaulle movement, a task Hitler hoped might eventually draw France into full participation in the war against England.[69]

In view of the importance of French co-operation for the German war effort and the fact that plans for action in the Mediterranean were taking final shape, it is impossible to understand Hitler's failure to make dramatic concessions to the French at this critical time or to take every precaution to avoid offending French sensibilities. Important military talks were scheduled in December with Laval, the vice-president of the Vichy Council of Ministers and minister of foreign affairs, talks made all the more important by Hitler's decision in November to seek Franco's permission to deploy German troops in Spain for an attack on Gibraltar.[70] As Hitler himself was repeatedly stressing at this time, such a campaign would have been enormously facilitated by the co-operation of the Vichy government. Yet throughout the autumn and winter of 1940 the expulsion of the French population from Alsace and Lorraine went on. Various absurdly petty concessions to the French were proposed, but none was ever actually made.[71] Hitler's only gesture toward France was the return of the ashes of Napoleon's son, the duke of Reichstadt, from Austria to France. But even this gesture was bungled, for Pétain was given only two days notice to attend the ceremony in Paris.[72]

Certainly Pétain was not mollified by German behavior. On December 13 he dismissed Laval, who was generally regarded as the most pro-German and collaborationist member of his cabinet. His motives for this action were many. Laval had achieved nothing substantial through his collaboration with the Germans; he was disliked and distrusted by French public opinion and by his colleagues; Pétain himself detested him. But the old marshal's basic reason for dismissing Laval at this particular time may very well have been his fear that Laval would make critical concessions to the Germans and involve France in an all-out policy of military collaboration.[73] Pétain was all the more unwilling to commit himself to such a course at this time because on December 6 he had received British assurances concerning the French colonial empire.[74] Meanwhile the policy of Laval was more than suspicious. His final words after a conference with high-level German military men at the Führer's headquarters on December 10 had been, "If you help us, we are ready to act, to act immediately." The Germans drew the conclusion that the French would now co-operate all the way.[75] Pétain, who had been informed of this and earlier discussions, presumably drew the same conclusion. Whether Laval, that devious, hardheaded peasant bargainer, actually meant what he said is another matter. In any case, he was given no further opportunity to attempt to cheat the Germans or anyone else.

It was a frustrating time for Hitler. On October 28 Mussolini had launched his campaign in Greece, thereby creating the prospect of Russian or British intervention in the Balkans. Early in November Hitler had long talks with Molotov, the Soviet commissar for foreign affairs, in which he attempted, without any success whatever, to secure a pledge of Russian disinterest in Finland and Southeastern Europe and to divert Russian attention instead to Persia and India.[76] On December 7 Franco turned down his request to permit the passage of German troops through Spain. Three days later, to prepare for any emergency, Hitler ordered his military leaders to draw up plans for the occupation of unoccupied France, the seizure of the French home fleet, and what was left of the French air force.[77] On December 13 Pétain dismissed Laval and subsequently evaded all German proposals for concessions and military collaboration in the Mediterranean area.[78]

Hitler was infuriated, not so much by the dismissal of Laval, whom he appears to have distrusted quite as much as did Pétain, but by France's refusal to co-operate further in the war against England. He therefore resolved to abandon his tactics of persuasion (lavieren). From now on he would state his demands plainly and show France that he had the power to enforce them. The armistice agreement gave Germany the right to demand everything it needed from France to continue the war against England. This pertained solely to unoccupied France, Hitler observed, for Germany was already taking everything it needed from occupied France.[79] German pressure produced the resignation of Flandin on February 9, 1941, and the appointment of Admiral Darlan as the new head of Pétain's Council of Ministers.

In the spring of 1941 the Germans again found themselves obliged to do some bargaining with the Vichy government. A coup d'état in Iraq at the beginning of April had brought to power the pro-Axis Rashid Ali Al-Gaylani, who promptly appealed to Germany for aid. The Germans were willing enough to provide such aid. They had long hoped to take

219

advantage of Arab anti-Semitism to bring the entire Arab world over to their side, a policy which if successful would have significantly improved their position in the Mediterranean. By giving effective support to Rashid Ali, they hoped they might entice other Arab leaders into the Axis camp, thereby facilitating their effort to gain control over such strategic points as the Suez Canal and enabling them to tap the oil resources of the Near East. Apart from sending supplies to Iraq by air, however, a costly and difficult operation, they could reach Iraq only via the French mandate of Syria, for Turkey was neutral and all other access routes to Iraq were controlled by the British.[80] The Germans therefore opened negotiations with Vichy to secure permission to send arms through Syria, or, better still, to persuade the French to release military supplies already in Syria for shipment to Iraq. On May 2 the Iraqi government declared war on Britain, bringing the problem to a crisis.[81]

Darlan was ready enough to bargain, especially since the Germans at last showed some willingness to make a few meaningful concessions. They agreed to allow the French to rearm seven French torpedo boats, to relax restrictions at the line of demarcation, and to negotiate a reduction of occupation costs. In return Darlan promised to permit the transport of arms across Syria, to permit German planes to land and refuel at Syrian bases, and to make available to Iraq French arms under Italian control in Syria as well as planes and bombs permitted to Syria under the armistice treaty. "These French concessions go considerably beyond what could have been expected on the German side," the German negotiators reported.[82]

Hitler, however, was not satisfied. All along he had been more concerned about getting supplies to the German armies in North Africa under the command of General Erwin Rommel than with shipments to Iraq, and for this purpose he needed concessions in France's North African territories. Above all he still hoped to secure France's actual involvement in the war on the side of Germany. This, at least, appears to have been his major object in summoning Darlan to Berchtesgaden on May 11. In response to Hitler's overtures, Darlan presented the usual French demand for German guarantees of French territory. These guarantees Hitler refused to give under the present circumstances; if France were to go to war against England, however, the points raised by Darlan would no longer present a problem. "Germany still needed a certain guarantee with respect to France. Not the least important reason for Laval's falling into disfavor [in France] was his policy of collaboration with Germany." Until France undertook some decisive action in order to confirm its policy toward Germany, Hitler saw no reason to confirm German policy toward France. France would be granted concessions and provided with guarantees to the extent that the French, for their part, made war against England easier for the Axis.[83]

What Hitler really wanted from France, Ribbentrop candidly told Mussolini in informing him of the Führer's talks with Darlan, was a maximum number of concessions "without binding himself in any way." [84] This purpose also must have been clear to Darlan. The French statesman was nevertheless generous with his professions of good will, and in subsequent negotiations with the Germans he actually agreed to many of the concessions demanded by Hitler. These included, in addition to previous concessions in Syria, an agreement to sell three-quarters of the entire stock of French military equipment in that country for shipment to Iraq, and to send military equipment and personnel from metropolitan France to Syria, presumably for future use against British forces in the Middle East. Even greater concessions were made with respect to North Africa. Germany was to be allowed to use French ports, preferably Toulon, for the shipment of supplies to North Africa, to charter French ships for this purpose, and to use the Tunesian harbor of Bizerte as an unloading port, while the French navy was to provide the convoy units required for transports of French ships from Toulon to Bizerte. France agreed further to sell to Germany a major part of the French arms and motor vehicles stock-piled in North Africa and to allow Germany to use French railways in North Africa for the transportation of military equipment. All these concessions were embodied in documents known as the Paris protocols, which were signed on May 27 and 28 by Darlan for the Vichy government and by General Walter Warlimont on behalf of the High Command of the Wehrmacht. [85]

The Germans were then dealt an unexpected blow. Pétain refused to ratify the Paris protocols, or rather he made their ratification dependent on conditions which he could be reasonably certain the Germans would not be prepared to accept. Whether blocking the treaty was Pétain's own policy, whether it was demanded of him by General Maxime Weygand, his delegate general in French Africa who had hurried to Vichy when he heard of the Darlan agreement, or whether Darlan himself had planned this maneuver from the beginning is impossible to determine. The only certain thing is that the Germans again found themselves thwarted. [86] In Iraq they were too late in any case. By May 31 Iraq resistance to Britain had ceased.

The German negotiators still hoped to exploit French concessions for the benefit of Rommel's forces in North Africa and, to secure the implementation of the Paris protocols, they attempted to meet Pétain's conditions. Even then, however, the French dragged their feet and in mid-June the German negotiators were obliged to report that virtually no progress had been made in their talks with the Vichy government. [87]

After the German attack on Russia on June 22, 1941, Hitler ordered the return to a policy of firmness in France. The French had evidently interpreted his attempts at negotiation as a sign of weakness, he told Otto Abetz in September, and he proposed to abandon these efforts. He had very little time to think about France in any case, since Russia was presenting so many difficulties that for the moment he was completely preoccupied. After the victory over Russia, which would come very soon, France would be compelled to align itself with the rest of Europe no matter what policy Germany pursued. But for Germany the French question would no longer be of much interest. "Germany would gain so much territory and so many raw materials in the east that she would not need France at all." [88]

The Russian campaign brought with it new unrest in France and a rapid growth of the French resistance movement. Hitler's response to these developments was to demand harsher measures in France and the execution of increasingly large numbers of French hostages for the murder of every German. The German military governor was instructed to take all steps necessary to preserve security "without regard for political considerations." [89]

In December 1941, with the breakdown of the German offensive in Russia, the retreat of Rommel's forces in North Africa, and the entry of the United States into the war, it was clear to all dispassionate observers that the chances of a German victory had sagged appreciably. The change in the military situation was reflected in the attitude of the French leaders. In that same month Göring initiated talks with Pétain and with General Alphonse-Pierre Juin, the commander in chief of French forces in North Africa, to secure greater French collaboration there. Again the French demanded concessions which the Germans refused to make and the negotiations broke down. [90] Goebbels summed up the situation in a diary entry for January 1942: "Our policies toward France have . . . just about failed." From an informant in France Goebbels had heard that Vichy desired neither a German nor a Bolshevik victory. Pétain, who was "absolutely vigorous in mind and body," was pursuing a policy of watchful waiting. "He would far prefer to have Germany and the Soviet Union grind each other to pieces and bleed each other white, thereby enabling France to resume the status of a great power, at least to a certain extent." [91]

The German position in France appeared to improve somewhat in April 1942 with the reinstatement of Laval in the Vichy government with all but absolute power. [92] Whether Laval, with all his talk of collaboration, actually conceded more to the Germans in the next two years than any French leader would have been compelled to do in the face of German pressure will never be known. In any case his appointment as virtual dictator of the Vichy government came too late for German purposes. Their great chance in the Mediterranean area in 1940 and 1941 had been missed. Rommel made a valiant effort to regain the initiative in North Africa in the spring of 1942, but he lacked fuel for his tanks and air support. His advance was halted at the beginning of July, in October came the German defeat at El Alamein, and by November the Axis forces in North Africa were in full retreat. [93] As a base for operations against Britain, the French African empire was permanently lost to Germany. On the night of November 7–8 United States forces landed in

North Africa. To protect their southern flank, the Germans occupied the rest of France on November 11, an operation which had been planned long in advance.[94] On November 23 Algeria, the last French overseas government recognizing the authority of the Vichy regime, renounced that authority. On November 26 the crews of the French fleet at Toulon scuttled their ships to prevent them falling into the hands of the Germans.[95]

The German occupation of previously unoccupied France was not intended to change the status of the Vichy regime, which the Germans still needed for the administration of the country.[96] Laval's authority was in fact increased by a constitutional act of November 18, which gave him the right to issue laws and decrees in his own name, thus conferring on him full legislative power.[97] The loss of the French Empire and the French fleet, however, stripped Vichy of most of its bargaining power. From then on, although Laval struggled and squirmed, the Vichy government was on the whole either an instrument of the German occupation or a hapless onlooker as the Germans implemented their own policies.

Total German Occupation

The German occupation of all of France (with the exception of an area in the southeast conceded to the Italians) did not make for any simplification of the German administration.[98] The authority of the military government was specifically excluded from the newly occupied territories, which were designated an operational zone and placed under the plenipotentiary authority of the supreme commander for the west (*Oberbefehlshaber West*), General Field Marshal Gerd von Rundstedt. Rundstedt in turn delegated administrative authority in this zone to a commander of the army area Southern France (*Kommandant des Heeresgebietes Südfrankreich*), General Heinrich Niehoff, who established his headquarters at Lyon. The only German administrative agency in France allowed to extend its operations to the newly occupied territories was the office of the senior SS and police officer. Thus, with the exception of that office, an entirely new German administration was established in Southern France.[99]

There followed the usual proliferation of German administrative agencies. Rundstedt appointed a plenipotentiary representative to the French government in Vichy, General Alexander von Neubronn, who promptly assembled a staff and set up his own office under his title as German general representing the supreme commander for the west in Vichy (*Deutscher General des Oberbefehlshabers West in Vichy*). In addition Rundstedt assembled a staff of his own to deal with political and administrative problems, the *Arbeitsstab Frankreich*. The headquarters of this office was in Paris, even though Paris was also the capital of the German military government of previously occupied France which already had a complete administrative apparatus at its disposal. Not to be outdone, the head of the administration for southern France, General Niehoff, also assembled a full-fledged administrative staff and set up liaison offices in the capitals of all French prefectures in the area under his jurisdiction. Besides these new military offices, there were the offices of the plethora of other government, party, and private agencies with interests in France, the largest being those of the Sauckel and Speer organizations. This host of new offices now had to be co-ordinated with the maze of offices already existing in France. The total result, in the words of a German historian, was "an almost impenetrable chaos of competencies." [100]

With the surrender of Italy on September 8, 1943, the Germans assumed responsibility for those territories of France previously occupied by the Italians. In this case no new administration was created. The territory was placed under the authority of the commander of the army area Southern France, who established liaison offices in the prefectures of this region as in the other areas under his command. Corsica, which the Germans had turned over to Italian administration after November 1942, was also placed under a German occupation administration, but was abandoned after less than a month because French guerrilla activity and the German lack of sea power made it impossible for the Germans to hold the island. [101]

The most immediate consequences of Germany's total occupation of France were intensified economic exploitation, harsher security and reprisal measures, and an extension of the campaign against the Jews. No German measures, however, directly affected so much of the French population as did their program for the recruitment of French labor.

In the spring of 1942 there were about one hundred and seventy thousand Frenchmen working for the German army in France, another two hundred and seventy-five thousand were employed on the construction of fortifications such as the Atlantic wall, while four hundred thousand were employed in French armaments industries which were working primarily in the German interest. There were still well over one million French prisoners of war in Germany, most of them working in war industries or agriculture. As of May 1942 almost one hundred and eighty-five thousand Frenchmen had volunteered for work in Germany. [102]

With Sauckel's appointment as plenipotentiary for labor in March 1942, the Germans sharply stepped up their requirements. Sauckel appeared in Paris in May with a demand that another quarter of a million French workers be recruited for work in Germany. The head of the German military government, General Karl von Stülpnagel, saw little chance that so many laborers could be recruited through voluntary enlistment; he warned that the introduction of compulsory labor would lead to dangerous popular unrest as well as awkward complications with the Vichy government. Sauckel, however, by allowing Vichy to believe that this would be the last German demand for French labor, persuaded the Vichy leaders to allow German recruiting in unoccupied France, where there was still a good deal of unemployment. Further, he persuaded Laval to co-operate actively with the recruitment program by promising the release of a French prisoner of war for every laborer sent to Germany. Although the Germans reduced the number of releases requested by Laval by one-third, Laval nevertheless supported their recruiting efforts, and by the end of the year they had almost met the goal set by Sauckel with the recruitment of two hundred and forty thousand French laborers.[103]

As so often in the case of the Nazis' "last" demands, the 1942 quota of a quarter of a million workers proved to be anything but final. Following their catastrophic defeat at Stalingrad and the loss of their forces in North Africa in late 1942 and early 1943, the Germans began inducting an ever-larger proportion of German workers into their armed forces, with the result that there was a new demand for foreign workers. Sauckel's program for the first three months of 1943 called for the recruitment of over one million foreign workers, and France was expected to supply one-quarter of this number. Although the Germans now occupied the whole of France, Sauckel again found it necessary to secure the co-operation of the Vichy government. Laval, who felt he had been duped by Sauckel's previous assurances, was not at all eager to please, and Sauckel complained angrily that Laval's ministry consisted exclusively of "artists in evasion." Under heavy German pressure Laval once again agreed to co-operate if French prisoners of war were released in exchange for laborers sent to Germany; once again he had to be satisfied with a ratio of one to three.[104]

By now it was evident that voluntary recruitment would no longer produce the number of workers demanded by Sauckel. On February 16, 1943, the Germans compelled the Vichy government to introduce a compulsory labor service law, with which German and French recruiters were once again able to meet Sauckel's quota. By March 31 another 250,259 French workers had been sent to Germany.[105]

Sauckel immediately set a new quota of 250,000 workers to be met by July 31, 1943; with the even more stringent provisions in the compulsory labor legislation, the recruitment program bogged down. As of July 31 only 156,246 workers had been recruited. Failure only led to a further increase in Sauckel's quota for France, which was now set at 100,000 workers a month.[106]

By this time labor recruitment had taken the form of gigantic round-ups of men, which were carried out by the German and French police forces—the head of the German military government refused to allow troops of the regular army to take part in these actions. Still Sauckel's quotas were not met. As in other occupied territories, men drafted for labor in Germany went into hiding, joined the underground resistance, or fled abroad, where many of them joined the armies of General de

Gaulle. It was labor recruitment more than any other single factor that turned the French resistance into something of a popular mass movement. After September 1943, instead of the one hundred thousand men a month demanded by Sauckel, Germany received an average of about five thousand.[107]

But the major reason for this dramatic drop in recruitment figures was not the flight of the French workers or even the changed attitude of the Laval government, which, confronted with constant new demands and given almost no concessions in return, virtually abandoned all co-operation with German recruitment authorities. Instead, the drop appears to have been due primarily to an agreement concluded in September 1943 between Albert Speer, the German minister of armaments and munitions, and Jean Bichelonne, Vichy's minister for industrial production, which provided that French industries were to assume greater responsibility for war production and that French workers employed in those industries would be exempt from recruitment for labor in Germany. This agreement brought labor recruitment in France to a sudden and almost complete halt, and led to a vicious altercation between Speer and Sauckel. On this question Hitler gave his support to Speer, while at the same time he demanded that Sauckel supply at least four million additional foreign workers for Germany in the course of 1944.

Sauckel did his best, but by August 1944 he had succeeded in recruiting only about fifty thousand workers in France, at which time the advance of the Allied armies put an end to his activities altogether.[108]

Hard as was the lot of the ordinary Frenchman under German occupation, the chief sufferers from German rule in France, as in all other occupied countries, were the Jews. There were about two hundred and seventy thousand Jews in France at the time of the German invasion, and approximately two hundred thousand of these lived in Paris. Many of the Jews in France were refugees who had left Germany after the Nazi seizure of power. An estimated forty thousand Jewish refugees fled to France after the invasion of the Low Countries in May 1940; in June some fifty thousand Jews fled from occupied to unoccupied France.[109] The Jewish population of unoccupied France was increased further when in October 1940 the Germans removed sixty-five hundred Jews from Baden and the Palatinate and unceremoniously dumped them in unoccupied France without informing or seeking the permission of the French authorities. This action was ordered by Hitler and was carried out, as the authorities in charge of the operation noted with some satisfaction, "without incident and almost unnoticed by the general public." [110]

During the first weeks of the occupation, the German military government in France arrested large numbers of Jews, for the most part refugees from Germany, for reasons of security. But otherwise the military government did nothing about the Jewish question. The initiative for further action against the Jews came from Otto Abetz and the Foreign Office—and from the French themselves.[111]

On August 20, 1940, Abetz requested Ribbentrop's approval to initiate an anti-Semitic campaign in occupied France "which might serve as a basis for the later removal of Jews from unoccupied France as well." All Jews were to be required to register and trustees were to be appointed for all Jewish economic enterprises whose owners had fled. Meanwhile Jews who had fled to the unoccupied zone were to be forbidden to return.[112] These proposals were approved by Ribbentrop and subsequently by Heydrich, but there was some fear that anti-Jewish measures might provoke an undesirable reaction in France because the necessary psychological preparations had not been made beforehand. On September 28 Abetz was instructed to proceed at once with the anti-Jewish program, but he was to do everything possible to arrange that anti-Jewish measures be carried out by the French authorities so they could be made to assume responsibility for them.[113]

The Germans soon found that they had no need to worry about psychological preparation. Although the documentary evidence makes it clear that the Vichy government's anti-Jewish legislation came as a result of German pressure, the Germans themselves were astonished by the virulence and extent of anti-Semitic sentiment that already existed in France. French anti-Semitism, however, differed significantly from the Nazi variety in that it was largely religious, political, or economic rather than racial. There was particular resentment against foreign and refugee Jews, whose presence was more obvious than that of native French Jews and who appear to have made many Frenchmen aware of a "Jewish problem." [114]

As early as July 22, 1940, the Vichy government ordered a revision of the naturalization of Jews who had acquired French citizenship since the promulgation of the nationality law of August 10, 1927. A Vichy law of August 27 abrogated the existing French law curbing anti-Semitic excesses of the press. Another Vichy law of October 3 defined the term *Jew* and excluded Jews from a variety of public and professional functions. On the following day an edict was issued permitting French prefects to intern foreign Jews. On the strength of this edict over forty thousand foreign Jews were interned by French authorities in unoccupied France by February 1941. In May and again in August 1941 the French police undertook further roundups of foreign male Jews in occupied France which produced 7,443 victims.[115]

Germany's anti-Semitic legislation in France also came as the result of pressure, in this case the pressure of Nazi authorities on the German military government. On September 27, 1940, the military governor issued a decree which corresponded almost exactly to the original anti-Semitic proposals submitted by Abetz to Ribbentrop. Jews who had fled from the occupied to the unoccupied zone were forbidden to return, all Jews who remained in the occupied zone were required to register and were no longer allowed to move from their present places of residence, all Jewish economic enterprises were to be designated as such. These regulations were supplemented by a decree of October 18 requiring the registration of all Jewish economic enterprises and authorizing the appointment of "administrative trustees" in all enterprises of any importance. A further German decree of April 26, 1941, was designed to remove Jews from all positions of influence in the French economy.[116]

Meanwhile Himmler's Jewish bureau in France under the direction of SS Obersturmführer Theodor Dannecker was preparing a file listing the name, residence, occupation, and nationality of all Jews living in France. Dannecker who, as the deputy of Adolf Eichmann, was to be responsible for the roundup and evacuation of all French Jews, took considerable pride in this file and the part it was to play in carrying out the final solution of the Jewish problem.[117]

Early in 1941, at the suggestion of Dannecker's office, the German embassy in Paris impressed on the Vichy government the desirability of creating a special French department for Jewish affairs. A French Jewish commissariat was duly set up on March 29 headed by the notorious French anti-Semite Xavier Vallet. The purpose of the new organization was to supervise the execution of Jewish laws already passed by the French government, to co-ordinate the French and German laws, and to propose new anti-Semitic legislation. From this time increasingly severe economic restrictions were imposed on Jews by the French government, culminating in a decree of July 22, 1941, which was intended to bring all Jewish economic assets under government control.[118]

A Vichy law of November 29, 1941, ordered the dissolution of all Jewish organizations, whose property was to be turned over to a new organization, the *Union générale des Israélites de France*, which was to serve as the Jewish Council, or Judenrat, for France. A census of Jews was undertaken shortly afterward, presumably to correct or supplement the list prepared by Dannecker's office. On December 12, 1941, Vichy issued a communiqué permitting the internment of all foreign Jews who had entered France since January 1, 1936.[119]

Up to this point Xavier Vallat appears to have co-operated with the Germans readily enough. He was prepared to eliminate Jewish political and economic influence and even to intern or deport foreign Jews, even though he was given fairly clear ideas of their future fate in Germany and Eastern Europe. Vallat objected, however, to the deportation of baptized French Jews, Jewish war veterans, or other Jews who could be considered assimilated into French national life. He refused to issue a decree requiring Jews in unoccupied France to wear a Jewish star. So recalcitrant did he become that Abetz brought pressure on the Vichy government to secure his dismissal. He was succeeded on May 6, 1942, by Louis Darquier de Pellepoix, an obscure official who had no scruples about co-operating with the Germans all the way on the Jewish question. So satisfied were the Germans with Darquier's attitude that at the end of June 1942 they demanded that he be given complete freedom of action in both the occupied and unoccupied zones to implement the anti-Semitic legislation already in effect.[120]

It was Laval who now fought a delaying action on behalf of the French Jews. He agreed to assist in the extradition of foreign Jews from unoccupied France, but only if the Germans would promise not to deport French Jews from the occupied zone. The Germans agreed to this condition, but they also made it clear to Laval that their ultimate intention was the removal of all Jews from France and that once all foreign Jews had been deported it would be the turn of the French Jews.[121]

Throughout the occupation the Germans purposefully sought to make the French government bear the brunt of the anti-Semitic campaign in France. In this they were more successful than they had believed possible, and they repeatedly expressed their surprise and satisfaction at the extent of French co-operation. After 1941, however, they found it necessary to increase significantly the size of their own anti-Jewish staff, in large part because their objectives concerning the Jews in France had broadened. Until May 1941 Jews were still permitted, even encouraged, to leave Europe. This policy was changed by a directive of May 20, 1941, from Walter Schellenberg, chief of the counterintelligence branch of the Central Office for Reich Security (RSHA), to the top German authorities in Belgium and France and to all senior police officials. "In view of the undoubtedly coming final solution of the Jewish question," the directive stated, "the emigration of Jews from France and Belgium is to be prohibited." [122]

Instructions to begin preparations for the final solution arrived soon afterward. In France this task was entrusted by Hitler to the Jewish section of Himmler's police organizations, which was still under the direction of Dannecker. It was Dannecker's office, operating in conjunction with Abetz and the German Embassy in Paris, which did most to bring pressure on the Vichy government to carry out Germany's anti-Jewish program.[123]

Despite Vallat's dismissal and his replacement by the more co-operative Darquier de Pellepoix, Dannecker was in no way satisfied with the progress of the final solution in France. At a conference with Adolf Eichmann in Berlin in March 1942 he urged the need to propose "something really positive to the French government, such as the deportation of several thousand Jews." Eichmann acted on this proposal by ordering the immediate deportation of six thousand Jews from France. This was only a preliminary measure, however. At another Eichmann conference on June 11 the decision was made to begin the deportation of Jews from Western Europe on a massive scale. Dannecker originally understood that one hundred thousand Jews from France would be involved, but Eichmann later fixed the first French quota at forty thousand.[124]

On June 26 Dannecker issued policy guidelines for carrying out these evacuation orders. All able-bodied Jews of both sexes between the ages of sixteen and forty-five were to be rounded up except partners in mixed marriages and citizens of certain countries Germany did not wish to offend. The next day he demanded the deportation of fifty thousand Jews from the unoccupied zone to the east as soon as possible. The German Embassy was instructed to ask Laval to deliver the required number and a conference was held among German officials concerned with the Jewish question to settle details about transportation.[125]

The German forces in the anti-Jewish campaign had meanwhile been strengthened by the appointment in April 1942 of Karl Oberg as senior SS and police officer in France with full authority over all German and French police. Oberg at once asserted his authority in the Jewish office by ousting Dannecker and replacing him by Heinz Röthke, an appointee of his own.[126]

Under Oberg's leadership large-scale roundups of Jews in both occupied and unoccupied France took place in the summer of 1942 with the collaboration of the French police. Statistics on the results of these actions vary widely, but by November 11, 1942, when the Germans occupied all of France, they had, according to their own figures, deported 41,911 Jews from occupied France. Well over 10,000 Jews, many of them refugees, had been delivered to them from unoccupied France.[127]

After the occupation of the whole of France in November 1942, the Germans were able to bring direct pressure to bear on French officials throughout the country to secure their co-operation in the roundup of Jews. In December Hitler ordered the arrest and deportation of all Jews and other enemies of Germany in France, an action he estimated would involve some six to seven hundred thousand Jews (a grossly exaggerated figure based on statistics supplied by Heydrich). This was only to be done after discussion with Laval, however.[128]

The roundup and deportation of Jews continued throughout the remaining years of the German occupation. But the number of deportees never came close to the figure mentioned by Hitler, and it fell far short of the relatively more modest expectations of German officials directly in charge of the operation. It has been estimated that of the well over three hundred thousand Jews, including refugees, in France at the beginning of the German occupation, only about sixty-five thousand—a horrible enough figure—were actually deported, mostly refugees.[129]

There were many reasons for the comparative success of French Jews in evading deportation. Much of the French population showed great courage in helping Jews, especially French Jews, to escape detection by German or French officials. Credit has also been given to Laval, by his critics and defenders alike, for employing delaying tactics which certainly saved the lives of many French-born Jews. Less attention has been paid to the role of the German army leaders in France in saving Jewish lives. The first German military governor, General Otto von Stülpnagel, signed anti-Jewish decrees and arrested Jews for reasons of security. But he avoided participation in the roundup of Jews and attempted to resist their deportation. Far more courageous was the position of his successor, the bitterly anti-Nazi General Karl Heinrich von Stülpnagel, who positively refused to have anything to do with the campaign againt the Jews, despite mounting pressure by Nazi officials. On July 21, 1943, the head of the German Jewish bureau in Paris reported to his superiors that Stülpnagel would not allow military units to assist in the roundup of Jews. The Jewish office was therefore obliged to depend exclusively on the German police forces in France, on the French police, and on a French militia, which was created in 1944 to aid in maintaining security and carrying out the Jewish program.[130]

The activity of those heroic French who gave asylum to Jews, the procrastination of Pierre Laval, and the conduct of German military leaders would all have been of no avail had Germany won the war, however. In France, as everywhere else in Europe, the ultimate intention of the Nazis was to eliminate the Jews altogether.

Allied forces landed in Normandy on June 6, 1944. A fortnight later the unsuccessful attempt was made to assassinate Hitler and overthrow the Nazi regime, a plot in which the head of the German military government in France, General Karl Heinrich von Stülpnagel, was irretrievably implicated. To the surprise and consternation of Himmler, Hitler did not take this opportunity to abolish the military government in France, but simply replaced Stülpnagel by another military commander, General Karl Kritzinger.[131]

By this time, however, there was no longer any opportunity to introduce significant changes in the organization or policy of the German occupation government. On August 1 the German defensive barrier around Normandy was broken. Six weeks later the Germans had evacuated almost all French territory, a retreat as rapid as had been their conquest of France four years earlier.

Alsace and Lorraine

In *Mein Kampf* and other works he had written before coming to power, Hitler had hardly mentioned Alsace and Lorraine; in fact, after 1933 he had steadfastly proclaimed his lack of interest in the two provinces. Nevertheless it became clear almost immediately after the German conquest of France that these areas were to be annexed to Germany.

Contrary to the provisions of the armistice agreement with France, the French government was deprived of all authority over the provinces. Moreover, like the departments Nord and Pas de Calais, they were removed from the authority of the German military government in France as well. Instead their administration was entrusted to two German civilian officials, Robert Wagner, Reichsstatthalter and Gauleiter of Baden, who was made head of the administration of Alsace and Josef Bürckel,

231

Reichsstatthalter and Gauleiter of the Saar-Palatinate, who assumed the same position in Lorraine. Thus the provinces were separated administratively not only from France but from each other.[132]

Both Wagner and Bürckel were among the earliest followers of Hitler. Wagner, an officer in the First World War, had taken part in the Munich Putsch and had shared Hitler's imprisonment in Landsberg am Lech. But it was the appointment of Bürckel in Lorraine that gave rise to the greatest misgivings among pro-French observers of Nazi policy, for Bürckel by now had a reputation as something of a specialist in annexation questions. He had been the Nazi party's plenipotentiary during the 1935 plebiscite in the Saar, which was subsequently annexed to his Gau. In 1938 he had supervised the plebiscite in Austria that had resulted in an overwhelming vote in favor of Anschluss to Germany, and shortly afterward he had been appointed Reichskommissar for the reunion of Austria with the German Reich.[133] Was he now to be given a similar assignment in Lorraine, apprehensive Frenchmen wondered? He was.

In mid-June 1940, before the armistice with France had been signed, Hitler summoned Wagner and Bürckel to his headquarters and informed them that Alsace and Lorraine no longer constituted a territorial problem. They were coming back to Germany and it would be the duty of the heads of the civil administration to win over the local population to National Socialism within ten years.[134] Hitler reinforced this order with intructions to his minister of finance that Alsace and Lorraine were to be restored to the German *Volk* in the shortest possible time and that the heads of the civil administration should not be hampered in this task because of inadequate funds.[135]

Wagner and Bürckel received their official appointments as heads of the civilian administrations on August 2, 1940. They were made directly responsible to Hitler, from whom they were to receive all orders for specific as well as general policies. The safeguarding of military security remained the task of the commander in chief of the army. The Reich Ministry of the Interior was to act as a co-ordinating agency between civilian, military, and central Reich authorities.[136]

The process of carrying out Hitler's orders to restore Alsace and Lorraine to Germany in the shortest possible time began at once. The administration of the provinces was thoroughly overhauled. After careful screening by the Germans, most of the rank and file administrative personnel were allowed to keep their jobs; but all leading French officials, including the prefects and mayors and all officials suspected of political unreliability, were dismissed or forbidden to return. They were replaced by German functionaries, many of them members of the regular administrative staffs of Germany's Gauleiter-governors.[137] So closely were the administrations of the conquered provinces and the adjoining German Gaus co-ordinated that Wagner soon gave up all pretense of maintaining Alsace's independent status and openly attached the party administration of Alsace to that of Baden. Baden and Alsace together were to be called the Gau Oberrhein, and their capital was to be at Strasbourg. Bürckel did the same for Lorraine and the Saar-Palatinate, which were to called the Gau Westmark after the frontier marches set up by Charlemagne, with their capital at Saarbrücken.[138] This party administrative amalgamation did not mean that Alsace and Lorraine were officially annexed to the Reich, for such a measure would have been an excessively flagrant violation of the armistice agreement with France. As it was, the French armistice delegation could only protest against this "disguised annexation." [139]

On July 4, 1940, State Secretary Wilhelm Stuckart of the Reich Ministry of the Interior proposed that the customs boundary of 1871 be restored, but that special steps be taken to keep up wages and prices in Alsace and Lorraine. Hans Lammers and Wilhelm Keitel agreed, recommending only that the necessary measures not be made public or the object of special legislation; the facts should be allowed to speak for themselves. The regulations re-establishing the German customs boundary of 1871 went into effect July 24. The German economic representative on the Armistice Commission was instructed not to discuss these measures with the French nor to reply to official French inquiries because "this could lead to superfluous discussions which would also be undesirable if they should be made public." [140]

The Germans soon gave up any attempt to conceal their Germanization and annexation policies in Alsace and Lorraine. After the official appointment of Wagner and Bürckel in August 1940, all German ordinances were published in the official legal bulletins for Alsace and Lorraine which were available to all members of the population.[141] Germanization measures were introduced at different times in the two provinces, but in all other respects the policies pursued by the German authorities were the same.

Laws on the "reintroduction of the mother tongue" made German the sole official language in Alsace and Lorraine. The names of all persons had to be Germanized, as did the names of all towns, streets, rivers, and so forth. All publications were to be in German. Signs on shops, inscriptions on buildings, even inscriptions on tombstones had to be rendered into German.[142]

Not only the language but the forms of all public activity were Germanized. German proceedings were introduced in state and municipal government and in the law courts. Legal judgments were to be handed down "in the name of the people," in the German manner. Gradually German laws, including racial legislation, were introduced, until by 1943 the entire legal system in both provinces had been reconstituted along German lines.[143]

A law of February 1941 defined the official terminology to be applied to a citizen of Alsace, Lorraine, or Luxembourg. He was no longer to be classified as a foreigner or member of an enemy state, but should be described in official documents as Racial German, Lorrainer (or Alsatian, or Luxembourger). In Alsace there was even an attempt to Germanize his appearance. The Basque berets, hitherto the headgear of most peasants and workmen and evidently regarded by the Germans as a sign of Gallicism, were forbidden.[144]

Special importance was attached to the Germanization of education, which was placed directly under the control and supervision of the political authorities. German was made the sole language of instruction; only National Socialist textbooks could be used. Teachers were rigorously screened to determine their racial and political suitability. Non-Germanic, clerical, and politically unreliable teachers were dismissed. The school system was remodeled along German lines; all private schools, clubs, and camps were closed. Attendance at elementary schools, and later at higher schools, trade schools, or their equivalents, was made compulsory for all children of Germanic blood. The German education law for Lorraine stated quite bluntly that its purpose was the training of youth in the spirit of National Socialism, and it enjoined school directors to operate their schools according to National Socialist principles.[145]

The economy of the provinces, too, was Germanized. In July 1940 Alsace and Lorraine had been reincorporated in the German customs area. At about the same time the railways were integrated into the German system, as were later the public utilities, the post, telegraph, and telephone offices. German was made the sole language of the economy. All business transactions and communications, all account books and registers, all advertising and public announcements had to be in German. German economic legislation, the German taxation system, German currency regulations were imposed on the provinces, as were Nazi agencies for the supervision and control of industry, agriculture, and labor. In March 1941 the French franc and all occupation currency used heretofore were called in and the German Reichsmark became sole legal tender. German authorities undertook the confiscation of property of "enemies of the Reich and the German people," a group that included the citizens of most enemy countries, Alsatians and Lorrainers who had persisted in their allegiance to France, Jews, and other non-Germanic peoples. Written into the legislation was the provision that much of this confiscated property was to be used to further projects for the resettlement of Germans on the lands vacated by these "enemies of the Reich." [146]

The Germans were at all times anxious to persuade racially suitable young citizens of Alsace and Lorraine to join their organizations. As voluntary enlistments did not progress satisfactorily, they soon made membership compulsory. In the spring of 1941 service in the Reich Labor Service, the Arbeitsdienst, was made compulsory for men and women between the ages of seventeen and twenty-five. A decree of the following year required that all boys join the Hitler Youth. This was followed by the introduction of compulsory military service for ethnic Germans in August 1942.[147]

Compulsory military service opened the way to granting Reich citizenship to all Alsatians and Lorrainers who served in the German armed forces, or who had otherwise demonstrated their loyalty to Germany. At the same time a majority of other ethnic Germans in the provinces were given the status of provisional German citizens.[148]

By 1942 everything had been done that legislation could achieve to incorporate Alsace and Lorraine into the German Reich, except the actual promulgation of decrees providing for their outright annexation to Germany. But the Nazis were not satisfied. What laws could do, laws could just as easily undo. The provinces had to be made German once and for all, and this could only be accomplished by the complete and thorough Germanization of their populations. Hitler recalled the inadequacy of the legislative efforts of the imperial German government after 1871. Far more effective in his opinion had been the policies adopted by the French after 1918. In de-Germanizing the provinces they had brutally thrust French customs and culture down the throats of the inhabitants. Hitler proposed to act in the same way, but to be even more ruthless. "If we want to make these into authentic German provinces," he said, "then we must drive out all those who do not voluntarily accept the fact that they are Germans." [149]

Wagner and Bürckel immediately began to carry out Hitler's instructions to rid Alsace and Lorraine of non-Germanic and hostile elements. Between July and December 1940 about one hundred five thousand Jews, Francophiles, and other undesirable persons were expelled from Alsace to unoccupied France or prevented from returning. Bürckel launched a similar campaign in Lorraine. There were, however, important differences between the principles of evacuation adopted in the two provinces. While in Alsace every effort was made to keep racially valuable persons if they could be tolerated at all politically, in Lorraine Bürckel had ordered the evacuation of one hundred thousand pro-French Lorrainers to unoccupied France regardless of their racial quality.[150]

Although Hitler himself had agreed to Bürckel's evacuation procedures, Himmler had serious reservations about this indiscriminate expulsion of pro-French elements from Lorraine. A fundamental aspect of Himmler's program was to regain all racially valuable persons for the Reich and, under no circumstances, to permit the escape of racially superior blood types who might some day lead an inferior people against their own race, as Germanic leaders in France and Eastern Europe had done for centuries. Himmler's policy for France, as for Eastern Europe, was to deprive these ancient enemies of Germany of German blood. France, like the Government General, was to be used as a dumping ground for racially undesirable persons. Instead of evacuating pro-

French persons indiscriminately to France, Himmler insisted that these people should be screened with the utmost care to make certain that no Germanic types were lost or given gratuitously to France. This same procedure should some day be applied to the whole of France, where the entire population should be subjected to rigid racial examinations. All Germanic types should then be brought to Germany.[151]

Himmler laid down the usual guidelines to be used in determining racial suitability. Physical fitness, documents of origin, and political record were all to be taken into account; but the ultimate criterion was that "anyone is to be acknowledged as a German who, in the light of all facts on which decisions are based, appears to be a desirable addition to the German Reich." [152]

Himmler also provided guidelines for future resettlement programs. Politically reliable citizens of Alsace and Lorraine who were also racially suitable might be left in the provinces. Racially desirable but politically unreliable persons, not only from Alsace and Lorraine but from any part of France, were to be resettled in the Reich or Eastern Europe. Racially undesirable persons were to be evacuated to France. To take the place of persons who had been evacuated, Germans from the Reich or Eastern Europe would be settled in Alsace and Lorraine and any other areas of France that were to be incorporated in the Reich. Himmler hoped that Germans resettled either in Eastern Europe or former French provinces would be politically reliable; but he also calculated that persons settled in these border areas, always face to face with a hostile population, would be forced to play the part of loyal Germans or perish.[153]

In May 1941 Himmler issued two decrees for the repatriation of Germans from France. As a first step he planned to move about seventy-four thousand ethnic Germans from occupied France to the Reich. This group would include many Alsatians and Lorrainers who had been deported so indiscriminately to France in 1940. At the same time he ordered the beginning of a large-scale resettlement program in Alsace and especially in Lorraine, whose large pro-French population was a matter of particular concern.[154]

Lorraine was also causing concern to its Gauleiter, who noted with pained surprise that the evacuation of "French-minded" Lorrainers in the autumn of 1940 had not resulted in a final pacification of the country. After consulting with high-ranking SS leaders, he decided to carry out further evacuations, especially of clergymen and intellectuals, but the decision as to where these persons were to be resettled was to be left up to Himmler.[155]

In September 1941 Bürckel and officials of Himmler's resettlement office were considering proposals to make the greater part of Lorraine a resettlement area for war veterans and other loyal Germans who could be counted on to guard this strategic border area for Germany. Plans included the building of new German cities and villages, a precise delimitation of fields and forests, and laws to regulate the entire resettlement procedure. The ideal ratio of German citizens (*Reichsdeutsche*) to ethnic Germans (*Volksdeutsche*) was put at sixty to forty by the SS director of the Lorraine resettlement program.[156]

While these plans were being made, actual resettlements were being carried out in Lorraine. On October 17, 1941, as the German armies were engaged in their desperate drive toward Moscow, a resettlement officer reported that one hundred forty thousand hectares of land in Lorraine had been confiscated and made available for German colonization within the past eleven days. In the course of the evacuation some seventy-seven thousand farm animals had perished because of inadequate care and feeding, but these losses were dismissed as "unavoidable." A graver problem was the difficulty in finding competent German farmers willing to move to Lorraine, especially since the resettlement office, which wanted to reserve this land for war veterans, refused to assign it to new settlers on a permanent basis. The lack of new settlers meant that some of the best land in Lorraine was not cultivated at all for long periods of time. Meanwhile the Lorrainers unfortunate enough to be selected for Germanization were herded onto Germany's already perilously overworked railways and sent to Eastern Europe, where for months and sometimes years they lived almost totally unproductive lives in Himmler's resettlement camps.[157]

Himmler's resettlement projects did not go uncriticized. There were sensible Germans, including members of Himmler's staff, who argued that resettlement projects should be undertaken after the war, if at all, but that manpower should under no circumstances be diverted from military tasks while the war continued. Such criticism did not deter Himmler, who went ahead with his projects, apparently confident that a proper application of racial principles would in itself ensure the triumph of German arms. Himmler was backed up by Hitler, who approved a major resettlement campaign in Alsace and Lorraine in August 1942. In Alsace, where no large-scale evacuations had taken place since December 1940, there was a second drive to remove racially undesirable elements. Jews, gypsies, Negroes, asocials (*Azosiale*), criminals, the mentally ill, "and all other trash which does not belong to us on the basis of blood" were to be expelled to France by order of the Führer. Politically unreliable persons of good blood were to be evacuated and resettled in Germany or Eastern Europe. At a resettlement conference on August 4, it was decided that the entire patois population of Alsace, that is, all people speaking French or a French dialect, should also be removed, but that this operation could be delayed until after the war.[158]

At the same time Hitler ordered the evacuation of an additional forty thousand persons from Lorraine. In this case too the racial "trash" was to be sent to France and the Germanic types to Germany and Eastern Europe.[159] Subsequent resistance on the part of Germanic Lorrainers provoked a decision from Himmler that all who refused to go to Germany and Eastern Europe and who persisted in their loyalty to France should be treated as Communist elements and sent at once to a concentration camp. The relatives of these "French-happy" individuals were to be resettled in the Government General, where their conduct would determine the fate of the concentration camp inmates.[160]

Even the head of Himmler's resettlement office, Ulrich Greifelt, balked at these orders. He pointed out that the evacuations would cause serious labor shortages in the provinces, that he lacked the manpower to carry them out effectively, that they would place additional burdens on Germany's already seriously overburdened transport system. "In these matters there is nothing that can be changed," Himmler replied. "This is a decision of the Führer." [161]

Practical difficulties proved stronger than the Führer's will, however. At a resettlement conference in October 1942 it was decided to restrict evacuations to racially undesirable and actively dangerous political elements. "The deportation of the indigenous population is to be postponed until after the war," the Resettlement Office reported. Hitler, however, wanted it clearly understood that this was merely a postponement. In May 1943 he informed Himmler that it was necessary to count on a future resettlement of a further two hundred to two hundred fifty thousand people from Alsace alone and a far larger number from Lorraine.[162]

Despite the decision for postponement, large numbers of persons in Alsace and Lorraine continued to be shifted about. Over 9,000 Lorrainers were scheduled for deportation in 1943. In January 1944 Gauleiter Robert Wagner reported that during the past year 3,549 Alsatians had been evacuated to the Reich, while 1,036 Alsatians and 84 Germans had been sent to education or concentration camps.[163]

In winning converts to the Germanic idea, Himmler's programs were as miserably unsuccessful in Alsace and Lorraine as in all other parts of Europe. His trusted lieutenant Gottlob Berger wrote a fitting epitaph for Nazi policies in Alsace in a letter to Himmler of June 21, 1944, after the Allied landings in Normandy: "The Alsatians are swine [*ein Sauvolk*]," he said. "They had already counted on the return of the French and the English, and were therefore particularly hostile and hateful when the retribution came. Reichsführer! I think we should deport half of them—anywhere. Stalin will undoubtedly be glad to have them." [164]

Of the territory under the administration of the German military government in France, Hitler left no doubt about his intentions with respect to the provinces of Alsace and Lorraine. At the very beginning of the German occupation he had given orders that these provinces were to be restored to Germany in the shortest possible time, and by 1942 all preparations had been made for their future incorporation into the Reich.

Equally clear was Hitler's intention to annex the area of the so-called Closed Zone, that broad strip of border territory from the mouth of the Somme to the lake of Geneva. For strategic purposes he also proposed to retain control over fortifications along the Atlantic coast. There was some talk among Nazi leaders about detaching Brittany from France and making it an independent state, but Hitler himself seems to have taken little interest in this project.

In speculating about the future of what was to be left of France in a Nazi-ordered world, a question that naturally arises is what Hitler's policies might have been if the Vichy government had co-operated more actively with Germany or had actually joined in the war on Germany's side. In commenting on this problem, Hitler had remarked in May of 1942 that, even if the French threw in their lot with the Axis, they must clearly understand that Germany intended to retain the strategic positions it now occupied along the Channel coast and that they must resign themselves to the idea of satisfying the territorial demands of Germany, Italy, and Spain in Europe and overseas.[165] In fact, all that Hitler appears to have been willing to concede to the French in return for their co-operation was an extension of French colonial territory in Central Africa at the expense of Britain, and presumably a guarantee of whatever territory remained to France in Europe after the demands of Germany, Italy, and Spain had been met.

After he had embarked on the conquest of Russia, Hitler stated that Germany would now acquire so much territory and so many resources in the east that in the future it would not need France at all. But this did not effect his plans for Alsace, Lorraine, the Closed Zone, and a large part of the French Atlantic coast. Further, as he told his associates in April 1942, Germany had legitimate claims to the former kingdom of Burgundy, which had been German territory from time immemorial and which the French had stolen in the period of Germany's weakness.[166]

What Hitler meant by the ancient kingdom of Burgundy and what territories he would have claimed under that title for purposes of annexation to Germany will never be known for certain. There is reason to wonder, however, whether Hitler would have allowed even a French rump state without Burgundy to exist indefinitely. Given Hitler's fear and hatred of France, combined with his insatiable greed, it seems probable that the Nazis would soon have begun to regard rump France, like rump Poland, as a desirable and necessary area for Germanic expansion and that this territory too would have been absorbed into the Germanic empire and subjected to a full-scale program of Germanization. As, by that time, a large proportion of the "Germanic" elements would have been removed from rump France already, the re-Germanization of this area would presumably have required its almost total resettlement.

CHAPTER 9

The Southeastern Flank

The countries of Southeastern Europe, like those of Scandinavia and the Low Countries, were not among Hitler's primary territorial or strategic objectives. He did, however, have vital economic interests in Southeastern Europe, above all in the Rumanian oil which was crucial to the German war economy, and a corresponding interest in preventing hostile powers from establishing their influence in this area. To safeguard the flow of the economic assets of Southeastern Europe to Germany and to exclude the influence of Germany's enemies, he pursued a policy designed to ensure Germany's own political as well as economic ascendancy in this region, and to prevent crises which might provide an excuse for other powers to intervene.[1]

In the years before the Second World War, but especially after Germany's victories over Poland and France, Hitler succeeded to a remarkable extent in gaining the ascendancy he desired by peaceful means. By the autumn of 1940, Hungary, Rumania, and Bulgaria had all been brought into the Nazi orbit; German troops had been granted rights of transit through Hungary and Bulgaria; and a large German force was stationed in Rumania to guard the oil fields in the German interest.

Hitler's campaign of peaceful political and economic conquest in Southeastern Europe was interrupted by Mussolini. Jealous of Hitler's successes and fearful that the Germans might deprive him of the preponderant influence in the Balkans which they had at one time promised him, the Italian dictator decided to take steps to ensure that influence. On October 28, 1940, he issued an ultimatum to Greece demanding that Italy be given strategic bases on Greek territory. Greece, backed up by a British guarantee, rejected the Italian demands, whereupon Mussolini launched an invasion of Greece from Italian bases in Albania. With that a situation was created which Hitler had hoped to avoid: the outbreak of war in the Balkans which offered an opportunity for Russian or British intervention. The threat which Russia posed to the Rumanian oil fields and other German economic interests in Southeastern Europe undoubtedly hastened Hitler's decision to attack the Soviet Union.[2] Hitler had little reason to fear the military power of Britain in the Balkans, but he did fear the establishment of British air bases in Greece from which the RAF might attack the Rumanian oil fields.

The Italian campaign against Greece was in trouble from the beginning. As early as November 12, 1940, Hitler gave orders to his army to make preparations to come to the aid of the Italians. At the same time he stepped up the pace of his negotiations with Yugoslavia, which had heretofore resisted closer political relations with Germany, to secure the co-operation or at least the neutrality of that country in case German military action against Greece should become necessary.

When, in December 1940, Hitler made his decision to attack the Soviet Union, the countries of Southeastern Europe assumed even greater importance for Germany, for these territories were then needed for the deployment of German troops and became vital avenues of strategic communication. Hitler also considered it essential to eliminate every possible threat on Germany's southeastern flank while the German armies were engaged in the conquest of Russia. Before the campaign against Russia could begin, therefore, he was resolved to knock out Greece, and with it the danger of British bombers operating from Greek air bases, and to make certain of the attitude of Yugoslavia.

By offering to guarantee the integrity of the Yugoslav state, as well as handsome extensions of Yugoslav territory at the expense of Greece, Hitler succeeded in persuading the Yugoslav government to join the alliance of Germany, Italy, and Japan (the Tripartite Pact) on March 25, 1941. Hardly had the Yugoslav representatives signed the pact, however, than their government was overthrown by a coup d'état. Convinced that the new Yugoslav government could not be trusted, Hitler decided that security in Southeastern Europe could only be achieved by force; thus he gave orders to his army to prepare for an invasion of Yugoslavia as well as Greece.

Operating from bases in Hungary, Rumania, and Bulgaria, the Germans launched their attack on Yugoslavia and Greece on April 6, 1941. By the end of that month all organized resistance to the Axis forces had been crushed and all of Southeastern Europe had come under Axis control.

Three Satellites

Hungary

Between 1938 and 1941 the Hungarians had been lured and coerced into the German camp, lured by promises of German support in regaining territory that had formerly been part of the kingdom of Hungary, coerced by the presence of overwhelming German power and the fear of being sold out to their Eastern European rivals.[3] In 1938 and 1939 Germany had secured large slices of Czechoslovak and Rumanian territory for Hungary; in return the Hungarians, in September 1939, had permitted the passage of German troops through their territory to enable the Germans to take over direct responsibility for the defense of the Rumanian oil fields. In April 1940, enticed by prospects of further territorial acquisitions, Hungary joined Germany in the attack on Yugoslavia. And in June 1941 Hungary joined in the German attack on the Soviet Union.[4]

Hungarian leaders did not participate with any enthusiasm in the war against the Soviet Union. They had no desire to dissipate their military strength in Russia, whose territories were not contiguous to Hungary and where they had little to expect by way of territorial gains. But they feared that failure to do so would give the Rumanians, who had also joined in the war against the Soviet Union, a critical advantage when the Germans made a final distribution of territory in Eastern Europe. Once the Hungarians were committed to war against the Soviet Union, the pressure of Germany, fear of their neighbors, and ultimately fear of Russian retribution and of Communism, kept Hungary in the war on Germany's side to the end.[5]

While participating in the war against Russia, the Hungarians did what they could to keep their military contribution to a minimum. When Admiral Miklós Horthy, the prince regent of Hungary, visited Hitler at his field headquarters in September 1941, accompanied by Prime Minister László Bárdossy and Field Marshal Ferenc Szombathelyi, the new chief of the Hungarian General Staff, the Germans were annoyed by the Hungarians' obvious reluctance to commit their forces to the Russian campaign. "The new chief of the General Staff takes the selfish view that what matters is to preserve Hungary's forces in consideration of her tasks in the Balkans," General Franz Halder remarked in his diary.[6] Under German pressure the Hungarians promised to increase the number of their troops on the eastern front, but in return the Germans were obliged to promise them a rectification of their Carpathian frontier in eastern Galicia (at this time part of the Government General). A German record of the conference with the Hungarians concluded by noting that "for the rest, the visit offered an opportunity for counteracting the strong influence exerted on Hungary by Anglo-American propaganda, which can normally be observed. In view of present and future successes of German arms we can at any event be sure of Hungary's continued co-operation with the Axis powers." [7]

While the successes of German arms continued, Hungary did indeed co-operate with the Axis. In November 1941 Hitler congratulated Bárdossy on the splendid services rendered by the Hungarian unit on the eastern front. "The Hungarians are good auxiliaries for us," he commented to his associates. "With proper stiffening, we find them very useful." [8]

On the economic front, too, the Hungarians were co-operating. "The Hungarian government has tried as far as possible to take account of German wishes in the economic field," an economic specialist of the German Foreign Office reported after negotiations in Budapest during the summer of 1941. In compliance with German requests, they had raised the value of the Reichsmark, provided a credit of two hundred million Reichsmarks for financing German purchases of strategic goods, and improved conditions for the activity of private German firms and German capital in Hungary. Fearful about losing their economic independence, the Hungarians tried to resist a German request to purchase controlling shares in Hungary's largest oil company, "Maort," which were owned by Americans. But Göring insisted that the Hungarians sell, and that all necessary pressure should be applied to make them do so. "The *Reichsmarschall* attached decisive importance to Germany's acquisition of 'Maort' because every oil deposit in Europe had to be utilized for German military purposes to the utmost limit of its capacity." The Hungarians procrastinated until at last Prime Minister Bárdossy himself assumed responsibility for complying with the German wishes "because he had become convinced that in the circumstances one could not act otherwise toward Germany, the ally to whom Hungary owed her large territorial expansion." For this service Bárdossy was given special thanks by Ribbentrop, who appealed to him to do everything in his power to increase deliveries to Germany, particularly oil. "The situation was such that relatively small quantities, such as an additional delivery of forty thousand tons, were of particular importance." [9]

With the halt of Germany's Russian offensive in December 1941, and especially after the German declaration of war on the United States, the Hungarians initiated efforts to loosen their ties with Germany. In March 1942 Horthy dismissed Bárdossy, the leading advocate of co-operation with Germany, and replaced him with the former minister of agriculture, Miklós Kállay. "His aim, as Premier, was to regain Hungary's freedom of action and to return, if possible, to a state of non-belligerence," Horthy wrote in his memoirs, "In the summer of 1942, our first contact was made with Great Britain." [10]

Hungary's nonbelligerence was evidently only intended to apply to major powers. In that same summer of 1942 Kállay went to see Hitler with a request from Horthy that he "should turn a benevolent blind eye if the Hungarians started a fight with the Rumanians." From the Hungarian point of view, Kállay said, such a fight would be part of the European struggle against Asia. Hitler at once put a stop to this idea, as he did to all Hungarian plans for territorial expansion that threatened the disruption of order in Eastern Europe. By this time his admiration for the fighting qualities of the Hungarians had declined sharply. "If the Hungarians go to war with the Rumanians," he said, "then, unless I am much mistaken, [Marshal Ion] Antonescu will knock the hell out of them!" [11]

Kállay's efforts to withdraw from the war were soon known to the Germans through intercepted telegrams and the reports of secret agents. "Fortunately we have never had any illusions about the Hungarians, so that now we are not disappointed," Goebbels remarked in his diary.[12] In mid-April 1943 Hitler summoned Horthy to Schloss Klessheim near Salzburg, where he confronted him with evidence of Kállay's duplicity and demanded his dismissal. Horthy defended his prime minister and his country's record as an ally, pointing out the considerable economic contribution Hungary was making to the joint war effort and appealing to Hitler to have faith in Hungary and its government.[13] Horthy's arguments can hardly have convinced Hitler, but the German leader was evidently too preoccupied with other problems to press matters in Hungary. For the time being he did no more than keep the country and its leadership under close observation.

With the surrender of Italy in September 1943, Hitler ordered that preparations be made for the occupation of Hungary and Rumania.[14] According to German intelligence reports, the governments of both countries were negotiating with the western Allies hoping to persuade the British and Americans to undertake a campaign in the Balkans which would liberate them from the Germans and at the same time protect them from the Russians. A Himmler agent considered the situation in Hungary to be particularly dangerous: The Hungarian government was now openly pro-West and German intervention imperative to prevent Hungary's defection. In any case, however, Germany could not tolerate that a regime based partly on "feudal concepts of individualism" and partly on "Jewish exploitation" should remain in the geographical center of its communications to the Balkans and the Near East.[15] A report Goebbels received from Hungary in November was also anything but encouraging. "Influential circles in Hungary are at work for a direct break with us," he wrote in his diary. "The Regent is trying to create the impression that he is neutral about these efforts. This is, however, in no way the case. I even regard him as the mainspring of this development. . . . If the English were to attempt an invasion of the Balkans, Hungary would be the first country to desert us. The Hungarians are also interested in keeping their army intact because they are still flirting with the idea of fighting the Rumanians." [16]

Unwilling to move against the present regime in Hungary without having another to put in its place, Hitler sent a special political agent to Budapest, Dr. Edmund Veesenmayer, who entered into negotiations with pro-German elements. Horthy, when he learned of Veesenmayer's activity through his own agents, demanded his expulsion from the country. But Veesenmayer had collected enough information to convince his government to take action, and in February 1944 Hitler issued orders for the military occupation of Hungary.[17]

To prepare the way politically for this move Hitler again summoned Horthy to Schloss Klessheim where, in a conference of March 18, he accused the Hungarian government of planning to make a separate peace. To forestall such treasonous behavior, he intended to occupy the country until a government acceptable to Germany had been formed. He assured Horthy that he had no intention of making Hungary a German province on the order of Bohemia, which after all had been part of Germany's Holy Roman Empire; but the best way the regent could safeguard Hungary's sovereignty and independence would be to name a government that would guarantee Hungary's loyalty to Germany. If Horthy dramatized his opposition to the German occupation by resigning or encouraged any kind of resistance, Hitler would feel justified in seeking the co-operation of Rumania, Croatia, and Slovakia. In Hungary itself he would install a government of the fanatic right-wing Arrow-Cross movement, Hungarian military units would be incorporated into the German army, and the Hungarian economy would be submitted to the ruthless exploitation of the occupation powers. On the other hand, if the regent remained at his post and did as the Germans requested, the German army of occupation would be withdrawn as soon as a government acceptable to Germany had been appointed.[18]

Horthy succumbed to this pressure. At a meeting of the Crown Council in Budapest on March 19, he expressed the conviction that if Hungary made any effort to resist, Hitler, with the aid of his Eastern European allies, would not only occupy Hungary but destroy the Hungarian race. To shield the people from this fate, he was resolved to remain at his post and to appoint a government dictated by Germany—in short, to provide the legal façade for the German occupation that Hitler desired.[19]

When German troops marched into Hungary on March 19, 1944, they met with no resistance. Horthy remained in office, and the entire government and administrative apparatus was placed at Germany's disposal.

On the day his troops entered Hungary, Hitler issued a decree that German interests were henceforth to be protected by a plenipotentiary of the Greater German Reich in Hungary, who would simultaneously bear the title of minister. To this post he appointed Dr. Edmund Veesenmayer, who had been expelled from Hungary two months earlier, and recalled the previous German minister to Hungary, Dietrich von Jagow. The Reich plenipotentiary was to be responsible for all political developments in Hungary; but his special task was to arrange the formation of a new national government "which will be resolved to fulfill loyally and until final victory is achieved the obligations imposed upon it by the Tripartite Pact." The Reich plenipotentiary was to advise this government on all important matters and to ensure the fullest use of all resources of the country for the joint conduct of the war. All German civilian offices were to be subordinated to the Reich plenipotentiary, who was to receive his directives through the Reich minister of foreign affairs. "To perform the tasks of the SS and police to be carried out by German agencies in Hungary, and especially police duties in connection with the Jewish problem, a senior SS and police officer will be appointed to the staff of the Reich plenipotentiary and will act in accordance with his directives." As long as German troops remained in Hungary, military sovereignty was to be exercised by the commander of those troops, who was immediately subordinated to the OKW and responsible for the internal military security of the country and its defense against threats from abroad.[20]

The seventy-six-year-old Horthy did what he could to hold the line against the Germans. The dismissal of Kállay was inevitable, but Horthy objected to Veesenmayer's suggestion of a government under the right-wing financier and former prime minister, Béla Imrédy. He declared that he could only tolerate a government of civil servants, either under Döme Sztójay, the Hungarian ambassador to Berlin, or Lajos Csatay, the minister of defense; any other solution would force him to violate his oath on the constitution and to the law. "His statements sound like a formula learned by heart," Veesenmayer reported to Berlin on March 20, "and I am afraid that he can hardly be convinced, let alone gained, for our cause." In the end Veesenmayer gave in to Horthy's objections, but the government of Sztójay that took office on March 23 was nevertheless far more to the taste of the Germans than that of the regent. It included Imrédy as minister of economics, and other right-wing elements, including two state secretaries in the ministry of the interior, László Endre and László Baky, both members of the Arrow-Cross movement, were placed in charge of the police and gendarmerie—and the Jewish question.[21]

The German occupation army in Hungary was accompanied by the usual civilian army of officials—policy makers; co-ordinators; advisers; the representatives of Speer, Sauckel, and Goebbels; the agents of private enterprise; and special task forces to liquidate the Jews. On March 31 Himmler appointed SS Obersturmbannführer and General of the Police Dr. Otto Winkelmann to the position of senior SS and police officer in Hungary. Unlike the situation in so many other occupied territories, Himmler's agent restricted himself to his police duties and left supreme political authority to the official who was supposed to exercise it, Reich Plenipotentiary Veesenmayer.[22]

Veesenmayer's basic policy was simple. He intended to secure Hungarian co-operation, opposing proposals to disarm the Hungarian army and other measures that might provoke the Hungarian government into denouncing its agreements with Germany or foster the development of passive resistance, in which the Hungarians were very skilled. Veesenmayer proposed instead to emphasize the importance of the common cause in which Hungary and Germany were engaged and the need to stand together to prevent the triumph of Bolshevism. On this basis he believed the Hungarians could be persuaded to accept all German demands—which he intended to augment steadily. Any danger from Hungarian troops could be eliminated by sending them to the Russian front; but to avoid all risks they should be sent out in small units and kept under constant German supervision.

Ribbentrop and other Nazi leaders wanted to deal more firmly with the Hungarians, but Veesenmayer had the support of Field Marshal Maximilian von Weichs, the commander of the German army of occupation, and of General Hans von Greiffenberg, the German military attaché in Budapest. Their arguments, combined with new German setbacks on the eastern front, persuaded Hitler to support Veesenmayer, who was informed on March 28 that from now on the official slogan of German-Hungarian relations was to be *Waffenbrüderschaft*—brotherhood-in-arms.[23]

The Veesenmayer policy worked well. During the summer of 1944 the Hungarians deployed all their effective troops in Russia, either in the fighting lines or as occupation forces. On June 2, 1944, the Germans concluded an economic agreement with Imrédy, the new minister of economics, which provided for the "integration of the Hungarian economy in the general European economic plan" and in effect totally subordinated the Hungarian economy to the German war effort. The Sztójay government also agreed to place all the facilities of the Hungarian state at Germany's disposal for the final solution of the Jewish problem.[24]

By the summer of 1944 the Hungarians had done everything to fulfill Hitler's conditions for the removal of German occupation forces, but these forces were not removed; or rather, the troops of the regular army were removed, but their place was taken by troops of the Waffen-SS and the German police. On July 7, 1944, Hitler summoned Sztójay to his headquarters and complimented him on the measures taken so far against the Jews. There was much more to be done, however, and German police units were to remain in Hungary "until the Jewish problem had been completely settled." [25]

With some justification Horthy felt he had been duped. He drafted two letters of protest to Hitler and resolved to dismiss Sztójay. Early in July he forbade further deportations of Jews and ordered the dismissal and arrest of Endre and Baky, the officials in charge of the Hungarian Jewish campaign. Hitler was infuriated, and on July 16 Veesenmayer was instructed to inform Horthy of the Führer's extreme disapproval of his most recent behavior, which he regarded as little less than treason. Hitler would not tolerate a weakening of the home front which failure to take action against the Jews would represent, and he would regard any move against the Sztójay regime as a revival of the intrigues that had led to German intervention in Hungary on March 19. Meanwhile, as a precautionary measure, he proposed to send two additional German armored units to Hungary.[26]

Faced with this kind of pressure Horthy was again intimidated. But the coup d'état in Rumania against the Antonescu regime on August 23, 1944, and the subsequent Rumanian declaration of war on Germany spurred him into action.[27] On August 25 he dismissed Sztójay and appointed a predominantly military government under the prime ministership of General Géza Lakatos, who was assigned the task of reasserting Hungary's sovereignty and concluding an armistice with the Allies—if necessary with Russia alone.[28]

Hitler did not react at once, but allowed Lakatos to carry on the business of government until plans could be completed for the ouster of Lakatos and the installation of a pro-German regime. Meanwhile he received accurate information about the progress of Hungarian negotiations with the Russians from his intelligence services. Toward the end of September he must have learned that an armistice with Russia was scheduled to be signed on October 16.[29]

By this time all possibility of collaboration with the old ruling groups in Hungary seemed at an end and the Germans were reduced to co-operating with Ferenc Szálasi, the head of the Arrow-Cross movement whose lack of popular support had heretofore rendered him unsuitable as an instrument of collaboration. In the first week of October Veesenmayer informed Szálasi that he had been designated by the Führer to take over power in Hungary; together they drew up a list of cabinet ministers and other leaders of the new government that was to be formed, as well as a list of persons to be arrested.[30]

The German preparations for the change of government in Hungary were carefully made. Otto Skorzeny, who had carried out a dramatic rescue of Mussolini in the previous year,[31] had been sent to Budapest at the end of September to arrest Horthy and other government leaders in the event of a premature move on the part of the Hungarians. Also sent to Hungary were SS General Erich von dem Bach-Zelewski, the head of Himmler's antipartisan units, and Rudolf Rahn, the German plenipotentiary and ambassador in Italy, who had recently scored notable successes in dealing with other trouble spots in the Nazi empire.

On October 14, 1944, the twenty-fourth German Panzer divison with forty tiger tanks moved into Budapest. The next day, when Hungary's withdrawal from the war was to be announced, Skorzeny's men kidnapped Horthy's son, while German troops surrounded the regent's residence. At noon, as scheduled, Horthy announced the conclusion of an armistice with Russia on the radio, but by this time, unknown to the regent, the radio station was in German hands. Immediately after Horthy had implicated himself, the Germans entered his residence and demanded that he sign a document naming Szálasi prime minister, thereby conferring on his appointment the appearance of legality. When Horthy refused, he was threatened with the death of his son. The appointment of Szálasi would go through in any case, Horthy was informed, and if necessary his signature would be forged. On the other hand if Horthy signed, the life of his son would be spared and he and his family would be placed in honorable detention in Germany. Horthy signed. The Germans kept their promises to him. Horthy and his family were deported to Germany, and his son, although sent to a concentration camp, was not killed.[32]

Otherwise the accession to power of the Szálasi regime took place almost without incident. From the start it was a government of illusions. Szálasi refused to recognize the fact that the war was hopelessly lost, or that he was a mere tool of the Germans. He and his ministers proceeded about the business of government as though they had every expectation of ruling indefinitely. Elaborate long-range plans were drawn up for the reorganization of political and economic life. To defend Hungary and hurl back the enemy, Szálasi proposed to raise fourteen new army divisions, not counting labor battalions, and during the last part of October he flooded the country with orders calling up various categories of the population for military or auxiliary services.[33]

The legislation enacted by the Szálasi government was of little practical importance since most of it could not be put into effect. Of far more immediate consequence was the government's policy of wreaking vengeance on political opponents and co-operating with the Germans in the final liquidation of the Jews. "Their rule was worse than the German domination in that it was baser and more immoral," the former prime minister Kállay wrote in his memoirs. "Szálasi was a madman; his followers were the dregs of the people." His government indulged in the wholesale arrest of "reactionaries," and the slaughter of Jews. "The only saving circumstance in those days was that the general disorganization of the Arrow-Cross regime made it incapable of carrying any undertaking to its logical conclusion." In the case of the Jews, "instead of systematic extermination, desultory and indiscriminate persecution took place. It was a period of private despicable enterprises, of atrocities inspired by individual revenge." [34]

The Szálasi regime kept Hungary in the war on the side of Germany; but otherwise the Germans derived little practical benefit from it. The administration of the country was soon reduced to chaos; neither labor nor troops were recruited on a scale the Germans had expected. In the economic field, Szlasi signed an agreement with Veesenmayer on October 17 giving Germany blanket rights to make use of Hungarian economic assets in the common war effort, with the costs to be credited to the account of the Hungarian government in Germany. But by this time German economic exploitation was merely a process of evacuating supplies from territories overrun or threatened by the Russians; the Germans took what they could and destroyed the rest.[35]

Budapest fell to the Russians on February 13, 1945, after a two-month siege during which most of the city was destroyed. The Germans continued to fight on in the west and it was not until April 1 that the last German troops, and with them the Szálasi regime, were driven out of the country.

The contrast in the status of Hungary before and after the German occupation of March 19, 1944, is most vividly seen in the fate of the Jews. Before that date the Hungarian government had passed stringent anti-Semitic legislation, and there had been two incidents of mass deportation and mass murder of Jews in territories recently acquired from Czechoslovakia and Yugoslavia. But the Hungarian government never sanctioned a policy of mass murder and steadfastly resisted German pressure on this matter. In March 1944 Hungary was the only country in the Nazi orbit where no systematic deportations or executions of Jews had taken place. Not only had the majority of Hungary's eight hundred and twenty-five thousand Jews survived, but thousands of Jews from other parts of Eastern Europe (the Germans estimated as many as one hundred thousand) had fled to Hungary as the last remaining refuge from the Nazi terror.[36]

This situation changed completely after the German occupation. Accompanying German occupation troops was a special task force for Jewish affairs under the the personal direction of Adolf Eichmann, which went into action immediately. The Sztójay government was persuaded to issue laws requiring Jews to wear the Star of David, restricting their freedom of movement, and crippling their economic existence. The Jews themselves, gulled by promises that they would not be harmed if they obeyed orders, were persuaded to place themselves under the jurisdiction of a Jewish Council and were thus brought under the control of a single organization.

Once the Jews had been identified and organized, Eichmann was ready to put his master plan into operation. Hungary was divided into six zones and a timetable was drawn for the roundup and deportation of Jews from each. The roundups were to be carried out by the Hungarian police and gendarmerie, with Eichmann and his staff acting as advisers. Deportations were to begin as soon as the roundups had been completed.

On April 23 Veesenmayer informed Berlin that the work of rounding up Jews in ghettos in the Carpathian zone had begun on April 16 and was scheduled to be completed by the end of the month, at which time approximately three hundred thousand Jews would have been secured. Roundups would then begin in Transylvania and the counties bordering on Serbia and Croatia, the counties of the interior, and finally the city of Budapest. Negotiations were in progress to secure the necessary transportation facilities to ship three thousand Jews daily to Auschwitz beginning May 15.[37]

Despite a shortage of freight cars and other transportation difficulties, Veesenmayer was able to report early in July that 437,402 Jews had been deported so far. The evacuation of the Budapest Jews was scheduled to take place in the course of that month.[38]

Before the roundup of Jews in Budapest could be carried out, Horthy, who had been shunted aside during the first weeks of the Sztójay regime, intervened. Under strong domestic and international pressure, and deeply disturbed in his own mind about the treatment of the Jews, the regent ordered that all deportations of Jews be stopped and demanded the dismissal and arrest of Endre and Baky, the officials in charge of Hungarian co-operation in the Jewish campaign.[39]

For the time being the systematic deportation of Jews came to a halt. In September Eichmann left Hungary in disgust and dissolved his task force there. But for the Jews it was only a reprieve. With the installation of the Szálasi regime in October, Eichmann returned to Hungary and the campaign against the Jews was renewed. All Jews capable of work were ordered placed in labor camps, the rest were to be confined in ghettos. This time Eichmann's plans for the deportation of Jews were frustrated by the breakdown of the transportation system. Although about forty thousand Jews were marched out of the country on foot, approximately one hundred sixty thousand Jews were left in Budapest when the Russians besieged the city in December. Of these, about thirty-six thousand were killed during the siege. Altogether an estimated five hundred seventy thousand of Hungary's eight hundred twenty-five thousand Jews died in the course of the German occupation.[40]

Rumania

Because of the decisive importance of Rumanian oil to the German war economy, German troops had assumed primary responsibility for the security of the Rumanian oil fields in September 1940, and after October a large German force was stationed in the country.[41] But Rumania was never, properly speaking, an occupied territory, for the government under General Ion Antonescu was left a large measure of control over the country's affairs, including the production and export of Rumanian oil.[42] German political interests were represented after 1941 by Obergruppenführer Manfred von Killinger, one of several SA men Ribbentrop employed in his diplomatic missions in Southeastern Europe to counter the influence of Himmler; German economic interests were represented by Dr. Hermann Neubacher, the special representative for economic questions at the German Legation in Bucharest; German military interests were represented by the various heads of the large military mission maintained in Rumania throughout the war.[43]

The Germans conceded the Rumanian government a large degree of independence because they thought they had a reliable instrument in Antonescu—Hitler regarded him as the strongest personality among his allies apart from Mussolini [44]—and because Rumanian troops proved to be valuable partners in the campaign against Russia. But their greatest reason for restraint in dealing with Rumania was probably their obsession with the lessons of the First World War. In that conflict the Germans had conquered and occupied Rumania, a success that had resulted in the destruction of Rumanian oil installations and the almost total loss of the Rumanian oil supply. Germany could not afford to repeat this experience in the Second World War, for, as Hitler never ceased reminding his colleagues, the life of the Axis depended on Rumanian oil.[45]

During the first period of the war, the Germans had no reason to regret their partnership with Antonescu. Despite the territorial losses imposed on his country by Hitler,[46] the Rumanian leader pursued an ostentatiously pro-German policy because he was convinced that the only means of preserving what was left of Rumania's independence was to co-operate with Germany and the only possibility of regaining the lost territories was to outbid his rivals for Hitler's favor. He joined from the first in the attack on the Soviet Union with the obvious motive of recovering the provinces ceded to Russia in 1940.[47] But with this step he also clearly intended to demonstrate the superior value of Rumania's friendship to Germany as compared with that of Bulgaria, which never declared war on Russia at all, and of Hungary, which hesitated for some time before doing so. Great as was the satisfaction of the Rumanians in the recovery of Bessarabia and Northern Bukovina and other territorial gains at Russia's expense, Antonescu made no secret of the fact that a major objective of his policy was the recovery of Transylvania and Southern Dobruja, which the Axis had compelled Rumania to yield to Hungary and Bulgaria; the future status of these territories was the question most persistently raised in conferences between the Rumanian and Nazi leaders. In addition, the Rumanians were anxious to acquire the Banat area of Yugoslavia.

While the war lasted, Hitler was more concerned with the prevention of conflict between his allies than with the distribution of territory among them, and he regularly side-stepped decisions about Transylvania and other areas coveted by the Rumanians. After the attack on Russia he evidently hoped to divert their attention from Translyvania by giving them additional territories in the east. During a conference on the future partition of Russia with his chief political and military leaders on July 16, 1941, he observed that Antonescu wanted not only the return of Bessarabia and Northern Bukovina, but the important harbor of Odessa and its hinterland—territory that had never belonged to Rumania. Despite the objections of Göring and Rosenberg, Hitler was prepared to meet Antonescu's wishes on this matter, all the more so because he desired Rumania's co-operation in occupying and administering the vast territories that were rapidly falling under German control.[48] On July 27 he wrote Antonescu congratulating Rumania on the recovery of Bessarabia and Northern Bukovina, "the only logical reward for you and your brave troops," and asking that Rumania also assume responsibility for the security and administration of territories further to the east. On August 14 he proposed that the Rumanian zone of occupation be extended as far as the Dnieper.[49]

Antonescu, although not averse to the acquisition of Russian territory,

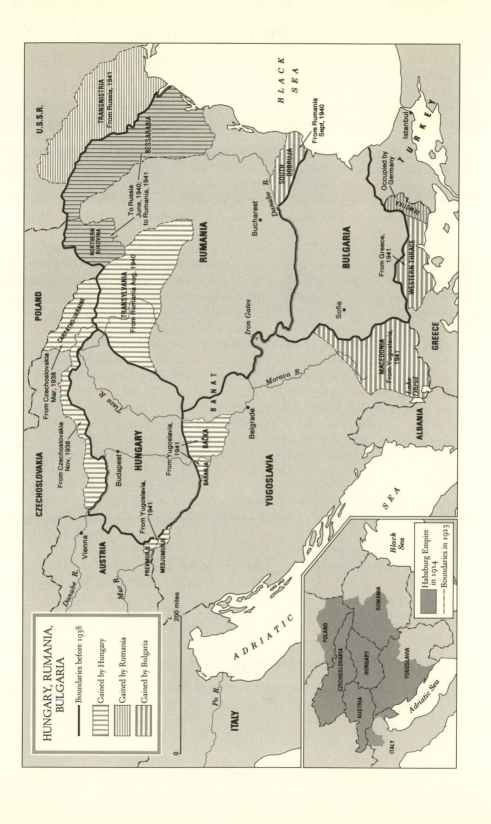

HUNGARY, RUMANIA,
BULGARIA

—— Boundaries before 1938

Gained by Hungary

Gained by Rumania

Gained by Bulgaria

U.S.S.R.

POLAND

CZECHOSLOVAKIA

AUSTRIA

Vienna

Budapest

HUNGARY

Danube R.

Mur R.

Tisza R.

PREKMURJE

MEDJUMURJE

From Yugoslavia, 1941

From Yugoslavia, 1941

BARANYA

BAČKA

From Yugoslavia, 1941

Belgrade

B A N A T

YUGOSLAVIA

CARPATHO-UKRAINE

From Czechoslovakia
Mar. 1938

From Czechoslovakia
Nov. 1938

TRANSYLVANIA
From Rumania Aug. 1940

NORTHERN
BUKOVINA

To Russia
June, 1940;
to Rumania, 1941

BESSARABIA

TRANSNISTRIA
From Russia, 1941

RUMANIA

Bucharest

Danube R.

Iron Gates

Mostrava R.

SOUTH
DOBRUJA

From Rumania
Sept. 1940

BULGARIA

Sofia

From Greece,
1941

B L A C K
S E A

Istanbul

T U R K E Y

Occupied by
Germany

DEMOTIKA

WESTERN THRACE

GREECE

MACEDONIA
From Yugoslavia,
1941

Lake
Ohrid

ALBANIA

0   200 miles

ITALY

Po R.

A D R I A T I C

S E A

Black
Sea

Habsburg Empire
in 1914

Boundaries in 1923

POLAND

CZECHOSLOVAKIA

AUSTRIA

HUNGARY

RUMANIA

YUGOSLAVIA

ITALY

Adriatic Sea

was obliged to admit that he lacked both the means and the trained personnel to administer and exploit so large an area. He was, however, prepared to assume full responsibility for the territory between the Dniester and the Bug, and on August 19 a Rumanian civil administration was established in this area, which was henceforth called the province of Transnistria. Following negotiations between Rumanian and German officials, a treaty was signed at Tighina [50] on August 30 whereby Rumania was officially assigned sole responsibility for the occupation, administration, and economic exploitation of Transnistria; in the area between the Bug and the Dnieper, on the other hand, Rumania was to be responsible solely for security and order, Germany for administration and economic exploitation.[51]

The Axis powers were somewhat premature in their division of the spoils of Russia, for despite a heavy commitment of Rumanian forces they failed to capture Odessa, which had been designated as the capital of Transnistria. It was not until the Germans came to Rumania's aid that the city fell on October 16, 1941. With that organized Russian resistance between the Dniester and Bug came to an end.[52]

Hitler was jubilant. He was convinced that the war was practically over for the Rumanians; all they had to do now was consolidate their position. "Antonescu now has the job of building up his state by basing it on agriculture," Hitler told his associates. "For industry he would need abilities that his peasant class (which is sober and honest) does not possess. On the other hand, a usable administration can be recruited amongst this class. But it must be small, and it must be adequately paid. Whoever in Rumania continues to abandon himself to corruption will have to be shot." An incorruptible army and police and a minimum number of administrators were the essential preconditions of an integral state. "But the first thing, above all, is to get rid of the Jew. Without that, it will be useless to clean the Augean stables. If Antonescu sets about the job in this manner, he will be the head of a thriving country, inwardly healthy and strong." [53]

Hitler still refused to make definite commitments about Transylvania. He did not believe any delimitation of frontiers in Southeastern Europe could do justice to all ethnic claims, he told the Rumanian deputy premier and foreign minister Mihai Antonescu in November 1941; but after the war both Rumania and Germany would have tremendous areas to colonize in the east and for this purpose he would make certain that Rumania regained as much of its ethnic population as possible.

> The Führer would understand it entirely if Rumania, in addition to the restoration of its old frontier, should demand an appropriate glacis, necessary for security, and Odessa. . . . In summary, the Führer remarked that Rumania could regard him as a sincere friend who desired a strong Rumania that could keep watch effectively against the east in order to protect Europe, whose culture had been created jointly by the Rumanians and the Germans, against its enemies.[54]

254

The Rumanians were willing enough to keep watch in the east, but they were by no means anxious to be relegated to the position of an agricultural hinterland of Germany, nor did Hitler's ethnic proposals in any way correspond with their own views on this question. They were not satisfied with regaining the Rumanian population from their lost territories in order to colonize new areas; they wanted to recover the lost territories themselves, especially Transylvania.[55]

In addition to differences about their conceptions of the future, the Rumanians and Germans began to have serious differences about more immediate problems. On the military front, neither German nor Rumanian generals were happy about the large role Hitler assigned Rumanian units in the Russian campaign. Rumanian leaders were particularly bitter about his failure to supply their troops with adequate materiel, a weakness that was to be glaringly exposed at Stalingrad. After that defeat, Antonescu, dubious about the possibility of a final German victory, attempted to negotiate with the Allies for the withdrawal of his country from the war, but he met with understandable mistrust and was forced back into Hitler's camp. From this time onward, however, he was a reluctant ally, ever on the lookout for means to extricate his country from its difficult position.[56]

In the economic sphere, the Germans became more dependent than ever on Rumanian oil after the first months of the Russian campaign, which virtually depleted Germany's oil reserves. Göring confessed as much to Mihai Antonescu in November 1941. Even if Germany succeeded in capturing the major Russian oil fields in the coming summer, it would be at least another year before Russian oil could be made available to the Axis in appreciable quantities. Meanwhile Germany would be compelled to rely heavily on Rumanian oil production, which had declined at an alarming rate in recent years—from 8.7 million tons in 1936 to 5.5 million tons in 1941. Göring assured the Rumanian minister that Germany did not intend an open or covert seizure of the Rumanian oil fields, but he appealed to him to remove all restrictions on the drilling of new wells and to stimulate maximum production by every conceivable means.[57]

The Rumanians, however, refused to permit maximum German exploitation of their oil fields, fearing that this would lead to a serious depletion or the total exhaustion of their oil reserves. After the war they intended to revive their claims to their lost territories in Central Europe, and when that time came they did not mean to be without their greatest source of economic power and most valuable bargaining counter. Nor were the Germans able to secure greater concessions by promises of compensation in the oil fields of Russia, especially as the prospects of conquering those oil fields grew more remote.[58]

In 1941, when chances of a German victory seemed brightest, the Rumanians exported almost three million tons of oil to Germany—the largest annual amount the Germans were to receive from Rumania in the course of the war. Total Rumanian production, however, had again declined in that year. Hitler made earnest representations to Antonescu about this situation, but was assured that no major increase in oil production could be achieved. By cutting domestic consumption to a minimum, the Rumanian leader hoped to be able to export another twenty-five thousand tons a month. Futher cuts, however, would depend on Germany. If Hitler sent sixty thousand tons of coal a month to Rumania, another twenty thousand tons of oil could be freed for export by substituting coal for oil in running the Rumanian railroads. And if Germany furnished pipelines to bring natural gas to Rumanian industrial centers, another twenty-five thousand tons of oil could be made available.[59]

Hitler did his best to meet Antonescu's conditions. German coal and a German pipeline were sent to Rumania, thereby achieving a substantial saving in Rumanian domestic oil consumption. Oil exports to Germany nevertheless declined sharply in 1942 (from 3 to 2.2 million tons), although total Rumanian production increased slightly in that year (from 5.57 to 5.66 million tons) and export deliveries were not yet seriously affected by enemy sabotage or bombing. In 1943 exports to Germany rose to 2.4 million tons, partly as a result of Italy's withdrawal from the war, while total production again declined. Still the Rumanians refused to give the Germans a free hand in drilling new wells, and in 1943 only 45 per cent of Germany's drilling projects were completed. At the same time, the Rumanians were raising all kinds of difficulties about payments for their oil exports, which again slowed the pace of oil deliveries. By 1944 Allied air attacks had become a major factor in cutting Rumanian oil production and slowing shipments to Germany. All in all, however, it can be said that the Rumanian government did far more than Allied bombing in the course of the war to cut down the supply of oil available to the German war economy. Yet to the end the Germans refrained from the outright seizure of the Rumanian oil fields. The co-operation of Rumania was too valuable, the practical difficulties of taking over the Rumanian economy too great, the danger of sabotage too dire to impel the Germans to take the extreme measures they had so frequently adopted elsewhere, often with far less provocation.[60]

In contrast to its procrastination in economic matters, the Rumanian government needed little encouragement from Hitler to move against the Jews.[61] On the contrary, Antonescu removed the Jews from the Rumanian economy with such haste and so indiscriminately that Dr. Hermann Neubacher, the chief German economic representative in Rumania, was alarmed about the effect of these actions on German economic interests. In August 1941 he obtained assurances from the Rumanian government that henceforth greater caution would be observed in dealing with the Jews, and that Jews essential to the war effort should be reinstated in their jobs.[62]

These assurances did not apply to Bessarabia, Northern Bukovina, and Transnistria, where Rumanian officials seemed as adamant as the most fanatic Nazis about liquidating the Jews. Reliable statistics on this subject are not available because of the large-scale population movements in these provinces, but it has been estimated that about two-thirds of the prewar Jewish population—well over a quarter of a million persons—were killed during the Rumanian occupation.[63]

During the summer of 1942 Nazi officials began to take an active interest in solving the Jewish problem in Rumania proper (the territory west of the Prut). In July Eichmann thought he had secured the co-operation of the Rumanian government in eliminating the Jews. But before the Eichmann program could be put into effect, the Rumanian government had begun to consider that the annhilation of the Rumanian Jews might be a poor background for peace negotiations with the Allies. Moreover, by this time many Rumanian officials were doing a profitable business in allowing Jews to purchase their safety. Thus, although the Rumanian Jews were constantly subject to official harassment, the majority of the approximately three hundred thousand Jews in the area west of the Prut survived the war.[64]

Apart from the Jews, Hitler's chief ethnic concern in Rumania was with the Germans. On the basis of treaties with Rumania and Russia, the German government arranged for the removal of ethnic Germans from Bessarabia, Bukovina, Transylvania, Dobruja, and Transnistria, with the population transfers to be carried out by Himmler's various racial organizations.[65] Racially suitable and politically reliable persons were to be settled in Germany's newly annexed eastern territories; racially suitable but politically unreliable persons in the Old Reich. A proposal to sterilize racially undesirable persons who opted to come to Germany does not appear to have been approved, presumably because it was easier not to admit such persons to German-controlled territory in the first place. The transfer of ethnic Germans from Bessarabia and Northern Bukovina continued even after the restoration of these territories to Rumania. At the end of June 1942 Himmler was informed that the resettlement of Bessarabian Germans in the Reichsgau Danzig-West Prussia was almost complete, an action that had involved almost eight thousand families and approximately forty thousand persons. The remaining Bessarabian Germans were scheduled for resettlement in the Warthegau.[66]

In Rumania, west of the Prut, although population treaties were arranged that permitted ethnic Germans to move to Reich territory with all their possessions, the majority of the over one-half million Rumanian Germans chose to remain in Rumania where they had been given a privileged position. A Rumanian government decree of November 20, 1940, conferred on the ethic German group the status of a public legal organization and recognized the Nazi party as the "bearer of the national will" of this body. A similar status was conferred on ethnic Germans in Transnistria, where they were conceded a large measure of self-government and given various means to extend and consolidate their land holdings.[67] A treaty of May 12, 1943, allowed Rumania's ethnic Germans to enlist in the Waffen-SS and thereby to gain German citizenship while still retaining that of Rumania. Approximately sixty thousand ethnic Germans took advantage of this opportunity rather than be drafted into the Rumanian army.[68]

After the surrender of Italy in September 1943, Hitler realized he had to count on the possible defection of his other allies, and plans were made for the occupation of Hungary and Rumania. At the end of February 1944 Hitler sounded out Antonescu about the attitude of Rumania, in case Germany took action against the present Hungarian regime. Hitler's objective at this time was not to destroy Hungary as a state, but to install a more reliable government there and to step up the country's contribution to the common war effort. He therefore appealed to Antonescu temporarily to renounce his program of territorial revisions. But Antonescu refused to co-operate with Germany on these terms, so that when Hitler moved into Hungary on March 19, 1944, he did so without Rumania's support. Afterward, Antonescu nevertheless demanded the withdrawal of Hungarian troops from Transylvania and its restoration to Rumania. Now it was Hitler's turn to refuse. He assured Antonescu privately that for him the Vienna treaty that had given Transylvania to Hungary had ceased to exist, but he would make no public concession.[69]

By this time Hitler's territorial awards were in any case of little consequence either for practical or propaganda purposes. Throughout the summer of 1944 the Russians continued their rapid advance on all fronts. On August 23 King Michael of Rumania, in a last-minute effort to save himself and his country, carried out a coup d'état against the Antonescu regime and declared war on Germany. Hitler responded by ordering all available German forces to smash the Putsch in Rumania and secure the Rumanian oil fields. On August 24 he offered the leadership of the Rumanian government to Horia Sima, the former head of the Iron Guard who had been interned in German concentration camps since the failure of his own Putsch against Antonescu in January 1941. But it was all too late. On August 31 Russian troops entered the Rumanian capital; by September 1 the greater part of Rumania was cleared of German troops. Rumania, Rumanian oil, and the war were irretrievably lost.[70]

Bulgaria

Bulgarian historians writing after the Second World War have maintained that the entry of six hundred eighty thousand German troops into Bulgaria on March 1, 1941, prior to the German attack on Yugoslavia and Greece, marked the beginning of the de facto occupation of their country by Germany. However justified this proposition may be, Bulgaria retained a greater degree of control over its domestic and foreign affairs during the war than any other country in Southeastern Europe. In contrast to Hungary and Rumania, Hitler did not call upon

Bulgaria to take an active part in the campaign against the Soviet Union. His primary concern was that Bulgaria should guard Germany's flank against Turkey; Bulgaria's participation in the war against Russia would have dissipated whatever value the country had in this respect.[71]

There was a German military mission in Bulgaria, but on the whole German interests were represented through regular diplomatic channels. In the spring of 1941 the career diplomat Herbert Freiherr von Richthofen was succeeded as minister to Sofia by SA Obergruppenführer Adolf Heinz Beckerle, a former member of the Free Corps and most recently police chief of Frankfurt. Attached to the German legation were specialists for economic, police, and other matters; but throughout the war the German government endeavored to restrict its military as well as civilian personnel in Bulgaria to a minimum.[72]

With Germany's initial victories in Russia in the summer of 1941, the Bulgarian government evidently thought some anti-Russian gesture would be opportune, but the Germans did nothing to encourage such a move. "In the question whether Bulgaria should maintain or break off diplomatic relations with the Soviet Union," Ribbentrop telegraphed his minister in Sofia, "please take a noncommital attitude and do not take a position in either one sense or the other." The Bulgarians accordingly went no further than to assure Germany of their good intentions. Bogdan Filov, the Bulgarian prime minister, informed the German minister on September 25, 1941, that Bulgaria would welcome a rupture of diplomatic relations with the Soviet Union, but that "she would not do the Russians the favor of breaking off relations of her own accord." [73] The Bulgarian government adhered to this policy until September 1944, when the Soviet Union declared war on Bulgaria. The gesture the Bulgarians did make, which seemed cheap enough at the time, was to declare war on Britain and the United States in December 1941.

Hitler felt a certain respect for King Boris of Bulgaria, whom he described on several occasions as a fox.[74] The description was apt, for the king and his government played an adroit game of restricting their aid to Germany to a minimum while constantly assuring the Germans of their admiration and good will. In response to Ribbentrop's appeal for additional grain deliveries in November 1941, the Bulgarian foreign minister Ivan Popov pleaded that the autumn harvests had been so poor that Bulgaria would have difficulty feeding its own population. While evading any definite commitments, he was lavish with good intentions and repeatedly promised that "Bulgaria would do everything possible, for she had not forgotten what Germany had done for Bulgaria. Bulgaria felt allied with Germany to the bitter end." [75]

Although Hitler too desired greater economic contributions from Bulgaria, his main object was still the preservation of order in Southeastern Europe and the neutralization of Turkey. In his own conversation with Popov he expressed his approval of Bulgaria's official position, "especially with respect to Turkey," and his satisfaction that Turkey had

259

stayed out of the war. According to an entry in Goebbels's diary, Hitler said much the same thing to King Boris four months later.

> He [the king] is very happy that the Führer does not expect more of him than that he be a stabilizing factor in the Balkans. The Führer is showing himself extremely liberal toward Bulgaria. Bulgaria, after all, cannot easily take an active part in the war, since it has almost never lived in peace throughout its young national history. It can, however, supply auxiliary troops here and there, as it indeed has done, for example, in Serbia.

To compensate for the frugality of his concrete aid to Germany, the king was liberal with personal flattery. He told Goebbels that he was "an impassioned devotee of Hitler's genius as a leader; he really looks upon him as a sort of emissary of God." Goebbels received his own portion of praise. He recorded in his diary that the king showed the greatest understanding for his work. "He follows what I do with such alert interest that I am simply astounded at what he knows and what he asks. My articles in the *Reich* are part of his required reading. Yes, he told me he even used the arguments advanced in these articles in all his diplomatic negotiations." [76]

Hitler's respect for the king of Bulgaria did not extend to the Bulgarian people. "As allies I prefer the Turks to the Bulgarians," he told his associates shortly after Boris's visit. The government of Bulgaria was unstable, the political attitude of its population uncertain.

> The fact is that Bulgaria is strongly affected by Panslavism, both on the political and on the sentimental level. She's attracted by Russia, even if Sovietized. I recognize that the king of Bulgaria is a very intelligent, even cunning man, but he doesn't seem to be capable of guaranteeing the stability of his regime. He himself confessed that he couldn't change a single minister or relieve a general of his command without endangering his crown. He has to act very cautiously, he says, beginning with granting sick leaves and then retaining these men's attachment with the help of numerous favors. [77]

It does not seem to have occurred to Hitler that Boris was stressing the weakness of his position as a tactic to evade excessive German pressure, whether in matters of policy or personnel. In any case, Hitler's attitude toward the southeastern states was anything but fixed. A few months later, disillusioned by Turkey's cool reception of his alliance offers and signs of a Turkish rapprochement with the Western powers, his views about the relative merits of Turkey and Bulgaria were reversed. "In the Bulgarians we have an ally on whom we can rely against the Turks," he said. [78]

Hitler's suspicions of Bulgaria revived when, on August 28, 1943, King Boris died suddenly under suspicious circumstances leaving his six-year-old son Simeon as heir to the throne. "The situation in Bulgaria is absolutely insecure," Goebeels wrote in his diary. "The Führer told me that it must now be regarded as certain that King Boris was poisoned." After the surrender of Italy early in September Goebbels suspected that Boris's death had been engineered by the Italians, whom he now believed capable of anything. For Germany the great danger in the situation was that the governments in Southeastern Europe might follow the example of Italy in surrendering to the Western Allies, for they all had an interest in encouraging an Anglo-American campaign through the Balkans that would liberate them from the Germans and at the same time protect them from the Russians. This danger was particularly great in Bulgaria, which was accessible to Allied armies via Turkey and by sea.

The Germans were somewhat reassured by the appointment on September 9 of a Regency Council in Bulgaria composed of Prime Minister Bogdan Filov, King Boris's brother Prince Cyril, and the former minister of war, General Mihov. "This Regency Council is positively on our side," Goebbels said. "We can go places with it." On September 24 Dobri Bojilov, the former minister of finance whom the Germans also regarded as reliable, succeeded Filov as prime minister.[79]

But the leaders of the new Bulgarian government were no more reliable than convinced opponents of Germany might have been as the probability of a German defeat grew greater. Like their counterparts in the other states of Southeastern Europe, they did what they could to come to terms with the Western Allies. As all moves on the part of the Bojilov government were unsuccessful, the Regency Council in June 1944 appointed a new government under Ivan Bagrianov, a former minister of agriculture and member of King Boris's personal staff, who had not been associated with the Bulgarian declaration of war on Britain and the United States and who was therefore deemed more suitable to conduct negotiations with these powers.

Until the coup d'état in Rumania in August 1944, the Bagrianov government continued to protest its loyalty to Germany. But following that event it announced its intention to maintain the strictest neutrality in the Russo-German conflict and to disarm all foreign troops that crossed the Bulgarian frontier. The Bulgarian government, however, did not move against German troops already stationed in Bulgaria, which by now had joined in the general withdrawal of German forces from the Balkans.

On September 2, as the Soviet armies pushed through Rumania to the Bulgarian frontier, the regents ousted Bagrianov in favor of Konstantin Muraviev, a liberal member of the Agrarian party. On appointing Muraviev prime minister, the regents declared they would agree to a complete reversal of their previous policy: the withdrawal of Bulgarian forces from territories occupied by Bulgaria since 1940, a general armistice, and the participation of a Communist representative in a coalition government. But the Russians no longer felt any need to bargain. On

September 5 they declared war on Bulgaria; three days later Russian troops crossed the Bulgarian frontier. On September 9 the old regime in Bulgaria was overthrown and a new government established in Sofia under Kimon Georgiev, the head of the Communist-dominated Fatherland Front, which promptly declared war on Germany. By this time all German forces had been withdrawn from Bulgaria. A Bulgarian puppet government established in Germany enjoyed no importance whatever.[80]

Germany's economic policy in Bulgaria during the Second World War has been described as pillage, and certainly the Germans did what they could to secure maximum deliveries from that country. But the Germans were also aware of the danger of jeopardizing the position of a friendly government in this area so close to the Turkish border and so exposed to British influence in the eastern Mediterranean, and they never carried out the kind of systematic spoliation practiced in other parts of Europe. They manipulated currency and exchange rates, they demanded that the Bulgarian government grant them exclusive rights to exploit certain mineral deposits and that Bulgaria bear the cost of German troops stationed in the country. Yet throughout the war the Bulgarian government was left the overall control of the country's economy, and was thus in a position to falsify production records and to withhold goods from delivery to Germany by official procrastination and delay. Altogether the economic losses sustained by Bulgaria during the war would seem to have been a small price to pay for the comparative immunity the country enjoyed from direct German occupation.[81]

Concerning the Jewish question, the Bulgarian government enacted anti-Semitic measures in January 1941 when German pressure in the Balkans was most intense and it subsequently set up governmental machinery to deal with the Jewish problem on the German model. Jews were dismissed from the government service, a quota was placed on the number of Jews allowed to participate in business and the professions, unemployed Jews were drafted for labor service, and in August 1942 all Jews were required to wear the Star of David. But the Bulgarian government procrastinated when it came to the actual deportation of Jews as desired by the Germans.[82] Early in 1943 SS Hauptsturmführer Theodor Dannecker was sent to Bulgaria from France to deal with the Jewish question; on February 22 he succeeded in concluding an agreement with Alexander Belev, the Bulgarian commissar for Jewish affairs, which provided for the immediate deportation of eight thousand Jews from Macedonia, six thousand from Thrace, and six thousand from Old Bulgaria. By early March eleven thousand three hundred and forty-three Jews were actually deported from Macedonia and Thrace, according to Bulgarian statistics.[83]

Ribbentrop, concerned that no Jews had as yet been evacuated from Bulgaria proper, raised this question with King Boris when the latter visited Hitler in April 1943. The king confessed that so far he had only given his consent to the deportation of Jews from the newly occupied provinces of Thrace and Macedonia. Of the Jews in Old Bulgaria, he proposed to deport only a small number of foreign elements. The rest, about twenty-five thousand, he intended to keep in Bulgaria because he needed them for road work. As Ribbentrop must have realized, the king was not being altogether candid, for the prewar Jewish population of Old Bulgaria had been about fifty thousand. But Ribbentrop did not draw attention to this discrepancy in figures and replied only that "in our opinion, the most radical solution of the Jewish question was the only correct one." [84]

Far from having been convinced by Ribbentrop's arguments, King Boris evidently returned from Berlin with the intention of stopping Jewish deportations altogether. When subjected to renewed pressure, he agreed to evacuate Jews from the cities of Bulgaria; but instead of shipping them east he would only allow them to be deported to the Bulgarian provinces. In June Beckerle reported to Berlin that these deportations were well under way; only two thousand Jews remained in Sofia, either because they were indispensable to the economy or had successfully bribed deportation officials.[85]

The German offices concerned with the Jewish question were not at all satisfied with these measures. This scattering of Jews over the Bulgarian countryside was no solution of the Jewish question and was, besides, a serious threat to domestic security. The Foreign Office should exert greater pressure on the Bulgarian government to secure the deportation of Jews to the east. Instructions to this effect were sent to Beckerle, but Beckerle's representations accomplished nothing. After talking to leaders of the Bulgarian government, he concluded that any German proposal for the deportation of Jews would be rejected no matter how much pressure were applied and that a renewal of such proposals at the present time would not only be useless but politically dangerous. They could only be put forward when German victories on the eastern front had once again consolidated Germany's political position in the Balkans.[86]

The necessary German victories were not forthcoming and the deportation of Bulgarian Jews to the east never took place. On August 30, 1944, the Bulgarian government revoked all anti-Semitic legislation. By the end of the war the majority of Jews in Old Bulgaria had survived.[87]

Yugoslavia

The kingdom of Yugoslavia was formed after the First World War as a political union of the south Slav peoples. It consisted of the former independent kingdoms of Serbia and Montenegro, and of numerous territories with a majority of Slavic inhabitants which had once formed part of the Austro-Hungarian Empire: parts of the Austrian lands of Styria, Carinthia, and Carniola, and the coastal territory of Dalmatia; the kingdom of Croatia and Slavonia, which for centuries had been integral with Hungary, as well as the Hungarian Banat; and the provinces of Bosnia and Herzegovina, under joint Austro-Hungarian administration since their detachment from the Ottoman Empire in 1878. In addition, the new Yugoslav state contained part of Macedonia, which Serbia had acquired from Turkey and Bulgaria following the Balkan wars of 1912–13 and the First World War.

Besides its south Slav population, Yugoslavia contained a large number of non-Slav peoples, including sizable groups of Germans, Magyars, Albanians, Turks, and Vlachs. Moreover the south Slavs themselves were by no means a homogeneous or harmonious national body. There was a long record of bitter hostility between the Serbs, who dominated the government of the new state, and the Croats, Slovenes, Macedonians, and other Slavic national groups, who in turn were frequently hostile to one another. From the time of the formation of Yugoslavia its history was marked by the efforts of the Serbs to establish a strong centralized government and by the resistance of other nationalities, particularly the Croats, to Serb domination.

Despite the legacy of Austrian as well as Hungarian claims to Yugoslav territory, Hitler had not originally planned to invade or occupy Yugoslavia. For several years, but especially after the Italian attack on Greece in October 1940, he had endeavored to safeguard German interests there by diplomacy. With Yugoslavia's adherence to the Tripartite Pact on March 25, 1941, he thought he had successfully brought that country into the Axis camp. It was only after the coup d'état in Yugoslavia on the following day that he decided to resort to military action. His plans for the occupation of Yugoslavia were therefore hasty improvisations, which were to be revised repeatedly in the ensuing weeks.[88]

The Division of the Spoils

On March 27 Hitler informed his generals of his intention to secure the active support of Italy, Hungary, and Bulgaria in the campaign against Yugoslavia by offering these states slices of Yugoslav territory, and to win over the large Croatian population of Yugoslavia by promises of national autonomy. A week later he released a memorandum embodying his guiding principles for the future organization of the Yugoslav area: The former Austrian crown lands bordering on the German Gaus of Carinthia and Styria were to be annexed to these Gaus and thus to the Reich; Croatia was to become an autonomous state, probably under Hungarian influence; the coastal areas of northwestern Yugoslavia, Dalmatia, and Montenegro, were to go to Italy; Yugoslav Macedonia would go to Bulgaria; Hungary was to receive its former territories north of the Danube; and Old Serbia (without Macedonia) was to be placed temporarily under German military administration.[89]

By April 12 Hitler's plans for the partition of Yugoslavia had become somewhat more precise. He had fixed the exact boundaries of the territories to be annexed by Germany, which were to be handed over district by district by the German army to the Gauleiters concerned as soon as the pacification of the country would permit. The adjacent territories on either side of the river Mur (Prekmurje and Medjumurje) were to go to Hungary, but Hitler changed his mind about giving Hungary the entire region north of the Danube. In this area both Hungary and Rumania laid claim to the territory east of the river Tisza (the Banat), where there was also a large ethnic German population. For the sake of these ethnic Germans, and to avoid offending either Hungary or Rumania, Hitler decided to keep this disputed area under German control, at least temporarily. Thus Hungary was to receive only the territory west of the Tisza (the Bačka and Baranja regions.) [90] Hitler's other plans for the partition of Yugoslavia remained the same.

The German armies invaded Yugoslavia on April 6; within just over a week organized resistance was virtually at an end; and, on April 17, the Yugoslav government surrendered unconditionally. By this time the Yugoslav state was already in the process of dissolution. On April 10 the establishment of an independent state of Croatia was proclaimed; the next day Hungarian troops moved into the territories promised to Hungary; on April 14 Hitler published decrees establishing a German civil administration in the territories he proposed to annex to Germany; and on April 17 the Bulgarians entered Yugoslav Macedonia.[91]

Following the collapse of organized Yugoslav resistance, Hitler informed his generals on April 16 of his basic decisions for the Balkan area. He intended to withdraw his forces as rapidly as possible, but to maintain bases in Yugoslavia, Greece, and the Aegean islands from which to attack British bases in the eastern Mediterranean. For this purpose the Salonika area in Greece was especially important. He would leave one German division to safeguard the copper mines of northeastern Serbia; two German divisions would temporarily occupy the Yugoslav territory between the Tisza, the Danube, and the Rumanian border (the Banat). "In Yugoslavia," Hitler said, "Germany is not interested in (a) Croatia as an independent state; (b) the Italian spheres of interest (the Albanian section of Yugoslavia, Montenegro, Dalmatia, Carniola, insofar as it does not come under German administration); (c) the former Hungarian territories west of the Tisza; (d) the Bulgarian sphere of interest (Macedonia)." From the successor states, Germany would assure itself of "(a) economic prerogatives and exports—at least as much as previously supplied by Yugoslavia—(bauxite from Dalmatia, grain, meat, raw materials); (b) transit rights and communication connections as far as Greece; (c) shipping rights on the Danube and its protection from Belgrade to the Bulgarian-Rumanian border." [92]

Up to this time the Italians, to whom Hitler had theoretically conceded a position of predominance in the southern Balkans, were not consulted or informed about Hitler's decisions with respect to Yugoslavia. Not until April 16, when Hitler's basic decisions had already been made, did Ribbentrop invite the Italian foreign minister, Count Galeazzo Ciano, to Vienna to discuss the future of the Yugoslav area, at which time he informed him of Hitler's intention to advance the frontiers of the Reich south of the Karawanken mountains into Slovenia to include the former Austrian crown lands of Lower Styria, Carinthia, and Upper Carniola. Ciano protested that German claims extended much farther south than Italy had anticipated; but Ribbentrop said the frontier had been fixed irrevocably by the Führer and must be considered final. Otherwise the Germans were generous enough. They agreed to Italy's annexation of the rest of Slovenia and the territory around Fiume, to the establishment of Italian dominion over the new state of Croatia and over a reconstituted state of Montenegro, and to an extension of the territory of Albania, which was already an Italian protectorate.[93]

A major difficulty facing the German and Italian negotiators was the question of the boundaries of the new state of Croatia. Hitler had already decided on the boundary between Croatia and Germany, which was to be fixed by treaty with the Croatian government on some suitable occasion; but the other boundaries of Croatia remained to be arranged. On the basis of unofficial requests by the Croatian government, Ribbentrop proposed that the new state include Bosnia and Herzegovina, together with large tracts of the Dalmatian coast. Ciano, however, claimed the entire Dalmatian coast for Italy. As Hitler saw no reason to mediate between Croatia and Italy—he may even have welcomed discord between them—he left it to Mussolini to negotiate directly with the Croatians on this matter. The Germans and Italians were able to agree that Croatia's frontier with Hungary in the east should follow the course of the Drava river, and that Croatia be given Syrmia, a district between the Danube and Sava rivers. In the south Croatia was to receive Bosnia and Herzegovina, the Italians reserving the right to advance the frontiers of their Montenegrin satellite state westward into Herzegovina if they should so desire.[94]

The problem of Croatia was not settled with a general agreement about boundaries. Although Hitler repeatedly emphasized his lack of interest in Croatia, he considered it imperative to safeguard German strategic and economic interests in the country. As he had no confidence in the ability of the Croatian government to provide such a safeguard, he proposed to leave a German army of occupation in Croatia and pointedly ignored Italian offers to replace German with Italian occupation troops. On April 24, the day the Germans and Italians reached a general agreement on the partition of Yugoslavia and the boundaries of Croatia, they signed a treaty dividing Croatia into German and Italian occupation zones which left the Germans in control of the entire eastern half of the country.[95] The Germans insisted that their occupation was merely temporary, but meanwhile the Italians were deprived of a large part of

YUGOSLAVIA, ALBANIA, GREECE
BEFORE THE SURRENDER OF ITALY

Boundaries before the
Axis invasions

Under German civil
administration

Under German military
administration

Croatia

To Italy

To Albania

To Hungary

To Bulgaria

0   300 miles

the sphere of influence that had purportedly been allotted to them.

By the end of 1941 the major provisions for the partition of Yugoslavia had been put into effect and formally ratified by treaty. Italy annexed its share of Slovenia on May 3 to form the new Italian province of Lubiana (Yugoslav: Ljubljana) and incorporated the territory around Fiume (Yugoslav: Rijeka) into the existing Italian province of Fiume on May 18. On that same day an Italian-Croatian treaty was signed which gave Italy the greater part of Dalmatia and the majority of islands off the coast.[96]

On May 13 the Germans signed a treaty with Croatia fixing their southern boundary with that state, and on October 10 they ceded Croatia the district of Syrmia, heretofore under German military occupation. The territories of the Italian satellite state of Albania were extended on June 29 to include the former Yugoslav provinces of Kosovo, Debar, and Struga. Bulgaria annexed Yugoslav Macedonia on May 18. On December 27 the Hungarians annexed the Bačka and Baranja regions, and the lands on either side of the river Mur.[97]

Lower Styria, Carinthia, and Upper Carniola

On April 14, 1941, three days before the German armistice with Yugoslavia, Hitler issued decrees establishing German civil governments in the former Austrian territories of Lower Styria, Carinthia, and Upper Carniola (Untersteiermark, Kärnten, and Oberkrain). As chief of the civil administration of Lower Styria he appointed Dr. Siegfried Uiberreither, the Reichsstatthalter and Gauleiter of Styria. For Carinthia and Carniola he selected Franz Kutschera, acting Gauleiter of Carinthia. In both areas the chiefs of the civil administration were made directly responsible to himself and were given full executive authority in the civil sector of the government. Military authority was to remain in the hands of the army. As in other occupied territories, the Reich Ministry of the Interior was to act as central office to ensure co-operation between the occupation administrations and the various administrative departments of the Reich. In further decrees of April 14, Hitler empowered Göring, as plenipotentiary for the Four-Year Plan, and Himmler, as Reich commissar for the consolidation of the German people, to issue orders directly to the heads of the occupation governments.[98]

The former Austrian territories of Yugoslavia that Hitler had placed under civil administration had been ancient Austrian crown lands, and Nazi theorists maintained that for this reason the Reich had a special claim to them. According to an article in *Reich, Volksordnung, Lebensraum*, the authoritative Nazi journal on Germany's ethnic and territorial claims, "the occupation of the land south of the Karawanken . . . was not only a political necessity, but signified politically the return of a land united by countless historic and natural conditions to the German Reich." This territory, the article went on, had been incorporated into the empire of Charlemagne and had been part of the Habsburg realm until 1918, when it was torn from Germany by the peace treaties following the First World War. In hardly any other area of German settlement was the role of the German as educator of the Slavic race more clearly discernible. "Flourishing cities and villages grew up under German leadership in areas where previously there had been swamps and wilderness; proud monuments of German creativity took the place of the previous nonculture." [99]

There can be no doubt that Hitler shared these views, and that he regarded it as his duty to restore Lower Styria, Carinthia, and Upper Carniola to the German Reich. "Make this land German once again," he instructed his civil administrators in sending them to their new posts.[100]

The heads of the German occupation governments did not hesitate to make public the nature of their assignment. On the day of his appointment Uiberreither issued a proclamation to the people of Lower Styria informing them that the Führer had "brought them home," and that their lands would shortly be reincorporated into the Greater German Reich. The time to declare themselves had now arrived, he said. All Styrians who acknowledged Adolf Hitler and his Reich would be allowed to apply for membership in a Styrian Home League (*Heimatbund*), an organization designed to include all right-minded (*gutgesinnten*) members of the population.

> We want to annex this country in such a way that there is no room here except for those Germans and Styrians who for years, for decades and centuries, have fought side by side as good comrades with our compatriots, and who, related to us by ties of blood, have been prepared during the past decades to desire with all their heart the reannexation to Germany. We are most willing to work with people like that. But all the rest, my compatriots—and we won't make any secret of it—will have to be thrown out.[101]

Kutschera took the same line in Carinthia and Upper Carniola. The ethnic German organization here was called the People's League (*Volksbund*), but like the Heimatbund it was intended to include

> all persons who on the basis of their Aryan-German blood come into consideration for restoration into the German ethnic community. The Volksbund is to lead these people spiritually, intellectually, and politically, to educate them to become citizens of the Reich, and to allow them to grow into the German ethnic community. . . . It is the goal of the Carinthian Volksbund to make this land, which was once a German cultural and colonization area, German once again.[102]

In November 1941 Hitler replaced Kutschera by Dr. Friedrich Rainer, Reichsstatthalter and Gauleiter of Salzburg, who was now transferred in the same capacity to the Reichsgau Carinthia with authority over the newly occupied sections of Carinthia and Upper Carniola. Speaking at the ceremony of Rainer's inauguration at Klagenfurt, the capital of Carinthia, Reich Minister of the Interior Wilhelm Frick said,

> Your most significant task will be to work indefatigably to integrate the new territories of Southern Carinthia and Upper Carniola and to make them valuable and equivalent parts of your Gau. . . . The superficial co-ordination with the Reich has already progressed so far that the formal incorporation of the occupied territory into the Reich can take place in the near future. After this incorporation, it will be your task to build on existing foundations to give depth to what has been achieved already and thereby to endow it with fresh vitality. But all these tasks take second place behind what in the last analysis is the decisive question of the ethnic incorporation of the territory south of the Karawanken. This task must always be the lodestar of your activity. For without the creation of a wall of German people in this land and without the political activization of these people, the most handsome administrative structure will be bound to collapse sooner or later.[103]

The superficial co-ordination of the provinces with the Reich had indeed already progressed far. Shortly after the German occupation began, regional administrative districts were reorganized to correspond with those of the neighboring German provinces in preparation for their eventual union with the Reich.[104] Over a thousand teachers were brought in from the Reich to give the educational system a German character. For adults a massive German language instruction program was inaugurated in what was designated as a "language offensive." In some districts the German language was made compulsory in both schools and administration. According to German statistics, 95 per cent of the ethnic Germans in Lower Styria enrolled in the Heimatbund, 97 per cent in Carinthia and Upper Carniola in the Volksbund, and a corresponding number of young people joined the various German youth organizations that were established. Laws of October 1941 and February 1942 required the use of the German form of all German names that had been Slavicized or otherwise corrupted under Yugoslav administration. All basically Slavic names on the other hand were to remain unchanged, presumably to facilitate distinguishing between German and Slavic members of the population. A law of October 1941, followed by a succession of qualifying ordinances, conferred German citizenship on all ethnic Germans living in the provinces at the time of the German occupation. Persons of German-related blood were given provisional citizenship. All non-Germans were designated wards (*Schutzangehörige*) of the Reich.[105]

In the economic sphere, too, the German intention of incorporating the Yugoslav territories under German civil administration was obvious. There were the usual ordinances requiring that all business enterprises resume operations and that all persons remain at their jobs; wages and prices were frozen, the rate of exchange fixed at twenty dinars to the mark; all important economic assets, including food, clothing, machinery, oil, and rare raw materials, were declared subject to confiscation and were to be at the disposal of the German administration. But the basic aim of German economic policy was clearly to co-ordinate the economy of the region with that of the Reich. In the last week of May 1941, the Reichsmark replaced the dinar as local currency, and the provinces were designated "inland, for purposes of currency regulations." In June came the first of a series of measures co-ordinating the taxation system with that of the Reich. In October the provinces were made part of the German customs area.[106]

As Wilhelm Frick and other Nazi leaders saw the problem, however, these legislative and economic measures were of minor significance compared to the program for the physical Germanization of the provinces. This program had been inaugurated simultaneously with the installation of the civil administrations. On April 14, the day the civil governments were established, Hitler authorized Himmler, in his capacity as Reich commissar for the consolidation of the German people, to issue orders directly to the chiefs of the civil administration. At the same time he instructed him to take steps immediately to solve the nationality question.[107]

Himmler delegated this task to his chief lieutenant, Reinhard Heydrich, who at once ordered the preparation of a population survey of the provinces. In a subsequent memorandum to all supreme Reich agencies, Heydrich noted that on the basis of a preliminary survey the main problem of Germanization would be the removal of the two hundred and sixty thousand Slovenes living in the area. At Heydrich's request a conference was held in Maribor on May 6 under Uiberreither's chairmanship to determine how this removal should be carried out. After some discussion the decision was made to evacuate as many Slovenes as possible to Old Serbia, despite the doubts expressed by the German military commander in Serbia about his ability to feed or house them, and his fears that such wholesale population transfers would have a disastrous effect on public security and order. The objections of the military commander were ignored, but because of the recent destruction of transportation routes the conference delegates agreed to delay the evacuation of Slovenes until July. After that it was to be carried out in three waves: first the Slovene intelligentsia, some six thousand persons; second, the thirty thousand Slovenes who had immigrated into the area since the First World War; and finally, the remainder.[108]

The plan to send the Slovenes to Old Serbia changed when the Germans learned that the leaders of the new state of Croatia would be willing to receive the majority of Slovenes to be evacuated if they could deport an equal number of Serbs from Croatia to Old Serbia. Hitler accepted the Croatian offer, and in June 1941 a German-Croatian treaty was concluded to implement the population transfer. In August the Germans concluded a similar treaty with Italy, which provided for the removal of ethnic Germans from the Italian-occupied provinces of Slovenia (most of them from the Gottschee, or Kočevje, area) to Germany and the shipment of an equal number of Slovenes from the German to the Italian-occupied area.[109]

Well before these treaties were arranged, the German authorities were faced with the familiar problem of racial classification. SS Gruppenführer Otto Hofmann, Himmler's deputy in charge of population transfers in Lower Styria and Carinthia, pointed out that many persons classified as being in an indeterminate racial category (*unausgeglichene Sippen*) had a high percentage of German blood and should not be shipped off to Serbia without further ado. Deputy Gauleiter Kutschera agreed. The indiscriminate evacuation of these people would send good German blood to the Serbs which would some day prove valuable to them and create difficulties for Germany. In response to these objections, Himmler amended the existing evacuation regulations in July 1941. All members of the Slovenian intelligentsia were henceforth to be subjected to a racial examination. Those deemed racially valuable should not be evacuated to Serbia, but sent to the Old Reich for Germanization. Other racially valuable persons who would not be an obstacle to Germanization would be allowed to remain.[110]

Even when the Germans could decide who should be evacuated, population transfers did not go smoothly. In September Heydrich complained to Ribbentrop that, while the Croats had dumped 118,000 persons in Serbia, legally or illegally, they had accepted only 26,341 persons from German territory. Their procrastination was all the more inconvenient because the German authorities needed space to make room for the 12,000 ethnic Germans who were to be evacuated from the Italian-occupied areas according to treaty arrangements with Italy. For political reasons, however, the Germans decided not to put pressure on the Croatian government. Instead, to make room for the new ethnic German arrivals, they decided to send the requisite number of Slovenes to Germany. Here they were to be allocated to labor camps from which only persons eligible for Germanization were to be released.[111]

The evacuation of Slovenes from the German-occupied territories was carried out first of all in the border areas, which Himmler proposed to resettle with ethnic Germans as part of his policy of building a racial wall along all the frontiers of Greater Germany. Gauleiter Uiberreither enthusiastically endorsed Himmler's program. Upon conferring documents of citizenship on new German settlers in Lower Styria in April 1942, he exorted them to "become soldier peasants [Wehrbauern] and guardians of the southern borders of our Greater German fatherland!"[112]

As for the rest of the territory under his administration, Uiberreither stated that it was the aim of his government to prepare for its reincorporation in the Reich at the latest by the end of the war. For this purpose he was evacuating political activists and racially undesirable persons, and conducting a systematic program of Germanization. Of the five hundred and fifty thousand inhabitants of Lower Styria, twenty-five thousand were ethnic Germans. The majority of the remainder were Wends, who were probably Slovenian in origin, but after much breeding with Germans and centuries of contact with them they had adopted many German customs and had shown themselves very receptive to German culture. In Uiberreither's opinion the Germanization of this race of Alpine farmers, most of whom were racially desirable, should be encouraged and advanced by every means at Germany's disposal. He had selected his Styrian Heimatbund as the principal instrument for this purpose, but Germanization was also being carried out through the schools and a wide variety of cultural activities. The nationality problem was more difficult in Carinthia and Upper Carniola, where there were only fifteen hundred ethnic Germans as compared to one hundred and eighty thousand Slovenes. Kutschera and his successor Rainer agreed with Uiberreither that the majority of these Slovenes were worthy of Germanization and that every effort should be made to bring about their conversion.

Whether the large-scale Germanization of the Slovenes could be achieved in the long run the German administrators did not know, but they were certain of one thing: In the future there would be no place in the German provinces south of the Karawanken for foreign racial elements. All Slovenian traits were to be eradicated, and wherever conscious Slovenian opposition was still at work German leadership was prepared to take radical measures.[113]

By the end of the war the provinces of Lower Styria, Carinthia, and Carniola had not yet been formally annexed to the Reich or effectively Germanized. But of the German intention to accomplish both purposes, and that as quickly as possible, there was never any doubt.

Croatia

At his conference with his generals on March 27, 1941, at which he announced his decision to destroy Yugoslavia, Hitler predicted that the Croats would take Germany's side when the attack began and gave orders that their reward for this action would be their eventual political autonomy. On March 31 Ribbentrop instructed his consul general in the Croatian capital of Zagreb (German: Agram) to inform Croatian leaders confidentially that Germany would provide for an independent Croat state within the framework of the new European order should the Yugoslav state collapse through its own mistakes. They could promote this goal most effectively by abstaining completely from further co-operation with Belgrade. The next day he sent a special emissary to Zagreb, Dr. Edmund Veesenmayer, to negotiate directly with Croatian leaders.[114]

Veesenmayer's mission was a failure in that he was unable to win over the leader of the largest and most influential political organization in Croatia, Dr. Vladko Maček, head of the Croat Peasant party. Maček cate-

273

gorically refused all discussion about an independent "greater Croatia" and on April 3 he accepted the position of deputy minister president in a new Yugoslav cabinet. His only concession to the Germans was an expression of willingness to undertake negotiations with the Reich on behalf of the Yugoslav government.[115] Disgusted with Maček, Veesenmayer secured Ribbentrop's approval to pursue a policy aimed at bringing about a union of other Croatian party leaders with members of the Peasant party who rejected Maček's recent behavior. For this purpose he entered into negotiations with Slavko Kvaternik, a former colonel in the Austro-Hungarian army and a leader of the Ustaša (revolutionary) movement, a Croatian nationalist-terrorist organization whose most prominent members were living in exile in Italy on subsidies from the Mussolini government. On April 5 Veesenmayer reported to Berlin that under his influence a union of Croatian national groups, including the right wing of the Peasant party, had been formed which advocated the establishment of an independent Croatian state to include "all areas that are Croatian from a historic and ethnic point of view." [116]

German policy in Croatia immediately following the invasion of Yugoslavia appears to have been entirely the work of Veesenmayer. Ostensibly to forestall a neutralist or pro-Yugoslav proclamation by Maček, and without waiting for authorization from Berlin, he proceeded on April 10 to install Kvaternik as head of the Croatian government and with some difficulty persuaded him to proclaim Croatia's independence. Developments during the last few days, Veesenmayer informed his superiors in Berlin, had made this action necessary. "The initiative and execution . . . were exclusively in my hands. . . . Since Kvaternik took over the government I have been at his side constantly and I am assisting him inconspicuously." Ribbentrop approved the actions of his emissary, and instructed him to remain with Kvaternik. "However, leave further measures entirely up to the Croatians, and remain yourself aloof. In the further treatment of the Croatian question, we now intend to let the Italians have precedence entirely." [117]

Mussolini was not happy about Germany's initiative in an area he considered to be an Italian sphere of influence, but he could hardly object to the installation of a government in Croatia under the leadership of a party that had been sponsored and subsidized by his own government for over a decade. On April 11, with Mussolini's blessing, Ante Pavelić, the *Poglavnik* or Führer of the Ustaša movement, left his exile in Rome with three hundred of his followers bound for Zagreb. Upon his arrival in the capital on April 14, Kvaternik turned over the leadership of the state and its government to him.[118]

Pavelić's first official move was to seek a conference with Veesenmayer, which took place on the evening of April 14. Pavelić used this occasion to assure the German emissary that he had no commitment of any kind to the Italians. He knew that the freedom of Croatia was exclusively due to the strength of the Führer, the Reich, and Europe, and he had only one wish: the earliest possible recognition of an independent Croatia by Germany. He did not propose to conduct a foreign policy of his own, but was willing to allow Croatia's relations with other powers to be determined by Germany. His one policy would be to seek the uplift of his people "and to prove that the Croatians were not Slavs, but professed themselves, in the last analysis, to be German by blood and manner." Hitler responded to this appeal by recognizing the independent state of Croatia on April 15. The next day Pavelić formed a government with himself as minister president and Kvaternik as deputy leader with control over the police and the armed forces.[119]

Pavelić had founded the Ustaša movement in 1929 following the proclamation of a royal dictatorship in Yugoslavia; almost immediately afterward he had gone into exile. After a brief sojourn in Vienna and Sofia, he settled in Rome, where he received support from the Italian government—Italy had been involved in territorial disputes with Yugoslavia since the end of the First World War, and was willing to use any means to weaken that state. The most spectacular act of the Ustaša organization was the assassination on October 9, 1934, of King Alexander I of Yugoslavia in Marseille. In response to international protest the Italian government interned Pavelić, but subsequently gave him a house in Siena and a monthly stipend of five thousand lira. With the signing of the Italian-Yugoslav friendship treaty in March 1937 during the Stojadinović era, the Italians promised to keep the Ustaša movement under control; they nevertheless held it in reserve in the event of another shift in Italy's relations with Yugoslavia.

According to the basic statutes of the Ustaša organization, the central task of the movement was armed revolution to free Croatia from the foreign rule of the Slavic Serbs and to create a completely independent state on the basis of Croatia's "entire ethnic and historic territory." In this new state the Croatian people, and only they, would be the masters of the material and spiritual assets of their realm. The nationalist-racist emphasis of the movement was supplemented by a strong admixture of traditional religion. The Ustaše were Roman Catholics, who regarded their movement as a new crusade against Orthodox heretics, Moslems, and Jews—a crusade that was to be waged relentlessly both within Croatia and abroad. Each member of the movement was obliged to take an oath to Almighty God to live according to the fundamental laws of the organization and to participate actively in its revolutionary activities.

The avowed program of the Ustaša movement did not change significantly after the party came to power in 1941, but there was a new emphasis on race that was obviously designed to curry favor with the Nazis. Article I of the party's program, for example, stated that the Croat people were not racially related to the Serbs. Articles III to VIII made the point that Croats had been the first settlers and landowners in the territories they inhabited and had exercised continuous sovereignty there since the early Middle Ages. Article XI demanded the exclusion of non-Croats from all positions of leadership and the delegation of authority only to persons of Croat race and blood, while Articles XIII to XVII required that the entire social, political, and economic fabric of the nation be subordinated to the welfare of the racial community.

What the program did not state openly was that the more fanatic Ustaše aimed at the outright extermination of peoples of other nationalities and religions. Very soon after coming to power the Pavelić government promulgated racial legislation based on the Nazi laws for the protection of people and state, the chief difference from the Nazis being the special position accorded the Roman Catholic Church and hierarchy in Croatia. The use of the Cyrillic alphabet was forbidden, and all evidence of Serbian nationality and culture in Croatia was to be eliminated. Jews were required to wear the Star of David. Following the Nazi example further, the Ustaše began a systematic roundup of Orthodox Serbs, Jews, and gypsies, who were expelled or exterminated in large numbers, and their property confiscated by the state.

The confiscation of the property of peoples of other religions or nationalities enriched the more unscrupulous members of the Croatian population. But for the majority of Croatians the rule of the Ustaše signified the breakup of the entire social and legal order to which they had been accustomed. Thousands of persons threatened with expulsion or extermination fled into the hills to join resistance groups. The Croatians who remained were frightened and alienated by the inhuman policies of the Ustaše, who had never had the support of more than 5 per cent of the population. The Germans thus found themselves backing a regime without popular support, and one which soon demonstrated its utter incapacity to deal with the massive unrest its policies had generated.[120]

Germany's position was made more difficult by Hitler's decision to regard Croatia as part of the Italian sphere of influence and to refrain from interference in the internal affairs of the newly independent state. His basic principle in the Balkans, he told his chief military representative in Croatia, was to keep the Italians in line by letting them have what they wanted in the area. As the Italians and Slavs had never been able to get along, he calculated that they would simply balance each other out. In the course of 1941 the German government repeatedly instructed its officials in Croatia to avoid supporting the Croatians against the Italians and to advise them to reach an amicable agreement with Italy. "In dealing with the whole matter," Ribbentrop telegraphed his representative in Zagreb in August, "please never lose sight of the fact that the alpha and omega of our foreign policy in the Mediterranean area is the preservation of our cordial alliance with Italy, and that in comparison the Croatian question can only have lesser importance for us." [121]

Hitler clung to this policy despite his personal sympathy for the Croatians, which was reinforced when Pavelić assured him when they first met in June 1941 that the Croatians were not Slavs at all. "They were descendants of the Goths, and the Panslav idea had been forced upon them as something artificial." [122] Hitler readily accepted this view. "The Croats are certainly more Germanic than Slav," he commented to his associates a short time later. He thought that if the Croats belonged to the Reich they would be faithful auxiliaries and that they certainly did not deserve the treatment they were getting from the Italians. They were a proud people, unshakable in friendship, their oath eternally binding. In 1942 Hitler regretted that he did not have them as his allies in Russia in place of the Rumanians, and thought that from an ethnic point of view it would even be highly desirable to Germanize them. "There are, however, political reasons which completely preclude any such measures." [123]

Hitler was correct in his expectation that the Italians and Croatians would not get along, but this typical example of his balance of power tactics hardly improved the position of the Axis in the Balkans. Certainly the Italians did nothing to strengthen the position or prestige of the Pavelić regime. From the start they undercut whatever popularity the creator of an independent Croatia might have enjoyed by taking what they wanted by way of territory and by reducing Croatia to the status of an Italian protectorate. Pavelić was obliged to cede to Italy almost the entire Dalmatian coast and the majority of offshore islands, territory which the Italians themselves admitted belonged to Croatia by right of nationality. In the small strip of Adriatic coast left to Croatia, the Croatian government was forced to renounce the right to build a navy or to construct military installations, while the Italians were to have free transit rights for civilian or military purposes. Pavelić agreed to accept an Italian prince as king of Croatia, he conceded the Italians the right to train and arm (and therewith control) the Croatian army, he guaranteed not to enter into international obligations conflicting with the spirit of friendship with Italy. On May 18, 1941, when the Italian-Croatian treaties embodying these concessions and guarantees were officially announced, Pavelić formally offered the crown of Croatia to the king of Italy, who accepted it on behalf of his relative the duke of Spoleto. Mussolini's installation of a member of the Italian royal house on the throne of Croatia was clearly intended to symbolize Italian dominion over the country. Although the duke of Spoleto never went to Croatia, this symbolism was perfectly obvious to the majority of Croatians, who dismissed their new independence as amounting to nothing more than subjugation to the Italians.[124]

Nor were the Italians satisfied with their treaties of May 18. Three months later they demanded that the Croatians give Italy executive authority in the Adriatic provinces still left to them, in the interest of maintaining security and order. "The Italians have gone mad," Hitler said, but again he subordinated his concern for Croatia to good relations with Italy and advised the Croatians to reach an amicable settlement with Italy. An Italian-Croatian treaty of August 21 provided that the civil administration in Croatia's Adriatic provinces should remain with Croatia, but that they should be occupied by Italian troops and that Croatian forces in the area be placed under Italian military command.[125]

Meanwhile the Germans themselves, for all their lip service to Croatian independence and Italy's preponderant position in the Balkans, safeguarded their own interests by maintaining an army of occupation in the eastern half of Croatia. Although the German military occupation was publicly declared to be temporary and the Croatian government was given full control over the civil administration and police in the German-occupied areas, the presence of Germany's physical authority could never be ignored. A German-Croatian treaty of May 16, 1941, provided that German economic interests were to be given special consideration and that the level of trade between the two countries was to remain at least as high as in the past. The Germans were conceded the right to continue the unrestricted exploitation of industrial raw materials wherever they already had concessions and they were to be given special consideration when new concessions were granted. The Croatian government was liable for all debts of the former Yugoslav state in territories now under Croatian control and was to pay the expenses for German military installations in German-occupied areas for the duration of the war.[126]

Despite the rights and concessions he extracted from the Croatian government, Hitler pursued a policy in Croatia that bore out his statements about his basic lack of interest in the country. He maintained just enough troops in the German area of occupation to protect transportation routes and economic installations, and he charged his principal military representative in Croatia with the task of building up a Croatian army capable of maintaining order without the need for German—or Italian—occupation forces.

This German military representative was General Edmund von Glaise-Horstenau, a former Austro-Hungarian staff officer, who had been a member of Schuschnigg's cabinet after 1936 and vice-chancellor and minister of the interior in the cabinet of Arthur Seyss-Inquart. On April 14, 1941, Hitler appointed Glaise military attaché in Agram (Zagreb) with the title of German general in Agram. In addition to his task of building up the Croatian army, he was responsible for presenting German military requirements to the Croatian government and assuring the cooperation of the German and Croatian armed forces whenever this should be necessary. The great weaknesses in Glaise's position were that he was not given authority to intervene in Croatian domestic affairs and that he lacked adequate manpower to take effective action independently. Hence all measures affecting the military situation had to be worked out in tedious negotiations with the Croatian government, which jealously guarded its prerogatives, with the result that military action in suppressing insurgent movements was often disastrously delayed or prevented altogether.[127]

Glaise's mission was not made easier by the chief German political representative in Croatia, Siegfried Kasche, who encouraged the independent stance of the Croatian government. Kasche was one of the SA men employed by Ribbentrop to replace career diplomats with loyal party men and to inject new blood into the German diplomatic service. A Free Corps soldier in the Baltic after the First World War, Kasche was an early member of the Nazi party and the SA. From 1928 to 1932 he had been acting Gauleiter of the Ostmark. At the time of his appointment in Croatia he had little experience in foreign affairs or diplomacy, he did not know the language of the country, and he knew almost nothing of its history and traditions. The German Foreign Office tried to make good Kasche's language and learning deficiencies by appointing the former Austrian consul general in Zagreb, Heribert von Troll-Obergfell, as his deputy, but Kasche relied more heavily on the advice of another SA leader he took with him to Zagreb named Willy Requard. He was contemptuous of traditional diplomats, disregarded the instructions he received from the "professionals" in Berlin, and conducted an independent Nazi party policy as he understood it. The essence of that policy was to build up the Pavelić regime, on which his own influence in Croatia depended, and to support that regime against the representatives of the German army and against the Italians.[128]

Pavelić for his part did what he could to ingratiate himself with Kasche and other Nazi party stalwarts in Croatia. Besides bringing his racial program into line with that of National Socialism and making numerous material concessions to the Germans, he went to some lengths to give a preferred status to the German ethnic minority in Croatia. A Croatian government decree of June 21, 1941, gave all individual German residents full rights of citizenship in the new state and conferred on the German ethnic group as a whole the legal status of a corporation. Subsequent decrees of July 31 and October 30, 1941, gave the ethnic Germans complete cultural autonomy, including their own schools, control of the local administration, and the right to establish their own units in the Croatian army and the Ustaša militia (later they were allowed to fulfill their compulsory military service duties in the Waffen-SS). Further, the Germans were permitted unrestricted communication with the Reich offices, the right to wear National Socialist uniforms and emblems, and freedom to acknowledge National Socialist ideology. The leader of the German ethnic group, Branimir Altgayer, was made a state secretary in the Croatian government with authority to issue decrees on matters affecting the German minority in Croatia. Following the promulgation of the decrees of October 30, 1941, Altgayer was inspired to declare that the clarification of the status of Germans in Croatia could be a model for the solution of ethnic problems in the rest of the Danube area. "The German ethnic group constitutes the living bridge leading from the

Croatian to the German people, and through its blood relationship with the German mother people constitutes a living transmitter of German culture and the German essence." [129]

The Germans and Italians were the only foreign peoples to whom the Croatian government conceded a preferred status. Otherwise the Croatian treatment of ethnic minorities was hardly a model for the solution of ethnic problems, unless that solution was to be expulsion or genocide. The Germans in Yugoslavia concerned with the preservation of security and order were dismayed by the effects of these policies. Glaise protested regularly against the ruthless persecution of the Serbs and other minority groups, pointing out that the country was seized with the gravest sense of insecurity. Troll, who had been sent to Croatia to make good the educational shortcomings of Kasche, concurred. "This resettlement, which is carried out harshly, and the many atrocities preceding it, will heap up tremendous amounts of incendiary material everywhere that Serbs live, and will create centers of unrest in the near future which will be difficult to control." Hitler, however, not only condoned but actively encouraged the Croatian government's racial policies. "If the Croatian state was to be really stable," he told Pavelić on June 7, 1941, "a nationally intolerant policy had to be pursued for fifty years, because only damage resulted from too much tolerance in these matters." [130]

The Pavelić regime never erred on the side of excessive tolerance, and unrest in Croatia steadily mounted. By the early autumn of 1942 German military authorities had become convinced that they could no longer afford to shield Croatian or Italian sensibilities and that order could only be restored in Croatia by uniting all Axis forces under German leadership and sending in massive reinforcements. But Hitler remained reluctant to put pressure on his allies or to send reinforcements into an area which was as yet of marginal strategic importance. Without such pressure the Italians could not be persuaded to subordinate their forces to German command, a situation that persisted until the collapse of the Mussolini regime and Italy's withdrawal from the war in September 1943. [131]

The moves Hitler did make to deal with the problems of Croatia were largely organizational—and ineffective. In October 1942 Glaise's title of German general in Agram was changed to that of German plenipotentiary general in Croatia and he was given unified control of all German military forces in the country. In December he was directly subordinated to the German commander in chief in the southeast who was given supreme command of all German forces in the Balkans. The situation nevertheless continued to deteriorate. General Alexander Löhr, Wilhelm List's successor as supreme German military commander in the southeast, wrote in a memorandum of February 27, 1943, that he considered the Pavelić regime to be a total failure. The army and the police, the railroad and munitions workers, the peasants and miners—all appeared to be uniformly hostile and were either not working at all, engaged in sabotage, or had fled into the hills. He noted that the Ustaša militia had murdered some four hundred thousand members of the Serbian population, that these atrocities had been cleverly exploited by the enemies of the regime, especially by the Communist leader Josip Broz Tito, whose forces already controlled the greater part of Bosnia and large sections of Croatia. To redeem the situation it was absolutely essential that the German Wehrmacht take over the government of the country to establish conditions in which the population could have confidence, and to remove the Ustaša regime which was hated by all sections of the population, especially the peasants. It was now too late to arrange a Maček government, but an attempt should be made to form a government under the followers of Maček. On the German side, Kasche, who continued to support Pavelić, should be recalled and Glaise should be named special Reich plenipotentiary with both political and administrative powers. Moreover he should be given an adequate staff to enable him to govern the country. If these reforms were not carried out, and soon, failure to do so would be paid for by the blood of German soldiers.[132]

The reforms recommended by Löhr were not adopted. On April 1, 1943, a small administrative staff was attached to the office of the German plenipotentiary in Croatia for the first time, but Glaise was still not given sufficient authority over the Pavelić government to bring about any improvement in the political situation, nor was he given enough reinforcements to suppress revolutionary movements and pacify the country. The intervention of the SS in the spring of 1943 was likewise ineffective, although Himmler's officials took command of all Croatian police forces and assumed major responsibility for protecting transportation routes.[133]

The Ustaša regime was not removed. On the contrary, following the surrender of Italy in September 1943 it was given new proof of German support by being allowed to denounce its boundary treaties with Italy of May 18, 1941; a Hitler order of September 7 specifically demanded a "positive attitude" toward the Croatian government on the part of all German officials. By this time, of course, Hitler could ill afford to discard any allies, no matter how ineffective, especially as he now faced the problem of administering the conquered territories previously occupied by Italy.[134]

Croatia's annexation of the former Italian-occupied province of Dalmatia was officially announced on September 9, but the Palvelić regime was never allowed to exercise any real authority there. The German military administrators, anxious to avoid the kind of unrest stirred up by the Ustaše in the rest of Croatia, declared that Dalmatia was still a zone of military operations under the executive authority of the local German military commander, and they refused to allow Croatian troops and administrators to enter the province. Claims on the part of Pavelić to those sections of the provinces of Lubiana and Fiume which had belonged to

Italy before 1941 were brusquely rejected by the Germans, who also ignored his objections to the formal retention of Italian sovereignty in these provinces under the restored government of Mussolini.

In fact, despite Hitler's demand for a positive attitude toward the Pavelić regime, German officials increasingly disregarded it. German army and SS units behaved in Croatia as though they were in enemy territory, which for all intents and purposes they were. They requisitioned whatever economic assets they required, and drafted the local population for labor. While virtually abandoning all pretense of trying to win over the Croatian people, they attempted to exploit national and religious differences in Croatia for immediate political or military advantages. Himmler, for example, set about organizing a Moslem division of the SS, unconcerned about the sensibilities of the Roman Catholic Croatians, while the army co-operated with anti-Communist Serbian forces despite Pavelić's denunciation of any German collaboration with the Serbs as a betrayal of the Croatian people.[135]

The advance of the Red Army to the Tisza river and the capture of Belgrade in October 1944 made Croatia an area of prime strategic importance, for the western Balkans were now the only line of retreat for the German forces still operating in Greece and Albania. Throughout the autumn and winter of 1944 the German army succeeded in defending the main road and railway lines from the south through the Sanjak of Novi Pazar and Bosnia to Brod and Zagreb. During this period the evacuation of the German troops from the southern Balkans was successfully carried out. The stronghold of the German position lay in the territory south of Zagreb, which the Germans managed to hold until the final capitulation of the German army on May 8, 1945. Up to that final day of the war in Europe, the Pavelić government, weak and discredited as it was, also continued to function.[136]

Serbia

On March 29, 1941, eight days before the German invasion of Yugoslavia began, the High Command of the Wehrmacht issued its first orders for the occupation of the country. As the occupied territory would be a sphere of military operations, the High Command of the Army would exercise supreme executive power. Especially urgent was the establishment of control over the main lines of transportation, in particular the Danube river and the railroad from Belgrade to Salonika. The army should also exert every effort to seize all available raw materials, which would be the subject of further directives from the plenipotentiary of the Four-Year Plan. Technicians and equipment needed to reactivate all important economic enterprises, for example the bauxite and copper mines, would be supplied by the army's office of military economy (Wi-Rü Amt.) [137]

On April 12 Hitler issued orders for the establishment of a German military government in Old Serbia, a territory roughly equivalent to that of the kingdom of Serbia before the Balkan wars of 1912–13. This government, installed in Belgrade on April 22 under General Helmuth Förster, was charged with the restoration of order and normal working conditions in the shortest possible time. To carry out these tasks, it was given supreme executive authority, including the power to issue decrees, to give orders to the native Serbian administration, and if necessary to take over the entire administrative apparatus. As long as Serbia remained a sphere of military operations, the military government was to be under the immediate authority of the Army High Command.[138]

On June 9, 1941, "in order to create a clear and unified chain of command in the occupied Balkan area," Hitler appointed Field Marshal Wilhelm List to the position of Wehrmacht commander for the southeast (*Wehrmachtbefehlshaber Südost*), with supreme executive authority in all Balkan territories occupied by German troops. His headquarters were to be in Salonika, and he was made immediately responsible to Hitler. At the same time Hitler named a new head of the military government in Serbia, General Ludwig von Schröder, who was made immediately responsible to the Wehrmacht commander southeast, thus only one step removed from the direct authority of Hitler. In this same order the title of the head of the military government in Serbia was changed from that of Wehrmacht commander in Serbia (*Wehrmachtbefehlshaber Serbien*) to commander in Serbia (*Befehlshaber Serbien*), to differentiate his functions from those of the more independent German military governors in Belgium and France.[139]

Hitler's order of June 9 gave him greater personal control over his military administrators, but it did not achieve its stated purpose of clarifying or unifying the German administration in the Balkans. In fact, in no part of German-occupied Europe was the administrative system more confused. In the first place, there was a problem about the relationship between the Wehrmacht commander southeast and the commander in Serbia. Because Field Marshal List and his successor, General Alexander Löhr, had their headquarters in Salonika, they were of necessity primarily concerned with the affairs of Greece. The major responsibility for the administration and military security of Serbia, therefore, devolved on the commander in Serbia, who was technically obliged to seek authorization for all policy decisions from the Wehrmacht commander southeast. As this process often took weeks, the commander in Serbia soon recognized that to carry on any kind of effective administration he would have to act with a good deal of independence. The result was a conflict of authority at the highest levels of the military administration.[140]

There was a further conflict of authority within the office of the military government in Serbia. This office was divided into two sections: a command staff, which was responsible for military affairs, and an administrative staff, which supervised both the German and serbian administrations. The chief of the administrative staff, SS Gruppenführer Harald Turner, was a doctrinaire Nazi who had previously been head of the German military administration in Paris. Like so many Nazi officials, Turner was anxious to inaugurate policies in line with Nazi party principles, while at the same time extending his personal authority at the expense of his colleagues, an attitude that did not make for harmonious relations between the military and administrative branches of the military government.[141]

The multitude of other German organizations that descended on Serbia in the first weeks of the occupation confused the administrative picture still further. Typically prominent among German occupation officials were the representatives of Göring and Himmler. Göring's agent was Dr. Franz Neuhausen, who was appointed plenipotentiary general for the economy of Serbia by a Göring order of April 13, over a week before the installation of the military government. As head of the economic administration, Neuhausen was empowered to issue directives on economic matters to all German and Serbian officials. Although subordinate to the military government in all military and noneconomic matters, he was immediately responsible to Göring for economic affairs. In December 1942 Göring made Neuhausen plenipotentiary for the mining of metal ores in the entire southeast, a position which enabled him to bypass the authority of the military government altogether.[142]

Himmler's original police unit in Serbia was a special task force (*Einsatzgruppe*) of the Security Service (SD) under SS Standartenführer Dr. Wilhelm Fuchs which was responsible for combatting subversive political elements. With the steady growth of insurrectionary activity throughout the summer and autumn of 1941, Hitler authorized the appointment in January 1942 of a senior SS and police officer for Serbia. To this post he named SS Gruppenführer and General of the Police August Meyszner, who was to be subordinate to the military commander in all military and administrative matters, but who was immediately responsible to Himmler for all police and racial questions.[143]

As in other areas under German occupation which might still be regarded as a foreign country, a special status was given the representative of Ribbentrop in Serbia. By a directive of April 28, 1941, Hitler appointed a plenipotentiary of the Foreign Office with the military government in Serbia, with responsibility for "all questions of a foreign policy nature." Far more important, and indeed surprising, was the fact that Hitler also charged the plenipotentiary of the Foreign Office with the task of preventing the activities of "Serbian elements harmful to the political interests of the Reich," an assignment that in effect authorized him to interfere in every sector of the German and Serbian administrations. To fill this position Ribbentrop selected Dr. Felix Benzler who, like Neuhausen, was technically subordinate to the head of the military government. But for all questions of foreign policy and the defense of German political interests he was immediately responsible to Ribbentrop.[144] Thus there were three senior German officials in Serbia who had been given critical assignments and who were virtually independent of the authority of the military government.

The overlapping and conflicting powers assigned to the top-ranking German officials in Serbia inevitably led to confusion and inefficiency. With the rise of unrest in Serbia in the summer of 1941, General List urged Hitler to unify German leadership in rebellious areas under a military commander, since the principal task in the suppression of revolt was military. To exercise this leadership he recommended General of the Infantry Franz Böhme, a former chief of the Austrian General Staff, who possessed an expert knowledge of conditions in the Balkans.[145]

In response to List's plea, Hitler, on September 14, appointed Böhme supreme commander of German forces in all areas of unrest in the southeast with the title plenipotentiary commanding general in Serbia. He was assigned full executive authority in all rebellious areas, with the right to issue orders to all military and administrative officials, including the head of the German military government in Serbia. On October 9, 1941, Böhme was also named head of the military government in Serbia and henceforth bore the title plenipotentiary commanding general and commander in Serbia (*Bevollmächtigter kommandierender General und Befehlshaber in Serbien*).[146]

While thus ostensibly unifying German leadership, Hitler still did nothing to curb the independent powers of other German officials in Serbia. Moreover in December 1941, with the insurrection in Serbia apparently crushed, he dissolved Böhme's position and made General Paul Bader head of the military government in Serbia. Bader, however, was given no more authority than his predecessors over the various rival German officials in the country.[147]

The appointment of Meyszner as senior SS and police officer in Serbia, with control of both the German and Serbian police forces, was regarded by the military leadership as "a very peremptory organizational change" and a serious weakening of the military government.[148] It was not Bader, however, but Turner, the Nazi chief of the military administrative staff, who suffered most from Meyszner's appointment. Perhaps recognizing in Turner his most serious political rival, Meyszner denounced him to Himmler as being primarily responsible for Germany's political failures in Serbia. Turner responded by accusing the military leadership of excessive leniency in dealing with rebellion. German troops had not been allowed to shoot Jews, Communists, and other undesirable elements, as recommended by Turner, on the ground that these people had done no wrong. Nor had the military commander yielded to Turner's demand to shoot the wives of partisans. But Turner's countercharges did him no good. By the end of the year he was dismissed and early in 1943 the administrative section of the military government was subordinated to the military section.[149]

The fall of Mussolini on July 25, 1943, which rendered doubtful the reliability of all Italian troops in the Balkans, led to another reorganization of the German administration in the southeast. On July 26 Hitler created the position of military commander southeast (Militärbefehlshaber Südost) who was to have authority over the German military governments in Serbia and Greece; over the German plenipotentiary in Croatia; and over the territories of Greece, Montenegro, and Albania still occupied by the Italians. But Hitler could never resist the temptation to overadminister. At the same time that he provided for the appointment of a single military commander for the southeast, he appointed a supreme commander southeast (Oberbefehlshaber Südost) with primary responsibility for military affairs, and a special plenipotentiary of the Foreign Office for the southeast with primary responsibility for political affairs. Because of the particularly serious military and political situation in Serbia, the headquarters of all three new officials were to be in Belgrade.[150]

Hitler's administrative reorganization, instead of establishing the single unified leadership in the southeast he ostensibly desired, in fact created three new authorities whose spheres of competence were defined only in the vaguest terms and whose activities were certain to overlap constantly. Hitler's only provision to deal with this difficulty was an order demanding "the closest comradely co-operation" among his officials. Hitler did not even clear the decks of other rival authorities. In transmitting Hitler's order of July 26, Hans Lammers stated that, although all nonmilitary agencies were to be subordinate to the military commander southeast, "the right of the central Reich agencies to give factual instructions to their subordinate offices will not be touched by this order," a ruling that in effect destroyed whatever unity Hitler's administrative reorganization might have achieved.[151]

The three new positions Hitler had created in the southeast were filled in the latter part of August 1943. As military commander southeast, Hitler appointed General of the Infantry Hans Gustav Felber; as supreme commander, Field Marshal Maximilian Freiherr von Weichs; and as Foreign Office plenipotentiary, Dr. Hermann Neubacher, who replaced Felix Benzler.[152]

Neubacher, a former official of the I. G. Farben Corporation and mayor of Vienna until 1939, had recently been in charge of German oil procurement in Rumania.[153] In 1941 he had been appointed plenipotentiary for oil questions in the southeast, and in October 1942 he was made special commissioner of the Reich for economic and financial questions in Greece. His tasks as Foreign Office plenipotentiary for the southeast were to be carried on in addition to his previous duties.

Aided by the fact that he had the special confidence of the Führer, Neubacher was even more successful than Benzler had been in extending his authority. On October 29, 1943, this authority was augmented still further by a Hitler order entrusting him with the unified political leadership of the fight against Communism in the southeast. He was to organize and co-ordinate anti-Communist forces in all the countries of the southeast; he alone was authorized to conduct negotiations with guerrilla leaders and to approve or forbid such negotiations. At the same time he was given full powers to conduct economic policy in the southeast, especially the feeding of the native population, as part of the anti-Communist campaign.[154]

With Neubacher given such broad political and economic powers and Weichs assigned primary responsibility for problems of military security, Felber appeared to be left with little more to do than deal with routine problems of administration. But even here the situation was confused. Unlike the German military administrators in Croatia, Greece, Albania, and Montenegro, who were given administrative without comparable military powers, Felber was placed in direct command of a substantial number of German troops so that he had some means of backing up his authority. But for all practical purposes that authority did not extend beyond Serbia. Just as previous military commanders for the southeast, with their headquarters in Salonika, had been forced to concede virtually independent powers to the commanders on the spot in Serbia, so Felber, with his headquarters in Belgrade, was obliged to concede similar independence to local commanders in other sectors of the Balkans and to confine his own attention to the desperate situation in Serbia. And within Serbia he confronted the same independent powers of rival German agencies that had frustrated his predecessors.

In order to cope more effectively with administrative problems, Felber reorganized his own office in Serbia by restoring the administrative section to a status of equality with the military. The big change he introduced here was an attempt to end the rivalry with Neuhausen's economic office by placing the administrative section of the military government under Neuhausen, whose large economic staff was now incorporated into that of the military administration.[155] The new arrangement satisfied no one. Military administrative personnel resented being subordinated to Neuhausen, a civilian, who for his part disliked giving up his previous status, which had not only been independent but lucrative. Neuhausen's sentiment was shared by many members of his staff who, like their leader, had used their foothold in the Serbian economy to make substantial personal fortunes. Nor did the new system achieve anything by way of administrative unity. Neuhausen escaped subordination to the chief of the military government through his position as plenipotentiary for mining, and he managed to arrange a similar dual position for favored members of his staff.[156]

August Meyszner, the senior SS and police officer in Serbia, resisted integration into the German military administration quite as effectively as Neuhausen. In his postwar testimony, Felber described them as being two "very independent [*selbstständige*] as well as very self-important [*selbstherrliche*] personalities, who besides were personally hostile to one another." In addition there was Hermann Neubacher, the Foreign

Office plenipotentiary, with his special powers in both the political and economic fields and his personal influence with Hitler. "From the beginning Neubacher took a stand against Neuhausen and Meyszner," Felber said. "It was soon obvious that he thought it his duty to get rid of both personalities because he considered them unsuitable." In his memoirs Neubacher maintained that his differences with Meyszner arose over the question of shooting hostages and similar reprisals. When Meyszner publicly criticized his position on the reprisal question, Neubacher accused the senior SS and police officer of undermining official discipline, "and with the help of Kaltenbrunner secured his immediate recall by Himmler." Whether or not Neubacher's account of the reason for his quarrel with Meyszner is trustworthy, he did succeed in getting rid of him, for Meyszner was recalled on April 1, 1944, and was succeeded by SS Brigadeführer Hermann Behrends.[157]

The rivalries among the top-ranking German officials in Serbia were but the most prominent of the feuds within the German occupation government. Other and, if possible, even more vicious conflicts were carried on between and within the large number of other German agencies. The proliferation of German administrative organizations, the independent status of so many of them, and the personal ambitions and personal animosities of their leaders created a situation which a contemporary German observer called a *Behördenkrieg*—a bureaucratic civil war—"in which each participant was primarily concerned with defending and extending his sphere of power." [158]

While engaged in a bureaucratic civil war among themselves, the German authorities were obliged to deal with the demands and mutual jealousies of their allies, whose territorial appetites they had endeavored to satisfy by ceding them large slices of Serbian territory. This policy did not increase the popularity of the Germans in what was left of Serbia, nor did it contribute to the popularity or prestige of the Serbian government set up under German auspices.

From the beginning of their occupation the Germans had recognized the need for such a government to carry on the routine business of administration, and on April 30, 1941, they established a provisional regime under the leadership of Milan Aćimović, minister of the interior in the Stojadinović cabinet and former chief of police in Belgrade.[159] With German support, the Aćimović regime succeeded in restoring normal administrative and economic life in a comparatively short time. But the truncation of Serbia, accompanied by brutal programs of population transfer, especially on the part of the Croatians, aroused widespread unrest, which grew into a major insurrection after the German attack on the Soviet Union on June 22, 1941. By August German authorities in Serbia were thoroughly alarmed by the general deterioration of the situation. There were large-scale defections from the Serbian police, nationally minded Serbians were joining forces with the Communists, and the most respected ministers had resigned from the Serbian provisional government, which was in the process of dissolution and clearly no longer capable of providing an effective or orderly administration.[160]

Heretofore the Germans had hesitated to concede a Serbian puppet government either strength or prestige for fear that it might turn against them. But now, lacking adequate administrative personnel and police of their own and confronted with a complete breakdown of governmental processes in a critical strategic area, they were made grimly aware of the degree of their dependence on Serbian co-operation. What was needed, the German military authorities became convinced, was a Serbian government that could command respect and regain the support of the national-conservative elements in the country who, for lack of any other alternative, had joined the Communists in rebelling against German rule. High-ranking officials in Berlin remained fearful, but the German commander in Serbia, General Heinrich Danckelmann, felt that procrastination was no longer possible. At the advice of Aćimović, and without waiting for approval from Berlin, he asked General Milan Nedić, Yugoslav minister of war until March 27, 1941, to form a government. Nedić was known as an energetic foe of Communism, but the compelling argument in his favor was that he was "the only powerful personality available." Nedić was given the title of minister president, he was allowed to select his own ministers and other government leaders, he was authorized to double the size of the Serbian police force (from five to ten thousand men) and to form auxiliary combat units up to the strength of five thousand men, and he was given the power to govern by decree under German supervision. The formation of his government was officially announced on August 29, 1941.[161]

For the Germans Nedić proved a fortunate choice. With his reputation as a staunch Serbian patriot and nationalist, he was able to persuade other nationalists to join his government. Whole units of nationalist troops previously in revolt rallied to his support. It was largely due to the co-operation of the Nedić regime that some progress was made in bringing the insurrectionary movement in Serbia under control and that by the end of 1941 an orderly administration was reestablished.[162]

Nedić does not appear to have collaborated with the Germans for reasons of personal ambition or ideological conviction, but because he was convinced Germany would win the war and saw no other alternative and because he hoped to be able to do something to improve the lot of his countrymen by accepting a position which seemed to offer him some means of exercising influence. Before taking office he had put conditions into writing in a letter to General Danckelmann of August 27, 1941. Besides the powers the Germans were willing to concede his Serbian government, including the right to build up an armed force of ten thousand men, Nedić demanded the release of all prisoners of war who were sick, over fifty-five years of age, or were needed for the reconstruction of the country, and he wanted the right to send food to those who were still in captivity. He wanted German support to improve the existing administrative and economic frontiers of Serbia and to put an end once and for all to the murder, persecution, and exploitation of the Serbs in Croatia, Bulgaria, and Hungary. He wanted German recognition of the fact that the fight against Communism in Serbia was primarily the responsibility of the Serbian people and that the Germans should assist in that struggle only when the Serbs lacked adequate means. In cases of sabotage against the German Wehrmacht, only the guilty should be punished, but never the innocent, whether as hostages or in acts of reprisal, and no punishment should be meted out until the Germans had sought the facts of the case from the Serbian government.[163]

The Germans accepted these conditions, but they did not live up to them. Instead they imposed increasingly onerous demands on the Nedić regime. Time and again Nedić tried to evade those demands by handing in his resignation or by pretending to be ill.[164] On each occasion the German authorities pressed him back into service and forced him to carry out the policies they required. Until the Germans were driven out of Serbia, the Nedić regime remained a valuable instrument of the German occupation government.

The Germans had a simple but effective means of putting pressure on Nedić. Refusals on his part to co-operate were countered by threats to turn still more Serbian territory over to Croatia, Bulgaria, or Hungary. This would have meant not only a further loss of territory, but, as the policy of these states had already demonstrated, the actual annihilation of the Serbian population in the lost areas. Even more alarming was the possibility that Nazi leaders, with their own fanatic attitude toward race, might be provoked by Serbian resistance to undertake a mass extermination program of their own. To reduce the danger of so terrible a prospect, Nedić evidently believed he had to convince the Germans that the Serbian people would be reliable and useful members of Hitler's New Order.[165]

Nedić's concept of a new Serbian state that would meet German requirements was inevitably influenced by the German example and the views of local German authorities. His program as it finally emerged called for the establishment of a national and socialist Serbian peasant state suitable to the predominantly agricultural character of the country and its population. To fulfill the national part of his program, Nedić proposed to emphasize the virtues of loyalty to the state and its institutions; socially he intended to improve the lot of the poor and eliminate class barriers by public works projects and the strict regulation of the national economy.

Nedić's measures to implement his program were likewise strongly influenced by Germany. He founded a National Reconstruction Service on the model of the Reich Labor Service, which was intended to awaken in all members of the population, but especially youth, an appreciation for the moral value of labor, remove class prejudices, and further mutual understanding. Special emphasis was placed on a reform of the education system. This was undertaken by Velibor Jonić, a former professor of German language and literature at the Belgrade Military Academy and minister of education in the Nedić government. The Communist influence was to be combatted by a rigorous "state-socialist teaching program," the removal of all unreliable teachers and textbooks, and the segregation of Communist-infected students in prison boarding schools. Apart from combatting Communism, the education program was chiefly concerned with the teaching of useful skills, above all the training of specialists in agriculture.

The Germans gave Nedić's policies every possible support. Both his labor and education programs kept young people occupied and off the streets and made their flight to the partisans more difficult. Moreover the labor service proved to be of great practical value in construction projects and repairing damage wrought by saboteurs.

As in all occupied areas, however, the principal value of a native government to the Germans was that it supplied the indispensable personnel for running the country. In Serbia as elsewhere the Germans maintained a tight control over the native regime. The administrative section of the German military government was divided into departments to supervise every sector of Serbian central and local government. The credentials of all Serbian personnel were carefully examined; Jews, Communists, Freemasons, and all persons suspected of political unreliability were dismissed. Special attention was devoted to the Serbian police, who were the responsibility of the military government until January 1942 and afterward of the senior SS and police officer. As a result of their rigorous selection of police personnel, the Germans succeeded in building up what they considered to be a reasonably reliable Serbian police force, but they always complained about the lack of initiative of its leaders. More satisfactory in this respect were the Serbian volunteer units organized after Nedić came to power which demonstrated drive and enterprise in carrying out campaigns against the partisans.[166]

In the beginning the Germans left the organization of Serbian local government intact, but by an order of December 18, 1941, they dissolved the Serbian local administrative districts (the *Banovinas*) and set up smaller districts on the German model (*Kreise*). These were in turn divided and subdivided, with the head of each administrative district responsible to the head of the next largest administrative unit. The center of gravity of the regional administration was the head of the Kreis (*Kreisvorsteher*), who held a position comparable to that of a Regierungspräsident in Germany. He was the sole local official responsible to the various ministries of the central government; the orders of all ministers went exclusively through him.

Other Serbian administrative institutions, such as the legal and judicial systems, were left intact so long as they met German needs. The

Serbian government was allowed to issue decrees in its own name, but all such decrees had to be submitted to the German authorities before publication. Moreover the Germans often compelled the Serbian government to issue decrees desired by themselves on matters for which the Serbian government was ostensibly responsible in order to escape blame for unpopular measures. This was done, for example, in the field of taxation; to pay the costs of the German occupation, the taxes on the Serbian population were screwed steadily higher.[167]

High taxes, however, were not the major or even a very important reason for the growing unrest in Serbia, where the suppression of rebellion would soon become the most serious problem of the German occuption government. The Serbian people, with their fierce national pride and independence, had never submitted easily to foreign rule. After the German attack on Russia, Communist agitators did their best to fan the flames of resistance. But the most obvious causes of rebellion were the ruthless racial policies pursued by the various governments to which portions of Yugoslav territory had been allotted. The worst offenders in this case were not the Germans, who were almost exclusively concerned with salvaging the small number of ethnic Germans in the area and with the elimination of the Jews, but the Hungarians, the Bulgars, and above all the Croats.

On September 3, 1941, the chief of the administrative section of the German military government reported to his commanding officer that up to that time thirty-seven thousand Serbs from Hungary, twenty thousand from Bulgaria, and one hundred thousand from Croatia had been pushed into German-occupied Serbia, contrary to all agreements. The miseries of these refugees, their tales of the cruelty they had endured and of the massacres of their fellow countrymen who had not been lucky enough to get away had stirred up the forces of unrest and driven thousands of men of widely different political views into the ranks of the partisans.[168]

It was in the hope of persuading Serbian nationalists and anti-Communists to abandon the cause of rebellion that the Germans set up the Nedić regime in August 1941. In that same month Hitler called for a moratorium on the resettlement of the ethnic Germans in the Balkans.[169] In response to Hitler's decision, the Germans shortly afterward convened a conference on population questions in the Croatian capital of Zagreb, where they concluded agreements with their allies to stop arbitrary population transfers.[170] These treaties were largely disregarded by the allies, however, and thus contributed little to Germany's pacification program.

Hitler, in any case, did not propose to rely primarily on statesmanship in dealing with recalcitrant subject populations. On September 16, 1941, he issued the first of many directives calling for the immediate restoration of order in Serbia by the harshest and most rigorous methods. All rebellion was to be represented as Communist, and reprisals were to be carried out at a ratio of fifty to one hundred Communists for the death of one German. "The only real deterrent here is the death penalty," Hitler said.[171] In an order of September 25, General Böhme, recently entrusted with the suppression of rebellion in the entire southeast, called upon German soldiers to avenge Serbia's betrayal of Germany in 1914 and again in March 1941, and to carry out reprisals with utter ruthlessness so as to discourage further attacks on German personnel. "An intimidating example must be set for the whole of Serbia which must hit the entire population with the utmost severity. Everyone who wishes to rule charitably sins against the lives of his comrades. He will be called to account without regard for his person and brought before a court-martial."[172]

The literal fulfillment of these orders produced results the Germans might have expected but did not necessarily desire. In October the plenipotentiary of the Foreign Office deplored the indiscriminate execution of large numbers of Serbs without trial by forces of the regular army, for in the process they had shot confidential agents, Croats, and the entire personnel of a German armaments factory. By far the largest number of victims of German reprisals had been peaceful citizens, who had engaged in no kind of opposition and who, relying on their innocence, had remained in their cities or villages. The behavior of German troops created the impression that no one was safe under German rule and drove everyone, regardless of personal inclination, into rebellion.[173]

By the end of December 1941 the Germans had succeeded in restoring comparative calm in Serbia, but they soon gave the Serbs new cause for discontent. On January 1, 1942, despite the objections of local German military commanders, the German government arranged that Bulgarian troops should occupy a portion of southern Serbia under German administration in order to ease the burden on German manpower. The employment of their hated Bulgarian rivals as occupation forces aroused bitter resentment and well-justified fears among the Serbs, for the Bulgars took advantage of their position to indulge in fresh acts of brutality against the Serbian population.[174]

New atrocities led to new unrest and to increasingly harsh reprisals. In March 1942 German soldiers were ordered to co-operate actively in nipping rebellion in the bud. Not only captured rebels, but all persons suspected of aiding rebels or illegally possessing arms were to be hanged or shot as a matter of principle. Villages which had harbored rebels or where illegal stores of arms or food were found were to be burned to the ground. For one German killed, one hundred Serbs were to be shot; for one German wounded, fifty Serbs killed. German troops should not be swayed by false sentiment. The more incisive and ruthless the retaliation measures at the beginning, the less necessary they would be later on. By December Hitler gave his troops blanket authority to use any methods whatever in their fight against the partisans, including reprisals against women and children. Restraint of any kind was to be considered a crime against the German people and German soldiers at the front.[175]

In terms of terror Hitler could go no further, but by this time terror had been used so indiscriminately against both innocent and guilty that it had lost much of its effect as an instrument of pacification. Instead it had aroused such implacable hostility toward the Germans and their puppet regime as to render any real pacification impossible, short of annihilating the greater part of the Serbian population. On the evidence of his orders, Hitler would have had no scruples about doing just that, but he never had sufficient manpower to carry out so drastic a program.

An exceptional position in the territory administered by the German military government in Serbia was accorded to the Banat, the area east of the Tisza which was claimed by both Hungary and Rumania and which Hitler decided on April 12, 1941, to place under temporary German control in order not to offend either ally.[176]

The Banat, ninety-three hundred square kilometers of rich agricultural land, had a population of six hundred and forty thousand, of whom ninety thousand were Hungarians, sixty-five thousand Rumanians, fifteen thousand Slovaks, two hundred and eighty thousand Serbs, and one hundred and thirty thousand Germans. It was the presence of this large number of ethnic Germans that accounted for the special treatment of the Banat by the Nazi government. On April 14 the commander of the German occupation forces, Lieutenant Colonel Wagner, issued the usual proclamation to the local population calling for the restoration of law and order, the resumption of economic activity, and the surrender of all unauthorized weapons. At the same time he began a process of transferring local administrative authority to ethnic German leaders.

This process was continued after April 29, when the Banat was transferred to the jurisdiction of the German military government of Serbia. On May 1 the military government appointed an ethnic German to the position of plenipotentiary for the civil administration of the Banat, with power to organize a civil administration office and to supervise the local administration under the control of the German district commander.[177]

The Germans soon recognized that by placing the Banat under their military government for Old Serbia, they had also theoretically placed it under the authority of the native Serbian government. To deal with this complication, they compelled the Serbian government to issue a decree in June 1941 making the Banat a separate administrative area under a vice-governor (*Vice-Banus*), and to appoint an ethnic German to this post. They stipulated further that all other principal administrative leaders in the Banat had to be nominated by the German vice-governor, a provision that in effect gave the ethnic Germans control of the civil administration.[178]

Despite the administrative authority conceded them in the Banat, ethnic German nationalists were not satisfied with their position. They had hoped the German government would establish a large German state in the Danube and Tisza valleys and were dismayed when Hitler conceded the Bačka region in the west to Hungary and Syrmia in the southwest to Croatia. Banat leaders went to Germany to address personal appeals to the Führer, but they met with no success. Indeed, they were not even assured that after the war the Banat would not be assigned to either Hungary or Rumania, for Hitler wished to keep both states more firmly bound to the Axis alliance through the prospect of acquiring this region.[179]

Left without promises about their future from the German government, the Banat Germans used their favored administrative status to consolidate their position and to weaken that of rival nationalities. They fostered the development of German national feeling through adult and youth organizations, they set up their own school system which was given marked advantages over other educational facilities. And all along they tried to convince Nazi authorities of the desirability of making them the nucleus of a new Gau in the Danube region.[180]

Whether this activity would have secured them the status they desired within a Greater German Reich after the war will never be known, but Hitler does not appear to have been much interested in the Banat. Had the Axis won the war, it is possible that he would have sacrificed the Banat in the interest of good relations with Hungary and Rumania, just as he renounced South Tyrol on behalf of good relations with Italy. In that event, the most the Banat Germans might have expected was a special status comparable to that of the ethnic Germans in Croatia. More probably they would have been uprooted altogether to aid in the colonization of the newly conquered eastern territories.

As in every other area under German occupation during the Second World War, the greatest sufferers in Serbia were the Jews. When the Germans first moved into Serbia, they took the line that the Jews were the principal fomenters of unrest and that for this reason they were justified in proceeding against them. By the end of May 1941 the military government had issued decrees based on Reich anti-Semitic legislation which defined Jews and which required the removal of Jews from all public services and professions, the registration of Jews and Jewish property, and the identification of Jews by the Star of David. The same legislation, without the provision about the Star of David, applied to gypsies.[181]

As unrest increased throughout the summer of 1941, Field Marshal List and other German leaders made it clear that they did not think Jews and Communists bore sole responsibility for the rebellion in Serbia. But Nazi fanatics among German occupation officials, whether or not they believed this explanation, used it as an excuse to carry on with their anti-Semitic campaign. Felix Benzler, the plenipotentiary of the Foreign Office, and Edmund Veesenmayer, who had been sent to Belgrade toward the end of July to help deal with the increased Communist activity in Serbia, informed Berlin on September 8 that it was absolutely essential to take steps immediately to seize at least all male Jews in Serbia, probably about eight thousand in all. A camp was being built to receive them, but Benzler thought it would be far preferable to remove the Jews entirely and recommended that they be shipped down the Danube on barges and dumped in Rumania.[182]

Ribbentrop rejected the suggestion of sending Jews to Rumania without Rumania's consent. The head of the Foreign Office bureau dealing with the Jewish question, Martin Luther, suggested instead that Jews be placed in labor camps and employed in public works; he did not see how Jews segregated in this way could make trouble if treated with sufficient determination and harshness. Benzler refused to be put off. The immediate solution of the Jewish problem was the most important political task in Serbia at the moment, he said, and it was the prerequisite for the elimination of Freemasons and the hostile intelligentsia. Moreover, both General Böhme and the military commander in Serbia had asked him to arrange for the removal of Jews as quickly as possible.[183]

Luther appears to have doubted Benzler's word on this point, and he remained opposed to dumping the Serbian Jews in Rumania. Instead of giving Benzler the authority he requested, he arranged with Heydrich to send a small commission to Serbia to investigate the Jewish menace and to make recommendations for solving the problem on the spot without disturbing Germany's relations with other states.[184]

German authorities in Serbia did not await the arrival of the Luther-Heydrich investigating commission before taking measures to eliminate the Jews. Hitler's order of September 9, 1941, demanding the execution of one hundred natives for the death of every German was carried out largely at the expense of native Jews. Harold Turner, the head of the administrative section of the German military government, described what was being done in a letter of October 17 to the senior SS and police officer in Danzig. The devil was abroad in Serbia, Turner said, and the German administration was confronted on every hand with sabotage, murder, and rebellion, which Turner was doing his best to put down. Five weeks earlier he had stood five hundred men against the wall, then two thousand, and more recently one thousand. Two thousand Jews and gypsies had been shot during the past week; another twenty-two hundred, almost exclusively Jews, were to be shot in the week to come. All this was not a pleasant task, Turner confessed, but the native population had to be taught what it meant to shoot a German soldier. Besides, the Jewish question was solved most easily that way.[185]

As a result of the mass execution of Jews during October, the members of the Luther-Heydrich commission found upon their arrival in Belgrade toward the end of the month that the problem of disposing of Jewish agitators was already well on the way to solution. The Foreign Office representative on the commission reported that the military administration, in carrying out reprisals, had first shot all active Communist leaders of Serbian nationality—about fifty—"and then regularly Jews as Communist agitators." [186]

Toward the end of October 1941, after detailed negotiations between members of the investigating commission and German officials in Serbia concerned with the Jewish problem, the decision was made to shoot what was left of Serbia's male Jews. The remaining twenty thousand Jews in Serbia (women, children, and old people), as well as fifteen hundred gypsies (of whom the males would likewise be shot) were to be sent to a concentration camp on an island in the Danube. From there, as soon as transportation facilities were available, they would be deported to camps in the east, where they would be dealt with "within the framework of the total solution of the Jewish question." This decision was implemented at once. On November 3 Turner ordered the immediate seizure of all Jews and gypsies. The men were shot and the women, children, and old men were sent to a temporary camp near Belgrade. Later, because the Danube island was temporarily under water, they were installed in a concentration camp at Zemun (Semlin) across the Sava river from Belgrade in what was then Croatian territory. They were never sent to the east, but were killed, group by group, in a gas van that had been sent from Germany for the purpose.[187]

On June 6, 1942, the chief of the German Security Service in Serbia, SS Obersturmbannführer Dr. Emanuel Schäfer, reported that there was no longer any Jewish problem in Serbia, the only remaining Jews being those in mixed marriages. The Serbian police had co-operated well in the solution of the Jewish question. Harald Turner of the German military administration reported the same result to General Löhr, the supreme military commander in the Southeast. In the interest of pacification, the German occupation government had eliminated the influence of Jews in the Serbian administration and economy, he said. "The Jewish problem as well as the gypsy problem was entirely liquidated (Serbia the only country in which *the Jewish problem and the gypsy problem is solved.*)" [188]

The elimination of the Jews in Serbia did not put an end to mass unrest and revolutionary activity in that country, notwithstanding the theories of Nazi officials on the subject. As in most occupied territories, the effectiveness of anti-German resistance forces was badly hampered by the lack of unity, which in Yugoslavia was exacerbated by national and ideological differences. Most serious was the split between Draža Mihailović, whose followers were for the most part Serbian nationalists, and the Communist leader Josip Broz Tito, who attempted to unite all anti-German elements no matter what their nationality or ideological orientation. In the course of the war Tito gradually had emerged as the most effective resistance leader, while Mihailović, in a desperate effort to save the Serbs from further massacre, not only failed to engage in all-out resistance but upon occasion found it expedient actually to co-operate with the Italians and the Germans.

With the defection of Rumania in August 1944, Tito's forces broke out of the mountains, where their guerrilla-type warfare had heretofore been most effective, and succeeded in establishing direct contact with the Soviet army. On October 18 the Germans evacuated Belgrade; although their forces succeeded in holding a line along the Drina and Drava rivers, by the end of October their effective control over Serbia had been broken.[189]

Montenegro

The former kingdom of Montenegro, part of the kingdom of Yugoslavia since the First World War, had been set up by the Italians as an independent satellite state in 1941. After the Italian surrender in 1943 it was occupied by the Germans, and on September 23 the German *Feldkommandantur* 1040 under the command of General Keiper officially took over the administration of the country from the Italian military governor. At this time Feldkommandantur 1040 was attached to the German regional command in Albania, Italy's other satellite state in the Balkans which had also been occupied by the Germans, but the Montenegrins objected so strongly to this apparent subordination of their country to the hated Albanians that the Germans decided for political reasons to transfer FK 1040 to another regional command. In the spring of 1944 it was made an independent military administration directly under the military commander southeast, General Hans Gustav Felber.[190]

Feldkommandantur 1040 did not exercise sole administrative responsibility, for in Montenegro there was the typical overlapping of official responsibilities. The principal political authority was Hermann Neubacher, who had just been appointed special plenipotentiary of the Foreign Office for the southeast. Because he had been assigned a comparable role in Serbia, Greece, and Albania, Neubacher was unable to devote much attention to Montenegro. Much of the political responsibility therefore devolved on General Keiper.[191]

In contrast to the Italians, who had staffed all principal administrative posts with their own officials, the Germans acknowledged Montenegro's independent status by permitting the establishment of a native government. Without adequate administrative or military personnel of their own, they saw that they were completely dependent on native co-operation for the establishment of any kind of control over this wild and mountainous country. At the end of October 1943 they had put together a National Administration Committee under the leadership of Ljubomir Vuksanović, a lawyer from the region of Andrejevica. "In voluntarily conceding the co-operation of the Montenegrin people in the administration of their land," General Keiper declared when officially installing the new government, "the German Reich wanted to express the fact that it had no interest in permanently occupying Montenegro."

For reasons of military necessity, however, the German military government reserved the right to supervise the Montenegrin government and to levy taxes until the war had been won and the Germans could safely withdraw from the country. Meanwhile, the primary concern of the National Administration Committee should be to secure the full co-operation of the Montenegrin people in maintaining security and order, for only those people who showed determination in defending their national honor deserved their freedom.

The National Administration Committee was never so effective as the Germans had hoped it might be. After repeated crises, it was reorganized in the summer of 1944, still under the leadership of Vuksanović, but by this time it had lost all appreciable popular support. Its police and security forces dissolved; in many cases entire units went over to the revolutionaries, taking their German-supplied weapons with them.[192]

On the German side, the administration was characterized by the familiar profusion of administrative agencies. In addition to the Feldkommandantur 1040 and the special plenipotentiary of the Foreign Office, there were the representatives of Himmler, Speer, Sauckel, Goebbels, and other Reich and private agencies. Unlike the usual situation in occupied areas, however, the German officials in Montenegro on the whole worked together harmoniously. They were scarcely given an opportunity to do otherwise, for from the time they entered the country they were obliged to devote their main efforts to combatting sabotage and rebellion. By the spring of 1944 their activities were restricted to protecting a limited number of strategic points and their routes of transportation and communication; by the autumn of that year they had withdrawn from the country altogether.[193]

Albania

On September 9, 1943, immediately after the Italian surrender, the Italian satellite state of Albania was occupied by the Germans. Hitler believed he could not afford to lose this strategic territory at the entrance of the Adriatic Sea, especially as the opposite coast of Italy was already in Allied hands. On September 11 Hermann Neubacher, who had just been appointed special plenipotentiary of the Foreign Office for the southeast, received orders from Ribbentrop to proceed at once to Albania where Hitler wanted him to arrange "an independent Albania, established on its own initiative (*ein aus eigener Initiative unabhängiges Albanien*)." Hitler conceded Albania this status because, as the only predominantly Moslem state in Europe, its treatment by the Germans was thought to be vital to Germany's good relations with the Moslem world in general and Turkey in particular.[194]

This rare attempt on the part of Hitler to be guided by political considerations in dealing with an occupied country could hardly have been

undertaken in less favorable circumstances. Albania had been made independent of Turkish rule in 1912; but Albanian governments, like those
of Turkey, had found it difficult to bring much of this wild and mountainous country under effective control. Albania had been made an Italian protectorate in the spring of 1939. Following the Axis victories in
the Balkans in 1941, the Italians extended the boundaries of Albania—
and therewith their own sphere of influence—at the expense of Yugoslavia and Greece. In contrast to the Germans, who governed all countries
under their occupation largely through local administrative personnel,
the Italians had introduced their own government in Albania and the
territories annexed to it; all higher ranks of the civil service had been
staffed by Italians. Now, after four years of Italian rule, there was no
longer an Albanian government of any kind, and the native bureaucracy
was demoralized.[195]

Undaunted, Neubacher established contact with various Albanian
leaders and informed them of Hitler's intention to grant their country independence. Then, to avoid all appearance of influencing the formation
of a new Albanian government, he flew back to Belgrade the day after
his arrival. He went even further in his policy of noninterference. When
he learned of the intention of the German army to establish a military
government in Albania, he protested that it was impossible for Germany
to recognize Albania's sovereignty and at the same time install its own
administration in the country. As a result of Neubacher's protest the
German military administration in Albania was relegated to the role it
played in Croatia. Its leader, General of the Artillery Geib, was given a
title equivalent to that of Edmund von Glaise-Horstenau, German general (later plenipotentiary) in Albania, and his duties were restricted to
representing the interests of the Wehrmacht with the Albanian government.[196]

On September 14 an Albanian National Committee was formed, consisting of twenty persons who still enjoyed a certain prestige. This committee proceeded to recall the National Assembly of 1939 and charged it
with the formation of a government on the basis of the last constitution
of an independent Albania. The newly constituted assembly met in the
royal palace of Tirana in October. To take the place of the king, who refused to return from exile, the assembly set up a three-man Regency
Council under the chairmanship of Mehdi Bey Frasheri, a former official
of the Ottoman Empire whom the Italians had interned in Rome because of his opposition to Italian rule and whose return to Albania was
arranged by Neubacher. As minister president the assembly elected
Redshep Mitrovica, who came from the Kossovo district, long an object
of dispute between Yugoslavia and Albania and which the Italians had
annexed to Albania in 1941. Djafar Deva, also from the Kossovo district,
was made minister of the interior; and Vehbi Frasheri, son of the chairman of the Regency Council, became state secretary for foreign affairs.

As one of its first acts, the new government officially dissolved all of Albania's ties with Italy, including its military alliance with the Axis, and secured Germany's recognition of Albanian sovereignty with a status of "relative neutrality." [197]

As many German officials in Albania feared might be the case, the new Albanian government proved incapable of controlling the country and unreliable as an instrument of German policy. The confidence of Neubacher in Mehdi Frasheri was not shared by members of the German military mission in Albania, who suspected him and his son of being in contact with the British and Americans via Ankara. Otherwise the only strong personality in the new regime was Djafar Deva, who had agitated against Yugoslav rule in his native province of Kossovo before 1941 and whose desire to retain this area for Albania seemed a guarantee of his loyalty to Germany. Deva believed that raw power was the only effective political weapon in Albania, and assembled a private army of mountain tribesmen in the capital to bolster his position. The reign of terror unleashed by these warriors did not contribute to the peace and order desired by the German authorities, and Deva's opponents, sensing that he did not enjoy full German support, secured his ouster from the government in June of 1944. As a German military historian analyzed the situation later, the fall of Deva removed the sole personality in the Albanian government who might have been capable of pursuing an effective policy in the German interest.[198]

Even less satisfactory than the Albanian leadership from the German point of view was the quality of the rank and file administrators. A German official described them as being "thoroughly corrupt, lazy, and incompetent," qualities which may have been fostered by their lack of enthusiasm for German rule. The Germans, in any event, complained that even during relatively calm times they did little or no work and that in periods of crisis they abandoned their duties altogether.[199]

Germany's own administration in Albania, however, was hardly a model of effectiveness.[200] German administrators were handicapped by Hitler's policy of treating Albania as an independent neutral state. But there were other weaknesses. Neubacher who, as special plenipotentiary of the Foreign Office in the southeast was primarily responsible for the formulation of German policy, was forced to divide his time between Albania and four other countries; he nevertheless insisted on making all major decisions. General Geib, the chief German military administrator, tried in vain to exercise some authority; but he had no troops under his command and only a small administrative staff. Additional administrative personnel assigned to him after his arrival were withdrawn in November 1943 at the instigation of Neubacher, who was still intent on avoiding any ostensible supervision of the Albanian government.

Greater influence was exercised by General Paul Bader and his successor, General Fehn, the commanders of the German troops in Albania, who had both personnel and power at their disposal. Also influential was Brigadeführer Fitzthum, the senior SS and police officer, who was sent to Albania as technical adviser for the organization of a native police force and gendarmerie. As there were almost no Jews in Albania, the Albanian government was spared his advice on this question.

The German consul general in Tirana, Schliep, who ordinarily should have been Germany's chief diplomatic representative in Albania, was completely overshadowed by Neubacher. Although raised to the rank of minister in June 1944, his duties were restricted to routine diplomatic and consular chores, such as the issuing of passports. German economic interests were represented by a plenipotentiary for economics with the German consul general in Tirana, Dr. Gstöttenbauer, who owed his appointment to Neubacher. Gstöttenbauer's effectiveness was hampered by the absence of a network of German regional economic officials, but to preserve his independence vis-à-vis the army he refused to operate through the army's regional administrative network and relied instead on local Albanian officials. This practice led to nasty altercations between the German military and economic leaders. The economic results, at least from the German point of view, were disastrous.

The German army could not long afford to observe the political restrictions imposed on its activities in Albania. In the spring of 1944 the commander of the German troops intervened decisively in Albanian domestic affairs for the first time, in order to set up defenses along the seacoast. As the military situation deteriorated, the need for military intervention increased. This necessity was officially recognized by Hitler in September 1944, when supreme executive authority in Albania was conferred on the commander of the German troops, General Fehn, and supreme administrative authority on the plenipotentiary general, a position now integrated with that of the senior SS and police officer in the person of Fitzthum.

The representatives of other German offices in Albania did not give up their struggle for influence, but their bureaucratic infighting was cut short when the spread of revolution to the capital of Tirana forced them to leave the country at the end of October 1944. What German authority still existed was exercised exclusively by the German army, which completed the evacuation of Albania by December 4.

The German military historian of the occupation of Albania summed up the German experience, "The practical effectiveness of Germany's policy in Albania suffered primarily from the fact that there was no unified leadership, that consequently there was frequently no clear-cut division of spheres of responsibility, and that therefore it was not always possible to pursue so consistent a course in dealing with acute problems as would have been desirable." [201] It was a criticism which could have been applied to the German adminstration in almost every country of Nazi-occupied Europe.

Greece

As was the case with Yugoslavia, Hitler had not originally planned to invade and occupy Greece. His primary purpose in the Balkans was to keep this region neutral under Axis influence, a source of raw materials for the German economy, and to exclude the influence of the British.[202] The ill-considered Italian campaign against Greece in October 1940 produced the situation Hitler most feared in the Balkans: the landing of British troops and the establishment of British air bases within striking distance of the Rumanian oil fields.

It was evident almost from the beginning that the Italian campaign was not going well. In December 1940 Hitler gave orders to prepare a German campaign against Greece with the principal aim of expelling the British forces from the eastern Mediterranean. After this purpose had been achieved, the mass of German units would be withdrawn from Greece *"for further use"* (the emphasis was Hitler's), and the greater part of the country would be turned over to the Italians. In planning an attack on Greece he counted on the active support of Bulgaria, which was to be promised Greek Macedonia.[203]

By March 22, 1941, Hitler had decided that because of the present attitude of the Greek government and the arrival of British forces on the Greek mainland, it would be necessary to invade and occupy the entire Greek mainland, including the Pelopennesus, as well as the islands of Thasos and Samothrace off the Aegean coast. Until the collapse of the entire Greek front, the initiative would probably have to be taken by German units. "When the Greek resistance has been broken, the further mopping up and security tasks will be left in the main to the Italians." [204]

On the morning of April 6, 1941, simultaneously with their attack on Yugoslavia, German troops began the invasion of Greece. In his proclamation to his soldiers on that day Hitler declared that the fight on Greek soil was not against the Greek people but against the universal enemy, England; however, those Greeks who stood by this enemy could expect to fall with him.[205]

Within three days after crossing the Greek frontier German troops had captured the vital harbor city of Salonika; by April 21 the bulk of the Greek forces had surrendered. Armistice negotiations were complicated by the fact that the Greeks, who felt nothing but contempt for the Italians, wished to deal exclusively with the Germans. But Hitler refused to bypass the Italians and on April 23 the Greeks signed an armistice with both the German and Italian governments.[206]

Immediately after the armistice, General Georgios Tsolákoglou, who had surrendered the Greek armies in Epirus and Macedonia to the Germans, approached Field Marshal Wilhelm List with an offer to form a government to take the place of the Greek government of King George

II that had left the country. Again Hitler refused to act without the participation of the Italians, and on April 27 Ribbentrop telephoned Rome to seek Mussolini's consent to accept Tsolákoglou's proposal. The offer, Ribbentrop said, was a gift from heaven for Germany and Italy, for it would place Greece under the leadership of a man whose name counted for something; Tsolákoglou would be in a position to call for the surrender of Greek forces still holding out in the mountains and islands and to facilitate Axis efforts to gain control of the Greek islands and shipping. Mussolini agreed at once that the offer should be accepted. On April 29 the establishment of a Tsolákoglou government was officially announced.[207]

In the belief that his government would be under a severe handicap if Greece were placed under Italian military occupation, Tsolákoglou tried to persuade the Germans to remain in control; in this endeavor he was strongly supported by local German officials. On May 9 German military leaders declared that they attached great importance to stabilizing the Greek political situation, for only then could the country be controlled with small forces. But such stability could only be achieved if the Greeks felt they were under German protection. If Greece were turned over to the despised Italians, the new Greek government would be doomed to unpopularity and impotence. German officials therefore recommended that the greater part of Greece remain under German occupation.[208]

Hitler, however, refused to alter his policy. On May 13 he announced his resolve to withdraw the bulk of the German forces from Greece as soon as possible and to leave the protection of the country to the Italians. Those German forces that remained for the defense of a few strategic areas were to be closely concentrated locally; German army headquarters were to be transferred from Athens back to Salonika. Under no circumstances were the Germans to act as arbitrators between the Greeks and the Italians. "It is none of our business whether the Italian occupation troops can cope with the Greek government or not." Ribbentrop followed up Hitler's instructions by reminding his diplomatic representative in Greece that the fundamental consideration of German policy in the Mediterranean area must be Germany's alliance with Italy. German interests in Greece might be defended against Italian claims in so far as possible through a friendly exchange of views; but any policy likely to bring Germany into conflict with Italy should be rejected out of hand. A strong Greek government was not even desirable, for it would only cause trouble. The Tsolákoglou government had been brought into existence to take the wind out of the sails of the Greek government in exile; it had fulfilled that purpose. The Germans now required nothing more from the Tsolákoglou government than that it keep the Greek administration going.[209]

A Hitler order of May 17, 1941, ended all doubt about his immediate intentions in Greece.

The aim of German intervention in the southeast—to drive the English out of the Balkans and to extend the bases for the employment of German air forces in the eastern Mediterranean—has been achieved, [he said.] The protection of the Greek area, apart from the exceptions listed below, henceforth devolves on the Italians. The German authorities are therefore not to intervene in general questions of the protection and administration of the country. In particular, any kind of mediatory activity that might be requested by the Greeks is to be declined.[210]

The exceptions to which Hitler referred were the Greek territories that were to be given to the Bulgarians as a reward for their co-operation in the campaign against Greece and a few strategically important areas that were to remain under German occupation. These included a buffer zone along the Turkish border, the city of Salonika and its hinterland, and bases in southern Greece needed for launching the forthcoming campaign against Crete, whose airfields were still available to the British for attacks on Balkan military and economic installations.[211]

Crete was captured at the end of May 1941. With that all immediate military goals in the Balkan area appeared to have been attained, and the Axis powers could proceed to the tasks of occupation and administration of the conquered Greek territories.[212]

The Greek provinces ceded to Bulgaria were not treated as occupied territory at all, but were incorporated into the state of Bulgaria. The Bulgarian language and administration were introduced to take the place of the Greek. Simultaneously the Bulgarian government inaugurated a policy of expelling the Greek population from the area and resettling it with Bulgarians. Before the war's end more than one hundred thousand Bulgarians had been moved into the annexed Greek territory.[213]

The Italians annexed the Ionian islands to Italy, and the Greek provinces of Yanina, Thesprotia, and Prenza to their satellite state of Albania. Otherwise they restricted themselves to carrying out the tasks of military occupation and supervising the native Greek administration. On July 2, 1941, Mussolini announced the appointment of an Italian high commissioner for Greece who was to be the top-ranking civil authority in the Italian occupied areas, with the power to appoint and dismiss Greek officials.[214]

The Germans too restricted themselves to a supervisory role. Shortly after the capture of Crete, the bulk of the German forces in the southeast were shifted to positions for the forthcoming attack on Russia. Henceforth Hitler adhered consistently to his policy of leaving primary responsibility for Greece to the Italians, until the spread of rebellion and the consequent threat to the Axis position compelled the Germans once again to come to the rescue of their allies.[215]

The Germans and Italians were fortunate in the system of government they found at hand in Greece and through which they exercised their supervision and control. In 1936 the Greek prime minister General

Joánnis Metaxás had dissolved the Greek parliament and established a dictatorship with full executive and legislative powers. In April 1941 General Tsolákoglou simply took over these powers, which gave the central government enough authority that the Germans and Italians could afford to leave the institutions of Greek central and local government essentially unchanged.

Faced with the problems of inflation, serious food shortages, and an ever-growing resistance movement, Tsolákoglou resigned in December 1942. He was succeeded by the former rector of the University of Athens, Constantin Logothetopoulos, who was sympathetic to the Axis cause but who proved to be a weak and ineffective leader. In April 1943 he gave way to Joánnis Rallis, a former cabinet minister, who was far less favorably disposed toward the Axis but was tolerated because of his energetic efforts to suppress Communism. None of these Greek governments was popular, none proved capable of dealing with the chronic economic crisis and revolution, but all fulfilled what Ribbentrop had named as the essential requirement of a native government: They kept the routine administration going, although with steadily declining effectiveness.[216]

The main lines of German military administration in Greece were laid down in the Hitler order of June 9, 1941, which was intended to establish a "clear and unified chain of command in the Balkans." Supreme military authority was vested in the Wehrmacht commander southeast, Field Marshal List, whose headquarters were to be at Salonika and who was to have full executive powers in all territory occupied by German troops. Subordinate to him were three major military governments: one for Serbia and two for Greece. In Greece the commander Salonika-Aegean was to have authority over the region around Salonika, the islands of Lemnos, Mytilene, Chios, and Skyros, and the Demotika frontier strip along the Turkish border; the commander southern Greece was responsible for the Athenian peninsula and the islands of Crete, Cerigo (Cythera), Anticythera, and Melos. Crete, whose defense and development as a major base for conducting the air war against Britain in the eastern Mediterranean Hitler regarded as the most important task in the southeast, was to be governed like a fortress under a commander of the Luftwaffe. The easternmost part of the island was assigned to an Italian occupation force which was to be under German military command where tactical questions were concerned.[217]

Despite Hitler's order of June 9, German administration in Greece was no more clear or unified than in other occupied areas. If anything it was less so, for the relinquishing of primary responsibility for Greece to the Italians deprived German military administrators of authority over matters affecting Greece as a whole, or indeed over anything beyond their immediate sphere of command. The power to deal with these broader questions was assigned to the representative of the German Foreign Office in Greece, presumably because they called for negotiation with foreign governments. To this position Hitler appointed Günther Altenburg, the former head of Ribbentrop's personal secretariat, who was given the title of Reich plenipotentiary for Greece. In this capacity he was to represent "the political, economic, and cultural interests of the Reich in Greece with the new Greek government until the resumption of formal diplomatic relations." In carrying out his tasks he was to maintain the necessary contacts with Italian authorities and to bear in mind constantly that the guiding principle of German policy in Greece was good relations with Italy.[218]

The powers conferred on the Reich plenipotentiary seriously hampered the effectiveness of the military administration. All general measures proposed by the military government had to be cleared with the Reich plenipotentiary and co-ordinated with his policies. As the headquarters of the military administration were in Salonika and those of the plenipotentiary in Athens, such co-ordination would have been difficult even if personal relations between the two offices had always been harmonious, which they were not.

The effectiveness of the military administration was undermined still further with the appointment on October 15, 1942, of Dr. Hermann Neubacher as special Reich plenipotentiary for economic and financial questions in Greece, with broad powers to deal with the problems of inflation and food shortages. The appointment of Neubacher left the military administration in the helpless position of being deprived of any real authority in either the political or economic spheres.[219]

As already noted in connection with Serbia, Hitler ordered a change in the German administration in the Balkans in August 1943 to deal with the growing problem of rebellion in the southeast and the possibility of Italy's defection after the fall of Mussolini. In that month he appointed a supreme military administrator for the entire area (General Hans Gustav Felber), a supreme military commander (Field Marshal Maximilain Freiherr von Weichs), and a supreme political co-ordinator (Dr. Neubacher, who was named Foreign Office plenipotentiary for the southeast in addition to his responsibilities as special Reich plenipotentiary for economic and financial questions in Greece). The headquarters of all three officials were to be in Belgrade.[220]

Further administrative changes were made after the surrender of the Italians a month later. Italian troops were disarmed with little difficulty and the Germans took over the administration of all territory formerly occupied by the Italians, with the exception of an area west of the Struma river which was given to the Bulgarians. The military commander for southern Greece, General Speidel, was now named military commander for Greece as a whole (Militärbefehlshaber Griechenland). His headquarters were to be in Athens and he was made immediately responsible to the new military commander southeast, General Felber. Serving under Speidel were a group of regional military adminsistrators, including the commander of Fortress Crete, who now assumed control of the whole of the island, and the commander of the Storm Division of Rhodes, who was responsible for the defense and administration of the Dodecanese islands and was later assigned independent administrative powers as commander for the eastern Aegean.[221]

As usual, the changes in the German administration in the southeast did not bring about the desired unification of German leadership. General Speidel, the supreme military administrator for Greece, was not given command of the German troops in Greece. These were entrusted to General Alexander Löhr, the commander of Army group E, whose headquarters were in Salonika and who was assigned primary responsibility for military security. As problems of administration and security could never be separated, the fields of the two commanders constantly overlapped. In the interest of security, the commander of Army Group E interfered more and more in administrative affairs, while frequently withholding military support requested by the administrative office. The dualism in military administration and command continued until September 1944, when the military situation became so serious that all of Greece was declared a battle area and placed under the authority of the supreme commander for the entire southeast, General Weichs.[222]

On September 7, 1943, yet another authority was introduced with the appointment of Gruppenführer Walter Schimana as senior SS and police officer for Greece. He was assigned primary responsibility for the suppression of rebellion and sabotage. Although nominally subordinate to the military commander, Schimana was empowered to supervise and give orders to all Greek officials and police forces. His own directives were to come from the Reichsführer SS and chief of the German police, Heinrich Himmler, and he was to carry out those orders independently and at any time he considered opportune. The military commander for his part could issue directives to the senior SS and police officer only when these seemed necessary to avoid direct conflict with the duties and operations of the Wehrmacht. As relations between the military commander and senior SS and police officer worked out in practice, the former eventually assumed responsibility for the legislative branch of the administration, the latter for the executive.[223]

At the beginning of November 1943, the office of Reich plenipotentiary for Greece, previously held by Günther Altenburg, and Neubacher's position as special Reich plenipotentiary for economic and financial questions were united under Neubacher who had been named special plenipotentiary of the Foreign Office for the southeast in August. To clarify their respective responsibilities, the military commander and the special plenipotentiary drew up a treaty whereby the military commander was left executive power and the sole right to promulgate laws and issue instructions to the Greek government (powers already usurped in large measure by the senior SS and police officer), while the special plenipotentiary reserved the right to lay down all political and economic guidelines and to appoint and dismiss leaders of the Greek government and administration (which would seem to have eliminated what was left of the authority of the military commander).[224]

Even the most efficiently organized German administration, however, would have had difficulty in dealing with the political and economic problems of wartime Greece—rebellion, inflation, and food shortages which reduced many areas to outright starvation. The measures of the German administration followed a familiar pattern. Decrees were issued forbidding the unauthorized possession of weapons, sabotage, direct or indirect support of rebels, and any other actions deemed a threat to public security and order. The Germans also resorted to their usual strategy of terror: shooting hostages, mass reprisals, burning villages suspected of harboring rebels or saboteurs. Yet rebellion continued to spread, until by mid-1944 a large part of the country was controlled by guerrilla bands. Only the bitter divisions between the various guerrilla movements themselves prevented them from overwhelming many of the weakly held German positions.

In the economic sphere the Germans were frustrated by the sheer poverty of the country and by the skill of the Greeks in evading their controls. German decrees required that all workers remain at their jobs and that all economic enterprises carry on as usual. Strikes or failure to work were punished by fines, imprisonment, or confiscation of property. But no amount of legislation could create jobs or reactivate an intrinsically weak economy now cut off from its major markets and sources of supply.[225]

The ineffectiveness of German legislation was most obvious in the field of labor, the only commodity Greece possessed in abundance. In January 1943 the Germans and Italians introduced compulsory labor for all Greeks between the ages of sixteen and forty-five (later sixty), with provisions that male laborers could be transferred to any part of the country where their services were required. But the compulsory labor laws could not be enforced. Greek officials explained that they could do nothing for fear of reprisals and that any attempt to coerce local laborers would result in their flight to the guerrillas in the hills. This is precisely what happened when the Germans themselves attempted to round up Greek workers. The Greeks had an uncanny way of knowing beforehand when such roundups were likely to take place; but even those workers unfortunate enough to be caught generally succeeded in escaping. The efforts of Sauckel's representative to recruit volunteers for labor in Germany were an almost total failure, despite the dire economic situation in Greece. Eventually he resorted to forceful recruiting with the aid of the army and SS. But even then his success was meager. Altogether no more than fifteen thousand Greek workers were sent to Germany during the entire course of the German occupation.[226]

The head of the Greek government during the period of German occupation was Minister President Joánnis Rallis whom the Germans admired, but also resented, for his tenacious defense of the interests of the Greek people. They found a more amenable instrument in his finance minister and later deputy minister president, Hector Tsironikos, who possessed the special confidence of Neubacher and was eventually entrusted with the ministries of economics, labor, agriculture, social welfare, and health. Tsironikos's influence, however, was limited because he possessed almost no personal following and was blamed for the country's chronic economic ills. The other Greek ministers were thoroughly undistinguished and had even less influence, but the Germans soon gave up efforts to replace them because new appointees generally proved to be even more incompetent or un-co-operative than their predecessors.

The declining influence of the Greek central government was in part the result of decay and demoralization in all ranks of the Greek administration. Inflation and the poor pay of government officials forced many of them to take other jobs and to accept bribes. As rebellion mounted and guerrilla bands gained control of large parts of the country, many provincial officials, including the police and gendarmerie, deserted their jobs altogether for fear of reprisals. By the summer of 1944 the authority of the Greek central government had ceased to exist altogether in areas not under the immediate control of German troops, and these areas were shrinking rapidly.[227]

Despite the undeniably harsh nature of their rule, the Germans on the whole treated Greece with greater restraint than other areas of Eastern Europe. Their behavior was undoubtedly influenced by a traditional German reverence for Greek civilization, which even Nazi education had been unable to eradicate.

German restraint toward the Greeks was not extended to the Greek Jews, however. Of the total Jewish population in Greece of about seventy-three thousand in 1941, approximately fifty-five thousand lived in the region of Salonika, which was under German occupation from the beginning. For over a year the German military administration took no action against the Jews; but on July 13, 1942, the German commander in the Salonika-Aegean area, General von Krenzki, ordered all male Jews between the ages of eighteen and forty-eight to register for labor. The campaign to destroy the Jews began in February of the following year with the arrival of two RSHA officials, who were sent to Salonika for this purpose. By an order of February 6, 1943, all Jews were obliged to register, to wear the Star of David, and to move into a ghetto area. By the end of the month the majority of Jews in the Salonika region had been rounded up; from mid-March trains carrying Jews via Belgrade to Auschwitz left Salonika almost daily. By the end of May approximately forty-six thousand Jews had been deported.[228]

On October 3, 1943, Walter Schimana, the senior SS and police officer, ordered the thirteen thousand Jews in Athens and the former Italian-occupied areas of Greece to register. By this time the Jews had learned what such registration meant. Of the eight thousand Jews in Athens, only twelve hundred registered; the percentage was even lower in the rest of the country. Even so, by March 1944 the Germans had succeeded in arresting and deporting some fifty-four hundred Jews from the Greek mainland. Altogether more than sixty thousand Jews were removed from Greece in the course of the German occupation.[229]

By August 1944, with the rapid advance of the Red Army into the Balkans following the collapse of Rumania and Bulgaria, the Germans initiated preparations for the evacuation of Greece. On August 26 the order was issued to withdraw from the country and by November 2 the last German forces had left the Greek mainland. The German garrisons on the islands of Rhodes, Crete, Melos, and Leros, which could not be evacuated because of the lack of German sea power, remained bastions of the Nazi empire in Southeastern Europe until the final German surrender.[230]

It is difficult to come to any firm conclusions about Hitler's war aims in Southeastern Europe because, as is evident from his inconsistent and often conflicting statements on the problem, he himself never made up his mind about what to do with much of this territory. Also here, even more than in other areas, his ideas and policies fluctuated with changes in the political situation.

In 1941, after the conquest of Yugoslavia and Greece, Hitler told his military representative in Croatia that his basic principle in the Balkans was to keep the Italians in line by letting them have what they wanted in this region, and his policies, at least in the western Balkans, reflected this attitude. His purpose was clearly to bolster his alliance with the Italians by giving them dominion over the Adriatic coast and its hinterland, which they wanted in order to consolidate their position in the Mediterranean, and at the same time to leave them the task of administering and controlling this turbulent and for the most part economically unproductive territory. Because of the important position Hitler had conceded to the Italians in Southeastern Europe, his plans for the future of this area were inevitably decisively affected by the Italian surrender in September 1943.

Long before the Italian surrender, however, Hitler had questioned the desirability of allowing the Italians to extend their influence into the eastern Balkans, for here important German interests were at stake, particularly in the valley of the Danube. Shortly after the beginning of the Russian campaign, Hitler spoke of the Danube as the river of the future, the major line of communication between West-Central Europe and the newly conquered territories that were to be colonized in the east. Along this great waterway the inexhaustible economic resources of the east, the petroleum and the grain, the metals and the rubber, would flow to Germany, transported down the great rivers of Russia and across the Black Sea. The canal from the Danube to the Main, which linked the waterways of Eastern and Western Europe, could never be too big. Together with the canal from the Danube to the Oder, it would give Germany an economic circuit of unprecedented dimensions.[231]

A major problem was how German control over the Danube was to be established. Hitler considered resettling the entire ethnic German population of Southeastern Europe along the Danube in order to make this river entirely German. He realized, however, that if he did so he would not have these 1.5 million ethnic Germans available for the resettlement of the conquered eastern territories, which was still his prime objective. "If one looks at the matter from that standpoint," he said in February 1942, "one comes to the conclusion that the north[east] is after all more important than the south[east]. But, the Danube is the Danube. We can never replace it. We should establish a firm foothold at the Iron Gate so that it can never be closed to us." The Danube was also Germany's chief link with Turkey, which Hitler hoped to make the guardian of Germany's southern flank in the same way as Finland was to be the guardian of Germany's flank in the north, for a country would never be able to conduct a global policy (*Weltpolitik*) until its flanks were completely secure.[232]

Despite the mounting difficulties of the Russian campaign, Hitler continued to mull over the problem of the Danube. In June 1942 he remarked that his Viennese compatriots were constantly asking whether, after the war, the Germans would be so foolish as to give up Belgrade once again; now that they had been forced to conquer it a third time they should really keep it for good. Hitler thought the Viennese were correct in this view insofar as it would be necessary to take special care in drawing up future boundaries in this corner of the Reich.

> However, there can surely be no doubt that we cannot give up the so-called Iron Gate of the Danube under any circumstances. The Danube was the waterway which led into the very heart of the continent, and for this reason, in a Europe united by us, would have to be regarded as a German stream and controlled by Germany. The organization of the entire east-west traffic in this great territory depends on whether the Danube is or is not German. Any canal construction would be superfluous, indeed stupid, if we do not succeed in keeping this main waterway under our unrestricted control.[233]

Hitler and his Viennese compatriots were not the only Germans concerned about the future of Belgrade and the Danube. Before and during the war, ethnic Germans in this region as well as numerous Reich agencies, public and private, formulated elaborate schemes for establishing permanent German control over the Danube region, and beyond. There were proposals to settle ethnic Germans on a broad strip of territory along both sides of the Danube from Mohács in southern Hungary to the Black Sea; to make Belgrade a fortress city of the Reich and the nucleus of a new Reichsgau; to extend the area of German dominion to the

Timok river so as to include the rich coal deposits of this region and the important copper mines at Bor; to control the valleys of the Morava and Vardar rivers so as to ensure German access to Salonika, and thence to Suez and the Far East.[234]

Despite the profusion of such proposals, no reliable evidence has so far come to light that Hitler himself, or any other top Nazi leader, had any specific plans as to how much of the Danube Germany should control, or how this control was to be effected. And about the Danube, too, Hitler was inconsistent. His various pronouncements about establishing permanent German dominion over the Danube seemed definite enough; but on occasion he took a more realistic view of Germany's capacity for controlling this region. "We must make sure that we do not assume the role of permanent guardians of the peace in the Danube basin," he said in August 1942, "but rather that of permanent referee, and for each decision which we give we must receive our little fee." [235] This suggests that Hitler envisaged the continued existence of a number of vassal states in the Danube basin, at least in the foreseeable future.

Hitler's policies in dealing with his Danubian satellites reinforce this supposition. He might resent the selfishness and opportunism of the satellite governments, or their skill in evading what he considered to be their share of the burden of the war, but on the whole he appears to have been prepared to allow them to maintain a large degree of administrative independence so long as their policies remained in line with those of Germany. At the time of the Italian surrender Hitler made plans to occupy both Hungary and Rumania, but he did so to prevent these countries from following the example of Italy, not to annex them to Germany. By 1943 German administrators were in short supply and Germany already had far too many other occupied territories to worry about.

Hitler was particularly doubtful about the Germans' capacity to deal with Hungary and he was not at all certain that, if ethnic Germans were settled along Hungary's sector of the Danube, they would be able to maintain their identity in that country. Of all peoples, he said, the Hungarians were the most passionately nationalistic; in the past they had succeeded in assimilating the ethnic Germans under their control with extraordinary speed. Moreover, they had known how to select the best of them for posts of command, which explained why the Hungarian aristocracy was primarily Germanic in its racial composition. If the ethnic German minority in Hungary were to be preserved, Germany would either have to take over the Hungarian state or remove the ethnic Germans.[236] Although Hitler never made a final decision on this matter, he was evidently inclined to the latter solution. During the Russian campaign he remarked that Admiral Miklós Horthy, the prince regent, was very clever to send his son to fight on the Eastern front, because if he won his spurs fighting with the Germans in Russia, Germany could hardly object if the Hungarians appointed him deputy to his father "and eventually even conferred on him the glory of the Crown of St. Stephen." [237] Even after the Germans moved into Hungary in force in March 1944, Horthy was retained as nominal chief of state. It was only after he actually announced his intention to conclude an armistice with the Allies that Hitler ousted him, and even then he installed another native Hungarian government in his place.

Hitler pursued a similar policy in dealing with Rumania, to which he assigned an important role in the administration of the occupied eastern territories. Although he at one time expressed a high opinion of the Rumanian peasantry, his regard for the Rumanian population sank appreciably during the course of the war. In February 1942 he denounced the Rumanian ruling class as being rotten to the marrow, the peasants nothing but wretched cattle, and he wished he had the Croats instead of the Rumanians as his allies in this strategic region of Eastern Europe. Hitler never lost his admiration for Marshal Ion Antonescu, however, whom he believed to be Germanic in origin and who in his opinion had the breadth of vision to perceive that this war would give Rumania the opportunity to become dominant in the Balkans. It was Antonescu's misfortune that he was obliged to rule over Rumanians, whose racial background Hitler never attempted to identify.[238] Despite his poor opinion of the Rumanians and the importance of Rumanian oil for the German war economy, Hitler left the Rumanians a remarkable amount of control over their own affairs until Antonescu was overthrown in August 1944, at which time the military situation in Rumania was in any case hopeless for the Germans.

Of all the states in Southeastern Europe, Hitler was most inconsistent about Bulgaria. During the Balkan campaign he assigned Bulgaria the task of guarding Germany's flank against Turkey. At the same time he took care to station German troops along the Turkish border to make certain that his flank would indeed be protected. He believed the Bulgarians were strongly affected by Panslavism, a sentiment which in the past had been nurtured by Russian propaganda and the Orthodox Church, and he feared that they continued to be attracted by Russia despite Russia's present anti-Christian regime. Given this situation, Hitler concluded that the Bulgarians would only remain loyal to Germany so long as Germany remained friendly with Turkey. A short time later, however, disillusioned by Turkey's rejection of his offers of friendship, Hitler declared that he looked upon the Bulgarians as allies against the Turks. It was impossible to generalize about the Slavs, he said. To label the Bulgarians as Slavs, for example, was arrant nonsense, for they were by origin Turkomans.[239] These vacillating opinions about Bulgaria and the Bulgarians reveal something of Hitler's ignorance about Southeastern Europe in general and may also be indicative of a general lack of interest in this area. In any event, his feelings about the Bulgarians appear to have had little effect on his policies toward that country. As in

314

the case of Hungary and Rumania, he allowed Bulgaria to retain its status of semiautonomy until he was no longer in a position to intervene in its affairs.

In Yugoslavia, Hitler's intentions were most clearly defined in the former Austrian crown lands of Lower Styria, Carinthia, and Upper Carniola. Here his policies were virtually identical with those he was pursuing in Alsace, Lorraine, and Luxembourg, and were obviously designed to prepare these territories for annexation to Germany. Although, by the end of the war, they had not been annexed officially to the Reich, they had been attached to Gaus of the National Socialist party; they were made part of the German customs and currency area; German administrative, economic, and educational systems had been introduced; and the ethnic German inhabitants had been granted full or provisional German citizenship. Further, all necessary preparations were under way to Germanize these lands, beginning with the border regions where a solid wall of ethnic Germans was to be established to guard these frontiers of the Greater German Reich. The most interesting feature of Nazi policy in these territories was the decision on the part of local Nazi officials that the majority of native inhabitants, for example, the Wends and the Slovenes, were suitable candidates for Germanization. Every trace of the Slavic tradition of these peoples was to be eradicated, however, and all persons who refused to accept Germanization or who otherwise opposed German dominion were to suffer the usual fate of expulsion or extermination.

Hitler's intentions toward Croatia had originally also seemed quite clear. Croatia was to be granted a nominal autonomy, but it was assigned to the Italian sphere of influence and was thus relegated to the status of an Italian satellite state. Although Germany maintained an army of occupation in the eastern half of the country, there is no evidence that Hitler intended to use these forces to retain permanent control over the German zone of occupation or retract his promise to turn the entire country over to Italy. Hitler made this concession with considerable regret, for he believed that the Croats were more Germanic than Slav and admired them as a proud people, unshakable in their friendship, their oaths eternally binding. If they were part of the Reich they would be valuable auxiliaries to police the frontier marches. In 1942 he expressed the wish that he had them as allies in Russia in place of the Rumanians. It would be highly desirable to Germanize them, but for political reasons—by which Hitler clearly meant Germany's relationship with Italy—this was "absolutely out of the question." [240]

Until the surrender of the Italians, Hitler continued to treat Croatia as part of the Italian sphere of influence. Afterward, however, he gave orders that the Croatian government of Ante Pavelić should be given positive support. Had Germany won the war he might well have inaugurated a program of Germanizing the Croats and making their country a frontier march or even an integral part of the Reich. But the rapid deterioration of the military situation after 1943 made it impossible for Hitler to undertake policies which might have given a more definite indication of his future plans for Croatia.

Hitler's policies also provide very few clues about his ultimate intentions in Serbia, although the Germans occupied the greater part of that country for well over three years. In his statements about policy Hitler made it plain that he regarded the Serbs as traditional enemies of the Germans, a treacherous and politically unstable people, who, like the French and the Poles, would always be a menace to German security. It may be assumed, therefore, that he would have gone ahead with plans to retain control of the strategic city of Belgrade and the Danube valley to the Iron Gate. This control would most likely have been extended to include Serbia's valuable bauxite and copper mines as well as the lines of communication along the Morava and Vardar valleys to Salonika and the Aegean. Whether he would have set up an actual Reichsgau in the Banat-Belgrade area, as many party officials and local ethnic Germans desired, is more doubtful, for Hitler believed in expansion into areas contiguous to the Reich; and between Belgrade and Germany lay Hungary—and Croatia. If Hitler had gone ahead with the idea of Germanizing the Croats, however, he might very well have given them a free hand to extend their dominion at the expense of the Serbs. In that case the Serbs would have been subjected to a program of extermination quite as brutal and ruthless as any conducted by the Germans in Poland and Russia.

Albania, Greece, and the former Yugoslav territory of Montenegro had all been assigned to the Italian sphere of influence in the Balkans, only becoming the responsibility of the Germans after the Italian surrender. The German ocupation of all three countries was too brief and the German officials there too preoccupied with problems of security to allow them much opportunity to reveal their plans for the future. It would appear, however, that they did not intend to annex these territories to Germany but rather to set up semiautonomous governments comparable to those in Hungary and Rumania which would be expected to keep their policies in line with those of the Reich and ensure Germany access to their economic resources. The only area over which Hitler would almost certainly have wished to retain direct control was the territory around the port of Salonika, the principal outlet of Southeastern Europe to the Aegean. The entire Adriatic coast, on the other hand, including the greater part of Greece, does not appear to have interested him very much. Hitler did not even propose to retain Crete as a German stronghold after the war, for that would have meant keeping a German fleet in the Mediterranean and created the danger of conflict with the Turks. Because Hitler wanted the Turks as allies after the war, the most he intended to do with Crete was to maintain a center for Germany's Strength Through Joy organization on the island.[241]

CHAPTER 10

Italy: The Defeated Ally

In political terms, Hitler's consistent advocacy of a German alliance with Italy can be explained as an application of the balance of power principle: If Germany dedicated a large proportion of its energies to the conquest of *Lebensraum* in Eastern Europe, a German alliance with Italy (and hopefully with Britain as well) would be essential as a counterweight to France. In terms of Hitler's racial ideology, however, his alliance with Italy remains something of an anomaly, for the racial qualities of the Italians could hardly be considered any more Germanic or Aryan than those of the French, who were regarded by Hitler as Germany's mortal enemies.

Yet in contrast to his alliance with Japan (which Hitler once defended by saying he would make an alliance with the devil himself in order to win the war),[1] Hitler's alliance with Italy was not simply a product of cynical calculation. Other racial theorists might classify the Italians as a Latin or Mediterranean people, but Hitler had quite different ideas on the subject. According to his racial doctrine, any culture worthy of admiration must a priori be the creation of an Aryan people. Thus the Greeks of the Golden Age, as well as the ancient Romans, had been Aryans. So, too, were the Italians, whose Renaissance was described by Hitler as "the dawn of a new era in which the Aryan man found himself anew." Hitler believed that, in terms of culture, the Germans were more closely linked to the Italians than to any other people, an opinion he considered to be confirmed by the art of northern Italy which was "nothing but pure German." Now, in the era of Mussolini's Italian Renaissance, the Germans and Italians not only shared common cultural values but common political values as well. "From the point of view of a world philosophy," Hitler declared, "[the Italians are] the only people on earth with whom we can see eye to eye." [2]

Hitler was by no means blind to the military deficiencies of his Italian

317

allies; but, apart from moments of pique when he described them as being better eaters than fighters, he tended to blame their miserable military showing on the poor quality of their military leadership and on the continued influence of the Italian court. Mussolini's failure to sweep away the monarchy was one of the few criticisms he leveled at the Italian dictator, whom he appears to have admired with real sincerity and for whom he seems to have felt a genuine friendship.[3] All available evidence suggests that until the downfall of the Mussolini regime Hitler honestly intended to concede Italy supremacy in the entire Mediterranean area, including North Africa and the Near East, and to renounce all German claims to the former Austrian territory of South Tyrol, from which the ethnic German population was to be removed.[4]

While Italy remained an ally of Germany, Hitler kept faith with the Italians, or at any rate with Mussolini, although that faith was often severely tried. Italy did not enter the war at the side of Germany until it was certain that France had been decisively beaten and it seemed equally certain that Germany would win a final victory over Britain as well. Once Italy did join in the war, the Italians demanded much by way of military equipment and raw materials and in general proved a serious drain on the German military economy. Yet, even with German economic support, the Italians fared badly. In the Balkans, Mussolini's ill-conceived and disastrous war against Greece badly tarnished the prestige of the Axis and undoubtedly contributed to the failure of Hitler's diplomatic efforts in Yugoslavia, thereby making a German military campaign in the Balkans necessary. In the war against British imperial forces in Africa, the Italians were soundly thrashed on every front and were only saved from total disaster in the spring of 1941 by the arrival of German troops under the command of General Erwin Rommel. The much-vaunted Italian navy and air force proved no match for the British in the Mediterranean, which they were never able to control in the Axis interest.

The Italian war effort broke down altogether in 1943. In November of the previous year, Anglo-American forces landed on the west coast of North Africa; by May of 1943 all Axis resistance in North Africa had collapsed. Two months later, on July 10, 1943, the Allies invaded Sicily and simultaneously launched heavy air attacks on Italian mainland cities. Within a fortnight half of Sicily, including the capital of Palermo, had fallen. On the evening of July 24 a majority of the Fascist Grand Council voted to censure Mussolini's conduct of the war; on the following day the king called for Mussolini's resignation. Upon leaving the royal palace, Mussolini was placed under arrest at the king's orders and was subsequently moved from one place of detention to another to frustrate possible attempts on the part of his followers or the Germans to liberate him.[5]

The king and the new head of the Italian government, Marshal Pietro Badoglio, assured the Germans that Italy would remain in the war on the side of Germany; but Hitler had no confidence whatever in the word of the Italian leaders. "They say they will fight, but it is certainly treachery," he told his generals on the evening of July 25. Hitler's first impulse upon hearing the news from Italy was to order German troops to Rome to capture the new Italian government and restore Mussolini, but the notable indifference of the Italian people to the downfall of the Fascist government persuaded him to abandon or at least postpone this project. Instead he ordered that preparations be made to implement Operation Alaric, a military plan formulated the previous May for the occupation of Italy in the event of Italy's withdrawal from the war. General Rommel, who had been placed in command of a new Army Group B for the purpose of covering Italy, was appointed commander of all German units in northern and central Italy. German forces already in Italy were regrouped and heavy German reinforcements were sent into the country.[6]

Hitler's lack of faith in the new Italian government soon proved justified. On September 3 the Badoglio regime signed a secret armistice with the Allies; five days later the unconditional surrender of Italy was publicly announced. The Germans were ready to cope with the situation. They immediately seized control of all strategic positions still held by Italian troops and disarmed all Italian forces that fell into their hands, meeting with remarkably little resistance as they did so. On September 9, the day after the announcement of Badoglio's surrender, the Germans proclaimed the formation of an Italian National Fascist government which was to be composed of Fascist leaders who had remained loyal to the German alliance. The question of the leadership of this government was still being debated—Mussolini's son Vittorio was proposed as a temporary figurehead—when, on September 12, Mussolini himself was dramatically rescued by an SS commando unit from his most recent place of detention on the Gran Sasso, the highest peak in the Abruzzi. He was at once flown to Germany, where he had several conferences with Hitler. On September 15 an official communiqué was issued in his name in Rome stating that "Benito Mussolini has today reassumed supreme direction of Fascism in Italy." This communiqué was followed by orders of the day reinstating Italian officials dismissed by Badoglio, instructing the Fascist party to support the German army, and absolving officers of the Italian armed forces from their oath of allegiance to the king.[7]

The Germans now faced the problem of putting together an Italian government over which Mussolini could preside. This task was undertaken by the chief German diplomatic representative in Italy, Rudolf Rahn, who had been sent to Rome at the end of July to negotiate with the Badoglio regime. By September 23 Rahn was able to announce the formation of a new Fascist ministry which included the respected Marshal Rodolfo Graziani as minister of war. "Reconstruction of the government completed at noon," Rahn reported to Berlin. "I was only able to persuade Graziani to enter the government one minute before the publication of the communiqué." [8]

The new Fascist Republican government was little more than a tool of the Germans. Tired and sick, Mussolini does not appear to have clung to power for its own sake so much as to use what small leverage he still possessed to act as a buffer between the Italian people and the Germans. His efforts, like those of other collaborationist leaders, were to be pitifully ineffective.

In the past, in the interest of his alliance with Italy, Hitler had persistently renounced all German political or ethnic claims to Italian territory, notably South Tyrol. All available evidence indicates that he was sincere in his assurances to Mussolini on that score. But with the Italian surrender, and even after the formation of the new Mussolini government, Hitler no longer felt any obligation to respect Italy's territorial integrity. He pursued a policy that left no doubt of his intention to incorporate a large part of northern Italy into the Greater German Reich.[9]

Propaganda Minister Joseph Goebbels had originally been opposed to any premature revelation of German intentions in northern Italy. "We cannot seize southern Tyrol now," he wrote in his diary on September 10, 1943, "because that would absolutely flabbergast the Italian people and condemn every neo-Fascist government to impotence." Goebbels's restraint was purely tactical, however. "We must not only get back South Tyrol," he said, "but I envisage the boundary line drawn south of Venetia. Whatever was once an Austrian possession we must get back into our own hands. The Italians by their infidelity and treachery have lost any claim to a national state of the modern type." Goebbels appears to have convinced Hitler of the desirability of the Venetian frontier, for on September 23 he recorded in his diary that Hitler now proposed to include Venetia in the Reich "in a sort of loose federation." Goebbels thought the boundary south of Venetia was "the only practical and right one. I only hope that the Führer will not let anything, especially his reawakening friendship for the Duce, divert him from this decision." [10] Goebbels had no need for concern. Hitler proceeded to reorganize Italy in the German interest with cavalier disregard of Mussolini's sensibilities or the prestige of his government.

Hitler's first orders for the German administration of Italy were issued on September 10, 1943.[11] All of Italy was placed under German military authority, and the occupied territory was divided into two general administrative spheres: operational zones (in the first instance the coastal and border regions), the boundaries of which were to be determined by military necessity and which were to be administered by German military commanders; and nonoperational areas (largely the territories of the interior), which Hitler subsequently turned over to the administration of Italian Fascist government. In the operational zones the military commanders were assigned as advisers civilian supreme commissars (*ob-*

erste Kommissare), who were empowered to appoint and dismiss all senior Italian officials and to install German advisers in all Italian administrative departments.

As usual in dealing with problems of administration, Hitler was not consistent. In a top secret supplementary protocol to his order of September 10, he set aside two sectors of the operational zones where German commissars directly responsible to himself were to have supreme administrative authority and where the military commanders would be responsible only for military affairs. The reason for Hitler's initial secrecy about these civilian-administered sectors was simple: These were territories he intended to annex to Germany; but because he still faced the problem of re-establishing an Italian Fascist government he could not yet afford to make his intentions too obvious.

The first of these civilian-administered sectors, which Hitler called the Lower Alps (Alpenvorland), consisted of the provinces of Bolzano (Bozen), Trent, and Belluno. This was the controversial South Tyrol area, until 1918 a part of Austria and still inhabited by a large body of ethnic Germans, which Hitler had previously renounced in the interest of his alliance with Italy. As his supreme commissar here he appointed the Reichsstatthalter and Gauleiter of Tyrol-Vorarlberg, Franz Hofer. In the other civilian-administered sector, the Adriatic Littoral (Adriatisches Küstenland), consisting of the provinces of Friuli (Udine), Gorizia, Trieste, Quarnero (Fiume), and Lubiana, Hitler's supreme commissar was Dr. Friedrich Rainer, Reichsstatthalter and Gauleiter of Carinthia.

Hofer, Rainer, and many of their deputies had been officials, or sons of officials, of the Austro-Hungarian Empire. They were now called upon to administer territories that had recently been part of that empire and in which they themselves often had connections or prior experience. Both Rainer and Hofer were known as fervent advocates of regaining these territories for a Germanic Reich. At the special request of Ribbentrop, Hitler delayed a public announcement of the appointment of Hofer and Rainer until after a clarification of the situation in Italy, but with the liberation of Mussolini and the subsequent formation of an Italian Fascist Republican government Hitler evidently saw no further reason for secrecy. Hofer was publicly installed in his new post on September 25, Rainer on September 29, 1943. Both officials were given supreme executive powers, the right to legislate by decree, and absolute authority over local officials, including the judiciary.[12]

The policies pursued by Hofer and Rainer removed whatever doubts the Italians may have had about the ultimate objective of the German administration. Upon taking over their duties they appointed new, and presumably more reliable, prefects as heads of the provinces within their administrative spheres. Except in the predominantly German-speaking province of Bolzano, all the new prefects were Italian. Each prefect, however, was assigned a German adviser who was empowered to issue orders to the prefect and whose approval was required for all administrative measures. This meant that the German advisers were the real rulers of the provinces, that the Italian prefects were mere figureheads.[13]

Apart from the appointment of Italian prefects, the German leadership made almost no concessions to Italian public opinion or to the Mussolini government. At a meeting with Hofer and Rainer soon after their appointment, Rudolf Rahn, Hitler's chief diplomatic representative to the Italian Fascist government, urged that they postpone or at least disguise their measures aimed at annexing Italian territory to Germany. Only those decrees vital to the war should be made public, and these should be negotiated with the Mussolini government whose prestige had to be preserved.[14] But neither supreme commissar heeded Rahn's advice. Decrees were published making the Alpine and Adriatic territories part of the Reich customs and currency area; frontier controls and customs barriers were set up along the borders of the new territories; neither territory could be entered from Italy without a passport or visa issued by the appropriate German authorities. Military conscription was introduced in the Alpine territory and German law replaced Italian for all ethnic Germans; in the Adriatic Italian law remained in force, provided it did not conflict with subsequent German decrees or with German military requirements. While Rainer allowed his prefects to establish contact with the Mussolini government, Hofer forbade all such relationships and proceeded to integrate his Italian provinces (with the exception of Belluno) into his German Gau. German was made the official language of the administration and the schools, Italian officials and teachers were systematically replaced by Germans. The continued use of Italian currency and postage stamps remained the only symbols of Italian sovereignty.[15]

Even in the nonoperational areas under the sovereignty of the Mussolini government the actual power of that government was minimal. Like the rest of German-occupied Italy, the nonoperational areas were under the supreme authority of the German army. In his order of September 10, however, Hitler appointed a special military commander for these areas (General Toussaint) with primary responsibility for their military security. In addition he named Rudolf Rahn plenipotentiary of the Greater German Reich with the Italian Fascist Republican government and as such special adviser for political affairs. SS Obergruppenführer and General of the Police Karl Wolff was appointed special adviser to the Italian Fascist government for police matters. And Hitler reserved the right to appoint further advisers as he saw fit. All Italian prefects in the nonoperational areas were also to have German advisers who were to receive their orders from Rahn in his capacity as Reich plenipotentiary. In October 1943, at the request of Mussolini, the title of General Toussaint was changed from German military commander in Italy to plenipotentiary general of the German Wehrmacht with the Italian Fascist Republican government. He remained responsible for military security and was authorized to assemble a full-scale administrative staff to supervise and control the Italian administration. As in the case of "independent" Croatia, "independent" Italy was treated like a con-

322

quered country; its manpower and other economic assets were ruthlessly exploited for German purposes. What had been left to the authority of the Fascist Republican government was not at all clear.[16]

Even less clear were the lines of authority of the German administration in Italy. Supreme military command was divided between Field Marshal Albert Kesselring in the south and Field Marshal Erwin Rommel in the center and north; but neither supreme military commander was given clear-cut authority over the other. Moreover, Kesselring and Rommel were unable to agree on major questions of policy or strategy, so that there was a command stalemate whenever questions affecting the whole of Italy had to be decided. Not until November 21, 1943, did Hitler accede to Kesselring's plea for a unified command in Italy, at which time Rommel was transferred to France and Kesselring appointed commander in chief southwest with responsibility for the whole of Italy.[17]

The unification of German military command in Italy did not put an end to administrative conflict and confusion. As in other occupied areas, Hitler assigned independent authority to a large number of Reich agencies to deal with their particular fields of competence. SS commands responsible for security and order were established in both the operational and nonoperational areas of Italy parallel to German military commands. On September 12 Hitler authorized Albert Speer to take whatever measures he considered necessary to mobilize the Italian economy for German war production. Later in the month Fritz Sauckel was given similar authority for the recruitment of Italian labor. Both officials built up a major administrative apparatus in Italy, as did other Reich leaders anxious to extend their administrative empires. Co-ordinating powers conferred on one office were generally ignored by other offices, or undercut by conflicting orders. Thus authority over German advisers to Italian officials, originally assigned to Rahn, was later delegated to Toussaint, but no orders were issued canceling the powers of Rahn. And so it went. All along there were protracted negotiations among German administrative agencies to clarify their various spheres of competence; but individual officials often seemed more interested in defending or extending their personal powers than in administrative efficiency.[18]

After Goebbels's appointment as plenipotentiary for total war in July 1944, Mussolini appealed to him to turn his attention to the problem of the German administration in Italy,

"where in a whole series of offices there are hundreds and thousands of Germans who could be better employed elsewhere. . . . There is a military administration, and this is understandable, but then there are other offices—economic, cultural, police, etc.—which constitute a superstructure, a series of small states within a state, with the result that . . . the [Italian Fascist] Republic's authority is continually being impaired." [19]

Goebbels was fully aware of the problem, but there was nothing he could do. The German military defense of Italy was stubborn and skillful; but behind the lines the confusion in the German administration persisted, the prestige of Mussolini's government steadily declined, sabotage and guerrilla warfare steadily increased.

Even with their backs to the wall, Nazi officials had time and manpower to devote to the Jewish question. Under pressure from the Germans, the Italian government had passed a certain amount of anti-Semitic legislation prior to the German occupation. Although this legislation caused a great deal of hardship, it was neither so thorough nor so rigorously enforced as similar legislation in the Reich. By the end of 1941 only about seven thousand of the fifty thousand Jews living in Italy at the beginning of the war had left the country; those who remained were by and large left in peace. As late as May 1943 a German diplomatic representative in Rome observed that the Italian government was simply not interested in the Jewish question; the Italian army was still permeated with Jews and countless half-Jews, and the Fascist party would do nothing against the Jews without direct orders from the Duce.[20]

The situation changed drastically after the German occupation. Early in October 1943 the head of the German police in Rome, SS Obersturmbannführer Kappler, received orders from Berlin to seize the eight thousand Jews living in Rome and to send them to northern Italy "where they are to be liquidated." German military and diplomatic officials in Rome argued that it would be far more sensible to use the Jews for construction work. They were informed, however, that Hitler himself had given the orders to remove the eight thousand Roman Jews; German diplomatic representatives were instructed on no account to interfere but to leave the whole matter to the SS.[21]

On October 17 Kappler reported to Senior SS and Police Officer Wolff that the "Jewish action was begun and concluded today on the basis of the best possible plan that could be worked out in an office." All available German police forces had been used because the Italians could not be trusted for this purpose. Altogether, 1,259 persons had been seized, of whom 1,007 would be shipped off on the following day. The reaction of the Italian population by and large had been one of passive resistance, in some cases of active resistance, but it had been possible to carry out the action without resorting to shooting.[22]

The Germans ascribed their failure to seize no more than one out of eight members of the Jewish population in Rome to the attitude of the Italian people, who showed no signs of anti-Semitic sentiments and who aided the Jews in escaping from the city or going into hiding. In other parts of Italy the action against the Jews was even less successful. In December 1943 Himmler's agents complained that the roundups of Jews had so far had no results worthy of mention, and they demanded more effective co-operation on the part of the Italian government. If Italian officials expressed scruples, they should be told that the ultimate purpose of the Jewish action was merely the internment of Jews, and not, as was actually the case, their complete extermination.[23]

At the behest of the Germans, the Italian government did indeed pass stringent anti-Semitic legislation, including a law requiring that all Jews be placed in concentration camps. But otherwise the Italians failed to provide the co-operation Himmler's agents desired. By the end of the war a large majority of Italian Jews had managed to escape arrest or deportation.[24]

As is hardly surprising, in no part of Europe were Hitler's war aims more drastically altered by the Italian surrender in September 1943 than in Italy itself. Before then he had been prepared to concede his Italian allies supremacy in the Mediterranean and the status of an equal partner (even if steadily less equal) in his New Order. After the Italian surrender, however, and even after the formation of Mussolini's Fascist Republic, he proceeded to deal with Italy as with a conquered country. In the territories of Italy which had been part of the Habsburg Empire before 1918 he pursued policies which left no doubt about his intention to annex them to the Reich. As Hitler already regarded the population of these regions to be Germanic, most of the native inhabitants would presumably have been considered suitable for Germanization; only non-Aryans and those who refused to recognize their Germanic heritage or who otherwise rejected Nazi dominion would have been expelled or exterminated.

Nazi territorial expansion in Italy would certainly not have stopped at the borders of South Tyrol, however. Goebbels had declared that the only logical German frontier in Italy should be drawn south of Venice. It can be assumed that the Nazis would also have claimed Lombardy, whether on the basis of its settlement by the Germanic Lombards or because Lombardy, like Venetia, had been a province of the Habsburg Empire until the mid-nineteenth century. As the ancient Romans were also considered to be a Nordic people, Nazi territorial claims at the expense of Italy could have been extended indefinitely. According to Nazi theorists, Sicily too had enjoyed its Golden Ages under Nordic organizers, be they Greek or Norman; as recently as the thirteenth century Sicily had been part of the Germanic Hohenstaufen Empire. Hitler, to be sure, had consistently condemned German expansion to the south as being misdirected and demoralizing, but neither he nor his satraps had shown notable restraint in this regard once the opportunities for expansion were present. German political and military leaders would have had no trouble making a case that the occupation of Sicily was essential to ensure German security and protect German interests in the Mediterranean; and German occupation would surely have been followed sooner or later by a program to Germanize the island in order to restore and preserve its Germanic character. The possibilities, and the justifications for them, were endless.

CHAPTER 11

Russia: The Promised Land

During the period of preparation for the invasion of Russia, Hitler had concentrated on military and diplomatic problems and devoted relatively little attention to long-range goals in the conquered territories of the east. He made up for this omission after the invasion began. At high-level conferences and in conversations with his closest associates he expressed views about German policy in the east which remained true in every essential feature to the doctrines expounded in *Mein Kampf*.

The Plans of Hitler

The main thing, he told Göring, Keitel, Rosenberg, Lammers, and Bormann at a conference on July 16, 1941, was that the Germans themselves should know what they wanted in the east.[1] This did not mean that they should make their task more difficult by premature announcements of their true intentions. On the contrary, as in the case of Scandinavia and the Low Countries they should disguise their aims by posing as liberators whose policies were designed solely to re-establish order and security in the best interests of the inhabitants. "Nobody should be able to recognize that they initiate a final settlement. This need not prevent us from taking all necessary measures—shooting, evacuations, etc.—and we shall take them."

After the collapse of the Red Army and the Bolshevik state, Germany would face the task of dealing with the immense territory west of the Urals according to its needs in order to dominate, administer, and exploit it. The first principle of German leadership should be to render impossible the establishment of another military power in this area. An accompanying principle should be that none but Germans should be allowed to bear arms. The apparent desirability of enlisting the aid of

326

subjugated peoples was a false illusion which was certain to redound to Germany's detriment if it were attempted.

The first necessity, of course, would be to pacify this gigantic territory as quickly as possible. "This could best be done by shooting everyone who looked in any way suspicious," Hitler said. He noted with satisfaction that the Soviet government had ordered the native population to conduct partisan warfare behind the German lines, for this would make it easier for German troops to identify and exterminate opposition elements. To speed the pacification process, he wanted to equip police regiments with armored vehicles and Göring was to move his training fields to the east so that airpower could be used against insurgents.

After conquest and pacification were complete, Hitler proposed to annex the Baltic states and the former Austrian part of Galicia to the Reich. The Crimea, together with a large hinterland, was to be cleared of foreign elements and colonized by Germans. This territory, too, was to become part of the Reich, as were the lands inhabited by the Volga Germans, the Baku oil district, and the Kola peninsula with its nickel mines.

In response to Göring's inquiry at the July 16 conference as to what promises had been made to other states, Hitler said that Ion Antonescu wanted Bessarabia and Odessa, plus a small strip to the northwest, which would extend Rumania's territory very little beyond its old boundaries. No specific promises had been made to the Hungarians, Turks, or Slovaks. The Finns wanted Eastern Karelia, which Hitler was willing to concede them with the exception of the Kola peninsula. The Finns also wanted the Leningrad area, which was to go to them after the city had been razed.

Hitler's ambitions expanded as he contemplated the manifold possibilities opening up before Germany in the east.[2] He soon rejected the Urals as the new German frontier.

> The real frontier, [he told his staff,] is the one that separates the Germanic world from the Slav world. It is our duty to place it where we want it to be. If anyone asks where we obtain the right to extend the Germanic space to the east, we reply that, for a nation, its awareness of what it represents carries this right with it. It is success that justifies everything. The reply to such questions can only be of an empirical nature.
>
> It is inconceivable, [Hitler continued,] that a higher people should painfully exist on a soil too narrow for it, whilst amorphous masses, which contribute nothing to civilization, occupy infinite tracts of a soil that is one of the richest in the world. . . . We must create conditions for our people that favor its multiplication, and we must at the same time build a dike against the Russian flood. . . . Since there is no natural protection against such a flood, we must meet it with a living wall. A permanent war on the eastern front will help form a sound race of men, and will prevent us from relapsing into the softness of a Europe thrown

RUSSIA, FINLAND,
AND THE BALTIC STATES

——————— Prewar boundaries

+ + + + + Russo-Finnish boundaries after
the Russo-Finnish war, Mar. 1940

· · · · · · · Russo-German boundary after
the destruction of Poland

Russian areas under Axis
military government

⊥⊥⊥⊥ Maximum extent of Axis
penetration

⚑ Oil fields

NORWAY

BARENTS
SEA

Petsamo

KOLA
PENINSULA

SWEDEN

WHITE
SEA

Onega Bay

Onega R.

KARELIA

FINLAND
Allied with Germany

Lake
Onega

Helsinki

Lake
Ladoga

Svir R.

Gulf of Finland

Leningrad

BALTIC SEA

Tallinn

Neva R.

ESTONIA

REICHSKOMMISSARIAT OSTLAND

Riga

LATVIA

LITHUANIA

Kaunas

Moscow

E. PRUSSIA

WHITE
RUTHENIA

Minsk

Smolensk

S O V I E T   U N I O N

Volga R.

GOVERNMENT GENERAL

VOLHYNIA-
PODOLIA

ZHITOMIR

Voronezh

Kiev

REICHSKOMMISSARIAT UKRAINE

KIEV

Kharkov

NORTHERN
BUKOVINA

TRANSNISTRIA
(Rumania)

NIKOLAEV

DNEPROPETROVSK

Stalingrad

BESSARABIA

Odessa

Melitopol

TAURIDA

Taganrog

Rostov

RUMANIA

Sea of
Azov

Isthmus
of Perekop

CRIMEA

CASPIAN SEA

BULGARIA

BLACK SEA

Maikop

Grozny

Batum

Tiflis

Baku

Istanbul

TURKEY

IRAN

0   500 miles

back upon itself. It should be possible for us to control this region to the east with two hundred and fifty thousand men plus a cadre of good administrators. . . . This space in Russia must always be dominated by Germans.

The Ukraine and the Volga basin were to become the granaries of Europe. Germany would also get oil and iron from the east. "Where is there a region capable of supplying iron of the quality of Ukrainian iron? Where can one find more nickel, more coal, more manganese, more molybdenum? . . . And, on top of that, so many other possibilities! The vegetable oils, the rubber plantations to be organized. With 100,000 acres devoted to the growing of rubber, our needs are covered." The rubber plantations would be established in the Crimea, which would also give Germany citrus fruits and cotton. "The Pripet marshes will supply us with reeds. . . . The Black Sea will be for us a sea whose wealth our fishermen will never exhaust. Thanks to the cultivation of the soya bean, we will increase our livestock. We will win from the soil several times as much as the Ukrainian peasant is winning at present."

In addition to the Crimea, Germany would take the southern part of the Ukraine and make the entire area an exclusively German colony. "There will be no harm in pushing out the population that is there now. The German colonist will be the soldier-peasant. . . . These soldier-peasants will be given arms, so that at the slightest danger they can be at their posts when we summon them." The Germans would have to constitute among themselves a closed society, like a fortress. The lowest German stable boy would be superior to any native. The opportunities for German youth would be limitless.

This Russian desert, we shall populate it. The immense spaces of the eastern front will have been the field of the greatest battles in history. We will give this country a past. We will take away its character of an Asiatic steppe, we will Europeanize it. With this object, we have undertaken the construction of roads that will lead to the southernmost point of the Crimea and to the Caucasus. These roads will be studded along their whole length with German towns, and around these towns our colonists will settle.

Railways would be extended through all parts of the country, with a four-track system along the principal lines of communication and new rolling stock capable of traveling at speeds of two hundred kilometers an hour. Inland waterways would be impractical because they would be icebound seven months of the year. "As for the two or three million men whom we need to accomplish this task, we will find them more quickly than we think. They will come from Germany, Scandinavia, the Western countries, and America. I shall no longer be here to see all that, but in twenty years the Ukraine will already be a home for twenty million inhabitants besides the natives. In three hundred years, the country will be one of the loveliest gardens in the world." The Germans would reforest the Ukraine to make the climate more equable and to control the rainfall. In the marshlands they would plant reeds to form barriers against the winds that swept the steppes.

> The German colonists ought to live on handsome, spacious farms. The German services will be lodged in marvelous buildings, the governors in palaces. Beneath the shelter of the administrative services, we shall gradually organize all that is indispensable to the maintenance of a certain standard of living. Around the city, to a depth of thirty to forty kilometers, we shall have a belt of handsome villages connected by the best roads. What exists beyond that will be another world, in which we mean to let the Russians live as they like. It is merely necessary that we should rule them.

There was but one supreme duty in the east: to pursue a methodical racial policy, "to Germanize this country by the immigration of Germans, and to look upon the natives as Redskins." Except in a few special areas the natives were not to be expelled from the occupied territories, for they would be needed as labor for the gigantic tasks that lay ahead. But they were to be screened carefully to make certain that all potential leaders and Jews were removed. Hitler had no intention of distributing land to the natives or giving them more than a rudimentary education. "Our guiding principle must be that these people have but one justification for existence—to be of use to us economically."

With the conquest of Russia, the German people would have been given what it needed to assert its position in the world. The possession of Russian space would make Europe an impregnable fortress, safe from all threat of blockade.

> My long-term policy aims at having eventually a hundred million Germans settled in these territories. It is therefore essential to set up machinery which will ensure constant progression, and we will see to it that million by million German penetration expands. In ten years' time we must be in a position to announce that twenty million Germans have been settled in the territories already incorporated in the Reich and in those which our troops are at present occupying. . . . We shall not succeed except by the application of the most severe measures. Nevertheless I am convinced that these territories will bear a profound Germanic imprint after fifty years of National Socialist history!

Military and political disasters had no effect on Hitler's war aims. Throughout the Russian campaign he stated and restated these same objectives with minor variations and embellishments. A speech to army group commanders in July 1943 might have been delivered in July 1941—or in 1924.

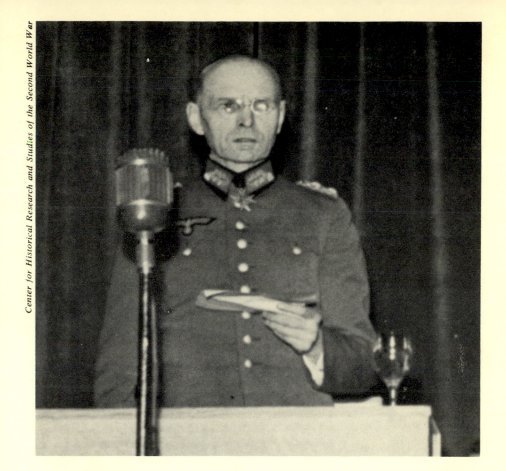

General Alexander von Falkenhausen, German military commander for Belgium and Northern France. *Below*, Eggert Reeder, chief of the administrative staff of the German military government of Belgium and Northern France, presenting a watch to the two hundred fifty thousandth Belgian worker departing to work in Germany, January 15, 1942.

Staf de Clercq, leader of the Flemish nationalist VNV party.

Joachim von Ribbentrop (left) and Léon Degrelle, the leader of the Belgian Rexist movement.

General Henri-Philippe Pétain with Admiral Jean François Darlan (left) and
General Laure (beside Darlan) talking with workers at a French steel factory.

Photo Harlingue-Viollet

Pierre Laval, the Vichy French leader, with Hitler.

Otto Abetz (left), the representative of the German Foreign Office in France, with Pierre Laval.

Reinhard Heydrich (center), acting Reich protector of Bohemia and Moravia, in Paris with the newly appointed senior SS and police officer for France, Karl Albrecht Oberg (left), and the previous head of the German police in France, Helmuth Knochen. Shortly after this picture was taken, Heydrich was assassinated in Prague.

Admiral Miklós Horthy, the regent of Hungary, with Hitler at a naval review in Kiel.

Marshal Ion Antonescu, the de facto head of the Rumanian government, on a visit to Hitler in Munich, June 6, 1941.

Staatsbibliothek Berlin

Hitler with the head of the puppet government of Croatia, Ante Pavelić, at the palace of Klessheim. Behind them, Siegfried Kasche, the German minister to Croatia (left) and Joachim von Ribbentrop; behind Ribbentrop, the head translator of the German Foreign Office, Dr. Paul Schmidt.

Wide World Photos

General Milan Nedić, head of the puppet government of Serbia.

Alfred Rosenberg, Reich minister for the occupied eastern territories, receiving Hitler's birthday congratulations.

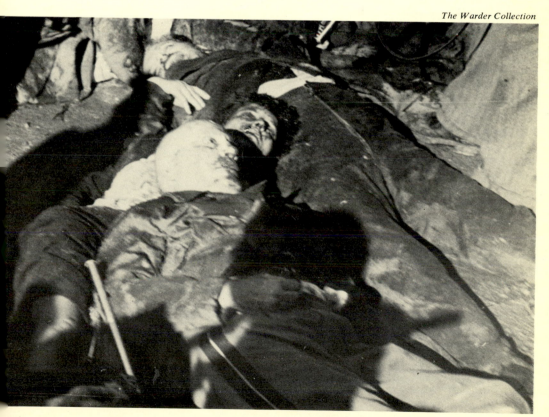

The corpses of Mussolini and his mistress, Clara Petacci.

Wilhelm Kube, Generalkommissar in White Ruthenia.

Hinrich Lohse, Reichskommissar of the Ostland.

Erich Koch, Gauleiter and Oberpräsident of East Prussia and Reichskommissar of the Ukraine.

The fight, gentlemen, is a fight for *Lebensraum*. Without this *Lebensraum* the German Reich and the German nation cannot endure. Germany must become the hegemonial power in Europe, but even if it does so, it cannot exist in such a ludicrous area as we inhabit today. In such an area one will not be able in the future to build up an army. . . . Whoever has his industry squeezed into such a small space runs the risk of having it destroyed, I might say, overnight. In that event fine ideas are of no use whatever, for in the end man lives from the earth and the earth is the prize which Providence gives to those people who fight for it.[3]

Given the nature of Hitler's program for Russia, there was a pathetic irony in the fact that in many parts of the country, but especially in the Baltic states and the Ukraine, the German invaders were greeted enthusiastically as liberators from Bolshevik tyranny. The first reports of German observers in Russia were unanimous on this point. They were equally unanimous in describing the rapid deterioration of this friendly attitude.[4] This change was due in part to the natural disillusionment that sets in soon after the establishment of any new regime. Liberators are never popular long. But it was far more due to the policies pursued by the various German leaders and organizations entrusted with the administration of the newly conquered territories.

Hitler's own policies for Russia were hardly calculated to endear the Germans to the native population. These policies were not endorsed by all German administrators in the east, to be sure, but the programs advocated by more moderate German leaders were either never adopted at all or were not pursued widely enough or consistently enough to offset the impression created by the activities of Hitler's more doctrinaire followers. Moreover the brutal nature of the conflict in the east, the almost constant fatigue and fear to which all German soldiers were subjected, made it inevitable that the ruthless measures ordered by Hitler should frequently be employed by men who otherwise had no sympathy or understanding for the program of their leader.

Among the more unfortunate of Hitler's policies from the point of view of the German administration in the east was his refusal on principle to enlist the aid of the Slavic peoples or to allow anyone but Germans to bear arms. This prohibition made it difficult—at first almost impossible—for the Germans to set up native nationalist or anti-Communist governments in the conquered areas as allies against Bolshevik Russia, or to recruit manpower in the east for service in the German armed forces. Because of Hitler's opposition, the Germans in the beginning made almost no use of the various *émigré* or nationalist leaders who had been cultivated by the German Counterintelligence, the Foreign Office, Rosenberg's Foreign Political Office, the Propaganda Ministry, and other German agencies seeking to exploit the national differences within the Soviet Union. This was the case, for example, with the Ukrainian nationalist leaders Andrei Melnyk and Stepan Bandera. Paradoxically, it was Himmler, the most literal exponent of Hitler's ideas, who from the first violated Hitler's principle about allowing the subject peoples of the east to bear arms; he consistently made use of native police as auxiliaries of his own police forces, he recruited natives as members of the Waffen-SS (without being overly punctilious about their racial qualifications), and it was he who finally persuaded Hitler to make use of the most famous Russian leader captured by the Wehrmacht, General Andrei Vlassov, who had offered to recruit an army of Russians to fight against Stalin and Bolshevism.[5]

So far as the efficiency of the German administration in the east was concerned, there was the further problem that Hitler had assigned broad, and quasi-independent, powers to four separate German administrative organizations—the army, the Göring economic offices, the Rosenberg ministry, and the Himmler offices—and that he had provided for the establishment of yet further administrative organizations in the form of civil governments which were to be set up as soon as the military situation would permit. Hence, from the beginning German rule in Russia was characterized by administrative conflict and confusion.[6]

The Military Administration

The first German organization on the scene in Russia was the German army, including the army's economic offices for the sequestration of Russian military equipment and raw materials. As in other occupied areas, the German military commanders were empowered to exercise supreme administrative as well as military authority during the initial period of occupation. The great difference in Russia was that a large part of the territory conquered by the Germans was never removed from the zone of military operations and thus remained under military government throughout the German occupation. This was true of the region south of Leningrad and of most of the territory east of the Dnieper river, a vast area. Thus in Russia the army appeared to have a unique opportunity to carry out its own policies as opposed to those of the Nazi leadership. The trouble was that, unlike Hitler, the Army High Command had no broadly conceived policies for dealing with Russia, nor was there any unanimity among German military leaders as to what Germany's ultimate aims in Russia should be.

The most obvious and important of the army's aims in Russia, of course, was the destruction of the Russian armed forces. After the first great German victories in the summer of 1941, the German High Command began to draw up plans for further conquests via Russia into the Near and Middle East.[7] But beyond purely military programs the army did not go. All administrative plans were based on the premise that Rus-

332

sia would be conquered quickly and that therewith the administration would be turned over to German civilian authorities.

Hitler did his best to see to it that the army pursued no independent administrative course in Russia. His basic decree on the powers of the military commanders in the newly occupied eastern territories of June 25, 1941, stipulated that the military commanders in the zones under military administration were to be appointed by himself and that their orders were to be drawn up according to his general directives. At the same time they were to remain part of the military hierarchy and were to be primarily concerned with military affairs. In Russia, as elsewhere, their main task was to safeguard the military security of the territory under their command against revolts from within and attacks from without. When a territory was transferred to a civil administration, they were to assist the civil leadership in its political and administrative tasks. Only in cases of military emergency were they empowered to resume supreme political as well as military authority.[8]

While assigning the army initial responsibility for the pacification of all conquered territory in the east, Hitler had also prescribed the methods to be used for carrying out this task. In his preinvasion directives he had demanded that his military commanders recognize the ideological nature of the struggle by wiping out all Bolshevik functionaries and Jews, and that they ruthlessly suppress every kind of opposition.[9] These directives were supplemented by a succession of almost identical orders after the campaign against Russia began.

"In view of the vast size of the conquered territories in the east," Hitler stated in an order of July 22, "the forces available for establishing security in these areas will be sufficient only if, instead of punishing resistance by sentences in a court of law, the occupying forces spread such terror as to crush every will to resist among the population." The commanders responsible for maintaining order in their respective territories should do so "not by demanding more security forces, but by applying suitable Draconian measures." [10]

A directive of September 8 on the treatment of Soviet prisoners of war reminded German commanders that "Bolshevism is the deadly enemy of National Socialist Germany," that they were now facing a foe steeped in this poisonous ideology. "He will make use of every means at his disposal: sabotage, morale-destroying propaganda, arson, murder." Because the Bolshevik soldier had forfeited every claim to be treated as an honorable foe, the most severe measures were justified in dealing with Russian prisoners of war. As Hitler still lacked confidence in the ruthlessness of his army leaders, he demanded that politically dangerous elements among the Russian prisoners of war be turned over to the SS and police for "special treatment." [11]

When Draconian measures, far from contributing to the pacification of the country, stirred up ever greater opposition and unrest, Hitler responded by calling for ever-greater ruthlessness. The unrest was part of a great mass movement directed by Moscow, he declared. *"Everywhere the harshest measures* are to be used to crush the resistance movement in the shortest possible time. . . . *Every case* of revolt against the German occupying power, no matter what the circumstances, must be ascribed to Communist origins." The most severe measures were to be applied immediately, at the first sign of revolt, to nip further unrest in the bud. Fifty to one hundred Communists should pay for the death of a single German soldier. "The manner of execution must intensify the intimidating effect." [12]

Further directives impressed on the military commanders the need to make every German soldier aware of the life-and-death nature of the current struggle, the necessity of exterminating the Jewish-Bolshevik system, and the justification of utter ruthlessness in dealing with insurrections behind the fighting lines "which experience has shown are always instigated by Jews." Any action likely to endanger the security of the German occupation forces was to be punished on principle with the death penalty. No pity should be shown to women and children. "Scruples of any sort whatsoever are a crime against the German people and against the front-line soldier who bears the consequences of the guerrilla attacks." [13]

Despite the bitter and often courageous protests of members of the German armed services of all ranks, the German army did indeed resort to brutal measures in its attempts to pacify the country, even if not always on the scale demanded by Hitler. There is ample evidence to suggest that the majority of German army leaders were as concerned as the most doctrinaire Nazis—a number of generals, of course, *were* doctrinaire Nazis—about the dangers of Russia and Bolshevism and, like them, they believed the major purpose of the present war should be to eliminate those dangers forever. It was presumably for this reason that some generals not only condoned the operations of Himmler's task forces in military administrative areas, as they had been ordered to do, but upon occasion actively supported these forces in their work of rooting out Communist functionaries and Jews who were supposed to be the principal bearers of the Bolshevik bacillus.[14]

Yet the actual policies of the various German military administrations in Russia were characterized not so much by brutal ruthlessness as by improvisation and expediency.[15] The nature of these military administrations varied widely in the immense territories under their jurisdiction and depended to a large extent on the character and political orientation of the local military commanders. Almost all army administrators, however, came to recognize that the most effective and least costly method of preserving order and reactivating the economy behind the fighting lines was to secure the confidence and co-operation of the local population. They were also to find that this could best be done, not by adhering firmly to a set of political and economic principles, but by dealing pragmatically with problems as they arose.

This was certainly the attitude of the German army administrators in the area around Leningrad, which remained under military government throughout the German occupation. The military authorities fostered local self government, for example, not for reasons of principle, but because they needed help in running the country and because they believed that men who held power under German auspices would have a stake in the German cause. By the beginning of 1942 almost all town and county districts in the Leningrad operational area were being administered by native governments under German supervision. The leaders of provinces and larger towns were appointed directly by the Germans; but all minor officials and the heads of small towns were selected by native administrators. The native governments were allowed to maintain their own police forces, local legal systems remained in effect, and minor offenses were tried in local courts according to local laws. Serious crimes and all political offenses, however, were handled by the German police and tried in German courts—if a trial was conducted at all.

The military government in the Leningrad area also removed many official economic restrictions, again not because of any theoretical belief in the principle of free trade, but because a free market proved to be the most effective way to reactivate the economy and bring goods into the market, where the Germans, too, might purchase them. Many forms of political and economic corruption were allowed to flourish if these seemed to contribute to an easing of political tensions and a rise in economic productivity. Thus a large-scale traffic in forged identity cards for Russian prisoners of war was condoned because it was recognized that these men would otherwise have no choice but to join the partisans. With forged identity cards, on the other hand, many escaped prisoners of war were able to return to their homes and contribute to the economic welfare of the community.[16]

One of the great difficulties of the German military administrators, as of all German administrators in the east, was that they did not exercise exclusive authority in the territories under their jurisdiction. In the areas under military government, Göring claimed overall economic authority, Himmler authority for all questions involving political security. Because Göring depended almost entirely on the army's own economic officials for the execution of his orders, his actual power to interfere in the affairs of the military government proved to be negligible. But Himmler had his own troops at his disposal which set about their task of combatting subversive elements and liquidating Communists and Jews (or suspected Communists and Jews) without restraint. As the measures of Himmler's forces, instead of pacifying the conquered territories, aroused steadily increasing hatred and popular opposition to German rule, many army leaders came to regard Himmler's agents as a greater menace to German

335

security than the partisans. Indeed it was they, these army leaders said, whose brutality and system of mass reprisals had driven thousands of previously well-disposed Russians into the partisan movement.

Hitler, of course, far from condemning tactics of terror, had himself given orders that terror be employed to the greatest possible extent. It was to Himmler, not to the army, that he entrusted ultimate responsibility for the pacification of the east. What was more, the military administrations themselves were living on borrowed time, for as soon as the military situation would permit they were to be replaced by Nazi civil governments in which only Nazi leaders would exercise authority.[17] For that reason, whatever conclusions may be drawn from the record of the military administrations in the east, they are of almost no significance as indications of Hitler's war aims.

Göring and the Administration of the Economy

The policies of Göring, Nazi though he was, resembled those of the military administrators in that they were shaped primarily by considerations of expediency. In the beginning, it seemed that Göring would exercise a decisive influence on the economic policies to be pursued in the newly occupied areas. Hitler, following up preinvasion provisions for the economic exploitation of Russia, issued a decree on June 29, 1941, empowering Göring as plenipotentiary of the Four-Year Plan to take all necessary measures to ensure the maximum exploitation of the conquered eastern territories. For this purpose he was authorized to issue direct orders to all military officials in the east and, after the establishment of civil governments there, to all civil officials as well.[18]

In subsequent decrees and policy statements, Göring emphasized that the Führer's decree had precluded all other government departments from issuing orders in the economic field in the east. He alone possessed the right to make fundamental decisions on economic policy; he alone was authorized to allocate the distribution of economic assets to other Reich agencies, which should henceforth channel all economic requests through his offices.[19]

Well before the invasion of Russia began, Göring had constructed an elaborate administrative apparatus and regional network to ensure his control over the economic exploitation in the east in areas under both military and civil administration.[20] To supplement his regional economic network, Göring issued a decree on July 27, 1941, providing for the establishment of giant monopoly companies to supervise entire sectors of the eastern economy. The Central Trading Company East (*Zentralhandelsgesellschaft Ost*), for example, was to be responsible for the production, collection, and distribution of all agricultural products; the Continental Oil Company (*Kontinentale Oel Aktiengesellschaft*) for the extraction, refining, and sale of petroleum products. Similar organizations were established for iron and steel, mining, textiles, leather goods, and tobacco. These monopoly companies, like the regional economic network, were to be under the central direction of Göring.[21]

In addition to his elaborate administrative organization, Göring had very clear ideas about Germany's economic aims in Russia. These amounted, quite simply, to a maximum exploitation of Russia's economic assets on behalf of the German war economy, regardless of the human or political factors involved, since the rapidity of the German conquest would render all political considerations unnecessary. It was only after it became obvious that the war would not be a short one that Göring saw the need, or allowed himself to be convinced of the need, to modify his original economic policies.

Göring's first directives for the conduct of economic policy in the newly occupied territories followed closely the line he had laid down before the invasion of Russia began. The aim of the economic leadership, he said on July 27, 1941, was not the early restoration of the economy. Instead, the vastness of Russian territory and the scarcity of skilled labor in the country necessitated a concentration on items essential to the German war economy—grain, vegetable oils, petroleum, light metals—and on industries for the production and distribution of such items as agricultural machinery and transportation equipment.

To avoid adding to the confusion caused by war, Göring proposed to retain the existing economic system in Russia, including the state factories and collective farms, which would be placed under German management. He even took state control a step further, establishing monopoly and trustee companies to manage entire sectors of the economy. In every case the decisive criterion for determining how any branch of the economy should be administered was to be expediency. If one system proved superior to another it was to be used. In the long run Göring thought that the best economic results could probably be obtained through private enterprise. "The system of collective economy shall, therefore, be continued only so long as it is absolutely essential to avoid the disruption of deliveries from Russian territory to the German army and the German economy which might result from sudden changes in economic methods." For the time being the order of the day was ruthless exploitation of Russian resources in which purely economic, not political, considerations should prevail. This policy was also to be pursued in the Baltic region (which the Germans called the Ostland), despite its special position as a future area of Germanization.[22]

Ruthless short-term exploitation was still the guiding principle when Göring reviewed German economic policies at a conference on November 8, 1941. For the duration of the war the requirements of the German war economy would continue to be the decisive consideration for all economic measures. The production of food and raw materials remained paramount. To feed the German army and at the same time to be able to send essential food supplies to the Reich, German authorities were instructed to cut deliveries of food to Russian urban centers to a minimum and to seize livestock for German use before the animals had lost too much weight. The consequences for the Russian townspeople would be hard, but unavoidable.

Of the raw materials, petroleum held first place among German requirements, but the mining of manganese ore had also become urgent. In the coal and iron mines the destruction by the Soviets should be repaired as soon as possible. Russian timber resources were to be exploited to the limit of available transportation facilities.

Manufacture was to be permitted only if it contributed directly to the production of food and raw material, or if it produced vehicles to relieve the burden on the transportation system. All manufacture of consumer goods was forbidden. Russian workers engaged in production essential to the German war effort were to receive higher rations. Russian prices and wage scales were to be kept as low as possible.[23]

When it became obvious after the failure of the German offensive in December 1941 that the war against Russia would not be a short one, Göring's policy underwent a change. He still insisted that the interests of the Reich remain paramount and that all measures were justified in furthering them, but short-term economic considerations now began to give way to long-range plans for economic reconstruction and to a consideration of the political and human factors involved in economic production.

Göring's change of attitude was reflected in his acceptance in January 1942 of a new agrarian program for Russia, which members of his and Rosenberg's economic staffs had long been advocating but which had been stoutly opposed by an influential body of German administrators in the east, including the heads of the civil government in the Ostland and the Ukraine. With the support of Göring, Rosenberg persuaded Hitler to agree to a liberalization of Germany's agricultural policies in the east. The problem, as German reformers saw it, was to reawaken private initiative and to win popular favor by promising a restoration of private property, while at the same time preserving the Communist system of state farms and factories, which were considered to be more efficient (at least in the short run) and easier to supervise.[24]

The decree on the New Agrarian Order, signed by Hitler on February 15, 1942, was an attempt to meet all these requirements.[25] It was hardly a radical reform. The collective farms were not abolished, but simply renamed communal farms. The bulk of the land was to be worked, as before, on a communal basis with state-owned equipment. Only one concrete concession was made to private enterprise: The private household plots belonging to every member of the community (*Hofland*) were declared to be tax-exempt. They were to be enlarged if the peasant owners gave proof of their capacity to work and gained the confidence of the occupation authorities. As soon as the necessary economic and technical prerequisites were at hand, however, all the land in the communal farms was to be distributed to their members for private development and use, but only when they had fulfilled their obligations to the German authorities—particularly the delivery of their quotas of produce.

In presenting the draft of this decree to Hitler, Rosenberg explained that "the transfer to private property was *not* envisaged, with the exception of the small amount of household property [*Hofland*] which already existed under Bolshevism and was now confirmed. Our hands are therefore not tied in any way and we are free to make any kind of decision for the postwar period." Thus the German promises to restore communal land to the peasant as private property were never more than a propagandistic maneuver.[26]

Meager as were the German concessions, even these met with delay and obstruction. Reichskommissar Erich Koch in the Ukraine opposed any kind of concession to the natives and did all he could to render the New Agrarian Order inoperable. On the local level the German managers of collective farms, many of whom hoped to retain them as private estates after the war, practiced an effective form of passive resistance. Yet in White Russia (which the Germans called White Ruthenia), where a substantial amount of land was turned over to the peasants for private use, the results in increased good will and production were often remarkable.[27]

Even before such results became apparent, Göring attempted to extend the economic liberalization program to other sectors of the economy. In a directive of May 20, 1942, he stated that the aim of German policy should be the restoration of maximum production in the east. To this end German administrators should seek to abolish Soviet economic restrictions so as to reawaken the entrepreneurial spirit and harness private initiative to the economic effort. Wherever possible economic enterprises should be turned over to individuals with the necessary business or technical experience who should be given every opportunity to make a reasonable profit. A final regulation of ownership, however, was to be avoided on principle, for all Russian property seized in the fight against Bolshevism belonged to the German Reich and was being held in trusteeship on a strictly temporary basis for the German people.[28]

The policies of economic liberalization never had a chance to prove their worth. In March 1942, just one month after the proclamation of the New Agrarian Order, Fritz Sauckel was placed in charge of labor recruitment in all occupied areas.[29] The labor recruitment of Göring and his representatives had been onerous enough, but it was Sauckel who made plain to every individual in the east that Hitler's statements about using the conquered Slavic population as slave labor were to be taken seriously.

The appointment of Sauckel was symptomatic of the decline of Göring's economic authority in all occupied territories. But that authority, despite Göring's elaborate organizations and the powers to which he laid claim, had never really been very great. In the field of economics, as in so many other sectors of the German administration, Hitler had delegated authority with a lavish hand. In competition with Göring there was above all the army, which was empowered to seize all economic assets of immediate use to the German war effort and which had the manpower to do so effectively. Besides the army there were Himmler's multifarious organizations, which took over property on a vast scale in the name of security, Germanization, or supplying the needs of police and SS units in Russia. The Reich Post Ministry had been assigned the task of administering the postal, telegraph, and telephone services in the east; the Reich Transport Ministry that of administering the railroads, highways, and canals, an assignment it shared with the Organisation Todt, which was also responsible for the construction of quarters for the German troops. Then there was the usual horde of other official and private agencies competing for the economic assets of a conquered territory.

Besides the competition of rival agencies, Göring suffered from the lack of a large corps of loyal officials to carry out his orders. His economic offices in the east in both military and civil administrative areas were staffed almost exclusively by army economic personnel, who tended to pay more heed to the orders of regional military commanders than to those issued by Göring's supervisory offices in Berlin. Nor could Göring count on the loyalty of his senior officials, who were often drawn from rival Reich offices with conflicting interests and overlapping authorities. For instance, Hans-Joachim Riecke, the head of the food and agriculture department in the office of his Four-Year Plan and in his Economic Staff East, was also a senior official in the Reich Ministry of Food and Agriculture as well as head of the food and agriculture department in the Rosenberg ministry. Similarly Gustav Schlotterer, the head of the department of industry and commerce in the office of the Four-Year Plan and the Economic Staff East, was the head of these same departments in the Rosenberg ministry, chief of the Eastern section in the Reich Ministry of Economics, and a director of the Flick Corporation, which had substantial government contracts in the east. Both Riecke and Schlotterer used their various positions to build up elaborate administrative organizations of their own, with central offices in Berlin and subsidiaries in the military and civil administrations in the east. Below Riecke and Schlotterer, and all along the line in the administrative hierarchy, were other officials who saw in their positions an opportunity to gain power and wealth and who were all too often more concerned with fostering their own interests than those of the Reich, much less those of the Reich marshal.[30]

As German difficulties in the east mounted and the ineffectiveness of Göring's economic administration became increasingly apparent, his rivals encroached ever-more freely on his authority and Hitler appointed other men to take over many of his functions, with the result that even more economic agencies in the east came into being. Fritz Sauckel, appointed plenipotentiary general for labor in the occupied territories in

March 1942, was technically subordinate to the plenipotentiary of the Four-Year Plan; but Hitler had empowered him to take over all labor organizations in the east and to issue orders directly to German civil and military administrators.[31] In June of the same year Hitler placed Albert Speer, the Reich minister for armaments and munitions, in charge of armaments, power, industries, building and highway construction, harbors and waterworks in the occupied eastern territories. He was to set up offices in the Ministry for the East and to keep Rosenberg informed of all important policy decisions. Hitler's decree made no mention at all of Göring.[32]

The chaos of the German economic administration in the east was the subject of bitter criticism by German civil and military officials. On September 4, 1942, Schwerin von Krosigk, the Reich minister of finance, complained directly to Göring and the heads of all other Reich economic offices. The original intention to unify German economic administration in the east had not been achieved, he said. On the contrary, the most obvious feature of the economic administration was its lack of unity. "The fact that new organizations, companies, and structures of all kinds spring up like mushrooms must give rise to serious anxiety. . . . People who are well qualified to judge tell me: 'We ourselves no longer know what constitutes an authority and what does not, what belongs to an authority, to a semiofficial company, or to the large group of selfish hyenas on the battlefield.'" Schwerin von Krosigk complained that the creation of new organizations and enterprises was often clearly motivated by the desire to escape the administrative and financial supervision of responsible Reich authorities, that unbridled economic egotism had taken the place of true entrepreneurial initiative. To rectify the situation, the Reich finance minister called for the elimination of all superfluous organizations and structures and the ouster of the loot-hungry adventurers who were managing them. But Schwerin von Krosigk's appeal, like those of other German critics, went unheeded and the economic chaos was allowed to continue. By that time, of course, the situation was probably beyond redemption in any case.[33]

As already indicated, a major reason that German policies of economic liberalization did not make the Nazi occupation more palatable to the native inhabitants was the labor recruitment program of Fritz Sauckel. From the beginning of their occupation, the Germans' policies for dealing with Russian labor were incredibly stupid. Confident of scoring a quick military victory over Russia, they failed to take into account that a longer war would impose a serious drain on German manpower and that they might some day be faced with a serious labor shortage. Consequently they were criminally negligent (from a national, not to mention human, point of view) about taking care of the almost four million prisoners of war who fell into their hands during the first six months of the Russian campaign. Admittedly the problems involved in guarding, housing, feeding, clothing, and transporting such a vast number of men were staggering, especially after the cold weather set in. The Germans did not even have enough winter clothing, materiel, or transport to supply their own troops adequately. But there were unconscionable delays in making use of the facilities for prisoners that were available. In many sectors Hitler's orders calling for brutal treatment or the outright extermination of prisoners of war were carried out with a terrible literalness or were used as an excuse for neglect. As a result of a combination of policy, negligence, and a genuine lack of facilities and supplies, almost three of the four million Russian prisoners of war had perished by February 1942.[34]

It was at about this same time that the Germans began to recognize the existence of an acute labor shortage. Having allowed millions of able-bodied men already under their control to perish, they now proceeded to disrupt the economy of the conquered eastern territories by a mass recruitment-conscription of eastern laborers. On February 24, 1942, Göring issued an order calling for the recruitment of three hundred and eighty thousand agricultural and two hundred and forty-seven thousand industrial workers in the east.[35] The following month, Sauckel was given supreme authority to co-ordinate the mass recruitment of labor in all occupied territories. In the east he appointed the regional Reich commissars as his deputies for the recruitment of labor and assigned them quotas which they were expected to fill regardless of local economic consequences.[36]

Sauckel pursued his recruitment policies not only with a complete disregard for the economic consequences, but for all political and human consequences as well. He realized that laborers, in order to work effectively, had to be adequately housed and fed; but his orders in this respect were not (and in many cases could not be) carried out satisfactorily. Thousands of eastern workers arrived in Germany so ill or undernourished that they had to be sent back. Those in Germany were often housed in compounds akin to concentration camps, their freedom of movement was severely restricted, and they were forced to wear insignia distinguishing them from workers recruited in other parts of Europe who were presumably racially superior to the easterners. Hitler, to be sure, had ordered that German recruiters do their best to secure workers suitable for Germanization, but the recruiters found they had little opportunity to exercise any kind of racial selectivity.

Word of the treatment of eastern workers in Germany quickly spread throughout the occupied eastern territories, with the result that voluntary recruitment had almost ceased by the time of Sauckel's appointment. Sauckel and his agents first resorted to compulsory conscription and subsequently to increasingly crude and violent methods of labor impressment. Entire villages were surrounded by press gangs, as were cinemas, dance halls, or other places where large groups of people might gather. All able-bodied men and women caught in such roundups were shipped off to work in the Reich.[37] A Nazi official in Russia complained

342

that Sauckel's agents had adopted "the whole bag of tricks" used by Arab slave hunters among the Negroes of Africa in previous centuries.[38]

Sauckel himself was proud of his ability to fill quotas and of the number of laborers he had recruited for Germany. But there was no mention in his reports of the quality of such laborers, or of the effectiveness of their work once they had arrived in Germany. Nor, needless to say, was there any mention of the number of men and women who had fled to the partisans to escape his press gangs, or of the disastrous consequences of his labor recruitment policies for the eastern economy, the morale of the native population, and the effectiveness of the German occupation governments in general.

As it was, the total number of laborers recruited by Sauckel in the east, even using his own padded statistics, was less than the number of prisoners of war who had been allowed to die or had been killed outright by Nazi extermination squads during the first months of the German occupation.[39]

The Rosenberg Ministry

From the beginning of the German occupation of Russia, German military administrators in the conquered eastern territories were clearly informed that they would be left in charge of political affairs in these territories only so long as was absolutely necessary for military reasons. Plans for the establishment of German civil governments in these areas had been under consideration long before the attack on Russia was launched. The final preparations for their implementation were made at a conference at the Führer's headquarters on July 16, 1941.[40] On the following day Hitler issued a series of secret decrees on the subject which were to be fundamental to Germany's subsequent government of Russia.[41]

At a time to be designated by Hitler, the former Polish territories of Bialystok and Galicia were to be removed from military control. Bialystok was to be placed under the personal administration of the Gauleiter and Oberpräsident of East Prussia, Erich Koch; Galicia under the personal administration of the governor general for the occupied Polish territories, Hans Frank. All other territory under civil administration in the east was to be placed under the jurisdiction of Alfred Rosenberg, who was now given the title of Reich minister for the occupied eastern territories. Hitler conferred on Rosenberg the power to legislate by decree and stipulated that his orders were to be binding for all officials in the areas under civil administration.

Hitler's decrees of July 17 provided for the division of the territory under Rosenberg's jurisdiction into Reich commissariats, which were to be subdivided into general and county districts under the authority of Reich, general, and county (Kreis) commissars. The Reich and general commissars were to be appointed by Hitler; the Kreis commissars and the heads of all other principal administrative districts in the east by Reich Minister Rosenberg. Although appointed by Hitler, the Reich and general commissars were to be immediately responsible to Rosenberg and were to receive their orders exclusively from him.

Rosenberg's powers, however, were not nearly so clear-cut as Hitler's decrees suggested. He was to have absolute and exclusive authority over officials in the civil administrative areas, but only when his orders did not conflict with those of the regional military commanders, the plenipotentiary of the Four-Year Plan, and the Reichsführer SS and chief of the German police, whose powers had already been defined in special decrees.[42] Moreover, to enable the Reich commissars to deal directly with matters of immediate concern in their provinces, Rosenberg was expected to delegate to them his power to legislate by decree. Thus his authority was subject to severe limitations from the start.

Because of the limitations of Rosenberg's authority, the manifold and elaborate plans for the east which he worked out before and during the German occupation of Russia proved to be of very little practical significance. They are nevertheless interesting because Rosenberg was almost alone among Nazi leaders in recognizing the desirability of exploiting the conflict among the many nationalities that made up the Soviet Union to facilitate Germany's conquest and control of the east.

Rosenberg's basic idea was that the Germans should seek to awaken the desire for freedom among the suppressed nationalities of the Soviet Union and encourage the formation of new national states as bulwarks against Moscow. Russia was to be divided according to historical and racial lines, with each unit bearing within itself a different political aim. By setting up a balance of power among the new states in the east, the Germans could effectively end all danger from that direction.

The Führer was to be represented as the liberator of the Soviet peoples from Bolshevik oppression, thereby gaining the co-operation of the millions of people inhabiting Eastern Europe for the work of European reconstruction. The most important precondition for this policy was a suitable treatment of the country and its inhabitants. The war against the Soviet Union was above all a political war, with the goal of establishing a permanent world order. The conquered territories could, therefore, not be regarded as objects of exploitation, even if German food and raw material requirements seemed to dictate such a policy. The war itself would impose on the natives hardships enough; but they would not hate their conquerors if they saw that German administrators were doing their best to overcome those hardships and had the interests of the local inhabitants at heart. Of overriding importance was Germany's agricultural policy. The Russian peasants were primarily concerned with eliminating the system of collective farming; this should be done forthwith. Without the co-operation of the peasants, as the German experience in 1917 and 1918 had demonstrated, it would be impossible to secure the grain of the conquered territories.[43]

Rosenberg's ideas were sound enough, at least from a German point of view; but they conflicted with the views of almost every other high-ranking Nazi leader. Civil governments were actually set up in the Baltic region (the Ostland) and in the Ukraine, and plans were made to establish similar governments in the Caucasus and Moscow areas. But the policies pursued in these provinces differed radically from those recommended by Rosenberg.

In anticipation of the invasion of Russia and in accordance with the powers Hitler had assigned him, Rosenberg had organized and staffed an office for the future administration of the east in the spring of 1941.[44] After his appointment as Reich minister he moved this office into the building of the former trade mission of the Soviet Union in Berlin, which he persuaded Hitler to release from the control of Ribbentrop's Foreign Office.[45]

The Reich Ministry for the East as finally constituted was an impressive organization with a full complement of departments, divisions, subdivisions, and all other attributes of a major government office.[46] But neither organization, building, nor his status as a Reich minister gave Rosenberg authority commensurate with the powers Hitler had assigned him and which he justifiably expected to exercise. He did not possess a loyal or experienced body of officials to carry out his orders; and the independent powers assigned to the army, to Göring, and to Himmler, a major concern to Rosenberg during the planning stages of the administration of the east, sapped his powers even more seriously than he had anticipated.

Rosenberg's first big difficulty arose with his attempts to staff his ministry. He was not already in charge of a large administrative apparatus whose personnel could be shifted to his new office or used in a dual capacity; rather, he had to recruit his personnel from other Reich offices, accept men who had been unemployable elsewhere, or train young men who were released from military service for this purpose. As training was a slow process, he was obliged to fill most of the top posts in his ministry with older officials of doubtful loyalty and competence.

Rosenberg's recruiting efforts met with varying reactions in rival departments. The Ministry of the Interior, for example, gave up personnel unwillingly and then only released men it was glad to lose. Göring, on the other hand, sent Rosenberg some of his most competent aides, not to get rid of them, but to plant his own men in key positions in the Rosenberg organization.

As his permanent deputy in the Reich Ministry for the East, Rosenberg selected Dr. Alfred Meyer, Gauleiter of Westphalia-North, Oberpräsident of Westphalia, and Reichsstatthalter of Lippe. Meyer, ineffectively mediocre, was described by Gottlob Berger as being "too weak to do any good and too cowardly to sin." [47] Rosenberg was more fortunate in the head of the political department of his ministry, Dr. Georg Leibbrandt, who succeeded in staffing his office with a number of competent men recruited from diplomatic and university circles. Rosenberg, however, failed to endow the political department with authority over other departments of his ministry so that, even within the ministry, it never had a chance to exercise any real political leadership.

The hapless Rosenberg, himself no model of energy or competence, soon found that he exercised almost no authority in the east. The army, Göring, and Himmler systematically ignored or overrode him. The Reich commissars, who were supposed to be directly responsible to Rosenberg and to take their orders exclusively from him, conducted themselves as independent potentates and openly defied him. They knew they owed their appointments to Hitler, and so long as they retained the confidence of the Führer they, too, felt safe in ignoring Rosenberg.[48]

Rosenberg protested to Hitler, but Hitler made no move to back him up. Here, of course, lay the crucial weakness of Rosenberg's position. Without a powerful or loyal organization behind him he was wholly dependent on the support of the Führer, which he failed to receive. In a desperate search for allies to bolster his position Rosenberg turned to Lammers, to Göring, to the army, and finally in 1942 to his archenemy Heinrich Himmler. From the beginning Rosenberg had complained about Himmler's abuse of his prerogatives in the east. He accused him of bypassing his ministry, of issuing orders that had nothing to do with security, of taking over economic enterprises and agricultural property on a vast scale without consulting or informing the local authorities or the Rosenberg ministry, of recruiting for his Waffen-SS in the east even before the National Socialist party had been established there. Such measures, Rosenberg declared, were sabotaging his efforts to impose unified direction over German policy in the east as ordered by the Führer.[49]

Unable to secure any kind of support in his struggle with Himmler, Rosenberg attempted to strike a bargain with him. He would allow SS and police forces free play in the occupied areas under civil administration and would see to it that their economic requirements were fulfilled on a generous scale if the SS in turn would close ranks with him against the economic encroachments of the Wehrmacht. This agreement only weakened Rosenberg's position further, for he now lost all right even to criticize the activities of Himmler's agents.[50]

Rosenberg fared no better in dealing with the question of race and resettlement. He argued that Himmler's RKFDV office was responsible only for the selection and actual transfer of populations and that his own ministry should have responsibility for the planning and political decisions involved. On this question Rosenberg was finally forced to settle for an agreement which permitted his ministry to maintain its own race and resettlement departments, but they were to issue no orders without the countersignature of Himmler's agents. Moreover, to avoid a duplication of effort, Himmler arranged that the officials responsible for race and resettlement in his own RKFDV offices should be the heads of these departments in the Rosenberg ministry. In other words, Rosenberg was to be allowed to have his own race and resettlement departments provided that they could do nothing without Himmler's sanction and were staffed by Himmler's men.[51]

Not surprisingly Rosenberg remained dissatisfied with the situation. But his protests were unavailing and he failed in all his efforts to conclude more favorable agreements with Himmler. As Rosenberg's position continued to deteriorate, his deputy Alfred Meyer suggested that he appoint Gottlob Berger, one of Himmler's most forceful lieutenants and one of the few Himmler officials who had heretofore maintained good relations with Rosenberg, as a liaison officer in the Ministry for the East so as to give Himmler a stake in that ministry and invest it with some part of his great authority. Rosenberg approved this suggestion; in July of 1942 Berger's appointment to his ministry was arranged.[52]

Once again the loser was Rosenberg, for Meyer now hastened to join forces with the Himmler party. He assured Berger that he would do everything possible to maintain peace with the SS and he promised to allow him to see all the files of the Rosenberg ministry for the personal and confidential information of the Reichsführer SS. Berger made full use of this right and henceforth Himmler was informed of Rosenberg's every move, or intended move. Rosenberg, for his part, was no better informed than before of Himmler's activities, nor did his orders carry greater weight.[53]

Even more serious from the point of view of Rosenberg's interests was the fact that Himmler encouraged Berger to use his influence in the Ministry for the East to oust officials loyal to Rosenberg (not many would be involved in that operation, it would seem) and replace them with Himmler men. Berger himself was to seek the post of state secretary (executive director) in the ministry, a position which would enable him to control it in Himmler's interest. Berger understood what was expected of him. He promised Himmler to clean up the Ministry for the East so that in one or two years that organization "would operate only according to the great principles and guidelines of the Reichsführer SS." [54]

By August 1943 Berger had succeeded in getting rid of Georg Leibbrandt, the chief of the political department of the Rosenberg ministry. He then transformed the political department into a Political Leadership Staff under his own direction. Berger was now in a position to control the Rosenberg ministry on Himmler's behalf, but the pressure of other duties left him little time or opportunity to do so. Further, the military situation was such that the exercise of authority in the east on the basis of the powers originally conferred on the Rosenberg ministry no longer had any significance.[55]

On October 12, 1944, with the east already lost in any case, Rosenberg sent in his resignation, which Hitler did not even bother to acknowledge. He was, as one writer has expressed it, the forgotten vassal at the head of a forgotten office.[56]

The Himmler Organizations and the
Germanization Program

The man who was to be the chief executor of Hitler's policies in Russia was not Rosenberg but Himmler who, well before the invasion of Russia, secured assurances from the Führer that he would be completely independent of Rosenberg's authority. "To work with, to say nothing of under, Rosenberg, is surely the most difficult task there is in the NSDAP," he said.[57]

In his preinvasion directives Hitler had demonstrated his confidence in Himmler by entrusting him with primary responsibility for dealing with problems of political security in territories under military administration in the east and giving him extraordinary powers to carry out "special tasks" that would be necessary for this purpose.[58] By a decree of July 17, 1941, he had extended these powers to areas under civil administration and authorized the Reichsführer SS to give orders directly to the heads of the civil governments. Whenever these orders were of a general nature or dealt with matters of political importance, they were to be issued through the Reich Ministry for the East, but this practice could be omitted in cases of emergency. A senior SS and police officer was assigned to each Reichskommissar, to whom the former was to be directly and personally subordinate. Lower-ranking SS and police officers were attached in similar fashion to the general and Kreis commissars.[59]

As in other occupied territories, Himmler stretched the terms *security* and *emergency* to cover every sphere of activity. Although he was supposed to send all politically important instructions to the Reich commissars through the Rosenberg ministry, a high official of that ministry stated after the war that this was not done in a single instance. Similarly, Himmler's senior SS and police officers, theoretically subordinate to the Reichskommissars, operated with almost complete independence.[60]

In September 1941 Hitler extended Himmler's powers still further by authorizing him to exercise the same authority in Russia as he did in Poland in his capacity as Reichskommissar for the consolidation of the German people. This meant that all resettlement and Germanization programs in Russia, and the manifold activities connected with them, also came within the sphere of authority of the Reichsführer SS.[61]

From an ideological standpoint Hitler's confidence was well placed; in Russia, as in other occupied territories, there was no more dogmatic or literal exponent of Hitler's theories on race and *Lebensraum* than Himmler. And in Russia, as elsewhere, there was no one who worked harder or with greater tenacity to secure a decisive position for himself and his organizations in attaining National Socialist racial and territorial goals.

Of all the great tasks of the future, Himmler told his SS leaders in 1943, the most important was the establishment of the SS as the foundation of the National Socialist New Order. The members of the SS, all products of a rigorous military, ideological, and political training, would provide the Germanic peoples of Europe with their superstratum of society, the elite from which Germany's military leaders, statesmen, and technicians would emerge. "In twenty or thirty years we must be able to furnish the whole of Europe with its leadership class." [62]

Difficult as had been the tasks undertaken and successfully carried out by the SS during the war, its real work would only begin after the war had been won. For this reason it was essential that every SS man should be fully aware of Germany's long-term goals. Himmler never allowed those goals to be forgotten. In speech after speech he tirelessly repeated the same formulas in drawing the features of the world which he and his SS men would create.[63] Their first great task would be to ensure the union of all Germanic peoples under the banner of the National Socialist Reich. Whatever existed by way of Germanic blood was to be brought under the control of the Reich. "We will bring these racial Germans home; the Germanic peoples, whether they like it or not, whether they understand it or not, will have to acknowledge their membership in the Reich because of the demands of the blood. All good blood that you encounter anywhere in the east—it is essential that you understand this fundamental principle—you must either win over or destroy." This might seem cruel, but nature was cruel. Because nature had provided that only members of the Germanic race possessed leadership or organizational qualities, it was the paramount duty of the present German rulers to avoid leaving potential leaders in the camp of the enemy who might some day lead that enemy against their own people. For, of all the dangers Germany faced, none was greater than that the hordes of the east might find a leader. This had already been demonstrated in the person of Stalin, "who was accidentally born in Russia" and who in twenty years had fashioned out of the stupid Russian masses the gigantic war machine which the Germans were now fighting. This Stalin might just as well have been born in China, with the result that instead of a mere two hundred million people, four hundred and fifty million would have been organized and all Asia would have been mobilized against European civilization. This was what had happened in the case of Attila, Genghis Khan, and Tamerlane, whom Himmler described as "lost Nordic-Germanic-Aryan blood types."

With all his emphasis on Germanic leadership qualities, Himmler showed remarkably little confidence in his Germanic successors. Like Hitler he envisaged the possibility that future leaders of the Reich might not understand the importance of blood, or that they might be weak or stupid. For this reason the Germanic Imperium would have to be established so firmly that it could survive any emergency.

The accomplishment of this purpose was the second great goal of Ger-

349

many's eastern policy. "The war would be pointless if within twenty years after its end Bohemia and Moravia, the German eastern provinces, Southeast Prussia, Danzig-West Prussia, the Warthegau, Upper Silesia, the Government General, the Ostland, the Crimea, and Ingermanland [the area around Leningrad] were not totally settled by Germans according to racial principles, the principles of the blood." In addition to their settlement in these territories, Germans would have to be settled along the great highways and railroads, around the airfields and garrison towns, as far as the Don, the Volga, and the Urals. The Germanic east would be the seedbed of Nordic blood. It would be the duty of Germans to foster this blood, to breed, to put it under cultivation in the east "as in a botanical garden, so to speak," so that in four or five centuries instead of one hundred and twenty million Germans there would be five to six hundred million. Here they would be born, here they would be raised as peasants, here the *Volk* would grow strong. All this was to be done for the blood, that sacred Nordic blood, "which gave this earth purpose, substance, *Kultur*."

Himmler had set himself the task of pushing the Germanic frontier five hundred kilometers to the east within the next twenty years. This meant a major resettlement of Germans and the exploitation of the Russian masses for Germanic tasks. It meant twenty years of untold labor, but also twenty years of untold beauty. For the lands of the east were not only to be settled by Germans; they were to be made to look like Germany and given the aspect of a German cultural landscape.

The Germans would also acquire overseas colonies—they would need them for many products—but their main colonies would be in the east. "Today colony, tomorrow settlement area, the day after tomorrow part of the Reich!" Germans would always be at home only in the Reich, never in some African colony where they would grow soft in an enervating climate and through contact with other racial influences. What had to be avoided at all costs was the disintegration of Germans as had taken place in South America and Spain (Catalonia had after all once been Gotalonia; Andalusia, Vandalusia).

The peoples of the east were to be mobilized as slave labor, a term Himmler did not hesitate to employ. "Among ourselves I can express myself very explicitly and very frankly on this point." They were to be used to build German cities, villages, and farms, and to lay the groundwork for a higher German standard of living. The loss of human life that might be involved in this process was completely inconsequential. The main thing was to prevent their breeding with Germans. "This is the task: to exploit them for Germany, to keep them weak so that they can never defeat or harm us, and so that we may at a given time drive them out and settle Germans in their place."

Finally there was the task of exterminating the Jews in the east. "The wanderings of the Jews will definitely be brought to an end within a year," Himmler said in June 1942.[64] "Then no Jew will ever wander again. For now we must really clean out the stables." This was not a matter of ideology but of cleanliness: getting rid of Jews was exactly the same as getting rid of lice. In a speech to Wehrmacht generals two years later Himmler expressed himself more soberly on this subject, referring to the solution of the Jewish problem "as the most horrible task that can be assigned to any organization." [65]

Merciless behavior was necessary, Himmler said, because this fight against the Jews was the absolutely crucial fight. For this was a racial war, a war against the Jews and against the races spewed out of Asia, all of which were linked through certain subhuman qualities.

> They know with animal instinct why they are fighting. They are strange, uncanny, we can never really understand them. Starting with the Russians, and all through Asia. For us Germans, for us Aryans, an incomprehensible thing. We never know exactly what is going on here. We only know one thing: this is the great danger! . . . From the invasion of the Huns to the era of Bolshevism: the danger came out of the east and the southeast, and it will always come from there.

It was to win for the German people the conditions for meeting and overcoming this danger that the present war was being fought, and it was for this purpose that the SS and police had been assigned "special tasks" in the occupied eastern territories. These "special tasks" of the Himmler organizations in Russia had been clearly defined before the invasion.[66] They were to be restated in oral and written directives many times thereafter.

The immediate goal, Heydrich told SS and police officers on July 2, 1941, was the political pacification of the newly occupied territories which was the prerequisite for the longer-term goal of economic pacification. In view of the two decades of Bolshevik rule in Russia, it would be necessary to carry out all measures for the attainment of these goals with ruthless severity. As the first step in political pacification, all high-ranking party officials, all members of central and district party committees, all Jews in party and state posts, and all other radical elements were to be singled out and executed forthwith. Exceptions were to be made only for persons who were needed for interrogation purposes or for doctors and other specialists whose skills were temporarily indispensable.[67]

Himmler and Heydrich did not altogether ignore political considerations in their pacification efforts. Both placed considerable emphasis on fostering anti-Bolshevik forces, such as the Orthodox Church, and on playing off the various nationalities in Russia against each other. But their principal weapon at all times was terror. On July 28, 1941, for example, Himmler laid down guidelines for the pacification of the swamp lands in the east. Whenever the local population in such areas appeared to be hostile or racially inferior, Himmler said, "all persons suspected of supporting partisans are to be shot; women and children are to be deported; livestock and food are to be confiscated and secured. The villages are to be burned to the ground." [68]

Himmler's indiscriminate use of terror destroyed whatever good will the Germans had ever enjoyed as liberators of the Russian people from Bolshevism, driving thousands of Russians into the ranks of the partisans. His methods (or at least their results) were bitterly criticized by other German officials; but Himmler received steady and consistent support from Hitler who, in July 1942, placed him in charge of all antipartisan operations in the east.[69]

A crucial step in Himmler's pacification program was the removal of all Jews from the occupied eastern territories.[70] In dealing with this problem he resisted all efforts to give more precise definition to the term *Jew*, for attempts at definition would only bind his hands with petty restrictions. The terrible responsibility of removing all Jews from Europe had been assigned him by the Führer, he said, and he refused to allow interference of any kind. The only thing that concerned him was that "the eastern territories are to be freed of Jews." [71]

Heydrich warned his chief that the continued importance of the Jews in the economic life in the east might endanger his Jewish program, for local administrators might object that Jews were essential to the economic productivity of a region. To counteract this danger an order was issued to German civil administrators that "in dealing with the Jewish problem, economic necessities are to be ignored on principle." [72] Himmler and Heydrich, however, did not propose to rely on local administrators for the destruction of the Jews, but on their own SS and police units.

In planning the campaign against the Jews in the east, Himmler had arranged before the attack on Russia began that his task forces should move into the country in conjunction with the troops of the regular army. He had reliable statistics showing that over four million of the approximately five million Jews in the Soviet Union were concentrated in the western part of the country; of these almost 90 per cent lived in urban areas. Thus the obvious strategy for Himmler's forces was to round up the Jews in the cities before they could escape to the countryside. About 1.5 million Jews succeeded in fleeing from western Russia before the arrival of the Germans, but so swift was the advance of the German forces that another 3.5 million remained trapped behind the German lines. Of these, approximately .5 million were killed by the Himmler task forces in the first five months of the German occupation.[73]

The number of Germans employed in these killing operations was surprisingly small. The combined strength of all Himmler's task forces in the first stage of the Russian campaign was no more than three thousand men, and individual detachments might consist of only three or four. These men, however, were well equipped, they acted quickly and ruthlessly, and they knew exactly what they were doing. The Jews on the other hand were stunned and disorganized, most of them were unarmed, and they received virtually no support from the local population. On the contrary, much of the success of Himmler's anti-Jewish operations was due to the co-operation of native auxiliary police who spoke the language of the country, were familiar with its terrain, and were thus far better prepared to round up Jews and flush them from their hiding places than the Germans.

Once the Jews had been rounded up, the procedure followed for dealing with them was simple. They were herded to the nearby countryside, forced to dig mass graves if no natural or previously dug ditches were available, and shot. Their bodies were then buried by Jews who had not yet been executed or other laborers. In some cases the Germans did not even bother with burial.[74]

After the partial stabilization of the Russian front in December 1941, the Himmler forces began a systematic roundup of the Jews who had been bypassed in the initial stage of the Jewish campaign. This operation was under the overall direction of the regional senior SS and police officers who exercised authority in both the military and civilian administrative areas. As the Jewish action was always made to appear as part of the pacification and antipartisan campaign, the senior SS and police officers were frequently able to secure the co-operation of regular army forces. But, above all, they depended on the native auxiliary police who were recruited in all occupied eastern territories and who made up two hundred and thirty-eight thousand of the two hundred and fifty thousand police forces available to the senior SS and police officers— approximately 95 per cent.

The tactics employed in the second stage of the anti-Jewish campaign in Russia were similar to those used in other occupied areas. The Jews were compelled to live in ghettos under the administration of their own Jewish councils. Once the Jews had been penned in, the local SS and police officer had only to move his forces from one town to another in carrying out the solution of the Jewish problem. The system of execution was essentially the same as that used in the initial stage of the Jewish campaign: The Jews were taken out of town, forced to dig their own graves, and shot. The ghettos were then combed for persons who had gone into hiding, a process carried out with such systematic ruthlessness that few were able to escape.[75]

At first the Himmler forces made little or no effort to conceal their slaughter of Jews from members of the regular army or the local population, who were frequently allowed to watch the proceedings and to satisfy their own sadistic impulses by assisting in the killing. It soon became evident, however, that the mass slaughter of helpless victims was having a deleterious effect on the morale of the German army and that it was arousing an anxiety amounting to panic among the non-Jewish natives, who feared, not without reason, that they might be the next ethnic group subjected to such treatment. The SS executioners themselves were not immune from morale problems, despite Himmler's repeated efforts to reassure them that they were carrying out an essential, if repulsive, task in ridding Europe of carriers of disease. Many members of his execution squads appear to have been able to go into action only when in a drunken stupor. Himmler became seriously alarmed about the number of his men who suffered mental breakdowns as a result of their experiences in the east. But Himmler did not allow problems of morale to deter him from his purpose. His only reaction to complaints about the activities of his troops was to issue increasingly stringent demands for secrecy in carrying out the execution of the Jews and providing for their burial. If German soldiers or natives asked awkward questions, they were to be told that the Jews were merely being resettled.[76]

As Heydrich had anticipated, some of the most vigorous protests against the extermination of the Jews were economic. In many areas the Jews constituted the greater part of the skilled labor force and were therefore essential to the economy of the region. Complaints about the disastrous economic consequences resulting from the removal of Jews came not only from military and economic officials, but from such sturdy Nazis as Gauleiter Hinrich Lohse, the head of the German civil government in the Ostland, and from Wilhelm Kube, the head of the civil government in White Ruthenia. Himmler, however, was prepared for such arguments; it was precisely to avoid obstructionism based on economic considerations that he had issued orders to ignore such considerations on principle. He suspected that some German officials were using economic arguments in an attempt to save the Jews, while others wanted to keep their Jews because they were a cheap source of labor. Both attitudes he regarded as pernicious, if not downright treasonous. The only skilled Jewish laborers Himmler would allow to survive were those working in his own concentration camps under constant SS and police supervision. When their labor was no longer essential to the German war economy, they too would be wiped out.[77]

Statistics on the slaughter of Jews in Russia vary widely. A conservative estimate is that 1.4 million were killed; but these statistics, grim as they are, are only a guide to intent. For, in Russia, as in all areas under their control, the ultimate aim of the Nazis was to eliminate the Jews entirely.[78]

For Himmler, however, the pacification of Russia and the elimination of the Jews were but preconditions for the main task to be undertaken in that country, namely, its Germanization. It was in Russia that Hitler had ordained that the Germans were to find the breeding grounds to guarantee their future for all time and it was above all in Russia that Himmler believed himself called upon to act as the chosen instrument of his leader of destiny.

Himmler's programs for the Germanization of the east had already been initiated in Czechoslovakia and Poland.[79] Inevitably, therefore, the work of his organizations in Russia was to a large extent modeled on the policies already inaugurated in these other Eastern European areas. The size and importance of Russia, however, required new and infinitely more grandiose plans, for Hitler's orders called for the Germanization of territories as widely separated as the Crimea (the future Gotengau) and the area around the former city of Leningrad (Ingermanland).[80] The problem for Himmler was to work out programs as to how this could be done most quickly and effectively, and at the same time to ensure his personal control over the entire operation.

To Himmler's annoyance, the first large-scale plan for the Germanization of Russia was not prepared in his own offices, but by Hans-Joachim Reicke of the Reich Ministry of Food and Agriculture, the head of the agricultural departments in the Rosenberg ministry and Göring's economic organizations. Worse yet, Reicke's plan was approved by Hitler.[81] Himmler, however, succeeded in delaying a Führer decision on the Riecke plan until he could submit a plan of his own. For the drafting of this plan, Himmler selected Professor Dr. Konrad Meyer-Hetling of the Institute for Agricultural Policies and Politics in the University of Berlin, an Obersturmbannführer in the SS and a department head in the central office of Himmler's Reich Commission for the Consolidation of the German People (RKFDV).

Fundamental in the Himmler-Meyer plan was the principle that all Germanization and resettlement programs in the incorporated eastern territories should be under the supervision of Himmler's consolidation office; that all other areas scheduled for German colonization should be under the direct administration of Himmler in his capacity as Reichskommissar for consolidation; and that all rights over the disposal of land in the east should be vested in the Reich, whose interests would be represented by the Reichsführer SS.

Areas of Germanic colonization not scheduled for immediate incorporation into the Reich were to be set up as *Siedlungsmarken*, frontier settlements or marches. These were to be removed from their former administrations and placed under the jurisdiction of the Reichsführer SS and Reichskommissar for consolidation. Under his supervision, a new administration would be set up in the frontier marches which would be responsible for overall planning, the selection and settlement of colonists, and the administration and financing of the entire operation. The first frontier marches would be established in the Crimea and the Leningrad area, as ordered by the Führer; perhaps another would be established in the Memel-Narev area. In addition to the frontier marches, thirty-six *Siedlungsstützpunkte*, or settlement strongholds, were to be established which would serve as nuclei for later full-scale marches. It was estimated that during the first twenty-five-year period of colonization, 50 per cent of the population of the marches and 25 per cent of the strongholds would be Germanized. The settlers themselves were to come from the Reich, from the other Germanic countries of Europe, from Germanic communities overseas, and would include native inhabitants suitable for Germanization.

The cost of the operation was to be borne as much as possible by the resettlement districts themselves, although the co-operation of the entire Reich would be indispensable. Substantial sums would have to be provided by the Reich government, but even greater sums were to be obtained from private investors who were to be given every opportunity to make handsome profits so as to attract capital to the east.[82]

Himmler approved Meyer's draft of a resettlement plan and in June 1942 he secured Meyer's appointment as planning commissioner for colonization and rural reorganization (*Planungsbeauftragter für die Siedlung und ländliche Neuordnung*). Meyer was now instructed to draw up a definitive plan, which was to serve as a basic blueprint for all future resettlement work, and to co-ordinate the plans of other Reich agencies concerned with the problem.[83]

The result was the *Generalplan Ost,* or General Plan for the East, which was subtitled The Legal, Economic, and Territorial Foundations of Eastern Development. This plan was little more than a detailed development of Meyer's original draft which followed Himmler's familiar policy line. "The Reich now views as its most noble task the building up of these areas in the shortest possible time into full-fledged Reich Gaus. For this purpose the first precondition is rural colonization and the creation of a healthy peasantry." Another precondition, it appeared, was that the entire operation should be under the direction of Heinrich Himmler in one or another of his many official capacities.[84]

In August 1942 the entire problem of Germanization and resettlement was discussed at a conference at Hitler's headquarters. Present were Himmler, Meyer, and the heads of Himmler's various Germanization and resettlement offices, but not Riecke or any of Himmler's other rivals in the resettlement field. Hitler now gave orders that the first territory to be colonized in the areas conquered since June 1941 should be the Ostland, where special attention should be paid to the possibility of Germanizing the Estonians. In Latvia, the Letts (Lettgallen) would have to be removed under all circumstances, as would the majority of Lithuanians, who were intellectually sluggish with a preposterous amount (*unerhört viel*) of Slavic blood. The task in White Ruthenia would be easier because there was no intelligentsia in this region and the people had no political pretensions.

In the Crimea German colonization was to be initiated with the establishment of a network of German strongholds, from which the Germanization of the surrounding agricultural areas would be conducted. Hitler also wanted parts of the Ukraine to be completely settled by Germans within the next twenty years. Here colonization was to take place along the main thoroughfares that were to be built: Cracow-Lvov-Zhitomir-Kiev; Leningrad-Mogilev-Kiev; Zhitomir-Vinnitsa-Odessa.[85]

Germanization and resettlement procedures in Russia closely resembled those already adopted in Poland: [86] the registration of Germans through the *Volksliste*, the racial examination of candidates for Germanization, and the removal of successful candidates to resettlement centers. By the end of 1942 well over three hundred and twenty-five thousand ethnic Germans had been registered in the Soviet Union, of whom seventeen thousand had been settled in the Reich or the Government General.[87] This work continued throughout the period of German occupation, and was actually accelerated during the great retreat of 1944.

In March of that year Himmler was informed that 113,490 Russian-Germans had been transported in 127 trains from the Ukraine to the Warthegau. The remaining 2,135, who could not be removed by train because of enemy action, were sent by armored convoy to Strjy where railroad transportation was again available. Altogether in the first three months of 1944, 116,625 Russian-Germans in the Ukraine, with 30,198 head of livestock and 8,962 horse-drawn vehicles had been evacuated. All this was done, it will be recalled, at a time when the Wehrmacht was fighting for its very existence.[88]

The Reichskommissariat Ostland

The Reichskommissariat Ostland, the first of the German civil administrative provinces in the newly conquered eastern territories, was officially created by one of the many secret decrees Hitler issued on July 17, 1941. The province was to be made up of the three Baltic states of Estonia, Latvia, and Lithuania, and of White Russia, which the Germans called White Ruthenia to sever even its semantic association with Muscovy. The exact boundaries of the province, as well as the date for the actual installation of the civil government, were to be determined later. As Reichskommissar for the Ostland, Hitler appointed Hinrich Lohse, Gauleiter and Oberpräsident of Schleswig-Holstein. His capital was to be at Riga. In his capacity as Reichskommissar, Lohse was to be directly and immediately responsible to Rosenberg, the Reich minister for the occupied eastern territories.[89]

In his first speculations about the future of the Baltic states Rosenberg was uncertain about what line to pursue. He had originally advocated that Germany should seek to reawaken the desire for freedom among the suppressed nationalities of the Soviet Union; but, if the Baltic region were to become an area of Germanization, a quite different policy would be required.[90] Hitler soon relieved Rosenberg of all doubt about his intentions in the Baltic area. As early as July 1940 he had decided that the Baltic states should be annexed to the Reich. At his conference on the future of Russia of July 16, 1941, he stated emphatically that "the entire Baltic area must become Reich territory." [91]

Following the line laid down by his Führer, Rosenberg's instructions to the Reichskommissar in the Ostland had an almost Himmlerian quality. "Seven hundred years of German activity had already made the Baltic region part of the *Lebensraum* of Greater Germany," he declared. "The goal of a Reichskommissar for Estonia, Latvia, Lithuania, and White Ruthenia must be to achieve the form of a German protectorate, and then to transform this region into part of the Greater German Reich by Germanizing suitable racial elements, colonizing with Germanic peoples, and banishing undesirable elements. The Baltic Sea must become a Germanic inland sea under the guardianship of Greater Germany." [92]

By this time Rosenberg had all necessary theories worked out on which to base a Germanization policy. The Estonians, originally a Finno-Ugric people, had become Germanized over the past seven hundred years, both intellectually and in blood, primarily as the result of the infusion of Swedish stock. So far as racial considerations were concerned, nothing stood in the way of including the majority of Estonians in the German racial state. More difficult was the problem of the Letts. While basically Germanized, they were more actively anti-German than the Estonians due to the influx of Russian intellectual groups. Here a large-scale population transfer would be necessary. The same was true of Lithuania, where the Jewish element had become a plague. The undesirable elements should be replaced by German rural settlers, including a large contingent of Volga Germans, as well as Danes, Norwegians, Dutch, and, after the war, English, so that within one or two generations the entire area would be Germanized.

White Ruthenia, to the east and south of the Baltic states, was culturally and economically backward and possessed the second largest Jewish community in the Soviet Union. This region was to be attached to the Baltic states as an agricultural hinterland and racial dumping ground for undesirable elements from the coastal areas and Poland. "Estonia, Latvia, and Lithuania form a historic unity geographically linked with Germany," Rosenberg said, "while White Ruthenia can be regarded as belonging to them." As envisaged by Rosenberg, White Ruthenia was to be far larger than the former Soviet Republic of White Russia and would include territory well to the east of Smolensk.[93]

In the same series of July 17 decrees in which Hitler had established the Reichskommissariat Ostland, he had also arranged for the administrative subdivision of the province into four general commissariats and for the appointment of the four Generalkommissars who were to govern them: SA Obergruppenführer Karl-Siegismund Litzmann in Estonia; Dr. Otto Heinrich Drechsler, the mayor of Lübeck, in Latvia; Dr. Adrian von Renteln, the head of the trade and craft section of the German Labor Front, in Lithuania; and Wilhelm Kube, the former Gauleiter and Oberpräsident of Brandenburg, in White Ruthenia.[94] All of these men, with the exception of Kube who had been dismissed from his positions in Brandenburg before the war for insinuating that Bormann's mother-in-law was partly Jewish, retained their former posts as well and remained responsible for carrying out the duties connected with them. Hitler never abandoned his romantic view that old party members were equal to any tasks.[95]

On July 18, 1941, Hitler issued a decree that on July 25 the first bloc of conquered territory in the east should be transferred to civil administration. This decree, like those of July 17, was not made public. Hitler wanted to dramatize the administrative reorganization of the east by announcing it in conjunction with a dramatic military victory such as the fall of Leningrad or Moscow. As no such success was achieved, the German civil administration operated in a haze of official secrecy until Hitler at last gave it public recognition on November 18, 1941.[96]

The greater part of Latvia and Lithuania was placed under civil administration on August 1, 1941; the rest of Latvia and the western part of White Ruthenia on September 1 and November 15 respectively. Finally, on December 5, after numerous appeals from Rosenberg, Estonia was placed under civil administration, with the exception of the border region around Leningrad which remained an area of military operations.[97]

Hinrich Lohse, the Reichskommissar of the Ostland, had been an early member of the Nazi party and was one of Hitler's tried and true band of Old Fighters. Although appointed by Hitler, Lohse had been recommended for the position in the Ostland by Rosenberg. He was president of Rosenberg's Nordic Society and a long-standing member of the SA, which led Rosenberg to believe that he could count on his personal loyalty and on his automatic hostility to Himmler. Rosenberg encountered a good deal of opposition to Lohse's appointment during the July 16 conference with Hitler, when so many fateful decisions with regard to Russia were made. He was obliged to emphasize "again and again that he had already approached Lohse, and that it would be very embarrassing if Lohse were not appointed." Later Hitler took full credit —or responsibility—for the selection of Lohse. He was having trouble finding personnel to take over positions of leadership on the East, he told his associates in May 1942, and had found himself obliged to turn once again to experienced Gauleiters like Lohse and Erich Koch, who was to be appointed Reichskommissar for the Ukraine.[98]

Lohse paid due homage to the ideas expressed by Nazi theorists about Germany's mission in Eastern Europe. His government, he said, was treading the fateful path of the Teutonic knights and the Hansa merchants in transmitting the great legacy of Western civilization to the east. In doing so it was deeply conscious of the magnitude and responsibility of its task.[99] Lohse, however, appears to have been less interested in the ideological aspects of German rule in the east than in the practical problem of building up his own administrative empire and accumulating the trappings of power. Upon hearing of his appointment, his first move was to appropriate palaces and luxury hotels as quarters for himself and his staff and to make certain that a fleet of motor cars would be at his disposal.

In accordance with Hitler's orders, Lohse established his headquarters in the Latvian capital of Riga, where he organized his offices along the usual German departmental lines. In theory he was directly responsible to Rosenberg, but in practice he acted as an independent ruler subject only to the orders of the Führer. Rosenberg had delegated to him the right to legislate by decree on matters of immediate concern to his province, a right Lohse interpreted as allowing him to legislate about anything he chose. Lohse also found that by co-operating with Göring or Himmler, or with any other officials who had been assigned special authority in his province, and by playing them off against Rosenberg and against each other, he was able to gain greater power and freedom of action for himself.

Yet with all his pretensions to personal authority, Lohse was fundamentally a petty bureaucrat who found his satisfaction in dealing with minor administrative details, such as fixing the price of geese, with or without a head, plucked or unplucked, and in having his signature affixed to public signs forbidding smoking in public buildings or regulating the disposal of garbage. Moreover, once the first thrill of authority in the east had worn off, he spent little of his time there. Part of his attention had to be devoted to the administration of Schleswig-Holstein, for which he was still responsible. But far more time appears to have been given to recuperating from overindulgence in food and drink in one or another of the spas of Greater Germany. In July 1944 he simply deserted his post in the Ostland and fled to the Reich.[100]

Lohse assembled a large administrative staff whose membership was drawn from the dregs of the manpower left in the Reich and whose work was duplicated and overlapped many times by the staffs of subordinate or parallel German authorities in the Ostland. In the city of Riga alone there were the regional headquarters of the three branches of the Wehrmacht, the offices of the Reichskommissar for the Ostland, the Generalkommissar for Lativia, the commissar for the city of Riga, the commissar for the county of Riga, the German mayor of Riga, and the German head of the communal administration. Besides these there were the offices of the Göring organizations, the senior SS and police officer for the Ostland, the SS and police officer for Latvia, the offices of the Reichsbahn, the Organisation Todt, and the usual spate of other state, party, and private agencies seeking power or profit in an occupied territory. It was the typical Nazi administrative confusion—an orgy of over-organization, Litzmann, the Generalkommissar for Estonia, called it—compounded in this case by the general incompetence of the Nazi administrators.[101]

The greatest confusion existed in White Ruthenia, much of which was never turned over to the civil government and where effective German control was often so slight that, in the words of one writer, "the real history of the country under German occupation must be sought in the annals of partisan warfare." [102]

The Generalkommissar here was Wilhelm Kube, who took a paternal, or more accurately seigneurial, interest in the "blondes and blue-eyed Aryans" in his province and who waged permanent bureaucratic warfare against Rosenberg, Lohse, Göring, and above all against Heinrich Himmler. So bitter was his feud with Himmler that when Kube was assassinated by a Russian servant girl on September 22, 1943, Himmler declared that only his death had saved him from a concentration camp.[103]

Kube was succeeded, ironically enough, by Himmler's agent in White Ruthenia, Senior SS and Police Officer Curt von Gottberg, an appointment which reflected the increased influence of Himmler (through Berger) in the Rosenberg ministry. Gottberg tried to rally support to the German cause by political and economic concessions, but by this time there was little room for political maneuver and Gottberg was almost exclusively engaged in the suppression of revolt.[104]

No matter how able the German administrators in the Ostland had been or how efficiently their government had been organized, the very size of the province would have made it impossible for the Germans alone to have administered it. Here, as in other occupied territories, they were dependent on the co-operation of the local inhabitants to carry on the routine business of government and exploit the economic resources of the region in the German interest.

The German military government had already acknowledged this dependence by permitting the establishment of native administrations in the three Baltic states. The German civil government not only retained these native administrations but was obliged to entrust them with ever-greater power and responsibility. Even Hitler, who had originally ordered the dissolution of the native administrations, reversed this decision by the end of September 1941.[105]

A curious feature of German rule in the Ostland was the failure to make use of the German Balts who had opted to go to the Reich after the Nazi-Soviet treaty on population transfers in this area.[106] Despite their shortage of administrative personnel, the Germans not only failed to tap this reservoir of experience, but specifically forbade the return of the Baltic refugees. The new administrators from the Reich evidently wished to forestall encroachments by these native Balts on their own authority. The decisive order prohibiting their return, however, was issued by Himmler, who wanted to use the Baltic Germans as settlers in the Warthegau, which had priority over the Ostland in his Germanization plans. Because of inadequate resettlement facilities, however, a large number of these Baltic Germans were not even used in the Warthegau, but spent the entire war in refugee camps.[107]

The form of the native administrations and the amount of authority conceded to each differed in every part of the Ostland. In Estonia there was a central administration composed of five directors; in Latvia there were six general directors; in Lithuania, seven general councilors. Below these there were different administrations for the counties, towns, and villages. In White Ruthenia there was no central administration, but a wide assortment of regional administrations. According to Dr. Otto Bräutigam, Rosenberg's liaison officer with the OKW, the leaders of the native governments in the Baltic were exceptionally competent. He regarded Dr. Hjalmar Mäe, head of the directorate in Estonia, as "an outstanding administrative specialist," and General Oskar Dankers, who held the same position in Latvia, as an "irreproachable character." There were also excellent men among the general councilors in Lithuania, but no regular administrative leader emerged in that country because General-kommissar Renteln was unable to establish lasting good relations with anybody. In general Bräutigam believed the Germans made a serious error in not conceding more authority to these native administrations.[108]

Besides the native administrations, the Germans arranged for the establishment of native advisory councils in all Reich, general, and Kreis commissariats, whose task it was to provide expert information on local problems. Council members were appointed by the Germans, but every effort was made to free them from the suspicion that they were merely German agents and to have them appear instead as the representatives of the local population.[109]

In March 1942 the native administrations in the Baltic states were given formal recognition in a series of published decrees and their functions were defined by Rosenberg in a secret directive to his Reich commissars. The lack of German personnel, Rosenberg said, required the widest possible use of reliable native administrators, who were to be given broad freedom of action and independence to encourage fruitful co-operation. The German administration should confine itself to supervision and co-ordination and was to interfere only when important German interests were at stake. In the selection of native personnel, the Germans should seek to control only the top appointments. All other officials should be chosen by native leaders, who would be held responsible for the personal and professional conduct of their subordinates. The Germans would, of course, reserve the right to appoint a candidate of their own to any office at any time. The heads of the native administration should not be allowed to form a central governing body, but were to remain simply heads of separate administrative departments. They would be empowered to issue decrees in their respective fields with the approval of the German leadership and to send directives to subordinate officials through channels regulated by the Germans.[110]

Because of the wide variations in political and economic conditions throughout the Ostland, Rosenberg urged the German authorities to place special emphasis on the development of native regional and local administrations—county, town, and village governments—which were uniquely competent to deal with local problems. A strong group of local governments would have the further advantage of balancing the power of the heads of the central administrative departments. In the interests of security, it was essential that native administrations maintain their own police forces, although these would have to be more closely supervised by the Germans than any other sector of the native governments. For all native administrations, the official language for dealing with the German authorities would be German, but within the native administrations the local language of the region might be used. Riga, the capital of the Ostland, with its ten to twelve thousand German officials, was excluded from the provisions of the self-government decrees and was to remain directly under a German mayor.[111]

Rosenberg felt obliged to explain to Hitler his motives for granting the Baltic peoples this measure of self-government. "In effect it was only the confirmation of an existing state of affairs and eliminated a certain uneasiness," Rosenberg said. "We had a shortage of officials and therefore had to economize greatly in our use of personnel." The entire procedure would demonstrate Germany's good will to the Baltic peoples. If they failed to respond to this kind of treatment by working harder and co-operating more fully in suppressing unrest, then the German authorities would have an "alibi to history" to justify the application of harsher measures.[112]

In May and June 1942 the Germans made further political concessions by restoring self-government in all districts and cities of the Ostland that had exercised this right prior to the Bolshevik occupation. All measures, however, had to conform to the laws and aims of the German administration and the head of each self-governing body was to have a German adviser who was to be consulted before any important decisions were made.[113]

Following the German defeats in the autumn and winter of 1942, a few German administrators saw that to survive in the east, Germany needed not only the co-operation, but the enthusiastic support of the native population. Litzmann, the Generalkommissar for Estonia, advocated that the Baltic peoples be granted a large measure of political autonomy immediately and that they be promised complete political independence after Germany had won the war. This policy had the support of Generalkommissar Drechsler in Latvia and of Field Marshal von Küchler, the German military commander in Reval, but it was resolutely opposed by Rosenberg and Lohse, the former because he knew the Führer demanded a German Ostland, the latter because he clung to his powers and prerogatives.[114]

Curiously enough, the idea of promising the Baltic states their independence was supported most energetically by Himmler's agent Gottlob Berger, largely, it would appear, because he believed it would facilitate recruiting for the Waffen-SS. Upon hearing of this proposal, Hitler is supposed to have asked what Germany should do if the Norwegians, Danes,

Dutch, Flemings, Walloons, and French sought a similar independent status. To this objection Berger replied that if these peoples had volunteered for the German armed forces in the same proportion as the Ests and Letts, Germany would have an additional million men under arms —and in return Germany would have given up nothing, for in the end all these areas would form part of the Reich.[115]

Hitler, however, refused to sanction any declarations of independence. In a conference with Bormann, Himmler, Rosenberg, and Lohse in November 1943, he remarked that he would never give up Estonia and Latvia; that therefore no promises should be made to these states. In any case, Hitler was opposed on principle to making concessions in such difficult times because they might be regarded as signs of weakness.[116]

The main emphasis of German rule in the Ostland, as in all other occupied territory, was on order, security, and control. In his initial proclamation as Reichskommissar of July 28, 1941, three days after the first transfer of Ostland territory to civil administration, Lohse declared that at the cost of their blood the German people had struck down the Bolshevik enemies of the world. "The German people therefore have the duty and the right to take measures so that a similar peril can never again threaten the heritage, indeed the very existence, of the European peoples." In the interest of safeguarding that existence, the German government demanded that its orders be obeyed absolutely and unconditionally.[117]

In the course of the next weeks, the German authorities published edicts demanding the surrender of all weapons; prohibiting public meetings, organizations, and political parties; calling upon local residents to co-operate in combatting sabotage, terrorists, and every other kind of disorder. When these orders failed in their effect, the Germans established the principle of collective responsibility for partisan and guerrilla activities.[118]

These general orders were accompanied by regulations to control the individual. All persons over fifteen were required to have an identity card, they were forbidden to change their address or place of work, and they could not leave the country without official permission. The procedure involved in securing an identity card gave the Germans the basic facts about every inhabitant of the Ostland: name, date and place of birth, address, profession, place of work (if any), race, citizenship, and religion. Such information was valuable to the Germans not only for purposes of security, but for the mobilization and allocation of labor, Germanization, and resettlement programs, and the campaign against the Jews.[119]

During the period of invasion and military government, German military and police courts took care of all cases involving security and related problems, if indeed they came before courts at all and were not dealt with by summary executions. In the Baltic states all other cases were turned over to native courts, which were allowed to resume operations shortly after the German occupation on the basis of local legal systems, unless these conflicted with German interests. In White Ruthenia, where neither trained non-Communist legal personnel nor a law code satisfactory to the Germans was available, the Germans temporarily administered the law themselves.[120]

After the introduction of German civil government, the native courts in the Baltic states were retained, but a separate system of German courts was introduced. A decree of October 6, 1941, established a German supreme court at the seat of the Reichskommissar, with German superior courts at the seats of each of the general commissars and regional courts wherever they were considered necessary. These German courts were to be staffed by Germans and to operate according to German legal procedures on the basis of German laws. They were to have jurisdiction over all criminal cases not referred to other courts (presumably military and police courts or, for minor offenses, native courts), over all civil cases in which ethnic Germans were involved, and over any cases designated by the Reichskommissar. Attached to each of these German courts were special courts to which all actions hostile to the Reich might be referred. There was to be no right of appeal against the decisions of these German courts except in minor criminal cases, or when this right was specifically granted in the judgment. The responsibilities of German military and police courts were not to be affected by this decree.[121]

In effect the October 6 decree divided the population of the Ostland into three legal categories: ethnic Germans, who would be judged by German courts; natives, who would go before their own courts unless Germans were involved or they were accused of political crimes; and Jews, gypsies, and other outcasts, who enjoyed no legal rights at all.

Because of the shortage of German legal personnel, and to foster the illusion of self-government in the Baltic states, the German civil authorities issued decrees in February and March 1942 giving precise definition to the status of native courts and specifically authorizing them to carry on their functions under their old laws.[122] The propagandistic effect of these decrees can hardly have been great, since the native courts were kept under close German supervision and everyone knew that all important cases, including all cases involving Germans, went before German courts. As if to eliminate all doubt that the laws of Germany had become the real law of the land, Rosenberg published another decree in February 1942 requiring all natives to conduct themselves according to German laws and the orders of the German authorities; all acts of violence in any form against the German state or people were to be punishable by death. To push the process of legal integration a step further, the Germans issued the first of a series of edicts in September 1942 on the "adaptation" of native laws to those of Germany which was supposed to standardize legal procedures but which in effect forced native courts to adopt the German legal system.[123]

The Germans were obliged to proceed somewhat differently in White Ruthenia. The severe burden placed on the German administration by the absence of native courts forced Generalkommissar Kube to recognize the need to build up a native legal apparatus. On September 12, 1942, after a year of preparation, a system of native courts staffed by native personnel was established and a simplified code of German law was drawn up to take the place of Soviet law. The jurisdiction of these courts was even more limited than those of the Baltic states, and German supervision and control even more rigid. All important cases continued to come before German courts. But whether in German or native courts, German law was the fundamental law of the land.[124]

In dealing with problems of elementary education in the Baltic states, the Nazis pursued a relatively moderate policy. They hardly changed the elementary school system, the curriculum reverted to that used before the Russian occupation, the native languages were the languages of instruction, and the old pre-1940 textbooks were used.[125]

The Nazis were less liberal in the field of higher education, perhaps because they regarded the Baltic intellectuals as a lost cause from an ideological point of view. On November 19, 1941, Rosenberg ordered the closing of all institutions of higher learning in the Ostland until further notice. Exempt from this decree were the "practical" disciplines such as medicine, agriculture, science, and technology. All other higher education was to cease immediately, even if students were in the middle of final examinations. They might have an opportunity of completing their studies later, but "the right to do this must be earned by exemplary behavior and by acting in the German interest." All faculty members of higher schools were to be dismissed. After a thorough examination they might fit into new educational programs if they were found to be politically and ideologically reliable. In the future all institutions of higher learning in the Ostland were to be German, among them the University of Dorpat, the Technical College in Riga, and the Agricultural College in Kaunas.[126]

In White Ruthenia Kube attempted to use education as a means of reawakening regional nationalism and of turning the population against Russians, Poles, and Bolshevism, while at the same time making the local population more valuable to the occupying power. "The cultivation of White Ruthenian culture, civilization, and education is an urgent task of the schools in the province of White Ruthenia," he declared. Poles and Russians living in the area would henceforth have to conform to White Ruthenian culture, the language of instruction would be White Ruthenian, and only qualified White Ruthenian teachers were to be employed under the supervision of the German authorities. Schools were to reopen October 1, 1941, with courses in reading, writing, mathematics, botany and zoology, geography, music, handicrafts, and athletics. At the beginning of each school day, all children were to receive instruction in the meaning of the New Europe of Adolf Hitler. Teaching of Bolshevik

366

doctrine was punishable by death, teachers were forbidden to use Russian or Polish textbooks, but should use instead material published in a journal called *The White Ruthenian School*.[127]

Some effort was made to harness religion to the German cause, for the Germans assumed that the churches in the Soviet Union would automatically be their allies in the struggle against Bolshevism. According to Rosenberg's guidelines on the question, religion was to be treated as a personal concern of each individual and all churches and ecclesiastical buildings were to be released for their original purposes. Church congresses and any other large ecclesiastical assemblies, on the other hand, were to be prohibited, as were ecclesiastical missions from other occupied territories or from abroad. Religious leaders were forbidden to engage in any kind of political activity.[128]

Perhaps the greatest opportunity of the Germans to win popular favor in the Ostland lay in the field of economics. By promising to restore private property and ease the economic restrictions imposed by the Soviet government they might have won over to their side the landowners and businessmen who still constituted an influential portion of the Baltic population. The Germans did in fact make some effort to exploit this possibility, but a policy of economic liberalization was never followed with any consistency; on the contrary, the actions and pronouncements of the German authorities often raised doubts as to the sincerity of their intentions.

"It is intended to restore private property completely," Lohse announced in a decree of August 19, 1941. The propagandistic effect of this declaration was badly tarnished, however; for this same decree provided that all property belonging to the Soviet Union, including all private property seized by the Russian government since its occupation of the Baltic states, was to be taken over by the German government and that former owners were to lose all legal claims to such property.[129]

A decree of October 17, 1941, "to liberate handicrafts, small business, and retail trade from the fetters of Bolshevism," contained equally unfortunate restrictions. Economic establishments which had been nationalized or incorporated into combines and trusts were to be decentralized and restored to private ownership, but only when such changes were not contrary to the public interest and the German war effort, a provision that allowed the Germans to maintain whatever combines and trusts they desired.[130]

German administrators who were convinced of the desirability of economic liberalization nevertheless kept up their efforts. In mid-August 1941 they decided to double the amount of land held as private property by peasants on state and collective farms, a measure that applied only to White Ruthenia because the farms in the Baltic states had never been collectivized. For the Baltic states, a decree of September 13 provided for the restoration of all agricultural property confiscated by the Bolshe-

367

viks, including livestock and all other inventory, to their former owners —unless these owners were Communists or Jews. Unclaimed property, or the property of owners who had fled, was to be administered by trustees appointed by the German authorities.[131]

In February 1942 came the New Agrarian Order with its provisions for an increase in the amount of land held as private property by peasants on state and collective farms and the eventual distribution of all communal land as private property—another measure that applied only to White Ruthenia.[132] A year later Rosenberg abolished all Soviet economic laws in the Baltic states and restored private property to its former owners, but again with the restriction that no changes take place that would be detrimental to the public interest or the war economy. German authorities were to decide on the validity of all claims and reserved the right to impose a tax on all property transfers.[133]

The most sweeping German concessions were embodied in a decree of June 3, 1943, announcing that all land turned over to the peasants for private use since the German occupation was to be given legal recognition as private property. According to this decree, all persons working the land had the right to the private possession of land, a right that extended to peasants who had been obliged to leave their land temporarily—including soldiers in the Red Army.[134]

In many parts of the Ostland, the restoration of private property yielded notable results in terms of good will and productivity, but more often the concessions came too late or were bounded by so many restrictions that local German administrators who opposed concessions to the natives on principle or who hoped to acquire much of the state-controlled property for themselves after the war found little difficulty in blocking private property restorations.[135]

Interesting as were the various German measures for economic liberalization, the most prominent features of German economic administration in the Ostland were the familiar policies of direct and indirect economic exploitation. Arms and scarce raw materials were seized by the German army and its economic task forces during the first stages of the German invasion, but sequestrations in one form or another took place throughout the occupation. Less obvious than the outright seizure of property but a nevertheless important form of sequestration was taxation, for the Germans not only continued to levy all taxes in force at the time of their invasion, including those imposed by the Soviet government, but added a variety of new ones.[136]

Mention has already been made of the German decree of August 19, 1941, empowering the German civil administration to take over all real and personal property that had belonged to the Soviet government, which meant all property the Russians had confiscated since the incorporation of the Baltic states in the Soviet Union.[137] To administer the confiscated property, Lohse, following the example of Göring, established a Trustee Administration for the Ostland, whose members were to be appointed by himself. Subsequent decrees expanded the control of the Trustee Administration to include the property of citizens of enemy countries and of all persons or organizations involved in anti-German activities. Exempt from this trusteeship was property already commandeered by the German army or brought under the control of other Reich authorities.[138]

Soon afterward a special Agricultural Trusteeship Association was set up under the Reichskommissar to administer agricultural property formerly owned by the state, by Jews and anti-German elements, or by persons who had fled. It was to exercise all rights of ownership and might order any measures "regarded as necessary in the interests of increased production, of the scientific operation of the property, or of the economic requirements of the Reich Commissariat for the Ostland."[139]

In January 1942, again following the example of Göring, Lohse assumed the right to declare certain industries in the Ostland government monopolies which were to be administered by a special monopoly department in the office of the Reichskommissar. This right was applied at once to salt and sweets, and subsequently to alcoholic beverages, tobacco, paper and pulp, textiles, and cellulose. The income from these monopolies, like that from the properties under trusteeship, became part of the budget of the Reichskommissar.[140]

Economic assets not seized outright by the Germans were brought under rigid control. Fundamental in this respect was a law on economic development of November 29, 1941, which was presented as an essential step from Bolshevik organization to private enterprise, but which in fact imposed restrictions quite as severe as anything introduced by the Russians. By the terms of this law, official sanction was required for almost every form of economic activity. All economic enterprises were to be judged on the basis of their usefulness to the community; the suitability of their location with respect to the availability of raw materials, power, and labor; their general effectiveness; and the reliability and competence of their management. Economic enterprises might be reorganized, closed, moved, or forced to continue in operation; the management, whether owners or trustees, might be changed. The Reichskommissar or his delegates were to be exclusively responsible for all decisions made on the basis of this law.[141]

A second decree of November 29 "on the self-government of manufacturing industries in the Ostland" eliminated the last vestiges of economic freedom by compelling all industries, whatever their legal status, to enroll in an Economic Chamber for the Ostland. This organization, which was to have its headquarters in Riga and branches in the other principal administrative centers, was to be directly under the Reichskommissar and was to carry out tasks assigned by him and his deputies.[142] A law of June 5, 1942, required that all economic enterprises not already included in monopoly or trustee organizations were to be brought into economic associations under the direction of the Reichskommissar for the purpose of increasing productivity and controlling production and distribution.[143]

Not content with these general laws, Lohse published special decrees putting key industries such as petroleum, iron and steel, and chemicals under the centralized direction of the Reichskommissar. The same was done for agriculture. A law of October 14, 1941, required that all grain be delivered and sold to government grain depots which would arrange for its subsequent distribution. In 1943 this law was extended to include every form of agricultural production and processing.[144]

A law of February 23, 1942, amalgamated all professional and labor organizations into a single, government-controlled labor union for the Ostland whose tasks included supervising, counseling, and channeling official orders to its members. A similar association was set up later for agricultural workers.[145]

Besides the policies of direct economic exploitation and control in the Ostland, there were the usual Nazi forms of indirect exploitation—currency manipulation, indirect taxation, the regulation of wages and prices, control of banks and insurance companies, control of the law courts, control over exports and imports. Although placed under German customs authority, the Ostland was not brought into a customs union with Germany for the simple reason that the Germans, while shipping their own products into the Ostland duty-free, wished to continue to collect customs and excise taxes on Ostland exports to Germany.[146]

Finally there was the exploitation of Ostland labor, which was mobilized at wages and hours fixed by the Germans. According to a decree of August 15, 1941, it was everyone's duty to help restore orderly conditions. Every inhabitant could be required to report in person to the official labor office with documents of his employment record; the labor office was empowered to assign him to another job, if necessary in another part of the country. When a mass labor force was needed, young people might be conscripted for work.[147]

Compulsory labor was introduced in White Ruthenia by a decree of September 10, 1941, which required that all persons take up some form of regular work immediately. Boys from fourteen to twenty and girls from seventeen to twenty-four were to be drafted into a Labor Service Organization unless they were otherwise employed. In December 1941 compulsory labor for all persons between eighteen and forty-five was introduced for the entire Ostland, a law extended in August of the following year to include persons of all ages. Later decrees demanded that every inhabitant of the Ostland secure a labor card to prove that he was working. Laborers might be retrained for different jobs and could be assigned to work abroad. "Everyone who is able to work is obliged to work" was the official slogan.[148]

After March 1942 the entire labor recruitment program came under the overall direction of Fritz Sauckel, who assigned the German Reichskommissars the task of serving as his deputies in the occupied eastern territories. Lohse, however, and many other German officials in the Ostland, resented the interference of Sauckel in their administrative domain and feared the political and economic consequences of his recruitment drives. Because of the un-co-operative attitude of German officials in the Ostland, fewer than two hundred and fifty thousand of the almost three million workers recruited in the east came from this province. Of these, almost half came from White Ruthenia.[149]

As inhabitants of an area scheduled for Germanization, the people of the Ostland were fortunate that their territory was low on the list of Himmler's priorities, for almost no Germanization was undertaken in the Baltic region. On the contrary, as previously mentioned, the Baltic Germans were not even allowed to return to their native lands because Himmler intended to use them for the Germanization of Poland.

The Jews, on the other hand, were top priority for Himmler in all oc cupied territories. In April 1942, on the basis of reports from his task forces in the field, Heydrich informed his chief that Estonia, with a pre-war population of 4,000 Jews, was now "free of Jews," and that almost all of the 70,000 Jews who had remained in Latvia at the time of the German occupation had been liquidated. All of Lithuania's 153,000 Jews except those urgently needed for work had likewise been eliminated and the purge of Jews in White Ruthenia was well under way, 33,210 having already been shot by his special forces. In July 1942 Kube informed Himmler that a further 55,000 Jews had been liquidated during the past ten weeks in the area under his jurisdiction and an additional 10,000 had been killed in the area under military administration.[150]

Although Kube co-operated readily enough in the liquidation of eastern Jews, he was seriously disturbed about the treatment of German Jews sent to his province. He was infuriated when Himmler's agents seized Jews working under his direction without bothering to consult or inform him. A particularly bitter dispute arose when, early on the morning of July 20, 1943, Himmler's agent Anton Brandt, acting on special orders from his chief, arrested seventy Jews working for the Generalkommissar "and sent them off for special treatment." According to Brandt's report of the incident, Kube summoned him to his headquarters the moment he heard of the matter and, in a state of greatest agitation, asked him how he dared arrest Jews in his employment; this was a serious incursion upon his executive authority and neither the Reichsführer SS nor his police officials had the right to meddle in his administration. As a result of this latest incident, Kube intended to end all co-operation with the German police, especially with members of the Sipo, who would no longer be permitted to enter his administrative offices.

Brandt was shocked by Kube's attitude and said it was incomprehensible to him that Germans should quarrel with one another about Jews. He himself was constantly being accused of barbarity and sadism, whereas he was only doing his duty. He had even been criticized about the fact that Jews "who were to be given the special treatment, had their gold fillings removed by professional dentists in accordance with instructions (*ordnungsmässig*)." These remarks, Brandt reported, had only made Kube more furious. Such behavior was unworthy of a German, he had said, and "if Germany's good name was today being undermined throughout the world, it was our own fault. Furthermore it was also true that [Brandt's] men positively reveled in these executions." Brandt protested, complaining "that it was deplorable that over and above this filthy work we should also have mud slung at us." But Kube refused to have anything more to do with him and issued orders that henceforth the members of his staff should sever all relations with the German police and give them no information.

Brandt and his colleague Curt von Gottberg, the senior SS and police officer in White Ruthenia, were now determined to destroy Kube. With the aid of documents in their police files, they built up a case that Kube was totally incompetent as a leader and administrator, that his attitude toward the SS and police had always been hostile—"the spirit of Himmler and Heydrich is undermining the Germanic people and is to be compared to the methods of Freemasonry" was one of his typical remarks—and "that finally he is taking an absolutely impossible attitude on the Jewish question." [151]

The dispute between Kube and the SS and police did not end until Kube's assassination in September 1943. Kube's successor as Generalkommissar, Senior SS and Police Officer von Gottberg, had no qualms about liquidating Jews, German or otherwise, a process which continued under his administration until the end of the German occupation. [152]

On April 1, 1944, the entire Ostland was again declared to be an area of military operations. As senior SS and police officer as well as Generalkommissar, Gottberg was left in charge of what remained of German administration in White Ruthenia. Early in July the Russians captured Minsk, the capital of the Generalkommissariat and with that German rule in White Ruthenia came to an end.

The Germans did not hold out much longer in the western part of the Ostland. After Lohse's abandonment of his position on July 28, Hitler appointed Reichskommissar Koch, who had meanwhile been driven out of the Ukraine, to take his place. Riga, the capital of the Ostland, fell to the Russians early in October; in that same month the entire Baltic region was effectively sealed off from Germany. By that time, although German troops continued to hold out in a few pockets in the Baltic, German rule in the Ostland had for all intents and purposes collapsed.

The Reichskommissariat Ukraine

The second great civil administrative province to be established in the newly occupied eastern territories was the Reichskommissariat Ukraine, which was created by a Hitler decree of August 20, 1941. This province was to encompass all lands inhabited by persons of Ukrainian nationality and was to include a large area that had been part of Poland before 1939. Two predominantly Ukrainian areas, however, were not incorporated into the new province. One of these was the former Polish district of Galicia, a province of the Habsburg Empire before 1918, which Hitler intended to annex to the Reich and which he placed temporarily under the personal administration of the governor general of occupied Poland. The other was the territory west of the river Bug, with the harbor of Odessa, which Hitler had promised to the Rumanians and which they subsequently organized as the province of Transnistria. The exact boundaries of the Reichskommissariat Ukraine were to be determined later, according to the progress of the fighting, as were the dates for the actual transfer of these territories to German civil administration.[153]

The first transfer of Ukrainian territory from military to civil administration took place on September 1, 1941. There were further transfers on October 20 and November 14, 1941, and a final transfer on September 1, 1942, which brought the boundaries of the province to beyond the Dnieper river.[154] At its greatest extent the Reichskommissariat Ukraine included some two hundred thirty thousand square kilometers of territory with a population of fifty million. The province was divded into the Generalkommissariats of Volhynia-Podolia, Zhitomir, Kiev, Nikolaev, Dnepropetrovsk, and Taurida. Scheduled for incorporation into the Reichskommissariat Ukraine but never transferred to civil administration were the Generalkommissariats of Kharkov, Stalino, Rostov, and Saratov, which would have brought the boundary of the province to the Volga. Also scheduled for incorporation into the Ukraine was the Crimean peninsula, a propaganda maneuver to give the Ukrainians the illusion that the Crimea would be part of a future Ukrainian national state. In fact Hitler had earmarked the Crimea, including the hinterland of Taurida, as one of the first areas to be settled by Germans.[155]

To Alfred Rosenberg the Ukraine was the key to German success or failure in Russia. As early as 1927 he had advocated an alliance with the people of the Ukraine against Greater Russia and Poland. At that time he had also favored an alliance with Britain to neutralize France in the west, in exchange for Germany's neutralization of the Russian-Bolshevik menace to the British Empire, especially India.[156]

By 1941 Britain and France were no longer factors in Rosenberg's calculations, but he was all the more convinced of the desirability of some kind of alliance with the people of the Ukraine. According to his version of the history of this region, the Ukraine had an almost unbroken tradition of independent national life which had been suppressed by years of Tsarist and Bolshevik terror. By encouraging the use of the Ukrainian language, fostering Ukrainian art and literature, giving fresh prestige to the great university at Kiev, Rosenberg believed it would be possible to reawaken Ukrainian national consciousness. The politically active elements of the population were to be encouraged to exercise maximum self-government with the object of creating an independent state which should be brought into "an indissoluble alliance with the German Reich." The Germans would thereby establish a formidable counter-weight to Moscow and they would win the co-operation of the Ukrainian people in securing the invaluable economic assets of the area. As German intentions toward the Ukraine were "absolutely honorable," there would be no harm in announcing these goals of German policy in the near future.

It was Rosenberg's conviction that, if Germany succeeded in creating a viable Ukrainian state as far east as Saratov, the pressure of Russia on Germany would be lifted and its supplies of food and raw materials would be safeguarded for all time. To carry out this policy, however, the essential precondition was to win the good will of the Ukrainian people and ensure their willingness to work.[157]

Rosenberg held to this policy after the German civil government was established in the Ukraine. Having freed the Ukrainian people from the Bolshevik terror, he said, the Germans must now under all circumstances remain true to their role as liberators. To treat them as Negroes or slaves would turn these potential allies into mortal enemies and would be the greatest error Germany could make. Whether the German army had forty million friends or foes at its back was, after all, a matter of vital importance. Instead of enslaving these people or treating them as racial inferiors, the Germans should seek to promote a political, economic, and cultural renaissance among them.[158]

The ideas of Rosenberg about the Ukraine were not shared by Hitler or his closest advisers. At the crucial conference with Hitler on July 16, 1941, Rosenberg's appeal on behalf of the Ukranian people was greeted with hostile suspicion by Martin Bormann. "It appeared several times that Rosenberg has a soft spot for the Ukrainians," he commented in his minutes of the meeting. Although Hitler agreed that the Ukraine would undoubtedly be the most critical area over the next three years, his own policy for this province called for nothing more than the exploitation of its economic resources and for the settlement of German in certain regions. Germany should certainly not foster the artificial intellectualization of the inhabitants, but seek only to maintain their working capacity. In all other respects Germany should remain aloof from Ukrainian internal affairs. This policy called for firm and, under certain circumstances, depending on the behavior of the natives, severe measures to safeguard German interests.[159]

During the initial stages of Germany's conquest and occupation of the Ukraine, it seemed that Rosenberg's fondest hopes and most sanguine prophecies would be fulfilled. For in the Ukraine, more than anywhere else in the Soviet Union, the German troops were welcomed as liberators from Russian-Bolshevik dominion.[160]

Almost immediately, however, Ukrainian nationalists became disillusioned about the Germans, because of the transfer of the Ukrainian portion of Galicia to the administration of the governor general of the occupied Polish territories and of Transnistria, with the harbor of Odessa, to the Rumanians. The probable effect of these actions was pointed out to Rosenberg, who was well aware of the sensibilities of the Ukrainians on these questions but who failed to register any kind of effective protest. On the contrary, in his guidelines for policy to be pursued in the Ukraine he ordered that "Ukrainian complaints about the transfer of certain areas of the Ukraine to the administration of the governor general and of Rumania, or similar complaints, are to be repulsed with the comment that the Ukraine has been saved by German blood and that Germany therefore reserves the right to dispose of the areas in accordance with general political requirements." [161]

The mistakes of high-level German policy in dealing with the Ukraine were not offset by the behavior of the German occupation forces. Himmler's men immediately set about their work of rounding up Jews and suspected Communists. They subsequently carried out mass executions in the most brutal manner, without making any attempt to conceal their operations.[162]

The behavior of the troops of the regular army was itself far from exemplary. A representative of the German Foreign Office with the army in the Ukraine reported shortly after the German invasion began that

> the frame of mind of the population generally became worse a few weeks after the occupation of the territory by our troops. The reasons for it? We display . . . inner hostility and even hatred toward this country, and arrogance toward the people. . . . How often it happened that, acting against the rules of psychology and committing mistakes that we could easily have avoided, we lost all sympathy of the population. The people cannot understand the shooting of exhausted prisoners of war in villages and larger localities and leaving their bodies there.

German troops were expected to live off the country, but the manner of requisitioning was another major error. "Psychologically, requisitioning the last hen is as unreasonable as it is economically unreasonable to kill the last pig or the last calf." [163]

Bad as was the situation in the Ukraine under the administration of the regular army, it grew dramatically worse after the introduction of the German civil government. As head of the German civil administration in the Ukraine, Hitler appointed Erich Koch, Gauleiter and Oberpräsident of the province of East Prussia, whose headquarters were to be in Rovno in the westernmost part of the Ukraine. As the German armies moved eastward, Koch wanted to transfer his headquarters to Kiev, but Hitler refused to restore the ancient capital of the Ukraine to a position of such eminence in the German New Order.[164]

Koch, a petty railroad official from the Rhineland, had joined the NSDAP in 1921 as its nineteenth member. Although he had served with the chauvinistic and violently anti-Communist Freikorps Rossbach after the First World War, Koch belonged to the left wing of the Nazi movement. As late as 1934 he had advocated co-operation with the peoples of Eastern Europe and the "hardened socialist youth" of Soviet Russia against the decadent capitalist West. It may have been to remove the obstreperous Koch from Berlin that Hitler appointed him Gauleiter of East Prussia in 1928. There he acquired a reputation for initiative and ruthlessness, as a man able to get things done. Through his position as Gauleiter, Koch had frequent occasion to work with Martin Bormann, with whom he developed a close personal friendship. He also worked closely with Göring on numerous economic projects, which appear to have been profitable if not always savory.[165]

It was Göring who pressed for Koch's appointment to a high administrative post in the east during the conference with Hitler on July 16, 1941, when so many fateful decisions regarding the future of Eastern Europe were made. Göring declared that Koch must be considered either for the Baltic (Ostland) because of his thorough knowledge of the region, or for the Ukraine, "simply because Koch was the personality with the strongest initiative and the best preparatory training." Rosenberg protested that Koch would not obey his orders—"Koch had, by the way, said this himself"—but Göring brushed aside this objection. Rosenberg could not expect to guide every footstep of Germany's administrators in the east. Because of the magnitude of the tasks these men would face, they would have to be allowed a great degree of freedom and independence. Hitler decided in favor of Göring. "The Führer emphasizes that the Ukraine will undoubtedly be the most important district for the next three years. Therefore it would be best to appoint Koch there." [166]

The appointment of Koch was a disaster. A man of monumental stupidity and arrogance, he approached his task with the attitude that the most suitable manner of ruling Slavs was with the Cossack whip. He instructed the German officials in the Ukraine to conduct themselves as befitted a master race in dealing with a thoroughly inferior people, and he forbade all social contact with Ukrainians. The sole task of the German administration was to make the Ukrainians work for Germany and to acquire the food and raw materials Germany lacked. The Führer had made him responsible for delivering three million tons of grain and seven hundred thousand tons of vegetable oil to the Reich; he meant to fulfill this obligation regardless of consequences. If the local population starved, that was totally irrelevant. "I will pump every last thing out of this country," he said. "I did not come here to spread bliss but to help the Führer." Koch did not wish to hear any mention of transportation or other difficulties that might be encountered in shipping goods to Germany. The only question that concerned him was that Germany needed the goods of the Ukraine and that therefore they were to be sent to Germany. How this was to be done was up to the ingenuity (*Phantasie*) of his administrators.

Koch insisted that severity and justice should be the twin principles of

German rule. As late as February 1943 he warned his officials against any relaxation of severity because of Germany's difficult military situation. The Slav always interpreted kindness as a sign of weakness. Whoever expected gratitude from the Slav had not learned about politics from experience in the NSDAP or from actual work in the east, but from bookbound intellectuals sitting in ivory towers.

In contrast to Rosenberg, Koch rejected the very idea of a Ukrainian national state and culture. There was no such thing as a Ukrainian nation, he said; he dismissed petitions of Ukrainian nationalists for self-determination or a greater measure of self-government as a "gross political impertinence." These people should be grateful that the Germans allowed them to live at all. In the future they were to be nothing more than helots, the slaves and laborers of the Greater German Reich. There was no need to give them education. Three grades of school were already too much. As a concession to their so-called culture they would be allowed to reopen two churches. Further cultural concessions were out of the question.

Koch made no attempt to hide his attitude from the Ukrainian population. In private conferences and even in public speeches he referred to them as colonial peoples, slaves, niggers, fit for nothing but menial labor.[167] So widely known did his attitude become and so great was the indignation his statements aroused that a story began to circulate that Stalin, in awarding a medal for supreme service to the Soviet state, regretted that the man who deserved it most was not yet in a position to receive it personally.[168]

Koch prided himself on the small size of his administrative staff, which he regarded as a supervisory agency only and which he actually cut down from over 800 to 252 persons between 1942 and 1943. Lacking personnel of his own, however, he was dependent on the manpower of other Reich offices, notably the army and the SS; but above all he was dependent on the despised Ukrainians. Koch nevertheless refused to have any Ukrainians in his office, even as advisers, and he forbade members of his staff to associate with them. It was a ludicrous order. Koch had manpower enough only to staff the very highest positions in his central and regional offices. He had no alternative but to fill all other positions with Ukrainians and to leave them in all but complete control of local government, under the thinnest kind of German supervision.[169]

Koch did not compensate for his hostility to the Ukrainians by cultivating close working relationships with his German colleagues. Lammers testified after the war that the records of Koch's quarrels with Rosenberg would fill many volumes—and they do.[170] Koch's relations with other German officials in the Ukraine were not much better. He was detested by German army leaders, whom he denounced in Berlin—undoubtedly with some justification—for having seized so many of the economic assets of the country that there was little left to swell the expropriation statistics of his own government.[171] Koch got along no better with the representatives of Himmler. He resented the fact that successive senior SS and police officers, who were supposed to be immediately and personally subordinate to him, were disregarding his authority and acting with a good deal of independence—very much, in fact, as Koch was behaving toward Rosenberg. In a violent scene with Senior SS and Police Officer Hans Adolf Prützmann in September 1942, Koch accused him of the most serious personal and professional lapses and threatened to have him shot. In reporting the scene to Himmler, Prützmann said the entire conversation had been conducted "in an unusually insulting and noisy manner" and that he found it impossible to discuss anything with the Reichskommissar in an objective or rational way. Gottlob Berger, who undertook negotiations with Koch on Himmler's behalf in the following year, wondered how he dared to act with such arrogance in view of his shockingly bad administration in the Ukraine, which was now evident to everyone. Koch, he said, was a drunkard, incapable of decent behavior.[172]

Without a large German administrative staff of his own, at loggerheads with his compatriots who had manpower at their disposal, and refusing to work with the Ukrainians, Koch appears to have had but limited means for exercising any real control over his government. His authority suffered further from his failure to be at the center of affairs in the Ukraine. At Hitler's orders he was obliged to maintain his headquarters at Rovno, at the very edge of his Reichskommissariat, whereas both the army and the SS had established their headquarters in Kiev. Not that the location of his capital mattered much, for Koch spent little time in the Ukraine. Like Lohse in the Ostland, he remained responsible for the administration of his German province and, again like Lohse, he appears to have spent much of his time indulging in rest cures in one or another of the spas of Greater Germany. Much of the administration of the Ukraine, therefore, appears to have been carried on without Koch's participation.[173]

The actual degree of Koch's authority, however, was far less important than his public posture, the extremism of his statements, and the crudity of his behavior when he condescended to appear in his satrapy. Moreover, Koch's attitude and the fact that he was known to have the support of the Führer encouraged the basest instincts of other German officials in the Ukraine, many of them products of Koch's training in East Prussia, others the dregs of what was left of the Reich's manpower. Koch's friend Bormann is supposed to have prevented most of the complaints about Koch's administration in the Ukraine from ever reaching the Führer. But Bormann's intercession can hardly have mattered much because fundamentally Hitler himself agreed with Koch's attitude and methods of dealing with the Slavic population. As late as August 1944, with the German armies in full retreat and the German civil administration driven out of the Ukraine altogether, he placed Koch, with his "proven capacity for action" and his "experienced personnel," in charge of new defenses in the Baltic region. After Lohse's flight from the Ostland, Hitler appointed Koch to take his place.[174]

Much of the German legislation enacted in the Ukraine was identical with that introduced in the Ostland, for the majority of decrees issued by Reich offices responsible for eastern affairs applied to all occupied territory in the east under civil administration. Thus in the Ukraine, as in the Ostland, all persons over fifteen were obliged to acquire an identity card, to keep the authorities informed of their addresses and places of work, and to co-operate in the preservation of order. Debolshevized adaptations of Soviet law were permitted in native courts; but all crimes involving Germans and all serious crimes came before German courts (if they came before a court at all) and were judged according to German laws.[175]

In the field of economic legislation, the Ukraine and the Ostland were subjected to similar laws on sequestrations, taxation, trusteeships and monopolies, wage and price restrictions, compulsory labor, and economic controls. All taxes levied by the Soviet government remained in force, the major difference between the Ostland and the Ukraine being that ethnic Germans were exempted from income, agricultural, and certain other taxes to encourage them to settle or to remain in the Ukraine. As in the Ostland, the entire revenue from taxation went into the budget of the Reichskommissar. A Central Bank of Issue for the Ukraine, with the right to issue currency, was established in March 1942. The Ukraine was declared to be an independent fiscal area (*Devisengebiet*) with its own currency, the Karbonvanetz, which was divided into one hundred kopeks. The Reichskommissar had the right to control the currency, to fix its value and official rate of exchange.[176]

Following the example of Göring and Lohse, Koch established trusteeship and monopoly organizations to control the production and distribution of economic assets. Like Lohse, he went beyond the original monopolies on liquor and tobacco sanctioned by Hitler and extended monopoly controls to sugar and salt, petroleum, the chemical industry, and mining. Each branch of the economy was organized into unions of associations, official permission was needed to conduct any kind of economic enterprise, and only those regarded as essential by the German authorities were allowed to remain in operation.[177]

Throughout the German occupation there was a steady flow of regulations fixing prices, wages, and hours of work. All laborers were required to register and were allocated to economic enterprises approved by the German authorities according to their particular skills and abilities. Large numbers were recruited or drafted for work in Germany. When Sauckel took over supreme direction of labor recruitment, Koch was appointed his deputy in the Ukraine.[178]

Koch objected on principle to any concessions to the native population, and he protested vigorously to Hitler against Rosenberg's New

379

Agrarian Order. Even after Lammers informed him that reasons of higher policy required its implementation, Koch did his best to sabotage the program. For this purpose he used his right to act as the trustee of all former Soviet property, which was now the property of the German people. On March 31, 1942, he created an Agricultural Management Association for the Ukraine (*Landbewirtschaftungsgesellschaft Ukraine*) which was to take over the trusteeship of all agricultural property in his commissariat and to organize production according to guidelines laid down by the Reichskommissar. Its tasks included the administration of all communal agricultural enterprises, agricultural associations, state and collective farms, which still required "rigid direction from the top" (*straffe Oberleitung*) to carry out "preparations for the colonization of agricultural property," presumably by ethnic Germans. Only after establishing his Agricultural Management Association did Koch issue a decree replacing collective farms by communal farms, as required by the New Agrarian Order; but he exempted all state or collective farms that were already occupied or under cultivation when the New Agrarian Order went into effect, thus completely nullifying Rosenberg's reform program.[179]

In response to protests from Rosenberg and other supporters of agrarian reform, Koch sent Hitler copious statistics to prove the effectiveness of his own economic policies. In 1942–43, he declared, he had secured six million tons of grain for the German army and Reich, a figure that compared well with production under Soviet management. Koch's critics found it significant that he should compare his achievements with those of the despised Soviet economic system. They also challenged the accuracy of his statistics. State Secretary Hans-Joachim Riecke of the Reich Ministry of Food and Agriculture, for example, maintained that from August 1941 to November 1943 Koch had delivered just over five million tons of grain, which was less than half the amount contributed by the other and far less productive occupied Soviet territories.[180]

The reports of Koch's critics give some idea of the nature of his regime in the Ukraine, where, it should be remembered, the agents of Himmler were also busily at work. On December 2, 1941, the head of the army economic office in the Ukraine sent a strictly confidential report to General Georg Thomas, the chief of the army's economic armaments office; confidential because he feared that wide dissemination of its contents among other Reich departments would only lead to further tensions and difficulties with the Koch administration. In the Ukraine itself, however, he had expressed his opinion about the errors of German policy with brutal frankness to the officials concerned and had tried time and again to have them rectified. The most obvious and most horrifying example of mistaken policy was the extermination of the Jews.

"The Jewish population remained unmolested temporarily shortly after the fighting. Only weeks, sometimes months, later, specially detached formations of the police [*Ordnungspolizei*] carried out a systematic shooting of Jews. This action . . . was taken entirely in public with the aid of the Ukrainian militia, and unfortunately in many instances also with members of the armed forces taking part voluntarily. The way these actions, which included men and old men as well as women and children of all ages, were carried out was horrifying. The great masses executed make this action more gigantic than any similar measure taken so far in the Soviet Union. So far about one hundred fifty to two hundred thousand Jews may have been executed in the part of the Ukraine belonging to the Reichskommissariat; no consideration was given to the interests of the economy.

Quite apart from sentiments of humanitarianism and common decency, the report continued, important economic interests were at stake. The Jews made up a large part of the industrial workers and tradesmen in the Ukrainian cities; their elimination was bound to have dire consequences for the entire economy, including industries badly needed for supplying the German troops. German administrators would have to begin to understand that they were utterly dependent on the Ukrainian population to produce the economic assets Germany so desperately needed. "If we shoot the Jews, let the prisoners of war perish, condemn considerable portions of the population to death by starvation, and also lose a part of the farming population by hunger . . . who in the world is then supposed to produce the economic values here?" [181]

With the beginning of Sauckel's great labor recruitment drives in March 1942, the situation in the Ukraine deteriorated still further. A report of July 1942, prepared by the German office for evaluating written communications exchanged among the Ukrainians, came to a very pessimistic conclusion. "There is hardly anything left today of the enthusiasm you could read about in all letters directly after the German troops liberated the Ukraine from Bolshevik oppression." As reasons for the deterioration of the German position, the report listed economic difficulties, forced labor, violations of personal and national pride, and German policy toward the Jews. The conclusions of the report were supported by direct quotations from Ukrainian letters. "The corn we harvest is taken away from us; one person receives ten kilograms monthly. Do not think this is the case here only; no, it is the same in all the villages." "They take the wheat away and write 'handed over voluntarily,' just the way they took you [presumably for forced labor in Germany]." "First the misery came from the east, now it comes from the west." "The situation has grown a hundred times worse. One lives like a chased dog. It is difficult to describe everything." "A meeting was called in the village and it was made known that everybody should register voluntarily for work in Germany; those who did not would be shot. Everyone is afraid now and reports voluntarily." "Now some other important news. On May 27, 1942, they shot all the Jews here. Only a small part of them consisting of skilled workers and doctors were left alive, but they were arrested. I went to town myself and saw how they were driven to the airport, where four big holes were already dug and where all of them were shot and killed." [182]

Old-guard Nazis joined in the criticism of the German administration in the Ukraine. Alfred Frauenfeld, the Generalkommissar of the Crimea, deplored the administrative confusion in the Ukraine resulting from the large number of quasi-independent and conflicting authorities. But his chief criticism was leveled at Koch. The stolid brutality and sledge-hammer techniques of the Reichskommissar had driven the friendly people of the Ukraine, who had enthusiastically welcomed the German troops upon their entry into the country, into the forests and swamps as partisans, thereby decisively influencing the course of events in the east. These methods were in no way necessitated by the harsh requirements of war. The gratuitous violence, the expressions of contempt for the native population, the constant blabbering in public about making the Ukrainians the slaves of the German master race "bear witness to a lack of instinct in handling foreign peoples which in view of its consequences cannot be called anything less than shattering and catastrophic." Moreover Koch and his various cohorts who talked most about their racial superiority were those who regularly got drunk and did not scruple about making a spectacle of themselves in public.

Frauenfeld regarded Koch's order forbidding all social contact with the native population to be as wrong as it was impossible to carry out. Equally stupid was his public pronouncement that the Ukrainians were henceforth to have a mimimum of education, a policy not only psychologically disastrous but one that was contrary to the interests of the Reich, for the Germans needed trained technicians, veterinarians, and agricultural experts to keep the economy going in so large an area. Most inane of all was the policy of cutting down on health measures so as to allow plague and disease to decimate the native population. "A quite unusual amount of stupidity and shortsightedness is required to believe that an occupied country can be exploited most effectively by allowing the population to sink into imbecility and to die out." [183]

But stupidity and shortsightedness remained the predominant characteristics of German rule in the Ukraine until the end. As Sauckel's deputy for the recruitment of labor in the Ukraine, Koch was the only high-level German administrator in the east to co-operate wholeheartedly with Sauckel's recruitment program. That co-operation proved most effective, for well over two-thirds of the almost three million workers recruited in the east came from the Ukraine.[184]

Despite feuds with Himmler and his deputies, Koch also co-operated in the destruction of the Jews in the Ukraine, where some four hundred thousand Jews were killed by Himmler's task forces and their Ukrainian auxiliaries in the course of the German occupation.[185]

The collapse of German rule in the Ukraine began almost exactly two years after the Reichskommissariat for the Ukraine was first officially established. In August 1943 the Red Army launched an offensive which was to end with the final expulsion of the Germans. Kharkov fell to the Russians on August 23, Taganrog in the south on August 30, Smolensk on September 25, and by October they had reached the Dnieper at several points. Kiev, the capital of the Ukraine, was captured on November 6; Zhitomir on December 31; and by May of the following year the entire Ukraine had been cleared of German forces.

The Crimea

The Crimea was originally scheduled to be one of the general commissariats of the Ukraine, although independent of the authority of Reichskommissar Koch, in order to allow the Ukrainians to believe that the Crimea would be part of a future Ukrainian national state. Hitler, however, had very different plans for the future of the Crimea. "The Crimea must be cleared of all foreign elements and colonized by Germans," he said in his conference of July 16, 1941. "In the same manner [as the Baltic area], the Crimea, with a substantial hinterland (the area north of the Crimea) must become Reich territory; the hinterland must be as large as possible."[186]

Hitler, who had never been to the Crimea, evidently believed the peninsula to be a tropical paradise. This was to be Germany's Riviera, a vast resort area for the party's Strength Through Joy programs, the center of Germany's citrus fruit and rubber plantations. In the interests of good relations with Turkey, he considered allowing the Turks to control the Black Sea, making it a Turkish sphere of influence. At the same time, however, he proposed to build forts on the Isthmus of Perekop and to construct a major German naval base in the Crimea to ensure that the peninsula should remain German for all time. German towns of fifteen to twenty thousand inhabitants would be founded throughout the area as service centers and seed depots for the German peasant colonists who would constitute the major portion of the population. In memory of the Germanic Ostrogoths who had first civilized this great land, the German Crimea was to be called Gotenland, the city of Sevastopol was to be renamed Theoderichshafen, and Simferopol was to be called Gotenburg.[187]

The German army launched its attack on the Crimean peninsula on September 25, 1941. It broke through the Russian defenses on the Isthmus of Perekop just over a month later. Simferopol, the capital of the Crimea, fell on November 1, Yalta on November 9; but not until July 2 of the following year did the Germans capture the fortress city and naval base of Sevastopol.[188]

The Crimea remained under German occupation until May 1944. Because of the strategic importance of the area the peninsula proper was left under military government throughout this period. Only the region of Taurida north of the Isthmus of Perekop, which was to form the hinterland of the future German colony, was transferred to German civil authority.

Hitler was anxious to implement his program for the colonization of the Crimea as soon as possible. He had counted on using the forty-nine thousand ethnic Germans already in the Crimea as a core group for further German colonization, but the Russians had removed them all as potential saboteurs before the German invasion.[189]

In February 1942 Hitler proposed moving one hundred and forty thousand ethnic Germans from Transnistria, now under Rumanian administration, to the Crimea; some months later he enthusiastically endorsed a suggestion to send the South Tyrol Germans there. In this way he would not only obtain valuable colonists for the Crimea, but the South Tyrol, which he had conceded to Italy, would be cleared of its German inhabitants. "I think the idea is an excellent one," Hitler said. Climatically and geographically the Crimea would be an admirable area of settlement, and there would be no transportation problem. "All they have to do is sail down one German waterway, the Danube, and there they are." [190]

For once Himmler did not enthusiastically endorse the ideas of his chief. He had hoped to use the South Tyrolese to re-Germanize the territory of Burgundy, and he foresaw numerous difficulties in transferring them to the Crimea. Hitler, however, clung to his idea, and Himmler could do no more than persuade him to postpone the resettlement of the South Tyrolese in the Crimea until after the war. "For Burgundy," he noted somewhat regretfully, "we will just have to find another [Germanic] ethnic group." [191]

Although Hitler agreed to postpone the settlement of the South Tyrolese in the Crimea, he demanded that there be as little delay as possible in ousting the indigenous population. On July 12, 1942, General Wilhelm Keitel informed army leaders in the Crimea of Hitler's intention to remove all Russians and Ukrainians from the peninsula as soon as the situation would permit. For the time being ethnic Germans, Tatars, Bulgarians, Greeks, and Armenians were to be allowed to remain, provided they were not Bolsheviks. As a first step the Reichsführer SS had ordered the security police to remove all active Bolshevik elements and "big city trash." Meanwhile, in preparing for the future, the entire population was to register with the German authorities to determine the ethnic status and profession of each inhabitant. The future evacuation of the area would be conducted by the Reichsführer SS in conjunction with the Ministry for the East. Until the peninsula was turned over to German civil administration, the forces of the Reichsführer SS were to receive every possible assistance and the fullest co-operation from the German army.[192]

The actual German administration in the Crimea was as confused as in other parts of occupied Russia. In theory the German army was in charge of the administration throughout the German occupation; but the first German military commander in the area, General Erich von Manstein, virtually abdicated his administrative responsibilities to be able to devote all his attention to military problems. Indeed the military situation was grim. Manstein lacked troops and supplies, there were immense areas where he was unable to establish any kind of front, and behind the lines there was constant partisan activity.[193]

Because of Manstein's preoccupation with military affairs, the actual administration of the Crimea appears to have devolved on the leaders of Himmler's SS and police troops, who had been assigned primary responsibility for dealing with problems of security and pacification. Manstein seems to have been only too willing to concede them these distasteful tasks and to allow them to cope with the problems of administration in general. After the war Otto Ohlendorf, the head of Himmler's task forces in the peninsula, not only admitted his administrative role, but even took some pride in it. "The army left it up to me to deal with the political situation in the Crimea," he testified at Nuremberg.[194]

Ohlendorf's first step was to remove dangerous elements—Communist party members and Jews—from positions of responsibility. He then attempted to carry out Hitler's orders to clear out all undesirable racial elements, including the Ukrainians, from the peninsula; but the practical difficulties involved in this project were so great that he never got beyond the elimination of Jews and gypsies. In the first place, the Germans never had adequate resources to remove the entire Slavic population. Secondly, here as in other occupied territories they were dependent on the indigenous population to carry on the government and the economy of the country.[195]

From the time they entered the Crimea, German military administrators began selecting local officials who appeared to be reliable to form the nucleus of native regional and local governments. Their selection, however, was dependent on the approval of the German police officials, who in cases of disagreement were empowered to choose the local administrative leaders themselves and who in the end took complete charge of setting up the native administrations. According to Ohlendorf, the selection of native administrative leaders was made on the basis of the predominant ethnic group in any given locality. Thus Ukrainian leaders were selected in a predominantly Ukrainian area, Russians in a Russian area, Tatars in a Tatar area.

Among the many ethnic groups in the Crimea, the Tatars were the only people in whom Ohlendorf placed any trust (the ethnic Germans, it will be recalled, had been removed before the arrival of the German armies). In contrast to the Russians and the Ukrainians, the Tatars were not only allowed to administer their own counties, towns, and villages, but were empowered to form a central government committee for education, religion, and culture. Under German auspices the Tatar language was introduced in predominantly Tatar schools, a Tatar newspaper and national magazine began publication, a Tatar national theater was founded, and fifty mosques were reopened. Only when the Tatars attempted to convert their central committee into something of a national government did Ohlendorf draw the line. The Tatars, for their part, on the whole co-operated loyally with the Germans; large numbers volunteered for the German army and auxiliary police.[196]

Ohlendorf's lack of confidence in the reliability of Slavic ethnic groups in the Crimea seemed justified when a Russian counteroffensive in January 1942 revealed the extent of their hostility to German rule. After the Russians had again been driven back, Ohlendorf engaged in wholesale "combing-out" operations by checking the credentials of every inhabitant of the peninsula; the entire region seemed permeated with enemy agents and sympathizers. With only very limited forces at his disposal, he employed typical German terror tactics in his attempts to control the native population, executing persons suspected of aiding the partisans and razing entire villages which had given them shelter. Ohlendorf's methods were sanctioned by General von Manstein, who himself ordered that the natives would have to be taught to fear German reprisals even more than they feared those of the partisans.[197]

Hitler's plan to place the Crimean peninsula under a German civil administration was never carried out. It was not until September 1, 1942, that five districts north of the Isthmus of Perekop, which Hitler had designated as the hinterland of the German Crimea, were transferred to a civil administration. To preserve the fiction that this entire region would one day form part of a Ukrainian national state, these five districts were attached to the Reichskommissariat of the Ukraine as the Generalkommissariat of Taurida, but they were made independent of the authority of the Reichskommissar of the Ukraine, Gauleiter Erich Koch.[198]

As the Generalkommissar of Taurida, Hitler, at Rosenberg's suggestion, selected the former Gauleiter of Vienna, Alfred Eduard Frauenfeld who, as a member of the Austrian Nazi party, had played an active role in the Anschluss movement. Frauenfeld attempted to prepare himself for his new position by learning all he could about the Crimea. He even wrote a book about the region which, not unexpectedly, placed heavy emphasis on the peninsula's Germanic heritage.[199] Unlike Koch in the Ukraine, Frauenfeld was sensible enough to recognize the absolute necessity of winning the confidence and good will of the local population, at least so long as the exigencies of war required it. After the war, he candidly admitted, the Germans could do what they pleased.

Frauenfeld never had much opportunity to demonstrate his abilities as an administrator. Installed in the Tauridian capital of Melitopol in September 1942, he was forced to flee just over a year later. During that time he tried to pursue a policy of "enlightened absolutism" to preserve order and stimulate economic productivity. In fact he appears to have done little more than sanction the continuation of the indigenous administrations that had been established before his arrival and, like the army, to have left much of the dirty work of security and pacification to the Himmler forces.[200]

From an economic point of view, the Crimea was a great disappointment to the Germans. A large part of the economy of the region had been destroyed by the retreating Russians; what the Russian armies had left behind had been plundered by the local population. The Germans were, therefore, confronted by such basic tasks as restoring the water supply, sewers, electric power, the transportation and communication systems. Instead of being able to exploit this productive region, they found they had to import food to prevent large-scale famine; food shortages remained their greatest problem during the first year of their occupation.

Economic recovery was slowed by bad weather and poor harvests, by partisan activity, and by the failure of the Germans to live up to their early promises to liberalize the economy. As in other parts of Russia, the Soviet collective farms and tractor stations were maintained, despite German promises to abolish them. The few concessions the Germans did make were largely nullified by laws requiring that all agricultural products, including those produced on private holdings, be sold at fixed prices, a policy that quickly drove agricultural produce out of the markets. Only gradually did the Germans adopt the system used by the military government in the north of abolishing price restrictions and allowing a black market to flourish. Prices might soar, but the food at least was made available.[201]

With the introduction of the New Agrarian Order in the spring of 1942, the majority of Crimean peasants were thoroughly skeptical. They recognized quite correctly that this was little more than a continuation of the collective farm system under another name. Miserable crops in the summer and autumn of 1942—only half the estimated grain crop and one-tenth the estimated potato crop were harvested—convinced the Germans that drastic policy changes were necessary. Already in 1942 they had converted the collective farms of the Tatars into agricultural co-operatives. On the south coast at least, where the weather had been good, the result had been a bumper fruit crop. Encouraged by this success, the Germans began the conversion of all collectives into co-operatives in September 1942, with the promise that the private holdings of reliable peasants would be enlarged 15 per cent. In December they removed all controls on most categories of agricultural products. By May of 1943 the increase in agricultural deliveries to urban markets was so great that the German economic authorities decided to permit a free market for all agricultural products except meat. The response was such that, despite the great demand for food, agricultural prices fell 10 to 20 per cent by the end of June in Simferopol, and they declined still farther by the end of the summer. After the harvests of 1943, for the first time since the German occupation began, the food situation was brought under control.[202]

But the Germans did not have long to enjoy the fruits of the new agricultural prosperity. Their labor recruitment policies and subsequent programs to conscript laborers for work in Germany drove more and more natives into the ranks of the partisans, while to the north the Soviet armies had already launched their great counteroffensive in the Ukraine. Early in 1944, with the Russian armies sweeping through the Ukraine, the Germans began their retreat from the Crimea. The fortress city and naval base of Sevastopol fell on May 9, and with that German rule in the peninsula came to an end.

The Caucasus

In addition to the Ostland and the Ukraine, Hitler planned to set up two further Reich commissariats in Russia during the first stage of his occupation of that country: one for the Caucasus and another for the region around Moscow. Reichskommissars were actually appointed for these provinces, but they were never brought under sufficiently firm military control to permit their transfer to civil administrations. The greater part of the Reichskommissariat Moscow, including the city of Moscow itself, was never occupied by the Germans at all; but they did succeed in occupying part of the Caucasus region.[203]

For the Caucasus, as for every other part of Russia west of the Urals, Reich Minister Alfred Rosenberg had drawn up detailed and fanciful plans. In his instructions to a Reichskommissar for the Caucasus, prepared before the invasion of Russia began, he stated that the "foremost and decisive task" of a German occupation government must be to secure the oil of the region for the Reich. To safeguard the oil supply, something akin to a German military colony would have to be established around the oil fields. Otherwise, however, Rosenberg recommended that the government of the Caucasus, like that of the Ukraine, be entrusted primarily to the indigenous population and that the Germans maintain a minimum number of their own officials in the area.

In contrast to the Ukraine, with its relatively homogeneous population, the Caucasus was inhabited by dozens of different nationalities and ethnic splinter groups, which meant that the formation of a national government here would be impossible. Instead Rosenberg proposed the formation of a federal union of the predominant nationalities in the Caucasus in which the culturally advanced Georgians would be allowed to play a leading role. But all nationalities would be expected to look to Germany as the ultimate safeguard of their political and cultural existence.

As envisaged by Rosenberg, the Reichskommissariat Caucasus, limited on the south by the borders of Turkey and Iran and on the east and west by the Caspian and Black seas, was to be extended in the north to include the territory east of the Volga and south of Rostov. The province was to be divided into seven general commissariats; its capital was to be at Tiflis. The Caucasus and Ukraine together were to form two giant connecting links between the Reich and the Black and Caspian seas. This entire region had formed part of a great Gothic empire which had been destroyed by the Huns in the fourth century, but which was to be reconstituted in the era of Adolf Hitler. Control of the Caucasus was vital for the establishment of such an empire, not only because of its oil but for political and geographic reasons as well. "The security of the German Reich will only be possible and the agriculture of the Ukraine can only exist if there is a secure connection between Kiev and Tiflis, if a common political attitude will in the future link the Caucasus and the Ukraine to Germany." [204]

As Reichskommissar for the Caucasus, Rosenberg proposed Arno Schickedanz, a Baltic German like himself who had been an editor of the *Völkischer Beobachter* and head of Rosenberg's office for foreign policy. Most recently he had served as Hans Lammers's representative to the Government General in Poland. In July 1941 Hitler approved Rosenberg's selection and formally appointed Schickedanz Reichskommissar for the Caucasus; but since the province was never turned over to the civil administration his appointment had almost no practical significance.[205]

Hitler's ideas about the Caucasus corresponded with those of Rosenberg on only one point: the importance of the Caucasus oil fields. "If I do not get the oil of Maikop and Groznyi, then I must end the war," he told his generals in June 1942.[206] To secure the Caucasus oil fields and ensure their profitable exploitation, Hitler had no intention of following Rosenberg's proposal to set up a federative state in the Caucasus with minimal German supervision. On the contrary, he believed that this region of warring tribes and blood feuds would have to be subjected to the most rigid kind of German control. Whether it should actually be annexed to Germany he did not yet know, nor did he have fixed ideas about how the administration of the province should be organized. Only one thing was certain: For military, political, and economic reasons, the Caucasus area was to be severed permanently from Russia.[207]

The German armies moved into the Caucasus region in August and September 1942, but they never succeeded in capturing more than a part of the northern sector of the province. They never reached Tiflis, their projected capital, or the Groznyi oil fields; they only reached the oil fields around Maikop after they had been effectively destroyed by the Russians. At the end of December 1942 the Germans began their retreat from the Caucasus, and by midsummer of the following year they held only a small area round the Kuban river delta and the Taman peninsula.

Since the German military administration in the northern Caucasus lasted less than a year in all and less than six months in most areas, it is almost meaningless as a guide to future German intentions. Yet it is interesting as an indication of what the Germans might have achieved by a more sensible policy in other parts of Russia.

The German military commander in the Caucasus was General Ewald von Kleist, who later succeeded Manstein in the Crimea and may have been responsible for the liberalization of German policies there during the final months of the German occupation. In the Caucasus, Kleist had the support of an able team of administrators. At the suggestion of Colonel Klaus von Stauffenberg, who was to plant the bomb in Hitler's headquarters in July 1944, the army appointed General Ernst Köstring as its chief military administrator in the Caucasus, with Colonel Hans Herwarth von Bittenfeld as his adjutant. Köstring, born in Moscow and German military attaché in that city from 1927 to 1930 and again from 1935 to the outbreak of war with Russia, was an outstanding specialist on Russian affairs, while Herwarth had been a Russian specialist at the German Foreign Office.[208]

The policies proposed by Köstring and Herwarth for the Caucasus did not differ substantially from those recommended earlier by Rosenberg. They, too, favored the establishment of a confederation of semiautonomous national states in the region with a minimum amount of German supervision. Indeed the only new idea they had to offer was the recruitment of a Caucasus legion among Russian prisoners of war which should aid in the struggle for national liberation against Muscovy and form the nucleus of a cadre of pro-German administrators when its members returned to their native districts after the war.[209]

Hitler had ignored Rosenberg's proposals for a Caucasus confederation of nationalities, but he gave his qualified approval to these proposals when they were put forward by the army. He demanded only that specific promises of national independence be deleted from army proclamations in the Caucasus because he did not wish to bind himself for the future or to make promises he could not keep. In response to army requests, he issued a directive on September 8, 1942, authorizing the establishment of indigenous governments in the Caucasus and conferring on the German military government absolute administrative authority in the area—limited as always by the independent powers granted to Göring, Rosenberg, and Himmler.[210]

The German military government in the Caucasus did its best to avoid the mistakes made by German occupation governments in other parts of Russia. German troops were given strict orders to treat the native population as friends, to respect private property and pay cash for all requisitioned goods, and in general to win the confidence of the people by model behavior. There was to be no conscription of labor in the Caucasus. If harsh measures were necessary, the reasons for them should be explained.

In its first public proclamations to the people of the Caucasus, the German army announced, "We bring you the right to own property, freedom from the Kolkhoz system, freedom to develop national culture, and freedom of religion." The German military administrators tried to live up to these promises. They permitted the prompt reopening of Moslem mosques and Christian churches; they encouraged the reopening of local schools with instruction in local languages and emphasis on regional cultures and traditions; and they granted a considerable degree of local autonomy and self-government. Complete self-government was to be introduced in three stages. During the initial stage, indigenous governments were to be formed in each ethnic district. In the second stage, which was to take place after the harvest in the autumn of 1942, the native governments were to take over authority from the German administration, but were to remain under German supervision. In the final stage, which was never reached, they were to be granted "full self-government." [211]

The New Agrarian Order, which nominally abolished collective farms, was introduced in the Caucasus as in other parts of occupied Russia, but the military administration intended to bypass the stage of communal farms and proceed at once to the distribution of land and livestock as private property. Due to opposition in Germany, the army was not allowed to go so far except in the mountain areas, where pasturelands and cattle were immediately transferred to private ownership. In the lowlands, 30 to 40 per cent of the collective farms (as compared to 10 per cent in the Ukraine) were transformed into agricultural co-operatives. The land held as private property by the peasants on these farms was immediately enlarged and the peasants were promised that all the land would be turned over to them as private property in the near future.

In the Karachai region, where the Germans received a particularly warm welcome from the Moslem mountaineers, the military government immediately confirmed the authority of a newly formed local native government and permitted the establishment of a Karachai National Committee to administer the entire "autonomous region." The Karachais were allowed to form their own police force and to recruit soldiers for a brigade that was to fight with the Wehrmacht. In October 1942 the Germans announced the dissolution of all collective farms in this region and the transfer of all land and livestock to private ownership.[212] Conditions under the German military government differed widely from region to region in the Caucasus, but in general it can be said that the policies pursued, while not always gaining the sympathy or support of the local population, at least avoided the evocation of fanatic hostility.

In the Caucasus the military administration was more successful than elsewhere in keeping the SS and police at bay, but even there the Himmler forces were able to set about their grisly work of eliminating Jews and other undesirable elements. How long the army administrators would have been allowed to pursue the political and economic policies they had inaugurated if the Germans had remained in control of the Caucasus will never be known, but to judge from the experiences of the army in other areas, it is safe to assume that the reign of relative reasonableness would have been brief.[213]

The army, of course, carried out harsh measures of its own in establishing order and requisitioning supplies; it is largely in contrast to other Nazi occupation administrations in Russia that its record appears impressive. During the German retreat, when the army was seized by panic and the life of every soldier was constantly at stake, the military authorities acted with a ruthlessness quite as extreme as any Nazi civil government in their struggle for self-preservation.[214]

In contrast to Southeastern Europe, Hitler's war aims in Russia were clear and consistent—and based squarely on the *Mein Kampf* program. Hitler's statements on policy, his directives, and the activities of his agents in Russia leave no doubt about his intention to fulfill that program to the letter, as rapidly as possible and on the broadest possible scale.

In the first instance Hitler proposed to establish German dominion over all Russian territory to the Urals, to annex the Baltic states and their hinterland and the Crimean peninsula and its hinterland (the southern Ukraine) to Germany, and to ensure German control over the nickel mines of the Kola peninsula and the oil fields of the Caucasus. But this was to be only the beginning. As the German population grew and new lands were required for German settlement, additional Russian territories would be annexed to the Reich as the Germans moved steadily and inexorably farther into the east. As there were no natural frontiers in this entire area, not even the Ural mountains, the only frontier that would exist in the future would be racial: the frontier between the Germanic and the Slavic-Asiatic populations.[215]

The first area of Russia scheduled to be colonized systematically was the Ostland, where special efforts were to be made to Germanize the Estonians. At the same time, however, German centers of colonization were to be established in the Crimea and the Ukraine, while in the countryside Germans were to be settled along the routes from Cracow to Kiev, Leningrad to Kiev, and Zhitomir to Odessa. Within ten years Hitler expected twenty million German colonists to be settled in the Russian territories incorporated into the Reich; by the time the colonization process was completed, there were to be ninety million Germans in the Ukraine alone.

The new Germanic settlers of the newly conquered eastern territories were to come not only from the Reich, but from all the Germanic countries of Europe—Denmark, Norway, Sweden, the Netherlands, Belgium, and, once the war was won, from England and overseas as well. One of the prime reasons for the conquest of the east was to make territory available for the settlement of Germanic peoples from every part of the world who had previously been forced to migrate abroad because there was no longer sufficient land at home to support them.

In the Russian territories annexed to Germany, Hitler did not intend to remove the indigenous population immediately. There was to be the usual combing-out process to find members of the population who were suitable for Germanization in order to use them as settlers in other parts of the Germanic empire and to deprive Slavs and Asiatics of a potential Germanic leadership class. Those not selected for Germanization, presumably a large majority of the native population, were to be retained temporarily as slave labor for the German master race to aid in the gigantic construction projects that lay ahead: building networks of motorways, railways, and canals; putting up model cities and villages in which the German colonists were to live; constructing new dams and hydroelectric plants, opening new mines, seeding new forests, and in general exploiting the natural resources of this vast area. While this work was going on, the non-Germans were to be strictly segregated from the Germanic population to prevent the contamination of Germanic by alien and inferior blood. The only alien races that would not be tolerated in the new Germanic colonization areas were the Jews and the gypsies, who were to be removed completely.

To his Finnish allies in the north, Hitler promised Karelia and the Leningrad area after Leningrad itself had been razed; to his Rumanian allies in the south, Bessarabia and Transnistria; to his Japanese allies in the Far East, supremacy in East Asia, which would presumably have meant Japan's annexation of a substantial amount of Russian territory in Siberia. Where the boundaries between the German and Japanese spheres of influence in Russia were to be drawn was never determined, but such boundaries would have been temporary in any case. When German settlement had reached the Japanese sphere of influence, the Japanese, too, would have been compelled to give way to Germanic *Lebensraum* requirements and presumably would have been subjected to the same fate as the Slavs or any other alien race that stood in the way of Germanic expansion. Such problems, however, lay far in the future and Hitler left it to later generations of Germanic leaders to deal with the.[216] But he had already indicated how they could and should be solved. "Nature recognizes no political frontiers," he wrote in *Mein Kampf*. "She first puts the living creatures on this globe and watches the free play of energies. He who is strongest in courage and industry then receives, as her favorite child, the right to be the master of existence." [217]

CHAPTER 12

Morgen die ganze Welt?

For the study of Hitler's war aims in territories not conquered or occupied by the Germans in the course of the Second World War, the historian is dependent on Hitler's own statements about his intentions, on plans prepared by state and party officials, and on speculation, with speculation often the major or sole resource available. For this reason the following discussion of many significant areas, including the greater part of Asia and the Western Hemisphere, is frequently cursory and almost all of it is inconclusive.

Britain, Finland, and the Neutrals

Britain

Of the European countries not conquered by Nazi Germany, the most critical and the one that most frequently occupied Hitler's thoughts was Britain. In *Mein Kampf* he had advocated an alliance with the racially related British as an essential prerequisite to any German effort to conquer territory in Eastern Europe. "For such a policy," he wrote, "there was only one single ally in Europe: England. With England alone, one's back being covered, could one begin the new Germanic invasion." To gain England's favor, no sacrifice would have been too great. But "only an unconditionally clear attitude could lead to such a goal: renouncing world trade and colonies; renouncing a German war fleet. Concentration of the state's entire means of power in the land army." [1]

After coming to power, Hitler did not change his opinion about the importance of Britain, and he worked hard to secure the kind of alliance with that country he deemed essential to the success of his expansionist program. By the autumn of 1937, however, he had become convinced that Britain as well as France would oppose any German attempt to

394

dominate Eastern Europe and that in all probability he would have to eliminate the threat of both countries before he could embark on the conquest of Russia. Britain's policy of appeasement, which gave Germany Austria and the Sudetenland (and with the Sudetenland, de facto control of Czechoslovakia), revived Hitler's hope that Britain might yet be willing to concede Germany a free hand in the east. Britain, after all, had every reason to welcome the destruction of Bolshevik Russia, which would eliminate the Russian threat to British interests from Asia Minor to the Far East while at the same time eliminating the political and social threat represented by international Bolshevism. This hope was shattered in September 1939 when Britain, instead of seeking means to evade its commitments to Poland, as it had done in the case of Czechoslovakia, responded to Hitler's invasion of Poland by declaring war on Germany.[2]

After Germany's victories in the west in the spring of 1940, Hitler again saw reason to hope that he could reach agreement with Britain. "We are seeking a rapprochement [*Fühlung*] with England on the basis of a partition of the world," he told his generals in May 1940.[3] He regarded it as a calamity that Germany had been obliged to fight Britain at all. The British decision for war had been in part the result of the shortsightedness and selfishness of Britain's leaders, but fundamentally it had been a product of the pressures and intrigues of the Jewish-capitalist clique which still dominated the British government. If Britain had only been willing to leave Germany a free hand in Russia and to offer Germany a few overseas colonies as a sop to German pride, Germany and England would still be living at peace. Even colonies would not have been necessary, for by compelling Germany to protect its lines of communications to overseas possessions, which would have involved the maintenance of a fleet and a network of naval and air bases, they would have created more problems for Germany than they were worth.[4]

With the refusal of the British to come to terms in the summer of 1940, Hitler ordered the preparation of plans for an actual invasion of Britain, for cutting off Britain's vital lines of supply, and for striking at strategic outposts of the British Empire. All such plans failed or were considered too dangerous to carry out, at least while Russia remained in a position to sever Germany's own economic lifelines in Eastern Europe. By this time Hitler had also become convinced that hope of Russian intervention was one of the major reasons the British continued to hold out. To crush this hope and at the same time knock out the Russian threat to Germany's own security on the continent, Hitler decided in December 1940 to destroy Russia in what he confidently expected would be a lightning campaign. Once Britain's last possibility of support on the continent had been eliminated, Hitler believed that even the stubborn British would at last come to terms with Germany. In that case he would be spared the need to invade England and destroy the British Empire, which he had never wanted to do. But if the British still refused to make peace, he could build up his forces at his leisure, without having to fear a flank attack and with all the resources of Europe and Asia at his disposal, and finally move against Britain with such overwhelming power that the outcome of the campaign would not be in doubt.[5]

Russia, of course, was not destroyed in a lightning campaign. As Germany's difficulties in Russia mounted, British air and naval operations in Western Europe, which had once been merely an awkward irritant, became a serious menace. Even then Hitler did not indulge in outbursts of anti-British fury or expressions of his determination to crush the British and their empire, as he so often did when thwarted by other nations. The destruction of the British Empire, he said, would only benefit the United States and Japan, which would then seize Canada and East Asia. "I could not even prevent the Americans from gaining a firm foothold in Africa." Hitler thought it possible that some day the British and Germans might actually march together against the Americans. "Germany and England will know what each can expect from its partner; then we should have found the ally we need. They have an unexampled cheek, those English! Which doesn't prevent me from admiring them." [6]

Most of all Hitler regretted that he had not gained the co-operation of the British in his war against Bolshevism. He compared the present rivalry between Britain and Germany to the rivalry between Prussia and Austria for the leadership of Germany in the previous century; it was a rivalry which he hoped would be resolved in a similar way. As a result of the Prussian victory over Austria in 1866, Austria had been excluded from German affairs; but only a few years later Prussia-Germany and Austria formed an alliance which endured through the rigors of the First World War. In similar fashion, Britain would be excluded from the affairs of continental Europe following Germany's victory over England in the present conflict; but afterward Hitler was prepared to offer Britain an alliance which would guarantee the lasting friendship of the two countries. In the future, with Germany guaranteeing the security of European civilization on land and Britain by sea, what might not yet be accomplished through the partnership of these Germanic peoples? [7]

There has been much speculation about what Hitler's policy would have been had he actually succeeded in conquering Britain. At the time a German invasion of Britain seemed imminent he appears to have had hopes that the duke of Windsor could be persuaded to return to his throne under German auspices and that Lloyd George, Chamberlain, or Hoare, would undertake the formation of a collaborationist government. This would have given the German occupation a most desirable appearance of legitimacy, and might have been expected to facilitate the reconciliation of the two peoples.[8]

Hitler himself issued no directives for a German occupation of Britain, or at least none has so far come to light. The memoranda on the subject prepared in German military, police, and economic offices, however, indicate that Britain's fate in the event of a German conquest would have been comparable to that of Denmark or the Netherlands, depending on the attitude of the British population and British leadership.[9] An army order of September 9, 1940, signed by General Walther von Brauchitsch, laid down principles for dealing with the British civilian population during the period of military operations. It was modeled on similar directives for other countries. "The welfare of the inhabitants and the interests of the country's national economy . . . will be considered insofar as they contribute directly or indirectly toward the maintenance of law and order and the security of the country's labor for the requirements of the German troops and the German war economy." British administrators were to be allowed to carry on their routine functions as long as they maintained a correct attitude. All firearms were to be surrendered within twenty-four hours, failure to do so to be punishable by death. A more unusual and severe army order was issued on September 23: "All male civilians between the ages of 17 and 45 will be arrested, insofar as this can be carried out, and dispatched with prisoners of war to transit camps on the continent. Later orders will follow about the establishment of internment camps for Englishmen." [10]

The most detailed plans for Britain were drawn up by German economic and police offices. A military-economic bureau for Britain, established July 27, 1940, soon developed into a full-blown administrative apparatus. Its plans called for the division of Britain into six military-economic commands, with headquarters in London, Birmingham, Newcastle, Liverpool, Glasgow, and Dublin—which indicates that Ireland, too, was to be brought into the Nazi orbit, at least for economic purposes.[11] The task of these commands would be to enable the invading armies to live off the country to the greatest possible extent, although Hitler himself had minimal expectations in this regard.[12]

As in all cases of German invasion operations, units of Himmler's police were assigned to accompany the German invasion army to Britain in order "to seize and combat effectively the numerous important organizations and societies in England which are hostile to Germany." On September 17, 1940, Heydrich appointed SS Standartenführer Professor Dr. Franz Alfred Six, the head of a new faculty for the study of foreign countries at the University of Berlin, to the position of representative of the Chief of the Sipo and SD in Britain. "Your task is to combat, with the requisite means, all anti-German organizations, institutions, opposition, and opposition groups which can be seized in England, to prevent the removal of all available material, and to centralize and safeguard it for future exploitation." Six's headquarters were to be in London, but he was authorized to set up special task forces as the situation required. Plans were subsequently made to establish headquarters for regional task forces in Birmingham, Liverpool, Manchester, and Edinburgh (or Glasgow, if the Forth bridge was blown up).

A secret information handbook on Britain, evidently prepared in Hey-

drich's office, contained a detailed description of the British police, secret service, and other critical organizations, as well as the location of
Britain's major industries, oil installations, and power supply systems.
Appended to this handbook was a list of every conceivable organization
that was likely to oppose the German authorities or which might be useful for political or propaganda purposes. This list also included the
names of twenty-seven hundred individuals living in Britain who were
believed to be anti-German, ranging from Winston Churchill and
Charles de Gaulle to H. G. Wells and Virginia Woolf, a group that included cabinet ministers, members of parliament, writers, artists, and
professors. All persons on this list were to be seized in the first wave of
German arrests. Heydrich's office also compiled card indexes of Jews,
Freemasons, German refugees, socialists, communists, and liberals. The
information on these cards was to be supplemented by data secured in
Britain itself. Each card purportedly contained the notation "immediate
arrest," "arrest," "immediate house search," or whatever other action was
to be taken.

By far the most interesting feature of German police plans for Britain
was that they envisaged the withdrawal of German occupation forces
and made provision for the postoccupation period. "Intelligence work
will be divided, according to its nature, on the one hand into making
normal situation and other reports on England during the occupation
period, and on the other into the establishment of intelligence cells in
England [for the period] when we leave the island." [13]

Thus Hitler may have contemplated conceding the British a quite unusual status of independence within the Germanic world if his plans had
succeeded—and if the British people had shown an appropriate willingness to participate in his New Order.

The Channel Islands

On June 30–July 1, 1940, the Germans actually did occupy some British
territory—the British Channel islands, an archipelago off the Normandy
coast consisting of the four principal islands of Jersey, Guernsey, Alderney, and Sark, which the British had decided not to defend.[14] These islands, which had been part of the duchy of Normandy when Duke William conquered England in 1066, were placed under the authority of the
German military government in France. By reattaching them to France,
Hitler may have hoped to aid history in repeating itself.

During the first two years of their occupation the Germans ruled with
a comparatively light hand. On August 23, 1940, the chief of the military
administration in France published a decree stating that "the general orders issued by the supreme commander of the army for the . . . military
administration in France are applicable, by way of analogy, to the occupied English Channel islands." [15] But in fact few of the measures taken
in France were put into effect. The islanders were allowed to govern

themselves under German supervision, French remained the principal official language of administration, English the principal language of business and religion. Administration, law, and the educational system were left much as they had been under British rule, the only change being that the German language was made a compulsory subject in the schools.[16]

Hitler, however, had major changes in mind. At a meeting with his naval commanders on August 22, 1941, and in a number of subsequent naval conferences, he announced his intention to annex the islands to Germany. They were to be fortified and made into permanent German bases, like Heligoland. On October 20, 1941, he issued an order enjoining his administrators "to press forward with maximum speed for permanent fortification of the Channel islands to convert them into an impregnable fortress." This order was followed up with such energy and resolution that by July of the following year Hitler was convinced the islands could never again fall into enemy hands.[17]

Hitler was not satisfied with fortifications alone. To ensure the security of the islands he demanded the removal of the entire British-born population, although the local German military commander protested that there had not been a single case of sabotage. The deportation order was issued on September 16, 1942. Shortly afterward some two thousand men and women between the ages of sixteen and seventy were evacuated and sent to camps in Germany. The remaining islanders were spared deportation and some of the worst aspects of a Nazi occupation, although they were forced to witness the inhuman treatment of thousands of workers brought in from the continent to build Hitler's fortifications.[18]

Hitler appears to have intended to deport the entire native population of the islands after the war, but he rejected the suggestion that they be resettled with Germans from Friesland and the Ems region. Instead he proposed to turn the islands over to his labor leader, Robert Ley, who was to make them into health resorts for his Strength Through Joy movement.[19]

But the Germans never got the opportunity to convert their barracks into hotels. At the end of the war the British regained Hitler's impregnable fortresses without having to fire a shot.

Some historians consider the German occupation of the British Channel islands significant as an indication of what German policy toward Britain itself might have been had Hitler succeeded in conquering Britain; but this analogy seems far-fetched. There is, after all, a difference between a major industrial power and center of a world empire and a sparsely inhabited rural archipelago. Hitler would hardly have squandered Britain's strategic and economic assets by turning the British Isles into a health resort, even had the climate of Britain been more suitable for that purpose.

399

Finland

By the terms of the Nazi-Soviet nonaggression pact of August 23, 1939, Germany recognized the preponderant interest of the Soviet Union in the Baltic states of Estonia, Latvia, and Lithuania, and in Finland, all of which had been part of the Russian Empire before 1914.[20] The Soviet government lost no time in seeking to establish firm control over these areas. In September and October, the Russians compelled the Baltic states to allow the Red Army to establish military bases within their territories and to conclude mutual assistance pacts with the Soviet Union. Similar Soviet demands were presented to Finland, but the Finns refused to make the desired concessions. On November 30, 1939, the Red Army attacked Finland. Although the Finns put up a valiant resistance, they were obliged to ask for an armistice early in the following year, and by the peace treaty of March 12, 1940, they ceded the Karelian isthmus, the city of Viipuri (Viborg), and the naval base of Hanko to the Soviet Union. It was to regain these lost territories—and improve their strategic position vis-à-vis the Soviet Union—that the Finns entered into an alliance with Hitler and joined his invasion of Russia in June 1941.[21]

In the late summer and early autumn of 1941, when it seemed that the German armies would soon achieve the decisive victory over the Soviet Union which the German leadership so confidently expected, President Ryti of Finland raised the question of his country's future boundaries in diplomatic discussions with the Germans. Ryti frankly acknowledged that he wished to reduce Finland's involvement in the war as soon as possible so as to be able to use Finnish manpower for the revival of the country's domestic economy. As for Finland's future frontiers, "the *small* Finnish nation with a large territory must lay emphasis on a *short* boundary. The Svir boundary with a glacis before it would fulfill this need. If Leningrad would not continue as a metropolis [Ryti must have been informed of Hitler's intention to destroy the former Russian capital], the Neva would form the best boundary on the Karelian isthmus." In addition Finland wanted all of Karelia, including the Kola peninsula, as well as territory in Eastern Karelia "with an eastern boundary following the coast of the White Sea to . . . where the Onega river flows into Onega Bay. From there . . . a general line to the southern shore of Lake Onega, then following the Svir river to the southern shore of Lake Ladoga, and thence along the Neva river to its mouth in the Gulf of Finland." [22]

Hitler was prepared to grant the Finns almost everything they requested. Finland was to be given the territory around Leningrad and a frontier that stretched from the White Sea to the Svir and the Neva, with the Neva as the future boundary between Finland and Germany. Germany reserved the right to participate in the exploitation of the nickel mines on the Kola peninsula, but apart from that Hitler asked nothing of Finland except that Germany be allowed to co-operate in the economic reconstruction of the country. To his associates Hitler acknowledged that he was all the more willing to concede Karelia to the Finns because the climate was not suitable for Germans and consequently this area could not be used for German colonization in any case.[23]

Hitler was filled with admiration for the heroic exploits of the Finns. In November 1942 he paid them what was for him the ultimate compliment by ordering that "from now on Finland and the Finnish people be treated and designated as a Nordic state and a Nordic people." [24] Yet in giving the Finns the status of Nordics, Hitler did not propose to incorporate them into his Germanic Reich. In 1942 he recalled how, after Finland's defeat by Russia in the winter war of 1939–40, Finnish leaders had asked him to make their country a protectorate of the Reich. He had never regretted turning down this request, Hitler said, because he believed that the Finnish people, who had spent six hundred years of their history in fighting, were worthy of the highest admiration and respect. It seemed to him more appropriate to have this nation of heroes as an ally rather than attempt to integrate them into the Reich. By far the best solution from the point of view of German security would be to preserve Finland as an ally and make it the guardian of Germany's flank in the north.[25]

The Neutrals

In considering the future of the European states that remained neutral in the Second World War, Hitler said very little about his intentions toward Sweden, except to veto the idea of a union between Sweden and Finland and to include the Swedes in the roster of Germanic peoples who would be encouraged to participate in the colonization of Eastern Europe.[26] The most obvious explanation for Hitler's reticence about Sweden is that he wished to avoid giving rise to rumors that might stir up Swedish fear and hostility and thereby jeopardize the vital shipments of Swedish iron ore to Germany.

It is of course possible that Hitler would have allowed Sweden, like Finland, to maintain an independent status after the war as an ally of Germany. However, in contrast to his attitude toward the Finns, whom he had accorded the status of honorary Nordics, Hitler clearly regarded the Swedes as Nordics by birthright. It is therefore more likely that he would have compelled the Swedes to accept membership in his Germanic Reich, and that the model of Nazi policy toward Austria would have served for Sweden, as it was to serve for Denmark, Norway, and the Netherlands.[27]

Hitler was more specific about his intentions toward Switzerland, which he described in August 1942 as a pimple on the face of Europe and a state that could not be allowed to endure. He was filled with hatred and contempt for the materialistic and democratic values of the

Swiss people, and he denounced them as a racial miscarriage, "a misbe-gotten branch of our *Volk*." Whereas he was anxious to attract Scandi-navians and Dutch as peasant colonizers to the newly conquered ter-ritories of the east, he believed the Swiss could be of use there only as innkeepers.[28]

Hitler did acknowledge the Swiss to be Germanic, however, much as he otherwise despised them. The probability is therefore great that when he carried out his intention to put an end to the existence of Switz-erland as a state, he would at the same time have initiated policies de-signed to regain the Swiss for Germandom and to incorporate the bulk of the Swiss population into his Germanic Reich. This was certainly the intention of Heinrich Himmler, Hitler's grand inquisitor for racial affairs who, in September 1941, was exchanging views with his faithful lieuten-ant Gottlob Berger about the suitability of various personalities for the position of Reichsstatthalter in Switzerland and the chances for a genu-ine amalgamation (*zusammenwachsen*) of the German and Swiss peo-ples. A document from the Himmler files bearing the letterhead Reichs-führer SS, SS Hauptamt, Aktion S[chweiz], contains a detailed plan for the establishment of Nazi rule in Switzerland. Although there is no evi-dence that this plan was endorsed by Himmler or any other high-level Nazi authorities, the fact that such a plan was drawn up at all may be interpreted as an indication of intent.[29]

Hitler was also quite definite about his future policy toward Turkey, a country which dominated some of the world's most important strategic waterways and overland routes between Europe, Asia, and Africa. As in the case of Japan, Hitler was evidently content to ignore the racial qual-ifications of the Turks for political reasons and because he had no inten-tion of incorporating Turkish territory into his Germanic Reich—at least not within the foreseeable future. The essence of Hitler's Turkish policy was that Germany should seek to form an alliance with Turkey in order to make that country the guardian of Germany's southeastern flank and thus the counterpart of Finland, the guardian of Germany's flank in the north. An alliance with Turkey should be easy to arrange, Hitler thought, because German and Turkish interests were nowhere in con-flict. As a Moslem state with a centuries-old tradition of hostility to Rus-sia, Turkey could be counted on to be a stable and reliable ally, and one which would have a vested interest in preventing all outside inter-ference in the region of the Straits and the Black Sea. Germany would thus be saved the trouble of having to defend the Straits or of having to maintain a fleet on the Black Sea or in the Eastern Mediterranean. An alliance with Turkey, in fact, would relieve Germany of all responsibil-ity in the Near East except that of keeping Turkey supplied with arms.[30]

More complicated was Hitler's attitude toward Spain and the regime of Francisco Franco, which he had done so much to put into power and which he might have been expected to support in the future as the guardian of Axis interest in the Southwest. But Hitler had become sorely disillusioned with Franco following the Spanish dictator's refusal to co-operate in the war against Britain and the conquest of Gibraltar, which might have enabled Germany to seal off the entrance to the western Mediterranean. Hitler believed that Franco, with the army behind him from the beginning, had started his rule in a far more favorable position than either Mussolini or Hitler himself when they became chiefs of state. Yet Franco had never carried out a truly comprehensive revolution in Spain and seemed unable to cope with the influence of the Roman Catholic Church or such dangerous agents of the church as his brother-in-law and foreign minister, Ramón Serrano-Suñer, who was playing a manifestly dishonest game with the Axis. While giving effusive assurances of his good will toward Germany, Serrano-Suñer was in fact attempting to form a Latin union composed of France, Italy, and Spain, and Hitler suspected that his next move would be to try to enlist this Latin alliance on the side of Britain. Hitler was confident, however, that Spain's eagerness to seize French territory had doomed all such efforts in advance.

While disgusted with Franco and his Roman Catholic entourage, Hitler had a high regard for the Spanish people, whom he described as being a mixture of Gothic, Frankish, and Moorish blood, and who in his opinion possessed the quality of "grandeza." They might seem inefficient or slovenly by German standards, but they had proven themselves to be tough and tenacious fighters. He had heard from Fritz Todt, the head of the immense Nazi construction organization, that "Red" Spaniards now working in German labor camps were not Reds at all in the German sense, but conscientious and decent fellows who protested that they had only co-operated with the Soviet Union because no other state had offered them support of any kind and they had been left with no alternative. Hitler thought it would be well to hold these Spanish Reds in readiness for the new civil war that was certain to break out in Spain, for they, together with old-guard Spanish Falangists, would constitute the most trustworthy force at Germany's disposal.

Hitler believed it would be a simple matter to find allies in Spain who would serve as German agents to topple the Franco regime. More difficult would be the task of finding a suitable personality to clean up the political situation in that country. Whether another general would have the necessary political capacities only the future would show. Meanwhile Hitler intended to do everything in his power to promote the popularity of Muñoz-Grande, the commander of the Spanish Blue Division fighting with the Germans in Russia, because he was a forceful and energetic personality who might someday play a decisive role in ousting Spain's present priest-ridden regime. He proposed to decorate Muñoz-Grande at the earliest opportunity; when the time came for the Blue Division to return to Spain, he would re-equip it on a grand scale with the very best in modern weaponry and accord it every possible honor and prestige.[31]

What Hitler meant by all this, it seems clear enough, is that he disliked the Franco regime and was prepared to co-operate in its overthrow if he could be certain that a coup d'état or another civil war would result in the installation of a more reliable friend of Germany as head of the Spanish government. If a new, pro-German, regime had been established, it is possible that Hitler would have offered Spain those extensions of territory in Europe and Africa at the expense of France which he had at one time offered to Franco in return for Spain's active participation in the war against Britain. If these territories had been accepted, Spain, with its pound of French flesh, could have been counted on as a reliable ally against what was left of France. It is also reasonable to assume that a pro-German Spain would have been allowed to take over Gibraltar and perhaps even permitted a free hand with Portugal in order to have a reliable power guarding the Iberian peninsula's entire Atlantic coast. But for this surmise there is no evidence whatever.

Overseas Colonies

In considering the question of Hitler's desire for colonies, it is necessary to distinguish between colonies to be established in territories contiguous to the Reich, which were Hitler's principal territorial objective throughout his career, and overseas colonies, which for him appear to have been at all times a peripheral concern. "It is not in the acquisition of [overseas] colonies that we should see the solution to this question [of *Lebensraum*]," Hitler wrote in *Mein Kampf*, "but exclusively in the winning of lands for settlement which extend the territorial base of the motherland." And again, "Make certain that the strength of our people is not based on [overseas] colonies, but on the soil of our European homeland." A demand for colonies was embodied in the Nazi party program, but this demand did not specify that these colonies should be overseas, although contemporary observers generally assumed that this was the case.[32]

After coming to power, Hitler seemed to confirm this assumption by persistently putting forward demands for the return of Germany's pre-1914 colonies as part of his propaganda campaign of securing justice for Germany and reversing the decisions of Versailles. While he still hoped for an alliance with Britain, Hitler toned down these demands somewhat; in the later 1930s he attempted to use colonies as bargain counters for a broad agreement between Britain and the Reich.[33] The British got the point, but they refused to make the kind of bargain Hitler clearly desired. After seeing the German dictator at Berchtesgaden in November 1937, the British cabinet minister Lord Halifax wrote, "The suggestion that we should try to do a bargain on the line of getting him to drop the demand for colonies as a return for a free hand in Europe is neither very moral nor very attractive. There might be more to be said for the more difficult but sounder bargain of a colonial agreement at the price of being a good European. But with what collateral security?" [34]

In outlining his policy to leaders of his own government later that month, Hitler left no doubt that his primary objective was still the acquisition of territory in Eastern Europe and that he would not be deflected from this goal by the offer of overseas colonies. This did not exclude the possibility that Germany would eventually seek such colonies once it was in a better position to defend and exploit them. At the present time, however, while the sea lanes around Europe were still controlled by foreign powers, overseas colonies would be of no use at all to Germany in case of emergency because Germany could not count on keeping open its lines of communication to overseas territories.[35] To his propaganda office Hitler issued orders that the agitation for colonies was to continue, but that colonial demands should not be pressed too acutely "because other foreign policy goals have priority." [36]

After the defeat of Poland in October 1939, Hitler appealed to Britain to make peace and declared that, apart from Poland, Germany desired no territorial revisions except the return of its former colonies, which Hitler demanded in the name of political justice and common sense.[37] Even now, overseas colonies appear to have been a very minor consideration, but Hitler evidently believed the British would be prepared to make colonial concessions as part of the price for peace. As usual he wanted to be certain that he acquired everything his opponents might be willing to concede. Although colonies were not a primary territorial aim, he told Mussolini later, they would be useful as sources of food and raw materials not available elsewhere and they would put an end to the degrading necessity of having "to beg for every pound of tea or coffee." [38]

Hitler's view that overseas colonies were of negligible value for purposes of national security was not shared by many of his compatriots, who, with the examples of the British and French empires before them, regarded colonies as major sources of national strength. The arguments of German colonial enthusiasts had no appreciable influence on the policies of Hitler, but after the fall of France and with the defeat of Britain seemingly imminent, German colonialists could no longer be restrained. Nor could numerous other Germans, for the prospects for conquest that seemed to have opened out before them were sufficient to stimulate the most prosaic imaginations. German territorial aspirations now began to assume world-wide proportions, as German planners from every kind of government and private office covered global maps with indicators and diagrams. Hemispheric defense lines were drawn from Iceland through

Britain and south to the Azores, the Canaries, and the Cape Verde islands, while arrows pointed the way for Nazi legions to the Caucasus,
the Persian Gulf, Afghanistan, and India.[39]

High on the list of attractions were the opportunities awaiting the
Germans in Africa. The German navy staked out claims to a unified colonial empire from French Guinea and Sierra Leone, via Togo, Nigeria,
the Cameroons, the French and Belgian Congos, to former German East
Africa, as well as to a large number of islands off the east and west
coasts of Africa (Ascension, St. Helena, Madagascar, the Seychelles,
among others), all of which was apparently indispensable to Germany
"for national and economic reasons." It was assumed that territory desired by the Germans which was now in the possession of Spain and
Portugal could be acquired "by friendly agreement." [40]

The colonial claims of the German navy in Africa were matched and
surpassed by the German Foreign Office. A memorandum of November
6, 1940, by Dr. Ernst Bielfeld, head of the Foreign Office department for
Central and South Africa, gives some idea of the heady effect of conquest on German planners and the extent of the territorial claims they
were prepared to make. The final objective to be aimed at, Bielfeld
wrote, was to bring as large a part as possible of the available colonial
territory in Africa under German influence so as to be able to explore,
cultivate, and exploit the entire African continent for the benefit of all of
Europe, with particular attention to the needs of Greater Germany. A
prerequisite for attaining this objective would be the acquisition of a
sufficiently large area in Central Africa, as compact as possible, which
could serve as a German base for opening up the entire continent. This
new German colonial empire in Central Africa should be built around
the nucleus of the former German colonies of the Cameroons, German
East Africa, and Togo. Indispensable as the link between the Cameroons and East Africa was the Belgian Congo, which Germany should
acquire no matter what Belgium's future status in Europe might be. Besides the Belgian Congo, Bielfeld recommended that Germany lay claim
to the greater part of French Equatorial Africa, including Dahomey and
the Lake Chad region; the greater part of British Nigeria; the harbor of
Ada in the Gold Coast; and the British territories of Kenya and Uganda.
The hinterland of German East Africa might perhaps be enlarged by the
inclusion of Northern and Southern Rhodesia, the latter one of the few
areas in Africa where a large-scale steel industry could be established.
For strategic reasons the German navy would require the naval bases of
Dakar in French West Africa, Conakry in French Guinea, and Freetown
in British Sierra Leone, together with a suitable amount of hinterland.
Also highly desirable for strategic reasons were the French islands of
Réunion, the Comoro group, and Madagascar, which was still being
considered as a future home for the Jews. Elsewhere in Africa Germany
should demand the return of its former colony of German Southwest Africa, now under the mandate of the Union of South Africa, a question

which Bielfeld believed could best be handled separately with the settlement of Germany's future relations with the Union of South Africa.[41]

Even Hitler caught the colonial fever in those intoxicating months after the fall of France. In recording the political observations of the Führer, General Halder wrote in his diary in July 1940, "In Africa we are laying claim to the coast. (Apparently in conjunction with Spain.) Italy wants hinterland. We are laying claim to the French and Belgian Congo." A month later Halder noted that German demands were now directed to the acquisition of a solid bloc of colonial territory from West to East Africa.[42]

But Hitler's fundamental attitude toward overseas colonies had not changed. "For a colonial policy to have any sense, one must first dominate Europe," he told his associates in 1941. "In any case, the only colony I'd like to have back would be our Cameroons—nothing else." Strength through colonies, he still insisted, was a mirage, and the acquisition of African territory remained for him a side issue.[43] Even in the summer of 1940 Hitler's chief interest in Africa and in colonial territories in general was their strategic value for carrying on his struggle against Britain, as well as their value as bargaining counters in negotiations with other powers, in the first instance with Britain itself.

The point has already been stressed that Hitler still wanted a peaceful settlement with Britain; he continued to hope that the British might yet be persuaded to come to terms with Germany in return for a German guarantee of the British Empire. To members of his entourage Hitler repeatedly declared that he had no desire to destroy that empire, for in doing so he would only benefit Japan and the United States. If Britain still had a European mission, it was to guarantee European security at sea as Germany would do by land; Hitler had been convinced by the spirit demonstrated by the British navy and air force during the present conflict that Britain was still capable of carrying out such a role.[44] Britain, however, steadfastly refused to make peace with Germany or give Hitler what he wanted most—a free hand in Eastern Europe.

With the failure of his overtures to Britain, but while still trying to leave open the possibility of a future settlement with that country, Hitler proceeded to use colonial territories as bait to consolidate old alliances and gain new ones. To convince the Italians of his good faith, he promised them Nice and the island of Corsica, Tunis and French Somaliland, and an extension of Italian territory south of Libya into French Equatorial Africa. From the spoils of the British Empire, the Italians were to receive Egypt and the Sudan, British Somaliland, Malta, and Cyprus, plus a preponderant position in the Arab Middle East. In addition he was prepared to consider Italian claims to Algeria and French Morocco.[45]

To draw Spain into the war against Britain and create the necessary conditions for the conquest of Gibraltar and the closure of the Western Mediterranean, Hitler dangled his colonial bait before Franco. The

Spanish dictator's price was high. He wanted an extension of Spanish territory at the expense of France in Europe, Gibraltar, French Morocco, Algeria as far as Oran, an extension of Spanish territory in the Sahara to the twentieth parallel, and an extension of the territory of Spanish New Guinea to Cape Lopez. Besides these territorial concessions, he would require massive military and economic aid if he were to participate in the war. But at no time would Franco set a date for his entry into the war or even for granting permission to German troops to cross Spanish territory.[46]

Hitler for his part was reluctant to make specific territorial commitments to Spain, because at the same time that he was negotiating with Franco he was trying to lure Vichy France into the war against Britain and he realized that breaking up the French colonial empire would hardly be the best means of doing so. In fact, one of the principal inducements he was able to offer the French in return for their participation in the war against Britain was a promise to allow them to retain the greater part of their colonial empire, or to offer them compensation at the expense of Britain for any colonial territories they might be asked to relinquish. Thus, in effect, the French, too, were to be lured into the Axis camp by colonial concessions.[47]

Juggling the conflicting colonial hopes and claims of Italy, Spain, and France, with the factor of Britain always in the background and the problem of Turkey and the Arab countries often very much to the fore, was a difficult task. Indeed it was hopeless; Hitler is supposed to have said that the only possible course for Germany under the circumstances was to engage in deceit on a grand scale.[48]

In November 1940, Hitler used the colonial gambit in dealing with Russia. When Vyacheslav Molotov, the Soviet commissar for foreign affairs, arrived in Berlin for a series of conferences, the Germans presented him with the draft of an alliance treaty whereby Germany, Italy, Japan, and the Soviet Union should undertake to respect one another's "natural" spheres of interest. By the terms of this treaty, Germany was to declare that, apart from territorial revisions in Europe to be carried out at the conclusion of peace, its territorial aspirations lay exclusively in Central Africa. The territorial aspirations of Italy were to lie in Northern and Eastern Africa; those of Japan in the area of East Asia south of the island empire of Japan; while Russia was to declare that its territorial aspirations lay in the area south of the Soviet Union in the direction of the Indian Ocean. Further, the four signatory powers would recognize the present extent of Turkey's possessions, but would endeavor to secure for the Soviet Union the right of unrestricted passage for its navy through the Straits at any time; whereas all other powers, except the Black Sea countries, but including Germany and Italy, would in principle renounce the right of passage through the Straits for their naval vessels.[49]

What Hitler was trying to accomplish with this tactic, and not too subtly at that, was to divert the attention of the Soviet Union from Eastern Europe, where it threatened the interests of Germany, to the British sphere of interest in the Middle East. This did not mean that Hitler had abandoned his resolve to conquer Russia; but if he could ease Russian pressure in Europe temporarily, or, better still, actually involve Russia in the struggle against Britain, he would be in a far more favorable position for waging war against Britain in his own right. If this tactic were successful, it would be all to the good; if not, it would give Hitler a valuable indication of Russia's intentions and of the nature of the Russian threat to Germany.

Hitler's negotiations with Molotov were a total failure. Even before the Russian statesman left Berlin Hitler realized that the Soviet Union would not rise to his colonial bait. By December he had come to the conclusion that the Russian threat would have to be removed even before a final victory over Britain had been achieved. A major factor in this decision, it will be recalled, was Hitler's belief that hope for Russian intervention was one of the principal reasons the British continued to fight.[50]

Hitler had better luck with his colonial bait in dealing with Japan. The Japanese, in fact, had not waited for Hitler to make offers. After the defeat of the Netherlands and France they had proceeded to take over Dutch and French colonial territories in East Asia. This Japanese behavior was not at all welcome to Hitler, who wanted to preserve as much territory as possible for the white race. In addition, he had hoped to exploit the concern of Dutch and French leaders about their colonial possessions to pressure them into closer co-operation with German occupation authorities. There was nothing he could do about the situation, however; and, in any case, he was far more concerned about securing Japan as an ally and preventing a possible rapprochement between Japan and the United States. For this purpose he was prepared to sacrifice all European colonial territory in East Asia.[51]

On September 27, 1940, representatives of Germany, Italy, and Japan signed an alliance (the Tripartite Pact) in which Germany and Italy recognized the leadership of Japan in establishing a new order in Greater East Asia. Further, in the interest of friendship with Japan, the Germans agreed to renounce their claims to the former German colonies in the South Seas now under Japanese mandate and to other former German possessions in this area under the mandate of Britain, Australia, and New Zealand, as well as to dispose of these territories in Japan's favor in return for compensation.[52] The Tripartite Pact in no way guaranteed that Japan would henceforth co-operate with Germany in international affairs, but it was to prove a significant landmark in the tense diplomatic struggle that was to culminate in the Japanese attack on the United States on December 7, 1941.

After the German attack on Russia in June 1941, Hitler seems to have lost almost all interest in overseas colonies for their own sake. As we have seen, however, various German offices had meanwhile laid claim to an immense overseas colonial empire; with the approval of Hitler they carried on preparations for taking over and administering this vast domain.

The nucleus of a colonial administrative apparatus had existed for some time. Within the Nazi party organization, a colonial department had formed part of the party's Military Policy Office (*Wehrpolitisches Amt*). On May 5, 1934, Rudolf Hess, the deputy of the Führer and head of the Nazi party administration, withdrew this colonial department from the Military Policy Office and established it as an independent Colonial Policy Office (*Kolonialpolitisches Amt*) under the leadership of Franz Ritter von Epp, the Reichsstatthalter of Bavaria. To this Colonial Policy Office, Hess assigned sole responsibility for handling all political and economic questions related to colonial problems within the National Socialist party and for representing Nazi colonial policy to the press. A few months later, however, Hess ordered that the Colonial Policy Office clear all official actions with the Führer's special delegate for foreign affairs, Joachim von Ribbentrop, and with the party's Organization for Germans Abroad. Any disagreements that might arise as the result of this order were to be submitted to the Führer's deputy for arbitration. Early in 1936 Hitler limited the powers of the Colonial Policy Office still further by entrusting Ribbentrop with the authority to ensure that the activities of the Colonial Policy Office, and of all other organizations concerned with colonial affairs, were in line with the foreign policy of the Reich. Later that same year all German colonial societies were dissolved and reorganized in a Reich Colonial League (*Reichskolonialbund*) under the immediate control and supervision of Ribbentrop.[53]

In February 1939 Hitler appeared to give Epp's Colonial Policy Office renewed authority by assigning it primary responsibility for making preparations for the future administration of German colonial territory. The task of acquiring that territory, however, was to remain the responsibility of the Foreign Office, since February 1938 under the direction of Ribbentrop, while the Organization for Germans Abroad was entrusted with the welfare of the German population and for building up the organization of the Nazi party in the colonies, where it was to have the same authority and functions as in the Reich. Further, all German troops in the colonies would be under the direction of the Wehrmacht, all police and racial offices under the direction of the Himmler organizations. Thus, even before the German colonial administration had colonies to administer, there were built into it the same overlapping of authority, conflict of competences, and opportunities for bureaucratic infighting that characterized the Nazi government as a whole.[54]

In February 1940, Epp's Colonial Policy Office was given its own budget for the first time to enable it to hire personnel for the future administration of the German colonies. After the fall of France Hitler issued orders to all Reich offices to give Epp all possible assistance so that his administrative preparations could be completed in the shortest possible time. Later the same year Hitler ordered that preparations be made for converting the Colonial Policy Office into a full-fledged Reich Ministry for Colonies, but he never signed the decree drawn up for this purpose, presumably because he wished to avoid prejudicing his relationship with other powers with colonial ambitions and the possibility of a peace settlement with Britain. In March 1941 Hitler again ordered preparations to reconstitute the Colonial Policy Office as a Reich Ministry. It was expected that the Russian campaign, which was to be launched that spring, would be over in a few weeks and when that time came Hitler wanted everything to be ready for the take-over and administration of colonial territory. As this order can hardly have referred to the colonial territory to be conquered from Russia, for which other and far more elaborate administrative preparations had been made, it must be assumed that Hitler had overseas colonies in mind and that he expected to acquire them in the near future, either as the result of an armistice with Britain or through further conquests.[55]

Elaborate plans were, in fact, being made to undertake such conquests. On June 11, 1941, before the campaign against Russia had even begun, a draft plan was prepared at the Führer's headquarters by his military staff for military campaigns that were to be conducted after the Red Army had been defeated. The emphasis in armaments was to be shifted from the army to the navy and the Luftwaffe. In the realm of diplomacy, efforts were to be intensified to secure the co-operation of Vichy France, Spain, and Turkey, and to mobilize the Arab world for the war against Britain. If Turkey and Iran refused to participate actively in the war, strong pressure was to be exerted on both countries to permit the passage of German troops through their territories. In the military sphere, the Germans proposed to mount a major attack on the Suez Canal by German and Italian forces operating from Cirenaica in the west, which was to be co-ordinated with a similar attack from the east. To prepare for this operation enough German troops would be concentrated in Bulgaria to make Turkey politically compliant or, if the Turks refused to yield to German pressure, to crush Turkey by force. Within the framework of the German army in Bulgaria, and also within the German army that would meanwhile have been established in the Caucasus, motorized forces were to be built up which would enable the Germans to strike swiftly and with overwhelming power through Turkey, Syria, and Palestine, and thence to the Suez Canal in the southwest and through Turkey and Iran to Basra and the Persian Gulf in the southeast.

Simultaneously with their campaign in the Near East, the Germans proposed to undertake the conquest of Gibraltar and the closure of the western Mediterranean, preparations for which were to be resumed during the final stages of the war against Russia. Once Russia had been defeated, Hitler was confident that both Spain and Vichy France would participate in this enterprise. If the French co-operated as expected, they were to be given full responsibility for the defense of the Atlantic coast of North and West Africa and for the reconquest of colonial territory now held by de Gaulle and the Free French movement. Meanwhile the Germans themselves, with naval bases along the Atlantic coast of Europe and Africa, could proceed to the conquest of strategic islands in the Atlantic and make all other necessary preparations for the final siege of Britain.[56]

The success of all these grandiose projects, of course, depended on a quick German victory over Russia. With the failure of their plans in Russia, all other plans, including those for acquiring a large colonial empire, went awry. In a communication to Lammers of September 6, 1941, Bormann noted that a large number of offices had begun to make detailed preparations for the administration of a German colonial empire, but in view of the military situation in the east he wondered whether such preparations still corresponded with the views of the Führer. Lammers took the hint and shortly afterward he informed Bormann that Epp had promised to reduce the total personnel of his colonial office by 32 per cent and all personnel liable to military service by 53 per cent. Still Bormann was not satisfied. In January 1942 he demanded a further and more drastic reduction in the personnel of the colonial office on the ground that "if we lose the war, even the most beautiful colonial administration will not be of any use." A year later, as the military situation in the east continued to deteriorate, Bormann transmitted a Hitler order to put an end to all activities not contributing directly to the war effort. "In the name of the Führer I herewith inform you that all activity on the part of the Colonial Policy Office as well as the Reich Colonial League is to cease completely by February 15, 1943." With that even the home front of the Nazi overseas colonial empire collapsed.[57]

Asia and the Western Hemisphere

The Near East

In contrast to the detailed and elaborate plans prepared by Nazi state and party offices for German territorial acquisitions in Africa, the Nazis made relatively few plans about Asia; at least very few have so far come to light. In the Near East, as in Africa, the Germans attempted to play a delicate balancing game. Turkey was to be made an ally of Germany, if the Turks fell in line with Nazi policies. But elsewhere in the Near East the situation was more complicated. To win over the Arab world to the Nazi cause, the Germans did their best to exploit Arab hatred for the Jews and resentment of British imperialism. And, in the manner of Britain during the First World War, they also allowed the Arabs to believe that, in the event of a German victory, Germany would take steps to ensure the independence and territorial integrity of the Arab states. While holding out these hopes to the Arabs, however, the Germans promised supremacy over the Arab world to the Italians, they promised the Turks an extension of territory at the expense of the Arab states, and they reserved substantial rights in the Arab Near East for themselves.[58]

The German government's decision to give the Italians supremacy in the Arab world was communicated to German diplomatic officials by a Foreign Office circular of August 20, 1940. "This consequently rules out any German claim to political leadership or the sharing of leadership with Italy in the Arab territories, which consist of the Arabian peninsula, Egypt, Palestine, Transjordan, Syria-Lebanon, and Iraq." This political disinterest, however, did not mean that Germany renounced all other interests in these areas. "First and foremost, Germany will assert, and settle in concert with Italy, her claims with respect to participation in the exploitation of the oil resources, the securing of her air routes, and the continuation of her archaeological activities." These policy guidelines, the Foreign Office circular stressed, were to be treated as strictly confidential, and in particular were to be kept secret from the leaders of the Arab world. While the war continued, the Germans should tell the Arabs only that they were fighting against England and speak of the "liberation of the Arab world" without detailed reference to specific future goals.[59]

With the failure of German efforts to seal off the western entrance of the Mediterranean, especially after the decision was made to attack Russia, Italy was rapidly displaced by Turkey as a factor in German calculations in the Near East. On June 18, 1941, just before the German invasion of Russia, Germany and Turkey signed a treaty in which they pledged to respect the integrity and inviolability of their territories and promised to consult one another on all questions affecting their common interests.[60] But Hitler and his military and diplomatic advisers were not satisfied with a defensive and consultative pact of this nature. As the war progressed they became increasingly anxious to secure active Turkish participation, or, failing that, permission to move German troops across Turkish territory to attack the Suez Canal and bring direct German pressure to bear on the power struggles in the Near East.

In August 1941 an official of the German Foreign Office put forward proposals designed to tempt Turkey into a closer partnership with Germany.

> In this context Turkey must be offered great prospects and must be persuaded that we do not want to assign her a second-class position in the New Europe, but rather important and honorable duties, possibly as the 'factor of stabilization' in the Near East and eastern Mediterranean, in

place of England, who will be forced out; in this way a certain balance with Italy would be established.

In order to prove to Turkey that Germany was sincere and wished to work with Turkey on a long-range basis, Germany should aid the Turks to gain territories they desired for reasons of security. These included Edirne (Adrianople) and a rectification of Turkish frontiers at the expense of Greece; the creation of buffer states in the Caucasus under Turkish influence; a rectification of the Turkish-Syrian frontier (the Bagdad Railway and Aleppo) and the Turkish-Iraq frontier (Mosul); and a solution to the question of the Aegean islands in order to give Turkey security against Italy after the removal of the Russian threat.

German diplomats recommended further that Turkey be assured about Germany's attitude toward the Arab world. As this region was a matter of vital concern to Turkey, Germany should make clear that it would make no move in the Arab lands without consulting Turkey and that no German declaration on behalf of the Arabs was intended to indicate a definite German stand on territorial questions. Ribbentrop was prepared to be even more specific; in April 1942 he informed the Turks that Germany would completely understand any desire on the part of Turkey to rectify its frontiers along the borders of the Arab world.[61]

Thus the Nazis, for all their lip service to the Arab cause, were using Arab territory in Asia Minor to purchase Italian or Turkish friendship just as they were using Arab territory in North Africa to purchase the friendship of Italy, Spain, and France. Germany's final territorial settlements in the Near East, of course, would have depended on future developments in that region; but whether the Germans would have conceded supremacy in the Arab world to Italy or Turkey, or even to the Arabs themselves, it may be taken for granted that German interests in the Near East, especially in Arabian oil, would have been safeguarded.

The Middle East and East Asia: The Problem of Japan

If Germany had won the Second World War, neither Italy nor Turkey, nor any state in the Near or Middle East could have withstood German pressure, and the extension of German influence in Asia would have been halted only at the boundaries of the Japanese sphere of interest. Where these boundaries would be drawn was never determined, but if negotiations on this question had ever taken place it is possible that they would have been based on the German-Japanese military agreement of December 1941, which provided for the division of the world into spheres of military operation along the seventieth degree of longitude, an agreement which left Germany and Italy responsible for the territory west of that line, Japan for the territory to the east. This would have meant that Siberia, China, India, and the greater part of Pakistan would have fallen to the Japanese, while the Arab countries, with Afghanistan, would have gone to the Axis. There is the further possibility that this agreement would have been modified to leave Afghanistan to the Japanese in exchange for an extension of the German sphere of influence in Russia, as the economic office of the OKW had recommended when the December agreement was under negotiation.[62]

Hitler himself speculated on this problem in January of 1942. "Where, in fact, is the frontier between East and West to be laid down?" he asked after the Japanese captured Singapore. To this question he could provide no consistent or satisfactory answer. As the Japanese overran one European territory after another in East Asia, he believed they would conquer Australia too and that the white race would disappear altogether from these regions. For Hitler this represented a turning point in history. "It means the loss of a whole continent, and one might regret it, for it's the white race which is the loser." It was nevertheless an immense relief to him that the Japanese had entered the war, for Japan was the only first-class military power on Germany's side and one on which he was certain he could rely. After the war, too, Hitler believed it would be in Germany's interest if Japan retained the preponderant position it was gaining in the Pacific, for Japan was Germany's chief safeguard for the future against the United States. He could feel no affinity with the Japanese, Hitler said, for their way of life and culture were entirely too foreign, but he felt real hatred and repugnance for the Americans.[63]

Some weeks later Hitler again spoke of the desirability for Germany of preserving its alliance with Japan. When the time came for making peace, he did not think the Japanese would create any serious difficulties if they were given all of Asia. He doubted whether they were capable of digesting India and he now wondered whether they would in fact be interested in taking over Australia and New Zealand. As a result of their alliance with Germany, they would feel a great sense of security and would have no further reason to fear anyone. But for Germany, too, this alliance would be an essential guarantee of tranquillity. "There's one thing Japan and Germany have in common," Hitler said. "That both of us need fifty to a hundred years for purposes of digestion: we for Russia, they for the Far East." [64]

Although Hitler was not certain whether Japan would seize Australia and New Zealand, it is obvious that he was prepared to concede these territories, like the rest of East Asia, to the Japanese sphere of interest. If the Japanese had indeed conquered Australia and New Zealand—and they would almost certainly have attempted to do so, if only for reasons of security—it may be assumed that Hitler would have offered the Anglo-Saxon inhabitants of these countries sanctuary in his Germanic Reich and would have attempted to recruit them as colonists in the newly won territories of the east. When Germanic settlement had reached the boundaries of the Japanese Empire in East Asia, the descendants of these Australians and New Zealanders would have the opportunity to take their revenge on Japan. But such possibilities lay many decades, perhaps centuries, in the future.

The Western Hemisphere

As in the case of Asia, Hitler devoted relatively little attention to plans for the future of the Western Hemisphere. There is ample evidence that before and during the Second World War Nazi agents in the Americas did their best to promote the Nazi cause and to stir up trouble for their adversaries, and that they engaged in espionage and sabotage. But no records of any kind have come to light of Nazi plans for an actual invasion of North or South America.[65] Hitler, after all, was not even able to strike effectively at Britain. What military plans he did make involving the Western Hemisphere were restricted to the campaign against Allied shipping and to the acquisition of bases from which he might attack the United States with long-range bombers or otherwise wage more effective warfare against America. Obsessed as he was with the lessons of the First World War, he always took into account the possibility of American intervention, and he wanted to be in the most favorable position possible to meet the American challenge.

As the Americans stepped up their aid to Britain during the summer of 1940, Hitler and the leaders of his armed forces became increasingly conscious of the threat posed by the United States. In September Admiral Erich Raeder impressed on Hitler the need to hasten preparations for the capture of Gibraltar and Suez so as to close the Mediterranean to the Allies "before the U.S.A. steps in." Raeder believed it might also be necessary to forestall a British or American seizure of the Spanish and Portuguese islands in the Atlantic—a distinct possibility if Spain or Portugal entered the war on the side of the Axis—because, from these bases, the Allies might establish control over French West Africa and the strategic harbor of Dakar. In response to these arguments Hitler ordered that plans be drawn up for the occupation of Spain's Canary islands by the Luftwaffe, an operation he considered both expedient and feasible.[66]

It was clearly in the context of these efforts to anticipate the American threat that on October 29 Major von Falkenstein, the head of a section of the OKW's department for national defense (*Landesverteidigung*), wrote to General von Waldau of the operations staff of the Luftwaffe.

"The Führer is occupied with the question of the Atlantic Islands with a view to the prosecution of war [*Kriegsführung*] against America at a later date. Deliberations on this subject have been started here. Essential conditions at present are: (a) no other operational commitment, (b) neutrality of Portugal, (c) support of France and Spain. A brief assessment on the part of the Luftwaffe is necessary about the possibility of seizing air bases, as well as holding and supplying them.[67]

At a conference with his naval leaders on November 14, Hitler again raised the question of occupying the Canaries; this time he placed special emphasis on the desirability of seizing the Portuguese Azores. "The Führer believes that the Azores would afford him the only facility for attacking America, if she should enter the war, with a modern plane of the Messerschmidt type, which has a range of 12,600 kilometers. Thereby America would be forced to build up her own antiaircraft defense, which is still completely lacking, instead of assisting Britain." By this time, however, the German navy and presumably the Luftwaffe as well had examined the possibilities of a German seizure of the Atlantic islands and had come to very negative conclusions. The occupation of the Azores would be a very risky operation, Raeder informed the Führer, although with luck it could succeed, but it was very doubtful whether the islands could be successfully supplied or defended.[68]

Undeterred by the pessimistic views of his naval leadership, Hitler reverted to the question of the Atlantic islands in a conference with Raeder in the spring of the following year. *"The Führer is still in favor of occupying the Azores,"* Raeder recorded in his minutes of this conference, *"in order to be able to operate long-range bombers from there against the U.S.A. The occasion for this may arise by autumn."* [69] It will be recalled that the attack on the Soviet Union was scheduled for June 1941 and that Hitler confidently expected Russia would be crushed in the course of the summer. By autumn, then, he could turn the bulk of his forces against Britain, if the British still refused to come to terms, and bomb the United States if the Americans continued to supply Britain with the wherewithal to continue the war or intervened directly. Meanwhile, however, Hitler's primary concern was to prevent American intervention. "He would . . . like to avoid having the U.S.A. declare war while the eastern campaign was still in progress. . . . After the eastern campaign he reserves the right to take severe measures against the U.S.A. as well." But Hitler did not really think such measures would be necessary; at a conference on July 25, 1941, he expressed confidence that the British would make peace after Russia was eliminated and they no longer saw any chance of winning.[70] With British bases no longer available, the United States would be deprived of every means to intervene effectively in the war in Europe and would, therefore, presumably not do so.

Although Hitler definitely considered the possibility of having to wage war against the United States at some future date, all evidence indicates that he was anxious to avoid such a conflict, at least for the time being. He was fully aware that he lacked the means even to contemplate an invasion of the Western Hemisphere and that it would be many years before the equipment necessary for such an enterprise could be assembled. Meanwhile he would need a long interval of peace to consolidate his gains in Europe.

Even if Germany were unable to invade the Western Hemisphere, however, the political and economic threat Germany would have represented if Hitler had brought all of Europe, and possibly much of Asia and Africa as well, under his dominion would have been very great indeed. Once solidly in control of Europe, the Nazis would undoubtedly have used the formidable political and economic power at their disposal to build up an anti-United States coalition among the countries of Latin America. By restricting or cutting off United States trade with the territories under German and Japanese influence, they could have dealt a serious blow to the American economy. While undermining the political and economic position of the United States, the Germans could have built up their own naval and air power, which by the late 1940s would have included intercontinental missiles, and constructed an armada which might have made an actual invasion of the Western Hemisphere feasible. If such an invasion had been co-ordinated with a Japanese invasion from the west, the military situation of the United States would have been precarious in the extreme.

Whether the operations of Nazi agents and organizations in the Americas represented a similar threat to the security of the Western Hemisphere, as many Americans feared, is more doubtful. The espionage and sabotage carried out by Nazi agents gave justifiable cause for alarm, as did the pro-Nazi demonstrations of German-American clubs and the activities of Nazi offices concerned with Germans abroad. Hitler and the more orthodox Nazis, however, were not interested in organizing the Germans in America. On the contrary, their primary concern about Germans in the Americas, as about Germans in all other parts of the world, was to regain these Germanic elements for Germany and at the same time to deprive potential enemies of Germany of their Germanic leadership class.

Hitler's views on this subject were a dominant theme in the guidelines and memoranda prepared by Nazi racial offices. In a top secret report submitted to Himmler in August 1940, Gottlob Berger, the head of recruiting for the Waffen-SS, calculated the number of ethnic Germans in every part of the world (he estimated that there were approximately 5.5 million in the United States and Canada), and urgently recommended that "a start should be made to recover these people, who would be exceptionally suitable as settlers later on." For this purpose he asked that Hitler personally authorize him to establish recruiting offices in foreign countries. Himmler fully concurred with Berger's view. In a memorandum on the need to regain the Germans now living in the United States and Africa, he observed with regret how many ethnic Germans had migrated overseas and how most of them were totally separated from Germany politically and ideologically, especially from the Greater German Reich of Adolf Hitler. "It is our task," Himmler said, "to bring back every person of German blood of any value at all to the German Reich to settle the acres that have been conquered." [71]

Once the Western Hemisphere had been deprived of its Germanic leadership class and the frontiers of the Reich had been extended far into Russia through German colonization and settlements, the time might have come to settle accounts with the United States.

> For me, [Hitler said,] the object is to exploit the advantage of continental hegemony. It is ridiculous to think of a world policy as long as one does not control the Continent. . . . When we are masters of Europe, we have a dominant position in the world. A hundred and thirty million people in the Reich, ninety in the Ukraine. Add to these the other states of the New Europe, and we'll be four hundred million, compared with the hundred and thirty million Americans.

It is interesting and highly significant that as his future ally against the United States, Hitler did not look to Japan or to some Latin American country, but to Britain, which he was certain would be embittered by the fact that the Americans would have taken advantage of Britain's defeat in Europe to annex Canada and probably a good deal of other British territory as well. He himself would not live to see it, Hitler told his associates several months before the Japanese attack on Pearl Harbor, but he was already glad for the German people that someday the Germans and the English together would move against America.[72]

A Summing Up
and Concluding Reflections

In making a final assessment of Hitler's war aims, it is important to bear in mind that the Nazi dictator was never an entirely free agent, that his aims were constantly affected by changes in Germany's political and military situation, and that his ambition expanded as new opportunities opened before him. Thus, although he professed not to be interested in the acquisition of overseas colonies, he did not hesitate to lay claim to an immense colonial empire in central Africa when it seemed likely that he would soon be able to acquire one. As Hitler never controlled this part of Africa, or the majority of other overseas territories coveted by German colonial enthusiasts, the ultimate extent of his colonial ambitions must remain a matter of speculation.

It was different with Europe, however, where Hitler's actual policies, viewed in conjunction with his policy statements, guidelines, and directives, give a very clear indication of his intentions. These policies demonstrate beyond all doubt that through all the vicissitudes of his career Hitler adhered with fanatic consistency to the two central objectives of his ideological program: the purification of the Germanic race through the removal of all non-Aryan racial elements; and the conquest of *Lebensraum* in Eastern Europe to ensure the security of the Germanic race for all time.

The entire business of racial purification was of course an anthropological absurdity, and the Nazi effort to put this program into effect was at all times a bizarre and thoroughly subjective procedure which could be dismissed as a farce had it not provided the rationale for the cold-blooded murder of millions of human beings. Yet, because of the inevitable vagueness of Nazi definitions of race and the broad interpretations

Nazi leaders frequently allowed themselves in selecting persons suitable for Germanization, it is impossible to estimate with any precision how large a proportion of the subject populations would eventually have been selected for Germanization and how many would have been expelled or exterminated. Apart from those groups which were to be removed entirely (Jews, gypsies, politically dangerous, and "asocial" persons), it would appear that the survival of members of the subject populations would have depended very largely on local conditions and on the judgment of local officials in charge of racial operations.

Hitler's policies give a far more precise indication of his territorial objectives in Europe, although here too his future plans for several important areas remained vague. Summarized in terms of regions, Hitler's Germanic empire would have included:

In the north: Denmark, Norway, and almost certainly Sweden, with Finland as an ally to guard Germany's flank in the northeast.

In the west: the Low Countries, Alsace, Lorraine, and Luxembourg, together with a broad strip of territory from the mouth of the Somme to Lake Geneva, fortifications along the French Channel coast, and the British Channel islands.

In the south: Austria, Switzerland (almost certainly), and northwestern Yugoslovia; and, after the Italian surrender, all Italian territory north of the Po, as well as a broad strip of territory along the Adriatic littoral.

In the east: Memelland, Danzig, all of Poland, the Sudetenland, and the Czech provinces of Bohemia and Moravia; the Baltic states, White Russia, and the Ukraine, with territorial claims staked out to the Urals and beyond.

In the regions of Central and Southeastern Europe there would have been a bloc of allied satellite states from Slovakia to Greece, where Germany would have made every provision to safeguard its strategic and economic interests. The future of Serbia remained indefinite. It might have been turned over to the Croatians, but more probably it would have been left under some form of German administration to ensure German dominion in the Danube area. Germany's flank in Southeastern Europe was to be guarded by another ally, Turkey.

Until the Italian surrender in September 1943, the task of safeguarding Axis interests in the south had been assigned to Italy, which was conceded supremacy over the Mediterranean region, including the greater part of North Africa, the Adriatic littoral, and the Arab Near East. After the Italian surrender, a large part of Northern Italy was scheduled for annexation to the Reich, while the Italy left under Mussolini's Fascist Republican government was relegated to the role of a satellite-ally. What was to become of rump Italy in the future was uncertain.

Also uncertain was the future fate of rump France, as well as those countries which did not fall under direct German dominion in the course of the Second World War: Spain, Portugal, Britain, and Ireland.

It may be assumed, however, that if Hitler had won the war all these countries would have been brought into the German power orbit, whether as satellites, allies, or integral parts of the Germanic empire.

Germany, however, did not win the war, and by 1945 Hitler's dream of empire, and with it Germany and a great part of Europe, lay in ruins. After the First World War the great powers of Europe, although weakened in terms of manpower and resources, had remained world powers. Aided by the withdrawal of the United States and the Soviet Union into isolationism, they had continued to make many of the major policy decisions affecting the world at large. It was Hitler's war which brought to an end the age of European global primacy, which placed a great part of Central and Eastern Europe under Soviet dominion, and which left the states of Western Europe perilously lodged between the millstones of Russian/Asiatic power in the east and American power in the west.

Apart from altering the power structure of the world, the Nazi catastrophe shattered whatever illusions men may have held about the moral progress of humankind, starkly revealing how thin was the veneer of humanitarian civilization in the modern world, even in countries which took great pride in their cultural achievements. More sinister still, the Nazis demonstrated how easy it is for man to find rational, even idealistic and moral, motives to carry out inhuman actions. In the words of Goethe's devil, "He calls it reason, yet uses it solely to behave more bestially than any beast."

The Nazis demonstrated further that, despite two centuries of democratic revolution and presumed political enlightenment in Europe, authoritarianism was by no means discredited as a form of government, for there were people in every part of Europe who had actually welcomed dictatorial rule as a means of solving the increasingly complex problems of industrial society. It would appear, moreover, that industrialization in itself had made it easier to impose and maintain an authoritarian regime, at least over the short run. The Nazis, at all events, seem to have had least difficulty controlling societies with a relatively high degree of industrial and technological development, whose predominantly urban populations were dependent for their very existence on the proper functioning of their industrial and technological apparatus. By contrast, the Nazis had somewhat greater difficulty controlling predominantly rural societies, whose populations were more scattered and had more direct access to the basic necessities of life.

Quite the most important reason for the effectiveness of Nazi rule, however, was the fact that the majority of people living under Nazi occupation, far from opposing the Nazi regime or joining the resistance, co-operated with the Nazi authorities, particularly during the early years of the occupation when a German victory seemed inevitable. This co-operation was in no way equivalent to the kind of notorious collaboration associated with the names of Quisling and Laval, but was simply a matter of carrying on with routine functions, whether as bureaucrats or policemen, industrial workers or peasants. By co-operating in this manner, the subject populations themselves kept the routine business of government and the economy going and thereby enabled the Nazis to rule, and to exploit, the occupied countries with a minimum investment of German personnel.

The response of the European peoples to Nazi dominion reflects an instinct of people everywhere to cling to life and to seek physical and economic security for themselves and their families. In any case, it is difficult to see what else the subject populations could have done. Militant or passive resistance, general strikes, attacks on German personnel, and any effort to disrupt the administration and economy of an occupied country provoked cruel and large-scale reprisals. Resistance activities were unquestionably inconvenient to the Germans and cut down the contribution of an occupied country to the German war effort, but it was the subject population which had to face the ultimate implications of resistance. Failure to produce for the Germans, after all, meant that the subject peoples would be unable to produce for themselves. In view of the fact that during the first years of the war it seemed probable that German rule would last indefinitely, the peoples under German occupation had considerable reason to believe that resistance would not only be futile but suicidal.

A case can be made, moreover, that in many areas a policy of co-operation with the Nazis "worked," meaning that it enabled a majority of a subject population to lead comparatively normal lives throughout the occupation and to survive. Until the last stages of the war the Danes, for example, escaped the worst rigors of Nazi oppression and managed to save almost their entire Jewish population; and it may be argued that only through their co-operation with the Germans did the non-Germanic Czechs avoid the pogroms carried out in Poland and Russia.

Similar arguments can be advanced on behalf of a number of collaborationist leaders, mixed as their motives may have been. Tiso undoubtedly saved the non-Germanic Slovaks from a Nazi occupation; and until March 1944 the government of Horthy protected not only the Magyar population but the Hungarian Jews as well from Nazi racial persecution. It is evident with hindsight that the degree of protection afforded a subject people by a policy of collaboration was dependent on the Nazis' willingness to permit collaboration, and that non-Germanic peoples were at best buying time through such a policy. But this fact was never clear to the collaborators; even if it had been, there was still much to be said for efforts to buy time. Certainly it would have been advantageous to the thousands of Hungarian Jews slaughtered after the overthrow of Horthy's regime had he been able to hold out for just a few more months.

In some countries, such as Yugoslovia, where the Nazis and their allies revealed through their policies that passive acceptance of their rule might in itself lead to extermination, a mass resistance took shape relatively early. Unfortunately, however, the history of the Nazi era does not bear out the popular belief that resistance was generally widespread. Not until the German attack on the Soviet Union did local Communist parties, which later claimed (and often deserved) major credit for leading anti-Nazi movements, begin to play a major role in the resistance. And not until the Nazis launched large-scale racial extermination and labor recruitment programs did the resistance itself become a mass and therewith relatively effective movement. Even then, however, the effectiveness of such resistance movements was not so much due to their inherent strength as to the fact that the bulk of Germany's military might was engaged in fighting the Allied armies. It was the power of those Allied armies, drawing on the resources and industrial strength of countries outside the Nazi orbit, which in fact put an end to the Nazi tyranny.

In only one country dominated by the Nazis does it seem likely that a resistance movement in itself might have played a decisive role in the overthrow of the Hitler regime. That country was Germany, where the resistance included high-ranking members of the government and the armed forces who would appear to have had the power and the opportunity to carry out a coup d'état. As we now know, a number of German generals and politicians were engaged for years in plots against the Nazi regime. Why all such plots failed and why so few attempts were actually made to assassinate Hitler or carry out a coup will long remain a subject of controversy. The most convincing argument is that the German conspirators lacked skilled and ruthless leadership, they lacked a clear sense of method and purpose, and above all, perhaps, they lacked luck.

Although members of the resistance in German-occupied territories had far less opportunity for effective action than their German counterparts, it is nevertheless remarkable that here too so little was done to strike at the obvious target of the Nazi leadership, to mount a campaign of terror against all German occupation personnel, especially against the heads of the occupation governments. During the entire Nazi era only two prominent Nazi leaders were assassinated: Reinhard Heydrich, the acting Reich protector of Bohemia and Moravia, whose custom of driving to his office each day along a regular route in an open car with only a chauffeur as bodyguard made him a ridiculously easy target; and Wilhelm Kube, the Generalkommissar of White Ruthenia, whose assassination by his servant-mistress was probably not motivated by political considerations at all.

This failure of the resistance in the occupied countries to undertake political assassinations of Nazi leaders is difficult to explain. The Nazis of course took measures to protect their personnel. One of the first moves of Nazi occupation governments was to confiscate all weapons in the hands of the local population and to impose rigorous penalties on persons caught with unauthorized weapons in their possession; German occupation forces and military police were supplemented by members of

Nazi police organizations; and Nazi officials generally took security precautions of their own. Yet none of these explanations is satisfactory. In all occupied territories resistance fighters were able to acquire weapons, often in large quantities; Nazi police were few in number and their records reveal an astonishing degree of incompetence; and German occupation officials, although they were not all so foolhardy as Heydrich, for the most part appeared regularly in public places and met with members of the local population. More convincing is the explanation that Nazi terror—the seizure of hostages and threats and acts of reprisal—was more effective than is generally acknowledged. But most effective of all, it would appear, were such prosaic measures as threats to curtail food rations or to cut off supplies of fuel or power which struck at the livelihood and ultimately at the very survival of a subject population.

Agonizing as are the moral and practical questions involved in the problems of resistance and collaboration, the most disturbing consideration of all, in the light of the Nazi experience, is the innate appeal of Nazism itself, not necessarily Nazism labeled as such, but the cult of racial nationalism which was the basic ingredient of the Nazi doctrine. On every continent we still find racial nationalist movements marshaled under the familiar slogans of national freedom and self-determination, sovereignty and independence—the very slogans which Nazism exploited so successfully. And in many cases these movements have been accompanied by programs of genocide, the compulsory relocation of entire racial or national communities, and acts of brutality that stun the imagination. Apart from the irrational passions and prejudices involved in all national-racial policies, or the even more incalculable factors of stupidity, panic, or sheer momentum, the common denominator of all of them appears to be a search for security, whether the government of a particular society be fascist, communist, or democratic. It remains one of the great misfortunes of mankind that this search is still so frequently conducted on the basis of the same simplistic logic that characterized the policies of Hitler, and that so many national-racial groups continue to seek the temporal salvation of their species of humanity at the risk of its dehumanization.

The basic fallacy in all such programs, as it was in Hitler's, is the belief that the racial-national community is somehow ordained by natural law to be the fundamental unit of human society, and the concomitant belief that once it achieves an adequate economic base and all domestic and external threats on the part of alien races and nations have been eliminated, the security of that community will be assured. Yet it is only necessary to look at the record of any national state, no matter how prosperous, powerful, or racially homogeneous, to realize how erroneous these assumptions are. For national states, like all human organizations, inevitably breed personal and political rivalries, class and social tensions, and other forces that are a constant threat to social stability and security. Perhaps an absolutely regimented totalitarian regime may

some day resolve such problems through drugs or programs of brain sur-
gery, but again it would be a matter of offering a nation security at the
expense of its humanity.

In the case of the Nazis, it is one of the great ironies of history (and
one of the few examples of the justice of fate in the historical process)
that Hitler's racial policies, which were supposed to provide the foundation of German national security, doomed the Nazi racial state from the
start. For non-Aryan scientists driven from Hitler's Europe played a
major role in the development of weapons which made an ultimate German victory impossible.

Even if Hitler had emerged triumphant from the Second World War,
however, the entire history of the Nazi movement suggests that his fundamental war aim—security for the German people—would have
eluded him. There was never any assurance that the Aryan race, or that
mélange of nationalities Hitler defined as Aryan, would have held together over the long or even the short run to form a stable society. Hitler himself constantly spoke of the possibility of his assassination and realized that his own person was at no time secure. This same lack of
security would even more have been the lot of his successors and their
lieutenants.

As for the masses of the German people, what kind of security did
Hitler in fact give them? The security to serve in his organizations from
the cradle to the grave; the security to be under the permanent surveil-
lance of state and party authorities, to be spied on by neighbors and
colleagues; the security of the gibbet or the concentration camp if they
deviated, or were suspected of deviating, from official orthodoxy; the security to be maimed or killed in the wars Hitler fought in the name of
national security, and which he believed would have to be waged in the
future to preserve the security already achieved.

A totalitarian form of security can appeal to intelligent and idealistic people, those who yearn for Utopia and believe it can be attained
by the logical and ruthless application of scientific or ideological principles to the problems of human society. But above all such security appeals to the perennial conformists who find security in regulations and
orders, in having no need to make decisions or judgments of their own.
Yet by any standard this remains a precarious and sterile security, a reg-
imentation of the minds and bodies of men which, in the Nazi experience at least, throttled the very cultural creativity which Hitler had declared to be the primary objective of his New Order. In the end, one of
the saddest features of the Nazi experience is that out of all the suffering, the bloodshed, and the destruction which Nazism inflicted on the
world, the Nazi movement contributed nothing whatever to human culture and civilization. Nothing except a terrible lesson about how fragile
and vulnerable human civilization is.

Appendices

A Note on the Spelling

The political and national upheavals that have taken place in Europe in the twentieth century have made the spelling of proper and geographical names a difficult as well as sensitive problem.

In the spelling of proper names, I have tried to use the spelling commonly used by the bearers of those names. When transliteration was required, I have adopted the system in most general use among contemporary American scholars.

In dealing with geographical names, I have used the spelling found in American atlases published during the period when the events described in this book were taking place. Thus I have used the name in common use in 1939 for Danzig, not the Polish Gdańsk; the Italian names for cities in the South Tyrol, for instance, Bolzano instead of Bozen; the Slovakian name for Bratislava instead of the German Pressburg or the Hungarian Pozsony. In some cases, however, I have used the German spelling of place names, with the local spelling in parentheses. The name Auschwitz, for example, loses much of its emotional impact when rendered by the Polish Oświeçem.

Whenever in doubt about spelling, I have tried to be clear rather than consistent.

Abbreviations

ABlGKKauen   *Amtsblatt des Generalkommissars in Kauen.* The official decrees of the German occupation government in Lithuania. Published in Kauen (Kaunas or Kovno).

ABlGKMinsk   *Amtsblatt des Generalkommissars in Minsk.* The official decrees of the German occupation government in White Ruthenia (White Russia). First published as *Amtsblatt des Generalkommissars für Weissruthenien.*

ABlGKReval   *Amtsblatt des Generalkommissars in Reval.* The official decrees of the German occupation government in Estonia. Published in Reval (Tallinn).

ABlGKRiga   *Amtsblatt des Generalkommissars in Riga.* The official decrees issued by the German occupation government in Latvia.

ADAP   *Akten zur deutschen auswärtigen Politik, 1918–1945* (Baden Baden and Göttingen). German text of *Documents on German Foreign Policy,* a series still in the process of publication.

AO   Auslandsorganisation. Organization for Germans Abroad. Officially a Gau of the Nazi party.

DAF   Deutsche Arbeitsfront. German Labor Front. The organization of all German workers including entrepreneurs and managers.

DDP   *Dokumente der deutschen Politik* (Berlin, 1937–44). A Nazi government document publication.

Devlag   Dietsch-Vlaamsche Arbeidsgemeenschap. The Society for German-Flemish Co-operation.

DGFP   *Documents on German Foreign Policy, 1918–1945* (Washington, 1949–). A publication of captured German documents.

DOT   *Documenta Occupationis Teutonicae.* 7 vols. (Poznań, 1945–59). A Polish government publication of captured German documents.

DUT   Deutsche Umsiedlungs-Treuhandgesellschaft. German Resettlement Trusteeship Corporation.

DVL   Deutsche Volksliste. German National List.

EC   Prefix of number of Nuremberg document. See NG, below.

EWZ   Einwandererzentralstelle. Central Immigration Office. For processing incoming settlers.

Gestapo. Geheime Staatspolizei. Secret State Police.

HJ   Hitler Jugend. Hitler Youth. For boys.

HSSPF   Höherer SS-und Polizeiführer. Senior SS and police officer.

ABBREVIATIONS

HTO Haupttreuhandstelle Ost. Main Trustee Office East. The public corporation created by Göring as plenipotentiary of the Four-Year Plan for the seizure and administration of Polish and Jewish property.

IMT International Military Tribunal. *Trial of the Major War Criminals before the International Military Tribunal. Proceedings and Documents.* 42 vols. (Nuremberg, 1947–49). The published records of the main Nuremberg trials.

NCA *Nazi Conspiracy and Aggression.* 8 vols. and 2 suppl. (Washington, 1946–48). A selection in English translation of documents presented in evidence at Nuremberg.

NG, NI, NID, NIK, NO, NOKW Prefixes of numbers of documents collected for the Nuremberg trials, most of them unpublished.

NS National Socialist, or Nazi.

NSB Nationaal-Socialistische Beweging der Nederlanden. The National Socialist Movement of the Netherlands.

NSDAP Nationalsozialistische Deutsche Arbeiterpartei. National Socialist German Workers party, i.e., the Nazi party.

NVV Nederlands Verbond van Vakvereenigingen. Netherlands Federation of Trade Unions.

OKH Oberkommando des Heeres. Army High Command.

OKW Oberkommando der Wehrmacht. High Command of the Armed Forces.

OSS Office of Strategic Services, Research and Analysis Branch. Under the auspices of this office, a large number of valuable studies of the German government, the Nazi party, and the countries under German occupation were prepared.

OT Organisation Todt. The armaments and construction organization under Dr. Fritz Todt.

PS Prefix of number of Nuremberg document. See NG, above.

RAD Reichsarbeitsdienst. Reich Labor Service.

RF Prefix of number of Nuremberg document. See NG, above.

RFSS Reichsführer SS. The title of Heinrich Himmler as head of the SS.

RGBl Reichsgesetzblatt. The official publication of German laws and treaties.

RHDGM Revue d'histoire de la deuxième guerre mondiale. A journal containing many useful articles and bibliographies of the Nazi era.

RK Reichskanzlei, or Reich Chancellery.

RKFDV Reichskommission für die Festigung des deutschen Volkstums. Reich Commission for the Consolidation of the German People. Himmler's main office for racial questions. The initials may also refer to the position of Himmler himself as head of that office: Reichskommissar für die Festigung des deutschen Volkstums. Reich commissar for the consolidation of the German people.

RSHA Reichssicherheitshauptamt. The Central Office for Reich Security. Another major office under Himmler, this one in charge of all state and party police organizations.

RuSHA Rasse-und Siedlungshauptamt. Central Office for Race and Resettlement.

RVL Reich, Volksordnung, Lebensraum. Official Nazi journal on occupation policies. Often astonishingly frank and revealing.

SA Sturm Abteilung. The Nazi storm troops, or more literally attack or assault division. Brown shirts.

SD Sicherheitsdienst. Security Service. The intelligence service of the SS.

SGV Sammlung der Gesetze und Verordnungen des Protektorates Böhmen und Mähren. The decrees of the Czech government under German occupation. See Bibliography, 6. Czechoslovakia and the Sudetenland.

Sipo. Sicherheitspolizei. Security Police.

SS Schutz Staffel. Literally "guard echelon," the elite guard of the Führer under the command of Himmler. Black shirts.

T Code letter prefix for microfilm serial and frame numbers of captured German documents filmed at Alexandria, Virginia. The films are now on deposit in the

National Archives, Washington. See Bibliography, 1. Guides and General Works, American Historical Association.

TWC   *Trials of the War Criminals before the Nuernberg Military Tribunals under Control Council Law N–10.* 15 vols. (Nuremberg, 1946–49). Includes trial records and documents in evidence of other Nuremberg trials.

UWZ   Umwandererzentralstelle. Central Office for Evacuation. Primarily for the deportation of Poles and Jews.

VBlB   *Verordnungsblatt des Militärbefehlshabers in Belgien und Nordfrankreich für die besetzten Gebiete Belgiens und Nordfrankreichs.* The official decrees of the German military government for Belgium and Northern France.

VBlDg   *Verordnungsblatt des Reichsstatthalters in Danzig-Westpreussen.* The official decrees of the German administration in the incorporated territories of Danzig and West Prussia (Poland).

VBlE   *Verordnungsblatt des Chefs der Zivilverwaltung im Elsass.* The official decrees of the German occupation government in Alsace.

VBlGG   *Verordnungsblatt für das Generalgouvernement.* The official decrees of the German occupation government in the so-called Government General of occupied Poland.

VBlF   *Verordnungsblatt des Militärbefehlshabers in Frankreich.* The official decrees of the German military government in France.

VBlKK   *Verordnungs-und Amtsblatt des Chefs der Zivilverwaltung in den besetzten Gebieten Kärntens und Krains.* The official decrees of the German occupation government in the Yugoslav territories of Carinthia and Carniola.

VBlL   *Verordungsblatt für Lothringen.* The official decrees of the German occupation government in Lorraine.

VBlLux   *Verordnungsblatt für Luxemburg.* The official decrees of the German occupation government in Luxembourg.

VBlN   *Verordnungsblatt für die besetzten niederländischen Gebiete.* The official decrees of the German occupation government in the Netherlands.

VBlNorw   *Verordnungsblatt für die besetzten norwegischen Gebiete.* The official decrees of the German occupation government in Norway.

VBlPolen   *Verordnungsblatt für die besetzten Gebiete in Polen.* The official decrees of the German occupation government in Poland. Later the *VBlGG*.

VBlRKO   *Verkündungsblatt* (later *Verordnungsblatt*) *des Reichskommissars für das Ostland.* The official decrees of the German occupation government in the Ostland (the Baltic states and White Ruthenia).

VBlRKU   *Verordnungsblatt des Reichskommissars für die Ukraine.* The official decrees of the German occupation government in the Ukraine.

VBlRMO   *Verordnungsblatt des Reichsministers für die besetzten Ostgebiete.* The official decrees of the Reich minister for the occupied eastern territories (the Baltic states and Russia).

VBlRProt   *Verordnungsblatt des Reichsprotektors in Böhmen und Mähren.* The official decrees of the German occupation government in Bohemia and Moravia (the Czech provinces of Czechoslovakia).

VBlUSt   *Verordnungs-und Amtsblatt des Chefs der Zivilverwaltung in der Untersteiermark.* The official decrees of the German occupation government in the Yugoslav territory of Lower Styria.

VBlW   *Verordnungsblatt des Reichsstatthalters im Warthegau.* The official decrees of the German occupation government in the incorporated Polish territory of Poznań, the so-called Wartheland.

VfZ   *Vierteljahrshefte für Zeitgeschichte.* A journal containing many useful articles and bibliographies on the Nazi era.

VNV   Vlaamsch National Verbond. The Flemish National Union. A Flemish nationalist organization.

VoMi   Volksdeutsche Mittelstelle. Liaison Office for Ethnic Germans.

ABBREVIATIONS

WF   Whaddon Film. Code letters I have used as a prefix to microfilm serial and frame numbers of captured German documents filmed at Whaddon Hall, England. The films are now on deposit in the Public Record Office, London, and the National Archives, Washington.

Wi-Rü Amt   Wehrwirtschaft-und Rüstungsamt. The German army's Military Economy and Armaments Office.

Zast   Zentralauftragstelle. Central Order Office. Clearing house for German orders in the occupied territories of Western Europe and general economic supervisory office.

ZBA   Zentralbodenamt. Central Land Office.

Biographical Sketches

ABETZ, OTTO. Specialist on French affairs in the Dienststelle Ribbentrop from 1935; ambassador to France, 1940–44; political adviser to the German military government in France, 1940–44.

ALTENBURG, DR. GÜNTHER. Head of the Political Department of the German Foreign Office dealing with Austria and Czechoslovakia, 1938; afterward in charge of Ribbentrop's personal secretariat; head of the Information Department of the Foreign Office, 1939; Reich plenipotentiary for Greece, 1941–43; head of the *Dienststelle Altenburg* in Vienna (dealing with Balkan questions), 1944–45.

ANTONESCU, MARSHAL ION. Rumanian general; minister president, September 4, 1940; chief of state, September 14, 1940–44.

ANTONESCU, MIHAI. Rumanian lawyer; minister of justice, September 14, 1940–January 27, 1941; minister of state attached to the minister president's office from January 27, 1941; deputy minister president, 1942–44.

BACH-ZELEWSKI, ERICH VON DEM. Senior SS and police officer for central Russia, 1941–42; chief of antipartisan operations, 1943–45; special plenipotentiary of Himmler for security and resettlement questions.

BACKE, HERBERT. State secretary in the Reich Ministry of Food and Agriculture, 1933–43; chief of the food division and member of the general council of the Four-Year Plan; acting Reich minister of food and agriculture, 1943–45.

BADER, GENERAL PAUL. Head of the German military government in Serbia, December 1941–August 1943; military commander in Albania, 1943.

BÁRDOSSY, LÁSZLÓ. Hungarian foreign minister from January 28, 1941; minister president and foreign minister, April 3, 1941–March 9, 1942.

BARGEN, WERNER VON. German Foreign Office representative with the military government in Belgium and Northern France, 1940–43.

BECKERLE, ADOLF HEINZ. SA Obergruppenführer; chief of police in Frankfurt to 1941; German minister to Bulgaria, 1941–44.

BEHRENDS, HERMANN. Senior SS and police officer in Serbia from April 1944.

BENE, OTTO. German Foreign Office representative with the Reichskommissariat of the occupied Netherlands, 1940–44.

BENOIST-MÉCHIN, JACQUES. Delegate general of the Vichy government in Berlin for the care of prisoners of war, December 10, 1940; attached to the office of the vice-president of the Vichy Council of Ministers as secretary-general, February 25, 1941; as state secretary, June 1941, April–September, 1942.

BENZLER, DR. FELIX. Plenipotentiary of the German Foreign Office with the military government in Serbia, April 28, 1941–August 1943.

BERGER, GOTTLOB. Chief of recruitment for the Waffen-SS; chief of the SS Central Office, April 1940–45; liaison officer of the Reichsführer SS to the Reich Ministry for the Occupied Eastern Territories, July 1942–45; chief of the Political Leadership Staff of that ministry, August 1943–45; chief of the prisoner of war staff of the Reichsführer SS, October 1944–45; military commander in Slovakia, September 1944.

BEST, DR. KARL RUDOLF WERNER. Chief of police in Hesse, 1933; senior counselor and department chief for administration and law in the Berlin office of the Gestapo, 1935; official in the SD department, Reich Ministry of the Interior, 1936–40; chief of the civil administration department of the German military administration in France, 1940; later attached to the Foreign Office; Reich plenipotentiary in Denmark, October 1942–45.

BILFINGER, DR. RUDOLF. Chief of the Department for Administration and Law in the office of the Sipo and SD in Cracow.

BÖHME, GENERAL FRANZ. Supreme commander of German forces in the southeast, plenipotentiary commanding general in Serbia, September 14, 1941; head of the military government in Serbia, October 9–December 1941.

BORIS III. King of Bulgaria, 1918–43.

BORMANN, MARTIN. Deputy chief of the Office of the Deputy of the Führer, 1933–41; head of the Party Chancellery, 1941–45; personal secretary to the Führer, April 1943–45.

BRÄUTIGAM, OTTO. Staff member of the German Embassy in Paris, 1936–39; member of the Economic Policy Department of the Foreign Office, 1939–40; consul general in Batum, 1940; liaison officer of the Reich minister for the occupied eastern territories to the High Command of the Army, June 1941–45; deputy head of the Political Department, Reich Ministry for the Occupied Eastern Territories, 1941–45.

BRANDT, ANTON. SS and police officer for Poznań, 1939–45.

BRANDT, RUDOLF. Himmler's personal adjutant.

BRAUCHITSCH, GENERAL WALTHER von. Commander in chief of the German army, February 1938–December 1941.

BRÜCKNER, HEINZ. Official in the Volksdeutsche Mittelstelle (VoMi).

BRUNNER, ANTON. Agent of Adolf Eichmann who operated in Vienna, Berlin, Salonika, Paris, and Bratislava.

BÜHLER, DR. JOSEF. State secretary and, from May 1940, deputy of the governor general of occupied Poland.

BÜRCKEL, JOSEF. Gauleiter of the Palatinate from 1926; Reichskommissar for the Saar, 1935; Reichskommissar for the reunion of Austria with the Reich, 1938–40; Gauleiter and Reichsstatthalter of Vienna, 1939–40; chief of the civil administration for Lorraine, 1940–44; Gauleiter and Reichsstatthalter for the Westmark (the Palatinate, the Saar, and Lorraine), 1941–44.

BURGSDORFF, DR. KURT von. Under state secretary in the Office of the Reich Protector of Bohemia and Moravia.

CANARIS, ADMIRAL WILHELM. Chief of the German counterintelligence service (Abwehr) of the OKW, 1938–44; hanged in March 1945 for complicity in the July 20, 1944, plot to assassinate Hitler.

CAROL II. King of Rumania, 1930–40.

ČATLÓŠ, FERDINAND. Minister of defense in the government of Slovakia, March 1939–September 1944.

CHAMBERLAIN, NEVILLE. British prime minister, May 28, 1937–May 10, 1940.

CHRISTIAN X. King of Denmark, 1912–47.

BIOGRAPHICAL SKETCHES

CIANO DI CORTELLAZZO, COUNT GALEAZZO. Son-in-law of Mussolini; Italian foreign minister, 1936–43.

CLAUSEN, DR. FRITS. Leader of the Danish Nazis.

CLERCQ, STAF DE. Leader of the Flemish National Union (VNV) to October 1942.

CLODIUS, CARL. Deputy chief of the Economic Policy Department, German Foreign Office, 1937–43.

CREUTZ, RUDOLF. Deputy head of the Central Office of the RKFDV.

DALUEGE, KURT. Chief of the *Ordnungspolizei*, 1936–44; acting Reich protector of Bohemia and Moravia, June 1942–August 1943.

DANNECKER, THEODOR. In charge of the deportation of Jews from France, 1942; Bulgaria, 1943; Italy, 1944.

DARLAN, ADMIRAL JEAN FRANÇOIS. Vice-president of the Vichy Council of Ministers and minister for foreign affairs, February 1940–April 1942.

DEGRELLE, LÉON. Head of the Rexist party in Belgium.

DIETRICH, DR. OTTO. Press chief of the Nazi party, 1932–45; press chief of the Reich government, 1937–45; state secretary in the Reich Ministry of Propaganda, 1937–45.

DIRLEWANGER, GENERAL OSKAR. Commander of the Dirlewanger Brigade, consisting of officers and men previously court-martialed for misconduct.

ĎURČANSKÝ, DR. FERDINAND. Member of the Slovak People's party; deputy minister president and minister of justice, social welfare, and health in the autonomous Slovak government, October 1938–March 10, 1939; Slovak foreign minister, March 14, 1939–July 1940; deputy minister president and minister of the interior, October 1939–July 1940.

EHLICH, HANS. Chief of the Nationality Section of the Department of Internal Security, RSHA.

EICHMANN, ADOLF. Chief of the Department for Jewish affairs in the RSHA.

ELIÁŠ, GENERAL ALOIS. Czech minister president, March 1939–September 1941.

ELIAS, DR. HENDRICK. Leader of the Flemish National Union (VNV) from October 1942.

EPP, GENERAL FRANZ XAVER, RITTER VON. Reichsstatthalter of Bavaria, 1933–45; head of the Colonial Policy Office of the Nazi party, 1934–43.

ETZDORF, DR. HASSO VON. Liaison officer of the German Foreign Office to the High Command of the Army (OKH), 1939–45.

FALKENHAUSEN, GENERAL ALEXANDER VON. Head of the German military government in Belgium and Northern France, May 1940–July 1944.

FALKENHORST, GENERAL NIKOLAUS VON. Commander in chief of the German armed forces during the Norwegian invasion and occupation.

FEINE, GERHARD. Counselor in the German legation in Belgrade.

FELBER, GENERAL HANS GUSTAV. German military commander for the southeast, August 1943–44.

FILOV, BOGDAN. Bulgarian archaeologist; minister president, February 1940–September 1944.

FLANDIN, PIERRE ÉTIENNE. Leader of the French Left Republican party; minister president, November 1934–May 1935; minister for foreign affairs, January–June 1936; minister for foreign affairs in the Pétain cabinet, December 1940–February 1941.

FORSTER, ALBERT. Gauleiter of Danzig, October 1930–1939; Gauleiter and Reichsstatthalter of Danzig-Westpreussen, 1939–45.

FRANCO Y BAHAMONDE, FRANCISCO. Chief of state, president of the government, and generalissimo of the armed forces in Spain from October 1936.

BIOGRAPHICAL SKETCHES

FRANK, HANS. Bavarian minister of justice, 1932; Reich minister without portfolio, 1934–45; president of the Academy of German Law; governor general of occupied Poland, 1939–45.

FRANK, KARL HERMANN. Deputy leader of the Sudeten German party from 1937; deputy Gauleiter of the Sudetenland, November 1938–April 1939; deputy Reich protector and state secretary in the Office of the Reich Protector of Bohemia and Moravia, 1939–43; senior SS and police officer for Bohemia and Moravia, 1939–45; Reich minister in Bohemia and Moravia, August 1943–45.

FRAUENFELD, ALFRED E. Member of the Austrian Nazi party and active on behalf of the Anschluss; Generalkommissar for the Crimea, September 1942–43.

FRICK, DR. WILHELM. Early member of the Nazi party; minister of the interior and of education in Thuringia, January 1930–April 1931; Reich minister of the interior, 1933–43; Reich protector of Bohemia and Moravia, 1943–45.

FRIDERICI, GENERAL ERICH. Wehrmacht representative in the Office of the Reich Protector of Bohemia and Moravia, 1939–45.

FUNK, DR. WALTHER. Reich press chief and under state secretary in the Ministry of Propaganda, 1933–37; Reich minister of economics, February 1938–45; president of the Reichsbank, January 1939–45; plenipotentiary general for military economy, February 1938–45.

GEORGE II. King of Greece, 1922–23, 1935–47.

GERSTEIN, KURT. In charge of the department for disinfectant gases, SS Health Institute.

GISEVIUS, HANS BERND. Gestapo and counterintelligence official who later joined the anti-Nazi opposition.

GLAISE-HORSTENAU, GENERAL EDMUND VON. Austrian vice-chancellor and minister of the interior in the cabinet of Arthur Seyss-Inquart, March 1938; German general in Agram (Zagreb), April 1941–October 1942; plenipotentiary general in Croatia, 1942–44.

GLOBOCNIK, ODILO. Gauleiter of Carinthia, 1933; of Vienna, 1938; SS and police officer for the Lublin province, 1939–43; senior SS and police officer for the Adriatisches Küstenland, 1943–45.

GOEBBELS, DR. PAUL JOSEPH. Gauleiter of Berlin; Reich minister of propaganda, 1933–45; Reich plenipotentiary for total war effort, 1944–45.

GÖRING, HERMANN WILHELM. President of the Reichstag, 1933–45; minister president of Prussia and Reich minister for air, 1933–45; commander in chief of the Luftwaffe, 1934–45; plenipotentiary for the Four-Year Plan, 1936–45; acting Reich minister of economics, December 1937–February 1938.

GOTTBERG, CURT VON. Head of the Land Office in the Protectorate of Bohemia and Moravia, 1939; SS and police officer for White Ruthenia, 1941–44; Generalkommissar of White Ruthenia, 1943–44.

GRAZIANI, GENERAL RODOLFO. Commander of the Italian forces in North Africa until February 1941; minister of war in Mussolini's Fascist Republican government from September 1943.

GREIFELT, ULRICH. Head of the central office of the RKFDV; head of the Office for Immigrants and Repatriates (*Leitstelle für Ein-und Rückwanderung*).

GREISER, ARTHUR. President of the Danzig Senate, November 1934–September 1, 1939; Gauleiter and Reichsstatthalter of the Wartheland (Poznań), 1939–45.

GROHÉ, JOSEF. Gauleiter of Köln-Aachen; Reichskommissar of Belgium and Northern France from July 18, 1944.

GROSS, THEODOR. Head of the Agriculture Department and Land Office in the Office of the Reich Protector of Bohemia and Moravia, 1939–41.

HAAKON VII. King of Norway, 1905–57.

HÁCHA, DR. EMIL. President of the Supreme Administrative Court of Czechoslovakia,

1925–38; president of Czechoslovakia, November 1938–March 1939; president of the Czech government in the Protectorate of Bohemia and Moravia, 1939–45.

HAGELIN, ALBERT VILJAM. Vidkun Quisling's representative in Germany, 1939–40; minister of commerce in Quisling's government in Norway, April 1940; head of the Department of the Interior in Norway, September 1940–45, with the title of minister from September 25, 1941.

HALDER, GENERAL FRANZ. Chief of the General Staff of the German army, August 1938–September 1942.

HALIFAX, VISCOUNT EDWARD WOOD. British secretary of state for war, 1935; lord privy seal, November 1935–May 1937; lord president of the Council, 1937–38; secretary of state for foreign affairs, February 1938–December 1940; subsequently British ambassador to the United States.

HANNEKEN, GENERAL HERMANN VON. Plenipotentiary for iron and steel production, Four-Year Plan, July 1937–April 1942; under state secretary and chief of the Raw Materials Division, Reich Ministry of Economics, January 1938–September 1942; military commander in Denmark, September 1942–January 1945.

HASSELL, ULRICH VON. German ambassador to Italy, 1932–38; later a member of the anti-Nazi resistance; executed in September 1944 for participation in the July 20, 1944, plot to assassinate Hitler.

HENLEIN, KONRAD. Founder of the Sudeten German *Heimatsfront*, 1933, which became the Sudeten German party in 1935; Reichskommissar for the Sudeten German territories, October 1, 1938; Gauleiter of the Sudetengau and Reichsstatthalter, May 1, 1939–45.

HERWARTH VON BITTENFELD, HANS. Specialist on Russia in the German Foreign Office; adjutant to General Ernst Köstring, chief of the military administration in the Caucasus region, 1942–43.

HESS, RUDOLF. Early member of the Nazi party; deputy of the Führer, 1933–41; head of the Central Party Committee (later called the Office of the Deputy of the Führer), 1932–41; flew to Britain in May 1941 in a futile effort to persuade the British to make peace and was interned for the duration of the war.

HEWEL, WALTHER. Participated in the Munich Putsch, 1923; later a member of the AO and the Dienststelle Ribbentrop; chief of the personal staff of the Reich foreign minister (Ribbentrop) and his personal representative with Hitler; ambassador for special duties since 1943.

HEYDRICH, REINHARD. Chief of the SD from 1931; chief of the Sipo and SD, 1936–42; chief of the RSHA, 1939–42; acting Reich protector of Bohemia and Moravia, September 1941–June 1942.

HIERL, KONSTANTIN. Reich labor leader, 1933–45.

HILDEBRANDT, RICHARD. SS and police officer for the Vistula district, 1939–43; chief of the Central Office for Race and Resettlement (RuSHA), April 1943–45.

HIMMLER, HEINRICH. Head of the SS, 1929–45; Reichsführer SS and chief of the German police, 1936–45; Reichskommissar for the consolidation of the German people, 1939–45; Reich minister of the interior, August 25, 1943–45.

HLINKA, ANDREJ. Roman Catholic priest; founder and leader of the Slovak People's party; died August 1938.

HOARE, SIR SAMUEL. British secretary of state for foreign affairs, 1935–36; first lord of the Admiralty, 1936–37; home secretary, May 1937–September 1939; secretary of state for air, 1940; ambassador to Spain, May 24, 1940–44; created Viscount Templewood in 1944.

HÖFFLE, HERMANN. Senior SS and police officer in Slovakia, August 1944.

HOESS, RUDOLF. Commander of the Auschwitz concentration camp, 1940–43.

HÖTTL, DR. WILHELM. Official in the Foreign Intelligence Department of the RSHA.

HOFER, FRANZ. Gauleiter of Tyrol, 1938–45; Reichsstatthalter, 1939–45; supreme commissar of the Alpenvorland, 1943–45.

HOFMANN, OTTO. Chief of the Central Office for Race and Resettlement (RuSHA), December 1939–April 1943.

HORTHY DE NAGYBÁNYA, MIKLÓS. Admiral in the Austro-Hungarian navy; regent of Hungary, 1920–October 15, 1944.

IMRÉDY, DR. BÉLA. Hungarian prime minister, May 14, 1938–February 15, 1939; minister of economics, March–August 1944.

JAGOW, DIETRICH VON. German minister to Hungary, 1941–44.

JODL, GENERAL ALFRED. Chief of the Wehrmacht Operations Staff of the OKW, 1939–45.

JUNGCLAUS, RICHARD. Deputy of the RFSS in Belgium, April 1942–44; senior SS and police officer in Belgium, July 1944; commander of the army and police in Belgium, August 1944.

JURY, DR. HUGO. Member of Seyss-Inquart's cabinet in Austria, March 1938; Gauleiter for the Lower Danube, 1938–45; Reichsstatthalter, 1939–45.

KÁLLAY, MIKLÓS. Minister president of Hungary, March 1942–March 19, 1944.

KALTENBRUNNER, DR. ERNST. State secretary for security in Seyss-Inquart's cabinet in Austria, March 1938; chief of the SS in Austria, 1935–38; senior SS and police officer in Vienna, 1938–43; chief of the Sipo and SD, 1943–45; chief of the RSHA, 1943–45.

KANSTEIN, DR. PAUL. Chief of the German police and entrusted with the Germanic program in Denmark, 1941–43.

KASCHE, SIEGFRIED. SA Obergruppenführer; German minister in Croatia, 1941–44.

KEITEL, GENERAL WILHELM. Chief of the OKW, February 4, 1938–45.

KERSTEN, DR. FELIX. Swedish physiotherapist, doctor, masseur, and confidant of Himmler.

KESSELRING, ALBERT. Military commander in the Mediterranean area, 1941–43; commander in chief for the southwest, November 1943–45.

KILLINGER, MANFRED VON. SA Obergruppenführer; minister in Slovakia, July 1940–January 1941; in Rumania, January 24, 1941–44.

KLEIST, GENERAL EWALD VON. Commander in chief of Army Group B in the Caucasus, the Crimea, and the Ukraine, 1942–43.

KOCH, ERICH. Gauleiter of East Prussia, 1928–45; Oberpräsident of East Prussia, 1933–45; Reichskommissar of the Ukraine, 1941–44; in charge of the defense of the Baltic region, August 1944.

KÖRNER, PAUL. State secretary in the Prussian Ministry of State, 1933–45; state secretary and chairman of the Central Office of the Four-Year Plan; deputy chief, Economic Executive Staff East; chairman of the supervisory board of the Hermann Göring Werke.

KÖSTRING, GENERAL ERNST. German military attaché in Moscow, 1927–30, 1935–41; chief of the military administration in the Caucasus region, September 1942–February 1943.

KOPPE, WILHELM. State secretary for security and senior SS and police officer in the Government General, November 1943–44.

KRÜGER, FRIEDRICH WILHELM. Senior SS and police officer in the Government General, 1939–43; state secretary for security, March 1942–October 1943.

KUBE, WILHELM. Gauleiter and Oberpräsident of Brandenburg, 1933–36; Generalkommissar of White Ruthenia, 1941–September 1943.

KUTSCHERA, FRANZ. Acting Gauleiter of Carinthia and head of the civil government of Carinthia and Upper Carniola, April–November 1941.

LAHOUSEN, GENERAL ERWIN. Official of the German counterintelligence (Abwehr) of the OKW.

LAMMERS, DR. HANS. State secretary in the Reich Chancellery from January 1933; chief of the Reich Chancellery, 1934–45.

BIOGRAPHICAL SKETCHES

LANDFRIED, DR. FRIEDRICH. State secretary in the Reich Ministry of Economics, 1939–43; member, General Council of the Four Year Plan.

LAVAL, PIERRE. French minister president, 1931–32; foreign minister, October 1934–May 1935; minister president and foreign minister, June 1935–January 1936; minister of state in the Pétain cabinet, June 1940; vice-president of Vichy's Council of Ministers, July 12–December 13, 1940; foreign minister, October 28–December 13, 1940; de facto head of the Vichy government, April 1942–August 1944.

LEAHY, ADMIRAL WILLIAM D. United States ambassador to Vichy France, January 1941–April 1942.

LEIBBRANDT, DR. GEORG. Chief of the Political Division of the Reich Ministry for the Occupied Eastern Territories, 1941–August 1943.

LEY, DR. ROBERT. Founder and chief of the German Labor Front (DAF), 1933–45.

LIE, JONAS. Chief (later minister) of police in Norway, September 1940–45.

LIST, GENERAL WILHELM. Commander of an army in the Polish and western campaigns; commander of the German forces in Rumania until May 21, 1941; Wehrmacht commander for the southeast, June 9, 1941–July 1942.

LÖHR, GENERAL ALEXANDER. Luftwaffe general; Wehrmacht commander for the southeast, August 1942–August 1943; commander of Army Group E, 1943–45.

LOHSE, HINRICH. SA Obergruppenführer; Gauleiter of Schleswig-Holstein, 1925–45; Oberpräsident of Schleswig-Holstein, 1933–45; president of the Nordic Society; Reichskommissar of the Ostland, 1941–44.

LORENZ, WERNER. Chief of the Liaison Office for Ethnic Germans (Volksdeutsche Mittelstelle or VoMi).

LUDIN, HANNS ELARD. SA Obergruppenführer; minister to Slovakia, January 1941–45.

LÜDKE, GENERAL ERICH. Military commander in Denmark, June 1940–September 1942.

LUTHER, MARTIN. Director of the Department for German Internal Affairs (including the Jewish question) in the Foreign Office, May 1940–April 1943.

MAČEK, VLADKO. Leader of the Croatian Peasant party; deputy minister president of Yugoslavia, August 26, 1939–March 27, 1941, April 3–7, 1941.

MACH, ŠAŇO. Leader of the Hlinka Guards, December 4, 1938–early 1940, July 1940–44; minister of the interior of Slovakia, July 1940–44.

MACKENSEN, HANS GEORG VON. German ambassador to Italy, April 1938–September 1943.

MANSFELD, DR. WERNER. Chief of the Division of Labor Law and Wage Policy, Reich Ministry of Labor, 1933–42; chief of the Division for Labor Allocation, Four-Year Plan, 1941–March 1942.

MANSTEIN, GENERAL ERICH VON. Commander of German armies in Russia, 1941–44.

MENDE, PROFESSOR GERHARD VON. Head of the department dealing with nationalities in the Caucasus, Reich Ministry for the Occupied Eastern Territories.

MEYER, DR. ALFRED. Gauleiter of Westphalia-North, 1931–45; Reichsstatthalter of Lippe and Schaumburg-Lippe, 1933–45; Oberpräsident of Westphalia, 1938–45; state secretary in the Reich Ministry for the Occupied Eastern Territories and permanent deputy of the Reich minister, 1941–45.

MEYER-HETLING, DR. KONRAD. Professor at the Institute for Agricultural Policies and Politics at the University of Berlin; chief of the planning section in the Central Office of the RKFDV; planning commissioner for colonization and rural reorganization.

MEYSZNER, AUGUST. Senior SS and police officer in Serbia, January 1942–April 1944.

MICHAEL I. King of Rumania, September 6, 1940–December 30, 1947.

MOLOTOV, VYACHESLAV. Chairman of the Council of People's Commissars of the Soviet Union; people's commissar for foreign affairs from May 1939.

MÜLLER, HEINRICH. Senior official in the Gestapo and SD; deputy director of the Reich Office for the Emigration of Jews, January–September 1939; chief of the Gestapo (Amt IV) in the RSHA, September 1939–1945.

MUSSERT, ANTON ADRIAAN. Leader of the Dutch National Socialist party.

MUSSOLINI, BENITO. Founder and head of the Italian Fascist party; head of the Italian government, prime minister, and commander of the armed forces to July 25, 1943; head of the Fascist Republican government, September 1943–April 1945.

NEDIĆ, GENERAL MILAN. Minister of war of Yugoslavia, February 1939–March 27, 1941; minister president of Serbia, August 1941–44.

NEUBACHER, DR. HERMANN. Engaged in illegal Nazi agitation in Austria before the Anschluss; official of the I. G. Farben Corporation, 1936; deputy mayor of Vienna, 1938–39; special plenipotentiary for economic questions in Rumania and plenipotentiary for oil questions in the southeast, 1941; plenipotentiary for economic questions in Greece, 1942; plenipotentiary of the Foreign Office in the Balkans, August 1943–44; entrusted with the unified political leadership for the fight against Communism in the southeast, October 1943–44.

NEUHAUSEN, DR. FRANZ. Plenipotentiary general for economic questions in Serbia, April 1941–44; plenipotentiary general for the mining of metal ores in the southeast, December 1942–44.

NEUMANN, DR. ERNST. The leader of the Memel Nazis.

NEURATH, CONSTANTIN VON. Reich foreign minister, 1932–February 4, 1938; Reich protector of Bohemia and Moravia, March 18, 1939–August 20, 1943.

OBERG, KARL ALBRECHT. SS and police officer in Radom (Poland), 1939–42; senior SS and police officer in France from April 1942.

PANCKE, GÜNTHER. Chief of the Central Office for Race and Resettlement (RuSHA), 1938–December 1939; senior SS and police officer for Denmark, November 1943–45.

PAULUS, GENERAL FRIEDRICH. Deputy chief of the Operations Section, Army General Staff; surrendered with the remains of his sixth army at Stalingrad, February 1943.

PAVELIĆ, ANTE. Poglavnik (Führer) of the Ustaša movement and, from 1941–45, chief of state of Croatia.

PÉTAIN, GENERAL HENRI-PHILIPPE. Chief of state in the Vichy government of France, June 1940–44.

PICKER, DR. HENRY. Representative of the Reich Ministry of the Interior at Hitler's headquarters, 1942.

POHL, OSWALD. Chief of the department of economics and administration, SS Central Office.

POPOV, IVAN. Bulgarian foreign minister from February 16, 1940.

PRÜTZMANN, HANS ADOLF. Senior SS and police officer attached to the Army Group South in Russia, October 1941–September 1943.

QUISLING, VIDKUN. Norwegian defense minister, 1931–33; founder and leader of the Nasjonal Samling party, 1933–45; chief of the Norwegian government, April 1940; minister president of Norway, February 1942–45.

RADEMACHER, FRANZ. Head of the department in the German Foreign Office dealing with the Jewish question, May 1940–April 1943.

RAEDER, ADMIRAL ERICH. Commander in chief of the German navy, May 1935–January 1943.

RAHN, RUDOLF. Senior counselor attached to the German embassy in Paris; on special mission in Syria, April–July 1941; on special mission in Tunis, 1942–43; ambassador to the Fascist Republican government of Italy, December 1943–May 1945.

BIOGRAPHICAL SKETCHES

RAINER, FRIEDRICH. Leader of the Austrian Nazi party before the Anschluss; Gauleiter of Salzburg, 1938–41; Reichsstatthalter of Salzburg, 1939–41; gauleiter and Reichsstatthalter of Carinthia, 1941–45; chief of the civil administration of Upper Carniola, 1941–45; supreme commissar of the Adriatisches Küstenland, September 1943–45.

RAUSCHNING, HERMANN. President of the Danzig Senate, June 20, 1933–November 24, 1934.

RAUTER, HANNS ALBIN. Senior SS and police officer in the Netherlands, May 1940–45.

REDIESS, WILHELM. Senior SS and police officer in Norway, June 1940–45.

REEDER, EGGERT. Regierungspräsident in Aachen, Cologne, and Düsseldorf, 1933–39; chief of the administrative staff of Army Group B, 1940; chief of the administrative staff of the German military administration in Belgium and Northern France, 1940–44.

RENTHE-FINK, CECIL VON. German minister to Denmark, 1936–40; minister and Reich plenipotentiary in Denmark, April 1940–October 1942.

RIBBENTROP, JOACHIM VON. Adviser to Hitler on foreign affairs and head of the Dienststelle Ribbentrop; ambassador to Britain, October 1936–February 1938; Reich foreign minister, February 1938–45.

RICHTHOFEN, HERBERT FREIHERR VON. German minister to Bulgaria, 1939–41.

RIECKE, HANS-JOACHIM. State secretary in the Reich Ministry of Food and Agriculture; head of the Food and Agriculture section in the Office of the Four-Year Plan and the Economic Staff East; head of the Food and Agriculture section in the Reich Ministry for the Occupied Eastern Territories.

RINTELEN, EMIL VON. Deputy chief of the Political Department of the German Foreign Office, 1941; member of the personal staff of the Reich foreign minister, 1941–43; ambassador for special assignments, 1943–45.

RITTER, KARL. Ambassador for special assignments in the German Foreign Office, 1939–45; liaison officer of the Foreign Office with the chief of the OKW, October 1940–44.

RÖTHKE, HEINZ. Head of the German office for Jewish affairs in France from July 1942.

ROMMEL, GENERAL ERWIN. Commander of the German Afrika Korps, February 1941–May 1943; commander in chief in northern Italy, 1943; commander of Army Group B in France, November 1943–July 1944.

ROSENBERG, ALFRED. Editor of the Nazi party newspaper, *Völkischer Beobachter*, 1921: Reichsleiter and head of the party office for foreign affairs, the Aussenpolitisches Amt; Reich minister for the occupied eastern territories, 1941–45.

RUNDSTEDT, GENERAL GERD VON. Commanded German army group during the occupation of the Sudetenland; commanded army groups during the Polish, western, and Russian campaigns; commander in chief in the west, July 1942–July 1944, September 1944–March 1945.

SAUCKEL, FRITZ. Gauleiter of Thuringia, 1927–45; Reichsstatthalter of Thuringia, 1933–45; plenipotentiary for labor, March 1942–45.

SCAVENIUS, ERIK. Danish foreign minister from July 1940; minister president and foreign minister, November 8, 1942–August 29, 1943.

SCHÄFER, DR. EMANUEL. Chief of the Sipo and SD in Serbia.

SCHELLENBERG, WALTER. Chief of the counterintelligence section of the RSHA.

SCHIMANA, WALTER. Senior SS and police officer for Greece, September 1943–44.

SCHIRACH, BALDUR VON. Reich youth leader, 1933–45; Gauleiter and Reichsstatthalter of Vienna, July 1940–45.

SCHLOTTERER, GUSTAV. Director in the Flick Corporation; head of the Department of Industry and Commerce in the Office of the Four-Year Plan and the Economic Staff East; head of the Department of Industry and Commerce in the Reich Ministry for the Occupied Eastern Territories.

443

SCHMIDT, FRITZ. Generalkommissar for special tasks in the Netherlands, 1940–June 1943; plenipotentiary for labor and propaganda, 1942–43.

SCHMIDT, DR. PAUL OTTO. Official interpreter of the German foreign minister; personal interpreter of Hitler, 1935–45.

SCHRÖDER, GENERAL LUDWIG. German commander in Serbia, June–July 1941.

SERRANO-SUÑER, RAMÓN. Spanish minister of the interior, January 1938–October 1940; foreign minister, October 1940–September 1942.

SEYSS-INQUART, ARTHUR. Austrian lawyer; councilor of state, May 1937; minister of the interior and security, February 16–March 15, 1938; chancellor, March 11–15, 1938; Reichsstatthalter of the Ostmark, March 15, 1938–May 1, 1939; Reich minister without portfolio, May 1939; deputy governor general of Poland, October 1939–May 1940; Reichskommissar of the Netherlands, May 1940–45.

SIMON, GUSTAV. Gauleiter of Koblenz-Trier (from 1940 called the Gau Moselland), 1931–45; chief of the civil administration in Luxembourg, 1940–45.

SKORZENY, OTTO. Chief of a department in the counterintelligence section of the RSHA, 1943; rescued Mussolini, September 1943; kidnapped Horthy's son, October 1944.

SOLLMANN, MAX. An official of the Lebensborn organization.

SPEER, ALBERT, German architect; Reich minister for armaments and munitions and head of the Organisation Todt, February 1942–45.

STEENGRACHT VON MOYLAND, GUSTAV FREIHERR. State secretary in the German Foreign Office, 1943–45.

STIER, GÜNTHER. Official in the RKFDV.

STUCKART, WILHELM. State secretary in the Reich Ministry of the Interior, March 1935–45; chief of staff of the plenipotentiary for the administration of the Reich, 1939–45.

STÜLPNAGEL, GENERAL KARL HEINRICH VON. Head of the German Armistice Commission in France, 1940–42; head of the German military government in France, February 1942–July 1944. Executed by the Nazis after the failure of the plot to assassinate Hitler.

STÜLPNAGEL, GENERAL OTTO VON. Head of the German military government in France, October 1940–February 1942.

STUTTERHEIM, HERMANN VON. Chief of the department in the Reich Chancellery dealing with the Foreign Office and occupied territories in Eastern Europe.

SZÁLASI, FERENC. Leader of the Hungarian Arrow Cross party; minister president of Hungary, October 1944–45.

SZTÓJAY, DÖME. Hungarian minister to Germany, December 19, 1935–44; minister president of Hungary, March 23–August 25, 1944.

TERBOVEN, JOSEF. Gauleiter of Essen, 1928–45; Reichskommissar of Norway, 1940–45.

THOMAS, GENERAL GEORG. Chief of the Military Economics Staff of the German armed forces (later the OKW), November 1934–39; chief of the Military Economy and Armaments Office (Wi-Rü Amt) of the OKW, September 1939–January 1943; general for special assignments with the chief of the OKW, January 1943–44; after the failure of the attempt to assassinate Hitler in July 1944, sent to a concentration camp.

TISO, DR. JOZEF. Roman Catholic priest; leader of the Slovak People's party from August 1938; minister president of the autonomous Slovak government, October 1938–March 10, 1939; minister president of Slovakia, March 14–October 26, 1939; president of Slovakia, October 26, 1939–45.

TODT, DR. FRITZ. Inspector general for German highways, 1933–42; founder and chief of the Organisation Todt; plenipotentiary for construction, Four-Year Plan, 1938–42; Reich minister for armaments and munitions, March 17, 1940–42; killed in air crash, February 8, 1942.

444

BIOGRAPHICAL SKETCHES

TUKA, DR. VOJTĚCH. Member of the Slovak People's party; deputy minister president and minister of the interior of Slovakia, March–October 1939; minister president, October 27, 1939–September 1944; foreign minister, July 1940–September 1944.

TURNER, HARALD. Chief of the German military administration in Paris, 1940; chief of the administrative staff of the German military government in Serbia, 1941–December 1942.

UIBERREITHER, DR. SIEGFRIED. Gauleiter of Styria, 1938–45; Reichsstatthalter, 1939–45; chief of the civil administration of Lower Styria, 1941–45.

VALLAT, XAVIER. Head of the Commissariat for Jewish Affairs of the Vichy government, March 1941–May 1942.

VEESENMAYER, EDMUND. Member of the Austrian Nazi party; assistant to Wilhelm Keppler, state secretary for special duties in the German Foreign Office, to 1944; German minister and Reich plenipotentiary in Hungary, March 19, 1944–45.

VICTOR EMMANUEL III. King of Italy, 1900–46.

VÖLKERS, DR. HANS HERMANN. Adviser to Neurath, 1932–33, 1939–42; head of the personal office of the Reich Protector.

WAGNER, ROBERT. Gauleiter of Baden, 1925–45; Reichsstatthalter, 1933–45; chief of the civil administration of Alsace, 1940–45.

WARLIMONT, GENERAL WALTER. Chief of the Department for National Defense (*Landesverteidigung*) in the OKW from November 1938; deputy chief, Armed Forces Operational Staff, January 1942–44.

WEICHS, GENERAL MAXIMILIAN FREIHERR VON. Supreme commander for the southeast, August 1943–March 1945.

WEITZEL, FRITZ. Senior SS and police officer in Norway, April–June 1940.

WEIZSÄCKER, ERNST VON. Head of the Political Department of the German Foreign Office, August 1936–38; state secretary, April 1, 1938–April 1943; ambassador to the Holy See, 1943–45.

WETZEL, DR. ERNST. Head of the Racial-Political Office of the Nazi party; assigned to the Reich Ministry for the Occupied Eastern Territories in 1941 as specialist for Jewish questions.

WIMMER, DR. FRIEDRICH. Generalkommissar for administration and justice in the Netherlands.

WINKELMANN, DR. OTTO. Senior SS and police officer in Hungary from March 1944.

WINKLER, MAX. Member of the Advisory Board of the Reichsbank; chief of the Combined Finance Boards (*Vereinigte Finanzkontore*); executive director of the Main Trustee Office East (Haupttreuhandstelle Ost) from October 1939; mayor of Lodz (Poland) under German occupation.

WISLICENY, DIETER. Eichmann's deputy in Slovakia, Greece, and Hungary.

WOERMANN, DR. ERNST. Under state secretary and head of the Political Department in the German Foreign Office, 1938–43; ambassador to China, 1943–45.

WOLFF, KARL. Chief of Himmler's personal staff, 1936–45; liaison officer of the Reichsführer SS at Hitler's headquarters, 1939–43; senior SS and police officer for Italy, 1943–45.

ZIMMERMANN, JOB. Chief of the propaganda section of the Reich Ministry for the Occupied Eastern Territories.

ZÖRNER, ERNST. Mayor of Dresden; governor of the Lublin province of Poland, 1939–44.

Notes

1. THE JEWS.

1   1. Adolf Hitler, *Mein Kampf* (New York, 1939), pp. 66 ff., esp. chap. 11, vol. 1. All citations are from the Reynal and Hitchcock American edition; on occasion I have amended this translation on the basis of the 1934 German edition. Gottfried Feder, *Hitler's Official Programme and Its Fundamental Ideas* (London, 1934), p. 39 (point four of the party's twenty-five points). For collections of Hitler's speeches and other writings on the Jewish question, see Norman H. Baynes, ed., *The Speeches of Adolf Hitler, April 1922–August 1939*, 2 vols. (Oxford, 1942), vol. 1, esp. chap. 24; Gordon W. Prange, ed., *Hitler's Words* (Washington, D.C., 1944), esp. chap. 5; and Raoul de Roussy de Sales, ed., *My New Order* (New York, 1941).

    2. Raul Hilberg, *The Destruction of the European Jews* (Chicago, 1961), the most thorough and comprehensive work on this subject; Gerald Reitlinger, *The Final Solution: The Attempt to Exterminate the Jews of Europe, 1939–1945* (New York, 1968), is briefer and more readable, but somewhat less reliable.

2   3. Quoted in Helmut Krausnick, Hans Buchheim, Martin Broszat, and Hans-Adolf Jacobsen, *Anatomy of the SS State* (New York, 1968), p. 21. An excellent work, on which I have relied heavily.

    4. *RGBl* (1933) 1:175, 195; Hilberg, *Destruction*, p. 45 and all of pt. 4.

3   5. *RGBl* (1935) 1:1146–47, 1333.

    6. The most important of the laws directed against the Jews have been assembled by Bruno Blau, *Das Ausnahmerecht für die Juden in Deutschland, 1933–1945* (Düsseldorf, 1954).

4   7. *IMT*, 374-PS, 25:376–81; 3051-PS, 31:515–19; 3058 and 3063-PS, 32:1–2, 20–29; Krausnick, *Anatomy*, p. 40; Hilberg, *Destruction*, pp. 23, 29.

    8. *RGBl* (1938) 1:1579–81, 1638, 1642, 1709; Göring conference on the Jewish problem, November 12, 1938, *IMT*, 1816-PS, 28:499–540; Göring testimony, *IMT* 9:276–78; Göring order of December 12, 1938, *IMT* 27:69–71.

    9. November 11, 1938, quoted in Krausnick, *Anatomy*, p. 43. The program of Julius Streicher's notorious anti-Semitic journal *Der Stürmer* went much further: "The Jewish problem is not yet solved, nor will it be solved on the day when the last Jew will have left Germany. Only when world Jewry has been annihilated will it have been solved" (January 1939, no. 4, p. 3; "The Jewish question will only be completely solved when the Jews have completely disappeared from amongst all nations" (May 1939, no. 18, p. 9).

    10. *TWC*, NG 2586A, 13:129; *DGFP*, D, 5:926, 933–36; Krausnick, *Anatomy*, pp. 46–49, 54, 68.

5   11. *RGBl* (1939) 1:1097; Hilberg, *Destruction*, p. 122; Krausnick, *Anatomy*, p. 47.

    12. *Fuehrer Conferences on Matters Dealing with the German Navy, 1939–1945*, 8 vols. (Washington, D.C. 1946–47), 1940, 1:54; Foreign Office memorandum, July 3, 1940, Nuremberg document NG 2586B; August 12, 1940, NG 2586C.

6   13. These Heydrich instructions were to apply to Danzig, West Prussia, Posen (Poznán), and Eastern Upper Silesia, *TWC*, 3363-PS, 4:119–23.

    14. *IMT* 4:350; 30:76, 79; 31:39; 37:672, 682, 687; NG 3104; NG 3933; affidavit of SS Standartenführer Walter Blume, June 26, 1947, NO 4145; Göring-Heydrich order, July 31, 1941, *TWC*, 2583E, 4:132; 13:169; *IMT* 26:266–67; Akten des SS Kav. Regt. 2, from the archives of the University of Freiburg im Breisgau (supplied through the kindness of Dr. Hans-Günther Seraphim); Krausnick, *Anatomy*, pp. 62–63, 67–68.

    15. On the decision to abandon the Madagascar project in favor of an eastern solution of the Jewish problem, see the German Foreign Office documents collected at Nuremberg under the numbers NG 3933, PS 2586, and PS 2184.

    16. Himmler files, quoted in Krausnick, *Anatomy*, pp. 69–70.

7   17. Nuremberg document NO 1209.

18. Göring order, July 31, 1941, *TWC* 4:132; *TWC*, 709-PS, 13:192; *IMT*, 3921-PS, 33:534–36; *TWC*, NG 2586F, 13:198.

8

19. Protocol of Wannsee conference, NG 2586G; extracts in *TWC* 13:210–17.

20. Himmler to Berger, *TWC*, NO 626, 13:240; 14:1011.

21. Hitler gave his approval for euthanasia operations as early as September 1, 1939, PS 630. See also the German manuscript record of the Nuremberg Doctors' Trial, pp. 7635 ff., 1885 ff., and documents NO 907, 2799, and PS 1151. The evidence on this complicated problem has been pulled together by Hans-Günther Seraphim in an unpublished manuscript, *Zum Problem der "Häftlingseuthanasie" in den nationalsozialistischen Konzentrationslagern*, which the author kindly made available to me.

22. *IMT* 11:398; G. M. Gilbert, *Nuremberg Diary* (New York, 1947), pp. 249–50; Rudolf Hoess, *Commandant of Auschwitz* (London, 1959).

9

23. NO 365; see also Brack's testimony in the German manuscript record of the Nuremberg Doctors' Trial.

24. Krausnick, *Anatomy*, pp. 96–101; Hoess, *Commandant of Auschwitz*, pp. 146–54, 183–200.

25. Greiser to Himmler, May 1, 1942, NO 246, T175/103/2625377–78; Brack to Himmler, June 23, 1942, Staatliches Archivlager, Göttingen, Lu 9, 23.

10

26. The blow to German morale was also evident among SS men. In February 1942, for example, SS Hauptsturmführer Kriegsheim, chief of staff of the commander of the Northern Army Group Rear, was denounced to Himmler by a fellow SS officer for his outspoken denunciation of the shooting of Jews, which he had stated was "unworthy of a German." "Similar statements, even if not quite so sharply worded, have been made by almost all officers [*Herren*] of the command of Northern Army Group Rear during the first months of the occupation of the east," Himmler's correspondent said, and were contributing to an overall defeatist attitude" (Staatliches Archivlager, Göttingen, Lu 2, 27b).

The most remarkable single case I have encountered on this question is that of SS Obergruppenführer Erich von dem Bach-Zelewski, Himmler's senior SS and police officer for central Russia and later the SS general in charge of all antipartisan operations in German-occupied territory. Early in 1942 Bach was hospitalized for a hemorrhoid operation from which he did not recover satisfactorily. His doctor informed Himmler on March 4 that one reason for the patient's unsatisfactory condition was his state of nervous exhaustion resulting from his assignments in Eastern Europe. "He is suffering especially from hallucinations in connection with the shooting of Jews, which he himself conducted, and from other agonizing experiences in the east," the doctor wrote, adding that he now considered Bach's moral rehabilitation to be a precondition for his physical recovery (NO 600).

27. Gerstein affidavit, citing the order of Globocnik; Party Chancellery documents, cited in *DOT* 6:596, 602–5; *IMT* 42:328–30; *The Goebbels Diaries, 1942–1943*, ed. Louis P. Lochner (New York, 1948), p. 147; Hoess testimony, *IMT* 11:50–54, 396 ff. Upon receiving a statistical report he had requested on the final solution of the Jewish problem, Himmler wrote to the chief of the Sipo and SD on April 9, 1943, "I consider this report to be very good as material for possible future use, especially for purposes of secrecy [*und zwar zu Tarnungszwecken*]" (T175/103/2625028).

28. Bormann circular, July 11, 1943, T175/18/1521542.

29. Brack to Himmler, June 23, 1942, Staatliches Archivlager, Göttingen, Lu 9, 23.

30. Himmler to Krüger, July 19, 1942, T175/122/2647914. On SS economic enterprises, see Enno Georg, *Die wirtschaftlichen Unternehmungen der SS* (Stuttgart, 1963).

31. T175/122/2647869; Krausnick, *Anatomy*, p. 111.

32. An army captain named Albert Battel, for example, tried to protect Jews working for the Wehrmacht by blocking off the bridges leading to the Jewish area of Przemysl and refusing to allow the SS and police to pass, but his orders were undercut by a subordinate officer and the Jews were removed after all. Meanwhile Himmler had assembled a file on Battel and on October 3, 1942, he sent the file to Hans Lammers with a covering note saying that "immediately after the war I propose to place Battel under arrest" (Staatliches Archivlager, Göttingen, Lu 2, 27a).

One of the most interesting cases of protecting Jews who were working for Germany was that of Gauleiter Wilhelm Kube, the head of the German civil administration (Generalkommissar) of White Ruthenia. See below, pp. 371–72.

11

33. NO 1611.

34. Foreign Office memorandum, February 20, 1943, NG 2586P; NG 2184; Staatliches Archivlager, Göttingen, Lu 3, 22; *IMT*, 3319-PS, 33:184–88.

35. Himmler memorandum on conference with Hitler, June 19, 1943, T175/94/2615096–97; Party Chancellery circular of October 9, 1942, *IMT* 42:328–30.

12

36. *Goebbels Diaries*, entry for March 27, 1942. The translation is based on the German edition, *Goebbels Tagebücher aus den Jahren 1942–1943, mit anderen Dokumenten*, ed. Louis P. Lochner (Zürich, 1948), pp. 142–43.

2. THE ETHNIC GERMANS

13 1. Hitler's racial and expansionist ideology is discussed in the first volume of this study, chap. 1.

2. *Mein Kampf* (New York, 1939), p. 3, which is the first page of the text.

14 3. On Hitler's campaign for the acquisition of Austria, see the first volume of this study, pp. 90–101, and its Bibliography, 13. Austria and the Anschluss.

4. *DDP* 6:145–46.

5. *DDP* 6:157–59.

15 6. *Bundesgesetzblatt für den Bundesstaat Österreich*, no. 75 (1938); *DDP* 6:147–48. Voting in the plebiscite was to be restricted to ethnic Germans, a procedure which in effect left the selection of voters up to the Nazis who controlled the election.

7. *RGBl* (1938) 1:237; *DDP* 6:148–49. See also the important work of Raphaël Lemkin, *Axis Rule in Occupied Europe: Laws of Occupation, Analysis of Government, Proposals for Redress* (Washington, D.C., 1944), pp. 108–16, 283–99.

8. *Gleichschaltung*, a term stemming from the science of electricity, meant more than co-ordination or synchronization when used in a political context; it implied a sort of leveling process; when used in connection with foreign countries, it meant the gearing of those countries to German needs and practices.

9. *DDP* 6:150; Gordon Brook-Shepherd, *Anschluss: The Rape of Austria* (London, 1963), pp. 198–99.

10. Kaltenbrunner testimony, *IMT* 9:237; Brook-Shepherd, *Anschluss*, pp. 197–98; Karl Stadler, *Österreich 1938–1945 im Spiegel der NS-Akten* (Vienna, 1966), p. 27 ff.; *Rot-Weiss-Rot-Buch. Darstellungen, Dokumente und Nachweise zur Vorgeschichte und Geschichte der Okkupation Österreichs* (Vienna, 1946), p. 160 (an Austrian government publication).

11. Law of March 18, 1938. *RGBl* (1938) 1:237.

16 12. *RGBl* (1938) 1:245, 247–49, 252–55, 257, 261, 301, 309, 350; Reich Minister of the Interior Frick to Supreme Reich Authorities, March 18, 1938. *TWC*, NG 2503, 12:739.

13. *DDP* 6:150; *RGBl* (1938) 1:257.

14. *DDP* 6:200–201.

15. *RGBl* (1938) 1:400, 413, 594, 607, 631, 790.

16. Recalling Bismarck's difficulties in dealing with the incorporation of Bavaria into the German union in 1871, Hitler informed his associates in April 1942 that in 1938 he had avoided telling the Austrians outright that he intended to incorporate them into Germany (Henry Picker, *Hitlers Tischgespräche im Führerhauptquartier, 1941–1942*, ed. Percy Ernst Schramm, and Andreas Hillgruber, Martin Vogt [Stuttgart, 1965], p. 254; *Hitler's Secret Conversations, 1941–1944* [paperback, New York, 1961], p. 383).

17 17. *RGBl* (1938) 1:407.

18. *DDP* 6:205–6.

19. *RGBl* (1938) 1:1333, 1338–39; *DDP* 6:210–13, 223–27; 7:686.

20. *DDP* 6:211, n. 4.

21. Bormann note, November 15, 1943. The problem is discussed in Stadler, *Österreich*, pp. 129–30, 392–401; Schirach testimony, *IMT* 14:409 ff.

19 22. *RGBl* (1939) 1:777; *DDP* 6:206, n. 1; 7:685–86, 692–701; Brook-Shepherd, *Anschluss*, p. 216.

23. *DDP* 7:685, 704–22.

24. *Hitler's Secret Conversations*, p. 55; Picker, *Hitlers Tischgespräche*, p. 146, where the date of Hitler's remarks is given as September 1941.

20 25. Remarks of October 1941 and June 1943, *Hitler's Secret Conversations*, pp. 73, 78, 655–57; Picker, *Hitlers Tischgespräche*, pp. 277, 299, 377. See also the memoirs of Hitler's architect and later minister of munitions, Albert Speer, *Inside the Third Reich* (New York, 1970), pp. 117–18.

26. Propaganda Ministry order, January 28, 1942, T70/3/3506288; Party Chancellery circular, February 13, 1942, T81/2/12184–85; Lammers circular, April 8, 1942, T70/10/3506289.

27. Statistical report on the final solution of the Jewish problem, April 1943, T175/103/2625029–45. Statistics on the subject vary widely. See Gerald Reitlinger, *The Final Solution: The Attempt to Exterminate the Jews of Europe, 1939–1945* (New York, 1968), p. 536.

28. Hermann Göring, *Reden und Aufsätze* (Munich, 1938), pp. 348–49.

29. Gestapo reports of October 21 and 25, 1939, T84/13/41022; T84/14/43421; Stadler, *Österreich*, pp. 285–90; Reitlinger, *Final Solution*, pp. 45–47; Jonny Moser, *Die Judenverfolgung in Österreich, 1938–1945* (Vienna, 1966).

30. See above, n. 27.

21 31. On Hitler's campaign for the acquisition of the Sudetenland, see the first volume of this study, pp. 101–10. Not until the last days of September 1938 did Hitler give orders to the Reich Ministry of the Interior to prepare for the establishment of a civil administra-

tion in the Sudetenland (State Secretary Stuckart of the Ministry of the Interior to Under State Secretary Woermann of the Foreign Office, September 23, 1938; Woermann note, September 29, 1938. NG 5638; NG 3089).

32. *RGBl* (1938) 1:1331, 1345, 1348.

22 33. *DDP* 6:376–77.

34. *DDP* 6:372, n. 1. A circular of the Reich minister of the interior to other Reich ministers of October 12, 1938, stressed that the civil administrative apparatus to be set up in the Sudetenland was as yet provisional (NG 3077).

35. *RGBl* (1938) 1:1392–93, 1397, 1418, 1430, 1446, 1453, 1524.

36. Stuckart had outlined some of the problems in his letter to Woermann of September 23, 1938 (NG 5638; see above n. 32).

37. *DDP* 6:378–79, and nn.

23 38. *DDP* 6:391–92; Christopher Thorne, *The Approach of War, 1938–1939* (London, 1968), p. 86.

39. *RGBl* (1938) 1:1641; 2:896.

40. On October 28, 1938, Stuckart sent Lammers a draft of a treaty on the citizenship question based on decisions Ribbentrop had received from Hitler (NG 903).

41. These elections had already been provided for by a Hitler decree of October 31 (*RGBl* [1938] 1:1567). A second decree on these elections provided that only those persons could vote who through the "homecoming" (*Heimkehr*) of the Sudeten German areas had acquired German citizenship, meaning persons of German or German-related blood (*RGBl* [1938] 1:1571). Thus, as was the case in Austria, the selection of voters was entirely in the hands of the Nazi authorities and the sentiments of the 676,478 Czechs in the Sudeten areas were not registered in the elections (*DGFP*, D, 4:152).

42. *RGBl* (1938) 1:1997; (1939) 1:358.

24 43. *RGBl* (1939) 1:745, 780; *DDP* 6:686–87; 7:701–4.

44. On the treaty status of Memel, see *DGFP*, D, 5:421, n. 3; on the German acquisition of Memel, *DGFP*, D, chap. 3; and vol. 1 of this study, pp. 118–20.

45. *RGBl* (1939) 1:559, 565, 763; 2: 608, 1000; *DDP* 7:538, 545–49, 552, n. 2, 554.

25 46. *RGBl* (1939) 1:1547, 1691, 2093; *Gesetzblatt für die freie Stadt Danzig* (1939) p. 413; *DGFP*, D, 7:207–8; *DDP* 7:593–97.

47. *VBlDg* (1939), p. 1; *DDP* 7:612.

48. *RGBl* (1939) 1:1567, 1621; *Gesetzblatt für die freie Stadt Danzig* (1939), p. 465; *VBlDg* (1939), pp. 11–12, 56, 111–12.

49. *RGBl* (1939) 1:2042, 2108, 2133, 2135; (1940) 1:832.

26 50. Picker, *Hitlers Tischgespräche*, pp. 144, 146, 254–56, 360; *Hitler's Secret Conversations*, pp. 55, 383.

3. THE SLAVS: CZECHOSLOVAKIA

27 1. On the background of Hitler's occupation of Bohemia and Moravia, see the first volume of this study, pp. 111–18. The best single account of the German occupation is Vojtech Mastny, *The Czechs under Nazi Rule: The Failure of National Resistance, 1939–1942* (New York, 1971); see also the same author's "Design or Improvisation: The Origins of the German Protectorate of Bohemia and Moravia in 1939," *Columbia Essays in International Affairs*, ed. A. W. Cordier (New York, 1966), pp. 127–53; and Heinrich Bodensieck, "Zur Vorgeschichte des 'Protektorats Böhmen und Mähren,'" *Geschichte in Wissenschaft und Unterricht* 19 (1968): 713–32.

29 2. *Hitler's Secret Book* (paperback, New York, 1961), p. 45.

3. Hermann Rauschning, *The Voice of Destruction* (New York, 1940), p. 38.

4. *Hitler's Secret Conversations, 1941–1944* (paperback, New York, 1961), p. 237.

5. Henry Picker, *Hitlers Tischgespräche im Führerhauptquartier, 1941–1942*, ed. Percy Ernst Schramm, Andreas Hillgruber, Martin Vogt (Stuttgart, 1965), pp. 162, 359, 434–35.

6. Decree of March 16, 1939 (*RGBl* [1939] 1:485). According to Karl Hermann Frank, the deputy leader of the Sudeten German party and later state secretary in the office of the Reich protector for Bohemia and Moravia, the decree was drafted on the night of March 15–16 by Hitler, Frick, Stuckart, and Ribbentrop (*IMT* 32:14). Further definitions of the status of the Protectorate were formulated by Frick and Stuckart (NG 2496, 3713). See also Mastny, *Czechs,* p. 47 ff.

30 7. See above, p. 27, and vol. 1 of this study, p. 116.

8. All these points were embodied in the decree of March 16. See above n. 6.

9. Mastny, *Czechs,* p. 86, citing Hitler directive no. 59/39 of March 21, 1939.

10. Mastny, *Czechs,* pp. 54–55; Sheila Grant Duff, *A German Protectorate: The Czechs under Nazi Rule* (London, 1942), pp. 77–78; OSS, *The Protectorate of Bohemia and Moravia* (Washington, D.C., 1944), pp. 3, 8, 24.

31 11. Decree on the authority of the Reich protector, March 22, 1939, *RGBl* (1939)

1:549; Stuckart essay on the Protectorate, April 1939 (?), NG 2496; *DDP* 7:496, 503, n. 6; *IMT* 40:525–26.

12. Albert Speer, *Inside the Third Reich* (New York, 1970), p. 176; *DDP* 7:508; Neurath testimony, *IMT* 16:654–71; 40:525–26.

13. *RGBl* (1939) 1:485, 549, 1039.

14. Neurath testimony, *IMT* 16:657.

32 15. Frank file, Berlin Document Center, cited in Mastny, *Czechs,* pp. 14, 53, 96; Grant Duff, *German Protectorate,* p. 166; Elizabeth Wiskemann, *Czechs and Germans: A Study of the Struggle in the Historic Provinces of Bohemia and Moravia* (London, 1938), pp. 44, 134, 159, 197; and by the same author, "Partitioned Czechoslovakia," in *Hitler's Europe,* ed. Arnold and Veronica Toynbee (London, 1954), p. 586.

16. Neurath testimony, *IMT* 16:657; Völkers testimony, *IMT* 17:129–30.

17. *RGBl* (1939) 1:1681; Neurath testimony, *IMT* 16:657–59; Frank statements, *IMT* 17:77–78, 89–90; 40:529; Burgsdorff testimony, *IMT* 12:58–59; Radomir Luža, *The Transfer of the Sudeten Germans: A Study of Czech-German Relations, 1933–1962* (London, 1964), pp. 180, 201; Gerhard Jacoby, *Racial State: The German Nationalities Policy in the Protectorate of Bohemia-Moravia* (New York, 1944), pp. 61–62; Grant Duff, *German Protectorate,* pp. 78–80; OSS, *Protectorate,* pp. 26–28.

33 18. Ulrich von Hassell, *Vom andern Deutschland. Aus den nachgelassenen Tagebüchern, 1938–1944* (Zürich, 1946), p. 112; Völkers testimony, *IMT* 17:129.

19. Hermann Hufnagel, "Organisation der Verwaltung im Protektorat Böhmen und Mähren," *Böhmen und Mähren,* (Prague, 1940), vol. 1; report of Dr. Werner Best on the administration of the Protectorate, August–September 1941, T501/101/1353–1667; Mastny, *Czechs,* pp. 92 ff.; Luža, *Transfer,* p. 200; Grant Duff, *German Protectorate,* pp. 97–98, 112–13; OSS, *Protectorate,* p. 16.

20. Frick and Lammers circular to all supreme Reich authorities, April 1, 1939, NG 3713.

21. *VBlRProt* (1939), pp. 1–2; OSS, *Protectorate,* pp. 2–3, 6–7.

34 22. *SGV* (1938), p. 1087; *VBlRProt* (1940), p. 604; Mastny, *Czechs,* 58–64; Hubert Ripka, *Munich: Before and After* (London, 1939), pp. 240–55.

23. Mastny, *Czechs,* pp. 153–65; Luža, *Transfer,* p. 200, 218–19; Grant Duff, *German Protectorate,* pp. 104–10, 172; OSS, *Protectorate,* pp. 38–39.

24. *RGBl* (1939) 1:485, 549, 1039, 1681; *SGV* (1940), pp. 259–60; Best report, T175/101/1353–66; Alfred Bohmann, "Die Stellung der Oberlandräte-Inspekteure: Zur deutschen Verwaltungsorganisation im ehemaligen Protektorat Böhmen und Mähren," *Zeitschrift für Ostforschung* 15 (1966): 118–26; Mastny, *Czechs,* p. 93; Grant Duff, *German Protectorate,* pp. 97–98, 110–13, 118, 121–22, 200; Luža, *Transfer,* pp. 200–201; OSS, *Protectorate,* pp. 6–7, 33, 38–40.

35 25. Best report, T175/101/1353–66; Mastny, *Czechs,* pp. 99–100.

26. Göring's views are reflected in an article on German economic policy in Bohemia and Moravia by Hans Kehrl, the head of the textiles section in the Office for German Raw Materials and Synthetics of the Four-Year Plan, published in *Der Vierjahresplan,* April 20, 1939; *TWC* 13:654–57; see also the record of the Göring economic conference of July 27, 1941, *IMT,* 133-R, 38:367–70.

27. Henlein memorandum for the Führer, November 1937, *DGFP,* D, 2:57; Mastny, *Czechs,* pp. 125–26; Václav Král, ed., *Die Vergangenheit warnt. Dokumente über die Germanisierungs-und Austilgungspolitik der Naziokkupanten in der Tschechoslowakei* (Prague, 1960), pp. 24–38, 163 (a valuable collection of documents).

28. Conrad F. Latour, *Südtirol und die Achse Berlin-Rom, 1938–1945* (Stuttgart, 1962), p. 34; Luža, *Transfer,* p. 188, n. 5.

36 29. Friderici memorandum of July 12, 1939, T77/869/5615851–57; Král, *Vergangenheit,* pp. 44–48.

30. Hitler appears to have overestimated the seriousness of the situation in the Protectorate at this time. *Hitler's Secret Conversations,* p. 210; Neurath testimony, *IMT* 16:663–65; 17:84–91; Völkers testimony, *IMT* 17:131–33; W. von Holleben (a member of Neurath's staff) statements, *IMT* 16:665–66; 40:533; Czech indictment, *IMT,* 998-PS, 26:467–69; K. H. Frank statement, *IMT* 40:527–28; Luža, *Transfer,* p. 206.

37 31. Ziemke, the representative of the German Foreign Office in Prague, to the Foreign Office, December 15, 1939, *DGFP,* D, 13:538–39.

32. Ziemke report on the future of the Protectorate, August 19, 1940, NG 5173; Král, *Vergangenheit,* pp. 51–58; Mastny, *Czechs,* pp. 125–27; OSS, *Protectorate,* pp. 29–31; Grant Duff, *German Protectorate,* p. 162.

33. Neurath testimony, *IMT* 16:672; 17:59–68, 95, 374–76; Neurath to Lammers, August 31, 1940, *IMT,* 3859-PS, 33:252–53; Luža, *Transfer,* pp. 188–90.

38 34. Neurath and Frank memoranda, *IMT,* 3859-PS, 33:253–71.

35. Ziemke report, October 5, 1940, *DGFP,* D, 11:266–67.

39 36. Neurath testimony, *IMT* 16:672–73.

37. K. H. Frank to Himmler, June 26, 1940. Král, *Vergangenheit*, p. 59, n. 13.

38. Friderici report, October 15, 1940, *IMT*, 862-PS, 26:375–77. This version of the document refers to a conference of *last* year, but this is clearly an error. See above, p. 38, n. 35.

39. Ziemke report, October 14, 1940. Král, *Vergangenheit*, p. 95.

40. Notes by SS Brigadeführer Hofmann of the Race and Resettlement Office on his talk with K. H. Frank and his visit to Prague, September 11–13. Král, *Vergangenheit*, pp. 83–85.

41. Neurath testimony, *IMT* 17:14; Gross affidavit, *IMT* 40:530–31; Král, *Vergangenheit*, pp. 83–87, 136–37; Mastny, *Czechs*, pp. 88–89, 120–21; Luža, *Transfer*, pp. 193–94.

42. See below, p. 80, on the Nazi occupation of Poland, where the first systematic efforts were made to deal with the problem of identifying ethnic Germans for purposes of inaugurating a large-scale Germanization program.

43. Heydrich to Frank, September 14, 1940. Král, *Vergangenheit*, pp. 74–75; also pp. 83–85, 109–17; Himmler to Hofmann, October 9, 1940; Hofmann to Himmler, October 24, 1940, T175/26/2531947–52; Race and Resettlement Office report, June 29, 1942, *IMT*, USSR-060(a), 39:362; Mastny, *Czechs*, pp. 128–33; Luža, *Transfer*, p. 190; Grant Duff, *German Protectorate*, p. 196.

44. Race and Resettlement Office memorandum, October 23, 1940. Král, *Vergangenheit*, pp. 76–77.

45. Král, *Vergangenheit*, pp. 109–21; Luža, *Transfer*, pp. 190–91.

46. *RGBl* (1940) 1:1488; Mastny, *Czechs*, pp. 134–36.

47. Friderici memorandum of October 15, 1940, on a conference with Frank on October 9, *IMT*, 862-PS, 26:376.

48. Neurath to his administrative offices, June 27, 1941, *IMT*, 3862-PS, 33:271–73; Neurath testimony, *IMT* 17:96; Vincent Urban, *Hitler's Spearhead* (London, 1945), pp. 33–34; Luža, *Transfer*, p. 204.

49. Král, *Vergangenheit*, pp. 16–17, 128–29; Mastny, *Czechs*, chap. 9; Luža, *Transfer*, p. 207.

50. *RGBl* (1941) 1:591; *VBlRProt* (1941), p. 535; Neurath testimony, *IMT* 17:16–17; Völkers testimony, *IMT* 17:134; Luža, *Transfer*, p. 207; Mastny, *Czechs*, pp. 179–80.

51. See vol. 1 of this work, p. 48.

52. On Heydrich, see the brief sketch in Joachim C. Fest, *The Face of the Third Reich: Portraits of the Nazi Leadership* (New York, 1970), pp. 98–110; Charles Wighton, *Heydrich: Hitler's Most Evil Henchman* (Philadelphia, 1962), pp. 21–28, 236–40; Felix Kersten (Himmler's doctor-masseur), *The Kersten Memoirs, 1940–1945* (London, 1956), pp. 90–99; Mastny, *Czechs*, pp. 183–87.

53. Heydrich speech to the German members of his staff, October 2, 1941. Král, *Vergangenheit*, pp. 122–33.

54. Heydrich speeches and conferences of October 2 and 17, 1941, February 4, 1942. Král, *Vergangenheit*, pp. 122–40, 145–48.

55. *VBlRProt* (1941), pp. 527–29, 535; Mastny, *Czechs*, pp. 187–91; Czech indictment, *IMT*, 998-PS, 26:505–11; Grant Duff, *German Protectorate*, p. 98; Luža, *Transfer*, pp. 208–9.

56. This is denied by some Czech writers, but contemporary German police records confirm Heydrich's own claims about the success of his policies. Even Luža, who tries to put Czech behavior in the best possible light, says that "the dose of Heydrich terror curbed the Czech nation but did not crush it. The Czech resistance movement was crippled, but not completely destroyed" (*Transfer*, p. 208).

57. Luža, *Transfer*, p. 209; Mastny, *Czechs*, pp. 194–96; Wighton, *Heydrich*, pp. 257–58.

58. Ziemke report, January 31, 1940, *DGFP*, D, 7:723–24; Helmut Heiber, "Zur Justiz im Dritten Reich. Der Fall Eliás," *VfZ*, 3 (1955): 275–96; Mastny, *Czechs*, pp. 187–91, 196–98; Luža, *Transfer*, pp. 203, 218, n. 60; OSS, *Protectorate*, p. 39.

59. *SGV* (1942), pp. 75–80, 551–52, 997–1003; *VBlRProt* (1942), p. 42; Jacoby, *Racial State*, pp. 65–67; Mastny, *Czechs*, pp. 158, 198–201; Luža, *Transfer*, p. 202; Král, *Vergangenheit*, pp. 141–44.

60. *SGV* (1942), pp. 792–96.

61. *RGBl* (1942) 1:329; *VBlRProt* (1942), pp. 117–22, 307–8; Mastny, *Czechs*, p. 201; Luža, *Transfer*, pp. 202–3; Jacoby, *Racial State*, pp. 67–69; OSS, *Protectorate*, p. 15.

62. *RGBl* (1941), 1:750, 913; (1942), 1:100; *VBlRProt* (1942), pp. 16–20, 61–62; Král, *Vergangenheit*, pp. 145–48, 152; Race and Resettlement Office report, June 29, 1942, *IMT*, USSR-060(a), 39:358–65; Mastny, *Czechs*, p. 202.

63. Gross affidavit, *IMT* 40:530–31; Luža, *Transfer*, pp. 190–94; Leopold Chmela, *The Economic Aspect of the German Occupation of Czechoslovakia* (Prague, 1948), p. 108; Václav Král, "The Policy of Germanization Enforced in Bohemia and Moravia by the Fascist Invaders during the Second World War," *Historica* 2 (1960):283, Grant Duff, *German Protectorate*, pp. 137, 202–3; *TWC* 13:608–9.

64. *SGV* (1942), pp. 509–18, 820–36; Czech indictment, *IMT*, 998-PS, 26:484–86; Luža, *Transfer*, 198.

452

65. *SGV* (1942), pp. 907–13, 1535–36; *VBIRProt* (1939), pp. 94–95; DDP 7:523; Král, "The Policy of Germanization," pp. 283–87; Nuremberg document NO 4021; Czech indictment, *IMT*, 998-PS, 26:470–71, 486; Luža, *Transfer*, pp. 192–93; Grant Duff, *German Protectorate*, pp. 190–91; OSS, *Protectorate*, pp. 42–44, 46.

66. *SGV* (1942), 905–13; the decrees are signed by Moravec. Jacoby, *Racial State*, p. 159.

67. *The Goebbels Diairies, 1942–1943*, ed. Louis P. Lochner (New York, 1948), pp. 35, 66, 88–89; also *Kersten Memoirs*, pp. 96–97; Mastny, *Czechs*, pp. 203–6.

68. Wighton, *Heydrich*, pp. 259–76; Alan Burgess, *Seven Men at Daybreak* (New York, 1960), pp. 134 ff.; Luža, *Transfer*, p. 210. On the problems involved in the Heydrich assassination, see Mastny, *Czechs*, pp. 207–10, a somewhat different interpretation.

69. Král, *Vergangenheit*, pp. 68, n. 14, 153, n. 40, 155, n. 41; Czech indictment, *IMT*, 998-PS, 26:511–13.

70. *VBIRProt* (1942), pp. 123, 181; report of the Reich protector's office for the period May to August 1942, *TWC*, NG 2068, 12:899–901; Mastny, *Czechs*, pp. 210–21.

71. *Hitler's Secret Conversations*, p. 522.

72. Reich protector's office report, May to August 1942, *TWC*, NG 2068, 12:899–901; Mastny, *Czechs*, p. 221.

73. Daluege arrived in Prague on May 27, 1942, after having been appointed on the basis of Hitler's oral instructions. The formal document of his appointment was not issued until May 30, 1942. Hitler's reasons for appointing Daluege are not clear. On this question, see Mastny, *Czechs*, pp. 211–12; Luža, *Transfer*, p. 213, n. 40.

74. Secret decree of August 29, 1943, on the reorganization of the office of the Reich protector, *IMT*, 1366-PS, 27:198–99; Lammers testimony, *IMT* 11:62–63; 18:187. According to a Lammers article on the government and administration of the Protectorate, dated March 1944, the changes in the German administration were initiated by a Hitler directive of August 20, 1943. The changes in the leading positions are also described in *Das Archiv*, August 1943, p. 347, partially printed in English translation in *NCA*, 3068-PS, 5:893; see also the Frick defense counsel statement, *IMT* 18:187; OSS, *Protectorate*, pp. 13, 16–20.

75. Luža, *Transfer*, p. 191; see also K. H. Frank's "secret" speech of April 1944 on Reich policy in Bohemia and Moravia. Král, *Vergangenheit*, pp. 163–73.

76. Friedrich Heiss, ed., *Das Böhmen und Mähren-Buch. Volkskampf und Reichsraum* (Prague, 1943), pp. 7, 11–12, 127–34, 412.

77. Himmler to Sollmann, June 21, 1943; Frank memorandum, June 22, 1943. Král, *Vergangenheit*, p. 159; Race and Resettlement Office report of June 29, 1942, *IMT*, USSR-060(9), 39:364; Luža, *Transfer*, p. 192.

78. Greifelt memorandum that Himmler had agreed to the settlement of one thousand German peasant families from the Dobruja in the Protectorate, May 28, 1942, T175/43/2554611–15; Steinacker to German peasant leaders in the Protectorate about the settlement of Germans from the Reich, Bessarabia, Bukovina (Buchenland), and the Dobruja in the Protectorate, August 17, 1942, T175/194/2733193–96; Luža, *Transfer*, pp. 192–94; Urban, *Hitler's Spearhead*, pp. 37–38; Král, *Vergangenheit*, pp. 19, n. 11, 160–61.

79. Korherr report, March 1943, NO 5194; *IMT* 8:299; 26:488–89; Raul Hilberg, *The Destruction of the European Jews* (Chicago, 1961), pp. 266–308; Gerald Reitlinger, *The Final Solution: The Attempt to Exterminate the Jews of Europe, 1939–1945* (New York, 1968), pp. 22–23; Heinrich Bodensieck, "Das Dritte Reich und die Lage der Juden in der Tschecho-Slowakei nach München," *VfZ* 9 (1961):249–61.

80. *VBIRProt* (1939), pp. 45–49, 281–84, 318–23; (1940), pp. 41–47, 81–82, 89, 146, 299, 507, 545; (1941), pp. 13, 35.

81. *DDP* 7:497; 8:587, 591–93; *VBIRProt* (1940), pp. 77–79; (1941), 469–70, 555–56, 642–44; (1942), pp. 91–92, 215.

82. The law of July 4, 1939, was published on April 24, 1940. *SGV* (1940), pp. 385–402, with supplements in 1942, pp. 565–70, 766–69, 1257–61; Luža, *Transfer*, p. 195, n. 34; *IMT* 26:488–89; Jacoby, *Racial State*, pp. 89–90, 118, 140–43.

83. *VBIRProt* (1942), pp. 38–40; Heydrich planning meeting, October 17, 1941, Král, *Vergangenheit*, pp. 135–36; *IMT* 26:488–89; Jacoby, *Racial State*, p. 241.

84. Korherr report, March 1943, NO 5194; Hilberg, *Destruction*, p. 283; Mastny, *Czechs*, pp. 90, 112, 191–92.

85. Decree of March 16, 1939. *RGBl* (1939) 1:485. On German economic policy, see Mastny, *Czechs*, chap. 4.

86. Article by Hans Kehrl, an official of the Reich Ministry of Economics and the Four-Year Plan, in *Der Vierjahresplan*, April 20, 1939; by the same author, "Das Protektorat im grossdeutschen Wirtschaftsraum," *Zeitschrift des Vereins Berliner Kaufleute und Industrieller* 22 (1941):19–23; Erich von Wedelstädt, "Die wirtschaftliche Eingliederung des Protektorats," *Die deutsche Volkswirtschaft* 9 (1940):290–83; see also the documents relating to economic policy on film in the National Archives, T77/657/1857841–76.

87. Göring conference, July 27, 1939, *IMT* 38:367–70.

88. For example, the remarkable proposal of Dr. Bernhard Adolf, chairman of the Federation of Industries in the Protectorate. Král, *Vergangenheit,* pp. 98–108.

53   89. *VBIRProt* (1939), pp. 56–57; OSS, *Protectorate,* pp. 6–8, 51–52; Král, *Vergangenheit,* p. 104, n. 23.

90. *VBIRProt* (1939), pp. 107–10; (1940), pp. 5–6, 85, 149; (1941), pp. 155–56; (1942), pp. 305–6; OSS, *Protectorate,* pp. 52–56.

91. *SGV* (1939), pp. 331–33, 371–72, 487, 538–43; (1940), pp. 481–524, 735–37; *VBIRProt* (1939), pp. 39–43, 227–28; (1940), pp. 6–12; *RGBl* (1939) 1:1012; (1940) 1:43; Jacoby, *Racial State,* chap. 10.

54   92. *SGV* (1939), pp. 385–93, 441–43, 658–59; (1940), pp. 425–31; OSS, *Protectorate,* pp. 54–55; Jacoby, *Racial State,* pp. 186–87; Raphaël Lemkin, *Axis Rule in Occupied Europe: Laws of Occupation, Analysis of Government, Proposals for Redress* (Washington, D.C., 1944), pp. 136–37; Luža, *Transfer,* pp. 196–97; *IMT* 26:485.

93. *SGV* (1942), pp. 75–80; Luža, *Transfer,* pp. 197, 202; *IMT* 26:484–86; OSS, *Protectorate,* p. 38.

94. *SGV* (1939), pp. 439, 523–24, 533–35; (1941), pp. 111, 1481–84; (1942), pp. 75–80, 757–60, 1427–28; *RGBl* (1939) 1:237, 1998; (1942) 1:179–80; *VBIRProt* (1939), pp. 181–83; *DGFP,* D, 4:215; Luža, *Transfer,* pp. 197, n. 45, 198, n. 50; Grant Duff, *German Protectorate,* pp. 135–50; Mastny, *Czechs,* p. 80.

95. *RGBl* (1939), 1:555; *SGV* (1939), pp. 367–69, 447–60; Luža, *Transfer,* pp. 195–96; Jacoby, *Racial State,* pp. 56–57, 180–81; Grant Duff, *German Protectorate,* pp. 132–35; Král, *Vergangenheit,* p. 104, n. 22; and especially Chmela, *Economic Aspect,* pp. 40–41.

55   96. Král, "The Policy of Germanization," pp. 295, 297, n. 53; Enno Georg, *Die Wirtschaftlichen Unternehmungen der SS* (Stuttgart, 1963), pp. 72–83.

97. *RGBl* (1940) 1:1238, 1240; *VBIRProt* (1939), p. 92; (1940), pp. 467–72; *DDP* 8:587, 594; Neurath testimony, *IMT* 17:12–13; Burgsdorff testimony, *IMT* 12:60–61; Chmela, *Economic Aspect,* pp. 141–59; Jacoby, *Racial State,* pp. 183–84.

98. Ministry of the Interior order, September 2, 1941. Reich Chancellery file RK 1340, WF 5246H/E311507–508.

99. In 1943 Karl Hermann Frank was annoyed to see that his senior SS and police officer for Bohemia and Moravia was included in the list of officials of occupied territories; he reminded police headquarters that the Protectorate was Reich territory and that, therefore, its police officials should be included on the list of the officials of the Reich. T175/119/2645220.

100. Picker, *Hitlers Tischgespräche,* pp. 162, 256, 333, 349, 359, 363, 434–35; *Hitler's Secret Conversations,* pp. 237–38, 263, 385, 464–65, 522.

56   101. This was the so-called Žilina (Sillein) agreement. Mastny, *Czechs,* p. 24.

102. *DGFP,* D, 4, chap. 1.

103. *DGFP,* D, 6:10–11. On the background of the breakup of Czechoslovakia, see the first volume of this work, pp. 101–18; on Germany's relations with Slovakia in particular, see Milan S. Ďurica, *La Slovacchia e le sue relazione politiche con la Germania, 1938–1945,* vol. 1, *Dagli Accordi di Monaco all'inizio della seconda Guerra Mondiale (Ottobre 1938–Settembre 1939)* (Padua, 1964); and Jörg K. Hoensch, *Die Slowakei und Hitlers Ostpolitik. Hlinkas Slowakische Volkspartei zwischen Autonomie und Separation, 1938/1939* (Cologne, 1965).

57   104. *DGFP,* D, 4:6, 118–27; 5:78–83.

105. Gilbert L. Oddo, *Slovakia and Its People* (New York, 1960), p. 261, drawing on the account of Sidor.

106. *DGFP,* D, 4:251–55; Jozef Lettrich, *History of Modern Slovakia* (New York, 1955), p. 142; Lemkin, *Axis Rule,* pp. 352–53.

58   107. *RGBl* (1939) 2:606; *DGFP,* D, 6:42–45; Lettrich, *Slovakia,* pp. 137–39.

108. Hitler directive, March 25, 1939. *IMT,* 100-R, 38:274–76; *DGFP,* D, 6:117–19.

109. Unsigned list of OKW requirements, April 15, 1939; unsigned memorandum on conference with Slovak ministers, April 19, 1939. *DGFP,* D, 6:254–55, 294–95.

110. *DGFP,* D, 6:890, n. 2.

111. Ibid., 7:50, where microfilm numbers of the complete document are cited. Film in the National Archives.

59   112. Ibid., 7:108, 172–74, 229–30, 252–53, 303, 395–96.

113. Ibid., 7:252–53, 458–59.

114. Ibid., 7:172–74, 395–96.

115. Hitler's instructions for the conduct of German troops in Slovakia, August 25, 1939. T77/545/1720388–93.

116. Lettrich, *Slovakia,* pp. 160–61.

60   117. Hewel memorandum, October 21, 1939. The treaty reuniting Slovakian territories lost to Poland in 1920, 1924, and 1938 was signed November 21, 1939. *DGFP,* D, 8:326–29, 436–37.

118. *DGFP,* D, 10:16–18, 375, n. 1; 11:870–71; Andreas Hillgruber, *Hitler, König Carol*

und Marschall Antonescu. Die deutsch-rumänischen Beziehungen, 1938–1944 (Wiesbaden, 1954), p. 117, nn. 39 and 40.

119. On this problem in general, see Hans-Adolf Jacobsen, *Nationalsozialistische Aussenpolitik, 1933–1938* (Frankfurt am Main, 1968), pp. 464–77.

61 120. *DGFP*, D, 6:114–15; 10:16–18.

121. Ibid., 6:254–55; 10:17, nn. 2 and 3; Lemkin, *Axis Rule*, pp. 357–58; Lettrich, *Slovakia*, pp. 171–73.

122. *DGFP*, D, 8:476–77; *IMT*, 2794-PS, 31:124–25; Lettrich, *Slovakia*, p. 168.

123. *DGFP*, D, 9:166, 420, 537–40; Lettrich, *Slovakia*, p. 165.

62 124. *DGFP*, D, 10:16–18.

125. July 22, 1940. Ibid., 10:268–69.

126. Ibid., 10:173, 268–69, 284. On German negotiations in Southeastern Europe at this time, see vol. 1 of this work, chap. 17.

63 127. *DGFP*, D, 10:284, n. 2, 345–48; Jozef Tiso, *Die Wahrheit über die Slowakei* (Munich, 1948), p. 41; Joseph Mikus, *Slovakia: A Political History, 1918–1950* (Milwaukee, Wisc., 1963), p. 120; Lettrich, *Slovakia*, pp. 165–66.

128. *DGFP*, D, 10:284, n. 2, 375, n. 1.

129. Ribbentrop to Killinger, July 29, 1940. Ibid., 10:375–76.

130. The alliance between Germany, Italy, and Japan, signed September 27, 1940; adhered to by Hungary, November 20, Rumania, November 23, and Slovakia, November 24.

131. Killinger report, August 19, 1940. NG 2674; Ribbentrop-Tuka conference, November 24, 1940. *DGFP*, D, 11:693–98.

64 132. Ludin to the Foreign Office, June 21, 1941; Ribbentrop to Ludin, June 22, 1941. *DGFP*, D, 12:1059–60, 1081. Slovakia's declaration of war on the United States and Britain of December 12, 1941, was officially ignored by the United States government. Lettrich, *Slovakia*, pp. 168–69, 302–3.

133. *DGFP*, D, 11:870–71.

134. T175/119/2644766.

135. On January 16, 1943, Berger had informed Himmler that a German SS officer had been entrusted with the supervision of the Hlinka Guard in Slovakia, a very necessary task at this moment, and that Ludin, who had "capitulated" to the Himmler faction, was co-operating in a very satisfactory manner. Minister of the Interior Mach, who had wanted to resign, had been persuaded by Berger to remain in office. NO 3068.

136. Berger to Himmler, September 2, 1944, NO 3063; Ludin affidavit, NO 3058; Berger affidavit, NO 1785; Oddo, *Slovakia*, pp. 298–301.

137. Höffle affidavit, NO 3056.

65 138. Lettrich, *Slovakia*, pp. 308–12.

139. Exchange of letters between Horst Wagner, Foreign Office liaison man with Himmler, and Himmler's personal adjutant, SS Gruppenführer Rudolf Brandt, December 1944. NG 3490; Brandt memorandum on conference with representatives of the German Foreign Office, January 25, 1945. NG 4340.

140. According to the Slovak government's census of December 12, 1938, taken after the 1938 territorial changes.

141. *DGFP*, D, 4:40, 82–83.

142. Hilberg, *Destruction*, p. 459; Lettrich, *Slovakia*, p. 177; Mikus, *Slovakia*, p. 96.

143. Killinger to Luther, August 1, 1940. NG 4399; Wisliceny affidavit, NG 2867; Reitlinger, *Final Solution*, p. 416; Hilberg, *Destruction*, p. 459; Lettrich, *Slovakia*, p. 180.

66 144. NG 4409, *TWC* 13:230; Hilberg, *Destruction*, p. 460; Reitlinger, *Final Solution*, p. 417; Lettrich, *Slovakia*, pp. 178–79; Oddo, *Slovakia*, p. 287.

145. Wisliceny testimony, *IMT* 4:357–58, 361–63; Reitlinger, *Final Solution*, pp. 418–20; Lettrich, *Slovakia*, pp. 182–84, 303; Oddo, *Slovakia*, pp. 290–92.

146. According to statistics compiled in Himmler's office, 56,691 Jews had been removed from Slovakia as of December 31, 1942, and a further 854 by the end of March 1943. T175/103/2625029–45; Korherr report, March 1943, NO 5194; Ludin-Foreign Office telegrams, NG 4407, *TWC* 13:231–32; Tuka conference with Ludin and Wisliceny, June 26, 1942, NG 4407, 4553; Hilberg, *Destruction*, pp. 467–68; Oddo, *Slovakia*, pp. 291–92; Lettrich, *Slovakia*, p. 183.

67 147. Veesenmayer memorandum, December 22, 1943, NG 4651; Höttl affidavit, NG 2317; Hilberg, *Destruction*, pp. 471–73; Reitlinger, *Final Solution*, pp. 421–25.

148. This figure, based on estimates given by Nazi officials, who generally exaggerated the effectiveness of their actions, is a good deal higher than the estimates in Hilberg, *Destruction*, p. 767, or in Reitlinger, *Final Solution*, p. 537. Estimates vary considerably depending on whether they are based on pre- or post-Munich Slovakia.

149. See above, p. 65.

4. THE SLAVS: POLAND

68   1. On the Nazi occupation of Poland, see the authoritative monograph of Martin Broszat, *Nationalsozialistische Polenpolitik, 1939–1945* (Stuttgart, 1961).
    2. See the first volume of this study, chap. 12.
    3. Schulenburg, the German ambassador to the Soviet Union, to the Foreign Office, September 17, 1939, *DGFP*, D, 8:79–80; treaty of September 28, 1939, with three additional secret protocols, ibid., pp. 164–66; supplementary protocol of October 4, 1939, defining the boundaries between the German and Russian sectors of Poland, ibid., pp. 208–12. See map, p. 69.

70   4. Broszat, *NS Polenpolitik*, p. 26. In his testimony at Nuremberg, Frank said that Hitler had appointed him civil governor of the occupied Polish territories on September 16 or 17, 1939 (*IMT* 12:6, 26); in January 1940 he informed his senior officials that Hitler had given him this assignment on September 15 (Frank diary, *IMT* 29:368–69).
    5. Führer directive no. 5, September 30, 1939, *DGFP*, D, 8:176–77.
    6. Hitler's original order called for the decree to go into effect November 1, a date changed later to October 26. Broszat, *NS Polenpolitik*, pp. 30–31.

71   7. Decree of October 8, 1939. *RGBl* (1939) 1:2042, 2057, 2108, 2133, 2135; (1940) 1:251, 832; *DDP* 7:668; Broszat, *NS Polenpolitik*, pp. 29–30, 33–34.
    8. *RGBl* (1939) 1:2077–78. On October 12 the British had brusquely rejected Hitler's peace offer, thereby evidently convincing him that, for the time being at least, there was no possibility of bargaining with the Western powers over Poland. Hitler did, however, leave the boundaries and the legal status of the Government General vague, perhaps in the hope that this territory might yet be used for purposes of negotiation.
    9. On November 21, 1939, a treaty was concluded between Slovakia and Germany giving Slovakia fifty-two communities (*Gemeinden*) which had been incorporated into Poland in 1920, 1924, and 1938, plus a narrow strip of territory along the Polish-Slovakian border (*DGFP*, D, 8:436–37). After the German attack on Russia, the Polish province of Bialystok was placed under the administration of the government of East Prussia (July 22, 1941. T77/545/1720437–38), while the district of Galicia was placed under the administration of the Government General (August 1, 1941. *VBlGG* [1941], p. 443). See below, p. 89.
    10. *RGBl* (1939) 1:3063; *VBlDg* (1939), p. 61; *VBlPolen* (1939), pp. 2–3, 7, 10–11, 21, 23; *VBlW* (1939), p. 9.

72   11. *RGBl* (1939) 1:2108, 2125, 2467; (1940) 1:707, 832, 844, 956; (1941) 1:297, 756–61; (1942) 1:166.
    12. *RGBl* (1940) 1:174; *VBlW* (1939), pp. 9, 12; *VBlGG* (1939), p. 55.
    13. *RGBl* (1939) 1:2133.
    14. On Himmler's Commission for the Consolidation of the German People, see the first volume of this work, pp. 55–56; and Robert L. Koehl, *RKFDV: German Resettlement and Population Policy, 1939–1945, A History of the Reich Commission for the Strengthening of Germandom* (Cambridge, Mass., 1957).
    15. Frick speech of November 2, 1939. *DDP* 7:599, n. 1, 687.
    16. The continued authority of the army in the realm of military affairs in areas under civil administration was specifically emphasized in all the decrees setting up these administrations.

73   17. Cited in document *TWC, EC-410*, 13:719.
    18. *TWC*, E-410, 13:718–21.
    19. *VBlGG* (1939), p. 36; Dr. Plodeck, "Die Treuhandstelle im Generalgouvernement," in Max du Prel, ed., *Das General-gouvernement* (Würzburg, 1942), pp. 110–14.
    20. Himmler order (not to be published) of December 16, 1939. T74/16/388187–89; *DOT* 5:207–9.
    21. June 12, 1940. *Deutsche Reichsanzeiger und Preussische Staatsanzeiger*, no. 260/39, of June 17, 1940; *VBlDg* (1940), pp. 441–42.
    22. Order of February 17, 1941. *VBlDg* (1941), p. 237.

74   23. See above, n. 14.
    24. *Mein Kampf* (New York, 1939), vol. 1, chap. 11; vol. 2, chap. 14; and elsewhere; *Hitler's Secret Book* (paperback, New York, 1961), pp. 45, 47–48, and elsewhere.
    25. Notes for the diary of Admiral Canaris, chief of the German counterintelligence (*Abwehr*), by General Erwin Lahousen, chief of Section 2 of the Abwehr, on a conference with Hitler in the Führer's train at Ilnau, September 12, 1939. Hitler's statements were recorded verbatim, but on the basis of notes written from memory. *NCA*, 3047-PS, 5:766–76 (English translation); German copy of document in Staatliches Archivlager, Göttingen, Lu 4, 14. See Lahousen's testimony, *IMT* 2:445–48. General Halder recorded in his diary on September 19 that Heydrich used almost the same words in describing the tasks of his forces: *"Flurbereinigung: Judentum, Intelligenz, Geistlichkeit, Adel* [Housecleaning: Jews, intelligentsia, clergy, nobility]" (Franz Halder, *Kriegstagebuch. Tägliche Aufzeichnungen*

des Chefs des Generalstabes des Heeres, 1939–1942, ed. Hans-Adolf Jacobsen, 3 vols. [Stuttgart, 1962–64], 1:79).

75   26. Oral report of September 22, 1939, by Major Radke of the Army General Staff on a conference with Brauchitsch and Heydrich (Staatliches Archivlager, Göttingen, Lu 4, 14b). See also Heydrich conference with senior SS officers, September 27, 1939 (Staatliches Archivlager, Göttingen, Lu 7, 1); army reports on the excesses of the SS (*IMT,* 419-D, 35:87–91); and a group of reports filed under Nuremberg document NO 3011.

   27. Alfred Rosenberg, *Das politische Tagebuch Alfred Rosenbergs aus den Jahren 1934/35 und 1939/40,* ed. Hans-Günther Seraphim (Göttingen, 1956), p. 81; Hitler's talk with Keitel, October 17, 1939, *IMT,* 864-PS, 26:378–79.

76   28. May 12, 1942. *Hitler's Secret Conversations, 1941–1944* (paperback, New York, 1961), pp. 441–46; Henry Picker, *Hitlers Tischgespräche im Führerhauptquartier, 1941–1942,* ed. Percy Ernst Schramm, Andreas Hillgruber, and Martin Vogt (Stuttgart, 1965), p. 330. In a speech to his officers of May 26, 1944, Hitler was still pursuing the same ideological line (T175/94/2614900–967).

   29. The following summary of Himmler's ideas is based on a memorandum entitled *Planungsgrundlagen für den Aufbau der Ostgebiete* (Basic Plans for the Reconstruction of the Eastern Territories) from the RFSS/RKFDV, with cover note dated March 8, 1940, stating that "these basic plans can be regarded as temporary guidelines for the future work of the Reichskommissar for the consolidation of the German people" (T77/4/717464–86); on a memorandum of May (?) 1940 entitled *Einige Gedanken über die Behandlung der Fremdvölkischen im Osten* (Some Reflections on the Treatment of Alien Races in the East), which Himmler forwarded to the Führer on May 25, 1940 (T175/119/2645113–22; *TWC,* NO 1880–81, 13:147–51); on a memorandum of November 26, 1940, entitled *Grundsätze und Richtlinien für den ländlichen Aufbau in den neuen Ostgebieten* (Principles and Guidelines for Rural Reconstruction in the new Eastern Territories) (T77/84/808340–42).

78   30. "*Sehr gut und richtig.*" This comment refers to the memorandum, Some Reflections on the Treatment of Alien Races in the East (see n. 29), and is reported in a Himmler memorandum of May 28, 1940 (T175/119/2645120–22).

79   31. See Broszat, *NS Polenpolitik,* p. 2.

   32. October 30, 1939. T175/194/2732983 ff.; Nuremberg documents NO 4059 and NO 5586; Frank diary, entry for October 31, 1939, *IMT* 29:358–59; Broszat, *NS Polenpolitik,* pp. 38–48, 86.

   33. This population transfer had been arranged by a confidential protocol of September 28, 1939, accompanying the German-Soviet boundary treaty of the same day. *DGFP,* D, 8:164–65.

   34. Weizsäcker telegram of September 28, 1939, *DGFP,* D, 8:162; H. von Rimscha, "Zur Umsiedlung der Deutschen aus den baltischen Staaten während des zweiten Weltkriegs," *Osteuropa* 11 (1961):134–36.

   35. Himmler orders of October 11, 1939 (NO 4613, NO 5026), and especially Himmler's order of December 16, 1939 (*DOT* 5:207–9).

80   36. Himmler's general orders and guidelines, October 1939 (NO 4059, a document certified by SS Sturmbannführer Rudolf Creutz); Himmler's order of November 3, 1939 (T175/194/2732969–70).

   37. See above, p. 40.

   38. The basic document on this entire problem is an official publication of the RKFDV of December 1940 entitled *Der Menscheneinsatz. Grundsätze, Anordnungen und Richtlinien,* published in part under document number 2916-PS, *IMT* 31:283–94, together with some of Himmler's most important decrees. The complete text of these documents is on film (T74/16/387840–967; T175/2733248 ff.). Many of Himmler's ideas and procedures appear to be based on a lengthy memorandum of November 25, 1939, prepared by members of the Racial-Political Office (*Rassenpolitisches Amt*) of the NSDAP (NO 3732).

81   39. The first order on the German National Register was published October 28, 1939, in the Warthegau (Posen), and was signed by Greiser. The drawing up of questionnaires and other procedures was described in a long memorandum which showed that the main problems were setting racial standards and securing accurate information about applicants (*DOT* 4:19–130). Two later decrees on the German National Register dealing with all incorporated Polish territories were published March 4, 1941, and January 31, 1942 (*RGBl* (1941) 1:118–20; (1942) 1:51). On February 16, 1942, Himmler issued an order that persons eligible to enroll in the German National Register and who failed to do so within eight days should be arrested and sent to a concentration camp (NO 3092, 4739, 5820; *IMT,* 112-R, 38:314–30).

   40. These procedures are described in Himmler's decree on the examination and selection (*Uberprüfung und Aussonderung*) of the population in the incorporated eastern territories of September 12, 1940 (*IMT,* 2916-PS, 31:290–94; T175/194/2733350–55).

   41. Guidelines for the Establishment and Procedures of the Supreme Examination Tribunal for Nationality Questions in the Incorporated Eastern Territories, October 31, 1941 (NO

4869); supplemented by an order of May 30, 1942 (*DOT* 5:140–42). As late as April 1943, however, Greiser was complaining to Himmler about the continued failure of these supreme racial tribunals to formulate fundamental principles for racial selection (*DOT* 5:67, n. 1, 122, n. 1).

82   42. The examination procedures were described in a memorandum sent with a covering letter of March 16, 1940, from SS Brigadeführer Otto Hofmann, acting head of the Racial Department of the Central Office for Race and Resettlement of the SS, to SS Sturmbannführer Kunzel of the Central Immigration Office (*Einwandererzentralstelle* or EWZ) (NO 4324–25). See also Himmler's directive of November 9, 1940, on the selection of Polish groups to be re-Germanized (NO 1682).

43. Greiser to Himmler, March 16, 1943, and SS Obersturmbannführer Brandt to SS Obergruppenführer Krüger, March 28, 1943, requesting guidelines on racial procedures (NO 3992); report of SS Oberführer Rudolf Creutz, deputy chief of the Central Office of the RKFDV, "On the Procedures for the Re-Germanization of Racially Valuable Persons," March 25, 1943 (NO 3996); instructions of Ulrich Greifelt, chief of the Central Office of the RKFDV, for the care of persons suitable for re-Germanization, May 17, 1943 (NO 2879).

44. See below, pp. 86–87, 90–96.

83   45. RKFDV statistics of December 1940 (NO 5150); further statistics printed in the *Völkischer Beobachter,* January 7, 1941. The figures on the number of these ethnic Germans is undoubtedly grossly exaggerated; as yet all refugees from the east claimed to be ethnic Germans and were classified as such, while Nazi officials made a habit of padding their statistics to make their work seem more effective.

46. Statistics of the chief of the Sipo and SD (Heydrich) of November 15, 1940 (T175/194/2733299). The statistics on the transfer of Poles appear to be far more reliable than those dealing with ethnic Germans.

47. Statistical survey on resettlements as of October 15, 1941 (NO 3688); of January 15, 1942 (NO 3570); Greifelt's reports to Himmler on the opposition of the Wehrmacht and other Reich agencies to resettlement policies, December 1941 and after (T175/123/2648444 ff.).

48. May 18, 1943 (T77/594/1775820). Reports of German agencies on increasing guerrilla activity, lower production, and protests against resettlement policies in general (T77/594/1775796–806).

49. Resettlement statistics as of May 1, 1942 (T175/43/2554663–92); of August 3, 1942 (T175/43/2554641–62; 2554693–724); of December 31, 1942 (T175/194/2732994–95; 2733087); of January 1944 (NO 3568). In a revealing letter to Greifelt of December 3, 1942, Himmler criticized the conduct of his resettlement officials in the Lublin district. "The entire procedure . . . also shows me that all the beautiful statistics and numbers which are submitted to me about the situation and the settlement of people [*Einsatz der Leute*] are more or less untrue" (NO 2416).

84   50. Statistics of the Central Office of the RKFDV, January 1944 (NO 3568); Greifelt-Himmler correspondence (NO 2772, 2784, 4004–6, 4867, 4878–79); Himmler speech, December 16, 1943 (T175/91/2613201–33). See also Greiser's letter to Himmler of March 7, 1944, claiming that through resettlement programs the German population of his Warthegau would soon have reached 1 million, the Jews had almost disappeared, while the Polish population had been reduced from 4.2 million to 3.5 million (NO 5503).

51. Hitler order of October 12, 1939, to come into effect October 26 (*RGBl* [1939] 1:2077); unpublished Hitler decree, October 19, 1939 (Reich Chancellery file RK 1340); Frank proclamation to the people of the Government General, October 26, 1939 (*VBlPolen* [1939], p. 1).

52. On Frank, see the brief sketch by Joachim C. Fest, *The Face of the Third Reich: Portraits of the Nazi Leadership* (New York, 1970), pp. 209–19. Frank's memoirs, *Im Angesicht des Galgens* (Munich, 1953), are unreliable but self-revealing. Far more important are the thirty-eight volumes of diaries (eleven thousand typewritten foolscap pages) which Frank kept throughout the war years. These "diaries" consist largely of transcripts of speeches, minutes of conferences, and other official records. Excerpts are printed under document number 2233-PS, *IMT* 29:356–724, and in Stanislaw Piotrowski, ed., *Hans Frank's Diary* (Warsaw, 1961). The original of the complete text is in the archives of the Polish Ministry of Justice, Warsaw. See also Frank's testimony at Nuremberg, *IMT* 12:2 ff., and Joseph Wulf, "Dr. Hans Frank, Generalgouverneur im besetzten Polen," *Das Parlament,* suppl., August 2, 1961.

53. Already on October 11, 1939, Frank informed German military administrators in Poland that in questions of planning he alone would make the decisions (T77/4–5/717433–34). In his diary, entry for October 31, 1939, Frank said that the Führer had given him full executive power in the Government General, in contrast to the limited, specialized powers of the army (*IMT* 29:361).

54. Frank speech on the authority conferred on him by Hitler, May 30, 1940 (*IMT* 29:440 ff.); *RGBl* (1939) 1:2077.

85   55. *The Goebbels Diaries, 1942–1943,* ed. Louis P. Lochner (New York, 1948), pp. 283–84; Ulrich von Hassell, *Vom andern Deutschland. Aus den nachgelassenen Tagebüchern, 1938–1944* (Zürich, 1946), pp. 112, 254.

56. Frank decree on the organization and administration of the Government General, October 26, 1939, with supplementary decrees of November 11, 1939, December 12, 1940, March 16, 1941 (*VBlGG* [1939], pp. 3, 71; [1940], 1:357–58; [1941], pp. 99–100, 561). On the administration in general, see Broszat, *NS Polenpolitik,* pp. 69–72, 81; Raul Hilberg, *The Destruction of the European Jews* (Chicago, 1961), pp. 131–32; also Seyss-Inquart's report on a journey of inspection to Poland, November 17–22, 1939, with his description of the administration of the Government General (*IMT,* 2278-PS, 30:84–101), and Seyss-Inquart's testimony, (*IMT* 15:640–41).

57. Polish law was to remain in force for the Polish population until superseded, or unless it proved contrary to the interests of the occupation government. All cases involving German citizens or German interests were to come before German courts and be judged according to German law. (*VBlGG* [1939], pp. 4, 34; [1940], pp. 57, 64). On the entire Nazi administration, see the revealing and informative work prepared under the auspices of the Frank administration, *Das General-Gouvernement,* edited by Max du Prel, which includes chapters by State Secretary Bühler, HSSPF Krüger, and other leaders of the Nazi occupation government. On the problems of law, see pp. 152–60. On the selection of Cracow as the capital of the Government General and Hitler's decision not to rebuild Warsaw, see Frank's diary (*IMT* 29:362; *DDP* 7:668).

86   58. *VBlGG* (1939), pp. 3, 7; (1940) 1:357–58; *DDP* 7:669, 682–83; du Prel, *General-Gouvernement,* pp. 51–55, 227 ff.; Broszat, *NS Polenpolitik,* pp. 72–74.

59. This problem is discussed by Broszat, *NS Polenpolitik,* pp. 30–31, 74–77.

60. *RGBl* (1939) 1:2077; *VBlGG* (1939), pp. 3, 29; Broszat, *NS Polenpolitik,* pp. 70, 80–84.

87   61. Record of Hitler's conference with Keitel on the future of Poland, October 17, 1939 (*IMT,* 864-PS, 26:377–83); Frank diary entry for January 19, 1940, describing Hitler's instructions of September 15, 1939 (*IMT* 29:368–69); Frank on Hitler's instructions for German economic policy in Poland, October 3, 1939 (*IMT,* 344-EC, 36:329–31).

62. Frank diary, May 26, 1943 (*IMT* 29:591).

63. Frank speech of May 30, 1940, describing Hitler's instructions of October and November 1939; conference of December 2, 1939 (*IMT* 29:365–66, 441).

64. In a speech to his police officers in May 1940, Frank said Hitler had informed him at the beginning of November that he intended to keep the Government General; he had purportedly discussed with Frank his intention that the future status of the Government General was not to be that of a protectorate or the like, but that it was to become an integral part of the German Reich and eventually be completely Germanized (*IMT* 29:441).

88   65. Frank to Lammers, June 25, 1940 (Reich Chancellery file RK 1343. WF 5246H/E311798–861); Broszat, *NS Polenpolitik,* p. 69; on Frank's protests about the dumping of Jews and Poles (*IMT* 29:371–73, 438–39; *DOT* 6:160, n. 6); record of conference with military leaders on March 2, 1940 (Nuremberg document EC 300).

66. The only records of Frank's conference with Hitler are Frank's descriptions of it to State Secretary Bühler and to his staff on July 10 and 12, 1940 (*DOT* 6:78–79; *IMT* 29:377–78). There is no further information about an American colony which Hitler was considering as another possible dumping ground for the Jews.

67. *DOT* 6:79–80; Hitler decree of July 31, 1940, on the reorganization of the Government General (*DDP* 8:598).

68. Frank staff conferences, September 12, October 9 and 31, 1940 (*IMT* 29:379, 408–9, 424–25); Bormann memorandum on conference with Hitler of October 2, 1940 (*IMT,* USSR-172, 39:425–29); Frank on the same conference (*IMT* 29:410–11); records of Frank's conference with Hitler, November 4, 1940 (*DOT* 6:80–83; *IMT* 29:380–81).

89   69. Frank diary, October 23, 1941 (*DOT* 6:17, n. 28; *IMT* 29:530, 538).

70. Frank diary, July 19, 1941 (*DOT* 6:20, n. 48; *IMT* 29:472, 540); on the annexation and administration of Galicia (*VBlGG* [1941], pp. 441–44).

71. Frank conferences and speeches, 1941–42 (*IMT* 29:500–505, 517, 529–30, 540–44, 570; *DOT* 6:161, n. 12).

72. Speech of December 16, 1941 (*IMT* 29:504–5).

90   73. *VBlGG* (1939), p. 1.

74. Seyss-Inquart inspection trip, November 1939 (*IMT,* 2278-PS, 30:84–101); Frank interview, February 6, 1940 (*IMT* 29:460–67; *DDP* 7:668–69); also du Prel, *General-Gouvernement,* pp. 51–55; Broszat, *NS Polenpolitik,* pp. 69–74.

75. Conferences of January 19 and March 8, 1940; comments on policy changes beginning in November 1939 (*IMT* 29:368–69, 371–73).

91   76. These views of Frank's are embodied in speeches, conference minutes, interviews, and similar records from January 1940 through 1944 (*IMT* 29:368–73, 377, 379, 381, 388, 402, 408–9, 428–38, etc.); Frank's conversations with Krüger of April 10, 1942, August 2, 1943, and January 12, 1944 (*IMT* 29:510–11, 608, 676); and the record of the con-

459

ference with the representatives of the army of March 8, 1940 (EC 300), from which the final quotation is taken.

92   77. Conferences of July 12, 1940, and December 9, 1942, and Frank's speech to administrators of the district of Lublin, July 25, 1940 (*IMT* 29:378, 405, 581–82).

78. October 11, 1939 (T77/4–5/717433–34).

79. Conferences of December 8, 1939, February 24–25, 1940 (*IMT* 29:366–67, 431–32); Göring-Frank, December 4 and 30, 1939 (Reich Chancellery file RK 1343. WF 5246H/E311760–63; DDP 7:669); Frank testimony (*IMT* 12:27–28). Göring subsequently confirmed Frank's authority in the Government General in a handsome manner (*IMT* 29:371, 438).

80. Broszat, *NS Polenpolitik*, pp. 71–77 and nn.

81. See especially the revealing record of Frank's conference with army leaders on March 8, 1940, in which he attempted to reassert his authority (EC 300).

93   82. Broszat, *NS Polenpolitik*, p. 76.

83. October 26, 1939 (*VBlGG* [1939], p. 5).

84. *VBlGG* (1939), p. 10, Broszat, *NS Polenpolitik*, pp. 77–84.

85. HSSPF proclamation of October 30, 1939 (*VBlGG* [1939], p. 16); Frank diary (*IMT*, 29:363; *DOT* 6:42, n. 23).

86. Decrees of May 6, 1940, May 7 and June 6, 1942 (*VBlGG* [1940] 1:186; [1942], pp. 263–64, 321–22); Frank testimony, *IMT* 12:8, 11, 28–29; Burgsdorff testimony, IMT 12:55–56; Bühler testimony, *IMT* 12:65–66; Bilfinger testimony, *IMT* 12:46–48.

94   87. Report of SS Brigadeführer Streckenbach on the desires of Himmler and statements of Krüger, October 31, 1939 (*IMT* 29:358–59).

88. Frank conference with his department chiefs, March 8, 1940 (*IMT* 29:371–73).

89. *IMT* 29:378, 405, 581; *DOT* 6:78–79.

90. Based on Frank's account of Hitler's statements at a conference with his department heads, November 6, 1940 (*DOT* 6:80–83).

91. Based on Krüger's oral report of the January 8 conference with Heydrich, January 15, 1941, and on a written report on the conference dated January 13, 1941, signed by *Abteilungspräsident* Westerkamp, a department chairman in the administration of the Government General, who had attended the conference with Krüger (*IMT* 29:482–91).

92. Conference of the Government General administration, January 15, 1941 (*IMT* 29:484–87).

95   93. *IMT* 29:470, 492, 498.

94. Krüger to Greifelt, November 25, 1941 (NO 5719). This claim followed an extensive effort on the part of Frank to reassert the authority of his own office over the Himmler organizations (Reich Chancellery file RK 1341, WF, serial 5246H).

95. Bühler letter of January 30, 1942 (Reich Chancellery file RK 1340. WF 5246H/E311561–62).

96. Lammers record of the conference of March 5, 1942 (RK file 1341. WF 5246H/E311654–55); Himmler record of the March 5 conference (NG 3333; Staatliches Archivlager, Göttingen, Lu 9, 8).

96   97. Frank conference with his department chairmen, March 13, 1942 (*DOT* 6:161, n. 12; *IMT* 29:506 ff.).

98. Lammers-Himmler letter of March 7, 1942, enclosing a draft of a Hitler decree corresponding to the agreement reached on March 5 (NG 3391); text of the decree, dated May 7, 1942 (*RGBl* [1942] 1:293–94; *VBlGG* [1942], pp. 263–64).

99. *IMT* 12:9–10.

100. Frank memorandum on conditions in the Government General since September 1, 1942 (*IMT* 29:559–61, 581–82); Frank testimony (*IMT* 12:144).

101. *DOT* 6:208–9. In letters to Himmler of July 7, 1942, Creutz made detailed proposals about the use of the Government General as a resettlement area (*TWC*, NO 4876, 4:867–69; T175/66/2582225–26).

102. Report on conferences of June 18 and August 4, 1942, IMT, 29:542–43, 569–72; *TWC*, NO 4876, 4:867–69; T175/66/258225–56.

97   103. Himmler order 17c, November 12, 1942 (NO 2785; T175/194/2733190–92); RKFDV order 83/I, December 9, 1942 (NO 4393; T175/194/2733124); report on conference of January 25, 1943 (*IMT* 29:635–54).

104. Letter of February 24, 1943 (NO 2418). A whole series of similar complaints from the top German administrators in the Government General are available on film (T77/594/1775757 ff.).

105. *Goebbels Diaries*, p. 396.

106. Berger to Himmler, June 17, 1942 (NO 2455).

98   107. Greifelt memorandum of May 12, 1943, on Himmler's decisions (NO 3173, 3181; T175/43/2554595–608); SS Obersturmbannführer Dr. Hans Weibgen to Brückner, June 30, 1943, on the campaign to regain ethnic Germans in the Government General (NO 5835). The estimates on the number of Jews and ethnic Germans were both grossly exaggerated.

108. Frank to Hitler, May 25, 1943 (NO 2202).

109. Lammers to Himmler, June 4, 1943 (NO 2202); Frank to Hitler, June 19, 1943 (*IMT*, 437-PS, 26:14–37).

99
110. Frank to Lammers, July 17, 1943 (Reich Chancellery file RK 1341. WF 5246H/E311632). In an oral report to a staff conference on July 22, 1943, Frank gave the date of his conference with Himmler as June 23 (*IMT* 29:628).
111. Himmler to Frank, July 3, 1943 (*TWC*, NO 2444, 4:868–70; T175/67/2583786–88).
112. Himmler to Frank, August 16, 1943 (Reich Chancellery file RK 1341. WF 5246H/E311636). On Frank's measures in the Warsaw ghetto, see below pp. 103–4.
113. Himmler to Koppe, October 22, 1943 (Reich Chancellery file RK 1341. WF 5246H/E311751). Koppe was to take over Krüger's positions officially on November 9, 1943. The official Hitler order was dated November 12, 1943 (WF 5246H/E311755). On the departure of Krüger, *IMT* 29:616–17.

100
114. Frank to Lammers, November 22, 1943 (RK 1341. WF 5246H/E311758).
115. On the tragic incident of the Warsaw uprising and the end of German rule, see Hans Roos, *A History of Modern Poland* (New York, 1966), pp. 194–208.
116. On June 11, 1943, Himmler had issued an order opposing the establishment of Polish formations to fight against the Russians. When Frank protested, Hitler informed Himmler that he agreed completely with his order of June 11 and authorized him to inform Frank to this effect (T175/94/2615096–97). Frank had suggested the possibility of enlisting Poles in the fight against Bolshevism in his letter to Hitler of June 19, 1943, to take advantage of Polish indignation over the discovery of the mass graves of Polish officers at Katyn, where, according to all available evidence, they were murdered by the Russians (*IMT*, 437-PS, 26:14–37).
117. SS report on resettlements, January 1944 (NO 3568); see also Frank's comments on the program (*IMT* 29:676, 679).
118. *VBlGG* (1939), p. 6; supplementary decrees of December 11 and 12, 1939, pp. 231, 246.

101
119. *VBlGG* (1939), pp. 61, 71–72, 231; (1940), 1:31–35, 231–32, 258, 288; (1940), 2:249, 387; (1941), pp. 211–12, 595; (1942), pp. 665–66, 683–86.
120. SS Brigadeführer Streckenbach reporting on Himmler's orders on the Jewish question, October 31, 1939 (*IMT* 29:358–59); Krüger statements on Jewish policy in the Government General, November and December 1939 (*IMT* 29:358–59, 363, 367).
121. Frank conference with his department chiefs, April 12, 1940 (*IMT* 29:374–75).
122. Frank conference with his department chiefs, July 12, 1940; speech to German officials, July 25, 1940 (*IMT* 29:378, 405).
123. *IMT* 29:378–80.
124. The reports of Krüger and Westerkamp on the conference in the RSHA of January 8, 1941 (*IMT* 29:482–85, 487–91).

102
125. See above, pp. 5–9.
126. The Ostland was one of the major German administrative districts in Eastern Europe consisting of the Baltic states (Estonia, Latvia, Lithuania) and White Russia. See below, pp. 357–59.
127. Frank's statements at conference of December 16, 1941 (*IMT* 29:502–3). Frank's figures on the number of Jews in the Government General were greatly exaggerated.
128. See above, pp. 7–8.

103
129. Bühler's statements at the Wannsee conference, January 20, 1942 (NG 2586G).
130. See above, pp. 8–9.
131. *Goebbels Diaries*, pp. 147–48; Helmut Krausnick, Hans Buchheim, Martin Broszat, Hans-Adolf Jacobsen, *Anatomy of the SS State* (New York, 1968), pp. 103–4.
132. Himmler-Krüger order, July 19, 1942 (T175/122/2647914).
133. Conference on police matters, June 18, 1942 (*IMT* 29:570–73); *Monatsberichte Distrikt Warschau*, August 15, 1942 (*DOT* 6:465, n. 49, 632); Theodor Ganzenmüller, state secretary of the Transport Ministry, to SS Obergruppenführer Karl Wolff, the head of Himmler's personal staff, July 28, 1942 (NO 2207); Krausnick, *Anatomy*, p. 104.

104
134. Himmler to Krüger, January 1943 (NO 1882; Staatliches Archivlager, Göttingen, Lu 2, 29a).
135. Report on the destruction of the Warsaw ghetto, May 16, 1943, with pictures (*IMT*, 1061-PS, 26:628–93); Himmler-Krüger order, February 16, 1943; Himmler-Pohl order, June 11, 1943 (NO 2494, 2496, 2514; *TWC* 5:621–23); Hilberg, *Destruction*, pp. 323–26; Gerald Reitlinger, *The Final Solution: The Attempt to Exterminate the Jews of Europe, 1939–1945* (New York, 1968), chap. 11, pt. 1.
136. Frank conference with SS Obergruppenführer von dem Bach-Zelewski, Himmler's special plenipotentiary for security and resettlement questions, August 2, 1943; Frank speech of January 25, 1944 (*IMT* 29:608, 678).

5. THE NORDICS: SCANDINAVIA

106
1. On Hitler's decision to control Scandinavia, see the first volume of this study, chap. 13; Walther Hubatsch, *"Weserübung." Die deutsche Besetzung von Dänemark und Norwegen, 1940* (Göttingen, 1962), which includes a valuable selection of documents; the somewhat different interpretation in the valuable study of Hans-Dietrich Loock, *Quisling,*

Rosenberg und Terboven. Zur Vorgeschichte und Geschichte der nationalsozialistischen Revolution in Norwegen (Stuttgart, 1970); and for military problems in general, Earl F. Ziemke, *The German Northern Theater of Operations, 1940–1945* (Washington, D.C., 1959).

2. Keitel directives of April 2, 1940 (*DGFP*, D, 9:67–72).

107 3. Falkenhorst directives for the occupation of Denmark and Norway, March 13, 1940 (*IMT*, 119-C, 34:365–80).

4. Renthe-Fink to the German Foreign Office, April 9 and 10, 1940 (*DGFP*, D, 9:102–3, 107–8, 127–28).

5. Keitel to the Führer's deputy and the highest Reich authorities, April 9, 1940 (*DGFP*, D, 9:112–15).

6. Memorandum by an official of the Cultural Policy Department, April 9, 1940 (*DGFP*, D, 9:115).

108 7. Ribbentrop to Renthe-Fink, April 12, 1940 (*DGFP*, D, 9:141–42).

8. Weizsäcker-Lammers letters to clarify the position of Renthe-Fink, December 20, 1940 (*Documents on International Affairs, 1939–1946*, vol. 2, *Hitler's Europe*, ed. Margaret Carlyle [London, 1954], pp. 213–14); analysis by Dr. Werner Best of the position of the German minister and plenipotentiary in Denmark, August–September 1941 (T501/101/1348–52).

9. Renthe-Fink reports of April 10 and 15, and May 10, 1940 (*DGFP*, D, 9:119–20, 177–81, 319–20); Sten Gudme, *Denmark: Hitler's "Model Protectorate"* (London, 1942), p. 40.

109 10. Renthe-Fink report, June 22, 1940 (*DGFP*, D, 9:685–87).

11. *DGFP*, D, 10:192–94, 234–37; 11:366–70, 909–10, 1103; 13:797, 887–91; Gudme, *Denmark*, pp. 53–54; OSS, *Denmark*, pp. 21–22.

12. March 22, 1941 (NO 029).

110 13. Raphaël Lemkin, *Axis Rule in Occupied Europe: Laws of Occupation, Analysis of Government, Proposals for Redress* (Washington, D.C., 1944), pp. 160, 381–83.

14. Ribbentrop memorandum for the Führer, November 11, 1941; Foreign Office memorandum, November 17, 1941 (*DGFP*, D, 13:795–98).

15. Wolff to Best, November 5, 1941 (T175/59/257562–63).

111 16. Remarks of February and June, 1942 (*Hitler's Secret Conversations, 1941–1944* [paperback, New York, 1961], pp. 332, 490).

17. Viscount Chilston, "Denmark," in *Hitler's Europe*, ed. Arnold and Veronica Toynbee (London, 1954), pp. 526–27.

18. Ulrich von Hassell, *Vom andern Deutschland. Aus den nachgelassenen Tagebüchern, 1938–1944* (Zürich, 1946), p. 362.

112 19. Foreign Office memorandum on Hanneken's account of the oral instructions he had received from Hitler on October 1, 1942 (NG 3918); Grundherr memorandum of October 3, 1942 (*Documents on International Affairs, 1939–1946* vol. 2, pp. 219–21).

20. Best's notification of his appointment, November 4, 1942 (NG 5335); Best personnel file (T175/59/2575550–51).

21. Best to Ribbentrop, November 8, 1942 (NG 5824).

22. Stutterheim memorandum explaining the position of Best to the head of the foreign affairs department of the Reich labor leader, January 8, 1943 (NG 3193).

23. Best testimony, *IMT* 20:123 ff.

113 24. Hans Bernd Gisevius, *To the Bitter End* (Boston, 1947), pp. 183–85; Hassell, *Vom andern Deutschland*, pp. 317, 362; *The Goebbels Diaries, 1942–1943*, ed. Louis P. Lochner (New York, 1948), pp. 426, 475.

25. Ribbentrop to Himmler, September 1, 1941 (T175/59/2575579); Best-Wolff correspondence, November 1941 (T175/59/2575562–63, 2575566–72); Himmler to Berger, November 21, 1942 (T175/59/2575554); Berger to Himmler, November 24, 1942 (NO 2215). It is possible that Ribbentrop selected Best for the position in Denmark because he knew of his quarrel with Himmler, but I have found no specific evidence on this point.

26. Berger-Himmler correspondence, November 1942 (T175/59/257552–54); Best to Himmler, April 3, 1943 (T175/59/2575538–39); cover letter and Best's report for Himmler of May 5, 1943 (T175/119/2644941–59).

27. T175/59/2575540; T175/67/2583301; *IMT* 26:263.

114 28. Best report of May 5, 1942, T175/118/2644959.

29. January 28, 1943 (NG 5121).

30. *IMT* 6:506; 38:669; T175/17/2521012; OSS, *Denmark* (Washington, D.C., 1945), p. 39.

31. May 5, 1943 (T175/119/2644941–59).

32. Best to Himmler, August 22, 1943 (T175/59/2575530–33); Lemkin, *Axis Rule*, p. 164; OSS, *Denmark*, pp. 68–76; *IMT* 38:631, 670.

115 33. T175/59/2575530–33.

34. Best to Himmler, August 30, 1943 (T175/59/2575534–37).

35. *IMT* 6:506–8; 38:633, 670–72; T175/67/2583198; OSS, *Denmark*, pp. 68–76.

116 36. Best to Himmler, August 30, 1943 (T175/59/2575534–37); Best to Ribbentrop,

August 30, 1943 (NG 5702); Ribbentrop's instructions to Best, August 31, 1943 (NG 5247); Best to Ribbentrop, September 1, 1943 (NG 4562).

37. OSS, *Denmark*, pp. 10–12; Lemkin, *Axis Rule*, p. 159; Berger to Himmler, July 19, 1941 (NG 5499); *IMT* 38:632.

38. Himmler to Best, draft of letter sent in October 1943 (T175/59/2575521); *IMT* 6:508; 35:211–12; 38:632.

39. Foreign Office memorandum, December 13, 1943 (NG 5455).

40. Best to the Foreign Office, October 6, 1943 (NG 5190); IMT 35:212, 506; 38:632, 639–73, 681–90.

117

41. Best affidavit, February 15, 1947 (NO 2225); OSS, *Denmark*, pp. 79–80.

42. *IMT* 38:640–41, 644–49, 651, 658; Nuremberg document PS 1211.

43. Ribbentrop to Steengracht, May 15, 1944 (NG 4562).

44. Best report to the Foreign Office, July 2, 1944 (NG 4562); *IMT* 38:642–43.

45. Steengracht memorandum, July 30, 1944 (NG 4880).

46. T175/67/2583199; *IMT* 6:508–10; 35:211; 38:635–36, 643–44, 661–63; OSS, *Denmark*, pp. 77–86.

47. Karl Brandt, Otto Schiller, Franz Ahlgrimm, *Management of Agriculture and Food in the German-Occupied and Other Areas of Fortress Europe: A Study in Military Government* (Stanford, Calif., 1953), pp. 299–311; OSS, *Denmark*, pp. 54–67; *IMT* 34:213–14.

119

48. *IMT* 5:536–41; 35:213–14; *NCA* 7:274–75; Lemkin, *Axis Rule*, pp. 161–62.

49. *DGFP*, D, 9:177–81; 10:248–49, 296–97, 385–89, 531–34.

50. George H. Stein, *The Waffen SS: Hitler's Elite Guard at War, 1939–45* (Ithaca, N.Y., 1966), pp. 94, 139, 153–57, 162, 208; OSS, *Denmark*, pp. 36–44; *DGFP*, D, 9:287; NG 5499; T175/104/2626381; T175/110/2634700.

51. Berger-Himmler reports (T175/67/2583353, 2583357–59); *DGFP*, D, 13:795–98.

120

52. Berger to Himmler, September 26, 1943 (T175/17/2521032–33).

53. Himmler to Müller, October 6 (?), 1942 (T175/18/2521976); Raul Hilberg, *The Destruction of the European Jews* (Chicago, 1961), pp. 357–63; Gerald Reitlinger, *The Final Solution: The Attempt to Exterminate the Jews of Europe, 1939–1945* (New York, 1968), pp. 370–76.

54. January 28, 1943 (NG 5121, 4807).

55. Memorandum on Best's attitude toward the Jewish question in Denmark, January 28, 1943; Best to Ribbentrop, September 8, 1943 (NG 5121; *IMT* 35:151–60; 39:117–18); Hanneken reports, September 23, 1943 (NOKW 356); Hanneken testimony, December 10, 1947 (NG 5208); Best to the Foreign Office, September 29, 1943; Ribbentrop to Best, September 30, 1943 (NG 5105); Hanneken affidavit (NG 5206).

121

56. Best report to the Foreign Office, October 5, 1943 (NG 3920); *IMT* 38:633–34, 674–75.

57. Ribbentrop's instructions to Bräuer, April 4, 1940 (*DGFP*, D, 9:84–93); Falkenhorst proclamation, April 9, 1940 (*Norway and the War: September 1939–December 1940*, ed. Monica Curtis [London, 1941] pp. 58–59).

58. Bräuer report, April 9, 1940 (*DGFP*, D, 9:102); Falkenhorst statement, July 3, 1946 (*Trial of Nikolaus von Falkenhorst*, ed. E. H. Stevens [London, 1949], p. 256); Hewel memorandum on Hagelin's conversation with Hitler, April 13, 1940 (*DGFP*, D, 9:144–47).

59. *DGFP*, D, 9:107, 118, n. 2. For a brief sketch of Quisling, see the first volume of this work, pp. 137–38; also Loock, *Quisling*, pp. 285–89; P. M. Hayes, "Brief aperçu de l'histoire de Quisling et du gouvernement de la Norvège de 1940 à 1945," *RHDGM* 66 (1967):11–30; and the apologia by Ralph Hewins, *Quisling: Prophet without Honour* (London, 1965).

60. Bräuer report, April 10, 1940 (*DGFP*, D, 9:123–25).

61. Bräuer to the Foreign Office, April 11, 1940 (*DGFP*, D, 9:129–30).

123

62. Bräuer reports of April 11 and 13, 1940 (*DGFP*, D, 9:136–39, 142–44).

63. Memorandum of telephone conversation between Bräuer and Ribbentrop of April 14, 1940 (*DGFP*, D, 9:159–60).

64. Ribbentrop to Bräuer, April 13, 1940; Bräuer telephone message to Ribbentrop, April 14; Habicht telephone conversation with Ribbentrop, April 14; Bräuer to the Foreign Office, April 15 (*DGFP*, D, 9:152, 161–64, 176–77).

65. *DGFP*, D, 9:162–64, 168–72; Loock, *Quisling*, p. 324; Lemkin, *Axis Rule*, p. 211; OSS, *Norway* (Washington, D.C., 1943), p. 3; Halvdan Koht, *Norway: Neutral and Invaded* (New York, 1941), pp. 131–35 (by the former Norwegian foreign minister, with a long chapter on German rule in Norway).

124

66. *DGFP*, D, 9:195–97.

67. Jodl diary, April 19, 1940 (Hubatsch, *Weserübung*, pp. 376–77); *DGFP*, D, 9:209, 214–15; *Falkenhorst Trial*, p. 258; Ziemke, *German Northern Theater*, pp. 57–58; *Fuehrer Conferences on Matters Dealing with the German Navy, 1939–1945* 8 vols. (Washington, D.C., 1946–47), 1940, 1:42–43.

68. On Terboven, see Loock, *Quisling*, pp. 335–39; OSS, *Norway*, p. 4; Åke Fen, *Nazis in Norway* (London, 1943), p. 63.

125   69. *RGBl* (1940) 1:677; *VBlNorw* (1940), pp. 1–2; *DGFP*, D, 9:230–31.
    70. Terboven report to Lammers, October 17, 1940 (NG 1583); Dr. Werner Best's analysis, August–September 1941 (T175/101/1339–47); Hans Reinhard Koch, "Der Aufbau der deutschen Verwaltung in Norwegen," *RVL* 3 (1942):40–59. Koch was the head of the central department for administration of the Reichskommissar. Also Loock, *Quisling,* pp. 341–47, 361–66, which describes Terboven's administrative apparatus and staff in some detail; Lemkin, *Axis Rule,* p. 210; OSS, *Norway,* pp. 19, 112–21.
    71. *Falkenhorst Trial,* p. 258; Hassell, *Vom andern Deutschland,* p. 300; Ziemke, *German Northern Theater,* pp. 220–21.
    72. Loock, *Quisling,* p. 460 ff.
126   73. Berger to Himmler, April 18, 1943 (T175/66/2582515–16). Weitzel was killed in Düsseldorf on June 19, 1940, during a bombing attack. On the position of the SS and police in Norway, see Loock, *Quisling,* pp. 356–60; OSS, *Norway,* pp. 34–36; *Falkenhorst Trial,* p. 264.
    74. Habicht-Ribbentrop telephone conversation, April 14, 1940 (*DGFP*, D, 9:162–64); Loock, *Quisling,* pp. 432–38.
    75. Himmler to Weitzel, April 26, 1940 (T175/103/2625520–22).
    76. Koch, "Verwaltung," *RVL* 3:45–50; Best analysis, T175/101/1339–47; OSS, *Norway,* pp. 18, 25, 47–49, 51–58, 74–82; *IMT* 38:716.
127   77. *IMT* 6:513–18; 14:100–101; 38:716.
    78. *DGFP*, D, 9:263–68, 528, 535; 10:93–94, 138–41; Loock, *Quisling,* pp. 366–69.
    79. The following account of Terboven's negotiations with the Norwegians is based on Loock, *Quisling,* p. 395 ff. See also Koht, *Norway,* pp. 136–43; Hayes, "Quisling," p. 18; OSS, *Norway,* pp. 5–7; Jacob Worm-Müller, *Norway Revolts against the Nazis* (London, 1941), pp. 30–31.
129   80. Loock, *Quisling,* pp. 480–81.
    81. Rosenberg memoranda of July 2, 6, and 22, 1940 (*DGFP*, D, 10:93–95, 138–41, 272–74); Loock, *Quisling,* pp. 432 ff., 483.
    82. Memorandum of Hitler's conversation with Quisling (*DGFP*, D, 10:491–95; NG 2948). This memorandum, dated September 4, 1940, is unsigned but was presumably prepared by Hans-Wilhelm Scheidt, the director of the department for Northern Europe in Rosenberg's Office for Foreign Affairs (*Aussenpolitisches Amt*).
130   83. Telegram of August 29, 1940, from the representative of the German Foreign Office on the staff of the Reichskommissar in Norway to the Foreign Office; Hitler's original orders have not been found (*DGFP*, D, 10:581); also Koht, *Norway,* pp. 152–60.
    84. The following account of Terboven's negotiations with the Norwegians is once again based on Loock, *Quisling,* pp. 517–41.
131   85. *VBlNorw* (1940), pp. 21–22; Koht, *Norway,* pp. 160–66; *IMT,* 39:209; OSS, *Norway,* pp. 8–9; Worm-Müller, *Norway,* pp. 137–46.
    86. *VBlNorw* (1940), pp. 19–20; *Deutsche Zeitung in Norwegen,* September 27, 1940. For an official explanation of the changes, Herbert Schneider, "Staatsrechtliche Entwicklung und Verwaltungsgesetzgebung Norwegens seit dem 9. April 1940," *RVL,* 2 (1942):390–91.
132   87. *VBlNorw* (1940), pp. 21–22, 24–25; *IMT* 6:514–15. On this point, see especially Koch, "Verwaltung," *RVL* 3:52–53.
    88. The following is again based on Loock, *Quisling,* pp. 546–58; also OSS, *Norway,* pp. 30–40, 70; and especially Schneider, "Entwicklung," *RVL* 2:389.
133   89. On Lie, see Loock, *Quisling,* pp. 430 ff., 547.
    90. Quisling to Lammers, complaining about Terboven (*DGFP*, D, 12:260).
    91. *DGFP*, D, 11:398–400, 814; 12:260–65; Nuremberg document PS 009.
134   92. *VBlNorw* (1941), pp. 17–20; (1942), pp. 3–4, 11, 35–36; Terboven report to Hitler suggesting measures for combatting sabotage (*IMT,* 870-PS, 26:387–90); Keitel-Falkenhorst directive, September 13, 1941 (*Fuehrer Directives and Other Top-Level Directives of the German Armed Forces,* vol. 1, *1939–1941* [Washington, D.C., 1948], 1:210–11); *IMT* 10:647; 38:718; OSS, *Norway,* p. 19.
    93. *Fuehrer Conferences,* 1941, 2:94–95; 1942, p. 6.
    94. *VBlNorw* (1941), p. 29; *IMT* 6:514–15; OSS, *Norway,* p. 29; and especially Koch, "Verwaltung," *RVL* 3:53.
    95. *IMT* 6:516; OSS, *Norway,* p. 49.
    96. *IMT* 39:209–10; OSS, *Norway,* pp. 72–74.
135   97. *ADAP,* E, 1:465–70, 494–95.
    98. Alfred Rosenberg, *Das politische Tagebuch Alfred Rosenbergs aus den Jahren 1934/35 und 1939/40,* ed. Hans-Günther Seraphim (Göttingen, 1956), pp. 110–11; *Fuehrer Conferences,* 1940, 1:65, 67; *DGFP*, D, 11:253; Woermann memorandum on a talk with Lammers, February 20, 1942 (*ADAP,* E, 1:494–95; NG 3948); *Goebbels Diaries,* p. 83.
    99. Remarks of February and April, 1942 (*Hitler's Secret Conversations,* pp. 316–17, 383–84) .
    100. Remarks of May 1942 (*Hitler's Secret Conversations,* p. 436).
136   101. SS Standartenführer Ehlich to Himmler, July 1, 1942 (T175/122/2647878–79);

Stuckart memorandum for Himmler, September 14, 1942 (NG 4006); Lammers to Quisling, September 17, 1942 (*IMT* 41:65–66; NG 3418).

102. *VBlNorw.* These decrees are cited and summarized in OSS, *Norway*, pp. 106–9.

103. Himmler to Rediess, March 1, 1943 (T175/66/2582416–17); Berger to Himmler, November 26, 1943 (T175/66/2582429–31).

104. Berger to Himmler, March 26, 1944 (T175/66/2582390); Rediess to Himmler, December 2 and 30, 1944 (T175/66/2582374; 2582379–80); Berger to Himmler, February 6, 1945 (NG 4643).

105. There is an excellent discussion of German economic policy in Norway in Loock, *Quisling*, pp. 460–80.

106. OSS, *Norway*, pp. 56–67; OSS, *Norway: Money and Banking*, pp. 23–39, 101–10; *IMT* 5:543–48.

137   107. OSS, *Norway: Labor*, pp. 6, 18–23, 25, 29–41, 49, 72–80; *IMT* 39:213.

108. *IMT* 5:541–42; *DGFP*, D, 9:114; *Hitler's Secret Conversations*, p. 51.

109. *NCA* 7:275–76. On this point, however, see Loock, *Quisling*, p. 464.

110. Koch, "Verwaltung," *RVL* 3:42–43.

138   111. Stein, *Waffen SS*, p. 94; OSS, *Norway*, p. 59; T175/104/2626350.

112. *Deutsche Zeitung in Norwegen*, June 14, 1941; T175/66/2582560; *IMT* 38:694; OSS, *Norway*, p. 20.

113. Quisling order of July 21, 1942 (*IMT* 926-RF, 38:694–95; 717); OSS, *Norway*, pp. 60–63.

114. T175/66/2582379; 2582560; *IMT* 38:694.

139   115. Stein, *Waffen SS*, pp. 139, 154–55; Hewins, *Quisling*, p. 308.

116. Hilberg, *Destruction*, pp. 355–57; Reitlinger, *Final Solution*, p. 377; *IMT* 39:210; and unpublished Nuremberg documents NG 5217, 2461, 3516, 5027, 5088, 2586E; NO 2861, 5193–94.

140   117. Henry Picker, *Hitlers Tischgespräche im Führerhauptquartier, 1941–1942*, ed. Percy Ernst Schramm, Andreas Hillgruber, and Martin Vogt (Stuttgart, 1965), pp. 144, 254–56, 397–98; *Hitler's Secret Conversations*, pp. 51–53, 383–84, 491–92; *DGFP*, D, 11:253; Albert Speer, *Inside the Third Reich* (New York, 1970), p. 218.

6. THE NORDICS: THE NETHERLANDS AND LUXEMBOURG

141   1. In addition to the Netherlands and Luxembourg, Nazi racial theorists held that Flanders, Alsace and Lorraine, and indeed the entire border region between France and Germany was primarily Nordic in character. Logically, therefore, the chapter dealing with the Nordics of Western Europe should discuss these areas as well. At the time of the Nazi conquest, however, Flanders was part of Belgium, and Alsace and Lorraine were part of France. As the occupation of these countries presents many special problems, the discussion of Nazi policies in these areas has been included in the chapters dealing with Belgium and France. See also the introductory paragraphs to Chapter 7, below.

2. On the background of the Nazi occupation of the Netherlands, see Werner Warmbrunn, *The Dutch under German Occupation, 1940–1945* (Stanford, Calif., 1963), chap. 1; Konrad Kwiet, *Reichskommissariat Niederlande. Versuch und Scheitern nationalsozialistischer Neuordnung* (Stuttgart, 1968), pts. 1 and 2; H. L. Mason, "War Comes to the Netherlands, September 1939–May 1940," *Political Science Quarterly* 78 (1963): 548–80.

3. Brauchitsch order of May 16, 1940 (T501/93/7–9). On the same film are other documents on the German military government in the Netherlands and the final report of its leader, General Alexander von Falkenhausen, later the head of the German military government in Belgium.

142   4. Hitler decree of May 18, 1940 (*RGBl* [1940] 1:778; *VBlN* [1940], pp. 2–4).

5. On Seyss-Inquart's activity in Austria, see the first volume of this study, pp. 95–96.

6. *The Goebbels Diaries, 1942–1943*, ed. Louis P. Lochner (New York, 1948), p. 426 (entry for September 8, 1943).

7. Kwiet, *RK Niederlande*, pp. 46–48; Warmbrunn, *Dutch*, pp. 29–30; Johannes Postma, *A Reichskommissariat: German Civil Government in the Netherlands* (unpublished M.A. thesis, University of Kansas, 1964), pp. 40–49.

8. Henry Picker, *Hitlers Tischgespräche im Führerhauptquartier, 1941–1942*, ed. Percy Ernst Schramm, Andreas Hillgruber, Martin Vogt (Stuttgart, 1965), p. 360; *Hitler's Secret Conversations, 1941–1944* (paperback, New York, 1961), p. 331.

143   9. Seyss-Inquart proclamation of May 25, 1940 (*VBlN* (1940), pp. 6–8); Seyss-Inquart testimony (*IMT* 15:647–48).

10. *Das Niederlandbuch. Sammlung deutscher und niederländischer Arbeiten*, ed. Walter Söchting, forward by Seyss-Inquart (Frankfurt am Main, 1942), pp. 57–64; Jac van Essen, *Mein Holland* (Amsterdam, 1944), who states in his forward, "The author has tried to seize upon the large number of connections, still largely unrecognized in Holland or in the Reich, which illustrate the strong folkish and historical connection between Holland and the Reich. Therefore his factual account is anything but objective."

11. The legend on a map in an article by E. Müller, "Der lotharingische Grenzraum," *Monatsschrifte für das deutsche Geistesleben*, March 1939.

12. Quoted on a picture of Marnix in W. Söchting, ed., *Das Niederlandbuch*, facing p. 81.

13. In a forward to a collective work, *Die Niederlande im Umbruch der Zeiten. Alte und neue Beziehungen zum Reich*, ed. Max du Prel and Willi Janke (Würzburg, 1942).

144   14. A. Seyss-Inquart, "Die politische Aufgabe des Reichskommissars," *RVL* 2 (1942):12; Wolfgang Ispert, "Der Bruch der niederländischen Entwicklungslinie," *RVL* 3 (1942):295–314.

15. Rudolf Kroiss, "Die Verwaltung des Reichskommissars," *RVL* 2 (1942):24. The Nazis published a book of documents to prove Anglo-French aggressive plans (*Allied Intrigue in the Low Countries*, German White Book No. 5 [New York, 1940]). On the basis of the captured German documents, it is possible to see that the documents in all German White Books were not only carefully edited, but were often redated or rewritten. In this case Ribbentrop ordered a further revision of the documents because the first draft did not make the German case strongly enough; if possible he wanted the fabrication of an Anglo-French order to invade Belgium and the Netherlands (Nuremberg document PS 700).

16. Seyss-Inquart, "Die politische Aufgabe," pp. 9–10, 14.

17. Speech of May 19, 1943 (*Vier Jahre in den Niederlanden. Gesammelte Reden* [Amsterdam, 1944] p. 144).

145   18. Seyss-Inquart's report to Berlin covering the period May 29–July 19, 1940 (*IMT*, 977-PS, 26:413–29).

19. Kroiss, "Verwaltung," p. 21.

146   20. Seyss-Inquart, "Die politische Aufgabe," p. 12; report to Berlin covering May 29–July 19, 1940 (*IMT*, 997-PS, 26:413–29).

21. Two orders of June 21, 1940 (*VBIN* [1940], pp. 54–56); Winkelman was arrested on July 7 and interned in Germany (Warmbrunn, *Dutch*, pp. 35–36).

22. March 1 and August 11, 1941 (*VBIN* [1941], pp. 137–39, 637–50); Seyss-Inquart report (*IMT*, 997-PS, 26:413–29); Seyss-Inquart testimony (*IMT* 15:643, 647–48; 16:28 ff.).

23. Quoted in L. de Jong and J. W. F. Stoppelman, *The Lion Rampant: The Story of Holland's Resistance to the Nazis* (New York, 1943), p. 45.

24. Speech of May 29, 1940 (*IMT*, 3430-PS, 15:643).

147   25. Kroiss, "Verwaltung," pp. 15–52. Several articles by German administrators in the Netherlands are included in "Die Verwaltung der besetzten niederländischen Gebiete" in du Prel and Janke, eds., *Die Niederlande*, pp. 83–130; also Warmbrunn, *Dutch*, pp. 34–38.

26. Orders of May 29 and June 3, 1940 (*VBIN* [1940], pp. 8–15); Seyss-Inquart to Lammers describing his government in the Netherlands, May 31, 1940 (NG 365); Seyss-Inquart report (*IMT*, 997-PS, 26:413–29); Seyss-Inquart testimony (*IMT* 15:646–47; 16:27); Lammers testimony (*IMT* 11:100).

27. Warmbrunn, *Dutch*, pp. 33–34; Postma, *Reichskommissariat*, p. 36.

148   28. Wimmer testimony (*IMT* 16:183 ff.); Postma, *Reichskommissariat*, pp. 55–57.

29. Kwiet, *RK Niederlande*, pp. 86–91; Warmbrunn, *Dutch*, pp. 32–33, 48, 73–75, 92–95; Postma, *Reichskommissariat*, pp. 31, 57–59, 96, 102–8; letter of the Dutch Nazi Rost van Tonningen to Himmler's agent Karl Wolff (NO 4894); Bethmann, Schmidt's deputy as labor leader in the Netherlands, to Reich Labor Leader Hierl, January 5, 1943 (T175/59/2575488).

30. Kwiet, *RK Niederlande*, p. 149.

149   31. Berger to Himmler, January 16, 1943 (T175/59/2575487); documents on the reaction to Schmidt's death and Himmler's orders to Rauter (T175/59/2575483–86); Warmbrunn, *Dutch*, pp. 32–33; Postma, *Reichskommissariat*, pp. 58–60, 102–9.

32. Hitler order of May 19, 1940 (EC 178); conference at the Foreign Office, May 25, 1940 (*DGFP*, D, 9:429–31); Seyss-Inquart testimony (*IMT* 16:6–7).

33. Report of General Thomas, chief of the Wi-Rü Amt, on Göring's conference with Hitler of May 25, 1940 (EC 469); final report of the armaments inspectorate for the Netherlands (EC 329); history of the armaments inspectorate for the Netherlands, May–September, 1940 (EC 473); Georg Thomas, *Geschichte der deutschen Wehr-und Rüstungswirtschaft (1918–1943/45)* ed. Wolfgang Birkenfeld (Boppard am Rhein, 1966), pp. 217–18.

34. Göring order establishing the Zast offices, August 26, 1940; the instructions for carrying out the order were signed by Thomas (T77/564/1741928–32).

35. History of the Zast offices by the German authorities, with a complete list of statistics (T77/131/635093–203).

150   36. T77/131/635098–100.

37. Postma, *Reichskommissariat*, pp. 29–31, 94–95.

38. *VBIN* (1941), pp. 152–54; (1942), pp. 155–56; *IMT* 5:393, 483; Seyss-Inquart testimony (*IMT* 15:662–64). On September 26, 1941, Hitler himself had decided that Germany should refrain from the compulsory transfer of Dutch workers to the Reich "because there would be no satisfactory results from such a measure in any case" (*DGFP*, D, 13:598).

39. *VBIN* (1943), pp. 173–76; *IMT*, 556-PS, 26:150–51, 158–59.

151   40. Warmbrunn, *Dutch*, pp. 72–77; Postma, *Reichskommissariat*, p. 96.

41. Landfried memorandum of September 7, 1940 (NID 8245). See also T77/575/1753285–88, which is the film of a document of May (?) 1941 describing German efforts to acquire control of Dutch business enterprises.

42. *VBIN* (1940), pp. 722–24; (1941), pp. 266–67.

43. Lammers memorandum of October 18, 1941; attached to this document is a memorandum which appears to be a record of Seyss's conference with Hitler on September 25, 1941, on German economic policy in the Netherlands. Seyss's representations on this occasion were approved by Hitler (T77/175/1753391–92).

44. Himmler report, May 22, 1940 (T175/94/2615221); Himmler to Rauter, May 23, 1940 (T175/123/2649360); Seyss-Inquart testimony (*IMT* 15:703; 16:4, 35); Wimmer testimony (*IMT* 16:183–84, 208, 229); Warmbrunn, *Dutch,* pp. 30–32; Postma, *Reichskommissariat,* pp. 31–32, 49–55, 102–8.

45. Kwiet, *RK Niederlande,* pp. 58, 85–86.

46. *VBIN* (1941), pp. 190–93; Seyss-Inquart testimony (*IMT* 16:35, 112–13).

47. Hitler order of May 25, 1940, setting up the *SS Verfügungstruppe Standarte Westland* in the Netherlands (NO 5743). On the recruitment and organization of SS units in the Netherlands, see Kwiet, *RK Niederlande,* pp. 109–13, 144–46; George H. Stein, *The Waffen SS: Hitler's Elite Guard at War, 1939–1945* (Ithaca, N.Y., 1966), p. 94.

48. Warmbrunn, *Dutch,* pp. 31–32.

49. Kwiet, *RK Niederlande,* p. 95.

50. Greifelt to Himmler, June 11, 1940; Himmler to Greifelt, June 28, 1940 (T175/63/2578835–39).

51. Himmler to Hildebrandt, January 7, 1941 (Kwiet, *RK Niederlande,* p. 111); Berger to Brandt, June 3, 1943 (NO 1340); and the article by H. W. van Etten, "Naar Oostland," in du Prel and Janke, eds., *Die Niederlande,* pp. 179–84. According to Himmlers' doctor-masseur, Felix Kersten, Hitler had been enraged by riots that took place in Amsterdam in February 1941 and had told Himmler, "I'll resettle the lot of them. I'll make an end of these parasites." Kersten says that Brandt actually showed him the documents, signed by Hitler and countersigned by Bormann, ordering the resettlement of the entire population of the Netherlands, 8.5 million people, in eastern Poland. The first scheduled to go were 3 million "irreconcilables," meaning all those who were likely to remain hostile to Germany. Kersten says that he persuaded Himmler, who in turn persuaded Hitler, to postpone the resettlement of the Dutch until after the war (*The Kersten Memoirs, 1940–1945* [London, 1956], pp. 172–73). Although Kersten's veracity has been vouched for by a number of distinguished scholars and humanitarians, his memoirs should nevertheless be treated with caution. See Warmbrunn, *Dutch,* p. 25.

52. Himmler to Rauter, March 7 and 23, 1942 (T175/63/2579361–62).

53. T175/63/2579468–70.

54. Memorandum on conference of a member of the German Foreign Office staff with Mussert, May 25, 1940 (*DGFP,* D, 9:406–8). In fact, the actual membership of the NSB appears to have been closer to thirty thousand (Kwiet, *RK Niederlande,* p. 72 ff.) See also Warmbrunn, *Dutch,* chap. 6.

55. Seyss-Inquart, "Die politische Aufgabe," pp. 12–13; report to Berlin (*IMT,* 997-PS, 26:413–29); testimony (*IMT* 15:644–45, 648); Wimmer testimony (*IMT* 16:185, 197–98); Kwiet, *RK Niederlande,* pp. 125–35, 144–45; Warmbrunn, *Dutch,* pp. 85, 89; Postma, *Reichskommissariat,* pp. 87–90.

56. Kwiet, *RK Niederlande,* pp. 133–34, 136–37; Warmbrunn, *Dutch,* p. 93 ff.

57. *VBIN* (1941), pp. 513–14; Seyss-Inquart, "Die politische Aufgabe," p. 13; testimony (*IMT* 15:645). Hitler's attitude toward Mussert and the NSB was still benevolent in September 1941 (*DGFP,* D, 13:599–602).

58. Rauter to Christiansen, December 1941 (T501/96/655–56); Rauter to Himmler, April 1, 1942 (NO 1463).

59. Himmler to Rauter, June 24, 1942 (T175/122/2647943).

60. Report of Otto Bene, Foreign Office representative in the Netherlands (NG 5078); Kwiet, *RK Niederlande,* p. 147.

61. *Hitler's Secret Conversations,* p. 232.

62. Memorandum of Hitler-Mussert conference (T175/126/2650973–83); report of Bethmann, the deputy of the Reich labor leader in the Netherlands, December 1942 (T175/63/2579350–60): Seyss-Inquart to the senior German officials in the Netherlands, December 15, 1942 (T175/59/257540).

63. De Jong and Stoppelman, *Lion Rampant,* pp. 163–67, 179–80.

64. Memorandum of Himmler-Mussert conversation, July 8, 1943 (T175/126/2651301–21); de Jong and Stoppelman, *Lion Rampant,* p. 154.

65. Seyss-Inquart report (*IMT,* 997-PS, 26:413–29).

66. Quoted in de Jong and Stoppelman, *Lion Rampant,* p. 262; *IMT* 16:183.

67. *Reichshauptstellenleiter* Sommer, "Die NSDAP in den Niederlanden," in du Prel and Janke, eds., *Die Niederlande,* p. 126.

68. *VBIN* (1941), pp. 559–60; Sommer, "NSDAP," pp. 126–27; Warmbrunn, *Dutch,* pp. 149–53; de Jong and Stoppelman, *Lion Rampant,* pp. 248–56, 261–65.

69. T175/63/2579320.

70. *Hitler's Secret Conversations*, pp. 327–28; Picker, *Hitlers Tischgespräche*, pp. 255–56.

71. Seyss-Inquart report (*IMT*, 997-PS, 26:413–29); *IMT* 3:433–34; 5:394, 402, 492, 506; 22:595–96; 36:651; Warmbrunn, *Dutch*, pp. 72–77.

72. Seyss-Inquart report (*IMT*, 997-PS, 26:413–29).

73. De Jong and Stoppelman, *Lion Rampant*, pp. 47–48, 102 ff.; N. W. Posthumus, ed., *The Netherlands during German Occupation* (Philadelphia, 1946), pp. 63–64.

74. *VBIN* (1941), pp. 898–915; Seyss-Inquart testimony (*IMT* 16:43).

75. De Jong and Stoppelman, *Lion Rampant*, pp. 110–11; Posthumus, *Netherlands*, p. 48 ff.

76. Quoted in de Jong and Stoppelman, *Lion Rampant*, p. 112. On this subject, see the Nazi tracts of van Etten, "Naar Ostland," pp. 179–84, and van Essen, *Mein Holland*.

77. Orders of July 25 and August 8, 1941 (*VBIN* [1941], pp. 548–50, 622–23).

78. *Vier Jahre in den Niederlanden*, p. 57; also Seyss's article, "Die politische Aufgabe," p. 13.

79. *Documents of the Persecution of Dutch Jewry, 1940–1945*, collected by the Jewish Historical Museum of Amsterdam (Amsterdam, 1965); Raul Hilberg, *The Destruction of the European Jews* (Chicago, 1961), pp. 366–71; Gerald Reitlinger, *The Final Solution: The Attempt to Exterminate the Jews of Europe, 1939–1945* (New York, 1968), pp. 352–67; Warmbrunn, *Dutch*, pp. 61–68, and chap. 9.

80. *VBIN* (1940), pp. 546–52; (1941), pp. 164–70, 624–28, 655–62, 841–44; (1942), pp. 289–300. The Nazi explanation for the dismissal of Jewish teachers and civil servants is quoted in de Jong and Stoppelman, *Lion Rampant*, pp. 212–16.

81. *VBIN* (1941), pp. 19–23; Seyss-Inquart testimony (*IMT*, 15:666 ff.; 27:536).

82. Warmbrunn, *Dutch*, pp. 63–64; Kwiet, *RK Niederlande*, p. 143.

83. Warmbrunn, *Dutch*, pp. 65–68; Hilberg, *Destruction*, pp. 372–73.

84. Rauter to Himmler, September 10, 1942 (NO 2256).

85. Rauter to Himmler, September 24 and October 7, 1942 (T175/63/2579234–36; NO 1155).

86. Himmler to Rauter, February 10–11, 1943 (T175/64/2579587–88, 2579699).

87. Hilberg, *Destruction*, pp. 377–79.

88. Speech of March 12, 1941 (*Vier Jahre in den Niederlanden*, p. 57).

89. Ribbentrop to Weizsäcker, May 16, 1940; Radowitz, the German minister in Luxembourg, to the Foreign Office, May 17 and 18, 1940 (*DGFP*, D, 9:356–57, 359, 367–68).

90. Final report of the German military administration in Luxembourg, August 6, 1940 (T501/94/355–83).

91. When Simon attached Luxembourg to his party administrative district, the name of the Gau was changed to Moselland.

92. As early as July 21 the army informed General Alexander von Falkenhausen, the military governor of Belgium, Luxembourg, and France, that a civil government under military authority would be established in Luxembourg on July 25. Hitler's order of August 2 was not immediately communicated to the army, and it was not until August 13 that the army was officially informed of an order of August 8 which withdrew Simon from the authority of the army and made him directly responsible to Hitler. Halder communications to Falkenhausen and Simon, July 25, 1940 (T501/93/126; T501/94/350–53, 489–90); Hitler order of August 2, 1940 (NOKW 3474).

93. *VBILux* (1940), p. 2. All decrees were signed by Simon, or in his name.

94. Decree of October 18, 1940 (NG 4297). Oral instructions to this effect were almost certainly issued earlier.

95. Simon proclamation of September 28, 1940 (T501/94/573).

96. *VBILux* (1940), p. 1, with many supplements.

97. Simon to the people of Luxembourg, August 7, 1940, published in the *Luxemburger Volksblatt*, August 8. The emphases are given in the newspaper version of the speech.

98. January 31, 1941 (*VBILux* [1941], p. 146).

99. *VBILux* (1940), pp. 3, 8, 278, 287–88.

100. Ibid. (1940), pp. 2, 290, 297, 335–39, 373, 440; (1941), pp. 311; (1942), pp. 77, 135.

101. Ibid. (1940), p. 241; (1941), pp. 18, 109, 213; (1942), pp. 33, 220; also the postwar report of the Luxembourg government, *IMT* 39:147.

102. *VBILux* (1940), pp. 6, 8, 13, 17, 21, 291, 295, 338, 347; (1941), pp. 67, 303; (1942), pp. 151, 154, 159–60.

103. Ibid. (1940), pp. 281, 297–98, 346; (1941), pp. 119, 132–33, 324, 343.

104. Ibid. (1941), pp. 98, 108–9, 232, 266; (1942), pp. 253–54, 409; (1943), p. 7.

105. *RGBl* (1942) 1:40, 533; *VBILux* (1942), pp. 254–55.

106. Simon to Himmler, May 31, 1941; Brandt, on behalf of Himmler, to the Volksdeutsche Mittelstelle (VoMi), June 26; Himmler to Simon, July 27; Himmler to the VoMi, July 21; Lorenz to Himmler, September 1; Himmler to Lorenz, September 19 (all collected under Nuremberg document NO 1792).

107. *VBILux* (1941), pp. 90, 125, 298; (1942), pp. 129, 277–78.

108. Simon to the OKW, July 6, 1943 (NO 1792).

109. Frick to Lammers, August 31, 1940; Reich Chancellery note on the decision of Hitler, September 6, 1940 (NG 2297); *VBlLux* (1940), pp. 10, 433–34; (1941), pp. 90, 298, 325, 407, 410, 420, 501; (1942), p. 134; Hilberg, *Destruction*, pp. 381–82.

110. Picker, *Hitlers Tischgespräche*, p. 183; *Hitler's Secret Conversations*, pp. 475, 479, 564. In October 1940 Hitler told Mussolini that he intended to leave the Netherlands semi-independent after the war because he wanted Holland to preserve its overseas empire (*DGFP*, D, 11:255). This consideration was evidently eliminated after the Japanese took over the greater part of that empire.

169 111. A law of October 31, 1941, speaks in paragraph two of the assimilation of Luxembourg territory into the Reich, and in paragraph three of Luxembourg citizens as Reich citizens (*VBlLux* (1941), p. 483). At a conference at Göring's headquarters on June 19, 1940, Hitler stated that Luxembourg was to be incorporated (*einverleibt*) into the Reich (T77/564/1741799–800).

7. THE LIMES OF LEBENSRAUM: BELGIUM AND NORTHERN FRANCE.

170 1. By the term *Limes* Nazi theorists referred to far more than Belgium, although there was some difference of opinion as to whether it should apply to the ancient empire of the Franks, the medieval state of Burgundy, or the entire border region between France and Germany. Nazi racial theorists, of course, laid claim to all territories which they believed had a predominantly Nordic character or those they thought should be Germanized in the interests of German security, a conception which could justify indefinite expansion in almost any direction. I have placed Belgium and Northern France under the rubric of Limes because, in the beginning at least, the Nazis themselves were uncertain about what to do with this area and its racially mixed population.

2. *Westland. Blätter für Landschaft, Geschichte und Kultur an Rhein, Mosel, Maas und Schelde* (Amsterdam, 1943 ff.) A review by K. Rabl summarizing the main theories embodied in the journal was published in *RVL* 5 (1943):366–72. The quotations in the text come from Rabl's review.

3. *"Sein Symbol ist der Limes: die Begrenzung nach Osten."*

172 4. *RGBl* (1940) 1:777, 803, 1222, 1301; (1941) 1:73, 584; memorandum of the Central Office for Race and Resettlement, September 28, 1942 (NO 1499).

So far as Belgium as a whole was concerned the provinces of Eupen, Malmédy, and Moresnet were a special case. Eupen and Malmédy had been part of Germany before the First World War; according to the provisions of the Treaty of Versailles their inhabitants were to have an opportunity to express their desire to remain with Germany. No regular plebiscite was held, but lists were provided on which the inhabitants could register their national preferences. These lists were public, there was no international supervision of the registration procedure, and during a six month period only 271 persons signed them. Accordingly the Council of the League of Nations, which had been entrusted with the final decision as to the fate of Eupen and Malmédy, confirmed the cession of the provinces to Belgium, rejecting German objections that the inhabitants had been subjected to pressure and intimidation. In 1940 Hitler was in a position to restate the German case more effectively. He declared that the provinces of Eupen and Malmédy had been wrested from Germany illegally and in violation of the principle of self-determination; in annexing the provinces to Germany he was therefore doing no more than righting an injustice.

The problem of Moresnet was somewhat more complicated. The boundaries of this border region had not been clearly defined by the Congress of Vienna in 1815 and were subsequently fixed by direct negotiation between Prussia and the Netherlands, which at that time included Belgium. The disputed territory was divided into three parts, one falling to Prussia, another to the Netherlands (and thus to Belgium after Belgium seceded from the Netherlands union in 1830), while a third part remained under the joint control of both states, the so-called Neutral Moresnet. After the First World War, Germany ceded both Prussian and Neutral Moresnet to Belgium; but in 1940 Hitler annexed both regions to the Reich, thus incorporating territory that had not been part of Germany in 1914. (Sarah Wambaugh, *Plebiscites since the World War*, 2 vols. [Washington, D.C., 1933], 1:518 ff.; Arnold H. Price, "The Belgian-German Frontier during World War II," *Maryland Historian* 1 [1970]:145–53).

5. Hitler explained to Abetz, his ambassador in France, that he needed the Calais region as a security zone against England which had to be kept under military control (September 16, 1941, *DGFP*, D, 13:519). But all of France occupied by the Germans, including the entire French coastal region, was also kept under German military government. Eberhard Jäckel, in his lucid and authoritative work *Frankreich in Hitlers Europa. Die deutsche Frankreichpolitik im zweiten Weltkrieg* (Stuttgart, 1966), makes a convincing case that Hitler's motives in separating these departments from France were primarily political and part of his pan-Germanic expansionist program. He quotes an April 1941 memorandum of Falkenhausen "that the German leadership wanted to create and preserve complete freedom of action in this German-Roman border region," which from ethnic, historical, cultural, economic, and geographic points of view had from time immemorial

been connected with the area of the Low Countries; even today the area between Dunkirk and Bailleul was ethnically entirely Flemish" (pp. 61–62).

173   6. Warlimont to Ausland Abwehr, January 11, 1940 (NG 5347).

    7. See above, p. 141.

    8. Himmler memorandum, May 22, 1940 (T175/94/2615215); Himmler to Rauter, May 23, 1940 (T175/123/2649360); Himmler handwritten notes on conferences with the Führer, May 25 and 31, 1940 (T175/94/2615215–18). On this problem see Thomas J. Knight, "Belgium leaves the War, 1940," *Journal of Modern History* 41, (1969):55–58.

    9. Falkenhausen, appointed military commander of the Netherlands on May 16, was subsequently appointed military commander for all occupied western territories. The Netherlands was placed under civil government on May 29; France, with the exception of the departments Nord and Pas de Calais, was detached from his administration on June 12; and Luxembourg was placed under a civil government on August 2, 1940 (T501/96/402, 462, 786–88; T501/93/9, 12, 37–46, 76, 82–83).

174   10. Jacques Willequet, "Le Procès Falkenhausen," *RHDGM* 3 (1951):59–65; Fernand Baudhuin, *L'Économie belge sous l'occupation, 1940–1944* (Brussels, 1945), pp. 127–29; Paul Delandsheere and Alphonse Ooms, *La Belgique sous les Nazis, 1940–44* (4 vols. Brussels, 1946–47), 4:195–96; Alexander von Falkenhausen, "Was ich dachte und was ich tat," *Die Zeit*, April 24, May 4 and 11, 1950; Falkenhausen affidavit, November 7, 1946 (NO 617).

    11. Ulrich von Hassell, *Vom andern Deutschland. Aus den nachgelassenen Tagebüchern 1938–1944* (Zürich, 1946), pp. 126, 146, 219, 221, 249, 317–19, 342–43; Gerhard Ritter, *Carl Goerdeler und die deutsche Widerstandsbewegung* (Stuttgart, 1954), pp. 340, 359, 387–88, 528–29.

    12. OKW order of May 31, 1940 (T501/93/37–39, 81–83; T501/96/786–88); Brauchitsch order of July 15, 1940 (T501/96/782–84); Walter Hailer, "Organisation der Militärverwaltung und ihr Verhältnis zu den landeseigenen Behörden," *RVL* 6 (1943):29.

175   13. OKW memorandum on Hitler's policy for Belgium, June 4, 1940 (T501/96/845); Keitel to Brauchitsch on Hitler's policy for Belgium, July 14, 1940 (T501/96/857); Falkenhausen report, July 31, 1940 (NG 2381). See also Reeder's letter to Berger of September 26, 1941, in which Hitler's guidelines for German policy in Belgium are described (T501/96/694–708).

    14. Report of Dr. Beyer of the German military economy administration staff in Belgium (T77/575/1754049–64). An entire Reich Chancellery file was devoted to criticisms of Falkenhausen and the efforts of Nazi leaders to replace the military government with a civil administration (WF serial 4839).

    15. Report of September 5, 1940 (T501/102/892–909).

176   16. Report of October 30, 1940 (T501/94/679 ff.).

    17. Falkenhausen order setting up the military government, June 25, 1940 (T501/96/825–26); Brauchitsch order defining the relationship between the army and the military government, July 15, 1940 (T501/96/782–84); Reeder reports describing the military administration, August 2 and 4, 1940 (T501/102/169, 191–802); report of Dr. Werner Best on the German military administration in Belgium (T501/101/1317–21); Hailer, "Militärverwaltung," pp. 28–46.

    18. On Reeder, see Thomas J. Knight, *The Establishment of German Military Government in Belgium, 1940–1941* (unpublished Ph.D. dissertation, University of Texas, 1967), pp. 20–27; and Edgar E. Knoebel, *Racial Illusion and Military Necessity: A Study of SS Political and Manpower Objectives in Occupied Belgium* (unpublished Ph.D. dissertation, University of Colorado, 1965), p. 79. I owe a deep debt of gratitude to both Knight and Knoebel for allowing me to use their manuscripts in the preparation of this chapter.

    19. Kraushaar testimony at Falkenhausen's trial, quoted in *La libre Belgique*, October 12, 1950, p. 5; cited in Knight, "Belgium," p. 53, n. 19.

177   20. Eggert Reeder, "Die Militärverwaltung in Belgien und Nordfrankreich. Grundsätze und politische Zielsetzung," *RVL* 6 (1943):7–23; Reeder report of August 4, 1940 (T501/102/191–802).

    21. See above, n. 8.

    22. Halder to Falkenhausen, July 20, 1940 (T501/96/858–59).

178   23. Lammers memorandum, October 21, 1941 (*DGFP*, D, 13:672–73).

    24. Keitel to Lammers, October 13, 1941 (*DGFP*, D, 13:643–44); Keitel to Lammers, December 9, 1941 (WF 4839/E245014–15); Witzleben to Brauchitsch, November 24, 1941 (T501/96/665–69).

179   25. Memoranda summarizing Stuckart's view, October 28 and November 4, 1941 (WF 4839/E244983–245005).

    26. Körner (Four-Year Plan) to Lammers, January 15, 1942 (WF 4839/E245021–23).

    27. Lammers to Keitel, October 24, 1941 (*DGFP*, D, 13:644, n. 1); Lammers note of January 5, 1942 (WF 4839/E245016); *Hitler's Secret Conversations, 1941–1944* (paperback, New York, 1961), p. 331.

    28. *Hitler's Secret Conversations,* May 5, 1942, p. 434; unpublished Goebbels diary frag-

ment, cited in Konrad Kwiet, *Reichskommisariat Niederlande. Versuch und Scheitern nationalsozialistischer Neuordnung* (Stuttgart, 1968), p. 67.

29. Lammers notes (WF 4839/E245029–31); *Hitler's Secret Conversations,* June 27, 1942, pp. 503–4.

180
30. Hitler communicated this decision to Seyss-Inquart (WF 4839/E245040).

31. Lammers memorandum, September 24, 1942; Stuckart to Lammers, October 9, 1942 (WF 4839/E245032–34).

32. Berger to Himmler, October 21, 1942 (T175/129/2654782–83).

181
33. Lammers notes of October 23 and 28, 1942 (WF 4839/E245048–49; E245501); Berger to Himmler, November 5, 1942 (NO 857). On the establishment of the German civil administration, see below, p. 195.

34. Hailer, "Militärverwaltung," pp. 28–46; Knight, *German Military Government,* pp. 14 ff., 85–88, 112–13; Knoebel, *Racial Illusion,* p. 91; Robert Capelle, *Au service du roi,* 2 vols. (Brussels, 1949).

35. See above, p. 176.

36. Hailer, "Militärverwaltung," pp. 28–46; Werner Best report (T501/101/1321); *Statistisches Handbuch der Militärverwaltung in Belgien und Nordfrankreich,* published by the Statistische Zentralstelle der Militärverwaltung, September 9, 1944 (T77/575/1754071 ff.).

37. The problem was extremely complicated and gave rise to much disagreement among the Belgians themselves. Following the king's orders to the Belgian people to work for the reconstruction of their country, the Belgian secretaries-general informed Reeder on June 5, 1940, that they would not oppose the occupation authorities, but neither would they do anything contrary to their patriotic duty. The Germans, however, required that these Belgian officials assume quasi-legislative powers; on June 9, after much debate, the secretaries-general agreed to assume what they called extended powers under the law of May 10 except in matters of language, political jurisdiction, and foreign relations (Knight, "Belgium," pp. 58–62; Louis Baillon, *La Résistance administrative. La Lutte secrète des pouvoirs publics contre les allemands en Belgique, 1940–1944* [Brussels, 1946], pp. 31 ff.).

38. Hailer, "Militärverwaltung," pp. 30–31, 38–40.

182
39. *VBlB* (1940), pp. 131–32, 273–74, 279–82; (1941), pp. 529–30; (1942), p. 76; T501/102/419, 799–800; T501/93/370; Hailer, "Militärverwaltung," pp. 30–37; Falkenhausen report of July 31, 1940 (NG 2381).

40. *VBlB* (1940), p. 31; German military government report, June 4, 1940 (T501/102/122–25); OSS, *Belgium* (Washington, D.C., 1944), pp. 31, 51–58.

41. Falkenhausen to Bach-Zelewski, August 26, 1943 (T501/96/53).

42. The OKW economic office in Belgium was set up by a Thomas order of June 13, 1940 (T501/93/102–4). Technically the head of this office was under the head of the German military administration for Belgium, but he received his orders from the Wi-Rü Amt (supplementary order of June 18, 1940, T501/93/109; Reeder report of August 2, 1940, T501/102/190); OSS, *Belgium,* p. 65; OSS, *Belgium: Money and Banking* (Washington, D.C., 1944).

183
43. *Heeresgruppen- und Verordnungsblatt für die besetzten Gebiete,* May 10, 1940, p. 4; *VBlB* (1940), pp. 29–30; *DGFP,* D, 9:476; currency regulations, *VBlB* (1940), pp. 11–12, 51–56, 58, 140–41; property confiscations, *VBlB* (1940), pp. 23–25, 32, 112–14; taxation, *VBlB* (1940), p. 34. Also the very important final German military government report (T501/107/168 ff.).

44. Report of the economic section of the German military government, August 31, 1940 (T501/102/1075–95); unsigned memorandum from the files of the German military government on economic goals in Belgium, September 30, 1940 (T501/96/796); German military government report on German economic goals, October 1, 1940 (T501/102/1322–79); Hailer, "Militärverwaltung," pp. 41–46.

45. Göring order of August 26, 1940 (*NCA,* 620-EC, 7:608–9).

46. See above, pp. 149–50.

184
47. The files on the activities of the Zast offices are on film T77/575/1753460 ff. See especially the report of January 1941 on the failures of the system (T77/575/1754035–37).

48. Report on the progress of the penetration of German capital in Belgium and the Netherlands (T77/575/1753288–90); Reeder report of December 1940 (*NCA,* 34-EC, 7:254–55).

49. German military government report of October 1, 1940 (T501/102/1359); report of May 1941 (T77/575/1753288–90).

50. *VBlB* (940), pp. 29–30; (1941), pp. 599, 605–6; (1942), p. 986; *Moniteur belge des arrêtés ministériels et autre arrêtés des secrétaires généraux,* September 4, 1940; Baudhuin, *L'Économie belge,* pp. 161–63.

185
51. *VBlB* (1940), pp. 47–48, 89, 96–102, 174–75. Also OSS, *Belgium: Money and Banking.*

52. *Moniteur belge,* August 30, 1940; *Belgisches Staatsblatt* (on film T77/575/1754099–101; T501/95/60); Hailer, "Militärverwaltung," pp. 41–46; Baudhuin, *L'Économie belge,* pp. 156–61.

53. Knight, *German Military Government*, pp. 269–70; T501/94/744; Robert Billiard, *La Collaboration industrielle et ouvrière avec l'occupant* (Brussels, 1945); and by the same author, *La Contrainte économique imposée aux industriels et aux ouvriers belges par l'autorité occupante allemande en 1940–1944* (Brussels, 1946).

54. *Moniteur belge*, February 13, 1941 (T77/575/1754123); Raphaël Lemkin, *Axis Rule in Occupied Europe: Laws of Occupation, Analysis of Government, Proposals for Redress* (Washington, D.C., 1944), pp. 128, 323–25; Baudhuin, *L'Économie belge*, pp. 168–72.

186 55. Report of the German military administration of January 1942 (NG 1946).

56. *VBlB* (1942), pp. 845, 1060.

57. Sauckel to Hitler, August 13, 1943 (*IMT*, 556(43)-PS, 26:158–59). On the Sauckel program, see the entire Nuremberg document PS 556; also *TWC*, NG 3388, 13:1000; *TWC*, 2:542, 608.

187 58. NG 2381; also OSS, *Belgium*, pp. 34–37, 45–47; *IMT* 6:537; Knight, *German Military Government*, pp. 168–69.

59. Bargen report, November 11, 1942 (NG 5219); Raul Hilberg, *The Destruction of the European Jews* (Chicago, 1961), pp. 383–84; Gerald Reitlinger, *The Final Solution: The Attempt to Exterminate the Jews of Europe, 1939–1945* (New York, 1968), p. 342.

60. *VBlB* (1940), pp. 279–82, 288; Hilberg, *Destruction*, pp. 383–84.

61. *VBlB* (1941), pp. 798–99; Eichmann to Rademacher, June 22, 1942 (NG 183); Hilberg, *Destruction*, p. 387.

188 62. Bargen report, July 9, 1942 (NG 5209); Luther to Eichmann, July 27, 1942 (NG 183); Luther to Brussels, June 28, 1942 (*TWC* 13:233–34).

63. Bargen report, November 11, 1942 (NG 5219); Reitlinger, *Final Solution*, pp. 343–44.

64. Bargen reports of September 24 and November 11, 1942; Luther to Brussels, December 3, 1942 (NG 5219).

65. Hilberg, *Destruction*, pp. 388–89; Reitlinger, *Final Solution*, p. 343.

189 66. Keitel to Brauchitsch, July 14, 1940 (T501/96/857); Falkenhausen report of July 31, 1940 (NG 2381).

67. Heydrich to Himmler, September 9, 1941, surveying the Flemish political movements (T175/68/2584736–42); Reeder to Berger, September 26, 1941, on the political problems involved in Flanders (T501/96/694–708).

68. Knoebel, *Racial Illusion*, pp. 88–90, 116; Knight, *German Military Government*, pp. 58–59; J. A. Wullus-Rudiger, *En marge de la politique belge, 1914–1956* (Paris, 1957), pp. 60–64, 243–45, 289; Shepard B. Clough, "The Flemish Movement," *Belgium*, ed. Jan-Albert Goris (Berkeley, Calif., 1946), pp. 108–26.

190 69. René Hislaire, "Political Parties," *Belgium*, ed. Jan-Albert Goris, pp. 105–7.

70. Degrelle memorandum, October 20, 1940 (*DGFP*, D, 11:339–46).

71. Reeder reports of January and March 1941 (T501/103/956–60; T501/104/178–80); Knoebel, *Racial Ilusion*, pp. 176–78.

72. Knoebel, *Racial Illusion*, pp. 211, 213; also see below, pp. 194–95.

191 73. Hitler's OKW adjutant to Falkenhausen, September 9, 1940 (T501/94/541); Himmler order of September 11, 1940 (T501/93/166); Harbou memorandum, September 26, 1940 (T501/94/570); Berger to Himmler, October 18, 1940 (No 1841); Berger to Heydrich, December 17, 1940 (T175/119/2644575–76).

192 74. Heydrich to Himmler, September 9, 1941 (T175/68/2584736–42); Reeder to Berger, September 26, 1941 (T501/96/694–708). Both letters survey in detail Germany's relations with Flemish national parties and their leaders.

75. Berger to Himmler, August 27 and September 17, 1941 (NO 3017, 2290; T175/68/2584756–59).

193 76. Berger to Himmler, October 29, 1941 (T175/128/2654533); Heydrich to Berger, November 4, 1941; Berger to Heydrich, November 5, 1941 (NO 1843); Hierl to Falkenhausen, November 18, 1942; Himmler to Berger, December 15, 1942; Berger to Himmler, December 16, 1942 (NO 5780–5783); Berger negotiations for the training of Flemish youth leaders, December 1941–January 1942 (T501/105/608); Heydrich circular of May 12, 1942, on the Devlag movement (NO 1408). The entire problem is surveyed in Knoebel, *Racial Illusion*, pp. 122–28.

77. Berger to Himmler, October 21, 1942 (T175/129/2654782–83).

78. Berger to Himmler, March 3 and September 8, 1942 (T175/126/2651720, 2651960–61).

79. T175/107/2630530, 2630564 ff.; Knoebel, *Racial Illusion*, pp. 125–26.

80. Berger to Himmler, November 4, 1942 (T501/126/2652109–11); Himmler to Keitel, January 15, 1943 (T175/80/2600746); Himmler to Reeder, February 16, 1943 (NO 2064; T175/56/2570560–61); Reeder to Himmler, February 20, 1943 (T175/56/2570548–57); Berger to Brandt, February 25, 1943 (T175/56/2570538–39); Berger to Himmler, June 25, 1943 (NO 1844; T175/119/2645137–39); Knoebel, *Racial Illusion*, pp. 135–36, 144.

194 81. Reeder to Himmler, August 28 and October 18, 1943 (T175/71/2588577–91, 2588611); Berger to Brandt, August 30, 1943 (T175/71/2588603); Knoebel, *Racial Illusion*, pp. 149–51.

82. Knoebel, *Racial Illusion*, pp. 181–92.

83. Berger to Himmler, January 5, 1943 (T175/80/2600745).

84. Quoted in Knoebel, *Racial Illusion,* pp. 193–96. Victor Matthys, who had led the Rexists while Degrelle was in Russia, took the same line. "The Walloons are a Germanic people who speak French," he said in October 1942, and they "undoubtedly belong to the Germanic realm by blood . . . history . . . geographical location . . . economic life . . . and ethics" (T501/105/1227).

85. Himmler to Berger, January 20, 1943 (T175/80/2600740–41); Berger to Himmler, February 10, 1943 (NO 1486; T175/59/2574738).

86. Himmler memorandum, May 24, 1943 (T175/53/2567726–30).

87. Hitler order of July 13, 1944 (PS 650; NG 3470); Berger to Himmler, July 31, 1944 (T175/80/2600653–54); Grohé to Himmler, July 29, 1944 (T175/80/2600655–56).

88. Jungclaus to Himmler, July 14, 1944; Himmler to Jungclaus, July 17, 1944 (NO 2402).

89. Henry Picker, *Hitlers Tischgespräche im Führerhauptquartier, 1941–1942,* ed. Percy Ernst Schramm, Andreas Hillgruber, and Martin Vogt (Stuttgart, 1965), pp. 144, 146, 183, 254–56, 417–18; *Hitler's Secret Conversations,* pp. 53, 79, 381–87, 434, 503–4.

8. FRANCE: THE MORTAL ENEMY

1. *Mein Kampf* (New York, 1939), pp. 889–90, 902, 966, 978.

2. Jodl diary, entry for May 20, 1940 (*IMT,* 513-F, 37:218–19).

3. Hitler order of June 18, 1940 (*DGFP,* D, 9:606).

4. Affidavits of Adolf Klas of the Reich Ministry of the Interior, November 18, 1947 (NG 3572); of Dr. Hans Globke of the Ministry of the Interior, September 25 and October 13, 1945 (*IMT,* 513-F, 37:218–19, 222–23); of Generals Keitel and Jodl, March 9 and 10, 1946 (*IMT* 40:385–94).

5. Remarks of April 25, 1942. Henry Picker, *Hitlers Tischgespräche im Führerhauptquartier, 1941–1942,* ed. Percy Ernst Schramm, Andreas Hillgruber, Martin Vogt (Stuttgart, 1965), p. 296; *Hitler's Secret Conversations, 1941–1944* (paperback, New York, 1961), pp. 418, 449–51.

6. In his diary, entry for April 30, 1942, Goebbels wrote, "If the French knew what the Fuehrer is one day going to demand of them their eyes would in all likelihood brim over" (*The Goebbels Diaries, 1942–1943,* ed. Louis P. Lochner [New York, 1948] p. 198).

7. Remarks of August 29, 1942 (*Hitler's Secret Conversations,* p. 624).

8. Memorandum of September 24, 1941, on a conversation between Hitler and Abetz (PS 1311).

9. Hitler's May 9, 1940, directive (*DGFP,* D, 9:300–301; T77/545/1720424–25).

10. See above p. 172.

11. *DGFP,* D, 9:671–76. The treaty did not go into effect until July 24, 1940, after the conclusion of the armistice between France and Italy.

12. The area was closed to prevent the return of French, and especially Jewish, inhabitants who had fled so as to facilitate its later Germanization (Eberhard Jäckel, *Frankreich in Hitlers Europa. Die deutsche Frankreichpolitik im zweiten Weltkrieg* (Stuttgart, 1966), pp. 89–90.

13. Jäckel, *Frankreich,* pp. 87–88; Günter Geschke, *Die deutsche Frankreichpolitik, 1940, von Compiègne bis Montoire. Das Problem einer deutsch-französischen Annäherung nach dem Frankreichfeldzug* (Frankfurt am Main, 1960), pp. 38, 57–61. On August 16, 1940, Ribbentrop telegraphed to Abetz, "Please continue to treat the transfer of the French government or individual ministries in a dilatory way. Such a transfer is out of the question at this time, since Paris and northern France are a theater of operations against England" (*DGFP,* D, 10:491).

14. See Keitel memorandum of August 12, 1940, on principles for the treatment of the demarcation line, approved by Hitler (*DGFP,* D, 10:468–70); Geschke, *Frankreichpolitik,* pp. 51–53.

15. Before the armistice, the German military administration for the occupied French territories was under General von Falkenhausen; from June 12 the military administration for occupied France (with the exception of the departments Nord and Pas de Calais) came under General Johannes Blaskowitz (T501/93/3–4).

16. Brauchitsch orders of June 26 and July 7, 1940 (T501/94/438–40; T501/96/818–24).

17. Brauchitsch order of October 18, 1940 (T501/94/702–10). On the German military government, see the articles by F. A. Medicus, the chief of the office of the military administration in Paris, "Militärverwaltung in Frankreich," *Archiv des öffentlichen Rechts* 34 (1944):86–96; by Dr. Werner Best, the head of the administrative department, "Die deutsche Militärverwaltung in Frankreich," *RVL* 1 (1941):29–76; and Best's report on the German military administration in France, August–September 1941 (T501/101/1304 ff.).

18. Jäckel, *Frankreich,* pp. 194–95.

19. Ulrich von Hassell, *Vom andern Deutschland. Aus den nachgelassenen Tagebüchern 1938–1944* (Zürich, 1946), pp. 181, 250–51, 318–19, 326, 336.

20. Gerhard Ritter, *Carl Goerdeler und die deutsche Widerstandsbewegung* (Stuttgart,

1954), pp. 239, 391, 478; Hans Rothfels, *The German Opposition to Hitler* (Chicago, 1964), pp. 73–74; Erich Weniger, "Zur Vorgeschichte des 20. Juli 1944. Heinrich von Stülpnagel," *Die Sammlung* 4 (1949):475–92; Harold C. Deutsch, *The Conspiracy against Hitler in the Twilight War* (Minneapolis, 1968), pp. 33, 175, 208–9, 218–19, 251, 256–57, 275, 359.

21. See the articles of Medicus and Best, cited in n. 17 above, and the description of the German military government by Dr. Gramsch of the Four-Year Plan (*DGFP*, D, 10:128–30); also Jäckel, *Frankreich*, pp. 62 ff.

22. Brauchitsch order of March 13, 1941 (T78/32/706265–71).

23. Armistice treaty of June 22, 1940 (*DGFP*, D, 9:672).

203   24. Werner Best, *Die deutschen Aufsichtsverwaltungen in Frankreich, Belgien, den Niederlanden, Norwegen, Dänemark, und im Protektorat Böhmen und Mähren. Vergleichende Übersicht* (unpublished manuscript; on film T501/101/1304); Best, "Militärverwaltung," p. 49; Jäckel, *Frankreich*, p. 64.

25. Best, "Militärverwaltung," pp. 37–38; *Aufsichtsverwaltungen* (T501/101/1304).

26. *VBIF* (1940), pp. 3–4, 6–7, 13, 59, 108, 144; (1941), p. 182; (1942), pp. 430–33, 458–59.

27. Hassell, *Vom andern Deutschland*, p. 181; Adrienne Hytier, *Two Years of French Foreign Policy: Vichy, 1940–1942* (Geneva, 1958), p. 110.

28. *La Délégation française auprès de la commission allemande d'armistice. Recueil de documents publié par le gouvernement français*, 5 vols. (Paris, 1947–59).

204   29. Jäckel, *Frankreich*, pp. 71–74.

30. *Délégation française d'armistice*, 1:166, 185; *DGFP*, D, 10:128–29, 170–73, 213–15; Geschke, *Frankreichpolitik*, pp. 52, 58–60.

31. *DGFP*, D, 6:886–88, 907–8, 913–14, 928, 946–47, 1043–44, 1062–63; 7:22, 58, 72; Jäckel, *Frankreich*, pp. 66–71; Geschke, *Frankreichpolitik*, pp. 63–65; see also Abetz's memoirs, *Das offene Problem. Ein Rückblick auf zwei Jahrzehnte deutscher Frankreichpolitik* (Cologne, 1951), pp. 41–107.

205   32. *DGFP*, D, 10:407–8; *IMT*, 3614-PS, 32:432–33; Hytier, *French Foreign Policy*, p. 114. On November 20, 1940, Hitler gave Abetz's office the title of German Embassy in Paris and confirmed his responsibility for dealing with all political questions in occupied and unoccupied France (*DGFP*, D, 11:638–39).

33. Abetz, *Das offene Problem*, pp. 132–285; Abetz affidavit, May 30, 1947 (NG 1838). See the interesting analysis of Hytier, *French Foreign Policy*, pp. 134–35; Jäckel, *Frankreich*, pp. 98, 268, 287, 294–95; and Robert Aron, *The Vichy Regime, 1940–1944* (New York, 1958), pp. 420, 460.

206   34. DGFP, D, 10:93. For Germany's economic policy in France, see Alan S. Milward, "German Economic Policy towards France, 1940–1944," *Studies in International History*, ed. K. Bourne and D. C. Watt (Hamden, Conn., 1967), pp. 423–43; by the same author, *The New Order and the French Economy* (London, 1969); Pierre Arnoult, *Les Finances de la France et l'occupation allemande, 1940–1944* (Paris, 1951); François Boudot, "Aspects économiques de l'occupation allemande en France," *RHDGM* 54 (1964):41–62; and Henri Michel, "Bibliographie. L'Économie française pendant la guerre (1939–1945)," *RHDGM* 57 (1965):119–28.

35. Army order of July 7, 1940 (T501/96/818–24); Brauchitsch order of October 18, 1940 (T501/94/702–10); affidavits of Keitel and Jodl (IMT 40:392–93); Boudot, "Aspects économiques," pp. 52–53.

36. Göring order of August 26, 1940 (T77/564/1741928–29). On the Zast offices, see above, pp. 149–50, 183.

37. Funk-Keitel-Speer order, July 25, 1942 (EC 600); Brauchitsch order of April 1, 1941 (T78/32/706259; T501/96/743–44).

38. Laws for the manipulation of currency, *VBIF* (1940), pp. 9–10, 16, 35, 67, 72–73; (1941), p. 252; (1942), pp. 338, 348; for the sequestration of enemy property, *VBIF* (1940), pp. 33–35, 97–102, 130–41; (1941), pp. 277–78, 288–91.

207   39. See the important reports and histories of the Wi-Rü Amt staff in France (EC 422 and EC 617). Very brief excerpts are published in *NCA* 7:482–84, 604.

40. Report of the Wi-Rü staff for France, August 5, 1940–April 3, 1941, p. 5 (EC 617); establishment of the German armaments inspectorate for France, June 20, 1940 (T77/564/1741500–503). Laws establishing a supervisory commission for the Bank of France, *VBIF* (1940), pp. 53–54, with numerous supplementary decrees; for agriculture, *VBIF* (1940), p. 143; for the armaments industry, *VBIF* (1940), p. 149; for the co-ordination of French industrial enterprises, *VBIF* (1940), pp. 149–52; for labor, *Journal officiel de l'état français* (in which the decrees of the Vichy government were published), October 4, 1941.

41. See the Wi-Rü Amt staff reports, cited in n. 39 above; also Hytier, *French Foreign Policy*, pp. 130, 168–69, 180; and Geschke, *Frankreichpolitik*, pp. 35–36. Various French authors, e.g., Aron, *Vichy Regime*, pp. 307–8, maintain that the Germans were in fact far less successful in buying into French firms than they claimed. So far as Germany's future intentions were concerned, however, the degree of success was not the important thing, but the policy itself.

42. See below, p. 223.

43. Jäckel, *Frankreich*, pp. 65, n. 25, 197, 226–27, 271–72; Michel de Boüard, "La Répression allemande en France de 1940 à 1944," *RHDGM* 54 (1964):63–90; Général Rivet, "Abwehr et Gestapo en France pendant la guerre," *RHDGM* 1 (1950):28–50; affidavits of Keitel and Jodl, *IMT* 40:386.

44. The following account is based on a report of the German military government's administration of the police, written after the German occupation had come to an end (T501/184/1044–83); see also the account of Best and Medicus, cited above, n. 17.

45. German military government report (T501/184/1061).

46. Ibid., T501/184/1044–83.

47. Memorandum of SD conference, March 18, 1942 (NG 4881); German military government report (T501/184/1047); Jäckel, *Frankreich*, pp. 196–98: affidavits of Keitel and Jodl (*IMT* 40:389–90).

48. Aron, *Vichy Regime*, pp. 373, 376–77; Jäckel, *Frankreich*, pp. 197–98; Boüard, "Répression allemande," pp. 69–71.

49. *VBIF* (1940), p. 86; (1941) p. 183.

50. German military government report (T501/184/1044–83); Jäckel, *Frankreich*, pp. 197–98, 257, 265, 271; Hans Luther, *Der französiche Widerstand gegen die deutsche Besatzungsmacht und seine Bekämpfung* (Tübingen, 1957).

51. Memorandum of December 16, 1942, on Himmler's moves against the intellectuals (*IMT*, 1238-RF, 39:8–9); on Marseille, Himmler to Oberg, January 18, 1943 (T175/123/2648868–69); Jäckel, *Frankreich*, p. 272; Aron, *Vichy Regime*, pp. 448–49. This action took place after the Germans had occupied the whole of France.

52. February 12, 1940, *RGBl* (1940), 1:355; subsequent unpublished decrees on the functions of this organization are summarized in Nuremberg document NI 4267.

53. *Délégation française d'armistice*, 4:188–93, 332, 342, 345, 361, 386–87; Hytier, *French Foreign Policy*, p. 125; Jacques Lorraine, *Les Allemands en France* (Paris, 1945), pp. 71–78. On the Germanization of Alsace and Lorraine and the campaign against the Jews, see below, pp. 226–38.

54. On Vichy, besides the works of Jäckel, Geschke, Aron, and Hytier, see Paul Farmer, *Vichy: Political Dilemma* (New York, 1955); Robert O. Paxton, *Parades and Politics at Vichy: The French Officer Corps under Marshal Pétain* (Princeton, N.J., 1966); William L. Langer, *Our Vichy Gamble* (New York, 1947); and the controversial work of Saint-Paulien, *Histoire de la collaboration* (published by L'Esprit Nouveau, Paris, 1964).

55. On Pétain, see the general works on Vichy, cited above, the collections of his writings and speeches listed in the bibliography, and his memoirs, *Quatre années au pouvoir* (Paris, 1949).

56. Quotations from Langer, *Vichy Gamble*, pp. 67–73, and Thomas Kernan (chief of the Condé Nast publications in Europe), *France on Berlin Time* (Philadelphia, 1941), pp. 109 ff., 133, 155 ff.

57. On Laval, see the general literature on Vichy cited above, n. 54; the now published *Unpublished Diary of Pierre Laval* (London, 1948); the statements for the defense collected by his daughter and son-in-law, Josée and René de Chambrun, *France during the German Occupation, 1940–1944* (Stanford, Calif., 1958–59); Paul Arnoult, ed., *La France sous l'occupation* (Paris, 1959); the works of Guy Bechtel, *Laval vingt ans après* (Paris, 1963); Alfred Mallet, *Pierre Laval*, 2 vols. (Paris, 1955); the record of Laval's trial, *Le Procès Laval. Compte rendu sténographique* (Paris, 1946); and above all Geoffrey Warner, *Pierre Laval and the Eclipse of France* (New York, 1968).

58. On Flandin, see Hytier, *French Foreign Policy*, pp. 229–31, 242–43.

59. The quotations are taken from Langer, *Vichy Gamble*, pp. 70, 117, 123. On Darlan, see Hytier, *French Foreign Policy*, pp. 247, 290; Jäckel, *Frankreich*, p. 159; the memoirs of Admiral William D. Leahy, *I Was There* (New York, 1950), pp. 13, 74, 92; and Darlan's own memoirs, *L'Admiral Darlan parle* (Paris, 1952).

60. See the first volume of this study, chap. 16, and, above all, the superb work of Andreas Hillgruber, *Hitlers Strategie. Politik und Kriegsführung, 1940–1941* (Frankfurt am Main, 1965).

61. Donald S. Detwiler, *Hitler, Franco und Gibraltar. Die Frage des spanischen Eintritts in den zweiten Weltkrieg* (Wiesbaden, 1962); Charles B. Burdick, *Germany's Military Strategy and Spain in World War II* (Syracuse, N.Y., 1968).

62. *DGFP*, D, 10:215, 274–75; *Délégation française d'armistice*, 1:463–64; Geschke, *Frankreichpolitik*, pp. 80–104.

63. See the first volume of this study, pp. 195–96.

64. Schmidt memorandum, October 4, 1940 (*DGFP*, D, 11:245–59); Jäckel, *Frankreich*, pp. 110, 114–23.

65. Unsigned, fragmentary memorandum of Hitler's conference with Franco, October 23, 1940; Schmidt memorandum of his conference with Pétain, October 24, 1940 (*DGFP*, D, 11:371–76, 385–92); see Paul Schmidt, *Statist auf diplomatischer Bühne, 1923–45. Erlebnisse des Chefdolmetschers im Auswärtigen Amt mit den Staatsmännern Europas* (Bonn, 1949), pp. 500–502.

66. See the first volume of this study, pp. 196–97.

67. *DGFP*, D, 11:444, 448–49, 456, 460, 570–71, 578–81, 885; *TWC* 13:164; NG 4933–34; *Délégation française d'armistice,* 2:244 ff.; Jäckel, *Frankreich,* pp. 128–31.

218

68. Schmidt memorandum of Hitler-Mussolini conference of October 28, 1940 (*DGFP*, D, 11:411–22); Schmidt, *Statist,* pp. 505–6.

69. Hitler directive 18 for the conduct of the war (*DGFP*, D, 11:527–31). Keitel summarized this policy in a communication to the chief of the Army General Staff of November 28, 1940 (T501/96/854–55).

70. Warlimont prepared a long memorandum for military talks with French leaders, November 29, 1940 (T77/884/5632730–47); see also *DGFP*, D, 11:812, 839–41, 860–63. On Hitler's policy toward Spain, see the first volume of this study, pp. 166–76, and the works of Detwiler and Burdick, cited above, n. 61.

71. Proposals for concessions to the French, October 21, 1940, and draft treaties (*DGFP*, D, 11:346–48, 350–51).

72. The occasion was the hundredth anniversary of the transfer of Napoleon's body from Saint Helena to Paris, where the duke of Reichstadt was now also buried. See Jäckel, *Frankreich,* pp. 140–44.

219

73. See Abetz's analysis, December 18, 1940 (*DGFP*, D, 11:891–98).

74. Prince Xavier de Bourbon-Parma, *Les Accords secrets franco-anglais de décembre, 1940* (Paris, 1949), pp. 213–23; Mallet, *Laval,* 1:290 ff.

75. Warlimont report of a conference of December 10, 1940 (*DGFP*, D, 11:860–63).

76. *DGFP*, D, 11:508–10, 533–49, 562–70, 594–95.

77. Canaris report on Franco's position; Hitler directive 19 for Operation Attila (*DGFP*, D, 11:816–17, 836–38, 852–53).

78. Pétain's letter to Hitler of December 13, 1940, thanking him for returning the body of the duke of Reichstadt and at the same time informing him of the dismissal of Laval is a good example of his method of dealing with the German dictator. It was his cherished intention, Pétain said, to make his co-operation with Germany more effective with each passing day. He had high praise for Laval; but, because Laval no longer possessed the confidence of the French people or sufficient authority in the country to carry out this policy of collaboration with Germany effectively, Pétain felt obliged to dismiss him. He proposed to replace him with Flandin, and hoped Hitler would approve (*DGFP*, D, 11:866–67). The German translation of this letter which was prepared for Hitler had an even more effusive tone (T77/78/5508390–91).

79. Keitel letter to Thomas, January 10, 1941, after Keitel had conferred with Hitler (T77/851/5596112–13).

220

80. Lukasz Hirszowicz, *The Third Reich and the Arab East* (Toronto, 1966); Joseph B. Schechtman, *The Mufti and the Fuehrer* (New York, 1965); Heinz Tillmann, *Deutschlands Araberpolitik im zweiten Weltkrieg* (East Berlin, 1965); S. Wiesenthal, *Grossmufti—Grossagent der Achse* (Salzburg, 1947).

81. *DGFP*, D, 12:497 ff., 655–56, 686, 862–64; Rudolf Rahn, *Ruheloses Leben. Aufzeichnungen und Erinnerungen eines deutschen Diplomaten* (Düsseldorf, 1949), pp. 152 ff. Hytier, *French Foreign Policy,* pp. 253 ff.; Jäckel, *Frankreich,* p. 161 ff.

82. May 8, 1941 (*DGFP*, D, 12:740–42; also pp. 718–20); Aron, *Vichy Regime,* pp. 312–17.

83. Schmidt memorandum of the Hitler-Darlan conference, May 11, 1941 (*DGFP*, D, 12:763–74); as reported by General Paul Doyen on the basis of Darlan's account of the conference (*Délégation française d'armistice,* 4:459–60); and Darlan's own account in his memoirs (*L'Admiral Darlan parle,* pp. 263–67).

221

84. Schmidt memorandum of the Ribbentrop-Darlan conference, May 13, 1941 (*DGFP*, D, 12:797–806).

85. *DGFP*, D, 12:892–900.

86. On this problem see Hytier, *French Foreign Policy,* pp. 253, 262–66; Jäckel, *Frankreich,* pp. 172–75; Aron, *Vichy Regime,* pp. 312–24.

87. *DGFP*, D, 12:991–92, 1033–34.

88. Unsigned memorandum of Hitler's talk with Abetz, September 16, 1941 (*DGFP*, D, 13:518–20); notes on Abetz's account to Hemmen of his talk with Hitler, September 24, 1941 (NG 1397; PS 1311); Jäckel, *Frankreich,* p. 180.

89. Keitel-Jodl affidavit, *IMT* 40:389; Jäckel, *Frankreich,* chap. 11; Hytier, *French Foreign Policy,* pp. 286, 296, 312.

90. Göring talks with Pétain and Darlan, December 1, 1941 (*DGFP*, D, 13:914–27, 930–34); with Juin, December 20, 1941 (T77/851/5595949–59).

91. *Goebbels Diaries,* pp. 39, 42.

92. It will be recalled that in February 1942 General Otto von Stülpnagel retired as head of the German military government in France, to be replaced after a short interval by his cousin, General Karl Heinrich von Stülpnagel, the former head of the Armistice Commission. In April SS Gruppenführer Karl Albrecht Oberg was appointed senior SS and police officer for France. The Germans, with the possible exception of Otto Abetz, appear to have had little interest in the reinstatement of Laval, but Laval evidently convinced

Pétain that only his appointment (with additional powers) would prevent the Germans from pursuing even harsher policies in France. On this question see Aron, *Vichy Regime,* pp. 348–59; Jäckel, *Frankreich,* pp. 220, 233.

93. Erwin Rommel, *The Rommel Papers,* ed. B. H. Liddell Hart (New York, 1953), pt. 3.

94. This was Operation Attila, plans for which had been prepared in accordance with a Hitler directive of December 10, 1940 (*DGFP,* D, 11:836–38); plans extended to include Corsica, February 13, 1941 (T77/777/5503731–36); co-ordinated with plans for the defense of the Iberian Peninsula (Operation Isabella), May 29, 1942 (T78/319/6273389–92).

95. Jäckel, *Frankreich,* pp. 250–53; Aron, *Vichy Regime,* pp. 420–23.

96. With the German occupation of Vichy France, Hitler instructed Stülpnagel to issue a special order to German troops to conduct themselves with dignity and restraint, especially in their relations with the French administration (T/78/32/706029).

97. Aron, *Vichy Regime,* pp. 419 ff.

98. With the total occupation of France in November 1942, the Italian zone of occupation had also been extended. The new line of demarcation between the German and Italian zones began southwest of Geneva, followed the course of the Rhone (leaving Lyon and Avignon in the German zone); south of Avignon it bent sharply to the east, reaching the Mediterranean coast at La Ciotat between Marseille and Toulon. The island of Corsica, too, was placed under an Italian occupation administration at this time. On the extension of the Italian occupation zone and the changes in the German administration in France, see Jäckel, pp. 254 ff.

99. Keitel's special order no. 1 for the newly occupied French territories of November 16, 1942 (NOKW 1005); Rundstedt order of January 25, 1943 (NOKW 1520).

224

100. Jäckel, *Frankreich,* p. 258; Medicus, "Militärverwaltung," pp. 93–96.

101. Jäckel, *Frankreich,* p. 278.

102. Statistics on French laborers in Germany, spring 1942, in Jäckel, *Frankreich,* pp. 223–24; report on the French economy by the German military commander for France, February 1, 1942 (EC 267); German Foreign Office memorandum of June 3, 1942, on the French contribution to the German war economy as of April 1, 1942 (NG 109).

225

103. The following account of German labor recruitment in France is based largely on Jäckel, *Frankreich,* pp. 222–24, 268–70, who draws on the final report of the economic section of the German military government. According to a letter of August 22, 1942, from Elmar Michel, the chief of the administrative staff of the German military administration, to Bernaud, the French liaison officer for French-German economic relations, Laval had promised Sauckel three hundred and fifty thousand workers, one hundred and fifty thousand of whom were to be metal workers. As it was now clear that voluntary recruitment would not produce the necessary number of workers, the Germans demanded the introduction of compulsory measures (*IMT* 5:484–85). On September 4, 1942, the Vichy government passed a law freezing all manpower and providing that all Frenchmen between eighteen and fifty who did not have a job occupying them more than thirty hours a week had to prove that they were usefully employed (*IMT* 5:392–93, 483).

104. Jäckel, *Frankreich,* p. 270. According to a Sauckel minute of January 5, 1943, Speer had called on him the previous evening to inform him of Hitler's order that it was no longer necessary to show special consideration to France in the future recruitment of labor and that recruitment in France was to proceed more energetically (*IMT,* 556(13)-PS, 26:150–51). Sauckel immediately expressed his intention to do so in a conference with the military commander on January 11, 1943 (*IMT,* 1342-PS, 15:173–78); Sauckel's quotas (pp. 178–80); Laval's complaints (*IMT* 15:85–86).

105. Law of February 16, 1943 (*Journal officiel;* reproduced in *TWC* 13:1003).

106. Jäckel, *Frankreich,* pp. 270–71. The quotas Sauckel set himself were even higher. On June 27 he asked Hitler's approval to make available over one million French workers for German war production in the second half of 1943 and to transfer an additional half-million French men and women to the Reich, a program Hitler authorized on July 28 (*IMT* 5:489–91; see also Sauckel's demands on the German military authorities of June 27, 1943 (NG 5172).

226

107. Jäckel, *Frankreich,* pp. 302–3; Sauckel to Hitler, August 13, 1943; Sauckel plans for the regional recruitment of labor, August 13, 1943 (*IMT* 5:491–92; 15:78, 96–97).

108. Jäckel, *Frankreich,* pp. 303–5.

109. Raul Hilberg, *The Destruction of the European Jews* (Chicago, 1961), pp. 389–421; Gerald Reitlinger, *The Final Solution: The Attempt to Exterminate the Jews of Europe, 1939–1945* (New York, 1968), chap. 12; J. Lubetzki, *La Condition des Juifs en France sous l'occupation allemande, 1940–1944. La Législation raciale* (Paris, 1945), a valuable analysis of French and German anti-Jewish legislation, with lists of the laws. Statistics in text based on Hilberg, *Destruction,* p. 392. As usual, statistics on the number of Jews in a particular area vary widely. Because of the various official definitions of the term *Jew* and the refugee problem, it is impossible to do more than arrive at rough estimates.

110. See above, p. 217. The quotation comes from a memorandum by the Foreign Office official Martin Luther of November 25, 1940 (NG 4934).

227   111. Final report on the military government written at the end of the occupation (T501/184/1080–81). Early in August 1940 Hitler informed Abetz of his intention to evacuate all Jews from Europe after the war (*DGFP*, D, 10:484). French anti-Jewish measures are summarized by Boüard, "Répression allemande," p. 87.

112. *DGFP*, D, 10:513.

113. *TWC*, NG 4893, 13:156–59; *NCA* 7:375–76.

114. Final report, German military government (T501/184/1080–81); Jäckel, *Frankreich*, p. 99.

115. *Journal officiel*, July 23, August 2 and 30, October 18 and 25, 1940; *DGFP*, D, 12:346–47, 437–39; *IMT* 38:740–46; Jäckel, *Frankreich*, pp. 99–100; Hilberg, *Destruction*, pp. 398, 400–403; Aron, *Vichy Regime*, pp. 166–69.

228   116. *VBIF* (1940), pp. 92–93, 112–14, 166; (1941), pp. 255–58, 263, 297; *DGFP*, D, 11:275–76.

117. Dannecker memorandum of February 22, 1942 (*IMT* 38:741).

118. *DGFP*, D, 12:346–47, 437–39; *IMT* 38:741–42; *Journal officiel*, July 23, 1941; Jäckel, *Frankreich*, p. 226; Hilberg, *Destruction*, pp. 398, 400–402; and especially the work of J. Billig, *Le Commissariat général aux questions juives (1941–1944)*, 3 vols. (Paris, 1955–60).

119. *Journal officiel*, December 2, 1941; *IMT* 38:741–44; Hilberg, *Destruction*, pp. 397–98; Aron, *Vichy Regime*, p. 305.

229   120. Billig, *Commissariat général*, 1:214–28; Aron, *Vichy Regime*, pp. 305, 371, 384; Hilberg, *Destruction*, pp. 400–402.

121. *IMT* 39:6–8; Aron, *Vichy Regime*, p. 385; Reitlinger, *Final Solution*, pp. 337–38.

122. Schellenberg directive (NG 3104; *IMT* 7:28); on Germany's Jewish policy in general, see above, Chap. 1.

123. *IMT* 7:29–30; 10:403; Jäckel, *Frankreich*, p. 226.

124. Conference of March 4, 1942 (*IMT* 38:746); Eichmann order (NG 4594C); conference of June 11, 1942 (*IMT* 7:37); *TWC* 13:233–36; Hilberg, *Destruction*, pp. 404–7.

230   125. Dannecker guidelines (*IMT* 39:2–4); demands of June 27 (*IMT* 7:38; 10:403–4; 39:2–6).

126. Röthke appears to have taken over the leadership of the Jewish office in France some time in July (RF 1225); Reitlinger, *Final Solution*, pp. 337, 339.

127. Official statistical report for Himmler (T175/103/2625029–45); *IMT* 7:40; 39:6–8.

128. Himmler note of December 10, 1942, on Hitler's orders (T175/103/2625558). At the famous Wannsee conference of January 20, 1942, Heydrich had estimated that there were still one hundred and sixty-five thousand Jews in the occupied territories of France, seven hundred thousand in unoccupied France (NG 2586; see above, Chap. 1).

129. Again it is necessary to bear in mind that all statistics can only be rough estimates. Hilberg, *Destruction*, pp. 416–19; Reitlinger, *Final Solution*, p. 538.

231   130. Jäckel, *Frankreich*, pp. 195–97, 332–34; Reitlinger, *Final Solution*, p. 349.

131. Jäckel, *Frankreich*, pp. 331–43.

232   132. On the German administration of Alsace and Lorraine and plans for the future, see the interrogations and affidavits of Dr. Hans Globke (*IMT* 37:218–23). The German civil administration in Alsace and Lorraine was established by mid-July, 1940, although no special orders to that effect had yet been issued (*DGFP*, D, 10:498). Also Jäckel, *Frankreich*, chap. 4; Marie-Joseph Bopp, *L'Alsace sous l'occupation allemande, 1940–1945* (Le Puys, Alsatia, 1945); Eugène Schaeffer, *L'Alsace et la Lorraine (1940–1945). Leur Occupation en droit et en fait* (Paris, 1953).

133. On Wagner and Bürckel, see Jäckel, *Frankreich*, pp. 76–77; Pierre Crénesse, *Le Procès de Wagner, bourreau de l'Alsace* (Paris, 1946).

134. According to Wagner's testimony (Crénesse, *Procès de Wagner*, p. 13), Hitler gave Wagner and Bürckel these instructions on June 20, a date that has been questioned by Jäckel, *Frankreich*, p. 76, n. 9.

135. Lammers to Schwerin von Krosigk, September 30, 1940 (NG 4302). An article by the Reich press chief, Dr. Otto Dietrich, described the impressions of Hitler's German retinue on the occasion of his entry into Strasbourg on June 28, 1940. "This city is German, and the farther we go, the more clearly did it reveal its German visage to us." At the end of his article Dietrich described French prisoners of war, who were exclaiming that Hitler had just come from Strasbourg. Yes, Dr. Dietrich said, the Führer *had* just come from Strasbourg—"the Strassburg which will now be German for evermore [*dem nun für immer deutschen Strassburg*]" (Hans Otto Meissner, ed., *Elsass und Lothringen. Deutsches Land* [Berlin, 1941], pp. 17–23).

136. Hitler's orders of August 2, 1942, were not published, although an official announcement about the appointments of Wagner and Bürckel was made on August 7 (NOKW 3474; NG 3587; *DGFP*, D, 10:498–99); Jäckel, *Frankreich*, pp. 79–80.

137. *DGFP*, D, 10:498–99; Geschke, *Frankreichpolitik*, p. 56; Schaeffer, *Alsace et Lorraine*, p. 66.

233   138. Hitler's orders of October 18, 1940, confirming the enlargement of the party administrative districts of Wagner and Bürckel were not published. The distinction be-

tween party and state administrations must be emphasized here. Both Wagner and Bürckel restricted their annexation measures to party offices; but as party and state offices frequently performed similar functions and were under the direction of the same official, this disguise of German intentions was thin at best. On this problem, see Schaeffer, *Alsace et Lorraine,* pp. 60–61; Jäckel, *Frankreich,* p. 83; and, above all, Pierre Cézard, "L'Annexion de fait de l'Alsace et de la Lorraine, Juin 1940–Septembre 1942," *RHDGM* 5 (1952):37–52.

139. Huntzinger to Stülpnagel, September 3, 1940 (*Délégation française d'armistice,* 1:239–41; 2:135–36; 3:90–103).

140. Stuckart to Schwerin von Krosigk and Himmler, July 4, 1940 (NG 1141; *Délégation française d'armistice,* 1:97; 2:135; *DGFP,* D, 10:498–99; *IMT* 6:436–37).

141. In the first issue of his legal gazette of August 24, 1940, Bürckel published an announcement of his appointment by Hitler as head of the civil administration for Lorraine under the date August 12, 1940 (*VBlL* [1940], p. 1).

142. Thus the name of the city of Nancy was to be Germanized as Nanzig; Besançon as Bisanz. Language Germanization decrees for Alsace, *VBlE* (1940), p. 2; for Lorraine, *VBlL* (1940), p. 60; (1941), pp. 139–49, 347–49, 358, 725; (1942), p. 423.

143. *VBlE* (1940), p. 22; (1941), pp. 35–37, 445–46, 490–91, 595–99, 659–61; (1942), pp. 64–65; *VBlL* (1940), p. 52; (1941), pp. 817–18, 909–14, 1076; (1942), pp. 145–46, 275; (1943), pp. 7–10, 37–43.

144. *VBlE* (1941), p. 744; *VBlL* (1941), p. 91.

145. *VBlE* (1940), pp. 26, 47, 62, 88–89; (1941), pp. 285, 429–31, 557–59; *VBlL* (1940), p. 69; (1941), pp. 100–101, 107, 109–10, 347–49; (1942), pp. 123–27.

146. *VBlE* (1940), pp. 2–3, 233–34, 325–26, 426–28, 494–96; (1941), pp. 106, 170, 414, 534, 602–3; (1942), pp. 283–84; *VBlL* (1940), pp. 92–93, 200, 216; (1941), pp. 2–4, 206–207, 437, 706–708, 1003, 1037–43; (1942), pp. 385–98.

147. *VBlE* (1941), p. 362; (1942), pp. 24, 252, 281; *VBlL* (1941), pp. 468, 1077; (1942), pp. 52, 357, 385, 501; (1943), p. 30; Jäckel, *Frankreich,* p. 229.

148. *RGBl* (1942), 1:533; *VBlE* (1942), pp. 251–52; *VBlL* (1942), pp. 413–22, 514; (1943), pp. 26, 242; Jäckel, *Frankreich,* pp. 231–32.

149. Remarks of May 12, 1942 (*Hitler's Secret Conversations,* p. 444; Picker, *Hitlers Tischgespräche,* pp. 331–32). See also Paul Kluke, "Nationalsozialistische Volkstumspolitik in Elsass-Lothringen, 1940 bis 1945," *Zur Geschichte und Problematik der Demokratie, Festgabe für Hans Herzfeld* (Berlin, 1958), pp. 619–36.

150. Stier memorandum of conference on evacuation problems, October 14, 1940 (NO 5589); and especially his memorandum of a similar conference of August 7, 1942 (PS 1470; *IMT* 38:330–36; *DGFP,* D, 11:448–49, 456, 460, 885; *Délégation française d'armistice,* 2:136–42; 3:223.

151. On this question, see especially Himmler to Lammers, June 10, 1942 (NO 2475); Himmler's order on evacuation and resettlement procedures of June 15, 1942 (NO 2559); Creutz to Himmler, July 30, 1941 (NO 5564); Brandt to Himmler, March 16, 1942 (NO 2474); Kaul to Himmler, with Himmler's marginalia, May 4, 1942 (T175/59/2574697); Kaul to Greifelt, May 27, 1942, informing him that one and a half years ago Himmler had ordered him not to evacuate racially sound but politically undesirable elements in Alsace to France "because it is not in the Reich's interests to provide France with racially valuable stock [*rassisch gutes Erbgut*]." Kaul, the senior SS and police officer in Württemberg and Baden as well as in Alsace, now wanted to settle these people in Württemberg (NO 2247; T175/59/2574691–92).

152. Greifelt to the representatives of the RKFDV in Strasbourg, Metz, and Luxembourg, May 15, 1941, forwarding two Himmler decrees on racial policy procedures (NO 3531c).

153. Himmler orders of May 1941 (NO 3531c); Himmler to Lammers, June 10, 1942 (NO 2475); Himmler directive of June 15, 1942 (NO 2559).

154. Himmler orders of May 1941 (NO 3531c).

155. Creutz to Himmler, July 30, 1941 (NO 5564).

156. Greifelt to Himmler, September 12, 1941, enclosing draft proposals, draft legislation, and memoranda of Bürckel's (T175/18/2522291–309).

157. Memorandum of October 22, 1941, on resettlement conference of October 17 (NO 5567).

158. Stier memorandum of August 7, 1942, on the August 4 conference (PS 1470; *IMT* 38:330–36). Objections to this program were raised at the conference and, later, by Ulrich Greifelt when he was informed of Hitler's decision to evacuate another forty thousand Lorrainers. German military authorities were on the whole appalled by the entire resettlement procedure. "The evacuations from Lorraine made a positively devastating impression," the German military government reported on November 30, 1940 (quoted in Geschke, *Frankreichpolitik,* pp. 117–18). On evacuation and resettlement plans, see also the detailed memorandum on the tasks of the RuSHA in the west of September 28, 1942 (NO 1499).

159. Greifelt to Himmler, August 28, 1942 (T175/18/2522257–62).

160. Brandt, on behalf of Himmler, to senior SS officers concerned with evacuation problems (T175/18/2522253–54).

161. Greifelt to Himmler, August 28; Himmler to Greifelt, September 7, 1942 (T175/18/2522256–62).

162. RuSHA memorandum of October 6, 1942 (NO 1600); Greifelt memorandum of May 12, 1943, recording Himmler's decisions based on orders received from Hitler (NO 3181; T175/43/2554595–608).

163. Memorandum of RKFDV conference on the evacuation of Lorrainers, November 28, 1942 (NO 5211); Wagner to Lammers, January 19, 1944 (NO 2244; T175/59/2574573–76).

164. Berger to Himmler, June 21, 1944 (T175/59/2574571). As late as August 28, 1944, with the German armies in full retreat, Himmler thought it necessary to evacuate all ethnic Germans from northern France immediately. All men who were physically fit were to be allocated as miners in the Aachen area, all women were to be used in the Reich for labor (NO 5652).

239 165. Picker, *Hitlers Tischgespräche*, pp. 337–38; *Hitler's Secret Conversations*, pp. 449–51.

166. Picker, *Hitlers Tischgespräche*, pp. 237–38, 295–96, 320; *Hitler's Secret Conversations*, p. 418; Felix Kersten, *The Kersten Memoirs, 1940–1945*. (London, 1956), pp. 184–86; see also the unsigned memorandum on new German boundaries in the west in the files of the military commander for Belgium and Northern France (T501/96/828–33).

9. THE SOUTHEASTERN FLANK

240
241 1. See the first volume of this study, pp. 180–95.
2. Henry Picker, *Hitlers Tischgespräche im Führerhauptquartier, 1941–1942*, ed. Percy
242 Ernst Schramm, Andreas Hillgruber, Martin Vogt (Stuttgart, 1965), pp. 354, 486–87.
3. See the first volume of this study, pp. 183–87; Martin Broszat, "Deutschland-Ungarn-Rumänien. Entwicklung und Grundfaktoren nationalsozialistischer Hegemonial-und Bündnispolitik, 1938–1941," *Historische Zeitschrift* 206 (1968):45–96; Andreas Hillgruber "Deutschland und Ungarn, 1933–1944. Ein überblick über die politischen und militärischen Beziehungen im Rahmen der europäischen Politik," *Wehrwissenschaftliche Rundschau 9* (1959):651–76; C. A. Macartney, *October Fifteenth: A History of Modern Hungary, 1929–1945*, 2 vols. (Edinburgh, 1956).
4. C. A. Macartney, "Hungary's Declaration of War on the U.S.S.R. in 1941," *Studies in Diplomatic History in Honour of G. P. Gooch*, ed. A. O. Sarkissian (London, 1961), pp. 152–65; G. Ránki, "Der Eintritt Ungarns in den zweiten Weltkrieg," *Der deutsche Imperialismus und der zweite Weltkrieg*, 3 vols. (East Berlin, 1962), vol. 3, pp. 415–37.
5. In his memoirs, the Hungarian statesman Nicholas (Miklós) Kállay wrote,

The Germans' chief instrument of pressure against the Hungarians was their citation of the example of Rumania and the probable consequences if we did not do as well: the Germans warned that, if Rumania fought with the Germans against the Soviet Union and we did not, Hitler would find it morally and practically impossible not to revise his stand on the Transylvania question in favor of the Rumanians (*Hungarian Premier: A Personal Account of a Nation's Struggle in the Second World War* [New York, 1954], pp. 64–65).

6. Franz Halder, *Kriegstagebuch. Tägliche Aufzeichnungen des Chefs des Generalstabes des Heeres, 1939–1942*, ed. Hans-Adolf Jacobsen, 3 vols. (Stuttgart, 1962–64), 3:218.
7. *DGFP*, D, 13:467.
8. Hewel memorandum of Hitler-Bárdossy conversation of November 27, 1941 (*DGFP*, D, 13:856–58); *Hitler's Secret Conversations, 1941–1944* (paperback, New York, 1961), p. 189.
243 9. Clodius report on economic relations with Hungary, August 16, 1941; Rintelen memorandum of Ribbentrop-Bárdossy conversation of November 26, 1941 (*DGFP*, D, 13:319–21, 835–39); G. Ránki, *Das ungarische Wirtschaftsleben im Dienste der deutschen Kriegswirtschaft zur Zeit des zweiten Weltkrieges* (East Berlin, 1958).
10. Nicholas (Miklós) Horthy, *Memoirs* (New York, 1957), pp. 203–4.
11. Remarks of June 7 and August 9, 1942 (*Hitler's Secret Conversations*, pp. 484–85, 580; Picker, *Hitlers Tischgespräche*, pp. 390–91).
244 12. *The Goebbels Diaries, 1942–1943*, ed. Louis P. Lochner (New York, 1948), p. 157 (entry for April 1, 1942).
13. Schmidt memorandum of Hitler's conversation with Horthy on April 17, 1943 (*IMT*, 736-D, 35:426–31); Horthy, *Memoirs*, pp. 204–6; *The Confidential Papers of Admiral Horthy*, ed. Miklós Szinai and László Szűcs (Budapest, 1965), pp. 248–49, 256, n. 2; *Goebbels Diaries*, p. 335 (entry for April 18, 1943).
14. *Kriegstagebuch des Oberkommandos der Wehrmacht (Wehrmachtführungsstab), 1940–1945*, ed. Percy Ernst Schramm, Andreas Hillgruber, Walter Hubatsch, and Hans-Adolf Jacobsen, 4 vols. in 7 (Frankfurt am Main, 1961–65), 4:180–93; G. Ránki, "L'Occupation de la Hongrie par les allemands," *RHDGM* 62 (1966):37.

245
15. Berger reports for Himmler, October–December 1943, incorporating information received from agents in Hungary (T175/119/2664757–74).
16. *Goebbels Diaries*, p. 507 (entry for November 10, 1943).
17. Hoettl affidavit (NG 2317); Horthy, *Memoirs*, p. 208; Elek Karsai, "Edmund Veesenmayer's Reports to Hitler on Hungary in 1943," *The New Hungarian Quarterly* 5 (1964): 146–53; *Kriegstagebuch OKW*, 4:193–200.
18. Horthy's report to the Crown Council of his talk with Hitler (*Confidential Papers*, pp. 280–85; Horthy, *Memoirs*, pp. 212–15); Ránki, "L'occupation," p. 38. Ránki points out that these sources of the Hitler-Horthy talks differ, but the main thing was that Hitler succeeded in persuading the regent to remain in office. See also *Kriegstagebuch OKW*, 4:200–205.
19. *Confidential Papers*, pp. 285, 289.

246
20. Hitler's appointment of Veesenmayer, March 19, 1944 (NG 1543; NG 2947; *TWC* 13:336–37); Horthy affidavit (NG 1828).
21. Veesenmayer report on negotiations with Horthy, March 20, 1944 (*TWC* 13:338–39); *Confidential Papers*, p. 288; Horthy, *Memoirs*, pp. 217–18.
22. Appointment of Winkelmann, March 31, 1944 (T175/119/2644800–801); affidavit of Kienast, Winkelmann's deputy in Hungary (NG 2528); Ránki, "L'occupation," pp. 42–44.

247
23. Ránki, "L'occupation," pp. 40–42, drawing on material in the German Foreign Office files.
24. *Confidential Papers*, p. 289; Ránki, "L'occupation," p. 45; Macartney, *October Fifteenth*, 2:297.
25. Horthy, *Memoirs*, p. 219. On the anti-Jewish campaign in Hungary, see below, pp. 250–51.
26. Horthy's draft letters, *Confidential Papers*, pp. 304–7, 316–19; Veesenmayer to Ribbentrop, July 6, 1944 (NG 5523); Ribbentrop to Veesenmayer, July 16, 1944 (NG 2739).

248
27. See below p. 258.
28. Lakatos affidavit (NG 1848); Horthy, *Memoirs*, pp. 221–28; *Confidential Papers*, pp. 314–15; Macartney, *October Fifteenth*, 2:306, 326; Ránki, "L'occupation," p. 50.
29. Horthy, *Memoirs*, pp. 227–29; Ránki, "L'occupation," pp. 51–52; Macartney, *October Fifteenth*, 2, chap. 18.
30. Miklós Lackó, "Les Croix-Flèchées (1935–1944)," *RHDGM* 62 (1966):53–68. Unfortunately the article breaks off at October 15, 1944; Ránki, "L'occupation," pp. 51–52.
31. See below, p. 319.

249
32. Winkelmann to Himmler, October 25, 1944 (NG 2540); Otto Skorzeny, *Skorzeny's Secret Missions: War Memoirs of the Most Dangerous Man in Europe* (New York, 1950), chap. 19; Rudolf Rahn, *Ruheloses Leben. Aufzeichnungen und Erinnerungen eines deutschen Diplomaten* (Düsseldorf, 1949), pp. 265–71; Horthy, *Memoirs*, pp. 229–37.
33. Macartney, *October Fifteenth*, 2, chap. 19.
34. Kállay, *Hungarian Premier*, pp. 470, 472–73.
35. Macartney, *October Fifteenth*, 2:452.

250
36. On this problem in general, see the three valuable works of Randolph L. Braham, *Eichmann and the Destruction of Hungarian Jewry* (New York, 1961); *The Destruction of Hungarian Jewry: A Documentary Account*, 2 vols. (New York, 1963); *The Hungarian Jewish Catastrophe: A Selected and Annotated Bibliography* (New York, 1963). My statistics come from Braham. Also Eugene Levai, *Black Book on the Martyrdom of Hungarian Jewry* (Zürich, 1948); Ránki, "L'occupation," pp. 46 ff.; Raul Hilberg, *The Destruction of the European Jews* (Chicago, 1961), pp. 509–54; Gerald Reitlinger, *The Final Solution: The Attempt to Exterminate the Jews of Europe, 1939–1945* (New York, 1968), pp. 447–87.
37. Veesenmayer to the Foreign Office, April 23 and 27, 1944 (*TWC*, NG 2233, 5535, 13:348–50); Ritter (Foreign Office) to Budapest, April 27, 1944 (*TWC*, NG 2196, 13:1071–72).
38. Veesenmayer to the Foreign Office, June 17 and 30, July 11, 1944 (*TWC*, NG 5567, 2263, 5586, 13:258–61).

251
39. Veesenmayer to Ribbentrop, July 6, 1944 (NG 5523); Ribbentrop to Veesenmayer, July 16, 1944 (NG 2739); Horthy, *Confidential Papers*, pp. 300–304; Horthy, *Memoirs*, pp. 219–20; Hilberg, *Destruction*, p. 550.
40. Hilberg, *Destruction*, pp. 553–54; Reitlinger, *Final Solution*, pp. 479–87, 542.
41. See the first volume of this study, pp. 187–92, and especially the excellent monograph of Andreas Hillgruber, *Hitler, König Carol und Marschall Antonescu. Die deutsch-rumänischen Beziehungen, 1938–1944* (Wiesbaden, 1954). Also *DGFP*, D, 11:126–28, 136–37, 144–56, 281–82.
42. Hillgruber, *Hitler, Carol, Antonescu*, pp. 207–8, 232; Henri Prost, "La Roumanie et la seconde guerre mondiale," *RHDGM* 6 (1952):26–49.
43. SA men remained bitter about the participation of Himmler's SS in the massacre of their leaders on June 30, 1934. On April 17 and 26, 1941, Berger wrote to Himmler that the Foreign Office had headed all the ministries in Southeastern Europe with SA men, and suspected that this was the result of an alliance between Joachim von Ribbentrop and Viktor Lutze, the chief of staff of the SA, which had been fostered by Martin Luther, the

head of the Foreign Office department for domestic affairs (T175/123/2648808–9; 2648944–47); on Neubacher, see his memoirs, *Sonderauftrag Südost, 1940–1945. Bericht eines fliegenden Diplomaten* (Göttingen, 1956); also *DGFP*, D, 9:467–70; 11: 870–71; Hillgruber, *Hitler, Carol, Antonescu*, pp. 85, 117, 121, 308, n. 39.

44. Remarks of October 17, 1941 (*Hitler's Secret Conversations*, p. 90); also Hitler's speech to Mussolini and senior German and Italian officials, January 20, 1941 (*NCA*, 134-C, 6:945).

45. On Hitler's conception of the importance of Rumanian oil, see his remarks to Ciano, November 18, 1940, and his letter to Mussolini of November 20, 1940 (*DGFP*, D, 11:606–10, 639–43).

46. On June 26, 1940, the Russians demanded the cession of the Rumanian territories of Bessarabia and Northern Bukovina, and at the advice of the Germans (at that time still adhering to their pact with the Soviet Union), Rumania yielded to the Russian ultimatum. Shortly afterward Bulgaria demanded Southern Dobruja, which Rumania· yielded by the treaty of Craiova, September 7, 1940, while Hungary demanded the greater part of Transylvania, which Rumania gave up under pressure from Germany and Italy (the Second Vienna Award, August 30, 1940). See the first volume of this study, pp. 184–86, 189, 193, 205–6.

47. Hitler to Antonescu, June 18, 1941; Antonescu to Hitler, July 1, 1941 (*DGFP*, D, 12:1047–49; 13:66–67); Hillgruber, *Hitler, Carol, Antonescu*, pp. 132–34.

48. Unsigned memorandum of Hitler's conference with Rosenberg, Lammers, Keitel, Göring, and Bormann, July 16, 1941 (*DGFP*, D, 13:149–56).

49. Hitler to Antonescu, July 27 and August 14, 1941 (*DGFP*, D, 13:225–27, 316–17). Bessarabia and Northern Bukovina were officially reunited with Rumania on July 25, 1941.

50. Russian, Bender; a city in Bessarabia, on the Dniester.

51. Antonescu to Hitler, August 17, 1941 (*DGFP*, D, 13:324–25 and footnotes); *NCA* 6:30–34; Hillgruber, *Hitler, Carol, Antonescu*, pp. 137, 139–40.

52. Hitler to Antonescu, October 5, 1941, offering German aid to Rumanian forces attacking Odessa (T78/335/6291837–38); Hillgruber, *Hitler, Carol, Antonescu*, pp. 138, 142.

53. Remarks of July 25 and October 17, 1941 (*Hitler's Secret Conversations*, pp. 43, 90–91). Within a few months Hitler's opinion of the Rumanians had changed drastically. The Rumanian peasants were merely wretched cattle, he said in February 1942, the ruling class rotten to the core (*Hitler's Secret Conversations*, p. 325; Picker, *Hitlers Tischgespräche*, p. 183).

54. Schmidt memorandum of Hitler's conversation with M. Antonescu, November 28, 1941 (*DGFP*, D, 13:891–94).

55. Hillgruber, *Hitler, Carol, Antonescu*, p. 145; Schmidt memoranda on Ion Antonescu's talks with Ribbentrop, Keitel, Göring, and Hitler in February 1942 (*ADAP*, E, 1:408–17; 422–25, 429–41, 443–56); Antonescu-Hitler talk of April 3, 1942 (*IMT* 7:322). In his diary, entry for April 16, 1942, Hassell recorded that according to Neubacher, the German official in charge of German economic interests in Rumania, the fear of Russia kept Rumania in the German camp, but that hatred for Hungary and desire for the return of Transylvania overshadowed everything (Ulrich von Hassell, *Vom andern Deutschland. Aus den nachgelassenen Tagebüchern 1938–1944* [Zürich, 1946], pp. 266–67).

56. *The Ciano Diaries, 1939–1943*, ed. Hugh Gibson (New York, 1946), pp. 568, 572; Neubacher, *Sonderauftrag Südost*, pp. 49–50; Hillgruber, *Hitler, Carol, Antonescu*, pp. 134–55, 167–99. Mihai Antonescu was particularly active in seeking to arrange an accord with Britain and the United States, and he tried to persuade the Italians to join him in overtures to the Western powers (Prost, "La Roumanie," p. 43).

57. Unsigned memorandum (from Schmidt's file) of Göring's conversation with M. Antonescu, November 26, 1941 (*DGFP*, D, 13:844–48).

58. Hillgruber, *Hitler, Carol, Antonescu*, pp. 156–64, with statistics on German-Rumanian economic relations, pp. 247–54. Detailed official German statistics on German oil needs, German oil production, and Rumanian oil exports, are available on film in the National Archives, T77, rolls 84, 438, and 594.

59. Antonescu to Hitler, December 5, 1941 (*DGFP*, D, 13:963–64); further documents on German-Rumanian economic negotiations, December 1941–February 1942 (*ADAP*, E, 1:7 ff.). In October 1942 the central planning department of the Four-Year Plan estimated that Germany needed 10 million tons of oil in 1942. To make up this amount, 3.2 million tons had to come from Rumania. The Reich Ministry of Economics estimated that Germany would need 15 millions tons for 1943, and only 11.7 million were available; therefore imports from abroad would be more necessary than ever (T77/10/721180–84).

60. Hillgruber, *Hitler, Carol, Antonescu*, pp. 200–208.

61. Ibid., pp. 236–46; Hilberg, *Destruction*, pp. 485–509; Reitlinger, *Final Solution*, pp. 425–38.

62. Neubacher to the Foreign Office, August 6, 1941 (*DGFP*, D, 13:287–88).

63. Hilberg, *Destruction*, pp. 491–97; Reitlinger, *Final Solution*, pp. 427–38.

64. Hilberg, *Destruction*, pp. 498–509; Reitlinger, *Final Solution*, pp. 438–46, 540–41.

65. Treaties on population transfers: with Russia, to remove ethnic Germans from Bessarabia and Northern Bukovina to the Reich, September 5, 1940 (T175/194/2732991); with Rumania on the resettlement of ethnic Germans from Southern Bukovina and Dobruja, October 22, 1940 (T175/194/2732991); with Rumania over the ethnic Germans in Transnistria, December 13, 1941 (T175/194/2733072–76); Hillgruber, *Hitler, Carol, Antonescu,* pp. 107–9.

66. Himmler orders of October 1940 to carry out the resettlement of ethnic Germans from Bessarabia and Northern Bukovina as soon as possible (T175/194/2733028, 2733139–41); Greifelt instructions of November 13, 1940, for the resettlement of ethnic Germans from Bessarabia in the new German provinces of Danzig-West Prussia and the Warthegau (NO 5138); notes on the RuSHA conference of January 11–12, 1941, on racial classification and resettlement problems (NO 1406); Hildebrandt-Himmler report of June 30, 1942, on the progress of the resettlement of ethnic Germans from Bessarabia (T175/66/2582229–30); Himmler to Hildebrandt, July 17, 1942, congratulating him on the conclusion of the settlement of Bessarabian Germans in Danzig-West Prussia (T175/66/2582241).

67. Hillgruber, *Hitler, Carol, Antonescu,* p. 110; German-Rumanian treaty of December 13, 1941, over the ethnic Germans in Transnistria (T175/194/2733072–76).

68. Berger to Himmler, May 17, 1943, reporting on the successful conclusion of the May 12 treaty (NO 2235–36); Hillgruber, *Hitler, Carol, Antonescu,* p. 111.

69. German plans for the occupation of Hungary with the co-operation of Slovakia and Rumania (code name, Margarethe I), of Rumania with the co-operation of Hungary and Bulgaria (code name, Margarethe II), Hillgruber, *Hitler, Carol, Antonescu,* pp. 177–82.

70. Ibid., pp. 209–31; Prost, "La Roumanie," pp. 45–49.

71. N. Gornenski and E. Kamenov, "Sur la Bulgarie en guerre. La Politique intérieure," *RHDGM* 72 (1968):23–41; G. Stefanov, "Sur la Bulgarie en guerre. La Politique extérieure," *RHDGM* 72 (1968):1–21; D. B. Cohen, "Le Pillage de l'économie bulgare par les allemands," *RHDGM,* 72 (1968):43–65.

72. Weizsäcker memorandum, April 5, 1941 (NG 2064).

73. Ribbentrop to Beckerle, September 20, 1941; Beckerle telegram of September 25, 1941 (*DGFP,* D, 13:537).

74. Remarks of April 2, 4, 9, 1941, *Hitler's Secret Conversations,* pp. 370–71, 376, 396; Picker, *Hitlers Tischgespräche,* pp. 239–42, 247, 265.

75. Rintelen memorandum of Ribbentrop-Popov conversation of November 26, 1941 (*DGFP,* D, 13:840–43). It will be recalled that in September 1940 Bulgaria acquired Southern Dobruja thanks to German and Italian mediation. After the German conquest of Greece and Yugoslavia, Bulgaria was allowed to occupy Greek Thrace, part of Yugoslav Macedonia, and part of Serbia. See below, pp. 264–68, 293, 305, 307.

76. Hewel memorandum of Hitler-Popov conversation of November 27, 1941 (*DGFP,* D, 13:858–61); *Goebbels Diaries,* pp. 151–52 (entry for March 28, 1942).

77. Remarks of March 31, 1942, *Hitler's Secret Conversations,* pp. 361–62; Picker, *Hitlers Tischgespräche,* pp. 227–29.

78. Remarks of August 8, 1942, *Hitler's Secret Conversations,* p. 579.

79. *Goebbels Diaries,* pp. 433, 442, 445 (entries for September 10 and 11, 1943); Gornenski and Kamenov, "Bulgarie, politique intérieure," pp. 23–41.

80. Stefanov, "Bulgarie, politique extérieure," pp. 14–21; Gornenski and Kamenov, "Bulgarie, politique intérieure," pp. 32–41.

81. Foreign Office memorandum of February 28, 1942, reviewing German-Bulgarian economic relations (*ADAP,* E, 1:553–54); Cohen, "Pillage," pp. 43–65.

82. Hilberg, *Destruction,* pp. 473–80; Reitlinger, *Final Solution,* pp. 408–14; Gornenski and Kamenov, "Bulgarie, politique intérieure," pp. 25, 27–29; and especially Lübomir Wladikin, "Die Judengesetzgebung in Bulgarien," *RVL* 5 (1943):295–333.

83. Hilberg, *Destruction,* pp. 482–84.

84. Ribbentrop-Beckerle, April 4, 1943 (NG 062).

85. Beckerle to the RSHA, June 7, 1943 (NG 2357).

86. Wagner to Kaltenbrunner, August 31, 1943 (NG 3302).

87. Hilberg, *Destruction,* p. 484.

88. See the first volume of this study, pp. 200–202, and especially J. B. Hoptner, *Yugoslavia in Crisis, 1934–1941* (New York, 1962).

89. Hitler conference of March 27, 1941; Hitler directive 26 of April 3, 1941; memorandum on Hitler's general plans for the organization and administration of the Yugoslav area, April 3, 1941 (not April 6, as given in document), (*DGFP,* D, 12:372–75, 440–42, 487; dating of document, *IMT* 27:61; NOKW 2542).

90. Hitler's provisional plans for the partition of Yugoslavia, April 12, 1941 (*IMT,* 1195-PS, 27:60–62).

91. See pp. 242, 268, 273–74; and Hoptner, *Yugoslavia,* pp. 285–92.

92. Keitel memorandum of April 18 embodying Hitler's decisions of April 16, 1941 (T501/269/308).

93. Ribbentrop to the German Embassy in Italy, April 16, 1941, sent April 17 (*DGFP,* D, 12:571–72).

258
259
260
261
262
263
264
265
266

94. Schmidt memoranda of the Ciano-Ribbentrop conversations, April 21 and 22, 1941, and Schmidt's memorandum of April 24 on the results of the German-Italian negotiations (*DGFP*, D, 12:594–98, 606–10, 630–32); Italian record (*Ciano's Diplomatic Papers*, ed. Malcolm Muggeridge [London, 1948], pp. 436–39).

95. Jovan Marjanović, "The German Occupation System in Serbia in 1941," *Les Systèmes d'occupation en Yougoslavie, 1941–1945* (Belgrade, 1963), pp. 270–71, 290; Ladislaus Hory and Martin Broszat, *Der kroatische Ustacha-Staat, 1941–1945* (Stuttgart, 1964), pp. 65–66.

268
96. Raphaël Lemkin, *Axis Rule in Occupied Europe: Laws of Occupation, Analysis of Government, Proposals for Redress* (Washington, D.C., 1944), pp. 584–85, 587–88; *DGFP*, D, 12:842–44; *DDP* 9:128; Hory and Broszat, *Ustacha-Staat*, pp. 67–68.

97. *RGB1* (1941) 2:264–65; *DGFP*, D, 12:696, n. 3, 658, n. 6; *DDP* 9:423–26; Lemkin, *Axis Rule*, pp. 269, 627, 631; Robert Herzog, *Grundzüge der deutschen Besatzungsverwaltung in den ost-und südosteuropäischen Ländern während des zweiten Weltkrieges* (Tübingen, 1955), pp. 47–48.

98. Hitler decrees of April 14, 1941 (T77/884/5633976–89; *DDP* 9:626–27); Frick to the supreme Reich authorities, April 22, 1941 (NG 3257). In his article on the German occupation of Slovenia, in which these territories were located, Tone Ferenc notes the similarity between the German administration here and those established in Alsace, Lorraine, and Luxembourg ("Le Système d'occupation des Nazis en Slovénie," *Les Systèmes d'occupation en Yougoslavie, 1941–1945* (Belgrade, 1963), p. 55.) A circular from the Nazi Party Chancellery of February 25, 1942, nevertheless insisted that party officials differentiate between territory of the Greater German Reich (including Bohemia and Moravia!) and *"Nebenländer,"* which included Alsace, Lorraine, Luxembourg, the Government General, as well as Lower Styria, Carinthia, and Upper Carniola; the incorporation of these last three territories in the Reich, however, was imminent *"steht bevor"* (T81/2/63497–98).

269
99. Herbert Friedl, "Oberkrain—Kärntens deutsche Markaufgabe," *RVL* 5 (1943):247–51; also Dr. Hermann Ibler, *Des Reiches Südgrenze in der Steiermark* (Graz, 1940), who said that Lower Styria must be considered an integral part of the vital living space of Germany. Among the many older German works on this subject were those of Doris Kraft, *Das untersteirische Drauland* (Munich, 1935), who maintained that the present frontiers dividing Carinthia and Styria from Upper Carniola and Lower Styria were totally artificial from geographical, economic, and cultural points of view; Dr. Gerhard Werner [Helmut Carstanjen], *Sprache und Volkstum in der Untersteiermark* (Stuttgart, 1935), who declared that Lower Styria had been German territory for centuries and had been allotted unjustly to Yugoslavia by the Treaty of St. Germain; Adraticus [F. Langer], *Deutschlands gerechte Grenze* (Berlin, 1925), who demanded the reunion of Lower Styria—and a good deal more—with Austria; and Hans Bruckner, *Der deutsch-slowenische Grenzraum* (Berlin, 1934).

100. *DDP* 9:628–29; Friedl, "Oberkrain," p. 248.

101. *DDP* 9:628–29, 633–34; *VB1USt* (1941), pp. 1–2, 31; *Marburger Zeitung*, April 15, 1941, quoted in Ferenc, "Slovénie," pp. 61–62.

102. *DDP* 9:645; *VB1KK* (1941), p. 63; Friedl, "Oberkrain," p. 264.

270
103. Second Hitler decree for the administration of Carinthia and Carniola (T77/884/5633895); Frick speech of December 16, 1941 (*DDP* 9:626–28).

104. *VB1USt* (1941), pp. 2, 196, 463; *VB1KK* (1941), p. 151; (1942), p. 42; *DDP* 9:624–25, 630–31; Ferenc, "Slovénie," pp. 56–58.

105. *RGB1* (1941) 1:648; *VB1USt* (1941), pp. 31, 351; *VB1KK* (1941), pp. 5, 63; (1942), p. 56; *DDP* 9:633–34, 636–40, 643–45; memorandum incorporating Uiberreither's ideas on the problems of citizenship, August 23, 1941 (NG 4898); Friedl, "Oberkrain," pp. 261–64; Ferenc, "Slovénie," pp. 69, 74–75, 94–95.

271
106. Uiberreither decree of April 14, 1941 (*VB1USt* [1941], p. 2); also *VB1USt* (1941), pp. 17, 41, 125, 405, 409–38; *VB1KK* (1941), pp. 1, 22–23; *DDP* 9:626, 629–31, 634, 641–42, 644–45; Ferenc, "Slovénie," pp. 83–84.

107. T77/884/5633976–89.

108. Heydrich to the supreme Reich authorities, April 21, 1941 (NG 4897); Maribor conference, May 6, 1941 (*DGFP*, D, 12:725–26); Luther memorandum of February 24, 1942, reviewing the entire problem (NG 5020).

272
109. *DGFP*, D, 12:830–31, 957–58; *DDP* 9:702–3, 729–33; Franjo Tudjman, "The Independent State of Croatia as an Instrument of the Policy of the Occupation Powers in Yugoslavia, and the People's Liberation Movement in Croatia from 1941 to 1945," *Les Systèmes d'occupation en Yougoslavie, 1941–1945* (Belgrade, 1963), p. 186.

110. Hofmann memorandum, May 24, 1941 (NO 3086); Greifelt, on behalf of Himmler, directives of July 7 and 14, 1941 (NO 5040, NO 3531 f; T175/194/2733077–79).

111. Heydrich to Ribbentrop, September 26, 1941 (*DGFP*, D, 12:570–71; NG 2671); Himmler order of October 18, 1941 (T175/194/2733132–36; NO 5562, 5247); Ferenc, "Slovénie," p. 65.

112. Himmler order November 1, 1941 (T175/194/2733080–82); *VB1USt* (1941), p. 453; *DDP* 9:625, 732.

273   113. Memoranda of August 23, 1941, and June 6, 1942 (NG 4898, 2500).
    114. Hitler conference of March 27; Ribbentrop and Rintelen to Zagreb, March 31 and April 1, 1941 (*DGFP*, D, 12:372–75, 425, 427–28). On Croatia, see Hory and Broszat, *Ustacha-Staat*, and Tudjman, "Croatia."

274   115. German negotiations with Maček (*DGFP*, D, 12:424–26, 430, 448–49); also Maček's memoirs, *In the Struggle for Freedom* (New York, 1957), pp. 218–23.
    116. Veesenmayer reports, April 4 and 5, 1941 (*DGFP*, D, 12:449–50, 461–62); Hoettl affidavit on the Veesenmayer mission (NG 2317).
    117. Two telegrams, Veesenmayer to Ribbentrop, April 11; Ribbentrop to Veesenmayer, April 12, 1941 (*DGFP*, D, 12:513–17, 533); DDP 9:421, 623; Lemkin, *Axis Rule*, p. 606.
    118. *DGFP*, D, 12:513, 520, 523–24, 535, 545–46, 549; Tudjman, "Croatia," pp. 163, 171, 174–75; Hory and Broszat, *Ustacha-Staat*, pp. 58–59.

275   119. *DGFP*, D, 12:544, 549–50, 552–58, 565–66; *DDP* 9:421–22; Lemkin, *Axis Rule*, pp. 606–7; Hory and Broszat, *Ustacha-Staat*, pp. 75–78.

276   120. Hory and Broszat, *Ustacha-Staat*, pp. 13–25, 77, 88, 93–106; Maček, *Struggle*, pp. 234–35.
    121. Halder, *Kriegstagebuch*, 2:370 (entry for April 17, 1941); *DGFP*, D, 12:578–79, 605–6; 13:342–43; Hassell, *Vom andern Deutschland* pp. 204–5, 208; Hory and Broszat, *Ustacha-Staat*, pp. 59 ff.

277   122. Hewel report of the Hitler-Pavelić conversation on June 7, 1941 (*DGFP*, D, 12:977–81).
    123. *Hitler's Secret Conversations*, pp. 38, 115, 326, 446; Picker, *Hitlers Tischgespräche*, pp. 183, 333 (remarks of July 11–12 and October 29, 1941, February 26 and May 12, 1942).
    124. *Ciano Diaries*, pp. 341–45, 348–49, 354 (entries for April 24–30, May 8, 10, and 18, 1941); *Ciano's Diplomatic Papers*, p. 439; treaties of May 18, 1941 (*DGFP*, D 12:844, n. 4, 851, n. 2; DDP 9:127–28; Maček, *Struggle*, pp. 232–33; Hory and Broszat, *Ustacha-Staat*, pp. 67–68; Tudjman, "Croatia," pp. 171, 181).

278   125. Ribbentrop memorandum of August 20, 1941, with Hitler's comments; Ribbentrop-Kasche telegrams, August 21, 1941 (*DGFP*, D, 13:341–44).
    126. German-Croatian treaty of May 16, 1941 (*DGFP*, D, 12:831–32).

279   127. Memorandum on German officials in Croatia and their assignments (NOKW 293); final German army report on German policy in Croatia (T501/258/716–17); Felber affidavit (NOKW 611). For a readily accessible example of Glaise's criticism of the Ustaša movement and the Pavelić regime, and Kasche's defense of both, see Glaise's report of January 5, 1944, and Kasche's comments on that report of January 14 (Karl Hnilicka, *Das Ende auf dem Balkan 1944/45. Die militärische Räumung Jugoslaviens durch die deutsche Wehrmacht* [Göttingen, 1970], pp. 279–83). Glaise himself was an able historian.
    128. Hory and Broszat, *Ustacha-Staat*, pp. 60–61; *DDP* 9:396; definition of Kasche's power and responsibilities, April 19, 1941 (T501/258/717).

280   129. The relevant documents in *DDP* 9:436–48; Hory and Broszat, *Ustacha-Staat*, pp. 70–71.
    130. Troll to the Foreign Office, July 10 and August 10, 1941; memorandum of Hitler-Pavelić conversation, June 7, 1941 (*DGFP*, D, 12:977–81; 13:113–15, 301–2);Maček, *Struggle*, pp. 239–40; Hory and Broszat, *Ustacha-Staat*, pp. 93–106.
    131. An entire file on the problems of Croatia consisting chiefly of letters and reports of Glaise is on film in the National Archives (T501/264).

281   132. Memorandum on German officials and their assignments in Croatia (NOKW 293); Hitler order no. 47 of December 28, 1942 (NOKW 1489); Löhr report of February 27, 1943 (NOKW 376); Johann Wüscht, *Jugoslawien und das dritte Reich. Eine dokumentierte Geschichte der deutsch-jugoslawischen Beziehungen von 1933 bis 1945* (Stuttgart, 1969), pp. 319–22.
    133. Final German army report on German activity in Croatia (T501/258/715–24).
    134. Order of September 7, 1943 (NOKW 293); Herzog, *Grundzüge*, p. 51.

282   135. Final German army report (T501/258/715–24); Hory and Broszat, *Ustacha-Staat*, pp. 162–63.
    136. Hory and Broszat, pp. 171–72; also final German army report.
    137. Keitel order, March 29, 1941 (*IMT*, 1746-PS, 28:31–42).

283   138. Hitler directives, through Keitel, of April 12, 1941 (*IMT*, 1195-PS, 27:62); Brauchitsch order of April 20 for the establishment of a German military government on April 22 (T501/264/302, 421).
    139. Hitler directive 31 of June 9, 1941 (*DGFP*, D, 12:988–90; T501/264/209).
    140. Final German army report on the German military administration in Serbia, April 10, 1945 (T501/264/205–6, 209–10, 219). The description of the German administrative apparatus by Hilberg (*Destruction*, pp. 433–34) is excellent. Schröder was killed in an air crash on July 24, 1941, and was succeeded by General Heinrich Danckelmann.

284   141. In February 1942 Turner's deputy, SS Sturmbannführer Georg Kiessel, specially selected for his post by Turner because of his SS affiliation, wrote two long letters to Karl Wolff of the RSHA to inform him (and through him, Himmler) of Turner's difficul-

ties with the German military administrators, whose catastrophic mistakes Turner had criticized and who were now trying to oust him from the military government in Serbia as they had previously ousted him from the military government in France. Turner, Kiessel said, not only refused to deny the principles of the party and the SS, but made them the foundation for all his activities. (Hnilicka, *Ende auf dem Balkan,* pp. 163–78).

142. Göring order of April 13, 1941 (T501/264/206); Brauchitsch order of May 12, 1941, on the organization of the economic administration, issued in agreement with Göring (T501/264/431–32); Göring order appointing Neuhausen plenipotentiary for mining, December 9, 1942 (T501/264/454).

143. Herzog, *Grundzüge,* p. 125; Hilberg, *Destruction,* p. 435; see below, n. 148.

144. Hitler directive of April 28, 1941 (T501/264/456; *DGFP,* D, 12:573–74). On Benzler's successor, Hermann Neubacher, see below, pp. 286–87.

285   145. List report of September 13, 1941 (NOKW 1424).

146. Hitler order of September 26, 1941 (NOKW 1492, 1334); assignment of October 9, 1941 (T501/264/209–10).

147. T501/264/209–10; NOKW 908.

148. Hitler order of January 22, 1942, installing a senior SS and police officer in Serbia (T77/777/5503675–77; T175/119/2644914); disapproval on the part of the military government (T501/264/210); Felber affidavit (NOKW 611, 1735).

149. Turner voiced his dismay about Meyszner's attitude in a tediously long letter to Meyszner himself of August 29, 1942, and to Himmler of August 30, 1942 (Hnilicka, *Ende auf dem Balkan,* pp. 179–83; NOKW 800). Kiessel followed these up with a letter to Wolff of October 13, 1942 (Hnilicka, pp. 184–85); dismissal of Turner (T501/264/211).

286   150. Hitler order of July 26, 1943, to go into effect August 26 (T501/264/211–12, 440–41).

151. Lammers to the supreme Reich authorities, August 5, 1941 (NG 4513).

152. On the reorganization of the German administration in the southeast at this time, there are several long and interesting postwar analyses, affidavits, and records of testimony by General Felber (NOKW 1735, 611, 1304, 1731).

287   153. See above, p. 251.

154. Hitler order of October 29, 1943 (NG 3439); Wüscht, *Jugoslawien,* pp. 322–33; Neubacher, *Sonderauftrag Südost,* pp. 13–15, 123–28; Felber memorandum (NOKW 1735).

155. Order of October 7, 1943 (T501/264/212, 442–46).

156. See above, p. 284.

288   157. Felber memorandum (NOKW 1735); Neubacher, *Sonderauftrag Südost,* pp. 143–45.

158. Final German army report on the German occupation of Serbia, April 10, 1945 (T501/264/205–6). In a letter to Himmler of April 28, 1944, Behrends reported that his relations with all members of the German administration in Serbia were excellent, but that certain regional military commanders were attempting to deal with matters that were actually the concern of the Reichsführer SS. Himmler replied on May 18 that Behrends should be particularly careful to remain on good terms with Neubacher, and that he should not put up with any encroachments on the part of the Wehrmacht (Hnilicka, *Ende auf dem Balkan,* pp. 307–11).

159. Feine report, April 27, 1941 (*DGFP,* D, 12:654); final German army report (T501/264/422–23).

289   160. Benzler reports of August 1941 (*DGFP,* D, 13:308, 400–401); Hory and Broszat, *Ustacha-Staat,* pp. 112–13.

161. Benzler report, August 29, 1941 (*DGFP,* D, 13:411–13); Hory and Broszat, *Ustacha-Staat,* p. 113; Nedić testimony (*IMT* 7:240–43); on the composition of the Nedić government and its later reorganization (T501/264/203–5, 235–39, 302, 424–26).

162. Final German army report (T501/264/209–10). The country was still far from pacified, however, as Feine reported on December 3, 1941 (*DGFP,* D, 13:944–48).

290   163. Nedić to Danckelmann, August 27, 1941 (Hnilicka, *Ende auf dem Balkan,* pp. 161–63). See also the records of the conference between the leaders of the German military administration and Nedić of February 7, 1942; between Benzler and Nedić, October 13, 1942; Nedić to General Bader, January 1, 1943, with two long memoranda on the need for a Serbian national organization and the reorganization of the Serbian administration, and the appraisals of his proposals by the German military administration and Meyszner; Meyszner's complaints about Nedić to Himmler, March 15, 1943; and in particular the long letter from Nedić to General Felber of February 22, 1944 (Hnilicka, pp. 160–63, 200–207, 226–30, 239–61, 312–20).

164. Neubacher speaks of Nedić's "chronic intentions to resign (*chronische Rücktrittsabsichten*)" (*Sonderauftrag Südost,* p. 134).

165. In December 1941 further Serbian territory was in fact turned over to the Bulgars, who promptly realized the worst fears of the Serbs by indulging in widespread massacres of the Serbian population (T501/264/210); on putting pressure on Nedić, see Ribbentrop's instructions to Benzler, October 9, 1942 (Wüscht, *Jugoslawien,* pp. 318–19).

291   166. Final German army report, T501/264/203–5, 231, 266–308, 341–46, 362 ff., 416 ff.
292   167. Ibid., T501/264/203 ff.

168. Hory and Broszat, *Ustacha-Staat,* p. 108; Turner's report of August 29, 1942, reviews the entire refugee problem and the unrest it engendered (NOKW 1486).
169. Steengracht memorandum, August 2, 1941 (*DGFP,* D, 13:295–96).
170. September 22, 1941 (*DGFP,* D, 13:552–55).

293   171. Hitler orders for List, September 16, 1941 (NOKW 1492); also the order for all occupied territories of September 16, 1941 (*DGFP,* D, 13:541–43).
172. Böhme order of September 25, 1941 (NOKW 1048).
173. Benzler report of October 29, 1941 (*DGFP,* D, 13:708–9).
174. Final German army report (T501/264/210, 233–34); Bader to List, January 19, 1942 (NOKW 1671).

294   175. Army order (General Kuntze) of March 19, 1942 (NOKW 835); Hitler order (through Keitel) of December 16, 1942 (NOKW 3401); Hory and Broszat, *Ustacha-Staat,* p. 118.
176. See above, p. 265; Vegh, "Banat Yougoslave," p. 496; final German army report (T501/264/214); Felber memorandum (NOKW 1735).
177. Vegh, "Banat Yougoslave," pp. 497, 505–6.
178. Lemkin, *Axis Rule,* pp. 602–6.

295   179. Vegh, "Banat Yougoslave," pp. 507, 547, n. 8.
180. Final German army report (T501/264/370); Benzler memorandum of September 7, 1942 (NG 139).
181. *Verordnungsblatt des Militärbefehlshabers in Serbien,* May 31, 1941; final German army report (T501/264/260); Sandor Vegh, "Le Système du pouvoir d'occupation allemand dans le Banat Yougoslave, 1941–1944," *Les Systèmes d'occupation en Yougoslavie, 1941–1945* (Belgrade, 1963), p. 512; Hilberg, *Destruction,* pp. 433–42; Reitlinger, *Final Solution,* pp. 385–92.

296   182. List report of September 13, 1941; Veesenmayer/Benzler telegrams of September 8 and 10, 1941 (*DGFP,* D, 13:463, 472–73).
183. Sonnleithner memorandum recording Ribbentrop's decision, September 11; Luther telegrams to Belgrade, September 12 and 18, 1941 (WF 482/231279, 231284, 231286); Benzler telegram of September 28, 1941 (*DGFP,* D, 13:582).
184. Luther memorandum, October 2, 1941; Luther telegrams to Belgrade, October 5 and 15, 1941 (*DGFP,* D, 13:605–6 and notes). The commission was to be composed of two representatives of the RSHA and Franz Rademacher, the head of the Foreign Office department dealing with the Jewish question.
185. Turner to Hildebrandt, October 17, 1941 (NO 5810). The orders for most of these executions went out under the name of Turner's superior officer, General Böhme (NOKW 192, 251, 567; NO 3402); Hilberg, *Destruction,* pp. 437–38.

297   186. Rademacher memorandum, October 25, 1941 (*DGFP,* D, 13:697–99).
187. Rademacher memorandum, October 25; Benzler report, December 8, 1941 (*DGFP,* D, 13:697–99, 990); Turner orders, November 3, 1941 (NOKW 800); Major Juppe memorandum, December 5, 1941 (NOKW 1150); Hilberg, *Destruction,* pp. 441–42.
188. Schäfer report of June 14, 1942 (NOKW 926); report on the return of the gas van to Berlin (PS 501); Turner to Löhr, August 29, 1942 (NOKW 1486).

298   189. Hnilicka, *Ende auf dem Balkan,* pp. 365–75. For the enormously important, but also enormously complicated and controversial, problem of the relationship between the Germans and the forces of Mihailović, see above all the work of F. W. Deakin, *The Embattled Mountain* (New York, 1971).
190. The following description of the German administration of Montenegro is based to a large extent on the final report of the German military administration in Montenegro, dated February 15, 1945 (T501/258/673–702); Felber memorandum (NOKW 1735); Herzog, *Grundzüge,* pp. 52, 90.
191. Neubacher, *Sonderauftrag Südost,* pp. 123, 132, 150.

299   192. Final German army report (T501/258/694–95); Neubacher, *Sonderauftrag Südost,* pp. 150, 159–64.
193. Final German army report (T501/258/695–702).
194. Final German army report/Albania (T501/258/613); Neubacher, *Sonderauftrag Südost,* p. 105.

300   195. Lemkin, *Axis Rule,* pp. 99–103, 267–82.
196. Final German army report (T501/258/465–66); Neubacher, *Sonderauftrag Südost,* pp. 107–11; Herzog, *Grundzüge,* p. 53.

301   197. Neubacher, *Sonderauftrag Südost,* pp. 107, 110–13.
198. Ibid., p. 117.
199. Final German army report (T501/258/613–72).
200. The following account of the German administration in Albania is based on the final German army report (T501/258/613–72); General Felber's affidavit and memorandum (NOKW 611, 1735); and the memoirs of Neubacher (*Sonderauftrag Südost,* p. 105).

302   201. T501/258/672.
303   202. On the background of the German occupation and the place of Greece in international affairs, see Ehrengard Schramm-von Thadden, *Griechenland und die Grossmächte*

im zweiten Weltkrieg (Wiesbaden, 1955), which unfortunately stops with the surrender of the Greek regular army and the beginning of the Axis occupation.

203. Hitler directive 20, Operation Marita, December 13, 1940 (*DGFP*, D, 11:867–69).

204. OKW order of March 22, 1941; also Hitler directive of April 13, 1941 (*DGFP*, D, 12:338–42, 538–41).

205. *DDP* 9:63; also the German army's proclamation to the Greek people (T501/258/470); Herzog, *Grundzüge*, p. 57.

206. Mackensen memorandum of April 21 and Rintelen memorandum of April 23, 1941, reviewing the course of German negotiations with the Italians (*DGFP*, D, 12:599–601, 643–47).

304   207. Mackensen memorandum of April 27, 1941 (*DGFP*, D, 12:648–51 and footnotes); Herzog, *Grundzüge*, pp. 151–54.

208. High Command of the Army to Keitel, May 9, 1941; also Altenburg's telegram to the Foreign Office of May 11 (*DGFP*, D, 12:747–48, 776 and footnotes).

209. Ritter memorandum of May 13, 1941, recording Hitler's decision; Ribbentrop to Altenburg, May 16, August 18 and 26, 1941 (*DGFP*, D, 12:796 and n. 1; 13:328, 394).

305   210. Hitler directive 29 of May 17, 1941; see also his directive of June 6, 1941 (*DGFP*, D, 12:845–47, 988–90).

211. The zones of occupation in Greece are described in Lemkin, *Axis Rule*, pp. 185–89, and Herzog, *Grundzüge*, pp. 57–59.

212. Hitler directive 28 of April 25, 1941, Operation Merkur, for the occupation of Crete; directive 29 of May 17 (*DGFP*, D, 12:636–37, 845–47); Herzog, *Grundzüge*, p. 89.

213. Lemkin, *Axis Rule*, pp. 187–89, 416–18.

214. Ibid., pp. 185–87, 415–16.

215. Final German army report on the German military administration in Greece (T501/258/467–598, pt. A); Herzog, *Grundzüge*, pp. 152–53.

306   216. Final German army report (T501/258/503); Herzog, *Grundzüge*, pp. 151–54; Neubacher, *Sonderauftrag Südost*, pp. 100–101; William H. McNeill, *The Greek Dilemma: War and Aftermath* (Philadelphia, 1947), pp. 50–60); and especially C. M. Woodhouse, *Apple of Discord: A Survey of Recent Greek Politics in Their International Setting* (London, 1948), pp. 27, 122–24, 133–36.

217. Hitler directive 31, June 9, 1941 (*DGFP*, D, 12:988–90). Although the German commander for southern Greece was to be responsible for the Athenian peninsula, the city and harbor of Athens (Piraeus) were to be occupied by the Italians.

307   218. Altenburg, who had originally been selected for Belgrade, was appointed Reich plenipotentiary for Greece by a Hitler directive of April 28, 1941. His office was to be in Athens, although Athens was under Italian occupation and administration (*DGFP*, D, 12:473–74, 696–97; 13:328, 394; T501/258/476).

219. Final German army report (T501/258/471–72, 476, 490); Neubacher, *Sonderauftrag Südost*, pp. 73–99; Herzog, *Grundzüge*, pp. 152–53.

220. See above, pp. 286–88. On the complicated organizational and personnel problems brought about by these changes, see in particular the postwar statements of General Felber (NOKW 611, 1735).

308   221. Final German army report (T501/258/473–80); General Speidel report to General Felber, October 4, 1943 (NOKW 1762).

222. Final German army report (T501/258/474–82, 597); Felber affidavit and memorandum (NOKW 611, 1735).

223. Keitel directive on the position of the senior SS and police officer, September 7, 1943 (NOKW 1438); final German army report (T501/258/509, 597).

309   224. Military government situation report, November 1943 (NOKW 1754); final German army report (T501/258/477, 597). After the Italian surrender, Altenburg had been transferred from Greece and his duties were taken over by Consul General Graevenitz. The powers of Neubacher who, since August 1943, had been responsible for problems in the entire southeast and whose headquarters had been shifted to Belgrade were in large part exercised by Graevenitz who served as his permanent representative and chargé d'affaires in Athens. "Basically," Neubacher wrote in his memoirs, "our policy in Greece was: money and food" (*Sonderauftrag Südost*, pp. 86, 101–2).

225. The final German army report summarizes and quotes from the principal German decrees for Greece after September 1943 and discusses the problems faced by the German administration (T501/258/512–18); also Neubacher, *Sonderauftrag Südost*, pp. 73–99; NOKW 1762.

226. Final German army report (T501/258/590–92).

310   227. Ibid. (T501/258/501–3); Neubacher, *Sonderauftrag Südost*, pp. 100–101.

228. Hilberg, *Destruction*, pp. 442–46.

311   229. Final German army report (T501/258/547); Neubacher report, June 28, 1944 (Staatliches Archivlager, Göttingen, Lu 7, 45 ff.); military government situation report, November 1943 (NOKW 1754); Hilberg, *Destruction*, pp. 449–52.

230. Hnilicka, *Ende auf dem Balkan*, pp. 370–71.

312   231. *Hitler's Secret Conversations*, p. 78.

232. Picker, *Hitlers Tischgespräche*, p. 184; *Hitler's Secret Conversations*, pp. 326–27.

233. Picker, *Hitlers Tischgespräche*, pp. 419–20; *Hitler's Secret Conversations*, pp. 505–6.

313   234. A good deal of material on this subject is pulled toether in Hans-Ulrich Wehler's article " 'Reichsfestung Belgrad.' Nationalsozialistische 'Raumordnung' in Südosteuropa," *VfZ* 11 (1963):72–84.

235. *Hitler's Secret Conversations*, p. 617.

236. Picker, *Hitlers Tischgespräche*, pp. 183–84, 298–99; *Hitler's Secret Conversations*, pp. 326, 620.

314   237. Picker, *Hitlers Tischgespräche*, pp. 390–91; *Hitler's Secret Conversations*, p. 485.

238. Picker, *Hitlers Tischgespräche*, pp. 157, 182–83; *Hitler's Secret Conversations*, pp. 74, 90–91, 138, 189, 227, 325–26, 644.

239. Picker, *Hitlers Tischgespräche*, pp. 227–29, 333; *Hitler's Secret Conversations*, pp. 361–62, 446, 579.

315   240. Picker, *Hitlers Tischgespräche*, pp. 183, 333; *Hitler's Secret Conversations*, pp. 38, 115, 326, 446.

316   241. Picker, *Hitlers Tischgespräche*, p. 319; *Hitler's Secret Conversations*, p. 439.

10. ITALY: THE DEFEATED ALLY

317   1. Henry Picker, *Hitlers Tischgespräche im Führerhauptquartier, 1941–1942*, ed. Percy Ernst Schramm, Andreas Hillgruber, and Martin Vogt (Stuttgart, 1965), p. 352; *Hitler's Secret Conversations, 1941–1944* (paperback, New York, 1961), p. 460.

2. Picker, *Hitlers Tischgespräche*, pp. 133–35; *Hitler's Secret Conversations*, pp. 39–40, 265–68, 572.

318   3. Picker, *Hitlers Tischgespräche*, pp. 290, 452–54, 466, 474; *Hitler's Secret Conversations*, pp. 74, 267–68, 303–4, 413, 434, 536–38, 553–54, 572.

4. At the time of the debacle of Italy's Balkan campaign, Hitler told Ciano in Vienna that "from this city . . . on the day of the Anschluss, I sent Mussolini a telegram to assure him that I would never forget his help. I confirm it today, and I am at his side with all my strength." Ciano noted that Hitler, in making this declaration, "had two big tears in his eyes. What a strange man!" (*The Ciano Diaries, 1939–1943* ed. Hugh Gibson [New York, 1946], p. 313).

5. F. W. Deakin, *The Brutal Friendship: Mussolini, Hitler, and the Fall of Italian Fascism* (paperback, New York, 1966), bk. 4; Dennison I. Rusinow, *Italy's Austrian Heritage, 1919–46* (Oxford, 1969); Ivone Kirkpatrick, *Mussolini: A Study in Power* (New York, 1964); and for the military aspects, A. N. Garland and H. M. Smyth, *Sicily and the Surrender of Italy* (Washington, D.C., 1965).

319   6. Josef Schröder, *Italiens Kriegsaustritt 1943. Die deutschen Gegenmassnahmen im italienischen Raum. Fall "Alarich" und "Achse"* (Göttingen, 1969); F. W. Deakin, *The Six Hundred Days of Mussolini* (paperback, New York, 1966), pp. 5–15; Erwin Rommel, *The Rommel Papers*, ed. B. H. Liddell Hart (New York, 1953), chap. 20.

7. Schröder, *Italiens Kriegsaustritt*, pt. 5; Deakin, *Six Hundred Days*, pp. 16–46, 94; Kirkpatrick, *Mussolini*, p. 583; *The Goebbels Diaries, 1942–1943*, ed. Louis P. Lochner (New York, 1948), p. 454); and especially Otto Skorzeny, *Skorzeny's Secret Missions: War Memoirs of the Most Dangerous Man in Europe* (New York, 1950), pp. 55–106.

320   8. Deakin, *Six Hundred Days*, pp. 35–45; Rudolf Rahn, *Ruheloses Leben. Aufzeichnungen und Erinnerungen eines deutschen Diplomaten* (Düsseldorf, 1949), pp. 222–61.

9. Rusinow, *Italy's Austrian Heritage*, chap. 15.

10. *Goebbels Diaries*, pp. 433, 445, 450, 452, 474.

11. Enzo Collotti, *L'amministrazione tedesca dell'Italia occupata, 1943–1945. Studio e documenti* (Milan, 1963), pp. 407–9; Lammers to supreme Reich authorities, September 11, 1943, transmitting Hitler's decree of September 10 (NG 3712; T175/126/2651192–93; 2651213–15); Albert Speer, *Inside the Third Reich* (New York, 1970), p. 367; Tone Ferenc, "Le Système d'occupation des Nazis en Slovénie," *Les Systèmes d'occupation en Yougoslavie, 1941–1945* (Belgrade, 1963), p. 111.

321   12. Rusinow, *Italy's Austrian Heritage*, pp. 297–302; Collotti, *L'amministrazione tedesca*, pp. 421–24, 427; Conrad F. Latour, *Südtirol und die Achse Berlin-Rom, 1938–1945* (Stuttgart, 1962), p. 118.

322   13. Robert Herzog, *Grundzüge der deutschen Besatzungsverwaltung in den ost-und südosteuropäischen Ländern während des zweiten Weltkrieges* (Tübingen, 1955), pp. 111–12.

14. Deakin, *Six Hundred Days*, pp. 96, 99.

15. The decrees of Hofer were published in *Verordnungsblatt des obersten Kommissars für die Operationszone Alpenvorland;* of Rainer in *Verordnungs-und Amtsblatt des obersten Kommissars in der Operationszone "Adriatisches Küstenland."* See Latour, *Südtirol*, pp. 118–20; Rusinow, *Italy's Austrian Heritage*, p. 302, n. 2.

323   16. Collotti, *L'amministrazione tedesca*, pp. 94–178, 407–27, 445, 450–53, 469, 494.

17. Deakin, *Six Hundred Days*, pp. 98–100; *Rommel Papers*, pp. 446–47; Collotti, *L'amministrazione tedesca*, pp. 450–53; Albert Kesselring, *The Memoirs of Field-Marshal Kesselring* (London, 1953), p. 191.

18. Collotti, *L'amministrazione tedesca*, pp. 419–21, 427, 446–50, 464, 469, 494–96; Deakin, *Six Hundred Days*, pp. 34, 56; Speer, *Inside the Third Reich*, p. 367.

19. Deakin, *Six Hundred Days*, p. 208.

324   20. Raul Hilberg, *The Destruction of the European Jews* (Chicago, 1961), pp. 421–26.

21. Moellhausen (counselor of embassy in Rome) to Ribbentrop, October 6, 1943, and Sonnleitner's telegram conveying Ribbentrop's decision on the question (NG 5027).

22. T175/53/2567133–34.

23. Wagner memorandum, December 4, 1943 (NG 5026).

325   24. Hilberg, *Destruction*, pp. 426–32.

11: RUSSIA: THE PROMISED LAND

326   1. Conference of July 16, 1941 (*IMT*, 221-L, 38:86–94).

327   2. The following quotations and summaries of Hitler's statements about Germany's future policy toward Russia are taken from the records of his conversations from July 1941 through September 1942, kept by Bormann, Picker, and Heinrich Heim while they served on his staff at his headquarters (Henry Picker, *Hitlers Tischgespräche im Führerhauptquartier, 1941–1942* ed. Percy Ernst Schramm, Andreas Hillgruber, and Martin Vogt (Stuttgart, 1965), p. 143 and passim; *Hitler's Secret Conversations, 1941–1944* (paperback, New York, 1961), p. 44 and passim); see also Hitler's remarks to Abetz, September 16, 1941; to Seyss-Inquart, September 26, 1941; Jodl's transmission of Hitler's directive of October 7, 1941 (*DGFP*, D, 13:520, 607–8, 623–24); Rosenberg memorandum of conversation with Hitler, December 14, 1941 (*IMT*, 1517-PS, 27:270–73); *The Goebbels Diaries, 1942–1943*, ed. Louis P. Lochner (New York, 1948), pp. 136, 143 (entries for March 20 and 21, 1942); *Fuehrer Conferences on Matters Dealing with the German Navy, 1939–1945*, 8 vols. (Washington, D.C., 1946–47), 1942, p. 98 (August 29, 1942); Hewel note on Hitler-Rosenberg conversation of May 19, 1943, on the basis of information supplied by Bormann (NG 3288).

331   3. Hitler speech to army group leaders, July 1, 1943 (T77/777/5503773–77).

4. "The German Wehrmacht was still regarded by the population as the emancipator and liberator from physical and spiritual oppression." Report from the Ukraine, concluded October 5, 1941, by Professor Hans Koch, an officer of the German Counterintelligence (PS 053). "There is hardly anything left today of the enthusiasm you could read about in all the letters right after the German troops liberated the Ukraine from Bolshevik oppression." Report of the German research bureau evaluating letters exchanged by the Russian population, mostly from the Ukraine, July 15, 1942 (PS 302). See also the report of Dr. Paul Thomsen of the Reich University of Posen, October 19, 1942 (PS 303); Rosenberg to Koch, December 14, 1942 (PS 194); Frauenfeld memorandum of February 10, 1944 (NO 5394). Not surprisingly, almost none of the many documents describing the enthusiastic reception accorded the Germans in the Soviet Union were introduced in evidence at Nuremberg, where the Russians were among the prosecutors.

332   5. On this problem, see the detailed work of John A. Armstrong, *Ukrainian Nationalism, 1939–1945* (New York, 1963); and above all Alexander Dallin, *German Rule in Russia 1941–1945: A Study of Occupation Policies* (London, 1957), pp. 111–14, 613–36.

6. See the first volume of this study, pp. 211–20. Dallin, *German Rule*, pp. 20–44, 84–106; Gerald Reitlinger, *The House Built on Sand: The Conflicts of German Policy in Russia, 1939–1945* (New York, 1960), pp. 66–77, 128 ff. A valuable analysis of this problem, based on firsthand knowledge of the situation, has been written by Otto Bräutigam, deputy head of the Political Department of the Reich Ministry for the Occupied Eastern Territories, *Überblick über die besetzten Ostgebiete während des 2. Weltkrieges* (Tübingen, 1954, pp. 4, 13).

7. Among many such plans, see for example the OKW memorandum of August 27, 1941 (*DGFP*, D, 13:422–33).

333   8. Hitler decree of June 25, 1941 (NG 1280; WF 5246H/E311494–95).

9. See the first volume of this study, pp. 212–14; Franz Halder, *Kriegstagebuch. Tägliche Aufzeichnungen des Chefs des Generalstabes des Heeres, 1939–1942*, ed. Hans-Adolf Jacobsen, 3 vols. (Stuttgart, 1962–64), 2:336–37; Walter Warlimont, *Inside Hitler's Headquarters, 1939–45* (New York, 1964), pp. 160–67; Helmuth Greiner, *Die oberste Wehrmachtführung, 1939–1943* (Wiesbaden, 1951), pp. 370–71; *IMT*, 877-PS, 26:401–8; 050-C, 34: 249–58; NOKW 3485.

10. Order of July 22, 1941 (T77/775/5500685–86).

11. Directive of September 8, 1941 (*IMT*, 1519-PS, 27:273–83); see the comments of Canaris (*IMT*, 338-EC, 36:317–20).

334   12. Keitel directive of September 16, 1941, transmitting Hitler's orders (*IMT*, 389-PS, 25:530–33).

13. Reichenau order of October 10, 1941; Manstein order of November 20, 1941; Keitel order of December 16, 1942, transmitting Hitler's order (*IMT*, 411-D, 35:84–86; 4064-PS, 34:129–32; *IMT* 9:220).

490

14. Dallin, *German Rule,* pp. 30–34, 70–74; Reitlinger, *House,* pp. 67–97.

15. Dallin, *German Rule,* pp. 95–98.

335   16. Oleg Anisimov, *The German Occupation in Northern Russia during World War II: Political and Administrative Aspects* (New York, 1954).

336   17. See the first volume of this study, pp. 214, 217–20.

18. Hitler order of June 29, 1941 (WF 5253H/E314300; T77/545/1720405); Bräutigam, *Überblick,* pp. 8–10.

19. Göring decree of July 30, 1941 (*TWC* 13:871–72); economic policy guidelines, July 1941 (*IMT,* 472-EC, 36:542–45); full text (WF 5253H/E314307–37); third edition, September 1942 (EC 347); Göring order of August 28, 1941 (WF 5083H/E292855–58); Göring to Himmler, August 26, 1941 (WF 5083H/E292860).

20. See the first volume of this study, pp. 214–17. Dallin, *German Rule,* pp. 38–40, 313–19; Karl Brandt, Otto Schiller, Franz Ahlgrimm, *Management of Agriculture and Food in the German-Occupied and Other Areas of Fortress Europe: A Study in Military Government* (Stanford, Calif., 1953), pp. 72–88.

337   21. *TWC,* NI 3777, 13:848–51; economic policy guidelines (EC 347, pp. 189–94); definition of the tasks of the Zentralhandelsgesellschaft Ost, December 3, 1941 (T454/16/738–41); Göring order of September 9, 1941, granting the Continental Oil Company a ninety-nine-year concession to oil rights in Russia (T454/91/484–88, 491–94); history of the Continental Oil Company, dated January 13, 1942 (NID 15425).

22. Economic policy guidelines, July 1941 (WF 5253H/E314307–37; EC 38; EC 472; PS 1743); Göring directive of July 27, 1941 (*TWC,* NI 3777, 13:848–51; T454/16/760–63); further directives of July 31, 1941, signed Körner (T454/16/764–65); of August 2, 1941 (T454/16/768); Burkart memorandum, August 13, 1941 (NI 5262): Göring to principal government departments, October 15, 1941 (T454/91/344–45); Bräutigam, *Überblick,* pp. 44–45.

338   23. General principles for economic policy in the newly occupied eastern territories, based on the conference of November 8, 1941 (*TWC,* 13:854–66); Bräutigam, *Überblick,* pp. 45, 49.

24. Guidelines for the treatment of collective farms (T454/16/698–99); Göring to Rosenberg, January 30, 1942, approving plans for a new agrarian policy (T454/91/325); second memorandum on the reform of the agrarian order, February 1942 (T84/114/1411610–705); directives for the economic administration of occupied Russia, April 1942 (NI 10119); Bräutigam, *Überblick,* pp. 33a–34. A liberalization had already taken place in the former Baltic states which now formed part of the Ostland. Rosenberg had spoken to Hitler on this subject on September 29, 1941, and had secured his agreement in principle to the gradual abolition of collective farms and a return to private enterprise, but "only to a limited degree" and not on large farms where food production might be jeopardized or in areas that were to be kept in reserve for German peasant settlements (*DGFP,* D, 13:596–97).

25. The actual decree is dated February 16, 1942 (*Documents on International Affairs, 1939–1946,* vol. 2, *Hitler's Europe,* ed. Margaret Carlyle [London, 1954], pp. 37–40).

339   26. Rosenberg memorandum of talk with Hitler about agricultural reform, February 15, 1942 (T454/94/819–28); Rosenberg to the heads of the German civil government in the Ostland and the Ukraine (T454/94/890–91).

27. Riecke testimony (*IMT* 11:590–91); Bräutigam, *Überblick,* pp. 34–36.

28. Göring directive of May 20, 1942 (EC 347, pp. 123–24).

29. Hitler decree of March 21 and Göring directive of March 27, 1942 (*RGBl* [1942] 1:179–80; *IMT,* 1666-PS, 27:432–33).

340   30. Economic policy guidelines (EC 347, pp. 185–86); Bräutigam, *Überblick,* p. 27 ff.; Dallin, *German Rule,* pp. 313–19; Brandt, *Management of Agriculture,* pp. 72–88; Peter Kleist, *Zwischen Hitler und Stalin, 1939–1945. Aufzeichnungen* (Bonn, 1950), pp. 148–49. Kleist, like Bräutigam, was an official of the Ministry for the Occupied Eastern Territories.

341   31. See above, p. 339.

32. Hitler order of June 9, 1942, transmitted by Lammers to the supreme Reich authorities, June 11 (WF 5246H/E311579–81); Bräutigam, *Überblick,* p. 12.

33. Schwerin von Krosigk to senior Reich officials, September 4, 1942 (*TWC,* NG 4900, 13:885–91).

342   34. Report of Dr. Werner Mansfeld, February 19, 1942 (PS 1201); Rosenberg to Keitel, February 28, 1942 (*IMT,* 076-PS, 25:156–61); Bräutigam memorandum, October 25, 1942 (PS 294); Dallin, *German Rule,* pp. 409–27.

35. Göring order of February 24, 1942, cited in a directive from Alfred Meyer of the Reich Ministry for the Occupied Eastern Territories to the Reichskommissars of the Ostland and the Ukraine, March 6, 1942 (*IMT,* 580-PS, 26:162).

36. Sauckel order of March 31; minutes of conference on labor recruitment, April 15; Sauckel's program, April 20, 1942 (IMT 15:168; 25:55–71; 36:310–16).

37. Sauckel program, April 20, 1942 (*IMT,* 016-PS, 25: 55–71); Dallin, *German Rule,* pp. 428–44; Reitlinger, *House,* pp. 261–76.

343   38. Frauenfeld memorandum, February 10, 1944 (NO 5394).
39. Sauckel to Hitler and Göring, July 27, 1942; Sauckel surveys for 1942; reports to Hitler, March–June 1943 (*IMT*, 26:2–14; 27:115–19, 573–612); statistics in Dallin, *German Rule*, pp. 451–53.
40. Conference of July 16, 1941 (*IMT*, 221-L, 38:86–94).
41. Decree of July 17 concerning the administration of the newly occupied eastern territories (*IMT*, 1997-PS, 29:234–37); first decree on the introduction of the civil administration in the newly occupied eastern territories (WF 34/24765; T77/545/1720411–12); a third decree dealt with the appointment of personnel to the top positions in the civil administration (NG 1325).

344   42. Decrees of June 25, 1941 (military commanders); June 29, 1941 (Göring in his capacity as plenipotentiary of the Four-Year Plan); and July 17, 1941 (Himmler in his capacity as Reichsführer SS and chief of the German police. *TWC* 12:1298–1304).
43. Several memoranda of plans for the administration of Russia before the German invasion from Rosenberg's "Russia" files have been published in *IMT* 26:547 ff. See especially his speech to those most immediately concerned with the eastern problem of June 20, 1941, in which most of the ideas expressed in previous memoranda on the subject were summed up (*IMT*, 1058-PS, 26:610–27).

345   44. See the first volume of this study, pp. 218–20, and the unsigned report from Rosenberg's files on the preparatory work for dealing with the problems of the east (*IMT*, 1039-PS, 26:584–92); Dallin, *German Rule*, pp. 24–26, 84–89.
45. *IMT*, 221-L, 38:93.
46. The Rosenberg ministry is described in detail in the so-called Brown Folder (*Braune Mappe*) of guidelines for German administration in the east (T454/16/674); Bräutigam, *Überblick*, pp. 22a–25; Walter Labs, "Die Verwaltung der besetzten Ostgebiete," *RVL 5* (1943):132–66.
47. Berger to Himmler, March 27, 1943 (NO 1488, cited in Dallin, *German Rule*, p. 86).

346   48. Bräutigam, *Überblick*, pp. 24–28; Kleist, *Zwischen Hitler und Stalin*, p. 144; Dallin, *German Rule*, pp. 84–89; Reitlinger, *House*, pp. 138–43; Roman Ilnytzkyj, *Deutschland und die Ukraine, 1934–1945. Tatsachen europäischer Ostpolitik*, 2 vols. (Munich, 1955–56), 2:407–8.
49. Rosenberg's complaints fill many volumes of files. See his letter to Lammers of August 27, 1941, complaining of Himmler's encroachments (NO 3726). Many pertinent documents are on film in the National Archives, T454/91, and WF 5083H.
50. Memorandum of Heydrich-Meyer conference, October 4, 1941 (T175/66/2582163–68; Staatliches Archivlager, Göttingen, Lu 1, 23a); Himmler minutes of conference with Rosenberg, November 15, 1941 (T175/128/2654511–13); Rosenberg's version (T454/102/17–21). In a letter to Heydrich of November 26, 1941, Himmler complained of the bureaucratic niggling of the Rosenberg ministry and said he had no intention of going through Rosenberg's ministerial channels in seizing what he needed to supply his forces in the east (T175/66/2582158–61).

347   51. Himmler to Rosenberg, August 17, 1942, rejecting his complaints about Himmler's activity in the field of resettlement (T175/68/2584086–88); Rosenberg to Lammers, September 21, 1942 (T175/68/2584147–49); Rosenberg to Himmler, September 28, 1942, saying he had approved all Himmler's measures and so had given them legality, but that in the future he wanted Himmler to secure his prior approval (T175/68/2584180–82); Greiser to Berger, October 9, 1942, enclosing Rosenberg's directive on the separation of spheres of authority between the civil administrations and police (T175/17/2521113–18).
52. Meyer to Himmler, July 1, 1942, suggesting that Berger go to the Rosenberg ministry (NO 2594); Himmler to Rosenberg, July 1942 (NO 3631); Berger affidavit (NO 3971); Kleist, *Zwischen Hitler und Stalin*, pp. 150–51; Bräutigam, *Überblick*, p. 32a; Dallin, *German Rule*, pp. 169–76.
53. Berger to Himmler, July 14 and August 27, 1942 (NO 3129; T175/122/2647654–55; NG 3511).
54. Berger to Himmler, March 9, 1943 (NO 031).
55. Himmler to Berger, October 25, 1942 (NO 737); Rosenberg to Berger, August 10, 1943 (NO 348–49); Berger affidavit (NO 3971); Berger to Himmler, January 12, 1945, asking to be relieved of his position with the Reich Ministry for the East (NO 1858).
56. Rosenberg letters to Hitler and Lammers, October 12, 1944 (*IMT* 11:508–9; 40:185–94); Rosenberg to Hitler, November 18, 1944, complaining that for an entire year he had not been allowed to see Hitler (NO 1815); Joachim C. Fest, *The Face of the Third Reich: Portraits of the Nazi Leadership* (New York, 1970), p. 173.

348   57. Himmler to Bormann, May 24, 1941 (T175/123/2648742–44); Dallin, *German Rule*, p. 37.
58. See the first volume of this study, pp. 217–18.
59. Hitler decree of July 17, 1941 (*TWC*, NG 1688, 12:1303–4; WF 5246H/E311497–98).
60. Bräutigam, *Überblick*, pp. 26–27.
61. Ibid., p. 11; Dallin, *German Rule*, p. 38, n. 1.

349   62. Speech to SS group leaders in Posen, October 4, 1943 (*IMT*, 1919-PS, 29:171).

   63. Collections of Himmler speeches from 1930 through 1945 are on film in the National Archives, T175/89–94; see especially roll 90. Some of these speeches have been printed, at least in part, in *IMT* 29:98 ff., and *NCA* 4:553 ff.

350   64. Himmler speech to senior SS officers, June 9, 1942 (T175/90/2612664 ff); also speech of October 4, 1943 (*IMT*, 1919-PS, 29:145–46).

351   65. Himmler speech of June 21, 1944 (T175/93/2613945–92).

   66. Keitel order of March 13, 1941 (*IMT*, 447-PS, 26:53–58); memorandum of conference of May 1, 1941 (PS 866). See the first volume of this study, pp. 217–18.

   67. Heydrich to senior SS and police officers, July 2, 1941. (Sipo and SD files, EK3, B No. IV-1100/41 gRs. Document made available to me through the courtesy of Dr. Hans-Günther Seraphim.) A large collection of field reports from Himmler's task forces in Russia from June 1941 to May 1943 is on film in the National Archives, T175/233–36. A particularly interesting report for the month of October 1941 is published as document 102-R, *IMT* 38:279–303.

352   68. Himmler order of July 28, 1941 (Staatliches Archivlager, Göttingen, Lu 2, 9d).

   69. Himmler directive of July 28, 1942 (NO 1662).

   70. The following account of the destruction of the Jews in Russia draws heavily on Raul Hilberg, *The Destruction of the European Jews* (Chicago, 1961), p. 177 ff., and Gerald Reitlinger, *The Final Solution: The Attempt to Exterminate the Jews of Europe, 1939–1945* (New York, 1968), p. 195 ff., as well as Reitlinger's *House*, p. 249 ff. The field reports of Himmler's task forces show that the destruction of the Jews was being carried on from the beginning of the Russian campaign and was not initiated at the famous Wannsee conference of January 1942 (see above, p. 7).

   71. Himmler to Berger, July 28, 1943 (NO 626).

   72. Memorandum of Heydrich-Meyer conference, October 4, 1941 (T175/66/2582163–68); Bräutigam to Lohse, December 18, 1941 (*IMT*, 3666-PS, 32:437).

   73. Hilberg, *Destruction*, p. 196.

353   74. Hilberg, *Destruction*, pp. 191–208.

   75. Ibid., pp. 242–56. The statistics on the auxiliaries come from Hilberg. How these auxiliaries were recruited and their motives for collaborating with the Germans are subjects that require much further investigation.

354   76. Hilberg, *Destruction*, pp. 208–19. See also above, pp. 9–10.

   77. Hilberg, *Destruction*, pp. 224–42, who describes the objections of Lohse and Kube. See above pp. 10–11, and below, pp. 371–72.

   78. These statistics are for pre-1939 Russia and the Baltic states. An SS report states that 633,300 Jews were evacuated from Russia and the Baltic states as of December 31, 1942. This figure does not include the Jews actually killed up to that time. Considering the fact that about .5 million were killed outright in the first five months after the German invasion began, the final total of 900,000 given by Hilberg (*Destruction*, p. 767) and of 700,000 to 750,000 given by Reitlinger (*Final Solution*, pp. 543–45) seems far too conservative. My own figure is based on the German task force reports which may have been exaggerated—but which did not include Jews who died from disease, exposure, or starvation as a result of the Nazi campaign. The extent of the failure of the Russian people and the Communist state to aid in protecting and evacuating Jews from Nazi-occupied areas appears to have been obscured in the Nuremberg trial and other official publications on German war crimes.

355   79. See above, pp. 40, 79–82.

   80. Hitler's orders described by Himmler in a conference with Riecke of February 19, 1942 (NG 1118).

   81. Himmler-Riecke conference of February 19, 1942, in which Riecke explained his ideas, which had been approved by Hitler, for the Germanization of Russia (NG 1118).

356   82. Meyer-Hetling memorandum, May 28, 1942 (NO 2255).

   83. Himmler to Greifelt, June 12, 1942 (NO 2255); appointment of Meyer-Hetling as planning commissioner (NO 5547–48).

   84. T84/73/1360137–239. The main part of the plan published by Helmut Heiber, "Der Generalplan Ost," *VfZ* 6 (1958):280–325.

   85. Berger memorandum of the conference at the Führer's headquarters, August 17, 1942 (T175/17/2521076–80; NO 2703). Hitler's orders on colonization were recorded in part 2 of Berger's memorandum. Hitler himself does not appear to have been present at this conference.

357   86. See above, pp. 79–82.

   87. Wetzel memorandum of a conference on Germanization and resettlement of February 2, 1942, attended by representatives of all major offices concerned with the occupied eastern territories (NO 2585). Statistics in Brückner to Brandt, April 10, 1943 (NO 5081).

   88. Lorenz to Himmler, March 30, 1944 (NO 5841). Copious statistics on resettlements are included in RKFDV reports of January 15, 1942 (NO 3570) and January 1944 (NO 3568).

89. Hitler decree of July 17, 1941 (T77/545/1720411–12: NG 1280).
90. Unsigned memorandum in Rosenberg's files, April 2, 1941 (*IMT*, 1017-PS, 26:547–54).
91. *IMT*, 221-L, 38:86–94.

358

92. Instructions for a Reichskommissar of the Ostland, May 8, 1941 (*IMT*, 1029-PS, 26:573–76).
93. Memorandum from Rosenberg's files of April 7, 1941 (PS 1018).
94. Hitler decrees of July 17, 1941. On administration (*IMT*, 1997-PS, 29:234–37); on personnel (NG 1325).

359

95. Hitler order of appointment, June 17, 1941 (NG 1325); Bräutigam, *Überblick*, pp. 7–8. For the spelling of the names of the Generalkommissars I have followed the official documents of appointment. On Kube, see Dallin, *German Rule*, pp. 203–9; Reitlinger, *House*, pp. 156–57; Kleist, *Zwischen Hitler und Stalin*, pp. 170–73.
96. Hitler order of July 18, 1941 (T77/545/1720436); Bräutigam, *Überblick*, p. 8.
97. For Latvia and Lithuania, Hitler orders of July 22, August 20, and November 4, 1941 (T77/545/1720437–38, 1720416); for Estonia, Hitler order of November 29, 1941 (WF 5083H/E292883–97); Rosenberg's appeals (*TWC* 13:875); Bräutigam, *Überblick*, pp. 13–16; Robert Herzog, *Grundzüge der deutschen Besatzungsverwaltung in den ost-und südosteuropäischen Landern während des zweiten Weltkrieges* (Tübingen, 1955), pp. 25–27.
98. *IMT*, 221-L, 38:86–94; Picker, *Hitlers Tischgespräche*, p. 314; *Hitler's Secret Conversations*, p. 345; Kleist, *Zwischen Hitler und Stalin*, p. 149.
99. H. Lohse, "Ostland baut auf," *Nationalsozialistische Monatshefte* 13 (1942):32–39.

360

100. Bräutigam, *Überblick*, pp. 13–14; Kleist, *Zwischen Hitler und Stalin*, pp. 149, 159, 166; Dallin, *German Rule*, pp. 186–89; Reitlinger, *House*, pp. 136–37.
101. Bräutigam, *Überblick*, p. 16; Dallin, *German Rule*, p. 187; Reitlinger, *House*, p. 147.

361

102. Reitlinger, *House*, p. 155.
103. Bräutigam, *Überblick*, p. 16; Dallin, *German Rule*, pp. 219–20. On Kube and his feud with Himmler, see below, pp. 371–72.
104. *ABlGKMinsk* (1943), p. 237; Dallin, *German Rule*, pp. 220–25.
105. Dallin, *German Rule*, pp. 189–90; Bräutigam, *Überblick*, pp. 15–17; Lammers memorandum of a Hitler-Rosenberg conference of September 29, 1941 (*DGFP*, D, 13:596–97); Reitlinger, *House*, p. 147; Lohse, "Ostland baut auf," p. 34.
106. Treaty of September 28, 1939 (*DGFP*, D, 8:165).
107. Himmler directive of August 19, 1941; Foreign Office circular of August 26, 1941 (*DGFP*, D, 13:395); Heydrich-Meyer conference of October 10; Heydrich to Wolff, October 21, 1941 (T175/66/258262–68); also Hitler's order of May 30, 1942, that Balts who had returned to the Ostland without permission were to be evacuated once again and that their return was to be prevented by all means (WF 5083H/E292901); Bräutigam, *Überblick*, pp. 79–80.

362

108. Bräutigam, *Überblick*, pp. 16–17; Dallin, *German Rule*, p. 190, n. 4; Litzmann proclamation of December 5, 1941 (*ABlGKReval* [1942], pp. 3–4); Alfred Bilmanis, *Latvia under German Occupation* (Washington, D.C., 1943), pp. 6–7.
109. Rosenberg's guidelines for the establishment of advisory councils, Brown folder (T454/16/692, 701–3; EC 347, p. 41).
110. Official announcement, March 7, 1942 (*RGBl* [1942] 1:844); Rosenberg directives and decrees of March 7, 18, and 23, 1942 (WF 5082H/E292628–41); Bräutigam, *Überblick*, p. 17.

363

111. Rosenberg guidelines for Estonia, Latvia, and Lithuania of March 7, 1941 (Reich Ministry for the East document no. II 1c 400/42 I/O, found in the German Foreign Office files).
112. Rosenberg memorandum of his conference with Hitler, May 8, 1942 (*IMT*, 1520-PS, 27:283–94).
113. Decree of May 15 on the introduction of local self-government (*VBIRKO* [1942], p. 99; *ABlGKRiga* [1942], pp. 293–94). This decree did not apply to White Ruthenia, where Kube installed native administrative advisers in June 1942 (Bräutigam, *Überblick*, p. 16). Further decrees on the introduction of local self-government in Estonia, June 20, 1942 (*ABlGKReval* [1942], pp. 497–501); in Latvia, June 27, 1942 (*ABlGKRiga* [1942], p. 43); in Lithuania the senior counselors were permitted to issue their own legislation (under German supervision) by a decree of September 9, 1942 (*ABlGKKauen* [1942], p. 634); in Estonia this right was conferred on the first director, December 22, 1942 (*ABlGKReval* [1943], p. 3).
114. Report of Windecker, the representative of the German Foreign Office in the Ostland, April 19, 1943 (NG 2721).

364

115. A large number of documents dealing with this problem, including the record of a conference on the subject under the chairmanship of Rosenberg of November 25, 1943, and the decisions of Hitler are on film in the National Arhcives (T175/126 and T454/92). Berger's views were supported by Dr. Ernst Kaltenbrunner, who feared that refusal of

promises of autonomy would lower morale still further in the Baltic states. Berger believed there would now be no prospect of securing the thirty thousand volunteers for the Waffen-SS he had expected to recruit (T175/126/2651045–47).

116. Conference of November 16–17, 1943 (PS 039); the final report of Generalkommisar Walter Schimana (White Ruthenia) of August 31, 1944, reviews the problem (T175/18/2521865–81). As late as September 1944, Rosenberg appealed to Hitler to issue proclamations to win the active support of the millions of people from the east who were now in the Reich for the German war effort, but Hitler still refused (NO 2995–97).

117. Lohse proclamation, July 28, 1941 (*VBIRKO* [1941], pp. 1–3; Raphaël Lemkin, *Axis Rule in Occupied Europe: Laws of Occupation, Analysis of Government, Proposals for Redress* (Washington, D.C., 1944), pp. 300–301. A similar proclamation was issued in White Ruthenia on September 1, 1941 (*ABIGKMinsk* [1941], pp. 1–2).

118. *VBIRKO* (1941), pp. 17, 20, 61; *ABIGKMinsk* (1941), pp. 5, 21–22; *VBIRKO* (1942), pp. 31–32.

119. *VBIRKO* (1941), p. 21; *VBIRMO* (1941), p. 5; (1942), pp. 10–11; (1943), pp. 77–78; *ABIGKMinsk* (1941), p. 64; (1942), pp. 71, 131–32; *VBIRKO* (1942), pp. 115, 133, 140; (1943), p. 13.

120. *ABIGKReval* (1942), p. 4; Lohse, "Ostland baut auf," p. 34; Bräutigam, *Überblick*, pp. 61–62, 65; Labs, "Verwaltung," pp. 154 ff.; Günther Moritz, *Gerichtsbarkeit in den von Deutschland besetzten Gebieten, 1939–1945* (Tübingen, 1955), pp. 214–18, 226.

121. *VBIRKO* (1941), pp. 31–32; Lemkin, *Axis Rule,* pp. 302–4; also Rosenberg decrees of December 19, 1941, and of April 27 and November 24, 1942 (*VBIRMO* [1941], pp. 3–4; [1942], pp. 18–19, 89); Lohse decree of January 26, 1942 (*VBIRKO* [1942], pp. 11–12); Brown folder, T454/16/682–83, 703–4; Moritz, *Gerichtsbarkeit,* pp. 219–24, 226–30, 332–33; Labs, "Verwaltung," p. 154.

122. In Lithuania, February 14, 1942 (*ABIGKKauen* [1942], pp. 242, 511); in Latvia, March 13, 1942 (*ABIGKRiga* [1942], pp. 141, 355); in Estonia, March 3, 1942 (*ABIGKReval* [1942], pp. 180–85, 699); Labs, "Verwaltung," p. 156; Moritz, *Gerichtsbarkeit,* pp. 226–30, 232–33.

123. Decree of February 17, 1942 (*VBIRMO* [1942], pp. 9–10); not published in Estonia until August 13, 1942 (*ABIGKReval* [1942], pp. 551–53); decree of September 28, 1942 (*VBIRKO* [1942], pp. 143–46).

124. *ABIGKMinsk* (1942), pp. 173–74; Labs, "Verwaltung," p. 157; Moritz, *Gerichtsbarkeit,* pp. 227, 230–34.

125. Bräutigam, *Überblick,* pp. 71–72; Dallin, *German Rule,* pp. 454 ff.

126. Rosenberg to Lohse, November 19, 1941 (T454/20/962–63; PS 300); Bräutigam, *Überblick,* p. 71; Dallin, *German Rule,* pp. 458–66.

127. Kube decrees of October 13 and December 2, 1941 (*ABIGKMinsk* [1941], pp. 6–8; [1942], p. 2).

128. Rosenberg guidelines, Green folder (EC 347, p. 43); Brown folder (T454/16/698); memoranda and directives on religious problems in Rosenberg's files of July and August 1941 (PS 1047, 1052, 1053); decree of June 19, 1942, on the legal status of religious organizations (*VBIRKO* [1942], p. 117); in general, Dallin, *German Rule,* pp. 472–93; Bräutigam, *Überblick,* pp. 66–69.

129. *VBIRKO* (1941), pp. 5–6.

130. *VBIRKO* (1941), pp. 29–30, 99–100; (1942), pp. 91–92.

131. Bräutigam, *Überblick,* p. 34; decree of September 13, 1941 (*VBIRKO* [1941], p. 16); published in Estonia, December 9, 1941 (*ABIGKReval* [1941], pp. 54–56).

132. See above, pp. 338–39.

133. Decrees of February 18 and 27, March 2, April 20, and June 28, 1943 (*VBIRMO* [1943], pp. 57–58; *VBIRKO* [1943], pp. 16–17, 18–21, 23–24, 74, 93–96).

134. Decree of June 3, 1943 (*VBIRMO* [1943], p. 83).

135. Riecke testimony (*IMT* 11:591); Bräutigam, *Überblick,* pp. 34–35, 51.

136. Guidelines on taxation (Brown folder), and Brauchitsch order (EC 347, pp. 101–3; T454/16/705–7); decree of October 18, 1941 (*VBIRKO* [1941], p. 41; [1942], pp. 14–15).

137. See above, p. 367.

138. Decree of October 24, 1941, and its successors (*VBIRKO* [1941], pp. 45–46, 84; [1942], pp. 19, 55–57; [1944], pp. 21–22); Göring to Lohse, November 7, 1941 (PS 1294); Göring to Rosenberg, May 5, 1942 (T454/20/318–19); Rosenberg guidelines of May 20, 1942 (PS 1294).

139. Decree of January 16, 1942, and its successors (*VBIRKO* [1942], pp. 7–8, 126–27, 141–42; [1943], pp. 59–61; *ABIGKMinsk* [1942], pp. 85–89; *VBIRMO* [1942], pp. 21, 78–82); Bräutigam, *Überblick,* pp. 37, 50.

140. *VBIRKO* (1942), pp. 5–6, 33–34; *VBIRMO* (1942), pp. 90–94; Bräutigam, *Überblick,* pp. 36–37, 47–51, 55.

141. *VBIRKO* (1941), pp. 82–83; Bräutigam, *Überblick,* p. 46.

142. *VBIRKO* (1941), pp. 83–84, 109.

370   143. Ibid. (1942), pp. 113–14, 137.
    144. Ibid. (1941), pp. 38–39; (1942), pp. 150–52; (1943), pp. 59–61.
    145. Ibid. (1942), p. 37; (1943), pp. 73–74.
    146. Ibid. (1941), pp. 7, 86–89; (1942), pp. 16–17, 35–37, 73, 85–88, 177–80; (1943), p. 15; *ABlGKMinsk* (1942), p. 91; EC 347, pp. 103–18; Bräutigam, *Überblick,* p. 47.
    147. *VBlRKO* (1941), pp. 4, 46–48, 52–55; (1942), pp. 19–20, 71–86; *ABlGKMinsk* (1942), pp. 2, 105–7.
    148. *ABlGKMinsk* (1941), p. 6; (1942), p. 192; *VBlRMO* (1941), pp. 5–6; (1942), p. 72; *ABlGKReval* (1942), pp. 26–28; *VBlRKO* (1942), pp. 125–26, 153–54; (1943), pp. 3–4, 71–72.

371   149. Bräutigam, *Überblick,* pp. 92–93; statistics in Dallin, *German Rule,* p. 452.
    150. Heydrich report, April 23, 1942 (*NCA,* 3876-PS, 8a:619); Kube report, July 31, 1942 (*IMT,* 3428-PS, 32:279–82).

372   151. Himmler order to the senior SS and police officer, Ostland, June 21, 1943 (NO 2403); Brandt memorandum, July 20, 1943 (Staatliches Archivlager, Göttingen, Lu 1, 11a); Brandt to Bach-Zelewski, July 25, 1943 (Lu 1, 11b); Gottberg to Himmler and Bach-Zelewski, July 21, 1943 (T176/59/2575281–82). The principal documents pertaining to this affair have been collected by Helmut Heiber, "Aus den Akten des Gauleiters Kube," *VfZ* 4 (1956):67–92; also Gerald Reitlinger, "The Doubts of Wilhelm Kube," *Wiener Library Bulletin* (September and December 1950).
    152. Hilberg, *Destruction,* pp. 254–56.

373   153. Hitler decree of August 20, 1941, unpublished (T77/545/1702414–15; 1702441–42; WF 5082H/E292736–37). On the transfer of Ukrainian territory to Rumania, see above, pp. 252–54; see also the memorandum of August 27, 1941, about preparations for the transfer of territory from military to civil administration (*NCA,* 197-PS, 3:210–14); Bräutigam, *Überblick,* p. 19.
    154. Hitler decrees of October 11 and November 4, 1941, and August 12, 1942, unpublished (T77/545/1702452–53; T454/91/438–39, 475–77, 482–83); Herzog, *Grundzüge,* pp. 28, 104.
    155. Brown folder, T454/16/681–82; on Hitler's plans for the Crimea, see the record of the conference of July 16, 1941 (*IMT,* 221-L, 38:87); also NOKW 1347; NG 1118; Bräutigam, *Überblick,* p. 19.
    156. Alfred Rosenberg, *Der Zukunftsweg einer deutschen Aussenpolitik* (Munich, 1927).

374   157. Unsigned memoranda of April 2 and 7 in Rosenberg's files on Russia (*IMT,* 1017-PS, 26:550–51; PS 1018); Rosenberg's instructions for a Reichskommissar in the Ukraine, May 7, and speech of June 20, 1941 (*IMT,* 1028-PS, 1058-PS, 26:567–73, 618–19).
    158. Rosenberg guidelines for German policy in the Ukraine, October 8, 1941 (found in the *Reichskanzlei* file RK 14392 B, 15082; Reich Ministry for the East no. I/182/41); Bräutigam to supreme Reich agencies, November 22, 1941 (T454/20/866–68); Rosenberg memorandum of March 16, 1942 (*IMT,* 045-PS, 25:97–98).
    159. July 16, 1941, conference (*IMT,* 221-L, 38:86–94).
    160. See above, p. 331.

375   161. Grosskopf report, August 6, 1941 (*DGFP,* D, 13:289–91 and footnotes); Rosenberg guidelines, quoted in Dallin, *German Rule,* p. 129; Bräutigam, *Überblick,* pp. 171–72.
    162. See above, pp. 348–54.
    163. Report of October 28, 1941 (*IMT* 8:248–49).
    164. Hitler decree of August 20, 1941 (see above, n. 153).

376   165. On Koch, see Dallin, *German Rule,* pp. 124–27; Reitlinger, *House,* pp. 174–83; Kleist, *Zwischen Hitler und Stalin,* pp. 180–92; Hans Gisevius, *To the Bitter End* (Boston, 1947), pp. 200–202.
    166. Conference of July 16, 1941 (*IMT,* 221-L, 38:86–94).

377   167. Because of the military situation and because Hitler had established the capital of the German civil administration of the Ukraine in the relatively unattractive city of Rovno, Koch spent very little time in the Ukraine. He made up for his neglect of the province by the forcefulness of his pronouncements when he resided there. See in particular his speeches of April 1942, as recorded by Dr. Friedrich Markull, head of the legal section of the Ministry for the East, who said that members of Koch's entourage were making similar statements "which every visitor and every member of the local civil administration can confirm from his own observation." (Markull report of August 19, 1942, *NCA,* 36-R, 8:52–59). Koch's policies of harshness appear to have been encouraged by Hitler and especially by Bormann, for after a visit to Hitler's headquarters in August 1942, he made some of his most extreme public statements on the subject. Report of Lieutenant von Engelbrechten, from the Etzdorff files, and unsigned reports (T454/92/895–97; NG 2720; *IMT,* 264-PS, 25:317–18); Koch's speech of November 1942, as reported by Riecke (*IMT* 41:196); Koch circular of February 20, 1943 (quoted by Koch in a memorandum to Rosenberg of March 16, 1943, *IMT* 25:283–84); Koch speech to Nazi party members, March 3, 1943, as reported by *Oberkriegsverwaltungsrat* Dr. Claassen (*IMT* 27:9–11); Koch memorandum for Rosenberg of March 16, 1943, justifying his policies (*IMT* 25:255–88);

Koch instructions to the heads of the German regional administrations in the Ukraine, August 25, 1943 (NO 2437).

168. Reitlinger, *House,* p. 175.

169. Koch to Rosenberg, March 16, 1943 (*IMT,* 192-PS, 25:256–57); Bräutigam, *Überblick,* pp. 19–20; Herzog, *Grundzüge,* p. 160.

170. Lammers testimony, *IMT* 11:48–49.

171. See for example the report to General Thomas on German policy in the Ukraine (*IMT* 3275-PS, 32:71–75); *Goebbels Diaries,* p. 202 (entry for May 2, 1942).

172. Prützmann to Himmler, March 27, 1943, and April 22, 1944 (NO 1488, 3974).

173. See above, n. 167; Bräutigam, *Überblick,* pp. 19–20.

174. Lammers to Rosenberg, August 24, 1944 (NG 1096); Dallin, *German Rule,* pp. 197–98.

175. *VBIRMO* (1942), pp. 3–5, 7–11, 18–19, 89; (1943), pp. 1–3, 78; *VBIRKU* (1943), pp. 67–68; Moritz, *Gerichtsbarkeit,* pp. 219–24; Bräutigam, *Überblick,* pp. 65–66.

176. *VBIRMO* (1942), pp. 5–6, 14–16, 19–21, 69, 72–73, 79–82, 90–94; (1943), pp. 49, 71–72, 80–82; *VBIRKU* (1941), pp. 45, 95, 145, 160; (1942), pp. 5, 30, 37, 43, 91, 115; (1943), pp. 71–72, 103.

177. Riecke memorandum, March 30, 1943 (*IMT* 41:200); *VBIRKU* (1942), pp. 11, 143; (1943), pp. 62–66, 103.

178. Decrees on price control are too numerous to record. On the control of wages and labor, see especially *VBRKU* (1941), p. 45; (1942), pp. 130, 160; (1943), pp. 61–62.

179. Lammers to Koch, February 16, 1942; Koch to Rosenberg, March 2, 1942, thanking him for the information that Hitler had read his objections to the New Agrarian Order and that Hitler had approved the scheme for political reasons (WF 5253H/E314353); Koch decree on the establishment of the Agricultural Management Association (*VBIRKU* [1942], p. 11); Koch decrees on communal farms, April 15, 1942, and February 27, 1943, published in *Zentralblatt des Reichskommissars für die Ukraine.*

180. Rosenberg to Koch, May 13, 1942; Koch to Rosenberg, June 2, 1942 (WF 5082H/ E292717–27). In his letter of June 2, Koch refuted Rosenberg's charges that he had permitted the public whipping of Ukrainian citizens; there had been little use of the whip, none of it in public, Koch said, and by an order of April 18, 1942 (WF 5082H/E292728) he had forbidden his officials to carry whips. On June 29, 1942, Koch sent the defense of his policies he had prepared for Rosenberg to Lammers, asking that it be submitted to Hitler (NG 1329), and shortly afterward he appeared at Hitler's headquarters to present his case personally. As his quarrel with Rosenberg continued to fester and criticisms continued to be leveled at his management of the economy of the Ukraine, Koch sent Hitler a long list of his economic accomplishments, replete with statistics, on July 6, 1943 (NO 1786). Koch's figures challenged by Riecke, November 17, 1943 (PS 1294) and by Rosenberg, October 18, 1944 (PS 327), among others.

181. Report of December 2, 1942 (*IMT,* 3257-PS, 32:71–75).

182. Report of July 15, 1942 (PS 302).

183. Frauenfeld memorandum, February 10, 1944 (NO 5394). Bitter criticisms were also voiced by Goebbels (*Diaries,* pp. 185, 246, 328, 330); by Bräutigam of Rosenberg's staff (*IMT,* 294-PS, 25:331–42); by Hildebrandt of Himmler's staff (T175/53/2567868–75); among many others. Although some of these criticisms were undoubtedly partly motivated by personal dislike or jealousy of Koch, they contain enough substantive material to make a thoroughly convincing case.

184. Bräutigam, *Überblick,* pp. 92–93; statistics in Dallin, *German Rule,* p. 452.

185. Again, statistics on this question vary widely, and the figure of four hundred thousand may be far too low. A German armaments inspectorate report of December 2, 1941, estimated that already at this time some one hundred fifty to two hundred thousand Jews had been killed in the RK Ukraine (PS 3257). My figures are based on German task force reports, see above n. 78.

186. *IMT,* 221-L, 38:87, 90–91.

187. *Hitler's Secret Conversations,* pp. 35, 44–45, 61–62, 93, 129, 451, 513, 559, 578–79; Picker, *Hitlers Tischgespräche,* pp. 145, 336, 429–30, 485–86; Rosenberg memorandum of conference with Hitler, December 14, 1941 (*IMT,* 1517-PS, 27:272); Michael Luther, *Die Krim unter deutscher Besatzung im zweiten Weltkrieg* (Berlin, 1956), pp. 38–40.

188. On the German conquest of the Crimea, see the memoirs of Erich von Manstein, the German general who conducted that operation, *Lost Victories* (London, 1958), pp. 204–59.

189. Luther, *Krim,* pp. 38–39.

190. Conference of February 19, 1942 (NG 1118); *Hitler's Secret Conversations,* p. 513; Picker, *Hitlers Tischgespräche,* pp. 429–30; Bräutigam, *Überblick,* p. 21; Luther, *Krim,* p. 40; Dallin, *German Rule,* pp. 253–56. The plan to move the South Tyrol Germans to the Crimea was proposed by Alfred Frauenfeld, who was designated to be head of the German civil administration in the Crimea. See below, p. 386.

191. Himmler to Frauenfeld, July 10, 1942 (NO 2417).

378
379
380
381
382
383
384

192. Keitel on Hitler's resettlement plans for the Crimea, July 12, 1942 (T175/122/2647917–18).

385   193. Dallin, *German Rule*, pp. 259–60; Manstein testimony, *IMT* 20:618–21.

194. Ohlendorf testimony, *TWC* 4:253–54. In his memoirs (*Lost Victories*) Manstein says almost nothing about the administration of the territory under his control and the name of Ohlendorf is not mentioned. In his defense of Manstein, R. T. Paget contends that Ohlendorf and other SS officers, condemned to death in 1947 for their actions in Russia, kept themselves alive by giving evidence for the prosecution at the trials of various German generals, Manstein among them. *Manstein: His Campaigns and His Trial* (London, 1951), pp. 97, 168–72.

195. Luther, *Krim*, 38, 44; Bräutigam, *Überblick*, p. 21; Dallin, *German Rule*, pp. 256–57. In his final report on the activity of the SS and police in the Crimea, SS Sturmbannführer Heinze stated that in October or November 1942 Himmler had instructed the senior SS and police officer in the Crimea to do everything necessary for planning the resettlement of the region with Germans and that a detailed plan submitted to Himmler in December 1942 was approved by him in January 1943 (NO 4009).

386   196. Ohlendorf testimony, *TWC* 4:253–54; Luther, *Krim*, pp. 44, 50–52, 62, 74–82 , 87 ff.; Dallin, *German Rule*, pp. 257–62.

197. Luther, *Krim*, pp. 63–64; Dallin, *German Rule*, pp. 259–60.

198. Luther, *Krim*, p. 42; Dallin, *German Rule*, pp. 264–66.

199. *Die Krim* (Berlin, 1942).

200. Luther, *Krim*, pp. 42–44. In his pamphlet *Ursache und Sinn unseres Kampfes. Bolschewismus-Kapitalismus. Das apokalyptische Tier mit zwei Köpfen* (Vienna, 1944), Frauenfeld declared that the war with Russia was a life and death struggle with Bolshevism and that anyone who failed to recognize his duty in aiding in this struggle was a pernicious person who would have to be eliminated in the same way as an any traitor. Through the destruction of Bolshevism, the German *Volk* would crown a thousand-year mission, a victory over the beast with two heads: western and eastern imperialism (pp. 62–63). In contrast to this propaganda brochure, Frauenfeld's long memorandum on the problems of administering the occupied eastern territories, dated February 10, 1944, and submitted to Himmler early in March, was on the whole an eminently sensible analysis from the point of view of German national interests and a devastating critique of the policies the Germans had actually pursued (NO 5394).

387   201. Luther, *Krim*, pp. 46–50; Kleist, *Zwischen Hitler und Stalin*, pp. 182–83.

202. Luther, *Krim*, pp. 66–74, 82–84.

388   203. OKW directive of March 13, 1941 (*IMT*, 447-PS, 26:53–58); conference of July 16, 1941 (*IMT*, 221-L, 38:86–94); Bräutigam, *Überblick*, pp. 4–5.

389   204. Unsigned memoranda of April 2 and 7, 1941, from Rosenberg's files (*IMT*, 1017-PS, 26:551–52; PS 1018); and above all Rosenberg's instructions for a Reichskommissar in the Caucasus (PS 1027) and his speech about plans for Russia of June 20, 1941 (*IMT*, 1058-PS, 26:620–21, 624); Dallin, *German Rule*, pp. 227–31; also Alexander Dallin "The North Caucasus," in John A. Armstrong, ed., *Soviet Partisans in World War II* (Madison, Wisc., 1964), p. 573.

205. Rosenberg's personnel proposals for the administration of Russia, April 7, 1941 (*IMT*, 1019-PS, 26:556). Rosenberg's first choice for the position in the Caucasus was State Secretary Herbert Backe, who spoke Russian fluently and who came from that region. Dallin, *German Rule*, pp. 88–89, 230–31.

206. Paulus testimony, *IMT* 7:260. In his military directive 41 of April 5, 1942, outlining his general plan for further operations in Russia, Hitler ordered that all available forces should first be concentrated in the southern sector "with the aim of destroying the enemy before the Don, in order to secure the Caucasian oil fields and the passes through the Caucasus mountains themselves" (*Hitler's War Directives, 1939–1945*, ed. H. R. Trevor-Roper [paperback, London, 1964], pp. 178–79). How the oil from the Caucasus was to be transported to Germany, even if the oil fields had been captured intact (a most unlikely possibility in view of past German experiences in Russia) was a problem Hitler does not appear to have faced. The High Command of the German Navy, in a memorandum of May 9, 1941, declared that the navy could do little or nothing about transporting oil from the Caucasus; even if it succeeded in gaining control of the Black Sea, there would be no ships available for transport purposes because all oil tankers were fully occupied with the transport of Rumanian oil (NOKW 2730).

207. Picker, *Hitlers Tischgespräche*, pp. 321–22; Dallin, *German Rule*, pp. 239–40.

390   208. Reitlinger, *House*, pp. 296–300; Dallin, *German Rule*, p. 239.

209. Rosenberg to Lammers asking for Hitler's decision about the policies of Köstring and Herwarth, July 21, 1942 (NG 1657). A memorandum of August 20, 1942, of guidelines for the treatment of the peoples of the Caucasus, prepared by a member of Rosenberg's staff and amended by Arno Schickedanz, showed that Rosenberg's ideas about the Caucasus did not change (T454/20/1140–44). A member of the Nazi administration in Poland, *Parteigenosse* Gloger, was horrified when he heard of the plans being concocted by the army and its allies in the Foreign Office. They were trying to find personnel among

Russian prisoners of war to set up a Caucasus legion and to serve as administrators after the German conquest, he wrote to a friend. Especially noteworthy, Gloger said, was his conversation with Herwarth about the future of the Caucasus, where independent states were to be set up within a Caucasus confederation. A German division was to be stationed there until these states could guarantee their own security, but afterward Germany would exercise only a tactful supervision so that the reality of German power should not be noticed. A speech by General Köstring to members of individual military units revealed that he, too, was thinking in terms of actually granting sovereignty to the people of the Caucasus. "You can imagine that I am appalled," Gloger wrote, the more so as Bräutigam and Mende seemed to have similar views (Gloger to Zimmermann, July 13, 1942, NG 1657).

391
210. Dallin, *German Rule*, p. 240; Dallin, "The North Caucasus," pp. 578–80, 583.
211. Dallin, *German Rule*, pp. 241, 244–49; "North Caucasus," pp. 575–78, 581–84.
212. Dallin, *German Rule*, pp. 244–49.
213. Ibid., p. 243.
392
214. Ibid., p. 249; "North Caucasus," pp. 584–86.
215. *Hitler's Secret Conversations*, p. 64.
393
216. Hossbach memorandum, conference of November 5, 1937, *IMT*, 386-PS, 25:402–13.
217. *Mein Kampf* (New York, 1939), p. 174.

12. MORGEN DIE GANZE WELT?

394
1. *Mein Kampf* (New York, 1939), pp. 183–84; also pp. 461, 902–903.
2. See the first volume of this study, pp. 129–31.
395
3. Franz Halder, *Kriegstagebuch. Tägliche Aufzeichnungen des Chefs des Generalstabes des Heeres, 1939–1942*, ed. Hans-Adolf Jacobsen, 3 vols. (Stuttgart, 1962–64), 1:308.
4. Henry Picker, *Hitlers Tischgespräche im Führerhauptquartier, 1941–1942*, ed. Percy Ernst Schramm, Andreas Hillgruber, and Martin Vogt (Stuttgart, 1965), pp. 479–80.
5. See the first volume of this study, pp. 157–63, 208–10.
396
6. Halder, *Kriegstagebuch*, 2:21; Picker, *Hitlers Tischgespräche*, pp. 63, 136, 145, 479–80; *Hitler's Secret Conversations, 1941–1944* (paperback, New York, 1961), pp. 42, 54, 75, 113–14, 580.
7. Picker, *Hitlers Tischgespräche*, pp. 244–45.
8. Ibid., pp. 169–71, 336–37; *Hitler's Secret Conversations*, pp. 260, 611, 629–30; Halder, *Kriegstagebuch*, 2:31; *DGFP*, D, 10 (see the index of documents on Britain, pp. xxiv–xxvi); also Norman Longmate, *If Britain Had Fallen* (London, 1972), p. 117.
397
9. For the following account, I have relied heavily on the excellent work of Ronald Wheatley, *Operation Sea Lion: German Plans for the Invasion of England, 1939–1942* (paperback, Oxford, 1962), chap. 5; and Peter Fleming, *Operation Sea Lion* (paperback, New York, 1956), chap. 18. See also Longmate, *If Britain Had Fallen*, chap. 8. David Lampe's work, *The Last Ditch* (London, 1968), which attempts to reconstruct German plans for the occupation of Britain, is unfortunately undocumented and imprecise; it adds little to the work of Wheatley and Fleming.
10. Wheatley, *Operation Sea Lion*, p. 117; Fleming, *Operation Sea Lion*, pp. 251–54; Longmate, *If Britain Had Fallen*, chap. 14.
11. One of the major gaps in the evidence on Hitler's war aims is the lack of references to Ireland. He appears to have done almost nothing to exploit the anti-English feeling in Ireland, nor did he make any specific comments on the position Ireland might occupy in a German-ordered world. At a conference with his naval leadership on December 3, 1940, Hitler stated that "a landing in Ireland can be attempted only if Ireland requests help." The German navy, however, came to the conclusion that "it *would not be possible* to follow up an Irish request for help by sending an expeditionary force and occupying the island, in view of the enemy's *superior naval force*, the *unfavorable geographical* conditions, and *the impossibility of forwarding supplies*" (*Fuehrer Conferences on Matters Dealing with the German Navy, 1939–1945*, 8 vols. [Washington, D.C., 1946–47], 1940, 2:59, 61–62).
12. Fleming, *Operation Sea Lion*, pp. 252–53; Longmate, *If Britain Had Fallen*, chap. 13.
398
13. Wheatley, *Operation Sea Lion*, pp. 122–24; Longmate, *If Britain Had Fallen*, chaps. 9 and 15.
14. Alan and Mary Wood, *Islands in Danger: The Story of the German Occupation of the Channel Islands, 1940–1945* (London, 1955).
15. *VBIF* (1940), p. 72.
399
16. Wood, *Islands in Danger*, pp. 64–72. C. W. Duret Aubin, "Enemy Legislation and Judgments in Jersey," *Journal of Comparative Legislation and International Law* 31 (1949), pts. 3 and 4, pp. 8–11, states that substantive law applied in the administration of criminal and civil justice during the German occupation was the same as before the occupation and that judgments were rendered by the courts in the name of the king!
17. *Fuehrer Conferences*, 1941, 2:27, 64; Warlimont-Ritter conference, October 24, 1941, PS 725; *Hitler's Secret Conversations*, p. 546; Wood, *Islands in Danger*, pp. 118–21.
18. Wood, *Islands in Danger*, p. 136; PS 725.

400

19. *Hitler's Secret Conversations,* pp. 545–46; Picker, *Hitlers Tischgespräche,* p. 466.
20. *DGFP,* D, 7:246–47.
21. See the first volume of this study, pp. 205–6.
22. *DGFP,* D, 13:477–78, 527, 719–22.

401

23. *DGFP,* D, 13:478, n. 3, 849–56; *ADAP,* E, 2:191; Picker, *Hitlers Tischgespräche,* p. 250; *Hitler's Secret Conversations,* pp. 380, 505.
24. *ADAP,* E, 2:446, n. 4.
25. Picker, *Hitlers Tischgespräche,* p. 250; *Hitler's Secret Conversations,* pp. 380–81.
26. Picker, *Hitlers Tischgespräche,* p. 144; Hitler-OKW conference, February 3, 1941, *IMT,* 872-PS, 26:394; Hewel memorandum on Hitler's conversation with the Swedish explorer Sven Hedin, December 5, 1940, *DGFP,* D, 11:783–87. See also *Sven Hedin's German Diary, 1939–1942* (Dublin, 1951), pp. 181–82.
27. In August 1942 Hitler is reported to have said, "As for the Swedish vermin, they must be swept away like the Danish vermin in 1848!" (*Hitler's Secret Conversations,* p. 614), a remark which surely referred to anti-German Swedes, not to the Swedish people as a whole. According to Himmler's doctor-masseur Felix Kersten, Himmler expressed regret that Germany had not occupied Sweden at the same time as Norway, but he obviously believed Germany would rectify this error after the war; in August 1942 he told Kersten he foresaw a great future for Sweden in the Greater German Reich (*The Kersten Memoirs, 1940–1945* [London, 1956], pp. 142–43, 146).

402

28. Picker, *Hitlers Tischgespräche,* pp. 144, 162, 441; *Hitler's Secret Conversations,* pp. 53, 525, 571, 614; *DGFP,* D, 12:951.
29. Berger to Himmler, September 8, 1941, T175/123/2648463; Swiss government report of December 28, 1945, on antidemocratic activities, 1939–45, NG 4137.
30. Picker, *Hitlers Tischgespräche,* pp. 144, 227–29, 250; *Hitler's Secret Conversations,* pp. 54, 293, 336, 361–62, 439–40, 451. For a detailed account of German-Turkish relations, see Lothar Krecker, *Deutschland und die Türkei im zweiten Weltkrieg* (Frankfurt am Main, 1964); see also below, pp. 412–14.

404

31. Picker, *Hitlers Tischgespräche,* pp. 338, 393–94, 439, 447–49; *Hitler's Secret Conversations,* pp. 188–89, 484, 488, 524, 530–33, 566–67, 618, 641–44. On the role of Muñoz-Grande in Spain, see Stanley G. Payne, *Falange: A History of Spanish Fascism* (paperback, Stanford, Calif., 1961), pp. 206, 209, 218, 225.
32. *Mein Kampf,* pp. 179, 181, 892, 949–50, 964; point three of the Nazi party's twenty-one demands, Gottfried Feder, *Das Programm der NSDAP* (Munich, 1927).
33. Klaus Hildebrand, *Vom Reich zum Weltreich. Hitler, NSDAP und koloniale Frage, 1919–1945* (Munich, 1969), provides an interesting analysis of the phases of Hitler's colonial policy, pp. 742–43; also pp. 770, 868–69, 894–902; Gerhard L. Weinberg, "German Colonial Plans and Policies, 1938–1942," *Geschichte und Gegenwartsbewusstsein. Festschrift für Hans Rothfels zum 70. Geburtstag,* ed. Waldemar Besson and Friedrich Freiherr Hiller von Gaertringen (Göttingen, 1963), pp. 462–63; Wolfe W. Schmokel, *Dream of Empire: German Colonialism, 1919–1945* (New Haven, Conn., 1964), pp. 89, 97–98, 120–22; Günther Moltmann, "Weltherrschaftsideen Hitlers." *Europa und Übersee. Festschrift für Egmont Zechlin,* ed. Otto Brunner and Dietrich Gerhard (Hamburg, 1961), pp. 214–15.

405

34. Lord Halifax, *Fulness of Days* (London, 1957), p. 190; *DGFP,* D, 1:54–71, 240–49; Schmokel, *Dream of Empire,* pp. 114–15.
35. Hossbach memorandum, *IMT,* 386-PS, 25:402–13; Schmokel, *Dream of Empire,* p. 106.
36. Memorandum of December 8, 1938, on the status of work on colonial questions on the part of the Wehrmacht and in the Reich, T77/642/1838567–69.
37. Reichstag speech of October 6, 1939, *Schulthess' Europäischer Geschichtskalender,* 1939, pp. 202–15: Hildebrand, *Vom Reich zum Weltreich,* pp. 632–39; Schmokel, *Dream of Empire,* pp. 127–29; Weinberg, "German Colonial Plans," p. 466.
38. Conference of March 18, 1940, *DGFP,* D, 9:8.

406

39. Foreign Office memoranda of May 30 and June 1, 1940, *DGFP,* D, 9:476–82, 496–501; report of the Reich Ministry of Economics to the Reichsgruppe Industrie, June 20, 1940, NIK 12050; Hitler order for the preparation of plans for a campaign in Afghanistan against India, *Kriegstagebuch des Oberkommandos der Wehrmacht (Wehrmachtführungsstab), 1940–1945,* ed. Percy Ernst Schramm, Andreas Hillgruber, Walter Hubatsch, and Hans-Adolf Jacobsen, 4 vols. in 7 (Frankfurt am Main, 1961–65), 1:328. See also Andreas Hillgruber, *Hitlers Strategie. Politik und Kriegsführung, 1940–1941* (Frankfurt am Main, 1965), pp. 242–55; Schmokel, *Dream of Empire,* pp. 140–42; Hildebrand, *Vom Reich zum Weltreich,* pp. 641, 703.
40. Admiral Fricke memorandum of June 3, 1940, *IMT,* 41-C, 34:240–42; *Fuehrer Conferences,* 1940, 1:65–66; proposals of the German navy for the acquisition of bases for the defense of a German colonial empire, July 27, 1940, C-40.

407

41. Bielfeld's memorandum of November 6, 1940, was placed by Ribbentrop in a special portfolio of documents to be submitted to the Führer, *DGFP,* D, 13:483–89. Early in 1940 Ribbentrop approved a communication to South African leaders who were thought to

be sympathetic to the Nazi cause, informing them that Germany intended to reclaim its former colony of German Southwest Africa, at this time under the mandate of the Union of South Africa. To compensate South Africa for the loss of its mandate territory, Germany would secure for South Africa the British protectorates of Swaziland, Basutoland, and Bechuanaland, and it would acquiesce in South Africa's annexation of Southern Rhodesia. Germany's only goal in Africa was to ensure its supply of tropical and subtropical raw materials; it was not contemplating the creation of a separate state on African soil and it recognized the Union of South Africa as the leading white state in the South African *Lebensraum. DGFP,* D, 8:711, 804–5; 9:45–48; 11:271–73.

42. Halder, *Kriegstagebuch,* 2:21, 74 (entries for July 13 and August 23, 1940).

43. Picker, *Hitlers Tischgespräche,* pp. 143–44; *Hitler's Secret Conversations,* pp. 35, 52, 93, 96; Halder, *Kriegstagebuch,* 3:29.

44. Picker, *Hitlers Tischgespräche,* pp. 136, 145, 479; *Hitler's Secret Conversations,* pp. 42, 54, 75, 114; Jodl memorandum on the continuation of the war against England, June 30, 1940, *IMT,* 1776-PS, 28:301–3; Halder, *Kriegstagebuch,* 2:21, 186; *The Ciano Diaries, 1939–1943,* ed. Hugh Gibson (New York, 1946), pp. 265–67; *Ciano's Diplomatic Papers,* ed. Malcolm Muggeridge (London, 1948), pp. 372–79; Hillgruber, *Hitlers Strategie,* pp. 145–46, 151, 208.

45. *Ciano's Diplomatic Papers,* pp. 372–79; *DGFP,* D, 9:608–11; 11:20–21, 245–59, 289–91; Hildebrand, *Vom Reich zum Weltreich,* pp. 649–50.

408   46. *DGFP,* D, 9:620–21; 10:15–16; 11:371–76, 380; Halder, *Kriegstagebuch,* 2:100, 136. See also the first volume of this study, pp. 171–76.

47. *DGFP,* D, 11:348–51, 354–61, 385–92.

48. Halder, *Kriegstagebuch,* 2:124; *DGFP,* D, 11:20–21.

49. *DGFP,* D, 11:508–10, 533–49, 562–70, 594–95.

409   50. See the first volume of the study, pp. 208–10.

51. Theo Sommer, *Deutschland und Japan zwischen den Mächten, 1935–1940* (Tübingen, 1962), pp. 324 ff. See also the first volume of this study, pp. 227–35.

52. *DGFP,* D, 11:204–5, 208.

410   53. Hildebrand, *Vom Reich zum Weltreich,* pp. 868, 873–75, 880–81; Weinberg, "German Colonial Plans," pp. 464–65.

54. Report of February 24, 1939, T77/642/1838557–58; Lammers to Epp, March 9, 1939, T77/642/1838579–80; Geldern report of June 6, 1939, T77/642/1835551–54. According to this report, Epp informed Geldern that after the clarification of the Danzig question, the Führer had no further demands to make on the European continent, so that the colonial question would then become acute. See also Weinberg, "German Colonial Plans," pp. 466–67; Hildebrand, *Vom Reich zum Weltreich,* pp. 904–5, 934; and Schmokel, *Dream of Empire,* chap. 4.

411   55. Lammers to top Reich offices, June 15, 1940, T77/642/1838547; OKW information bulletin on colonies, July 8, 1940, T77/643/1838852–53; Hitler order for a future Ministry of Colonies, July 13, 1940, T77/642/1838238–39; Geldern memorandum of August 1, 1940, T77/642/1838524–30; Reichsgruppe Industrie conference, September 9, 1940, NI 3491; OKW information bulletin on colonies, September 6, 1940, T77/643/1838840.

412   56. Draft plan of June 11, 1941, *DGFP,* D, 12:1012–16; memorandum of July 2, 1941, on possibilities of operations through the Near East, T78/346/6303870–73; OKW memorandum of August 27, 1941, *DGFP,* D, 13:423–33; Hillgruber, *Hitlers Strategie,* pp. 377–88; Hildebrand, *Vom Reich zum Weltreich,* p. 703.

57. Hildebrand, *Vom Reich zum Weltreich,* pp. 638–40, 934, 940–42; Schmokel, *Dream of Empire,* pp. 149–54.

413   58. See Lukasz Hirszowicz, *The Third Reich and the Arab East* (Toronto, 1966), an excellent monograph.

59. *DGFP,* D, 10:261–62, 515–16; also 11:238–39, 241–43; 13:188–89, 885.

60. *DGFP,* D, 12:1051.

414   61. *DGFP,* D, 13:368–70; *ADAP,* E, 1:99–100; 2:59–61, 203–4.
415   62. *ADAP,* E, 1:23–26, 97–98, 133–34, 257, 260–62; Johanna Menzel Meskill, *Hitler and Japan: The Hollow Alliance* (New York, 1967), pp. 103–5, 109–113. See the interesting affidavit of Friedrich Gaus, director of the Legal Department of the Foreign Office, January 25, 1948, NG 4556; also the first volume of this study, p. 235.

63. *Hitler's Secret Conversations,* pp. 165, 190, 195–96.

64. *Hitler's Secret Conversations,* pp. 293, 460; Picker, *Hitlers Tischgespräche,* pp. 352, 431; *The Goebbels Diaries, 1942–1943,* ed. Louis P. Lochner (New York, 1948), pp. 137–38.

416   65. According to Hermann Rauschning, Hitler spoke at some length early in 1933 about plans to create a "new Germany" in Brazil and of German possibilities in the Western Hemisphere in general (*The Voice of Destruction* [New York, 1940], pp. 61–72). As I have found no corroborating evidence on this question, I did not feel justified in using Rauschning's records. For a different opinion, see Alton Frye, *Nazi Germany and the American Hemisphere, 1933–1941* (New Haven, Conn., 1967), chap. 11. But see also Louis de Jong, *Die deutsche fünfte Kolonne im zweiten Weltkrieg* (Stuttgart, 1959), who con-

cludes that there is not a single piece of evidence that Hitler ever had any concrete plans for a military attack on South America (p. 209); and Moltmann, "Weltherrschaftsideen Hitlers," p. 221.

66. *Fuehrer Conferences,* 1940, 2:19–20, 25.

67. *IMT,* 376-PS, 25:393; *Kriegstagebuch des OKW,* 1:135; Göring testimony, *IMT,* 9:347; Jodl testimony, *IMT,* 15:397.

417   68. *Fuehrer Conferences,* 1940, 2:40–41, 53–57.

69. Conference of May 22, 1941, Ibid., 1941, 1:65.

70. Conference of July 25, 1941, Ibid., 1941, 2:13–15.

418   71. Berger to Himmler, August 7, 1940, NO 1825; Himmler memorandum, April 23, 1942, NO 5629.

419   72. Picker, *Hitlers Tischgespräche,* p. 145; *Hitler's Secret Conversations,* pp. 43, 54, 113–14, 635–36.

Bibliography

Materials already listed in the bibliography to Volume One have not been included here unless specifically cited in this volume. A Note on the Sources, including a brief description of the unpublished materials used, will be found in Volume One, pages 313–14.

1. GUIDES AND GENERAL WORKS

American Historical Association, Committee for the Study of War Documents, and National Archives and Records Service. *Guides to German Documents Microfilmed at Alexandria, Virginia.* Washington, D.C., 1958–. Over fifty volumes of catalogue guides have appeared so far. Indispensable aids for the study of the Nazi era. The films are deposited in the National Archives, Washington, D.C.

Bengston, John R. *Nazi War Aims: The Plans for the Thousand Year Reich.* Rock Island, Ill., 1962. An interesting but somewhat simplistic survey.

Best, Werner. *Die deutschen Aufsichtsverwaltungen in Frankreich, Belgien, den Niederlanden, Norwegen, Dänemark, und im Protektorat Böhmen und Mähren. Vergleichende Übersicht.* Unpublished manuscript by a Nazi legal and administrative expert who, in October 1942, became Reich plenipotentiary in Denmark. The manuscript is available on film. T501/101/1292ff.

Bräutigam, Otto, *Überblick über die besetzten Ostgebiete während des 2. Welt-*

503

krieges. Tübingen, 1954. An interesting and useful work by a member of Rosenberg's Reich Ministry for the Occupied Eastern Territories.

Brandt, Karl; Schiller, Otto; and Ahlgrimm, Franz. *Management of Agriculture and Food in the German-Occupied and Other Areas of Fortress Europe: A Study in Military Government.* Stanford, Calif., 1953. An important work.

Buchheim, Hans. "Die Höheren SS-und Polizeiführer." *VfZ* 11 (1963):362–91.

Deutsch, Harold C. *The Conspiracy against Hitler in the Twilight War.* Minneapolis, 1968.

Fest, Joachim C. *The Face of the Third Reich: Portraits of the Nazi Leadership.* New York, 1970. Interesting vignettes.

Georg, Enno. *Die wirtschaftlichen Unternehmungen der SS.* Stuttgart, 1963.

Gerber, Berthold. *Staatliche Wirtschaftslenkung in den besetzten und annektierten Ostgebieten während des zweiten Weltkrieges unter besonderer Berücksichtigung der treuhänderishen Verwaltung von Unternehmungen und der Ostgesellschaften.* Tübingen, 1959.

Grassmann, Gerhard Otto. *Die deutsche Besatzungsgesetzgebung während des zweiten Weltkrieges.* Tübingen, 1958.

Gruchmann, Lothar. *Nationalsozialistische Grossraumordnung. Die Konstruktion einer "deutschen Monroe-Doktrin."* Stuttgart, 1962. Valuable and suggestive.

Herdeg, Walter. *Grundzüge der deutschen Besatzungsverwaltung in den west-und nordeuropäischen Ländern während des zweiten Weltkrieges.* Tübingen, 1954.

Herzog, Robert. *Grundzüge der deutschen Besatzungsverwaltung in den ost-und südosteuropäischen Ländern während des zweiten Weltkrieges.* Tübingen, 1955.

Hillgruber, Andreas. *Hitlers Strategie. Politik und Kriegsführung, 1940–1941.* Frankfurt am Main, 1965. A masterful work analyzing Hitler's policy during the most critical period of the war, with full consideration of the difficulties and subtleties of the situation.

Jacobsen, Hans-Adolf. *Nationalsozialistische Aussenpolitik, 1933–1938.* Frankfurt am Main, 1968. Primarily a study of the machinery of government and the decision-making process, with important sections on ideology and efforts to spread Nazism to other parts of the world.

Jong, Louis de. *Die deutsche fünfte Kolonne im zweiten Weltkrieg.* Stuttgart, 1959.

Kamenetsky, Ihor. *Secret Nazi Plans for Eastern Europe: A Study of Lebensraum Policies.* New York, 1961.

Kent, George O. *A Catalog of Files and Microfilms of the German Foreign Ministry Archives, 1920–1945.* Stanford, Calif., 1962–72. Indispensable for the use of the microfilms of the German Foreign Office documents.

Koehl, Robert L. *RKFDV: German Resettlement and Population Policy, 1939–1945: A History of the Reich Commission for the Strengthening of Germandom.* Cambridge, Mass., 1957. Full of important information, but leaves much to be done on this enormous and complicated subject.

Krausnick, Helmut; Buchheim, Hans; Broszat, Martin; and Jacobsen, Hans-Adolf. *Anatomy of the SS State.* New York, 1968. A collection of excellent essays, on which I have drawn heavily.

Kulischer, Eugene M. *Europe on the Move: War and Population Changes, 1917–1947.* New York, 1948.

Labs, Walter. "Die Verwaltung der besetzten Ostgebiete." *RVL* 5 (1943):92–166. An official Nazi analysis.

Littlejohn, David. *The Patriotic Traitors: A History of Collaboration in German Occupied Europe, 1940–1945.* London, 1972. Unfortunately I was not able to get a copy of this book in time for use in my own study. The subject is fascinating.

Loock, Hans-Dietrich. "Zur 'Grossgermanischen Politik' des Dritten Reiches." *VfZ* 8 (1960):37–63.

Moltmann, Günther. "Weltherrschaftsideen Hitlers." *Europa und Übersee. Festschrift für Egmont Zechlin,* pp. 197–240, edited by Otto Brunner and Dietrich Gerhard. Hamburg, 1961. An intelligent analysis.

Moret, Claude. *L'Allemagne et la réorganisation de l'Europe, 1940–1943.* Neuchâtel, 1944.

Moritz, Günther, *Gerichtsbarkeit in den von Deutschland besetzten Gebieten, 1939–1945.* Tübingen, 1955.

Mourin, Maxime. *Le drame des états satellites de l'axe, de 1939 à 1945.* Paris, 1957.

Office of Strategic Services, Research and Analysis Branch. *German Military Government over Europe*. Washington, D.C., 1943–45. Under this general title the OSS published a series of Army Service Forces Manuals during the final years of the war on many aspects of German government, instruments of control, and German occupation administrations, including special volumes on the army, the SS and police, military and police tribunals, the Nazi party, technical and economic troops, labor controls, and others. An invaluable series pulling together a remarkable amount of information.

Proudfoot, Malcolm J. *European Refugees, 1939–1952: A Study in Forced Population Movement*. Evanston, Ill., 1956.

Reitlinger, Gerald. *The SS: Alibi of a Nation, 1922–1945*. London, 1956. A readable and authoritative study.

Ritter, Gerhard. *Carl Goerdeler und die deutsche Widerstandsbewegung*. Stuttgart, 1954.

Rothfels, Hans. *The German Opposition to Hitler*. Chicago, 1964.

Schechtman, J. B. *European Population Transfers, 1939–1945*. New York, 1946.

Schürmann, A. "Festigung deutschen Volkstums in den eingegliederten Ostgebieten." *RVL* 6 (1943):475–538. An official Nazi account.

Schumann, W., and Lozek, G. "Die faschistische Okkupationspolitik im Spiegel der Historiographie der beiden deutschen Staaten." *Zeitschrift für Geschichtswissenschaft* (1964):213–30.

Seraphim, Hans-Günther. *Zum Problem der "Häftlingseuthanasie" in den nationalsozialistischen Konzentrationslagern*. Unpublished manuscript, made available to me through the kindness of the author.

Stein, George H. *The Waffen SS: Hitler's Elite Guard at War, 1939–45*. Ithaca, N.Y., 1966.

Thorne, Christopher. *The Approach of War, 1938–1939*. London, 1968. Excellent brief synthesis.

Toynbee, Arnold, and Toynbee, Veronica, eds. *Hitler's Europe*. London, 1954. A volume in the Survey of International Affairs series. The first major attempt to analyze the government of Germany and the German occupation administrations, with contributions from numerous authors. Still of great value.

Wambaugh, Sarah. *Plebiscites since the World War*. 2 vols. Washington, D.C., 1933.

Wright, Gordon. *The Ordeal of Total War, 1939–1945*. New York, 1968. An excellent comprehensive survey, with a splendid bibliography.

2. PUBLISHED DOCUMENTS, GENERAL

Akten zur deutschen auswärtigen Politik, 1918–1945. Baden Baden and Göttingen. The German text of *Documents on German Foreign Policy* (see below). Series E, covering the years 1941–45, has so far been published only in German. Indispensable for the study of German foreign policy, although the peripheral character of the German Foreign Office during the Nazi era must be borne in mind.

Ciano's Diplomatic Papers. Edited by Malcolm Muggeridge. London, 1948. Important documents from the files of the Italian foreign minister.

Documenta Occupationis Teutonicae. 7 vols. Poznań, 1945–59. A very important source.

Documents on German Foreign Policy, 1918–1945. Washington, D.C., 1949–. Series C covers the years 1933–36; Series D, 1936–41. For Series E, see *Akten zur deutschen auswärtigen Politik*.

Documents on International Affairs, 1939–1946. Vol. 2, *Hitler's Europe*. Edited by Margaret Carlyle. Prepared under the auspices of the Royal Institute of International Affairs. London, 1954. A selection of important documents.

Dokumente der deutschen Politik. Berlin, 1937–44. Only nine volumes covering the year 1933–41 were published. A valuable collection of documents with commentaries reflecting the official Nazi point of view.

Feder, Gottfried. *Hitler's Official Programme and Its Fundamental Ideas*. London, 1934.

Fuehrer Conferences on Matters Dealing with the German Navy, 1939–1945. 8 vols. Washington, D.C., 1946–47. Enormously valuable source.

Fuehrer Directives and Other Top-Level Directives of the German Armed Forces. Vol. 1, *1939–1941*. Washington, D.C., 1948. Another valuable source, although much of this material has also been published in other collections. So far as I can ascertain, only one volume of this collection was ever published.

Hitler, Adolf. *Hitler's Secret Conversations, 1941–1944*. New York, 1953; paperback, New York, 1961. Martin Bormann's notes of Hitler's table talk. Available only in English and French translations. Of fundamental importance.

——. *Hitlers Tischgespräche im Führerhauptquartier, 1941–1942*. Edited by Percy Ernst Schramm, Andreas Hillgruber, and Martin Vogt. Stuttgart, 1965. The notes of Dr. Henry Picker, an official assigned to Hitler's headquarters. Comparable to the notes of Bormann, who probably drew on them for his own records.

——. *Hitler's War Directives, 1939–1945*. Edited by H. R. Trevor-Roper. London, 1964; paperback, 1966.

——. *Hitler's Words*. Edited by Gordon W. Prange. Washington, D.C., 1944. A collection of speeches and public statements.

——. *Hitlers zweites Buch. Ein Dokument aus dem Jahre 1928*. Edited by G. L. Weinberg. Stuttgart, 1961. English translation, *Hitler's Secret Book*. Paperback, New York, 1961. A valuable supplement to *Mein Kampf*, not published in the Nazi era.

——. *Mein Kampf*. 2 vols. Munich, 1925–27; English translation, New York, 1939. A memoir which is at the same time an invaluable document of Hitler's ideas and program.

——. *My New Order*. Edited by Raoul de Roussy de Sales. New York, 1941. A collection of Hitler's speeches and writings.

——. *The Speeches of Adolf Hitler, April 1922–August 1939*. Edited by Norman H. Baynes. 2 vols. Oxford, 1942.

——. *The Testament of Adolf Hitler: The Hitler-Bormann Documents, February–April 1945*. Edited by F. Genoud. London, 1961.

International Military Tribunal. *Trial of the Major War Criminals before the International Military Tribunal: Proceedings and Documents*. 42 vols. Nuremberg, 1947–49. Enormously important records of the trials. Unfortunately only a small number of the documents assembled at Nuremberg is published in this collection. Microfilms and mimeographed copies of the unpublished documents are available in major libraries in the United States and Europe.

Kriegstagebuch des Oberkommandos der Wehrmacht (*Wehrmachtführungsstab*), *1940–1945*. Edited by P. E. Schramm, A. Hillgruber, W. Hubatsch, and H.-A. Jacobsen. 4 vols. in 7. Frankfurt am Main, 1961–65. An important source for military decisions.

Lemkin, Raphaël. *Axis Rule in Occupied Europe: Laws of Occupation, Analysis of Government, Proposals for Redress*. Washington, D.C., 1944. A valuable document collection.

Nazi Conspiracy and Aggression. 8 vols. and 2 suppls. Washington, D.C., 1946–48. A selection in English translation of documents and affidavits presented in evidence at the Nuremberg trials, including some not published in the *IMT* collection.

Probleme des Ostraumes. Berlin, 1942. A collection of essays by Alfred Rosenberg, Georg Leibbrandt, and other leading German administrators in Eastern Europe. Interesting as public statements of official policy.

Reichsgesetzblatt. Published annually in two volumes in Berlin. Contains laws and treaties pertaining not only to Germany, but also to all the occupied countries.

Trials of the War Criminals before the Nuernberg Military Tribunals under Control Council Law N-10. 15 vols. Nuremberg, 1946–49. Includes trial records and documents in evidence of Nazi doctors, industrialists, diplomats. Unfortunately only excerpts of many important testimonies and documents are printed.

3. DIARIES, LETTERS, AND MEMOIRS

Principally German. For materials in this category by non-Germans,
see under individual countries or areas.

Abetz, Otto. *Das offene Problem. Ein Rückblick auf zwei Jahrzehnte deutscher Frankreichpolitik*. Cologne, 1951. By the German ambassador to France during the occupation.

Frank, Hans. *Im Angesicht des Galgens. Deutung Hitlers und seiner Zeit auf Grund eigener Erlebnisse und Erkenntnisse.* Munich, 1953. Unreliable, but revealing memoirs by a Nazi legal expert and the governor general of occupied Poland.

Frauenfeld, Alfred. *Ursache und Sinn unseres Kampfes. Bolschewismus-Kapitalismus. Das apokalyptische Tier mit zwei Köpfen.* Vienna, 1944. Pamphlet by the Nazi Generalkommissar for the Crimea.

Gilbert, G. M. *Nuremberg Diary.* New York, 1947. Interesting records of conversations with the Nazi defendants, recorded by the prison psychologist.

Gisevius, Hans. *To the Bitter End.* Boston, 1947. The memoirs of a former member of the Gestapo who joined the anti-Nazi resistance. Often the sole source on governmental infighting, so that it is difficult to check the author's reliability.

Goebbels, Joseph. *The Goebbels Diaries, 1942–1943.* Edited by Louis P. Lochner. New York, 1948. Valuable source.

Greifelt, Ulrich. "Die Aufgabe der Festigung deutschen Volkstums in den neuen deutschen Ostgebieten." *Siedlung und Wirtschaft.* Berlin, February 1941. By the head of the Central Office of the RKFDV.

———. "Einsatz im Osten. Wirtschaftliche Festigung des deutschen Volkstums." *Die deutsche Volkswirtschaft* 28 (1941):1110–12.

———. "Festigung deutschen Volkstums in den Ostgebieten." *Deutsche Verwaltung* 17 (1940):17–18.

———. "Das Reichskommissariat für die Festigung des deutschen Volkstums." *Deutsche Verwaltung.* Berlin, January 2, 1940.

Greiner, Helmuth. *Die oberste Wehrmachtführung, 1939–1943.* Wiesbaden, 1951. Based on Greiner's war diary of the German high command.

Greiser, Arthur. *Der Aufbau im Osten.* Jena, 1942. By the head of the German occupation government in the Wartheland (Poznań).

Halder, Franz. *Kriegstagebuch. Tägliche Aufzeichnungen des Chefs des Generalstabes des Heeres, 1939–1942.* Edited by Hans-Adolf Jacobsen. 3 vols. Stuttgart, 1962–64. Invaluable source.

Hassell, Ulrich von. *Vom andern Deutschland. Aus den nachgelassenen Tagebüchern, 1938–1944.* Zürich, 1946. By the former German ambassador to Italy and a leader of the anti-Nazi resistance. Full of interesting observations and insights.

Himmler, Heinrich. "Denkschrift Himmlers über die Behandlung der Fremdvölkischen im Osten (Mai 1940)." Edited by Helmut Krausnick. *VfZ* 2 (1957):194–98.

———. *Reichsführer! Briefe an und von Himmler.* Edited by Helmut Heiber. Stuttgart, 1968.

Hoess, Rudolf. *Kommandant in Auschwitz. Autobiographische Aufzeichnungen.* Edited by Martin Broszat. Stuttgart, 1958. Memoirs of the master exterminator.

Kersten, Felix. *The Kersten Memoirs, 1940–1945.* London, 1956. A remarkable record of observations by and about Himmler and his entourage by Himmler's Swedish doctor-masseur.

Kesselring, Albert. *The Memoirs of Field-Marshal Kesselring.* London, 1953.

Kleist, Peter. *Zwischen Hitler und Stalin, 1939–1945. Aufzeichnungen.* Bonn, 1950. By a member of the Dienststelle Ribbentrop, assigned in July 1941 to Rosenberg's Reich Ministry for the Occupied Eastern Territories. Interesting comments.

Manstein, Erich von. *Lost Victories.* Chicago, 1958. Especially valuable for German campaigns in the east.

Neubacher, Hermann. *Sonderauftrag Südost, 1940–1945. Bericht eines fliegenden Diplomaten.* Göttingen, 1956. Valuable memoirs of the chief German diplomatic representative in the Balkans.

Rahn, Rudolf. *Ruheloses Leben. Aufzeichnungen und Erinnerungen eines deutschen Diplomaten.* Düsseldorf, 1949. Fascinating memoirs of Germany's trouble shooter in the Near East and North Africa, and ambassador to Italy after the official Italian surrender.

Rauschning, Hermann. *The Voice of Destruction.* New York, 1940. The records of conversations with Hitler between 1932 and 1934 by the former president of the Danzig Senate. Should be used with caution.

Rintelen, Enno von. *Mussolini als Bundesgenosse. Erinnerungen des deutschen Militärattaches in Rom, 1936–1943.* Tübingen, 1951.

Rommel, Erwin. *The Rommel Papers.* Edited by B. H. Liddell Hart, assisted by L. M. Rommel and F. Bayerlein. New York, 1953. Of great interest.

507

Rosenberg, Alfred. *Das politische Tagebuch Alfred Rosenbergs aus den Jahren 1934/35 und 1939/40.* Edited by Hans-Günther Seraphim. Göttingen, 1956. Gossipy, with only occasional bits of historical interest. Breaks off before Rosenberg's appointment as Reich minister for the occupied eastern territories.
———. *Der Zukunftsweg einer deutschen Aussenpolitik.* Munich, 1927. Revealing pamphlet.
Schmidt, Paul. *Statist auf diplomatischer Bühne, 1923–45. Erlebnisse des Chefdolmetschers im Auswärtigen Amt mit den Staatsmännern Europas.* Bonn, 1949. Valuable comments on some of Hitler's major conversations with foreign statesmen.
Skorzeny, Otto. *Skorzeny's Secret Missions: War Memoirs of the Most Dangerous Man in Europe.* New York, 1950. By the man who, among other things, "rescued" Mussolini in September 1943.
Speer, Albert. *Inside the Third Reich.* New York, 1970. The memoirs of Hitler's architect and minister of armaments and munitions. Fascinating descriptions of the personality and working methods of Hitler, and of his entire entourage.
Thomas, Georg. *Geschichte der deutschen Wehr-und Rüstungswirtschaft (1918–1943/45).* Edited by Wolfgang Birkenfeld. Boppard am Rhein, 1966. Important source.
Warlimont, Walter. *Inside Hitler's Headquarters, 1939–45.* New York, 1964. A valuable source, although like most military memoirs it attempts to blame Hitler for military mistakes and exonerate the army with respect to military atrocities.

4. THE JEWS

Arendt, Hannah. *Eichmann in Jerusalem: A Report on the Banality of Evil.* New York, 1963. Suggestive and controversial.
Ball-Kaduri, Kurt Jakob. *Das Leben der Juden in Deutschland im Jahre 1933; ein Zeitbericht.* Frankfurt am Main, 1963.
Blau, Bruno. *Das Ausnahmerecht für die Juden in Deutschland, 1933–1945.* Düsseldorf, 1954.
Genschel, Helmut. *Die Verdrängung der Juden aus der Wirtschaft im dritten Reich.* Göttingen, 1966. With an excellent bibliography.
Graml, H. "Die Auswanderung der Juden aus Deutschland zwischen 1933 und 1939." *Gutachten des Instituts für Zeitgeschichte.* Munich, 1958, pp. 79–85.
Hilberg, Raul. *The Destruction of the European Jews.* Chicago, 1961. A detailed and authoritative work, which also deals extensively with Nazi occupation administrations and policies.
Kochan, Lionel. *Pogrom: 10. November 1938.* London, 1957.
Manvell, Roger, and Fraenkel, Heinrich. *The Incomparable Crime. Mass Extermination in the Twentieth Century: The Legacy of Guilt.* New York, 1967.
Mommsen, Hans. "Der nationalsozialistische Polizeistaat und die Judenverfolgung vor 1938." *VfZ* 10 (1962):68–87.
Poliakov, Léon. "Note sur le chiffre total des victimes Juives des persécutions raciales pendant la deuxième guerre." *RHDGM* 24 (1956):88–92.
———. and Wulf, Josef. *Das Dritte Reich und die Juden. Dokumente und Aufsätze.* Berlin, 1955.
Pulzer, Peter G. J. *The Rise of Political Anti-Semitism in Germany and Austria.* New York, 1964.
Reichmann, E. G. *Die Flucht in den Hass. Die Ursachen der deutschen Judenkatastrophe.* Frankfurt am Main, 1956.
Reitlinger, Gerald. *The Final Solution: The Attempt to Exterminate the Jews of Europe, 1939–1945.* New York, 1968. Authoritative and readable.
Scheffler, Wolfgang. *Judenverfolgung im Dritten Reich, 1933–1945.* Berlin, 1960.
Seraphim, Peter Heinz. *Bevölkerungs-und wirtschaftspolitische Probleme einer europäischen Gesamtlösung der Judenfrage.* Munich, 1943.
———. *Das Judentum. Seine Rolle in der Vergangenheit und Gegenwart.* Munich, 1942. Two Nazi tracts on the subject.

BIBLIOGRAPHY

5. AUSTRIA, MEMEL, DANZIG

For the Sudentenland, see under Czechoslovakia; for Danzig, see also under Poland.

Brook-Shepherd, Gordon. *Anschluss: The Rape of Austria.* London, 1963. An able account by a British journalist.

Bundesgesetzblatt für den Bundesstaat Österreich. The laws of the state of Austria, published annually in Vienna. Title before May 1934, *Bundesgesetzblatt für die Republik Österreich;* after the Anschluss, *Gesetzblatt für das Land Österreich.* Final publication, March 31, 1940.

Fried, Jakob. *Nationalsozialismus und katholische Kirche in Österreich.* Vienna, 1947.

Gehl, Jürgen. *Austria, Germany, and the Anschluss, 1931–1938.* London, 1963. A solid study taking the story to the day of the Anschluss.

Gesetzblatt für die freie Stadt Danzig. Published annually to 1939. For the publication of laws after the German occupation, see Bibliography, 7. Poland.

Grayson, Cary Travers. *Austria's International Position, 1939–1953: The Re-establishment of an Independent Austria.* Geneva, 1953.

Latour, Conrad F. *Südtirol und die Achse Berlin-Rom, 1938–1945.* Stuttgart, 1962. A valuable monograph.

Loebsack, Wilhelm. *Danzigs Gauleiter Albert Forster.* Hamburg, 1934. A eulogy written long before Forster became head of the government of Danzig-Westpreussen.

Moser, Jonny. *Die Judenverfolgung in Österreich, 1938–1945.* Vienna, 1966. Brief, but informative.

Pfeifer, Helfried. *Die Ostmark. Eingliederung und Neugestaltung.* Vienna, 1941. A Nazi tract.

Romanik, Felix. *Österreichs wirtschaftliche Ausbeutung, 1939–1945.* Vienna, 1966.

Rot-Weiss-Rot-Buch. Darstellungen, Dokumente und Nachweise zur Vorgeschichte und Geschichte der Okkupation Österreichs. Vienna, 1946. An Austrian government publication.

Rusinow, Dennison I. *Italy's Austrian Heritage, 1919–46.* Oxford, 1969. An important monograph, full of important information.

Stadler, Karl. *Österreich 1938–1945 im Spiegel der NS-Akten.* Vienna, 1966. Unsystematic and, on the whole, rather trivial.

Steinmetz, Selma. *Österreichs Zigeuner im NS-Staat.* Vienna, 1966. On these generally neglected victims of Nazi persecution.

Sündermann, Helmut. *Die Grenzen fallen. Von der Ostmark zum Sudetenland.* Munich, 1939. A rapturous Nazi chronicle.

Szecsi, Maria, and Stadler, Karl. *Die NS-Justiz in Österreich und ihre Opfer.* Vienna, 1962. An examination of the operation of Nazi law in Austria, with main emphasis on resistance groups.

Verordnungsblatt für den Reichsgau Kärnten. A collection of regional legislation. Of enormous value for studying Nazi administration.

Verordnungsblatt-und Amtsblatt für den Reichsgau Niederdonau. (March 1940–45). Replaces *Verordnungsblatt für den Reichsgau Niederdonau* (September 1939–March 1940); *Verordnungsblatt für den Amtsbereich des Landeshauptmannes von Niederdonau* (1938–September 1939); *Verordnungsblatt für den Amtsbereich des Landeshauptmannes des Burgenlandes* (August–October, 1938); and *Landesgesetzblatt für das Burgenland.*

Verordnungs-und Amtsblatt für den Reichsgau Steiermark (February 1940–1944). Replaces *Verordnungsblatt für den Amtsbereich des Landeshauptmannes für Steiermark* (August 1939–February 1940); *Landesgesetzblatt für das Land Steiermark* (1920–May 1938); and absorbing *Amtliche Nachrichten für Steiermark* (1938–February 1940).

Verordnungs-und Amtsblatt für den Reichsgau Wien (1940–March 1945). Replaces *Verordnungsblatt für den Reichsgau Wien* (August 1939–January 1940).

6. CZECHOSLOVAKIA AND THE SUDETENLAND

Amtsblatt des Protektorates Böhmen und Mähren. Amtsblatt der čechoslovakischen Republik. (September 1939–December 1944). Official announcements of the Czech administration.

BIBLIOGRAPHY

Bodensieck, Heinrich. "Das dritte Reich und die Lage der Juden in der Tschecho-Slowakei nach München." *VfZ* 9 (1961):249–61. Deals only with the period to March 1939.

——. "Die Politik der zweiten Tschecho-Slowakischen Republik (Herbst 1938–Frühjahr 1939)." *Zeitschrift für Ostforschung* 16 (1964):79–101.

——. "Zur Vorgeschichte des 'Protektorats Böhmen und Mähren.'" *Geschichte in Wissenschaft und Unterricht* 19 (1968):713–32.

Bohmann, Alfred. "Die Stellung der Oberlandräte-Inspekteure: Zur deutschen Verwaltungsorganisation im ehemaligen Protektorat Böhmen und Mähren." *Zeitschrift für Ostforschung* 15 (1966): 118–26.

Brügel, Johann Wolfgang. "Die Aussiedlung der Deutschen aus der Tschechoslowakei." *VfZ* 8 (1960):134–64. Very little here on the German administration.

Burgess, Alan. *Seven Men at Daybreak*. New York, 1960. The reconstruction by a British journalist of the assassination of Heydrich, showing how it was planned in Britain and carried out by Czech refugees. To be used with caution.

Chmela, Leopold. *The Economic Aspect of the German Occupation of Czechoslovakia*. Prague, 1948. A survey of German methods of economic exploitation. Undocumented.

Ďurčanský, Ferdinand. "Mit Tiso bei Hitler." *Politische Studien* 7 (1950):1–10.

Ďurica, Milan Stanislao. *La Slovacchia e le sue relazioni politiche con la Germania, 1938–1945*. Vol. 1, *Dagli accordi di monaco all'inizio della seconda guerra mondiale (Ottobre 1938–Settembre 1939)*. Padua, 1964. So far as I can ascertain, only one volume has been published.

Fichelle, A. "La crise interne de la Tshécoslovaquie." *RHDGM* 52 (1963):21–38.

Grant Duff, Sheila. *A German Protectorate: The Czechs under Nazi Rule*. London, 1942. Full of important information.

Heiber, Helmut. "Zur Justiz im Dritten Reich. Der Fall Eliáš." *VfZ* 3 (1955):275–96.

Heiss, Friedrich, ed. *Das Böhmen und Mähren-Buch. Volkskampf und Reichsraum.* Prague, 1943. A book of texts and photographs by many contributors designed to show that racially, geographically, economically, and culturally these areas belong to and should be part of the Greater German Reich.

Hoensch, Jörg K. *Geschichte der Tschechoslowakischen Republik, 1918–1965.* Stuttgart, 1966.

——. *Die Slowakei und Hitlers Ostpolitik. Hlinkas Slowakische Volkspartei zwischen Autonomie und Separation, 1938/1939.* Cologne, 1965. A valuable monograph.

——. *Der ungarische Revisionismus und die Zerschlagung der Tschechoslowakei.* Tübingen, 1967.

Hufnagel, Hermann. "Organisation der Verwaltung im Protektorat Böhmen und Mähren." *Böhmen und Mähren.* Prague, 1940. An official Nazi account.

Jacoby, Gerhard. *Racial State: The German Nationalities Policy in the Protectorate of Bohemia-Moravia.* New York, 1944. Valuable, well-researched monograph, based on all the sources available at that time, including the laws promulgated by the German and Czech administrations.

Kehrl, Hans. "Das Protektorat im grossdeutschen Wirtschaftsraum." *Zeitschrift des Vereins Berliner Kaufleute und Industrieller* 22 (1941):19–23. By a senior official of the Reich Ministry of Economics and the Four-Year Plan.

Kennan, George F. *From Prague after Munich: Diplomatic Papers, 1938–1940.* Princeton, N.J., 1968.

Král, Václav. *Die Deutschen in der Tschechoslowakei, 1933–1947.* Prague, 1964. A collection of documents.

——. "The Policy of Germanization Enforced in Bohemia and Moravia by the Fascist Invaders during the Second World War." *Historica* 2 (1960):273–303. An interpretation of Nazi policy in Marxist terms. Despite frequent uncritical use of evidence and errors, full of important information.

——, ed. *Die Vergangenheit warnt. Dokumente über die Germanisierungs-und Austilgungspolitik der Naziokkupanten in der Tschechoslowakei.* Prague, 1960. A valuable collection of documents.

Landesverordnungsblatt für Mähren und Schlesien. Official publication of laws for Moravia. Published in Brno (Brünn).

510

BIBLIOGRAPHY

Lettrich, Jozef. *History of Modern Slovakia*. New York, 1955. Pro-Czech and bitterly hostile to Tiso, with a valuable appendix of documents.

Luža, Radomír. *The Transfer of the Sudeten Germans: A Study of Czech-German Relations, 1933–1962*. London, 1964. Contains a brief and accurate description of German policy toward Czechoslovakia before 1945. Valuable notes and bibliography.

Mastny, Vojtech. *The Czechs under Nazi Rule: The Failure of National Resistance, 1939–1942*. New York, 1971. An admirable brief study, judicious and fair, with a good bibliography.

Mikus, Joseph A. *Slovakia: A Political History, 1918–1950*. Milwaukee, Wisc., 1963. Translated from the French. Full of interesting information, but curiously organized. Written from a Slovak nationalist point of view, anti-Czech, and sympathetic to Tiso.

Neurath, Konstantin von. "Die Neuordnung der europäischen Mitte." *Europäische Revue*. April 1939, pp. 327–28.

Oddo, Gilbert L. *Slovakia and Its People*. New York, 1960. Pro-Slovak, sympathetic to Tiso.

OSS. *The Protectorate of Bohemia and Moravia*. Washington, D.C., 1944.

———. *Slovakia*. Washington, D.C., 1945.

Průcha, Václav, and Olšovský, Rudolf. "L'occupazione nazista e l'economia cecoslovacca." *L'occupazione nazista in Europa*, Edited by Enzo Collotti. Rome, 1964, pp. 311–66.

Rabl, Kurt. "Vier Jahre freie Slowakei." *RVL* 5 (1943):45–56. A Nazi tract, of little value except for the use of the term *Gefolgslandschaft* to describe Slovakia's status in the German *Lebensraum*.

Rhode, Gotthold. "Das Protektorat Böhmen und Mähren." *Das Parlament* 11 (1964):3–15.

Ripka, Hubert. *Munich: Before and After*. London, 1939. A Czech account.

Sammlung der Gesetze und Verordnungen der čecho-slovakischen Republik. Official publication of the decrees of the Czecho-Slovak and, after March 1939, of the Czech government. Title changed with the issue of March 15, 1939, to *Sammlung der Gesetze und Verordnungen;* with the issue of September 20, 1939, to *Sammlung der Gesetze und Verordnungen des Protektorates Böhmen und Mähren*. Last issue, April 20, 1945.

Schiefer, Hans. "Deutschland und die Tschechoslowakei von September 1938 bis März 1939." *Zeitschrift für Ostforschung* 4 (1955):48–66.

Schubert, Erich, ed. *Deutscher Sozialaufbau in Böhmen und Mähren*. Prague, 1943. Contributions by Nazi writers.

Statistisches Jahrbuch für das Protektorat Böhmen und Mähren. Prague, 1942.

Taborsky, Eduard. "Local Government in Czechoslovakia, 1918–1948." *American Slavic and East European Review* 10 (1951):202–15.

Urban, Vincent. *Hitler's Spearhead*. London, 1945. On the Nazi occupation of Bohemia and Moravia.

Verordnungsblatt für Böhmen und Mähren. First issue March 15, 1939, published in Berlin; published in Prague after April 14, 1939. Title changed, July 7, 1939, to *Verordnungsblatt des Reichsprotektors in Böhmen und Mähren;* in 1943, when Karl Hermann Frank was named German minister of state in Bohemia and Moravia, the title was changed to *Verordnungsblatt des deutschen Staatsministers in Böhmen und Mähren*. The official German statutes for the Czech provinces.

Verordnungsblatt für die Sudetendeutschen Gebiete. The first issue published in Berlin, October 8, 1938; from April 15, 1939, published in Reichenberg. With the issue of May 3, 1939, title changed to *Verordnungsblatt für den Reichsgau Sudetenland*.

Vietor, Martin. "Aperçu de l'évolution de l'état Slovaque." *RHDGM* 52 (1963):39–60. Too brief to be of much use. Communist point of view.

Wedelstädt, Erich von. "Die wirtschaftliche Eingliederung des Protektorats." *Die deutsche Volkswirtschaft* 9 (1940):290–93.

Weizsäcker, Wilhelm. *Geschichte der Deutschen in Böhmen und Mähren*. Hamburg, 1950. A brief survey by a German refugee and former professor at the German university in Prague.

Wighton, Charles. *Heydrich: Hitler's Most Evil Henchman*. Philadelphia, 1962.

Wiskemann, Elizabeth. *Czechs and Germans: A Study of the Struggle in the Historic Provinces of Bohemia and Moravia*. London, 1938.

——. "Partitioned Czechoslovakia." *Hitler's Europe*. Edited by Arnold and Veronica Toynbee. London, 1954. Oversimplified analysis of issues and marred by many errors, major and minor.

——. "Slovakia, March 1939 to March 1945." *Hitler's Europe*.

7. POLAND

Amtsblatt des Militärbefehlshabers Danzig-Westpreussen. Collection of official German announcements. First issue, September 18, 1939. Title changed November 4, 1939, to *Amtsblatt des Reichsstatthalters, Reichsgau Danzig;* November 15, 1939, to *Amtsblatt des Reichsstatthalters, Reichsgau Danzig-Westpreussen;* April 3, 1940, to *Amtsblatt des Reichsstatthalters in Danzig-Westpreussen*.

Amtsblatt des Oberpräsidenten der Provinz Ostpreussen, Zivilverwaltung für den Bezirk Bialystok. Title until September 21, 1941, was *Der Zivilkommissar*. Official publication of German announcements for the Polish areas annexed to the province of East Prussia.

Apenszlak, Jakób; Kenner, Jacob; Lewin, Issac; and Polakiewicz, Moses, eds. *The Black Book of Polish Jewry: An Account of the Martyrdom of Polish Jewry under the Nazi Occupation*. New York, 1943.

Berenstein, Tatiana, ed. *Faschismus-Getto-Massenmord. Dokumentation über Ausrottung und Widerstand der Juden in Polen während des zweiten Weltkrieges*. Berlin, 1961.

Best, Werner. *Die Verwaltung in Polen vor und nach dem Zusammenbruch der polnischen Republik*. Berlin, 1942. By the Nazi legal and administrative specialist, from October 1942 Reich plenipotentiary in Denmark.

Broszat, Martin. *Nationalsozialistische Polenpolitik, 1939–1945*. Stuttgart, 1961. A readable and authoritative monograph, the best single work on the subject.

Bühler, Josef. *Das Generalgouvernement. Seine Verwaltung und Wirtschaft*. Cracow, 1943. By the state secretary and later deputy of the governor general of occupied Poland.

Diewerge, Wolfgang. *Der neue Reichsgau Danzig-Westpreussen. Ein Arbeitsbericht vom Aufbauwerk im deutschen Osten*. Berlin, 1940. By the Gau's chief of propaganda.

Documenta Occupationis Teutonicae. 7 vols. Poznań, 1945–59. An important document collection.

Drzewieniecki, W. M. *The German-Polish Frontier*. Chicago, 1959.

Forster, Albert. "Bewährung bestanden. Ein Jahr Reichsgau Danzig-Westpreussen." *Der Schulungsbrief* 8 (1941):47–59. By the Gauleiter.

Frank, Hans. "Deutsche Ordnung und polnische Wirtschaft. Die straffe deutsche Führung im Generalgouvernement." *Der Schulungsbrief* 8 (1941):88–90. By the governor general.

——. *Hans Frank's Diary*. Edited by Stanislaw Piotrowski. Warsaw, 1961. Very brief excerpts from this massive collection.

——. *Im Angesicht des Galgens. Deutung Hitlers und seiner Zeit auf Grund eigener Erlebnisse und Erkenntnisse*. Munich, 1953. Frank's memoirs.

Gollert, F. *Warschau unter deutscher Herrschaft. Zwei Jahre Aufbauarbeit im Distrikt Warschau*. Cracow, 1942.

Hohenstein, Alexander. *Wartheländisches Tagebuch aus den Jahren 1941/42*. Stuttgart, 1961. Much interesting material.

Koch, Erich. "Aufbau im neuen Ostpreussen." *Der Schulungsbrief* 8 (1941):39–41. Deals with the newly annexed Polish areas; by the head of the administration of East Prussia.

Krannhals, Hanns von. *Der Warschauer Aufstand, 1944*. Frankfurt am Main, 1962.

Krausnick, Helmut. "Hitler und die Morde in Polen. Ein Beitrag zum Konflikt zwischen Heer und SS um die Verwaltung der besetzten Gebiete." *VfZ* 11 (1963):196–209. Important article.

Kundt, E. "Entstehung, Probleme, Grundsätze und Form der Verwaltung des Generalgouvernements." *Die Burg* 5 (1944):47–67.

Lange, Friedrich. *Ostland kehrt Heim*. Berlin, 1940. Refers to Memel, Danzig, West

Prussia, the Wartheland, and Upper Silesia, not to the later province of that name. Anti-Polish tract, of little interest.

Madajczyk, Czeslaw. "Deportation in the Zamość Region in 1942 and 1943 in the light of German documents." *Acta Poloniae Historica* 1 (1958):75–106.

Die Neuordnung des Rechts in den Ostgebieten. Sammlung der Reichsgesetze, der Verordnungen der Militärbefehlshaber, der Reichsstatthalter Danzig-Westpreussen und Wartheland, des Generalgouverneurs für das Gouvernement Polen mit kurzen Anmerkungen. Edited by Theodor Rohlfing and Rudolf Schraut. Berlin, 1940. Valuable collection.

OSS. *Eastern Territories Incorporated into the Reich.* Washington, 1945. Deals with the Reichsgaus Danzig-Westpreussen and the Wartheland.

———. *The General Government.* Washington, D.C., 1945.

Prel, Max du, ed. *Das General-gouvernement.* Würzburg, 1942. Contains contributions from leaders of the German administration in the Government General.

Das Recht des Generalgouvernements. Die Verordnungen des Generalgouverneurs für die besetzten polnischen Gebiete und die Durchführungsbestimmungen hierzu nach Sachgebieten geordnet. Edited by Albert Weh. Cracow, 1940. Valuable collection. Weh was head of the legal department in the Government General.

Roos, Hans. *A History of Modern Poland.* New York, 1966.

———. "Polen in der Besatzungszeit." *Osteuropa-Handbuch.* Edited by Werner Markert. Cologne, 1959, pp. 167–93.

Rothfels, Hans. "Zur 'Umsiedlung' der Juden im Generalgouvernement." *VfZ* 7 (1959):333–36.

Streng, H. von. *Die Landwirtschaft im Generalgouvernement.* Tübingen, 1955.

Sukiennicki, Wiktor. "The Establishment of the Soviet Regime in Eastern Poland in 1939." *Journal of Central European Affairs* 23 (1963):191–218.

Verordnungsblatt des Chefs der Zivilverwaltung beim Militärbefehlshaber von Posen. Official collection of German decrees, published in Posen (Poznań). Title changed November 14, 1939, to *Verordnungsblatt des Reichsstatthalters im Reichsgau Wartheland;* title changed October 15, 1940, to *Verordnungsblatt des Reichsstatthalters im Warthegau.*

Verordnungsblatt für die besetzten Gebiete in Polen, published in Berlin; title changed by Hitler decree of October 12, 1939 to *Verordnungsblatt für die besetzten polnischen Gebiete;* in 1940 published in Cracow in two parts under the titles *Verordnungsblatt für das Generalgouvernement,* which contained decrees of the governor general, and *Verordnungsblatt des Generalgouverneurs für die besetzten polnischen Gebiete,* which contained all other decrees and announcements; from 1941 all decrees were once again contained in one publication, the *Verordnungsblatt für das Generalgouvernement.*

Verordnungsblatt für die Zivilverwaltung in den dem Gauleiter Forster als Chef der Zivilverwaltung unterstellten besetzten Gebieten, first issue published in Danzig, September 7, 1939; title changed September 18, 1939, to *Verordnungsblatt des Militärbefehlshabers Danzig-Westpreussen;* title changed November 1, 1941, to *Verordnungsblatt des Reichsstatthalters, Reichsgau Danzig-Westpreussen;* title changed April 3, 1940, to *Verordnungsblatt des Reichsstatthalters in Danzig-Westpreussen.*

Wulf, Joseph. "Dr. Hans Frank, Generalgouverneur im besetzten Polen." *Das Parlament,* suppl. August 2, 1961, pp. 453–63.

Der Zivilkommissar. See *Amtsblatt des Oberpräsidenten der Provinz Ostpreussen.*

8. SCANDINAVIA AND FINLAND

Brandt, Willy [pseud. for Karl Frahm]. *Norwegens Freiheitskampf, 1940–1945.* Hamburg, 1948.

Chilston, Viscount. "Denmark." *Hitler's Europe.* Edited by Arnold and Veronica Toynbee. London, 1954.

———. "Norway." *Hitler's Europe.*

Erfurth, Waldemar. *Der Finnische Krieg, 1941–44.* Wiesbaden, 1950.

Fen, Åke. *Nazis in Norway.* London, 1943.

Gudme, Sten. *Denmark: Hitler's "Model Protectorate."* London, 1942.

Hambro, C. J. *I Saw It Happen in Norway.* New York, 1943. By the president of the

Norwegian parliament, with interesting material on the German invasion, negotiations, and the efforts of Quisling to form a government.

Hayes, Paul M. "Brief aperçu de l'histoire de Quisling et du gouvernement de la Norvège de 1940 à 1945." *RHDGM* 66 (1967):11–30. An intelligent, balanced analysis.

———. *Quisling: The Career and Political Ideas of Vidkun Quisling, 1887–1945.* Bloomington, Ind., 1972. A valuable work, which unfortunately reached me too late to be used in this study.

Hedin, Sven. *Sven Hedin's German Diary, 1935–1942.* Dublin, 1951. Includes accounts of interviews with Nazi leaders, including Hitler.

Hewins, Ralph. *Quisling: Prophet without Honour.* London, 1965. A defense of Quisling, with much interesting information.

Hubatsch, Walther. *"Weserübung." Die deutsche Besetzung von Dänemark und Norwegen, 1940.* Göttingen, 1960. Includes the most important documents on the subject. Unfortunately only takes the story to the beginning of the German occupation.

Johnson, Amanda. *Norway: Her Invasion and Occupation.* Decatur, Ga., 1948. Based largely on periodicals, with numerous errors.

Karlbom, Rolf. "Sweden's Iron Ore Exports to Germany, 1933–1944," *Scandinavian Economic History Review* 13 (1965):65–93.

Karup-Pedersen, Ole. "Les recherches sur l'histoire du Danemark pendant la deuxième guerre mondiale." *RHDGM* 48 (1962):39–44.

Koch, Hans Reinhard. "Der Aufbau der deutschen Verwaltung in Norwegen." *RVL* 3 (1942):40–59. Koch was head of the administrative section of the German occupation government.

Koht, Halvdan. *Norway: Neutral and Invaded.* New York, 1941. By the former Norwegian foreign minister, with an excellent account of the German invasion and a long chapter on German rule.

La Ruche, F. *La Neutralité de la Suède. Dix années d'une politique, 1939–1949.* Paris, 1953.

Leistikow, Gunnar. "Denmark under the Nazi Heel." *Foreign Affairs* 21 (1943):340–53.

Loock, Hans-Dietrich. *Quisling, Rosenberg und Terboven. Zur Vorgeschichte und Geschichte der nationalsozialistischen Revolution in Norwegen.* Stuttgart, 1970. A thorough, scholarly study, which takes the story in detail to September 25, 1940. An excellent final chapter deals briefly with the last years of the occupation.

Lundin, C. Leonard. *Finland in the Second World War.* Bloomington, Ind., 1956.

Milward, Alan S. *The Fascist Economy in Norway.* New York, 1972. Unfortunately reached me too late for this study.

Mohr, Andreas. "Der norwegische Oberste Gerichtshof und seine Zuständigkeit." *RVL* 6 (1943):539–44. Mohr was president of the supreme court.

Norway and the War: September 1939–December 1940. Edited by Monica Curtis. London, 1941. Useful collection of documents.

OSS. *Denmark.* Washington, D.C., 1945.

———. *Norway.* Washington, D.C., 1943. Two separate pamphlets on Norway deal with *Money and Banking* (Washington, D.C., 1945); and *Labor* (Washington, D.C., 1943).

Quisling, Vidkun. *Die nationale Revolution in Norwegen. Reden.* Oslo, 1944.

Riste, Olaf, ed. *Norway and the Second World War.* Oslo, 1966.

Satz, Margot. "Enemy Legislation and Judgments in Denmark." *Journal of Comparative Legislation and International Law* 31 (1949), pts. 3 and 4, pp. 1 ff.

Schneider, Herbert. "Staatsrechtliche Entwicklung und Verwaltungsgesetzgebung Norwegens seit dem 9. April 1940." *RVL* 2 (1942):379–405.

Stabell, Peter O. "Enemy Legislation and Judgments in Norway." *Journal of Comparative Legislation and International Law* 31 (1949), pts. 3 and 4, pp. 3 ff.

Stuckart, Wilhelm, ed. *Verfassungs-, Verwaltungs- und Wirtschaftsgesetze Norwegens.* Darmstadt, 1942.

Thomsen, Erich. *Deutsche Besatzungspolitik in Dänemark, 1940–1945.* Düsseldorf, 1971. Unfortunately reached me too late to be used for the present study.

Trial of Nikolaus von Falkenhorst: Formerly Generalobserst in the German Army.

514

Edited by E. H. Stevens. London, 1949. Chiefly concerned with Falkenhorst's complicity in shooting prisoners of war.

Verordnungsblatt für die besetzten norwegischen Gebiete. Oslo, 1940–45. The official publication of German decrees.

Worm-Müller, Jacob. *Norway Revolts against the Nazis.* London, 1941. Contains much valuable information.

Ziemke, Earl F. *The German Northern Theater of Operations, 1940–1945.* Washington, D.C., 1959. Based on German military and diplomatic documents.

9. THE NETHERLANDS AND LUXEMBOURG

Althaus, Ernst. *Die Behandlung der Personalangelegenheiten in den besetzten niederländischen Gebieten. Im Auftrage des Reichskommissars für die besetzten niederländischen Gebiete zusammengestellt.* The Hague, 1941.

Documents of the Persecution of Dutch Jewry, 1940–1945. Amsterdam, 1965. Collected by the Jewish Historical Museum of Amsterdam.

Essen, Jac van. *Mein Holland.* Amsterdam, 1944. A propaganda tract attempting to fit the Dutch into *Deutschtum.*

Ispert, Wolfgang. "Der Bruch der niederländischen Entwicklungslinie," *RVL,* 3 (1942):295–314.

Jong, Louis de. "Documentation et recherches concernant l'histoire des Pays-Bas pendant la seconde guerre mondiale." *RHDGM* 50 (1963):37–42.

——. "Jews and Non-Jews in Nazi-Occupied Holland." *On the Track of Tyranny: Essays Presented by the Wiener Library to Leonard G. Montefiore.* London, 1960, pp. 139–55.

——. "Les Pays-Bas dans la seconde guerre mondiale." *RHDGM* 50 (1963):1–26.

——, and Stoppelman, J. W. F. *The Lion Rampant: The Story of Holland's Resistance to the Nazis.* New York, 1943. Full of important information.

Kitz, Wilhelm, and Gross, Heinrich. *Die Organisation der niederländischen Verwaltung.* Düsseldorf, 1941.

Kroiss, Rudolf. "Die Verwaltung des Reichskommissars." *RVL* 2 (1942):15–52.

Kwiet, Konrad. *Reichskommissariat Niederlande. Versuch und Scheitern nationalsozialistischer Neuordnung.* Stuttgart, 1968. An excellent monograph, focusing on the first months of the German occupation. Good bibliography.

The Luxembourg Grey Book: Luxembourg and the German Invasion: Before and After. London, 1942. Brief wartime volume, no longer of much value.

Maass, Walter B. *The Netherlands at War, 1940–1945.* London, 1970. A firsthand account by a member of the resistance, drawing on documentary materials now available.

Mason, Henry L. "War Comes to the Netherlands, September 1939–May 1940." *Political Science Quarterly* 78 (1963):548–80.

Mussert, Anton Andriaan. *Vijf Nota's van Mussert aan Hitler over de Samenwerking von Duitsland en Nederland in een Bond van Germaansche Volkeren, 1940–1944.* The Hague, 1947.

Nationaal Socialistisch Jaarboek. Utrecht. Calendar-date book, filled with NSB propaganda in slogans and pictures.

Neumann, H. J. *Arthur Seyss-Inquart.* Graz, 1970.

OSS. *The Netherlands.* Washington, D.C., 1944.

Paape, A. H. "Le Mouvement national-socialiste en Hollande." *RHDGM* 66 (1967):31–60.

Posthumus, N. W., ed. *The Netherlands during German Occupation.* Philadelphia, 1946.

Postma, Johannes. *A Reichskommissariat: German Civil Government in the Netherlands.* Unpublished M.A. thesis, University of Kansas, 1964. Full of useful information.

Prel, Max du, and Janke, Willi, eds. *Die Niederlande im Umbruch der Zeiten. Alte und neue Beziehungen zum Reich.* Würzburg, 1942. With a forward by Seyss-Inquart.

Het Proces Mussert. The Hague, 1948. The record of the trial of the Dutch Nazi leader.

Het Proces Rauter. The Hague, 1952. The record of the trial of the senior SS and police officer in the Netherlands.

Rauter, Hanns Albin. "Cinq Lettres de Rauter à Himmler." *RHDGM* 50 (1963):43–56.

Schöffer, I. *Het nationaal-socialistische beeld van de geschiedenis der Nederlanden. Een historiografische en bibliografische studie.* Amsterdam, 1956.

Seyss-Inquart, Arthur. "Die politische Aufgabe des Reichskommissars." *RVL* 2 (1942):9–14.

———. *Vier Jahre in den Niederlanden. Gesammelte Reden.* Amsterdam, 1944.

Simon, Gustav. "Luxemburgs Weg ins Reich." *Der Schulungsbrief* 8 (1941):179–82.

Söchting, Walter, ed. *Das Niederlandbuch. Sammlung deutscher und niederländischer Arbeiten.* Frankfurt am Main, 1942. With a forward by Seyss-Inquart. A work designed to demonstrate the racial and spiritual unity of the Dutch and German peoples.

Verordnungsblatt für die besetzten niederländischen Gebiete. The Hague, June 5, 1940–March 8, 1945. The German legislation for the Netherlands.

Verordnungsblatt für Luxemburg. Luxembourg, September 1, 1940–45. Laws promulgated by the German military administration in Luxembourg were first published in *Verordnungsblatt für das besetzte Gebiet des Grossherzogtums Luxemburg* and from June until the takeover by the civil administration in *Verordnungsblatt des Militärbefehlshabers in Belgien und Nordfrankreich für die besetzten Gebiete Belgiens, Luxemburgs, und Nordfrankreichs.*

Warmbrunn, Werner. *The Dutch under German Occupation, 1940–1945.* Stanford, Calif., 1963. An authoritative account, with an excellent bibliography.

Westland: Blätter für Landschaft, Geschichte und Kultur an Rhein, Mosel, Maas und Schelde. A journal published in Amsterdam (1943 ff.) under the auspices of Seyss-Inquart. A valuable source for the study of Nazi attitudes toward the lands of Western Europe.

10. BELGIUM

Ardenne, R. [pseud.]. *German Exploitation of Belgium.* Washington, D.C., 1942. Useful short pamphlet.

Bährens, Kurt. *Die flämische Bewegung. Europäisches Problem oder innerbelgische Frage.* Berlin, 1935.

Baillon, Louis. *La Résistance administrative. La Lutte secrète des pouvoirs publics contre les allemands en Belgique, 1940–1944.* Brussels, 1946.

Baudhuin, Fernand. *L'Économie belge sous l'occupation, 1940–1944.* Brussels, 1945. Scholarly and well balanced.

———. *Les Finances de 1939 à 1949. La Belgique et la Hollande.* Paris, 1951.

Billiard, Robert. *La Collaboration industrielle et ouvrière avec l'occupant.* Brussels, 1945.

———. *La Contrainte économique imposée aux industriels et aux ouvriers belges par l'autorité occupante allemande en 1940–1944.* Brussels, 1946.

Bronchkhart, Joseph. *Cinq Ans d'occupation. Verviers pendant la guerre, 1940–1945.* 3 vols. Verviers, no date.

Capelle, Count Robert. *Au service du roi.* 2 vols. Brussels, 1949.

Clough, Shepard B. "The Flemish Movement." *Belgium.* Edited by Jan-Albert Goris. Berkeley, Calif., 1946, pp. 108–26.

———. *A History of the Flemish Movement in Belgium: A Study in Nationalism.* New York, 1930.

Dantinne, Father L. G. *The Catholic Church in Belgium under the German Occupation.* London, 1944.

Degrelle, Léon. *La Cohue de 1940.* Lausanne, 1950. By the leading Walloon collaborationist and head of the Rexist movement.

———. *Die verlorene Legion.* Stuttgart, 1955. Refers to the Belgian legion Degrelle commanded in Russia.

Delandsheere, Paul, and Ooms, Alphonse. *La Belgique sous les Nazis, 1940–44.* 4 vols. Brussels, 1946–47. A day-by-day account, full of interesting information.

Falkenhausen, Alexander von. "Was ich dachte und was ich tat." *Die Zeit,* April 24, May 4 and 11, 1950. By the head of the German military administration.

BIBLIOGRAPHY

Hailer, Walter. "Organisation der Militärverwaltung und ihr Verhältnis zu den land-eseigenen Behörden." *RVL* 6 (1943):24–52. An official German account.

Heeresgruppen-und Verordnungsblatt für die besetzten Gebiete. The first publication of German laws for the West, May 10, 1940. See under *Verordnungsblatt.*

Hislaire, René. "Political Parties." *Belgium.* Edited by Jan-Albert Goris. Berkeley, Calif., 1946, pp. 93–107.

Jacquemyns, Guillaume. "Quelques Attitudes et réactions travailleurs belges sous l'occupation allemande (1940–1944)." *RHDGM* 31 (1958):24–30.

——. *La Société belge sous l'occupation allemande, 1940–1944.* 3 vols. Brussels, 1950. Deals primarily with such problems as labor conditions, rationing, heating, social welfare.

Knight, Thomas J. "Belgium Leaves the War, 1940." *Journal of Modern History* 41 (1969):46–67. An excellent article.

——. *The Establishment of German Military Government in Belgium, 1940–1941.* Unpublished doctoral dissertation, University of Texas, 1967. A work on which I have drawn heavily.

Knoebel, Edgar Erwin. *Racial Illusion and Military Necessity: A Study of SS Political and Manpower Objectives in Occupied Belgium.* Unpublished doctoral dissertation, University of Colorado, 1965. Another work on which I have drawn heavily.

Lejeune, L. "Tableau de la résistance belge (1940–1945)." *RHDGM* 31 (1958):31–43.

Liebrecht, Henri. *L'Université de Bruxelles et la guerre.* Brussels, 1944.

Lousse, E. *L'Université de Louvain pendant la seconde guerre mondiale.* Bruges, 1945.

Moniteur belge des arrêtés ministériels et autre arrêtés des secrétaires généraux. The official publication of decrees of the Belgian government. Note that there were two versions during the war, one published in London by the Belgian government in exile, the other in Brussels.

Narváez, Luisa. *Degrelle m'a dit.* Paris, 1961. By Luisa María Narváez y Macías, duchess of Valencia, on the leader of the Rexist movement.

OSS. *Belgium.* Washington, D.C., 1944. There is also an OSS pamphlet on Belgium dealing with *Money and Banking.* Washington, D.C., 1944.

Otto, Helmut. *Die flämischen und holländischen Nationalbewegungen. Ihre staats-politische Ziele nach dem Weltkrieg.* Leipzig, 1936.

Price, Arnold H. "The Belgian-German Frontier during World War II." *Maryland Historian* 1 (1970):145–53.

Reeder, Eggert. "Die Militärverwaltung in Belgien und Nordfrankreich. Grundsätze und politische Zielsetzung." *RVL* 6 (1943):7–23. By the chief of the administrative staff of the German military administration.

Smolders, Theodore, ed. *La Législation belge depuis le 10 mai 1940.* 6 vols. Brussels, 1941 ff.

Struye, Paul. *L'Évolution du sentiment public en Belgique sous l'occupation allemande.* Brussels, 1945. A collection of documents.

Thiry, Marcel. *La Belgique pendant la guerre.* Paris, 1947. A book of impressions. Of little value.

Vauthier, Marcel. *L'Université de Bruxelles sous l'occupation allemande, 1940–1944.* Brussels, 1944.

Verordnungsblatt des Militärbefehlshabers in Belgien und Nordfrankreich für die besetzten Gebiete Belgiens und Nordfrankreichs (VBlB). The official decrees of the German military government, published in Brussels from August 17, 1940. Replaced the *Verordnungsblatt des Militärbefehlshabers in Belgien und Nordfrankreich für die besetzten Gebiete Belgiens, Luxemburgs, und Nordfrankreichs* (May–August, 1940), which in turn replaced the *Heeresgruppen-und Verordnungsblatt für die besetzten Gebiete,* published May 10, 1940.

Wauters, Arthur. "Belgium under the Occupation." *Belgium.* Edited by Jan-Albert Goris. Berkeley, Calif., 1946, pp. 415–28.

Willequet, Jacques. "Le Procès Falkenhausen." *RHDGM* 3 (1951):59–65.

——. "Regards sur la politique belge d'indépendance (1936–1940)." *RHDGM* 31 (1958):3–11.

——. "Les Fascismes belges." *RHDGM* 66 (1967):85–109.

Wullus-Rudiger, J. A. [pseud. for Armand Wullus]. *La Belgique et la crise européenne, 1914–1945.* 2 vols. Paris, 1945. Full of errors and on the whole not very useful.

——. *En marge de la politique belge, 1914–1956.* Paris, 1957. Contains much useful information, especially about Belgian collaborationist groups.

Zeck, Hans F. *Die flämische Frage. Ein germanisches Volk kämpft um sein Lebensrecht.* Leipzig, 1938.

11. FRANCE

Abetz, Otto. *Das offene Problem. Ein Rückblick auf zwei Jahrzehnte deutscher Frankreichpolitik.* Cologne, 1951. By the German ambassador to France during the occupation.

Anrich, Ernst. *Die Geschichte der deutschen Westgrenze.* Leipzig, 1940. The author was made rector of the University of Strasbourg by the Germans.

Arnoult, Pierre. *Les Finances de la France et l'occupation allemande, 1940–44.* Paris, 1951.

——, ed. *La France sous l'occupation.* Paris, 1959. A critical analysis of the content and implications of the Chambrun publication (see below).

Aron, Robert. *The Vichy Regime, 1940–1944.* New York, 1958. Based largely on the postwar trials.

Bechtel, Guy. *Laval vingt ans après.* Paris, 1963.

Best, Dr. Werner. "Die deutsche Militärverwaltung in Frankreich." *RVL* 1 (1941):29–76. By the chief of the department of civil administration in the German military government, 1940.

——. "Frankreich. Schuld und Schicksal." *RVL* 1 (1941):291–313.

Billig, Joseph. *Le Commissariat général aux questions juives (1941–1944).* 3 vols. Paris, 1955–60.

Boehm, Max Hildebert. *Geheimnisvolles Burgund. Werden und Vergehen eines europäischen Schicksalslandes.* Munich, 1944.

——. *Lothringerland. Anderthalb Jahrtausende Grenzlandschicksal zwischen Argonnen und Vogesen.* Munich, 1942.

Böhme, Hermann. *Der deutsch-französische Waffenstillstand im Zweiten Weltkrieg.* Erster Teil. *Entstehung und Grundlagen des Waffenstillstandes von 1940.* Stuttgart, 1966.

Bogdatsch, R. "Politische und militärische Probleme nach dem Frankreichfeldzug." *Das Parlament* 14 (1962):149–87.

Bopp, Marie-Joseph. *L'Alsace sous l'occupation allemande, 1940–1945.* Le Puys, Alsatia, 1945. A contemporary study containing much interesting material.

Boüard, Michel de. "La Répression allemande en France de 1940 à 1944." *RHDGM* 54 (1964):63–90.

Boudot, François. "Aspects économiques de l'occupation allemande en France." *RHDGM* 54 (1964):41–62.

Bourbon-Parma, Prince Xavier de. *Les Accords secrets franco-anglais de décembre, 1940.* Paris, 1949.

Brinon, Fernand de. *Mémoires.* Paris, 1949. By the representative of the Vichy government in the German-occupied territories.

Cernay, Louis. *Le Maréchal Pétain, l'Alsace et la Lorraine. Faits et documents (1940–1944).* Paris, 1955. Documents showing Pétain's efforts on behalf of the provinces: protests, diplomatic actions, interventions.

Cézard, Pierre. "L'Annexion de fait de l'Alsace et de la Lorraine, Juin 1940–Septembre 1942." *RHDGM* 5 (1952):37–52. Based on obvious published materials. Good brief survey.

Chambrun, René and Josée de, eds. *France during the German Occupation, 1940–1944.* Stanford, Calif., 1958–59. Documents collected by the daughter and son-in-law of Laval.

Cobban, Alfred. "Vichy France." *Hitler's Europe.* Edited by Arnold and Veronica Toynbee. London, 1954, pp. 338–434.

Crénesse, Pierre, ed. *Le Procès de Wagner, bourreau de l'Alsace.* Paris, 1946.

Darlan, Alain. *L'Admiral Darlan parle.* Paris, 1952. By the vice-president of the Vichy Council of Ministers, 1940–42.

BIBLIOGRAPHY

La Délégation française auprès de la commission allemande d'armistice. Recueil de documents publié par le gouvernement français. 5 vols. Paris, 1947–59. Valuable source, admirably edited. Although the reports of transactions only go to December 1941, the volumes include documents covering the entire period of the German occupation.

Denzel, Rosemarie. *Die chemische Industrie Frankreichs unter der deutschen Besetzung im zweiten Weltkrieg.* Tübingen, 1959.

Dommages subis par la France et l'union française du fait de la guerre et de l'occupation ennemie (1939–1945). Part imputable à l'Allemagne. 9 vols. Paris, 1947–51. Published by the Commission Consultative des Dommages et des Réparations. Includes some very important material.

Duquesne, Jacques. *Les Catholiques français sous l'occupation.* Paris, 1966.

Emmrich, Hermann. "Westmark des Reichs. Von der Sehnsucht zur geschichtlichen Wirklichkeit." *Der Schulungsbrief,* 8 (1941):164–66.

Farmer, Paul. *Vichy: Political Dilemma.* New York, 1955. A valuable analysis.

Geschke, Günter. *Die deutsche Frankreichpolitik, 1940, von Compiègne bis Montoire. Das Problem einer deutsch-französichen Annäherung nach dem Frankreichfeldzug.* Frankfurt am Main, 1960. A valuable monograph.

Hallier, Christian. *Das Elsass. Deutsches Kern-und Grenzland.* Frankfurt am Main, 1941. One of the many works to prove that in every respect—architecture, costumes, names—Alsace was originally a Germanic country.

——. *Vom Selbstbehauptungskampf des deutschen Volkstums im Elsass und in Lothringen, 1918–1940.* Berlin, 1940.

Hoffmann, Stanley. "Aspects du regime de Vichy." *Revue française de science politique* 6 (1956):44–69.

——. "Collaborationism in France during World War II." *Journal of Modern History* 40 (1968):375–95.

Huddleston, Sisley. *France: The Tragic Years, 1939–1947: An Eyewitness Account of War, Occupation, and Liberation.* New York, 1955.

Hytier, Adrienne. *Two Years of French Foreign Policy: Vichy, 1940–1942.* Geneva, 1958. An admirable monograph.

Jäckel, Eberhard. *Frankreich in Hitlers Europa. Die deutsche Frankreichpolitik im zweiten Weltkrieg.* Stuttgart, 1966. An exemplary monograph, scholarly, well written, with eminently sensible conclusions.

Jacob, Paul. *Les Lois de l'occupation en France.* New York, 1942. Brief pamphlet.

Journal officiel de l'état français. The official publication of the Vichy government, replacing the *Journal officiel de la République Française.*

Juin, Marshal Alphonse. *Mémoires.* 2 vols. Paris, 1959–60. By a French leader who played a critical and often equivocal role during the German occupation.

Kernan, Thomas, *France on Berlin Time.* Philadelphia, 1941. By the chief of the Condé Nast publications in Europe.

Kistenmacher, Hans. *Die Auswirkungen der deutschen Besetzung auf die Ernährungswirtschaft Frankreichs während des 2. Weltkrieges.* Tübingen, 1959.

Kluke, Paul. "Nationalsozialistische Volkstumspolitik in Elsass-Lothringen, 1940 bis 1945." *Zur Geschichte und Problematik der Demokratie. Festgabe für Hans Herzfeld.* Berlin, 1958, pp. 619–36. A fairly skimpy treatment.

Laferrière, Julien. *Le Nouveau Gouvernement de la France. Les Actes constitutionnels de 1940–1942 à l'usage de la license en droit et de la préparation aux concours administratifs.* Paris, 1942.

Langer, William L. *Our Vichy Gamble.* New York, 1947. An intelligent defense of American policy in negotiating with the Vichy regime.

Laval, Pierre. *Laval parle. Notes et mémoires.* Paris, 1948.

——. *The Unpublished Diary of Pierre Laval.* London, 1948.

Leahy, William D. *I Was There.* New York, 1950. By the American ambassador to Vichy.

Législation de l'occupation. Recueil des principaux textes de lois, décrets, ordonnances, arrêtés, et circulaires des autorités allemandes et françaises, promulgués depuis l'occupation. 16 vols. Paris, 1940–44.

Lubetzki, J. *La Condition des Juifs en France sous l'occupation allemande, 1940–1944. La Législation raciale.* Paris, 1945. A valuable analysis of French and German anti-Jewish legislation, with lists of the laws.

519

BIBLIOGRAPHY

Luther, Hans. *Der französiche Widerstand gegen die deutsche Besatzungsmacht und seine Bekämpfung. Tübingen, 1957.*

Mallet, Alfred. *Pierre Laval.* 2 vols. Paris, 1955. By a close friend of the French statesman.

Martin du Gard, Maurice. *La Chronique de Vichy, 1940–1944.* Paris, 1948.

Medicus, F. A. "Militärverwaltung in Frankreich," *Archiv des öffentlichen Rechts,* 34 (1944):86–96. By the chief of the office of the military administration in Paris.

Meissner, Hans Otto, ed. *Elsass und Lothringen. Deutsches Land.* Berlin, 1941. A handsome book of essays commemorating the German occupation of Alsace and Lorraine and leaving no doubt that the German government regarded the provinces as German and intended to annex them to the Reich.

Michel, Henri. "Aspects politiques de l'occupation de la France par les allemands (juin 1940–décembre 1944)." *RHDGM* 54 (1964):1–40.

———. "Bibliographie. L'Économie française pendant la guerre (1939–1945)." *RHDGM* 57 (1965):119–28.

———. *Vichy. Année 40.* Paris, 1966.

Milward, Alan S. "German Economic Policy towards France, 1940–1944." *Studies in International History.* Edited by K. Bourne and D. C. Watt. Hamden, Conn., 1967, pp. 423–43.

———. *The New Order and the French Economy.* London, 1969. A valuable monograph.

Müller, E. "Der lotharingische Grenzraum." *Monatsschrift fur das deutsche Geistesleben.* March 1939.

Munz, Alfred. *Die Auswirkungen der deutschen Besetzung auf Währung und Finanzen Frankreichs.* Tübingen, 1957.

Noguères, Louis. *Le Véritable Procès du Maréchal Pétain.* Paris, 1955.

OSS. *France.* Washington, D.C., 1944.

Paxton, Robert O. *Parades and Politics at Vichy: The French Officer Corps under Marshal Pétain.* Princeton, N.J., 1966.

———. *Vichy France: Old Guard and New Order, 1940–1944.* New York, 1972. Perceptive and scholarly study, which unfortunately reached me too late to be used for my own work. The author may take too literally the statements of Vichy leaders about their desire for collaboration as recorded in German documents.

Pétain, Henri-Philippe. *Appels aux français, 1940.* Paris, 1941.

———. *Dictionnaire du maréchal.* Paris, 1942.

———. *La France nouvelle. Appels et messages.* 2 vols. Montrouge, 1941.

———. *La France nouvelle. Principes de la communauté.* Paris, 1941.

———. *Paroles aux français: Messages et écrits, 1934–1941.* Lyon, 1941.

———. *Quatre Années au pouvoir.* Paris, 1949. Dictated in prison.

Poliakov, Léon. *Le condition des Juifs en France sous l'occupation italienne.* Paris, 1946.

Le Procès du Maréchal Pétain. Compte rendu sténographique. 2 vols. Paris, 1945.

Le Procès Laval. Compte rendu stenographique. Paris, 1946.

Renault-Roulier, Gilbert. *La Ligne de démarcation.* Paris, 1969.

Rivet, Général. "Abwehr et Gestapo en France pendant la guerre." *RHDGM* 1 (1950):28–50.

Rougier, Louis. *Les accords Pétain-Churchill. Histoire d'une mission secrète.* Montreal, 1945.

———. *Les accords secrets franco-brittaniques de l'automne 1940. Histoire et imposture.* Paris, 1954.

Saint-Paulien [pseud. for Maurice-Yvan Sicard]. *Histoire de la collaboration.* Paris, 1964. Detailed but not particularly informative treatment of this difficult and controversial subject. To be used with care.

Schaeffer, Eugène. *L'Alsace et la Lorraine (1940–1945). Leur Occupation en droit et en fait.* Paris, 1953. Emphasis on legal aspects.

Steinberg, Lucien. *Les Autorités allemandes en France occupée.* Paris, 1966. Useful survey of materials on the subject.

———. "Statistiques de la déportation des Juifs de France." *Monde Juif* 21 (1966):26–30.

Thomson, David. *Two Frenchmen: Pierre Laval and Charles de Gaulle.* London, 1951. A suggestive study.

Vernoux, M. *Wiesbaden, 1940–1944.* Paris, 1954.

BIBLIOGRAPHY

Verordnungsblatt des Chefs der Zivilverwaltung im Elsass (VBlE). Strasbourg. First issue published August 24, 1940. The legislation of the German civil administration.

Verordnungsblatt für die besetzten französichen Gebiete. First issue published July 4, 1940. Title changed October 29, 1940, to *Verordnungsblatt des Militärbefehlshabers in Frankreich (VBlF)*. The legislation of the German military government.

Verordnungsblatt für Lothringen (VBlL). Saarbrücken. First issue published August 24, 1940. The legislation of the German civil administration.

Wagner, Robert. "Elsässischer Schicksalsweg." *Der Schulungsbrief* 8 (1941):132–37. By the head of the German civil administration.

Warner, Geoffrey. *Pierre Laval and the Eclipse of France*. London, 1968. The best of the biographies of this controversial figure.

Weinmann, Manfred. *Die Landwirtschaft in Frankreich während des 2. Weltkrieges unter dem Einfluss der deutschen Besatzungsmacht*. Tübingen, 1961.

Weniger, Erich. "Zur Vorgeschichte des 20. Juli 1944. Heinrich von Stülpnagel." *Die Sammlung* 4 (1949):475–92. On the head of the German military government who was deeply involved in the July 20 plot to assassinate Hitler and take over the German government.

Werth, Alexander. *France, 1940–1955*. London, 1956. Full of interesting insights.

12. SOUTHEASTERN EUROPE: HUNGARY AND THE BALKANS.

Adriaticus [F. Langer]. *Deutschlands gerechte Grenze*. Berlin, 1925. A plea for the reunion of Lower Styria, and a good deal more, with Austria/Germany.

Argenti, Philip P. *The Occupation of Chios by the Germans and Their Administration of the Island*. Cambridge, Eng., 1966. A superficial study based largely on oral evidence, with no attempt to relate Chios to the general pattern of German administration in Greece and no satisfactory description of the German administration in Chios itself.

Braham, Randolph L. *The Destruction of Hungarian Jewry: A Documentary Account*. 2 vols. New York, 1963.

———. *Eichmann and the Destruction of Hungarian Jewry*. New York, 1961. Clear, thoroughly documented account.

———. *The Hungarian Jewish Catastrophe: A Selected and Annotated Bibliography*. New York, 1963.

Broszat, Martin. "Deutschland-Ungarn-Rumänien. Entwicklung und Grundfaktoren nationalsozialistischer Hegemonial-und Bündnispolitik, 1938–1941," *Historische Zeitschrift* 206 (1968):45–96. Excellent article.

Bruckner, Hans. *Der deutsch-slowenische Grenzraum*. Berlin, 1934.

Cohen, David B. "Le Pillage de l'économie bulgare par les allemands." *RHDGM* 72 (1968):43–65.

The Crimes of the Fascist Occupants and their Collaborators against the Jews in Yugoslavia. Edited by Zdenka Löwenthal. Belgrade, 1957. The first section is a summary in English. Based largely on oral evidence. No documentation.

Dolaptchieva, J. "Bibliographie sur la guerre et la résistance." *RHDGM* 72 (1968):83–93. Citing materials chiefly from the point of view of the Communist bloc, on the impact of war on Bulgaria.

Dukar, Erwin, "Der Aufbau des Schulwesens in der Untersteiermark." *Marburger Zeitung*, April 12, 1943.

Eudes, Dominique. *Les Kapetanios. La Guerre civile grecque de 1943 à 1949*. Paris(?), 1970. Communist point of view.

Fabry, Philipp W. *Balkan-Wirren, 1940–1941. Diplomatische und militärische Vorbereitungen des deutschen Donauüberganges*. Darmstadt, 1966.

Ferenc, Tone. "Le Système d'occupation des Nazis en Slovénie." *Les Systèmes d'occupation en Yougoslavie, 1941–1945*. Belgrade, 1963, pp. 47–133. Full of important information.

Friedl, Herbert. "Oberkrain—Kärntens deutsche Markaufgabe." *RVL* 5 (1943): 247–67.

Gornenski, N. and Kamenov, E. "Sur la Bulgarie en guerre. La Politique intérieure." *RHDGM* 72 (1968):23–41.

Grünberg, L. *Die deutsche Südostgrenze*. Leipzig, 1941. A Nazi historical review of the changes in the political boundaries in Southeastern Europe. Of little interest.

Hillgruber, Andreas. "Deutschland und Ungarn, 1933–1944. Ein Überblick über die politischen und militärischen Beziehungen im Rahmen der europäischen Politik." *Wehrwissenschaftliche Rundschau* 9 (1959):651–76. Valuable article.

——. *Hitler, König Carol und Marschall Antonescu. Die deutsch-rumänischen Beziehungen, 1938–1944.* Wiesbaden, 1954. Important monograph, with tables of statistics on Rumanian oil production and deliveries.

——. *Südosteuropa im zweiten Weltkrieg. Literaturbericht und Bibliographie.* Frankfurt am Main, 1962.

Hnilicka, Karl. *Das Ende auf dem Balkan, 1944/45. Die militärische Räumung Jugoslawiens durch die deutsche Wehrmacht.* Göttingen, 1970. Includes valuable documents, 1941 to 1945.

Hoptner, J. B. *Yugoslavia in Crisis, 1934–1941.* New York, 1962. Excellent monograph on the background of the German occupation.

Horthy, Nicholas. *The Confidential Papers of Admiral Horthy.* Edited by Miklós Szinai and László Szűcs. Budapest, 1965. Captured by the Russians from the Germans and returned to Hungary. The editors make no pretense to objectivity.

——. *Memoirs.* New York, 1957. By the regent of Hungary. Although Horthy did not have his private papers at his disposal when he wrote these memoirs, he undoubtedly used material published in the many war crimes trials, for his account rarely conflicts with the evidence presented at those trials.

Hory, Ladislaus, and Broszat, Martin. *Der kroatische Ustacha-Staat, 1941–1945.* Stuttgart, 1964. Valuable study.

Ibler, Hermann. *Des Reiches Südgrenze in der Steiermark.* Graz, 1940.

Juhász, Gyula. "La Politique extérieure de la Hongrie de 1939 à 1943." *RHDGM* 62 (1966):19–36.

Kállay, Nicholas. *Hungarian Premier: A Personal Account of a Nation's Struggle in the Second World War.* New York, 1954. By the minister president from March 1942 to March 1944, who appears to have done his best to resist German pressure.

Karsai, Elek. "Edmund Veesenmayer's Reports to Hitler on Hungary in 1943." *The New Hungarian Quarterly* 5 (1964):146–53.

Kerekes, Lajos, ed. *Allianz Hitler-Horthy-Mussolini.* Budapest, 1966. Documents from Horthy's papers and the Hungarian Foreign Ministry.

Kiszling, R. *Die Kroaten. Der Schicksalsweg eines Südslawenvolkes.* Graz, 1956.

Kraft, Doris. *Das untersteierische Drauland.* Munich, 1935. Calls for reunion of these areas with Austria/Germany.

Lackó, Miklós. "Les Croix-Fléchées (1935–1944)." *RHDGM* 62 (1966):53–68. Unfortunately the article breaks off at October 15, 1944, when the Arrow Cross leaders assumed power in Hungary.

Leibrock, Otto. *Der Südosten, Grossdeutschland, und das neue Europa.* Berlin, 1941. On Germany's mission to organize and dominate this area.

Levai, Eugene. *Black Book on the Martyrdom of Hungarian Jewry.* Zürich, 1948. Based on survivors' accounts, Hungarian and Jewish documents. Packed with information, but poorly organized and often confusing.

——. *Eichmann in Hungary.* Budapest, 1961. Documents.

Macartney, C. A. "Hungary's Declaration of War on the U.S.S.R. in 1941." *Studies in Diplomatic History in Honour of G. P. Gooch.* Edited by A. O. Sarkissian. London, 1961, pp. 152–65.

——. *October Fifteenth: A History of Modern Hungary, 1929–1945.* 2 vols. Edinburgh, 1956–57. Full of important information, but so cluttered with detail that major problems and events are often obscured.

——. "Ungarns Weg aus dem zweiten Weltkrieg." *VfZ* 14 (1966):78–103.

Maček, Vladko. *In the Struggle for Freedom.* New York, 1957. By the leader of the Croatian Peasant party and deputy minister president of Yugoslavia before the German occupation.

McNeill, William H. *The Greek Dilemma: War and Aftermath.* Philadelphia, 1947. Makes the Greek government under Axis auspices appear more effective, at least during the first years of the occupation, than does Woodhouse (see below), an analysis which corresponds more closely with that of German observers on the scene.

Manning, Clarence A. *The Axis Satellites and Greece Our Ally.* New York, 1946.

Marjanović, Jovan. "The German Occupation System in Serbia in 1941." *Les Systèmes d'occupation en Yougoslavie, 1941–1945.* Belgrade, 1963, pp. 263–301.

BIBLIOGRAPHY

Matl, Josef. "Jugoslawien im zweiten Weltkrieg." *Osteuropa Handbuch*. Edited by Werner Markert. Cologne, 1954.

Müller-Haccius, Dr. Otto. "Zwei Jahre deutscher Verwaltung in Untersteier." *Marburger Zeitung*, April 12, 1943.

Neubacher, Hermann. *Sonderauftrag Südost, 1940–1945. Bericht eines fliegenden Diplomaten*. Göttingen, 1956. By one of Germany's most influential agents in the Balkans. Includes much interesting information.

O'Ballance, Edgar. *The Greek Civil War, 1944–1949*. New York, 1966. Includes a brief and unsatisfactory chapter on the Axis occupation, based largely on Woodhouse (see below).

Orlow, Dietrich. *The Nazis in the Balkans: A Case Study in Totalitarian Politics*. Pittsburgh, Pa., 1968. The title is somewhat misleading, for this is primarily a study of the Southeast Europe Society (*Südost-Europa Gesellschaft*); it includes little on Hitler's plans or actual Nazi policy in the Balkans.

OSS. *Greece*. Washington, D.C., 1943.

Paris, Edmond. *Genocide in Satellite Croatia, 1941–1945: A Record of Racial and Religious Persecutions and Massacres*. Chicago, 1962.

Pock, Friedrich. *Grenzwacht im Südosten. Ein halbes Jahrhundert Südmark*. Graz, 1940.

Presseisen, Ernest L. "Prelude to 'Barbarossa': Germany and the Balkans, 1940–1941." *Journal of Modern History* 22 (1960):358–70.

Prost, Henri. "La Roumanie et la seconde guerre mondiale." *RHDGM* 6 (1952):26–49. Valuable article.

Ránki, György. "L'Occupation de la Hongrie par les allemands." *RHDGM* 62 (1966):37–52. An excellent article based on German military and diplomatic sources covering the period March 19 to October 15, 1944.

———. *Das ungarische Wirtschaftsleben im Dienste der deutschen Kriegswirtschaft zur Zeit des zweiten Weltkrieges*. East Berlin, 1958.

Ronneberger, Franz. "Der politische Südosteuropabegriff." *RVL* 6 (1943):53–107.

Roth, Cecil. "The Last Days of Jewish Salonika." *Commentary* 10 (1950):49–55.

Rusinow, Dennison I. *Italy's Austrian Heritage, 1919–46*. Oxford, 1969. An important monograph.

Sattler, Wilhelm. *Die deutsche Volksgruppe im unabhängigen Staat Kroatien*. Graz, 1943.

Schneefuss, Walter. *Donauräume und Donaureiche*. Vienna, 1944.

Schramm-von Thadden, Ehrengard. *Griechenland und die Grossmächte im zweiten Weltkrieg*. Wiesbaden, 1955. Unfortunately only takes the story to the German attack and the Greek surrender.

Schreiber, Thomas. "Historiographie hongroise de la deuxième guerre mondiale." *RHDGM* 44 (1961):39–56.

Šepić, Dragovan. "La Politique italienne d'occupation en Dalmatie, 1941–1943." *Les Systèmes d'occupation en Yougoslavie, 1941–1945*. Belgrade, 1963, pp. 377–424.

Stefanov, Gueorgui. "Sur la Bulgarie en guerre. La Politique extérieure." *RHDGM* 72 (1968):1–21.

Tudjman, Franjo. "The Independent State of Croatia as an Instrument of the Policy of the Occupation Powers in Yugoslavia, and the People's Liberation Movement in Croatia from 1941 to 1945." *Les Systèmes d'occupation en Yougoslavie, 1941–1945*. Belgrade, 1963, pp. 135–261.

Vegh, Sandor. "Le Système du pouvoir d'occupation allemand dans le Banat Yougoslave, 1941–1944." *Les Systèmes d'occupation en Yougoslavie, 1941–1945*. Belgrade, 1963, pp. 495–561.

Verordnungsblatt des Befehlshabers Saloniki-Ägäis. Unfortunately this publication was never available to me.

Verordnungsblatt für das besetzte griechische Gebiet. Published after the installation of the Wehrmachtbefehlshaber Südost. After the Italian surrender and the German takeover of Greece, the title of the German journal of legislation was changed to *Verordnungsblatt für Griechenland*.

Verordnungs-und Amtsblatt des Chefs der Zivilverwaltung in den besetzten Gebieten Kärntens und Krains (VBlKK). Klagenfurt.

Verordnungs-und Amtsblatt des Chefs der Zivilverwaltung in der Untersteiermark (VBlUSt). Published in Marburg (Maribor) and later in Graz.

BIBLIOGRAPHY

Verordnungsblatt für das besetzte jugoslawische Gebiet. Title changed May 16, 1941, to *Verordnungsblatt des Militärbefehlshabers in Serbien,* which later became *Verordnungsblatt des Befehlshabers Serbien.* Belgrade.

Wehler, Hans-Ulrich. " 'Reichsfestung Belgrad.' Nationalsozialistische 'Raumordnung' in Südosteuropa." *VfZ* 11 (1963):72–84. An interesting article, which may exaggerate the importance of the various German plans for this region.

Werner, Gerhard [Helmut Carstanjen]. *Sprache und Volkstum in der Untersteiermark.* Stuttgart, 1935. Makes case that the territory belongs to Germany.

Wladikin, Lübomir. "Die Judengesetzgebung in Bulgarien." *RVL* 5 (1943):295–333.

Woodhouse, C. M. *Apple of Discord: A Survey of Recent Greek Politics in Their International Setting.* London, 1948. A well-informed and balanced appraisal. Makes the case that the Greek government and administration under Axis rule was virtually nonexistent.

Wüscht, Johann. *Jugoslawien und das Dritte Reich. Eine dokumentierte Geschichte der deutsch-jugoslawischen Beziehungen von 1933 bis 1945.* Stuttgart, 1969. Contains important materials, but the entire work is an apologia for German policy.

———. "Pläne des Dritten Reichs zur Neuordnung des jugoslawischen Raumes nach 1941." *Der donauschwäbische Lehrer* 1 (1959).

Xydis, Stephen G. *The Economy and Finances of Greece under Occupation.* New York, no date. Brief and superficial.

Zsigmond, L. "La Politique extérieure de la Hongrie de 1933 à 1939." *RHDGM* 62 (1966):7–17.

13. ITALY

Alfieri, Dino. *Dictators Face to Face.* New York, 1954. By the Italian ambassador to Germany, 1940–43, who fled to Switzerland in October 1943.

Anfuso, Filippo. *Du Palais de Venise au lac du Garde.* Paris, 1949. By Ciano's *chef de cabinet,* later Italian ambassador to Berlin and under secretary for foreign affairs in Mussolini's Fascist National government.

Badoglio, Pietro. *Italien im zweiten Weltkrieg. Erinnerungen und Dokumente.* Munich, 1947. By Mussolini's successor as de facto head of the Italian government.

Ciano, Count Galeazzo. *The Ciano Diaries, 1939–1943.* Edited by Hugh Gibson. New York, 1946. Important source.

Ciano's Diplomatic Papers. Edited by Malcolm Muggeridge. London, 1948.

Collotti, Enzo. *L'amministrazione tedesca dell'Italia occupata, 1943–1945. Studio e documenti.* Milan, 1963. Valuable study, with important documents.

Deakin, F. W. *The Brutal Friendship: Mussolini, Hitler, and the Fall of Italian Fascism.* Paperback, New York, 1966. A valuable monograph.

———. *The Six Hundred Days of Mussolini.* Paperback, New York, 1966. Part 3 of *The Brutal Friendship.*

Dollmann, Eugen. *Dolmetscher der Diktatoren.* Bayreuth, 1963.

———. *Roma nazista.* Milan, 1949.

Faldella, Emilio. *L'Italia nella seconda guerra mondiale. Revisione di giudizi.* Bologna, 1960.

Favagrosso, Carlo. *Perchè perdemmo la guerra. Mussolini e la produzione bellica.* Milan, 1947. By the head of Italian war production, who describes the inefficiency of Italian efforts. With a large appendix of documents.

Fogar, Galliano. *Sotto l'occupazione nazista nelle provincie orientali.* Udine, 1961.

Garland, A. N., and Smyth, H. M. *Sicily and the Surrender of Italy.* Washington, D.C., 1965.

Hitler, Adolf. *Hitler e Mussolini. Lettere e documenti.* Milan, 1946. French translation, *Les Lettres secrètes échangées par Hitler et Mussolini.* Paris, 1946.

Kirkpatrick, Ivone. *Mussolini: A Study in Power.* New York, 1964.

Latour, Conrad F. *Südtirol und die Achse Berlin-Rom, 1938–1945.* Stuttgart, 1962. Valuable monograph.

Möllhausen, Eitel von. *Die gebrochene Achse.* Alfeld, 1949. By the deputy of Rudolf Rahn, the German ambassador to Mussolini's Fascist National government.

Mourin, Maxime. *Ciano contre Mussolini.* Paris, 1960.

Mussolini, Benito. *Memoirs, 1942–1943.* London, 1949.

OSS. *Italy.* Washington, D.C., 1944.

Rahn, Rudolf. *Ruheloses Leben. Aufzeichnungen und Erinnerungen eines deutschen*

Diplomaten. Düsseldorf, 1949. By the German ambassador to Mussolini's Fascist National government.

Rintelen, Enno von. *Mussolini als Bundesgenosse. Erinnerungen des deutschen Militärattaches in Rom, 1936–1943*. Tübingen, 1951.

Rusinow, Dennison I. *Italy's Austrian Heritage, 1919–46*. Oxford, 1969. Important monograph.

Sala, Teodoro. *La crisi finale nel litorale adriatico, 1944–1945*. Udine, 1962.

Schneider-Bosgard, Hanns. *Bandenkampf in der Operationszone Adriatisches Küstenland*. Trieste, no date, probably end of 1944. An SS manual.

Schröder, Josef. *Italiens Kriegsaustritt 1943. Die deutschen Gegenmassnahmen im italienischen Raum. Fall "Alarich" und "Achse."* Göttingen, 1969.

Verordnungsblatt des obersten Kommissars für die Operationszone Alpenvorland.

Verordnungs-und Amtsblatt des obersten Kommissars in der Operationszone "Adriatisches Küstenland." Trieste.

14. RUSSIA AND THE BALTIC STATES

Allen, W. E. D. *The Ukraine: A History*. Cambridge, Eng., 1940.

Amtliche Mitteilungen des Reichskommissars für die Ukraine. See *Verordnungsblatt des Reichskommissars für die Ukraine (VBlRKU)*.

Amtsblatt des Generalkommissars für den Generalbezirk Dnjepropetrowsk. Dnepropetrovsk, 1942–43.

Amtsblatt des Generalkommissars für den Generalbezirk Kiew. Kiev, 1942–43.

Amtsblatt des Generalkommissars für den Generalbezirk Nikolajew. Nikolaev, 1942–43.

Amtsblatt des Generalkommissars für den Generalbezirk Wolhynien-Podolien. Lutsk, 1942–43.

Amtsblatt des Generalkommissars für Weissruthenien. Minsk. First issue September 30, 1941. Title changed with issue of July 21, 1942 to *Amtsblatt des Generalkommissars in Minsk (ABlGKMinsk)*. Publication continued until March 1944.

Amtsblatt des Generalkommissars in Kauen (ABlGKKauen). Kaunas (Kovno), 1941–44.

Amtsblatt des Generalkommissars in Reval (ABlGKReval). Tallinn. First issue February 2, 1942. Publication continued until June 1944.

Amtsblatt des Generalkommissars in Riga (ABlGKRiga). Riga, 1941 to June 1944.

Anisimov, Oleg. *The German Occupation in Northern Russia during World War II: Political and Administrative Aspects*. New York, 1954. Valuable, but more work needs to be done on this subject.

Armstong, John A. *Ukrainian Nationalism, 1939–1945*. New York, 1963. Enormously detailed monograph.

——, ed. *Soviet Partisans in World War II*. Madison, Wisc., 1964. Contains numerous important articles.

Backe, Herbert. *Die russische Getreidewirtschaft als Grundlage der Land-und Volkswirtschaft Russlands*. Berlin, 1941. By a senior German official responsible for food and agriculture problems.

Bilmanis, Alfred. *Latvia under German Occupation*. Washington, D.C., 1943.

Blau, George E. *The German Campaign in Russia: Planning and Operations, 1940–1942*. Washington, D.C., 1955.

Bräutigam, Otto. *Überblick über die besetzten Ostgebiete während des 2. Weltkrieges*. Tübingen, 1954. By a senior official in the Reich Ministry for the Occupied Eastern Territories. Full of important information.

Carrell, Paul. *Hitler's War in Russia: The Story of the German Defeat in the East*. London, 1964.

Child, Clifton J. "The Ukraine under German Occupation." *Hitler's Europe*. Edited by Arnold and Veronica Toynbee. London, 1954, pp. 632–48.

Clark, Alan. *Barbarossa: The Russian-German Conflict, 1941–1945*. New York, 1965.

Le Crime méthodique. Documents éclairant la politique de l'Allemagne nazie en territoire soviétique. Moscow, 1963. Published by the Soviet government.

Dallin, Alexander. *The German Occupation of the U.S.S.R. in World War II: A Bibliography*. Washington, D.C., 1955. Very useful.

——. *German Rule in Russia, 1941–1945: A Study of Occupation Policies*. New York, 1957. Basic and indispensable.

BIBLIOGRAPHY

——. "The North Caucasus." *Soviet Partisans in World War II.* Edited by John A. Armstrong. Madison, Wisc., 1964.

Erickson, John. *The Soviet High Command: A Military-Political History, 1918–1941.* New York, 1962. A very important work.

Fischer, George. *Soviet Opposition to Stalin: A Case Study of World War II.* Cambridge, Mass., 1952.

Frauenfeld, Alfred. *Die Krim.* Berlin, 1942. By the Generalkommissar for the Crimea.

——. *Ursache und Sinn unseres Kampfes. Bolschewismus-Kapitalismus. Das apokalyptische Tier mit zwei Köpfen.* Vienna, 1944. A hysterical tract, which contrasts with the more sensible official memoranda he wrote about Nazi policy in Russia.

Heiber, Helmut. "Aus den Akten des Gauleiters Kube." *VfZ* 4 (1956):67–92.

——. "Der Generalplan Ost." *VfZ* 6 (1958):280–325.

Howell, E. M. *The Soviet Partisan Movement, 1941–1944.* Washington, D.C., 1956.

Ilnytzkyj, Roman. *Deutschland und die Ukraine, 1934–1945. Tatsachen europäischer Ostpolitik.* 2 vols. Munich, 1955–56.

Kamenetsky, Ihor. *Hitler's Occupation of the Ukraine, 1941–1944.* Milwaukee, Wisc., 1956.

Kleist, Peter. *Zwischen Hitler und Stalin, 1939–1945. Aufzeichnungen.* Bonn. 1950. By an official of the Reich Ministry for the Occupied Eastern Territories. Contains much interesting information.

Koch, Erich. *Aufbau im Osten.* Breslau, 1934. By the future Reichkommissar for the Ukraine. Refers to his work in East Prussia.

Krausnick, Helmut. "Zu Hitlers Ostpolitik im Sommer 1943." *VfZ* 2 (1954):305–12.

Labs, Walter. "Die Verwaltung der besetzten Ostgebiete." *RVL* 5 (1943):92–166. By an official of the Reich Ministry for the Occupied Eastern Territories.

Lacquer, Walter. *Russia and Germany: A Century of Conflict.* London, 1965.

Leibbrandt, Georg, ed. *Ukraine.* Berlin, 1942. Compiled by a senior official of the Reich Ministry for the Occupied Eastern Territories.

Lohse, Hinrich. "Ostland baut auf." *Nationalsozialistische Monatshefte* 13 (1942):32–39. By the Reichskommissar for the Ostland.

Lowery, Sidney. "The Ostland." *Hitler's Europe.* Edited by Arnold and Veronica Toynbee. London, 1954, pp. 568–75.

Lundin, C. Leonard. "Nazification of Baltic German Minorities: A Contribution to the Study of the Diplomacy of 1939." *Journal of Central European Affairs* 7 (1947):1–28. Makes the case that the Baltic Germans were thoroughly Nazified and organized, and that they constituted a real threat to Russia.

Luther, Michael. *Die Krim unter deutscher Besatzung im zweiten Weltkrieg.* Berlin, 1956. Valuable, but here, too, more remains to be done.

Manstein, Erich von. *Lost Victories.* Chicago, 1958. By the German military commander in the Crimea. Little on German administration.

Mende, Gerhard von. *Die Völker der Sowjetunion.* Reichenau, 1939. By a later official of the Reich Ministry for the Occupied Eastern Territories.

Meyer, Alfred, ed. *Das Recht der besetzten Ostgebiete. Estland, Lettland, Litauen, Weissruthenien, Ukraine.* Munich, 1943. An important collection of laws.

Paget, R. T. *Manstein: His Campaigns and His Trial.* London, 1951. A defense of the military commander in the Crimea.

Philippi, Alfred, and Heim, Ferdinand. *Der Feldzug gegen Sowjetrussland, 1941 bis 1945. Ein Operativer Überblick.* Stuttgart, 1962.

Pottgieser, Hans. *Die deutsche Reichsbahn im Ostfeldzug, 1939–1944.* Neckargemünd, 1960.

Reitlinger, Gerald. "The Doubts of Wilhelm Kube." *Wiener Library Bulletin,* September and December 1950.

——. *The House Built on Sand: The Conflicts of German Policy in Russia, 1939–1945.* New York, 1960. Readable and, on the whole, excellent analysis.

Riecke, Hans-Joachim. "Aufgaben der Landwirtschaft im Osten." *Probleme des Ostraumes.* Berlin, 1942. By the head of the food and agriculture section in the Reich Ministry for the Occupied Eastern Territories.

Rimscha, H. von. "Zur Umsiedlung der Deutschen aus den baltischen Staaten während des zweiten Weltkriegs." *Osteuropa* 11 (1961):134–36.

BIBLIOGRAPHY

———. *Die Umsiedlung der Deutschbalten aus Lettland im Jahre 1939. Eine Betrachtung.* Hanover, 1959.

Rosenberg, Alfred. *Letzte Aufzeichnungen. Ideale und Idole der nationalsozialistischen Revolution.* Göttingen, 1955. Of little interest.

———. *Der Zukunftsweg einer deutschen Aussenpolitik.* Munich, 1927. Interesting for the early views of the later Reich minister for the occupied eastern territories.

Samarin, Vladimir. *Civilian Life under the German Occupation, 1942–1944.* New York, 1954.

Sammlung der Anordnungen und Bekanntmachungen zur Regelung des Wirtschaftslebens. Riga, 1941–42. An official publication of the Generalkommissar for Latvia.

Schiller, Otto. *Ziele und Ergebnisse der Agrarordnung in den besetzten Ostgebieten.* Berlin, 1944. By the consultant on land distribution for the Economic Staff East.

Shankowsky, Lev. "Nazi Occupation of Ukraine." *The Ukrainian Review* 2 (1955):8–18.

Thorwald, Juergen. *Wen sie verderben wollen. Bericht des grossen Verrats.* Stuttgart, 1952. Full of important material, much of it based on interviews.

Verkündungsblatt des Reichskommissars für das Ostland. Riga, first issue published August 30, 1941. Title changed, April 23, 1942, to *Verordnungsblatt des Reichskommissars für das Ostland (VBlRKO).* Publication continued until August 1944.

Verordnungsblatt des Reichskommissars für die Ukraine (VBlRKU). Rovno, 1941–44. Title changed after first issues from *Amtliche Mitteilungen des Reichskommissars für die Ukraine.*

Verordnungsblatt des Reichsministers für die besetzten Ostgebiete (VBlRMO). Berlin, 1942–44.

Völker, Volksgruppen und Volksstämme auf dem ehemaligen Gebiet der UdSSR. Leipzig, 1941. A publication of the racial office of the Reichsführer SS.

Zentralblatt des Reichskommissars für die Ukraine. Rovno, 1942–43. A publication of official announcements.

15. BRITAIN, THE CHANNEL ISLANDS, SPAIN, AND SWITZERLAND.

Aubin, C. W. Duret. "Enemy Legislation and Judgments in Jersey." *Journal of Comparative Legislation and International Law* 31 (1949), pts. 3 and 4, pp. 8–11.

British Foreign Office, Research Department. "The Connection of Albrecht Haushofer with the Flight of Rudolf Hess and German Plans for Negotiated Peace with Britain." Mimeographed report. London, 1946.

Burdick, Charles B. *Germany's Military Strategy and Spain in World War II.* Syracuse, N.Y., 1968.

Cadogan, Alexander. *The Diaries of Sir Alexander Cadogan, 1939–1945.* Edited by David Dilks. London, 1971.

Coysh, Victor. *Swastika over Guernsey.* Guernsey, 1955.

Detwiler, Donald S. *Hitler, Franco und Gibraltar. Die Frage des spanischen Eintritts in den zweiten Weltkrieg.* Wiesbaden, 1962.

Durand, Ralph. *Guernsey under German Rule.* London, 1946.

Fleming, Peter. *Operation Sea Lion.* Paperback, New York, 1957. A lively account, giving both the British and German sides of the story.

Halifax, Edward Wood, Viscount. *Fulness of Days.* London, 1957.

Hayes, Carlton J. H. *Wartime Mission in Spain, 1942–1945.* New York, 1945. By the United States ambassador.

Henderson, Nevile. *Failure of a Mission: Berlin, 1937–1939.* London, 1939. By the British ambassador.

Hoare, Sir Samuel (Viscount Templewood). *Complacent Dictator.* New York, 1947. By the British ambassador to Spain, 1940–44.

Lachmann, Günter. *Der Nationalsozialismus in der Schweiz, 1931–1945. Ein Beitrag zur Geschichte des Auslandsorganisation der NSDAP.* Berlin, 1962. Throws little light on Hitler's intentions.

Lampe, David. *The Last Ditch.* London, 1968. German plans for the occupation of Britain. Contains little of importance that is new.

Longmate, Norman. *If Britain Had Fallen.* London, 1972. Based largely on the research for a BBC television film on the subject. Has unearthed little new material of importance. The book's defense of the men the Nazis had picked out as potential Quislings may be more spirited than is justified.

Meyer, Alice. *Anpassung oder Widerstand. Die Schweiz zur Zeit des deutschen Nationalsozialismus.* Frauenfeld, 1965. Well-documented study of the struggle between the advocates of accommodation and resistance.

Mosley, Oswald. *My Life.* London, 1968. By the leading British fascist during the Nazi era.

Payne, Stanley G. *Falange: A History of Spanish Fascism.* Paperback, Stanford, Calif., 1961.

Sinel, Leslie P. *Swastika over Jersey: An Outline of the German Occupation and Liberation of the Island.* Guernsey, 1958.

———, ed. *The German Occupation of Jersey.* London, 1969.

Uhlmann, H. "Angriffspläne gegen die Schweiz." *Allgemeine Schweizerische Militärzeitung* 115 (1949):841–42.

Uttley, John. *A Short History of the Channel Islands.* New York, 1967.

Wheatley, Ronald. *Operation Sea Lion: German Plans for the Invasion of England, 1939–1942.* Paperback, Oxford, 1962. The best work in English on the subject.

Wood, Alan and Mary. *Islands in Danger: The Story of the German Occupation of the Channel Islands, 1940–1945.* London, 1955.

16. COLONIAL PLANS, ASIA, AND THE WESTERN HEMISPHERE.

Friedländer, Saul. *Prelude to Downfall: Hitler and the United States, 1939–1941.* New York, 1967. The best work on the subject.

Frye, Alton. *Nazi Germany and the American Hemisphere, 1933–1941.* New Haven, Conn., 1967. Well-documented study of Nazi subversion.

Glasneck, J., and Kircheisen, I. *Türkei und Afghanistan. Brennpunkte der Orientpolitik im zweiten Weltkrieg.* Berlin, 1968.

Groehler, Olaf. "Kolonialforderungen als Teil der faschistischen Kriegszielplanung." *Zeitschrift für Militärgeschichte* 4 (1965):547–73.

Hildebrand, Klaus. *Vom Reich zum Weltreich. Hitler, NSDAP und koloniale Frage, 1919–1945.* Munich, 1969. Intelligent, scholarly, and thoroughly convincing treatise, although annoyingly verbose and repetitious. Massive bibliography and valuable document appendix.

Hirszowicz, Lukasz. *The Third Reich and the Arab East.* Toronto, 1966. A thorough and scholarly monograph.

Jones, F. C. *Japan's New Order in East Asia: Its Rise and Fall, 1937–1945.* London, 1954. A fascinating and valuable work.

Kirk, George E. *The Middle East in the War.* London, 1952.

Krecker, Lothar. *Deutschland und die Türkei im zweiten Weltkrieg.* Frankfurt am Main, 1964. Competent monograph.

Kühne, Horst. *Faschistische Kolonialideologie und zweiter Weltkrieg.* East Berlin, 1962.

———. "Zur Kolonialpolitik des faschistischen deutschen Imperialismus, 1933–1939." *Zeitschrift für Geschichtswissenschaft* 9 (1961):514–37.

Martin, Bernd. *Deutschland und Japan im zweiten Weltkrieg. Von Pearl Harbor bis zur deutschen Kapitulation.* Göttingen, 1969.

Meskill, Johanna Menzel. *Hitler and Japan: The Hollow Alliance.* New York, 1967.

Moltmann, Günther. *Amerikas Deutschlandpolitik im zweiten Weltkrieg. Kriegs-und Friedensziele, 1941–1945.* Heidelberg, 1958.

———. "Weltherrschaftsideen Hitlers." *Europa und Übersee. Festschrift für Egmont Zechlin.* Edited by Otto Brunner and Dietrich Gerhard. Hamburg, 1961. Sober, intelligent analysis.

Oestereich, Heinrich. "Japanisches Reich und Ostasiatischer Grossraum." *RVL* 5 (1943):337–66.

Remak, Joachim. "Hitlers Amerikapolitik." *Aussenpolitik* 6 (1955):706–14.

Romeril, P.E.A. *War Diplomacy and the Turkish Republic: A Study in Neutrality, 1939–1945.* Leiden, 1963.

Schechtman, Joseph B. *The Mufti and the Fuehrer.* New York, 1965.

Schmokel, Wolfe W. *Dream of Empire: German Colonialism, 1919–45.* New Haven, Conn., 1964. Important monograph.

BIBLIOGRAPHY

Sommer, Theo. *Deutschland und Japan zwischen den Mächten, 1935–1940. Vom Antikominternpakt zum Dreimächtepakt.* Tübingen, 1962.

Tillmann, Heinz. *Deutschlands Araberpolitik im zweiten Weltkrieg.* East Berlin, 1965.

Weinberg, Gerhard L. "German Colonial Plans and Policies, 1938–1942." *Geschichte und Gegenwartsbewusstsein. Festschrift für Hans Rothfels zum 70. Geburtstag.* Edited by Waldemar Besson and Friedrich Freiherr Hiller von Gaertringen. Göttingen, 1963, pp. 462–91. Excellent article based primarily on microfilms of German documents in the National Archives.

Index

Aachen, 172, 176, 195
Abetz, Otto, 204–5, 221–22, 227, 228
Aćimović, Milan, 289
Ada, harbor of, 406
Adriatic Littoral (Adriatisches Küstenland), 321
Afghanistan, 406, 414–15
Africa, 217, 402, 420; German colonial claims in, 406–7. *See also* names of countries
Agadir, 217
Agrarian party (Czechoslovakia), 34
Aisne, department of, 210, 238
Albania, 240, 265; boundaries, 300; economic policies in, 302; evacuation of (1944), 302; German administration, 299–302, 316; Italian rule, 300–301, 305; Nazi occupation of Yugoslavia and, 265, 266, 267, 282, 286, 287, 300; Regency Council, 300; SS and police units, 302
Albanian National Committee, 300
Alderney, island of, 398
Aleppo (Syria), 414
Alexander I, King (Yugoslavia), 275
Algeria, 407, 408
Alsace and Lorraine, 17, 171, 200, 210, 212, 217, 218, 231–39, 421; banning of Basque berets, 234; citizenship (1941), 233–34; de-Germanizing (after 1918), 235; deportations, 238; economic program,
234; educational system, 224; expulsion of French population, 218; German administration, 231–39, 315; Jews, 234, 235, 237; legal system, 233; racial policies, 235–37; resettlement project, 237–38; separation from France (1940), 232
Altenburg, Günther, 307, 308
Altgayer, Branimir, 279
Amiens, 210
Andalusia, province of, 350
Anschluss, 15–16, 20, 152, 191, 232, 386
Anti-Bolshevik Legion, 160
Anticythera, island of, 306
Antonescu, General Ion, 243, 248, 251, 252–53, 255, 256, 258, 314, 327
Antonescu, Mihai, 254, 255
Arab world, xiii, 407, 408, 421; hatred of Jews, 412–13; oil industry, 414; proposed Italian supremacy in, 413, 414; resentment of British imperialism, 413; Vichy government and, 219–20. *See also* names of countries
Arbeitsdienst. *See* Reich Labor Service
Arbeitsstab Frankreich, 223–24
Ardennes, department of, 210, 238
Armenians, 384
Arrow-Cross movement, 245, 248–49
Ascension Island, 406
Asia, 396, 402; Nazi plans for, 412–16. *See also* names of countries

531

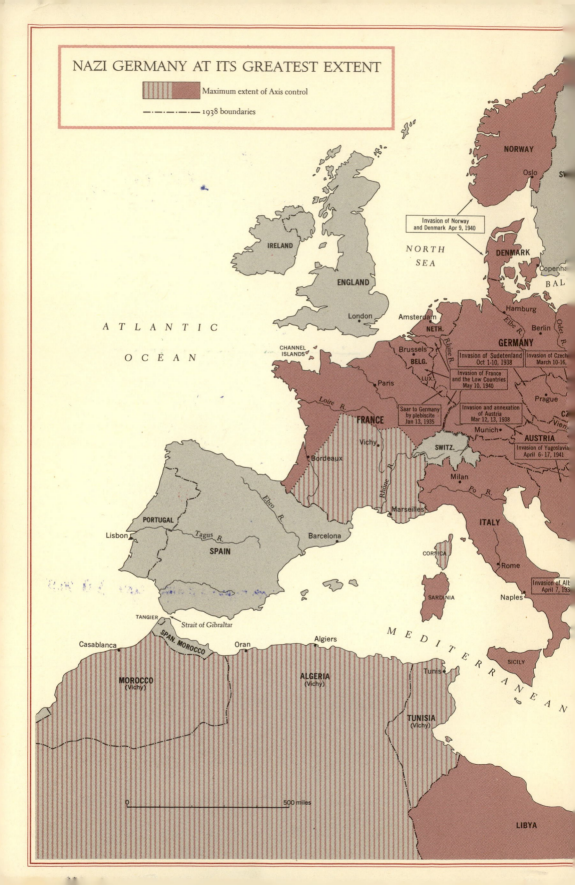

NAZI GERMANY AT ITS GREATEST EXTENT

Maximum extent of Axis control

—·—·—·— 1938 boundaries

NORWAY

Oslo

SW

NORTH
SEA

Invasion of Norway
and Denmark Apr 9, 1940

DENMARK

Copenha

BAL

Hamburg

Berlin

Elbe R.

Oder R.

GERMANY

IRELAND

ENGLAND

London

Amsterdam

NETH.

Brussels

Invasion of Sudetenland
Oct 1-10, 1938

Invasion of Czech
March 10-16.

ATLANTIC

OCEAN

CHANNEL
ISLANDS

BELG.

Rhine R.

LUX.

Invasion of France
and the Low Countries
May 10, 1940

Prague

Paris

Loire R.

Saar to Germany
by plebiscite
Jan 13, 1935

Invasion and annexation
of Austria
Mar 12, 13, 1938

CZ

Vien

FRANCE

Vichy

Munich

AUSTRIA

Bordeaux

SWITZ.

Invasion of Yugoslavia
April 6-17, 1941

Rhône R.

Milan

Po R.

Ebro R.

Marseilles

PORTUGAL

ITALY

Lisbon

Tagus R.

Barcelona

CORSICA

Rome

SPAIN

Invasion of Alb
April 7, 193

Naples

SARDINIA

TANGIER

Strait of Gibraltar

M E D I T E R R A N E A N

SICILY

Casablanca

SPAN. MOROCCO

Oran

Algiers

Tunis

MOROCCO
(Vichy)

ALGERIA
(Vichy)

TUNISIA
(Vichy)

0   500 miles

LIBYA

FINLAND

Russo-Finnish War
Nov 30, 1939-Mar 12, 1940

• Helsinki   • Leningrad

ckholm

ESTONIA

SEA   LATVIA

• Moscow

ation of
emel
21, 1939

LITHUANIA

Danzig   EAST
PRUSSIA

SOVIET   UNION

Volga R.

Ural R.

Invasion of Russia
June 22, 1941

stula R.

• Warsaw   POLAND

Poland invaded and divided
by Germany and Russia
Sept 1-Sept 29, 1939

Don R.

• Stalingrad

• Kiev

Dnieper R.

Volga R.

VAKIA

• Rostov

CASPIAN SEA

udapest

NGARY

RUMANIA

BLACK   SEA

anube R.

grade

• Bucharest

• Baku

VIA

Invasion of Greece
June 6-23, 1941

BULGARIA

• Sofia

Bosporus

• Ankara

ANIA

Istanbul

TURKEY

Dardanelles

IRAN

GREECE

SYRIA

Euphrates R.   Tigris R.

• Athens

CYPRUS

IRAQ

SEA

CRETE

PALESTINE

Bengasi   Tobruk

• Alexandria

TRANS-
JORDAN

SAUDI ARABIA

Nile R.

EGYPT